the secondary school principal in action

the secondary school principal

in Action

Leonard E. Kraft

University of Georgia

WM. C. BROWN COMPANY PUBLISHERS

contents

PART THREE

The Principal and Instructional Leadership

PART FOUR

The Principal and Personnel

Contents   ix

preface

These are exciting times for those who are interested in studying the role of the secondary school principal. Few administrative roles are more vulnerable to the changing demands of society. The articles found in this book were carefully chosen to give the reader insight into the emerging role of the secondary school principal. The numerous articles of the last decade reflect profound changes in the philosophy and practice of administering a secondary school.

In order to fully comprehend the changing role of the secondary school principal, the editor feels it is of utmost importance to focus attention on recent writings which provide assistance to the beleaguered practitioner. In addition, the book will enable prospective secondary principals, professors of educational administration, and others to better perceive the principal in action. Since all articles are intact, their references, bibliographical listings, and footnotes provide additional reading sources. The intent of the editor is to create a book that will be optimally useful to students and practitioners at various levels of sophistication.

The Secondary School Principal in Action systematically focuses on several functions of the role. The comprehensive overview is organized around five major parts: America's Educational Challenge; The Principal; The Principal and Instructional Leadership; The Principal and Personnel; and The Principal, the Student, and the Community. Each part is divided into one or more chapters. An overview at the beginning of each chapter offers the reader a brief introduction to the chapter and to each article.

The editor wishes to express his gratitude to the many authors and their publishers who gave permission to reprint the articles in this volume.

part one

AMERICA'S EDUCATIONAL CHALLENGE

part one

The Challenge
Facing Secondary
Schools

I

chapter overview

The direction in which education starts a man will determine his future life.

—PLATO

American secondary schools must provide the necessary conditions for change or be destroyed by the forces for change. The magnitude of the challenge is etched in almost every aspect of our daily lives. No longer is the American society content to permit its educational institutions the luxury of indifference to the educational needs of all its citizens. No longer is the American society willing to support inferior educational programs. The jury is in, the verdict is clear, educational leaders are challenged to provide a humane environment for conducting the educational affairs of the people.

"One small step for man, one giant step for mankind." These were the words dramatically portrayed to our nation and to the world when an American, Neil Armstrong, set foot upon the moon for the first time in 1969. Leonard Kraft contemplated this and other achievements when he identified two major challenges confronting our educational systems: (1) the changing concept of the world in which we live and (2) the development of the ability to cope with change.

America's progress is dependent upon its ability to provide quality education for all of her people. Edward W. Brooke views the ferment pulsing through American education as an opportunity for significant educational progress. He discusses "some of the key dimensions in which further progress is imperative, if American education is to retain an effective instrument for individual development and social evaluation."

Harl R. Douglass projects the kind of quality expected of our secondary schools of the future by parents, educators, and the general public. The future is here. We must seriously consider the words of John Ruskin, who wrote in his *The Crown of the Wild Olives* in 1866, "Education is not so much coming to know what we ought to know as it is coming to behave as we ought to behave."

3

1 | America's Educational Challenge

Leonard Kraft

What are some of the challenges facing our public school educational programs? What is the scope of these pressing issues which permeate our society? What are some of the questions that must be pondered in the formulation of public school programs? Can we expect the public schools to educate the people in a manner which enables the individual to realize his full potential as a responsible citizen?

In this paper, observations are delimited to education in the "formal" sense. Specifically, these comments are directed to that education which takes place in our public educational systems. This approach is not an attempt to minimize the work of informal agencies in transmitting the cultural traditions of our country or the contributions of the non-public school in the United States. Furthermore, it is not the belief of the writer that our social problems, i.e., juvenile delinquency, anti-Semitism, Negro-and-white relations, war and peace, etc., can be solved only through "formal" education.

John Wahlquist very clearly stated what he thinks the American public schools contribute to our society:

The American public schools are the very center of American life. No doubt, other schools, private and parochial, have their place in American life, but the public school is the hub of democracy. Under the principle of reciprocity, democracy countenances schools sponsored and supported by minority groups, but the entire public has a special obligation to the common school system. Traditions peculiar to certain sects, classes, and minority groups may be preserved, often times to the advantage of the public, in church, proprietary, and special schools, but the common heritage is primarily the responsibility of the American public school system. It is doubtful if another institution in American life is so influential; that is the one major institution, aside from the federal government, that binds all people.[1]

This instrument of our society finds itself in a much different world today than it has at any other time in our history. Not only is education facing many domestic challenges, but urgent and vital challenges from around the world are placing great demands upon it.

From *Contemporary Education*, Vol. 40 (November 1968), pp. 69-71. Reprinted by permission of the publisher.

1. John Wahlquist, *The Administration of Public Education* (New York: Roland Press, 1952), p. 36.

TWO MAJOR CHALLENGES

Two major challenges confront our public schools today, (1) the changing concept of the world in which we live, and (2) the development of the ability to cope with change.

Challenge Number I—The changing concept of the world in which we live.

One of our fallacious assumptions has been the belief that we could separate ourselves from Europe, Asia, Middle East, Far East, etc., that our oceans would keep us "safe," etc., and that our domestic and foreign policies were not interdependent. This belief still persists in some segments of our society.

Alexis de Tocqueville in 1831 recognized the geographical position of the United States and remarked that we had "no neighbors."[2] Today, more than ever before, we realize that the whole world is one neighborhood. The world has shrunk in effective size as distance has been conquered by communication and transportation achievements. Perhaps these achievements in communication and transportation are bringing people together faster than they are ready for the change.

It is now clear that our educational programs must reflect the total world scene. Our people must be realistically informed about the issues both home and abroad. Recent political campaigns have concentrated upon world affairs, as well as upon domestic issues. Foreign affairs have become most important in our everyday lives. Most of our mass media, radio, television, newspaper, etc., give considerably increased attention to world affairs. This is not to say that we would or should ignore our domestic affairs, but only to point out beyond them the need to educate for total world understanding. The schools must evaluate their programs in light of this changing conceptualization of the world.

Adlai Stevenson stated America's education challenge in the following way:

Looking for the long pull—not just to missiles and rockets—the American problem in education is to prepare citizens not merely to live in American society but to live in an America caught up inextricably in an evolving world community, which, in turn, is sized by both technological and political revolution.

This means new dimensions for education. It means the training of innovators, not organization men, in both science and humanities. It means the understanding of other societies and it means a deeper understanding of American history and society not merely as a unique and

2. Cited in George S. Counts, "Education and the Foundations of Liberty," *Teachers College Record*, February, 1958.

treasured saga but as a part of universal experience. Instinctive knowledge of the American life as it is lived at home is no longer enough.[3]

This is an awesome responsibility placed upon our people.
American teachers, as well as other American citizens, need to be engaged in the task of developing the role appropriate to education
in these very dynamic times. As Max Lerner points out,

Education has to perform a dual function in any civilization. It must
transmit the cultural heritage, and it must also provide each generation
with the intellectual and moral tools for assessing itself, calculating the
forces that confront it, and making the necessary changes. In this sense
it must be at once conservative and innovating, transmissive and unsettled.[4]

The educational system has an enormous task in educating the
youth to an understanding of the cultural backgrounds of all the
people of the world. Among other things, we must become fully
aware that the white race is only a minority race, and a small minority at that, and that over three-fourths of the world's population is
colored, mostly brown. The Negro race could also be classified as
a minority race. Whether we like it or not, some notions about the
superiority of the white race must change, if we, as a nation, are to
survive. But more than that, if we believe in democratic ideals and
aspire to lead the world to just and lasting peace and to freedom,
we must demonstrate by deeds. Prejudice is taught; it is not born.

Ashley Montagu states, "If civilization is to survive we must
cultivate the science of human relationship—the ability of all peoples, of all kinds, to live together in the same world at peace."[5]

Challenge Number II—The development of the ability to cope
with change.

Over the years we have moved from a highly agricultural society
to a highly complex technological society. Approximately one hundred years ago eighty-five percent of our people were at work producing food for themselves and others. Today, only fifteen percent
or less are so employed. In this revolution can be noted the shift
from the small rural communities to the large urban centers. It is
the view of some experts that the bulk of the population of our country in the near future will be concentrated in just six large metropolitan areas. The large city life atmosphere is often characterized
by its bigness, coldness, and lack of neighborliness. This is of course
in contrast with our earlier history as a nation. The community was

3. Cited by Ernest O. Melby, *Education for Renewed Faith in Freedom* (Columbus:
Ohio University Press, 1959), p. 5.
4. Max Lerner, *America As a Civilization* (New York: Simon and Schuster, 1957),
p. 737.
5. Ashley Montagu, *Education and Human Relations* (New York: Grove Press, 1948).

a far greater force in the life of the individual prior to our industrial movement. The human community atmosphere has played a very important role in the development of our country. There seems to be a decided shift of the American character as we moved from an agricultural society to a highly industrialized society. The passing of time brings about changes of values in cultures, and our society is no exception.

Today our educational system is being challenged to fill the gap between our social inventiveness and our moral responsibilities to ourselves and our neighbors (the world). James T. Shotwell very vividly points out the need for an alert society to meet the demands of a scientific age when he says,

Scientific discovery remakes time and space, and invention enables man to assume the mastery of the material world. For the future it holds promise of ever-increasing betterment and man's ultimate release from unremitting toil as well as from want and poverty. And yet, if we consider the past, the present and the immediate future, we must admit that the first effects of this still-young revolution are by no means reassuring. The emergence of this new power, by disturbing the accustomed ways of living, brings new problems of adjustment and will continue to do so throughout the future, because the force for change, intelligence in action, has started upon a career which will never cease.[6]

The force for change is being felt in almost all aspects of our everyday life. Change does not necessarily mean progress, but all progress stems from change.

CONCLUSION

In our evaluation of programs, we must observe the following directional signals: (1) that we know what effects various kinds of educational programs have on values and beliefs, (2) that our school programs be the best expression of our culture, (3) that the programs provide opportunity for cross-cultural experiences, and (4) that our educational programs contain the necessary experiences to meet the technological and political revolution of the present and future.

Undergirding these four directional signals is the need to develop the kind of educational program which will educate individuals effectively in the ability to change.

6. James T. Shotwell, *The Long Way to Freedom* (New York: Bobbs-Merrill, 1960), p. 397.

Education for Progress
2 | Social Change and the
American School

Edward W. Brooke

It is always a thrill to be in this exciting city, but even the lure of San Francisco would not have drawn me if this had not been such an important occasion, for some of our country's most vital work is being done in this meeting and others like it. The ferment now pulsing through American education is yielding a heady brew of self-criticism and innovation. I am very pleased to be with you today.

Horace Mann, that Massachusetts patron who admonished America to "build schools to abolish ignorance, crime, and misery," would be proud to behold the labors of his successors. Not satisfied with the results, but proud of the effort. Ignorance, crime, and misery persist in the United States, but there has been a great awakening to the truth Mann spoke when he described education as the "balance wheel of social machinery." The last decade has seen an unprecedented attempt to bring that wheel into play as the central instrument in relieving the compound problems of our society. So far, the results have been uneven and often disappointing. But the conviction remains that this country's salvation as a free society which nourishes inquiry and achievement must lie through better, more dynamic education for all our people.

The difficulties of achieving such quality education have become more and more apparent. What we have learned is how little we know. Consider, for example, the shocking results of one recent study. In analyzing school records in a Pennsylvania city, the study revealed that if a first-grader came from a home where the father was not working and where there was no phone, the chances were eight out of ten that he would become a dropout. By another measure, it was found that children who were not achieving academically after the end of the first grade and who had to repeat either the first or second grade had only a 20 percent probability of completing high school. It would appear that youngsters such as these were virtually condemned to failure at age six. What dreary testimony to the feeble power of the schools to equip these children for productive lives!

Findings of this sort abound. They make it clear that we must take a more comprehensive view of the entire educational process,

From *The NASSP Bulletin* (May 1969), pp. 95-103. Reprinted by permission of the publisher.

indeed the total environment from pre-school years through secondary and higher education. Such findings also have induced a new sense of the limitations of present educational techniques.

"The mood of American education," someone has said, "is like that of the starlet who has been pleading for a dramatic lead and, suddenly thrust to the center of the stage, is paralyzed with fright."

KIND WORDS NOT ENOUGH

The simile is apt. Education and educators have always been blessed with kind words of encouragement, but somehow, for all the glowing praise Americans have heaped on the role of education, our schools and teachers were for generations taken for granted or treated like neglected stepchildren. The spare and ill-equipped school house and the dedicated, but wretchedly underpaid, teacher became part of native folklore.

But in recent years, especially since 1958, education has moved front and center in the ranks of America's public institutions. Interest in every level and facet of the educational process has soared to unknown heights. Resources have become available on a scale no one would have been willing to predict before Sputnik shocked the nation into grave concern over our educational capabilities. Between 1967 and 1968, total expenditures on public and private education jumped $3 billion to an annual total of $52 billion, nearly 7 percent of the gross national product. Yet the seeming largesse which education has come to enjoy has proved ephemeral when compared to the soaring demands being placed upon the system.

Certainly the increased public attention being lavished on our schools and colleges accounts for some of the tensions which have appeared in this field. More people are getting into the act now. Parents' and citizens' groups are probing more deeply into the methods and purposes of the professionals who have long dominated education in our society. Vigorous and varied challenges have arisen to test the traditional authority and functions of the classroom teacher.

The relative privacy in which teachers normally operated has faded, as the close and quiet relationship of mentor and pupil has come under the scrutiny of many parties. Such scrutiny often helps to energize that relationship; but it can also breed conflict, as teachers come to resent the intrusions of the new observers, as students learn to enlist outside support in contesting the judgment and prerogatives of the teachers, as parents become involved in a competition for greater influence over the formal education of their children.

POSSIBLE PERVERSION OF THE EDUCATIONAL PROCESS

I believe we must be wary, lest such conflicts pervert the educational process into a direct struggle for power over a valuable social tool. We must never forget that education is more than a means; for creatures blessed with the gift of reason, it is a worthy end, in and of itself. It suffers if conceived solely in instrumental terms. Political contests bearing on education can be healthy and constructive; America's familiar practice of local school board elections offers one example. But the purpose of education is not the purpose of politics. In some recent episodes, I fear the distinction has been forgotten or overlooked. The contest for control over the schools has sometimes degenerated into a battle for personal or group power, instead of a struggle over educational issues.

What is worse, in my own state and elsewhere we have recently seen more than one instance in which persons seeking power in the wider political arena have exploited, in the most calculating manner, educational issues which should have been considered purely on their merits, not as political platforms. This intensified political competition has undoubtedly generated some of the tensions now surrounding education in the United States.

Yet none of these developments is the full explanation for the rising anxieties concerning our present educational system. Indeed they are minor and tangential elements in a far more complicated set of trends. The larger trends which produce the fundamental apprehensions now surging through our educational establishment relate to the mammoth and diverse tasks now confronting it. Money for education has increased, to be sure, but the mission for education has grown at an even more rapid rate.

EXPECTATIONS INCREASE

Our educational institutions are expected not only to perform their traditional functions of basic instruction in the three "r's" but to transmit new knowledge in a constantly widening range of study. They are expected not only to nourish the individual qualities and unique talents of each student, but to prepare vast numbers of students to meet the socially determined requirements of our complex labor market. They are expected not only to play the part of auxiliary parent, but to provide the setting and instruction through which the parent's prejudices and preferences will be subordinated to society's higher values. They are expected not only to equip each student with the necessary skills to earn his way in a competitive economy, but to instill a philosophy which transcends the materialistic emphases which clamor for his allegiance in an affluent society.

In such an environment, laden with multiple and intense pressures, those charged with basic responsibility for the education of

America's children face hard and urgent choices. Indeed, many of them might prefer to trade their new-found prominence in our national life for the more sheltered existence of earlier generations. But I, for one, am tremendously impressed by the manner in which American educators are striving to cope with the enormous job before them. I tend to share the view of Harold Howe that American teachers and schools deserve more praise than condemnation for their recent attempts to cope with their added responsibilities. In this and other areas, Commissioner Howe contended that "perhaps we have more critics and mourners than we need, too many who assert the American problem and not enough who assert the signs of progress toward the American dream." I can appreciate his feeling, although I must add that the clearest sign that we are still making progress toward that dream is our recognition of how far we have to go.

I would like to spend the rest of our time together today discussing some of the key dimensions in which further progress is imperative, if American education is to remain an effective instrument for individual development and social evolution. While the priorities I will state are personal ones, I do not pretend that they are either original or exclusively my own. In fact, I believe they represent elements of an emerging consensus among educators, the public, and their elected officials at all levels of government.

The National Advisory Commission on Civil Disorders, on which I served, highlighted a number of bleak and disturbing trends already visible to many acute students of urban education. We came to see, in poignant and painful detail, the effects of our national failure to create a humane and hospitable environment for millions of our urban residents. One of the principal factors in our urban crisis, at once a cause and a consequence of our wider failure, has been the total inadequacy of our educational effort in most of the urban ghettos.

As many of you know, the work of James Coleman, Thomas Pettigrew, and others had already made evident the grave shortcomings of public education in such areas. Indeed, they had pointed to the likely impossibility of effective learning on the part of pupils attending schools under the conditions that prevail in the ghetto. The data on student performance offer grim evidence for this thesis. On standard achievement tests Negro students scored 1.6 grades behind white students by the time they reached the sixth grade, and the gap widened to 3.3 grades by the 12th grade. Some critics have even argued from these and related findings that ghetto schools are doing more harm than good.

At the very least, it must be said that the relatively better accomplishment of students in other schools is a convincing measure of the fact that schools in urban slums, if they do not actually contribute to the poor achievement of their students, are doing woefully little to overcome the initial handicaps under which the children labor. No doubt the picture varies from school to school and city to city, but on a national basis the scene is one of consistent failure.

The results of this failure appear on every hand—in the wreckage of individual lives and in the added burdens society must bear when many of its members are unprepared to carry a full share of the community's obligations. No one here needs to be told of the adverse consequences poor education has on an individual's job prospects in an economy of growing complexity and technological sophistication. It is enough to note that students concentrated in the inferior schools of our urban centers are three times as likely as other youngsters to drop out by the time they reach the ages of 16 and 17.

These are the kinds of patterns and trends which have prompted the fierce criticism recently heaped on our urban educational system. Paul Briggs, superintendent of schools in Cleveland, has stated:

Many of those whose recent acts threaten the domestic safety and tear at the roots of the American democracy are the products of yesterday's inadequate and neglected inner-city schools. The greatest unused and underdeveloped human resources in America are to be found in the deteriorating cores of America's urban centers.

That is certainly true. Moreover, an inadequate education that arouses desire but frustrates fulfillment may fuel the most destructive impulses of which human beings are capable.

EDUCATIONAL RESULTS OF RESIDENTIAL SEGREGATION

As we gain greater appreciation of these relationships, the problems of urban education are coming to occupy a central position on the agenda of our society's unfinished business. The sheer magnitude of these challenges is greatly complicated by some serious distortions in our society, in particular by the pronounced residential segregation of our population along racial lines. Because such residential patterns have developed, our commendable tradition of neighborhood schools under local control has had some undesirable side effects. Segregated neighborhoods have guaranteed segregated schools.

The extremes which such patterns have now reached are truly staggering. In 75 cities surveyed by the U. S. Civil Rights Commission, 75 percent of all Negro students in elementary grades were enrolled in schools that were 90 percent or more Negro. Nine out of ten Negro students attended schools with Negro majorities. This distorted result was matched in other neighborhoods where virtually all white students were studying in schools with more than 90 percent white enrollment. And these trends are growing, not declining. In less than a decade, unless corrective action is taken, 80 percent of all Negro students in the 20 largest cities, containing nearly one-half of the country's entire Negro population, will be attending schools whose student bodies are more than 90 percent Negro.

These are grim prospects for America. They would be grim even if every Negro family in the urban centers were white-collar and middle-class in social standing, for racial isolation of this character is incompatible with the fundamental values of a variegated and free society. More and more Americans are coming to hold the conviction that an integral and necessary part of education in a heterogeneous community must be mutual exposure between majority and minority groups. On this ground alone I believe most thoughtful Americans would be concerned about the persistence of such trends. But these developments are made even more disastrous by the fact that those congregating in the ghettos constitute the most disadvantaged groups in society.

THREAT TO PUBLIC EDUCATION

It is very important that we recognize what is at stake in the current crisis in urban education. It is not only the lives of the millions who inhabit the ghetto that are in jeopardy; in major respects, it is the public school system itself, the system which has been such an invaluable means for assimilating our nation's diverse social groups. Already in the 20 largest American cities, four out of every ten white students have fled the public schools. The Negro middle class is also deserting the public systems in record numbers; one in ten Negro children is now enrolled in a private school. If those whose social origins enable them to shape a positive climate for public education continue to leave the public schools, further deterioration of general education in the cities will be assured.

Is it possible to reverse these disintegrative forces in our city schools? I believe it is, and I am encouraged by the early effort to do so. No doubt we need more and deeper studies of many aspects of the phenomena which I have traced briefly, but I am convinced that we already possess enough knowledge to forge wiser and more effective policies and programs. The remedy, if not self-evident, is strongly implied by the evidence now in hand.

We must relieve the exaggerated and debilitating concentration of under-privileged students in the urban schools. The goal is obviously a long-term one, but we must be on with the job. Compensatory efforts to reduce the gap between the children of the slums and those of other neighborhoods must be continued and intensified, but they must serve the larger purpose, not become a substitute for action toward it.

Eventually, if we are successful in lowering the barriers which impede mobility out of the ghetto, natural forces alone should help to reduce the disproportionate burdens now levied on the central city schools. A major feature of the total program must be an end to discrimination in the sale or rental of housing. Last year, the Congress took historic action in this direction by passing potent legislation to curtail such discrimination. Gradually the opportunity for ghetto residents with adequate resources to acquire decent housing on equal terms with other citizens can do much to reduce the crushing pressures on housing and schools in the inner cities. But more immediate measures must also be taken.

PROMISE IN PRESENT EXPERIMENTS

I am hopeful that a variety of present experiments will prove useful in meeting these educational dilemmas. In several cities and states, cooperative arrangements are being explored through which individual schools or entire school districts in more fortunate areas will assist culturally deprived students and schools in the urban cores.

Ambitious efforts of this sort have been under way for some years in the Los Angeles Transport-a-Child program. In my own state of Massachusetts, the basis for similar efforts was laid by the passage, during my term as attorney general, of the Racial Imbalance Law, a statute designed to prevent perpetual de facto segregation. In the Boston area, organizations like the Metropolitan Council for Educational Opportunities and Project EXODUS have begun promising campaigns to correct such imbalances by placing disadvantaged children in better schools which have excess capacity.

Bussing remains a controversial notion, as the recurrent disputes across the country remind us, and the benefits and liabilities of such efforts are not yet adequately understood. But I believe that the initial experience with experiments of this kind justifies further trial. Most authorities who have examined these programs appear to share the view that they do no harm to children from social backgrounds which are supportive of educational attainment, and that they do substantial good for children from more deprived backgrounds.

In general it is preferable for programs of this nature to originate at the local level and to proceed on the basis of local initiative and leadership. The psychological environment is critical to the success of such ventures and there can be no substitute for sympathetic cooperation between the institutions and jurisdictions involved. However, I think we should give serious consideration to various incentives that the higher levels of government might offer to local school districts which undertake these efforts. Among other things, the superior fiscal resources of the federal government might reasonably be tapped to cover some of the additional costs engendered by bussing programs.

This is, of course, only one facet of a cluster of related problems, both educational and otherwise, which must be attacked as a whole. Yet, it is one of the cardinal issues with which you and your associates throughout our land must come to grips. Few challenges could provide so worthy a test of our mettle as a people and of our justice as a society.

When weighty problems mount and threaten to overwhelm an institution, there is always a danger that first principles will be forgotten in the momentary preoccupation with present difficulties. I believe this to be the case with the educational system today. There is a danger that too many of those with responsible roles may drift into disillusionment or cynicism. Contemplating hordes of deprived students, some teachers may begin to wonder whether education is destined to become merely "the opium of the people," as Marx once judged religion to be.

Such bitter judgments may be personally satisfying to some who relish a reputation for so-called "toughmindedness," but they miss the noble essence which persists in American education. Our education enterprise is at the very heart of our social mission. We need to recognize that, though vast and complex, this undertaking has shown progress, and the new knowledge we are acquiring reflects successes as well as failures.

A generation ago, for example, of every 1,000 children reaching the fifth grade, barely 300 finally graduated. By the 1960's, that balance had been decisively reversed. In 1967, 721 students graduated from high school for every 1,000 who had been fifth graders in 1959. Thus, the dropout problem is grave, but far less grave than it would have been without the intensive efforts and sizeable investment of the intervening years. Certainly no one should cite these figures as an indication that things are automatically improving. Quite the contrary. We still face a 35 to 40 percent dropout rate, which means that we are losing over *three-quarters of a million* potential graduates from each class. And, needless to say, dropouts fare poorly in our complicated, skill-oriented economy.

Similarly, there are some positive elements even in the picture of inner-city schools. Surveys by Johns Hopkins University personnel found that, in the 15 cities studied, ghetto schools were actually drawing teachers of above average qualifications. The teachers themselves were generally satisfied with their working conditions and rejected the demoralizing notion that youngsters in these schools were uneducable. They also reported that the parents of the students were fully as concerned about education, if not more so, than other parents, and that the parents considered teachers allies. To these educators, the poor environment and weak preparation were the main factors hindering their students. Discipline was not considered a paramount and all-consuming burden. In short, they saw their schools, not as blackboard jungles, but as institutions of limited but affirmative influence in a terribly difficult setting. That, it seems to me, is the kind of modest, hopeful attitude that must prevail if we are to identify and apply the reforms necessary to make our urban schools more effective.

They say that James Conant used to keep a figure of a turtle on his desk with a little sign that read: "The turtle never gets anywhere unless he sticks his neck out." Education, like the turtle, is embarked on a risky path and it, too, will have to stick its neck out, to take chances, to experiment with different concepts and techniques.

The task is formidable. Faint hearts will insist that it cannot be done. But we know better, for it is in accepting this challenge that we will rescue order and progress from the strife and reaction which threaten. It is in performing this task that we will replace social dissonance with domestic harmony. It is in educating our populace that we will raise a nation humane in outlook, exceptional in competence, and blessed with the self-respect which only a just society can provide.

The Quality Secondary School of the Future | 3

Harl R. Douglass

Never before in the history of American education has there been so much ferment in the minds of the public, so many proposals for new practices and so much criticism of current programs, so much experimentation, so much money available from the government or foundations or other sources for experimentation and new ideas, or so much controversy between the groups who urge different kinds of changes. Extremely vigorous campaigns are conducted for the use of team teaching, of teaching machines, programmed materials and closed circuit television. In many schools there have been more changes in the last ten or twelve years than in the fifty or sixty years previously.

Just where all the discussion, controversy, experimentations and changes of practice will lead no one is able to say with a great degree of certainty and accuracy. Nevertheless, out of the confusion, there seems to be strong trends, some of which will almost certainly be projected into the future but with different slopes—accelerated or decelerated. To identify these and to assign them to categories of different possibilities one must in addition to having studied them all somewhat carefully as they function in the school, view them with respect to their relative effectiveness and desirable modifications in different types of schools and different situations. One must also evaluate ideas and practices on the basis of a fairly complete knowledge of human nature—adolescents and adults—and upon a fairly sound and clear picture of current trends and probable changes in the next few decades in important areas of American life.

The secondary schools of the future will in many respects vary from one another. Excepting a few fundamental characteristics, they will not all be alike.

Sound predictions made on the basis of trends in 1966 are not merely linear projections of the 1966 trends, but must be constructed in the mind of the close student of current trends in the light of such things as follows:

1. the degree to which the practice has been successful in various types of schools, communities, grade levels and subjects;
2. the possibility that the trend has about spent itself;
3. the trend has proven or will prove eventually to be unwise and will be replaced by a counter trend.

From *Contemporary Education*, Vol. 39, No. 2 (November 1967), pp. 75-80. Reprinted by permission of the publisher and author.

The rapidity with which the sound trends will affect practice in different schools will vary because some schools are much more likely than others to take up and put into practice, effectively, new trends. These will be, as some are today, *pioneer quality* schools; they will be affected by most of these trends by 1970 or the early 1970's. Many sound or permanent trends will not be put into practice in these *cautious* quality schools until the early 1980's.

There are many ordinary schools which are fairly progressive but which do not wish to become conspicuous by reason of having a different program from better schools and with fewer modern features. Most current trends will be incorporated into practice in most of these schools only in the late 1980's or early 1990's.

SHIFTS IN PHILOSOPHY OF EDUCATION

There has been ferment, new interest, division, and shift and reverse shift with respect to the basic philosophy of education and its purposes, not only among educators, but among people in general, and a great division has developed. Parents are no longer content to send their children to school to learn only what is contained in school books, but they want the school to help their boys and girls grow in a variety of ways which will insure success and happiness in all respects of their life.

Many parents have given ostentatious lip service at least to great emphasis upon learning of facts of the types used on television and radio contests. Nevertheless, while not so ostentatiously, parents have in large numbers especially recently also become insistent upon more effective preparation for vocational success, for college, for good health, for the expenditure, pleasurably and honorably, of a great amount of time in leisure pursuits, for loyal and intelligent citizenship and for home life which contributes to developing wholesome ideals and character, intellectual skills, and wholesome interests.

More and more parents, educators, and the general public are coming to agree with John Ruskin, the great English essayist, who wrote in his *The Crown of the Wild Olives* in 1866, "Education is not so much coming to know what we ought to know as it is coming to behave as we ought to behave."

BETTER ADAPTATION TO THE INDIVIDUAL

There will be, as there are already in an increasing number of schools, a variety of types of adaptation of the instructional and learning materials to the individual.

1. *Ability grouping with class sections for the abler student, and class sections for the least able students.* (Not possible in the

smallest schools.) In most of the larger schools, there will be separate class sections of five levels of ability with the top level containing very outstanding students quite capable of studying with very little direction on the part of teachers, and in the lowest level group there will be students who will be taught in what we think of today as special education classes for "dull-normals."

2. *Special provision for the student of unusual creative ability in any field, e.g., art, science, shop, home economics, and mathematics, with a variety of plans employed in different schools.* In general, in schools the student will be permitted, encouraged, guided and helped to spend at least a third of his time in the field of his unusual creative ability and unusual creative interest and the rest of the time in subjects selected by him in conference with the counselor. The unusually creative student will not be required to meet the conventional requirements for graduation in terms of Carnegie units, but will be held to a passable standard of work in written and oral expression, in basic knowledge necessary for good citizenship, health, home living, leisure and elementary mathematics (arithmetic) along with very superior creative work in some field.

IDENTIFICATION OF THE BRIGHT, LEADER, CREATIVE, DULL AND NON-ACHIEVER

The secondary school of the future will do something that the typical school of twenty or thirty years ago was unable to do and in many districts today seems to be unable to do—*accurate identification of the learners who are deviates* from the great mass of ordinary students, since in the secondary school of the future there will be more and better trained counselors, who have had training in psychometry. A teacher of the subject and a counselor will consider carefully borderline and doubtful cases individually in a clinical fashion, considering a variety of pertinent information about these cases.

ENRICHMENT AND ACCELERATION

In the secondary school of the future there will be both enrichment and acceleration. Enrichment and acceleration will take the form of providing for the abler learner much appropriate material of a type only a bright child can do well, materials which challenge his superior abilities to learn, which provide learning experiences which will develop his unusual and precious potentiality. Acceleration will also provide for abler students the opportunity to go more rapidly through the schools. In the secondary school of the future there will be a great many bright youngsters completing the requirements for graduation at the age of sixteen and soon thereafter—some even earlier—and entering college or taking college subjects in high school at that age.

Educators in secondary schools will have discarded the superstition that the bright student who goes to college before the age of seventeen years is too immature, and that something bad is likely to happen to him. They will be building their practices in view of the findings of research which definitely proves that such is rarely the case.

Programmed learning materials and activities for teaching machines are not prepared for dull children nor for bright children. Educators working in the high school of the future will have realized that adequate provision for bright children cannot be made by rushing them through material selected primarily for average and slightly superior students and that adequate provision cannot be made either for dull or bright children by having them go slowly through such learning materials.

SPECIAL ATTENTION TO STUDENTS OF LOW CULTURAL LEVELS

Resulting in large part from federal interest and funds much experimentation is going on which will greatly improve the curriculum and methods of teaching for the young people coming from homes of low cultural levels. There will be new and different, especially adapted, content of courses in English, history, social studies, mathematics, and science and special counseling service for these underprivileged boys and girls who will otherwise be integrated with the other students in such school experiences as extra class activities and home rooms.

TEACHERS OF CLASSES OF EXCEPTIONAL YOUNGSTERS

Because of the great amount of time required for planning, teachers of the bright classes will have only four classes to teach, in five shorter periods a week, or five classes meeting only four times a week for longer periods. For similar reasons the teacher of classes of dull children will also be assigned fewer classes, probably only three classes, certainly no more than four, meeting five times a week for 60 to 65 minutes. For both types of students, appropriate teachers would be carefully selected on the basis of appropriate training and appropriate personalities for teaching that type of youngster.

To insure effective adjustment of learning materials and methods, all sections of abler students and all sections of dull students will be taught by teachers with personalities better suited than those of the average teacher and who have special training for teaching bright or for leading dull students.

MORE AND BETTER COUNSELING

The high school of the future will have at least one counselor for every 200 students or major fraction thereof with greatly improved counseling, as compared to the primitive concept of counseling that exists widely today, i.e., counseling is helping students select a vocation or get admitted to college.

All counselors will do things that only a minority of counselors do now. They will be doing much home visitation, conferring with parents, and acting as curriculum consultants to the various departments by reason of what they have learned from the students and information they have discovered at their homes.

In all but the schools enrolling less than 100 pupils per grade, there will be a variety of counselors specialized in different fields such as military service, jobs and placement, mental and physical health, problems of sex relationships, college selection and going, appearance and popularity problems, religious conflict problems, and miscellaneous personal problems, e.g., relations with parents, and fears.

BETTER PREPARATION FOR COLLEGE

Another characteristic of the high school of the future will be much more effective preparation for college Definitely abandoned will be the old superstition used as an alibi for not really doing the job of preparing young people for college, that preparation may be made by the accumulation of enough credits in designated subjects such as mathematics and foreign languages to meet the entrance requirements of colleges and universities. In recent years more than half of those who entered colleges or universities dropped out before they got a degree, and more than one-third completed no more than two years, and one-fifth no more than one year.

In the high school of the future, students will acquire (1) in each of a number of subject fields, e.g., science, mathematics and social studies, very definite and effective training in study skills and habits, (2) accurate and precise meanings of words which are important in the various areas of college subject matter, (3) a high level skill in numerical computation and mathematical problem solving, (4) skills in the use of resources of the library, (5) the abilities to express themselves well orally and in writing, (6) the ability to acquire accurately the ideas and facts as expressed by a lecturer, the use of individual tape recorders will have taken the place of note taking and (7) an interest in several subject matter fields. Furthermore, the teacher in the high school of the future will regard as a major responsibility the extension and encouragement of the interests of the students in his particular subject rather than to diminish the interest by undue pressure to get the subject matter facts and skills "learned" at least temporarily.

NATIONAL TESTING DE-EMPHASIZED

Students in few schools will take part in state or national testing or "assessment" programs, for administrators will then know what some have known for 25 or 30 years, (1) that *scores on such examinations have no significant relationships to the quality of the work done or grades made in college,* (2) *preparing students to do well on written tests causes leaders to abandon their role as educators to follow the will-o-wisp in the form of coaching youngsters to make good scores on tests.*

BETTER TRAINING IN STUDY SKILLS

In the high school of the future there will be more free periods for the youngsters to improve their skills in study and in using the library. The school day will be longer, 6 to 6½ hours exclusive of the lunch period, and more and more schools will have more free periods for the pupil to study at school.

Many more students will be doing more study of the type that can be done best in the library. Study rooms as well as libraries will be furnished with individual study carrels. Most of the study rooms will not be supervised by teachers but by non-certified aides at greatly reduced costs. An "after school" study period will be available for all students as will one or two teachers for each subject field.

VOCATIONAL STUDENTS AND GENERAL EDUCATION

The high school of the future will prepare all students except the least able to go to some college. Most of those following a vocational curriculum will earn at least twelve units of credits above the eighth grade in academic subjects. There will be no use made of such terms as "college-bound." The undemocratic and rather futile attempts to separate the sheep from the goats will have gone down memory lane along with fortune telling and astrology.

BETTER PREPARATION FOR JOBS

In the high school of the future there will be preparation for more types of jobs. Administrators will no longer be reluctant to offer vocational courses not subsidized by state and federal funds. Most schools of the future will prepare for at least ten or twelve, the larger schools for twenty or more, types of jobs for which potential dropouts and others can be prepared, including clerical and sales service, various types of food service, cosmetic services, and the lower level of occupations related to electronics. Furthermore, enrollments in diversified occupations and distributive education and in auto mechanics will also be greatly increased, probably quadrupled.

THE TEACHER OF THE FUTURE

The teacher in the high school of the future will have been much better prepared for first class professional work than the teacher of previous generations. Not only will he have finished at least thirty-five semester hours in his broad field of specialization such as history and the social studies, English, physics and mathematics, physical and biological science, physics and chemistry, but some ten to fifteen hours of work in each of several areas of the broad fields, e.g., English grammar, speech and forensics or dramatics, English literature and American literature, although in some narrower fields such as mathematics or a foreign language some will have only twenty-five to thirty semester hours of college work, beyond two years in high school.

The teacher in the high school of the future will have a good broad general education including many courses which were taught as *general education* as opposed to specialized education, rather than for the purpose of preparing underclassmen to major and become a specialist in some narrow field.

Furthermore, the teacher in the high school of the future will have been better and more broadly prepared professionally to discharge his responsibilities and his opportunities as an educator. He will have acquired a carefully conceived concept of the objectives of education both for the benefit of the individual and for the benefit of his nation, an extensive knowledge of the nature of the adolescent and his interests, of his social habits, of his methods of learning, testing, and evaluation of growth and progress in general and in his field of specialization.

REMUNERATION

The teacher in the quality high school of the future will have started his work at a salary not less than $6,000 in 1970, $7,000 in 1980. He will have increases at least $1,000 every four or five years until his salary reaches $10,000 to $12,000, $15,000 to $18,000 for the most outstanding teachers in wealthy districts, regardless of where he teaches—North or South—large school or small school—unless a majority of a committee appointed to make recommendations consisting of another teacher in the same field, the head of the department, a counselor, and the principal or assistant principal and the director of secondary education or the director of instruction or assistant superintendent of schools in secondary education recommends against promotion to the next five year bracket.

NEW FEATURES OF MASTER SCHEDULES

In the secondary school of the future the master schedule will look quite different. In the first place, there will be more periods per week and per day. The school day of six periods of approximately 55 minutes each will be retained in only a few schools—a vestigial relic of days gone by.

There will also have disappeared the illogical practice of scheduling practically all classes for five periods a week, an outmoded practice for which the schools of the United States have been unique. Bright students will be taught in shorter or in fewer periods per week, as we now know that for bright students to work well they need to be in the presence of the teacher for a smaller amount of time than do the other students. For dull students, however, the class periods will be longer.

In the large schools the use of computers will be used in the construction of the master school schedule and in a much smaller number of schools—very large ones—in construction of student individual schedules.

In the typical high school of the future there will be an opportunity period as part of the longer school day in which special attention will be given by designated teachers for assistance to students in each field of study who are in need of much help in connection with their work, e.g., dull students, under-achievers, returned absentees, potential drop-outs, and some bright students working on projects rather independently. Teachers to whom this responsibility will be assigned will be selected on the basis of their ability to adapt to the needs of the student and the quality and quantity of the help which they are able to give. In this opportunity period there will be offered special instructions by specially qualified teachers for designated students in reading vocabulary development, and in mathematical computation.

STUDENT LOAD AND TEACHER LOAD

In the high school of the future the students of average learning ability will carry at least five full units of work, some five-and-a-half, the abler students six, and some even six-and-a-half, and thus provide for acceleration through school. This heavier student load will be practical in a day when few students work after school and the social day is longer.

Being relieved in the future high school of supervision of study rooms, supervision of halls and given generous aid in connection with mimeographing and other clerical help, the instructor teaching twenty-two to twenty-five periods a week, depending upon the subject taught, with classes of not more than twenty-five students will most likely have a lighter load than the typical secondary school teacher of today.

There will be some larger sections, some with as many as 40 to 50 students, maybe 75 to 100 in typewriting, in each of which there will be at least an effective non-certified aid to assist as a specialist in routine tasks and in assistance to the individual student. Occasional well-prepared lectures will be given to much larger groups, e.g., seventy five to two hundred students.

BETTER RELATIONS WITH THE PUBLIC

For certain rather obvious reasons there will be a much greatly improved program of public relations. By 1980 more than 40 billion dollars a year will be spent by the public on their schools and the people will want to know and to understand what they are getting for the $500 per adult they will pay annually in local, state and federal taxes for education. As more new materials and methods of learning are employed it will be necessary to spend great efforts in developing understanding, confidence and good will.

Very few of the parochial schools and only a small minority of the private schools will be able to find the financial backing to produce a school equal to greatly improved secondary public schools. Even if tuition is raised to the point of excluding the great majority of young people, there will not be enough funds except in very heavily endowed schools available to provide a school equal to the typical high schools of the future In many of the high schools of the future there will be students from parochial schools in attendance on a half-time basis.

The nonpublic school of the future will serve chiefly "problem" students whose parents think that they need to attend a boarding school with close supervision, who attach more importance to religious bias than to better education, who attach excessive importance to very small ratio of students to teachers, or who wish to have attendance at a nonpublic school serve a social and economic status symbol though even many well-to-do fathers will want their sons to attend public high schools.

Teachers and counselors of the secondary school of the future will visit homes at times when both parents can be present, especially those who cannot be persuaded to come to school. Home visitation will have become an important part of guidance and public relations, much of it in the evening when daddy is home.

part two

The PRINCIPAL

The Secondary
School
Principalship

II

chapter overview

As goes the principal, so goes the school

As the secondary school principalship emerges in the seventies, it is undergoing rapid and turbulent change. Those serving in the position might feel as if it is the "eye" of the educational hurricane. One thing for certain, it's a new ball game. This is where the action is.

The first article in this chapter vividly demonstrates the unique demands of urban education. Luvern L. Cunningham reports it as he saw it. It causes one to pause and reflect on the competencies necessary to successfully function in the principalship.

The administrative hierarchy in American public education is being severely challenged in a period of unprecedented change. Fenwick English analyzes the current trends in education and their effects on the principalship. He emphatically declares the need for administrative leadership to "clean its own house and recognize its own recalcitrance as a major obstacle to the maintenance of that leadership."

Identification, recruitment, and training of competent administrative leaders is essential for the attainment of America's educational goals. Donald C. Weaver examines some of the conditions affecting change in our secondary schools. He predicts that competent leadership in this new era will exemplify to a high degree technical, human, and conceptual skills, especially the latter.

The role of the black school administrator in our educational system is not a new one, but it too is caught up in the swirl of change. Hugh J. Scott probes the underlying problems and concerns of the black school administrator. He offers thirteen commandments for black administrators. Many of his "Do's and Don'ts" provide a handy and practical reference for white school administrators.

Do you have the IFD Disease—"from Idealization to Frustration, to Demoralization"? Robert T. McGee is alerting all school administrators to the possible causes of the disease (administrator's syndrome). His thoughts are not a panacea for curing the disease, but a guide to more effective administrative leadership.

"Don't worry—only the worst become administrators." Thomas Ford Hoult describes his personal experience in a meeting with a group of secondary school administrators. The author challenges administrators to "assess themselves and their policies in the light of meaningful democratic standards and to institute needed reform."

Food for thought for educators is provided in the article by Robert S. Thurman. Must the principal be replaced? If so, why?

Hey, Man, You Our Principal? Urban Education as I Saw It

4

Luvern L. Cunningham

This is a report. It is as objective as I can make it. The remarks that follow are based on a few days' experience as principal of an inner-city junior high school—a problem-saturated place.

I want it known that although what I say here is critical, it is not intended to be critical of any person or group of persons. But it is an indictment of us all—educators and laymen, critics and the criticized.

The notion of an exchange cropped up out of the woodwork. Someone had an idea that this would be a good thing to do. The big-city people agreed and we agreed and so we were off and running. We didn't have the luxury of much advanced planning time. Had we had a chance to contemplate the event in Columbus (in the peace and quiet and solitude of the ivory tower) we could have lost our courage and copped out on the whole deal. We didn't have that time, so we did appear at our respective schools at the appointed hour, Monday, May 5. On that fateful morning (like little kids going to kindergarten) we picked up our pencil boxes and marched off to the school house.

I arrived at about 7:45 A.M. I had read about the city's riots in 1966 and I knew it was near here that they had started. I was aware too that this was a junior high that had been having its share of trouble. I knew that the faculty had walked out in January in protest of school conditions. Most of the faculty stayed away for two days, saying that this school was an unfit place in which to carry on professional activity.

My first several minutes as the new helmsman were exciting, to say the least. I walked in through the front door and introduced myself to the regular principal's secretary. She was most cordial and smiled knowingly. I think she chuckled to herself, thinking that this guy is really in for an education. If those were her feelings she was quite right.

I walked into the office and was about to set my briefcase down. I looked up and there must have been 20 faces, most of them black, all around. And others were coming through the office door. Some were students, some were faculty members with students in tow, others were clerks who wanted me to make some monumental decisions about events of the day.

From *Phi Delta Kappan* (November 1969), pp. 123-128. Reprinted by permission of the publisher and author.

They weren't even in line. They were all just kind of standing around there competing for attention. And to make life more exciting a little black fellow with a flat hat and a cane about two feet long came up to me. He whipped that cane around on his arm and stuck it in my stomach and said, "Hey, man, you our principal?" I began thinking longingly of Columbus and said, "Well, no, I'm not. But I'm here for a week and I'm going to be taking his place." I was backpeddling and trying to think of some answer that would make sense to this eighth-grade student.

A number of youngsters who were crowding around were just curious; others had problems. One was a girl who had recently been released from a correctional institution and was under court order to come back to school. She was there for an appointment, but she didn't want to come back to this or any other school. She was openly hostile, asking harshly that she not be made to come back. I had no file. I didn't have any background on this young lady. I was unprepared to make a decision. So instead of displaying administrative genius, I said, "Would you sit down over there and I'll talk to you later." She sat—head down, sullen, oblivious to the confusion surrounding us. It was an hour before I got back to her problem.

There was tragedy and comedy. A teacher who was obviously disturbed about something had a very attractive 16-year-old girl by the hand. She came in and said, "I understand you're the new principal, Mr. Cunningham. Look at that skirt. Look at that mini-skirt. It's entirely too short. Just look at that thing. I think we ought to send her home. Aren't you going to send her home?"

She turned to the girl and said, "Is your mother home?" The girl said "No." "When will she be home?" "Well, she'll be home about 6:15 tonight."

The teacher turned to me and said, "We can't send her home." Then she marched the girl over in front of me, rolled that brief skirt up several inches and said, "Look at that, it's got a hem in it. It's got a hem in it that long. We ought to be able to take that hem out. Let's go back to the classroom." I didn't have a chance to say a word.

In the meantime other kids were still clustered around. They had their own brand of problems so I said, "Would you go and wait outside the office please and come in one at a time?" They kept coming in with their questions, some that I could answer, most that I could not.

When the first bell rang and the students had to go to their homerooms, faces disappeared, the corridors cleared a bit, and there was an atmosphere of temporary calm. I was able to sit down and try to get my bearings. It was an inauspicious beginning, to say the least.

Let me comment a bit about Lester Butler. Lester was assigned to the principal's office. His responsibility was to be available during free periods for phone calls, delivery of messages, and any other tasks that might appropriately be handled by an eager, intelligent seventh-grader. After quiet had been established in the office on that first day he gave me a quick tour of the building. He took me to the obvious places like the library, the auditorium, the gymnasium, and special classrooms, but he also pointed out the nooks and crannies, the special recesses, the hideaways of the old structure. With his special brand of radar he was able to track me down and bring messages to me during the week when I was about the building. We became unusually fine friends.

This junior high school building is old. The oldest part was built 65 years ago. It has had two additions. Despite its age the building has been refurbished from time to time; it was painted and the windows were in. It's not particularly unattractive from the inside, but as a structure to house education it's a nightmare of inefficiency. Traffic patterns are unbelievable. You have to go upstairs to get downstairs. You go upstairs across a kind of plateau and down the other side to reach another part of the building. The arrangements for science and home economics facilities, as well as classrooms housing other particular specialized aspects of the curriculum, do not accommodate decent traffic patterns. When the bell sounds and classes pass it is a wild place. It's wild in between times, too, for that matter.

The absentee rate is very high. Of the nearly 1,800 enrolled, between 350 and 400 were absent every day. Where they were no one really knows. There was no apparent relationship between my presence and the absentee rate; that's the way it is every day. During my first day a counselor took me in his car and just crisscrossed the neighborhood. He wanted to point out the housing, the neighborhood, the fact that the streets were crowded with humanity just milling around. It was a warm week, the first week in May. People were outside. Kids of all ages were all over. There appeared to be as many youngsters on the street as there were in the elementary school and the junior and senior highs.

Ironically, everybody shows up during the lunch period. The lunches are partly financed with federal funds and the youngsters are admitted to the lunchroom by ticket. Kids who are truant get into the building (despite door guards) and into the cafeteria. They have something to eat and then melt into the community.

The building is a sea of motion—people are moving about all the time. Adults (teachers, teaching assistants, observers, student teachers, door guards, other people who get in through the doors despite the guards) and students are in the halls all the time. Some of the students have passes to go somewhere given by somebody, but most students are just there. Those who don't have passes have excuses. As a newcomer seeing all of this motion, what should I have done?

Should I have gotten tough? Should I have tried to shout them back to class? Should I have threatened such and such? Or should I have turned my head and let them go on about their own purposes? I turned my head.

When I was in my office students would come in with all sorts of questions, grievances, or requests for excuses. Apparently the pattern in the building is that if you can't get a hearing for your complaint anywhere else you end up in the principal's office. I had a steady flow of customers.

The school has 85 teachers. There is a high absence rate each day among teachers too. They fail to show up for many reasons. The teacher absentee numbers (while I was there) would range from 11 to 14 per day. If you have a faculty of 85 and 14 teachers fail to show (and you don't get substitutes), you have to make some kind of ad hoc arrangements quickly to handle the crises. Each day three to five substitutes would appear and they would be assigned quickly to cover classes. But they were not enough. Furthermore, there was little relation between the substitutes' teaching fields and their assignments. The first priority is to put live people in classes to maintain some semblance of order.

The youngsters, as I said, were in motion. I had the feeling that I was walking on a live volcano. Classes were often noisy and rowdy. Fights and squabbles broke out frequently. Fights between girls occurred about five to one more often than fights among boys. But the fights among the girls were often over boys. The adult population was on pins and needles from the time the building opened in the morning until school was out at 3:30 in the afternoon. Everyone hoped to make it through the day without large-scale violence.

The day is organized around eight periods. Students have a number of free periods, during which time they are assigned to study halls. Some go to a large auditorium; others go to classrooms with teachers assigned to study hall duty there. Large numbers congregate in the cafeteria on the ground floor for "study." The cafeteria accommodates around 300 youngsters. Teachers are reluctant to supervise the cafeteria study halls. When they do it is with fear and trembling. The place is noisy. Kids move around despite the efforts of several teachers to keep them seated. They shoot craps. Some play other games. There is bickering and fighting. Kids pick up chairs and fling them across the room at one another. It's dirty and hot.

The whole building is hot, because the custodians cannot shut off the heat. It is the only way to provide hot water for the lunch program. So they keep the stokers going to have hot water for the federally subsidized lunches. Everybody complains about it: the principal, the assistant principals, the teachers, the students, and the PTA.

The lunchroom study halls are unbearable. The undermanned custodial staff is unable to keep the table tops clean; a slimy film covers them. They are neither attractive for eating nor for study purposes. Because of the danger of intruders coming in off the streets, the major cafeteria emergency exit has been nailed shut. Teachers asked the principal to have the custodians do this. The custodians refused because of fire regulations. In desperation the principal himself nailed it shut. Each day he lives in fear that a fire will break out and students will be trapped. Large numbers might not get out through the narrow passageways that serve as entrances and exits. Thus a measure taken to protect the teachers could lead to another type of disaster.

We called the police only once during my stay. It was different at another junior high school where my colleague Lew Hess served as principal. At night following his first day a fire bomb was thrown through his office window. It was a dud and didn't go off. On his last day three fire bombs were thrown inside the building and they did go off. The police and fire department had to be summoned each time.

On the second day, in a classroom study hall right across from my office, a young boy was late. His name was Willy Denton. He was about a minute and a half tardy and his excuse was that he had been next door signing up for a special program of summer employment. The study hall supervisor had obviously had a hectic morning. As Willy entered the room a few words were exchanged. The supervisor grabbed Willy, put a hammerlock around his neck, kind of choked him, and wrestled him out into the corridor. The noise attracted other kids. Immediately there were about 40 students as well as door guards right around the teacher and Willy. Willy got free for a moment but the supervisor caught him again, this time grabbing him by the shoulders. He shook him against the lockers and that was like whomping a big bass drum. The sound reverberated around that part of the building and more people came. The supervisor got a fresh hammerlock on Willy, dragged him over to my office, threw him in and across to the other side, and said, "Take charge."

I suppose that I turned whiter in that sea of black, but I took charge. I closed the door and asked Willy to sit down. All of a sudden another teacher opened the door about six inches and shouted, "Willy's got a good head on his shoulders," slammed the door, and left.

It was about 12 noon. The period had just started. There were nearly 35 minutes until Willy was to go to another class. So Willy and I just talked. I didn't think that lining him up for swats would make much difference. He was livid. If he had been white he would have been purple. He was furious, and so we just sat and talked.

We talked about what he liked and what he disliked. I asked him if he had worked last summer, since he was going to be employed this coming summer. He said that he had. I asked where and he said, "I worked in a church." And he added, "You know I teach Sunday school." I asked how old his class members were and he said, "Well they're about the same age as I am." "How many do you have?" "About 15, and sometimes I teach on Saturdays too." "Do you like to teach?" He said, "Well, it's okay. But boy those first Sundays my stomach just kind of turned around and I didn't know what I was doing. But it's better now. Like last Sunday, did you hear about that plane that was shot down in Korea? You know, we just talked about that. I sat down and we talked about that."

It was clear that Willy loved what he was doing in Sunday School. He liked math too and he planned to go to high school. But he was so angry at that study hall supervisor. He trembled for several minutes; he just couldn't get control. We talked through the balance of the hour till the bell rang. I sent him on to his next class sans swats.

The PTA leaders same in to meet with me on Wednesday. They shared their definitions of the school's problems. I held a faculty meeting on Thursday. And I was amazed at the similarity between faculty and parent sentiments on the issues facing the school.

The teachers, by and large, are a very dedicated lot. Many of them are young; some of them are coming out of MAT programs. Despite their youth they, like the rest of the faculty, are tired, disheartened, even despondent. But they don't want to fail.

One of the teachers was shot 10 days before I arrived on the scene. He missed his lunch break and went across the street to get a coke and a bag of potato chips. Coming back he was held up on the street and shot with a pellet gun. He came back into the building, walked into the principal's office, with his hand pressed against his side. Blood was spewing between his fingers and he said, "I'm shot, I'm shot, I'm shot." The principal called an ambulance and got him to the hospital. But he was back teaching while I was there, with the pellet still in him. He hadn't had time to have it taken out. He was going to the hospital that weekend to have the bullet removed.

I tried to visit classes and meet teachers. As I became known around the building, it was rather like walking down the hall and being attacked by aardvarks. Teachers would come out, grab me by the arm, pull me back into the teachers' lounge or their classrooms, and say, "Let me tell it like it is here." Every one of them had deep feelings for the school and for the kids, but an inability to define the specific changes that would make a difference. Their intense desire to solve the school's problems mixed with overwhelming despair is one of the powerful impressions that remains with me as a consequence of those days.

In many ways it is an overmotivated but underprepared staff. As one young fellow who came in March said, "This is an overpeopled and understaffed school. We've got lots of special people running around under federal grants doing their particular thing. But they don't fit into any kind of mosaic that has meaning for solving the problems of the school."

Many teachers have the too-little-and-too-late kind of feeling. No one is apologetic about it. There is no sense of humiliation about being assigned to the school. But most of them want to get out because they feel that it is an absolutely hopeless situation, that they can't afford to spend whatever psychic energy they have in fighting a losing battle. Even though they are emotionally committed to the place they still want to leave. So the turnover rate is high. Some youngsters had had several different teachers in some of their classes since the beginning of the year.

After the early chaos of my first morning I was able to visit a class being taught by a Peace Corps returnee. She was a young woman with an MAT degree. She had two adults with her in the room assisting with the youngsters. And it was pandemonium. She was trying to teach social studies. She was obviously searching desperately to locate something that might motivate or have some interest for 15 seventh-graders. Her Peace Corps assignment had been in Africa, so she was showing slides of how people construct thatched cottages there. It was something she knew about first-hand—she had been on the scene. But the kids tuned her out. They were making funny remarks and fighting.

One of the other adults in that room was a young man, a practice teacher who had arrived that morning. He had already been slugged twice by students before my 11 A.M. visit. I talked with him later in the week trying to find out whether he was going to give up or stick around. I had to admire his tenacity. He was going to stay; he wasn't going to be licked by that set of events.

During the lunch hour a group of seventh-grade teachers who were cooperating in a transitional program (transitional from the sixth grade into junior high) were meeting for a planning session. I was invited to sit in. The young Peace Corps returnee came in with a tear-stained face. She just couldn't manage her situation. She didn't know what to do. She had to go back and face those classes that afternoon and the next day and the next. She had been advised by the principal and by others to turn in her chips and move to another school. But she just wouldn't do it. She had been fighting it since September, facing failure all year long, but she just would not give up. Others like her were having similar experiences.

The curriculum at this junior high is archaic, outmoded, irrelevant, and unimportant in the minds of the kids who are there. The faculty has agreed for the most part that this is true. But no one is able to design a pattern of change which will remedy or act upon all of the deficiencies that are so prominent in the program of studies. Because of the way the building is constructed (room sizes, locations, and the like) they are locked into an eight-period day. There just are not enough classrooms to handle a six-period organization. Furthermore, there is ambiguity about who is responsible for curriculum reform. Everyone wants change but no one knows how to achieve it.

They were administering the Stanford Achievement Test the week I was there. Large numbers of kids couldn't read it. Many couldn't even read the name of the test. Some of them would mark all of the alternative responses; some wouldn't mark any; some would just casually draw pictures on the test; some would stare; others would raise their hands and ask for help from those who were monitoring the testing.

A few teachers raised the question with me, "Why test?" It is a good question. Or why use that kind of testing for youngsters in a junior high school like this one? Apparently standardized testing is a system-wide requirement which may have had historical significance and is continued merely because no one has considered not doing it.

As I have said, most of the teachers' energy goes into control. I found few classrooms where I could say with any confidence that there was excitement relative to learning. The only place where I saw interest and motivation and product was in home economics, which enrolls both boys and girls. In other areas interest and motivation appeared to be near zero. It seems to me that the traditional school "subjects" have to be very carefully analyzed in terms of some relevancy criterion.

We toss that word around a great deal—relevance. It's in everybody's language. It has reached cliché status more rapidly than most similar words in our professional jargon. Nevertheless, there is some meaning there.

When I ask myself what would be relevant to the young people at this school I reach an impasse very quickly. It is hard to know what is relevant. Certainly it ties to motivation. If we were insightful enough to know what the prominent motivations are among such young people, then maybe we could organize a program of studies in keeping with interest areas. The program might look quite unlike the traditional subject-centered arrangement in these schools.

I mentioned earlier the "leakage" of the building, both inside out and outside in. The staff walkout in January, 1969, took place because the school was an unsafe place in which to teach. The Board of Education responded by putting door guards on the doors. The measure was to protect teachers and student from a range of intruder types. It was also to control students coming in and going out during the day. The guards have helped a bit in keeping invaders out of the building, but this move hasn't solved the pupil "leakage" problem. An outsider (or an insider for that matter) will cause a disturbance at one of the doors. Door guards come quickly from their posts to help out, leaving their own stations unattended. Other kids will then open the unprotected doors and run out or run in, whichever suits their fancy.

Administrators and teachers resort to corporal punishment. The chief vehicle for control is the swat system. The teachers worked out a scheme to improve control following the January walkout. Teachers volunteer to help with discipline in the "gym balcony," a little area overlooking the gymnasium. During free periods kids who have misbehaved, for whatever reason, are brought there. They queue up, outside, both boys and girls, waiting to be swatted. Teachers take their turns up there in the gym balcony. Similar disciplinary lineups occur outside of the office doors of the three assistant principals, who have paddles or razor straps hanging from their belts. If they need to use them in the corridors they do.

Disciplinary cases are brought first to their door. If they or the principal are too busy, in juvenile court or at home with a case of nerves or whatever it might be, then the students go to the gym balcony to get their swats. Afterward they go back to class or study hall or library or get out of the building.

I didn't administer corporal punishment. I don't know whether I was psychologically capable of it. I don't think I could have forced myself. Teachers on a few occasions brought students to my office. One teacher just threw them in, saying "Take charge" and leaving.

There doesn't seem to be any intrinsic motivation, any way of appealing to the interests of pupils to stay and learn. So everyone (adults and students) adjusts to the corporal punishment routine. No one likes it; no one wants it. Teachers hate it; the principals hate it. But they have no other alternative. They have not been able to discover any better control measure.

And now about death. There is an astonishing callousness about death among the students here. One of them had been killed a few days earlier. He was shot in a car wash down the street. I have mentioned the shooting of the teacher; fortunately that did not end in death. There were other shoot-outs in the neighborhood ending in fatalities. Lester Butler, on my last day, sought an excuse to attend a funeral. I asked for particulars. He said, "It's for my friend's father. He was killed a week ago. He was shot right outside the school. I want to attend the funeral. I'll come right back after it's over." I wrote the excuse.

Lester described the event without emotion, with placidness, with matter-of-factness. Death is a part of life here. Life is filled with its own brand of violence. Its violence is routine. It is not necessarily racial. It is grounded in hate which feeds upon itself. It is cancerous and spreads and spreads and spreads.

The cancer of hate is latent within the student body. You sense its power. You sense its presence and the prospect for its release at any moment. You do not know when it will burst forth and cascade around you. It is everywhere; it is nowhere. Lester sensed that the school was a powder keg. He would even try to describe it to me in his own way.

In many ways life at this junior high is a charade. People go about the business of routine schooling. Teachers laugh and smile. They walk through the corridors ignoring the rowdiness. They try at times, half-heartedly, to establish a bit of order. The administrative staff takes the problem more seriously; they shout and cajole and urge and plead. The counselors do their thing. They talk with students. They describe worlds of glitter and gold. The students squirm and stare and ignore. The counselors' cubicles, tucked away here and there, are temporary refuges from the storm.

I was impressed with the door guards. They try. They understand the charade. Many of them have played the game for a lifetime. They represent well the male image. They are for the most part young, strong, handsome. They are on the side of the angels. That is, they try to support the purposes of the school. They work closely with teachers and administrative officials. They do their job. It involves keeping hoodlums off the street out of the building, avoiding physical encounters but not turning away from them. There is no training for their positions. They must exercise amazing discretion every minute of the day. Most of them have little formal education. But they have established a bond with the professional staff that is harmonious and marked by mutual respect. Each day I issued up a silent prayer of thanks that they were there.

What to do about this school? And other similar junior highs in other places? An archaic building, a largely uncaring community, an irrelevant program of studies, a student population that is out of hand, an underprepared, overpressured staff, a sympathetic but essentially frustrated central administration, a city that wishes such schools would go away. A proposal from the staff and administrators was to burn the school down. Destroy it. Get the symbol out of the neighborhood. This was more than a half-serious proposal.

Short of that, what can be done? This question haunted me during my stay. What could be done? Only a few feeble proposals occurred to me.

I would argue for complete building-level autonomy. The principal and faculty should run the show without concern for other places. They should be allowed to organize the program of studies without adherence to district-wide curriculum guides and the like. The principal should be free to select his own faculty without reference to certification. He should look for talented people anywhere and everywhere. They could be found across the street or across the nation. The principal should build his own budget and make internal allocations in terms of the faculty and staff's definition of need.

More radically, I would ask that the principal be given complete control over time. That is, he should be able to open and close the school at will. If in his judgment events are getting out of hand, he should have the power—indeed be expected—to close the school down for a day, a week, or a month. During the time the building is closed, all of the adults in the school, in cooperation with students and community leaders, should focus on the problems that are over-whelming them. They should develop a problem-solving ethos. They should include genuine and substantial neighborhood participation. They should zero in on questions one by one, work them through and seek solutions. The state, the city, and the central school ad-ministration should support but not interfere. What is required in schools like these is a set of solutions. There is no justification for keeping the building open simply to observe the state code.

The staff should be kept on during the summer. Give them an air-conditioned retreat; allow them to plan for the year ahead. Work on the program of studies, work on motivation, work on community linkage, work on patterns of staffing, work on everything.

It occurred to me that it might be wise for the boys and girls to be separated—have boys' schools and girls' schools. There are some research data to support this recommendation. I remembered a study in Illinois that I directed a few years ago. There we tried to discover the impact of segregated learning on achievement. We ex-amined a small district where youngsters were feeding into one junior high school out of white schools, black schools, and integrated schools. We were interested in such factors as pupil alienation, atti-tudes toward schooling, and achievement in the traditional subject fields. We discovered some significant differences, but the over-whelming difference was how boys responded to the learning en-vironments in contrast with how girls responded. The boys were getting the short end of the stick on most things.

Systems should depress the emphasis on attendance. I would even support abandoning compulsory education for this part of the city. Emphasize programs of interest and attractiveness; de-empha-size regimentation. Much of the faculty's energy goes into keeping kids in school. And once in school, keeping them in class. Why fight it? Jettison the pressure toward control. Enroll students on the basis of interest only. Such policies violate the rich American tradi-tion of education for everyone, but why carry on the charade? Why?

Again I want it understood that I came away from this school with profound admiration and respect for the regular principal, the three assistant principals, the several counselors, the many teachers, and the many special staff members, as well as the central admini-stration. And I came away with respect for the students. The adults in the building are struggling feverishly. They are dedicated. They are in their own way in love with the school. But they are shell-shocked, exhausted, and desperate. They need help but they are not sure what kind of help. And I am not sure. I have advanced a few notions but they need careful scrutiny and considerable elaboration.

It is clear that we have no experts in this sort of urban education anywhere. The most expert may be those professionals who are there every day engaging in the fray. But they are reaching out, and it is for this reason that some kind of liaison with universities and other sources of ideas is critical. Refined, umbilical relationships need to be developed. We are just scratching the surface at Ohio State. No one has *the* answer. Anyone who thinks he has is a fool. At best there are only partial answers—pieces of a larger mosiac that could at some point in the future fit together in a more productive fashion than today's mosaic.

There are many schools in America like the one I have described. We don't want to admit it but there are. And all of us who bear professional credentials must carry that cross.

Such educational institutions are an indictment of presidents and senators; of justices and teachers; of governors and legislators. It is ludicrous the way we behave. Our pathetic politicians wailing and wringing their hands, spouting platitudes and diatribes. They advance shallow excuses. They say that bold acts will not find favor with unnamed constituencies. And we educators stand impotent, frightened, disheveled in the face of such tragedy.

The Ailing Principalship

5

Fenwick English

Extraordinary pressures buffeting educational systems today have cast the principalship into troubled waters, with the distinct possibility that given the present trends it will become little more than a figurehead role in the future. Some of these trends are teacher boycotts, urban rioting and the demands by minority groups for equal educational opportunities, the explosion of knowledge, the insatiable appetite of the educational system for technical expertise and specialization, and the paralysis of large-city school systems in dealing with these issues.

The nature of the conflict suggests that the organizational structure of American public education is undergoing tremendous strains in a period of unprecedented transition and controversy. Principals have been the target of militant teachers and organized parent groups advocating all types of changes in their schools; they have been treated like ugly ducklings in negotiations between lay boards and teachers. Generally, principals and principals' professional associations have reacted defensively and negatively to the winds of change. Both the NASSP (National Association of Secondary School Principals) and DESP (Department of Elementary School Principals) are currently considering withdrawal from the NEA over that organization's emerging militancy. At the state level, many principals' groups are separating from the mother teacher associations, or are considering such changes.

Principals do not seem to understand that many of the urgent reforms of public education mean changing the bureaucratic structure to allow it to respond to societal pressures which it is currently unable or unwilling to meet. They find themselves, on one hand, cheering for teachers in their battles for better working conditions and pay; on the other they are deeply anxious about their own position in the struggle. It is difficult for principals to realize that it is their position which holds the old autocratic organization together and thus provides it stability. It is also a barrier of the first magnitude to democratization and reform when the structure exhibits senility. By continuing to withdraw towards entrenched positions and away from teacher demands to be involved in the decision-making process, principals fall into the trap of defending the status quo and abandoning any claims for leadership. By denying the necessity

From *Phi Delta Kappan*, Vol. 50 (November 1968), pp. 158-161. Reprinted by permission of the publisher and author.

for changing themselves, they preserve the rigor mortis of the educational bureaucracy.

One of the greatest shocks to principals, one gathers from the backroom and assembly conversations at their conventions and meetings, has been the fact that they have been left out of the negotiating process while new links of power have been formed within the educational structure. Discovering their impotence has come as a severe psychological blow. Principals were actually ignorant of their value to the educational enterprise. Rather than forge new organizational links that would strengthen and enhance their leadership capabilities, they have turned their backs upon answers provided by research and have fought for legal sanctions and immunity from reform by polishing up negotiating procedures to preserve their positions. Thus they are severed from being partners in organizational transition and run the risk of becoming obsolete. One cannot lead by isolating himself from his constituents and the issues of the day.

The development of education in this country was once tightly controlled by private corporations or church groups. Lay citizens possessed and exercised direct authority over their schools. As school systems expanded, it became impossible to control the emerging tasks of the schools directly, and the superintendency was created from the principalship to deal with the board of education. Superintendents in turn delegated many of their administrative chores to the principal, who was called a "headmaster" or principal teacher. These duties consisted of regulation of pupil discipline and grade progression, distribution of materials, school safety and cleanliness, and enforcement of various rules and regulations upon the teaching staff. The model or organization which developed is an example of what Gouldner has labeled the "punishment-centered" type of bureaucracy.[1] Its chief characteristic is that authority within the system rests solely in the hands of the administration. Authority within this system becomes attached to positions, not to individuals,[2] and is called "formal" by Anderson.[3] It is not rooted in technical competence and is limited to hierarchical position within the organization. The desire for absolute control by lay boards and their administrative leaders, plus the generally low level of technical competence possessed by teachers when entering the profession, produced a "formal " bureaucracy. As it grew it crystallized around the concept of the teacher as a subprofessional. Various other roles were created to "help" the teacher, such as supervisors, consultants, coordinators, vice-principals, and principals.

1. Alvin W. Gouldner, *Patterns of Industrial Bureaucracy* (Glencoe, Ill.: The Free Press, 1954).
2. Robert Bierstadt, "An Analysis of Social Power," *American Sociological Review*, December, 1950.
3. James G. Anderson, "Bureaucratic Rules: Bearers of Organizational Authority," *Educational Administration Quarterly*, Winter, 1966.

In reviewing one of the problems of bureaucracies, that of adaptability, Bennis[4] notes that it "thrives in a highly competitive undifferentiated, and stable environment." The administration provides the stability via organizational rules and task routinization, the undifferentiated teaching positions provide the raw material, and the competition for administrative positions assures organizational conformity. We have built-in candidates for the pyramidal authority structure. "Actions of teachers become directed toward the maintenance of vested interests, which means adhering to exisiting procedures and resisting innovations or changes inimical to the status or advantage of the individual teacher."[5]

The American teacher today works in an undifferentiated organization. He is advanced not by expertise but by time served. He is considered an interchangeable part. Regardless of competence, teachers are rewarded in exactly the same manner and receive exactly the same instructional responsibilities no matter what their training or experience. The structure of education is indifferent to the individual talents of teachers. This is so despite occasional merit pay plans, which reward teachers for being "superior" but leave untouched their organizational responsibilities.

But two major events have forced educators to consider changes in the organizational structure of public education. The first has been the fact that the system has failed to provide the means of social mobility for Negroes, Puerto Ricans and Mexican-Americans that it did for the masses of white, European immigrants at the turn of the century. For these millions of Americans, rapid changes in society have left behind the old educational organization. The results are so appalling that responsible citizen groups at the national level have called for the creation of a private educational system to replace the public system.

The other major counterforce agitating the established bureaucracy of education has been the updating and increased sophistication of teacher training and preparation, an updating demanded by the public and, ironically, by school administrators. It has produced the highest caliber of teaching excellence in public education the nation has yet known. This advanced training has provided the impetus for teachers to challenge the organizational rules which lock them out of the decision-making process and ignore their specialization. The increasing complexity of educational problems is inimical to the elite approach to problem solving characteristic of most school systems today. Teachers resent decisions being made in their behalf by generalists; they resent being evaluated wholly by generalists considerably less well prepared in their fields than they are themselves.

4. Warren G. Bennis, *Changing Organizations: Essays on the Development and Evolution of Human Organizations* (New York: McGraw-Hill, 1966).
5. Anderson, *op. cit.*

Teachers have challenged the administrative hierarchy in their recent nationwide strikes and resignations by going outside the educational bureaucracy. They did so because they were unable to initiate change or be considered as integral and equal partners in the deliberations of new policy or programs within the bureaucracy. They have realized the hardrock resistance of administrators to any *real* changes in the line-staff setup. The reasons why this movement has been vicious and anti-administration are not hard to understand. "The most dramatic, violent, and drastic changes have always taken place under autocratic regimes, for such changes usually require prolonged periods of self-denial. . . ."[6]

The emerging link of power in the educational organization is the straight line relationship to boards of education and state legislatures which neutralizes the administration. The endless communication channels and the petty administrative policies aimed at teacher control are thus negated within the bureaucracy. This strategy on the part of teachers may be compared with the German attack on the rear of France's Maginot Line in the Second World War. Whether one likes or dislikes the consequences of that strategy, it has proven to be effective.

The bureaucracy itself must share much of the blame for these developments, blame, because by going outside, the centralization of administrative power is preserved; there is no real decentralization. Much of the "down-town" staff of middle-sized and large city school districts continues to support an archaic and self-defeating force of supervisory personnel which teachers greatly resent and which is a major area of contention. The teacher has changed and so has the need for supervisors. Yet the educational superstructure still insists they are necessary. The bureaucracy is unable to accept the new teacher and his new competence. The organization is unable to welcome the desire by teachers for more involvement in decision making as a sign that the profession is maturing. Rather than react arrogantly and negatively, the organization should make sure that teachers assume the responsibilities concomitant with their newly found authority. The administrative lament of "I've been good to my staff, why should they feel this way" is nothing more than a paternalistic master-servant attitude that teachers abhor and are attempting to eliminate.

The forecast appears bleak. In large cities the die may be cast. But the emerging trends are not irrevocable. Two things must occur if we are to avoid complete neutralization of the principalship. First, principals must work for new organizational relationships with teachers in the decision-making process at the school level. Teachers must become partners; they must be involved with their principals in the shaping of school policies, curriculum decisions, and mutual

6. Bennis, *op. cit.*

evaluation of colleagues. Perhaps the concept of the academic senate may be modified and used with success in this function. Second, differentiated staffing must be employed to release teachers to serve in varying capacities within the organization. Until the organization can hold much of its talented personnel, it will find them continuing to leave education for better salaries and more freedom, or else they will be subverted onto the administrative ladder. The basic motivation inherent in differentiated staffing is the creation of the collegial relationship between students and teachers, and between teachers and administrators. Differentiated staffing can dissolve much of the authoritarian superstructure of the educational bureaucracy and provide the means for democratic participation of teachers in the decision-making machinery.

In such an atmosphere, the role of the principal changes to that of a skilled social manager. This cannot be another cloak for dogmatism, because the role can only be successfully realized when there is mutual professional respect between the participants, not the superior-subordinate relationship. Popper[7] foresees the manager as possessing "mastery of the discrete skills which are required for effective role performance at each subsystem level of public school organization and mutual confidence in the quality of professional preparation for these roles. For the professional quality or conceptual frames in which value orientations to role tasks are shaped will be of equal importance with technical skills that are required for these tasks."

The competence of the changed principal will be measured in the interpersonal skills with which he works with a team of teacher specialists. These are the real "change agents" of education. The principal is responsible, then, for the quality of professional relations within the social system of the school. He is an intergroup specialist. Relations on a staff will be made collegial and highly interrelated by the principal's coordination. That he should be able to do this without reverting to coercion, fear, or paternalism suggests the quality of preparation he will need.

The principal will no longer dictate curriculum or books, nor will he evaluate teachers all by himself. He will not adopt staff policy unilaterally, or be the single arbiter of issues involving decision making. He may still be an executive, but what will change is the quality of relationships with his teaching colleagues. Although he may still bear legal accountability for the school, his authority will be diffused throughout the teaching staff. Teachers as technical specialists may equal or surpass the principal in status. The emphasis of the central office and superintendent will be upon promoting instructional excellence in the classroom. This is not accomplished

7. Samuel H. Popper, *The American Middle School: An Organizational Analysis* (Waltham, Mass.: Blaisdell, 1967).

through the maintenance of "experts" completely detached from regular teaching.

Excellent classroom teachers may influence the decision-making process at many levels within the organization without having to become administrators. This will require an overhauling and remodeling of the educational hierarchy, emphasizing flexibility and competence. If such an organizational system is possible, and differentiated staffing offers one alternative, the system may be able to become self-generating. Then it need not suffer the painful trauma of extensive change to maintain its social viability.

Before administrative leadership, as exemplified in the principalship, can work within the emerging new constraints and demands, it must first clean its own house and recognize its own recalcitrance as a major obstacle to the maintenance of that leadership. A frank appraisal of existing limitations and extensive training for new functions and skills must be an integral part of furthering the strength and case for public education in the latter half of this century.

Competent Leadership for an Explosive Era   6

Donald C. Weaver

During the past year virtually every secondary school administrator has been admonished to adjust to changes in the attitudes and behaviors of the present student population, to make the curriculum relevant to the learner, to open up channels of communication, to assure the rights of all students and to provide positive leadership. Lectures and articles addressed to the professional school administrator at this point in time are replete with the above admonitions; yet, few, if any of such lecturers and writers offer specific information and/or suggested behaviors for the beleaguered administrator who is already well aware that to exercise educational leadership in 1969 is to "play a new ball game."

The present article assumes that the secondary schools of this country can contribute significantly to the management of the current social malaise and that successful management of conflicts present in the secondary school requires that those who provide leadership in secondary education have pertinent information regarding the nature of the present youth culture and specific skills in the area of student involvement. To exhort a change in the direction of positive student involvement in secondary education without recognizing the need for specific skills on the part of the leaders who initiate and manage such change is to engage in meaningless didactics.

Furthermore, a discussion of whether or not students should be directly involved in the management of the secondary school in the immediate future is an equally unproductive educational exercise. Events of recent months have demonstrated clearly that they *will* be involved. The task of the educational leader is, therefore, to perfect the process by which students are to be involved—a process which maximizes the thrust of student participation in the direction of positive attitudinal and behavioral change, relevant curriculum, open communication and assured recognition of legal and extra-legal student rights.

The process of student involvement must, at the same time, insure the maintenance of the school as an organized social system;[1] for, the organization is essential to the management of human behavior particularly where the protection of individual rights and responsibilities is at issue. Regardless of the powerful forces bent

From *Michigan Journal of Secondary Education*, Vol. 10 (Summer 1969), pp. 19-30. Reprinted by permission of the publisher.

1. Jacob Getzels and Egon Guba, "Social Behavior and the Administrative Process," *School Review*, March, 1957.

upon the destruction of the secondary school as an institution, the secondary administrator must not permit such destruction; for, to do so is to invite chaos—a situation in which those responsible are powerless to manage current social conflicts.

To argue that the school as an institution must be maintained is not to contend that its present organizational structure, policies and programs are appropriate to the effective management of human behavior. In fact, it is clearly evident that the secondary school must change substantially if it is to provide for meaningful student involvement thus becoming a laboratory for the management of human behavior.

What, then, are current conditions which influence the direction of the change in the secondary school? What changes must be made *now* to insure that the secondary school becomes a laboratory for the management of human behavior? What are the specific leadership skills and behaviors required to expedite the necessary changes?

CONDITIONS WHICH INFLUENCE THE DIRECTION OF CHANGE IN THE SECONDARY SCHOOL

There are at this point in time two prime factors influencing the direction of change in secondary education; namely, conditions within the society which have created a serious conflict over control of secondary education and a marked change in the nature of the present youth culture.

There was a time when the authority of the board of education to determine school policy and to delegate to the school personnel the right to administer the policy was unquestioned. Under such conditions it was thought to be a desirable public relations gesture to ask organized groups periodically to advise the school regarding the appropriateness of its policies and program. Yet, few educational leaders felt obligated to change policy or program on the basis of "suggestions" from such groups. Further, these groups were usually thought to represent majority opinion from within the educational "community"—opinion which need not be validated by reference to groups representing opposing points of view. Every educational leader worthy of the title is aware that such is no longer the case.

Recent events in New York City[2] and in a number of local school districts in Michigan[3] and elsewhere serve to confirm the commitment of the American people to the goal of cultural pluralism. These events further indicate that the battle to achieve cultural pluralism

2. Article appearing in the Education Section of *Time*, November 29, 1968, describing the conflict over local control in the New York City Schools, pp. 89-90.
3. Edward Cushman and Damon Keith, "Report of the Detroit High School Study Commission," Board of Education Detroit, Michigan, June, 1968.

may well be fought in the school. The educational leader must now recognize:

1. All groups affected by an educational decision demand to be involved in the decision-making process.
2. Minority opinion can no longer go unheeded or ignored.
3. Groups heretofore believed to be powerless to affect the decision-making process have found legitimate though often disruptive, means of intervening in the process.
4. In the face of powerful opposing forces the educational leader cannot hope to *resolve* conflict; he may be able only to *manage* the conflict.

A second factor influencing the direction of secondary education is the nature of the present youth culture. Despite the tendency by many to rationalize away the threat of the present group of secondary school youth on the basis that they are passing through the usual adolescent phase of development and given time the threat will be diminished, there are clear signs to indicate that the group of young people presently enrolled in our secondary schools are indeed different from past generations and that they are not likely to pass easily through the present phase thus permitting the secondary school to return to business as usual.[4] Convincing evidence to support this contention is before us:

1. The leaders in the present high school sub-cultures are products of affluent and permissive home environments. Either they were treated by their parents as developing young citizens subject to a minimum of adult-imposed restrictions or they were manipulated into particular behavior patterns by their parents. Those treated by their parents as developing young adults resent many of the rules and regulations imposed by the school, while those manipulated by their parents recognize similar attempts by the school personnel to cajole them into acceptance of school policies and procedures. Such students prefer genuine treatment by school personnel and tend to resent further attempts at manipulation. Both groups are prominent in student leadership positions and are not interested in playing leadership games or in being "used" further by school authorities.
2. Another important characteristic of today's young people, also related to the affluent society in which they were raised, is their lack of specific vocational orientation and a general lack of concern for "making a living." During their lifetime there has been little need for concern for the provision of the basic economic necessities.

4. S. L. Halleck, "Twelve Hypotheses of Student Unrest," in *Stress and Campus Response*, edited by G. Kerry Smith. Published by American Association for Higher Education, Washington, D. C., 1968, pp. 115-133.

3. Because the present youth group has not been preoccupied with economic matters, it has concentrated its effort upon social concerns of the society. There is, consequently, an impatience with the older generation which still insists that economic concerns must take precedence over social problems. Young people of high school and college age are particularly intolerant of the curriculum which does not deal realistically with the social issues of our time.

4. Our young people live in what McLuhan has described as an "instantaneous electronic environment." Consequently, such events as the Viet Nam war, confrontations between police and demonstrators and high school and college riots and sit-ins are to the young viewer real and emotion-laden.

5. This "instantaneous electronic environment" provides a realistic communication link which makes it possible for the young person to join not only a national youth culture but an international one as well. A student demonstration in a high school anywhere in the world is viewed by young people via television in a matter of hours.

6. At the same time that the present youth group recognizes its tremendous potential for power, it is reminded in subtle ways that it has no legitimate means for exercising that power. Our youth are constantly reminded that educational decisions are made by those empowered to do so—namely, the adults to whom such power has been delegated. As a result young people often resort to means of expressing their concerns which to adults seem irrelevant and irrational. The response from a student leader at the University of British Columbia to a challenge from the writer that student behavior at a "sit-in" in the Faculty Club last fall was totally irrelevant serves to illustrate the rationale behind such behavior. Having failed to accomplish what they viewed as a satisfactory hearing on legitimate requests to the university representatives, the students took over the faculty club. "We were well aware" replied the student leader "that control of the Faculty Club was not the real issue. This act was only the means by which we got a hearing. When we took over the Faculty Club, they listened to us!"

CHANGES REQUIRED IN THE SECONDARY SCHOOL

While he must defend the necessity for an institution through which the rights to an education for all citizens is guaranteed, the educational leader must now recognize that the changing societal expectations for the school and the changing nature of the high school student population require an immediate re-structuring of secondary education in this country if the school as an institution is to avoid complete chaos. While the addition of course offerings and the proliferation of co-curricular opportunities may be desirable, such efforts are not likely to meet the demands for change. Much more is required:

1. *The secondary school program must include provision for the extra-legal rights of students.* The explosive nature of much of the conflict in secondary education has focused attention upon the *legal* aspects of students' rights[5] with the result that the *extra-legal* rights of students are relegated to a position of secondary importance. Yet, it is in the provision for the guarantee of *extra-legal* rights of the student that the school demonstrates its interest in helping the student to become a fully-functioning, self-actualizing member of society. Further, it is from his observation of the school staff as it provides for his *extra-legal* rights that the student decides whether or not the school staff constitutes a legitimate authority in his life.

Extra-legal rights of students include:
a. The right to make mistakes and thereby to learn.
b. The right to be taken seriously.
c. The right to know the specific expectations held for him.
d. The right to be accepted as a citizen with all the rights pertaining thereto.
e. The right to a share in the control of his environment.
f. The right to be involved in the substantive issues relating to his education—the curriculum, the schedule, the methods of instruction and the co-curricular program.
g. The right to a relevant curriculum—one from which he can make some sense.

It may well be on the basis of his treatment by the school personnel in the area of his *extra-legal* rights that the student decides whether or not he is likely to experience success in working through the legitimate channels within the education establishment. Studies conducted at the Brandeis University Center for the Study of Violence[6] indicate that it is when a group becomes convinced that the channels of legitimate communication are, in fact, closed that the group resorts to violence. High school student groups are no exception. In fact, such activist organizations as the Students for a Democratic Society[7] have as one of their goals to convince increasing numbers of students that "To expect that a movement would have any success radically altering our educational system is absurd. We should be in the forefront of any student protest against administrative action." When large numbers of secondary school students be-

5. American Civil Liberties Union, *Academic Freedom in the Secondary Schools*, 1963.
6. Ralph W. Conant, *Riot, Insurrection and Civil Disobedience* (Boston: Lemberg Center for the Study of Violence, Brandeis University, 1968).
7. Mark Kleiman, Editorial *Michigan Journal of Secondary Education*, Spring, 1968.

come convinced that the education establishment is closed to any legitimate student requests the secondary school has lost its authority to manage student conflict.

Obviously, the school demonstrates to students that it is concerned with their rights when it institutionalizes such rights—that is, when school policy and practice require that the rights of every school citizen be respected. Similarly, the school is more likely to avoid arbitrary confrontations with students when it has demonstrated its role as a legitimate authority capable of enforcing a code which respects the rights of all its citizens.

Until every staff member in the secondary school can attest to the guarantee of *extra-legal* rights of students, the secondary school is vulnerable to attack from organizations already at work to force such guarantees—peaceably or otherwise.

2. *The secondary school must be decentralized.* The goal of such decentralization is to provide a significant unit within the secondary school with which every student and faculty member may feel an identity. The unit must be sufficiently small to permit an open climate among the members and the focus of much of student and faculty programming must be based in the unit. Grouping of faculty and students within the unit upon the basis of "teachability criteria" such as those recommended by Thelen[8] would be a feature of any feasible decentralization plan. Also, such units would be organized across departmental and grade lines to provide maximum heterogeneity within the group. Present grouping practices in the secondary school based upon homogeneity or administrative convenience (viz., home rooms, remedial groups, tracks, phases, etc.) do not provide an open climate in which social and personal problems may be managed. Until it is generally recognized that there are inherent flaws in the secondary school structure itself which prevent both students and faculty from meaningful involvement we are likely to continue to face the problems of alienated students and faculty members.

3. *Increased opportunity must be provided for communication among all groups affected by the secondary school program.* An interrelatedness among all groups involved in decision-making must now be recognized. Faculty decisions about the school program affect students and student decisions regarding matters of dress and behavior affect the faculty; hence, provision must be made for both vertical and horizontal communication within the system. The resolution of personal and social issues facing the secondary school requires an awareness of feelings, attitudes and desires within one's own group and among outside groups as well. Therefore, if the real

8. Herbert Thelen, *Classroom Grouping for Teachability* (New York: John Wiley and Sons, 1967).

issues are to be resolved, communication between both allies and adversaries is essential.

Deliberate structuring to increase communication throughout the secondary school assumes that every unit within the system has something to say to every other unit. If such is to be the case, it must be recognized that worthwhile ideas may be generated at any level within the school—especially among student groups. The secondary school leader would do well to recognize that many of the most creative ideas for the improvement of secondary education are likely to originate within student groups.[9]

Current problems facing the secondary school require a communication system within the school which permits:

a. A school-wide, organized, small confrontation involving all faculty and students called, if necessary, upon an hour's notice.
b. Regularly scheduled, small group unit (see number two above) meetings involving the entire faculty and student body for discussion of substantive issues in the school. The planning of new school facilities and subsequent changes in the school program and schedule provides a natural stimulus to such communication.
c. Training for all participants in the educational process in the techniques of inter-group communication with particular emphasis upon listening as a technical skill.
d. Knowledge on the part of all students and faculty members regarding the specific procedure by which decisions are made.
e. The maximum use of all communication media available within the school free of censorship but subject to community standards of "good taste."

4. *There must be provided within the secondary school a student-controlled organization which trains student leadership and coordinates student involvement in the area of social and organizational problem solving.* It is clear that secondary school students demand to be involved in the resolution of social and organizational problems within the school; however, it is equally clear that to be constructively involved requires on their part specific training in group leadership and in the techniques of social problem solving.[10] It has been generally assumed that the student council provided the laboratory for student involvement in problem solving and the preparation for leadership. However, there is considerable evidence to suggest that such is not the case.[11] The student council has failed as a laboratory for a number of reasons not the least of which is its

---

9. John D. Rockefeller 3rd, "In Praise of Young Revolutionaries," *Saturday Review*, December 14, 1968, pp. 18-78.

10. Donald C. Weaver, *The Student Council—Laboratory for Leadership Development.* Unpublished Syllabus used in Student Involvement Seminar, Western Michigan University, 1968, pp. 1-51.

11. *Ibid.*, pp. 17-27.

relegation to dealing with the trivia associated with the school's social activity program and to policing the student body. If one didn't know better he might assume that there had been a deliberate attempt over the years to involve the student council in the trivial lest there be a request to be involved with something substantial. Needless to say, students are asking for a "bigger piece of the action" and it seems reasonable to involve them in such a way that they might contribute to the resolution of the social problems within the school and at the same time develop the leadership skills required to resolve the social issues of the society at large.

Whether it be the student council or a newly created vehicle for student involvement, the student organization which is to serve as a laboratory for social problem solving and leadership development must:

1. Be broadly representative
2. Be assigned competent faculty leadership
3. Be scheduled to meet regularly on school time.
4. Be trained in the specifics of group leadership
5. Be free to communicate with all groups within the system
6. Be involved with the faculty and administration in discussion and decision-making
7. Be free to delegate trivia to other student organizations
8. Be considered capable of originating ideas for the improvement of secondary education.

THE LEADERSHIP ROLE IN SECONDARY EDUCATION

What is the role of the educational leader in today's secondary school?

Whereas his energies were once in the direction of *administration*—the management of resources, the efforts of the secondary educator must now be directed toward the larger process of exercising *leadership*—organizing and directing groups toward mutually acceptable goals. The nature of the present youth culture within the secondary school and conditions in the society outside the school require a re-examination of the leadership roles in secondary education. Assuming that the changes in the secondary school proposed earlier are appropriate, it follows that specific skills are required of those who would exercise leadership to implement the proposed changes. The educational leader must now organize groups for the resolution and/or management of conflict, decentralize the education establishment and provide for maximum student involvement in the educative process. The exercise of leadership in today's secondary school, therefore, requires skills beyond those required of the administrator of a former era.

Leadership skills may be grouped roughly into the following three categories first used by Katz[12] to describe managerial skills:

Technical skills are defined as those involving specialized knowledge, analytical ability within the specialty and facility in the use of tools and techniques of the specific discipline—in this case, administration.

Human skills include those necessary to working effectively as a group member and building cooperative effort within the team. Human skill, according to Katz, is contrasted with technical skill: working with people versus working with things.

Conceptual skills involve the ability to see the enterprise as a whole. These skills include recognizing how various functions of the organization depend on one another and how changes in any one part affect all the others.

Although the successful leader in the secondary school today must be skilled in all areas—conceptual, human and technical, it is essential that he possess a high degree of *conceptual* skill for it is his conceptual ability which enables him to "see the whole picture," analyze the elements in the situation and initiate the structure through which the secondary school accomplishes its task. The following *conceptual* skills are essential to satisfactory performance as a secondary school leader:

1. Organization and management of a complicated system of communication—one in which the delegation of decision-making to proper sub-groups within the school is required.
2. Analysis of the school as a social system delineating the personal and organizational dynamics of the situation.
3. Assignment of priorities within a personal schedule and within the program of the school.
4. Analysis of the relationship of the parts of the organization to each other and to the whole.
5. Prediction of outcomes based upon anticipated actions.
6. Identification of power groups which affect the school and recognition of the relationships among the power forces which bear upon the operation of the secondary school.
7. Prediction of anticipated behaviors based upon knowledge of perceptions of various groups involved in the program of the secondary school.

Also of considerable importance in the exercise of leadership are the *human* skills. Given the conceptual ability to analyze the situation and structure a plan of action, the educational leader must set the human machinery in motion to accomplish his goal. The follow-

12. Robert L. Katz, "Skills of an Effective Administrator," *Harvard Business Review*, January-February, 1955, pp. 33-42.

ing *human* skills are important to successful performance as a leader in the secondary school:

1. Projection of empathy for the other person.
2. Acceptance of others as they are—permitting them their separateness.
3. Demonstration of consistently predictable behavior in the leadership role.
4. Provision of positive support for groups and individuals in their efforts to reach the goal.
5. Delineation between personal and professional goals in the group leadership situation.

The use of the "team approach" to leadership in the secondary school provides a variety of *technical* skills among members of the team thus requiring fewer *technical* skills of each individual member. There are, however, certain *technical* skills considered desirable for all persons involved in leadership at the secondary school level whether they operate as part of a leadership team or independently. *Technical* skills required are:

1. Direction of group leadership activities
2. Communication—including both oral and written
3. Listening
4. Organization of routine administrative details
5. Allocation and utilization of time

It seems clear that certain conditions within the secondary school and in the society outside the school are demanding immediate changes in secondary education. The educational leader who would effect such changes must recognize that different conceptual, human and technical skills will be required of those who are to provide leadership in the immediate future. Hopefully, those in positions of leadership will turn their attention to the development of the required skills while there is still time to avoid the inevitable chaos resulting from the absence of leadership in these explosive times.

The Black School Administrator   7
and the Black Community

Hugh J. Scott

A considerable portion of the explosive force of the historic Negro protest has been directed at the public schools and their representatives. Never in the history of the public schools have they and their representatives experienced such a collective demonstration of public dissatisfaction and distrust as is now being directed at them by the Black community.

At present, many public school administrators appear bewildered by the issues and related events. They are seemingly incapable or unwilling to respond actively and realistically to the Negro indictment against the public schools.

On the other hand, the Black community has displayed unprecedented solidarity in its belief that the public schools have historically and systematically operated in such a manner as to impose and to perpetuate a second-class citizenship, a menial existence, and an ignoble status upon the Black American.

POSITION OF THE BLACK SCHOOL ADMINISTRATOR

The issues raised and the charges made by the Negro community have placed the Negro school administrator in a most sensitive and crucial role. The Black community demands that he give his complete support to their efforts and proposed programs to attain quality education for all Negro students. The expertise, knowledge, and position of the Black school administrator is invaluable to the efforts of the Negro community. But, in his interactions with the Black community, the Black school administrator has more at stake than his professional integrity and effectiveness—his identification with and acceptance in the Negro community. Society, with its restrictive and oppressive racial attitudes and practices, openly discriminates against and extensively segregates the Negro from the mainstream of American life. No Black can view lightly concurrent isolation from and ostracism by the Black community in part or in total.

As the Negro school administrator weighs the relative merits of any proposed actions on his part, in response to the demands of the Negro community, he must also keep in proper prospective his professional obligations to the school system and to his colleagues. The

From *Integrated Education*, Vol. 7 (July-August 1969), pp. 52-56. Reprinted by permission of the publisher and author.

school system expects him to be professionally responsible in his interactions with colleagues and the Negro community.

Many issues confronting public school educators, related to the needs of Black students, strike at the heart of policies, practices, and programs which cannot and should not be defended or continued. The Negro school administrator must participate in the revelation, clarification, and resolution of the issues raised by the Negro community and other concerned citizens. The immediate future of the public schools will be shaped largely by pertinent, open and constructive dialogue and resultant action of representatives of the public schools and the Negro community.

IMPLICATIONS OF PROFESSIONALISM

The Black school administrator, not unlike his white colleagues, likes to think of himself and to be viewed by the public as a professional. In the current confrontations between Black groups and representatives of the public schools, what are the implications for the Black school administrator who seeks to be professional? To what degree does adherence to a professional code of conduct discipline his interactions with colleagues and with the Negro community? To what extent does professionalism determine the scope and impact of the utilization of his skills and understandings in the identification, clarification and resolution of the issues in the crisis? The answers to the questions presented are critical and are dependent on how one defines professionalism and identifies the professional.

Professionalism perceived here not only implies but requires commitment of one's full resources to establish and to maintain quality education for all students. The educator who accepts an assignment to a school position must demonstrate the degree of expertise and awareness, appropriate to the internal and external problems and needs of the assignment. If he does not have the required expertise and awareness or if he cannot utilize them, he must be judged incompetent and/or inadequate. The educator so judged should be removed from the ranks of school administrators. The school administrator judged to have the professional competency, but whose level of performance indicates that he is inadequate for the assignment, should be placed on probation and/or transferred to an assignment more in line with his professional capabilities.

The degree to which the professional school administrator should be supportive of his school system and colleagues has to be flexible and conditional. Yet he must oppose constructively policies, practices and programs detrimental to students and which are in conflict with the standards and dictates of his profession.

SOCIAL AND PROFESSIONAL COMMITMENT

The Black school administrator must recognize and withstand the negative forces and influences present in the Negro community and among his colleagues, white and Negro; forces and influences which are covertly and overtly determined to control his acts as a school administrator. Despite such pressures, the Black school administrator must play a major role in presenting and resolving the issues.

The professional views of the Black school administrator and the degree he is committed to such views are important factors in shaping the evolution of his ultimate position and role in the crisis. His professional views and commitment cannot be demonstrated in isolation from his personal perceptions of the major social, political and economic problems and needs of the Black American.

It should be abundantly evident to any observer of this current crisis in the public schools that the Black school administrator's role cannot be one of passive compliance or non-active coexistence. The Black school administrator, if he is to be effective, has no choice but to lend openly, actively and professionally his expertise, knowledge and status to the equitable and efficient resolution of the issues raised in the confrontations between the public schools and the Negro community. In reality, the question should not be: Should the Negro school administrator become an active and constructive participant, but how can he best participate in the identification, clarification and resolution of the issues?

At the same time, the Negro community or its representatives cannot expect the Negro school administrator to give responsible support to programs and recommendations which are educationally unsound and racist in nature and intent. The Black school administrator is socially and professionally obligated to combine his knowledge and understanding of public school education and of the Black community in an active effort leading to positive and constructive interaction between the schools and the Black community.

GUIDELINES FOR COMMITMENT

Negro school administrators who are assigned to administrative positions in the public school systems of the major cities in America are facing intense pressures and criticism from a very vocal and influential segment of the Negro community. Combined with the static from the Black community, Black school administrators are viewed with a considerable amount of uncertainty by a significant number of their white colleagues. Many of the latter are suspicious of the Negro educator's contacts and relationships with representatives of the Negro community, especially that segment of it which is vocal and vehement in its demands and criticism of the public schools.

The Negro school administrator can only be effective in providing guidance and assistance in resolving the issues raised by the Negro community and his colleagues if he can avoid many unnecessary pitfalls. The "Do's and Don'ts" offered here are designed to provide the Black school administrator with a handy and practical reference and to serve as a general guide for the utilization of his expertise in the resolution of the issues associated with the Negro indictment against public school education and educators.

13 COMMANDMENTS

1. Promote coordinated effort on the part of your Black colleagues to identify, present and resolve the educational issues and needs of the Black community.
2. Within the structure of the school system, voice constructive criticisms and recommendations for changing school policies, practices and programs detrimental to the Negro community.
3. Singly and collectively, participate in discussion and investigation of the issues raised by the Black community and by your colleagues regarding Black educational policy, practice or program affecting the Negro community.
4. Review objectively and thoroughly the contrasting statements and views of conflicting individuals and groups.
5. Provide professional assistance to individuals and groups in the Negro community for the establishment and maintenance of effective channels for communication and action between representatives of community and schools so as to promote a collective approach to issues.
6. Confine public criticism of and disagreements with existing and proposed school policies, practices and programs to principles related to specific issues rather than specific personalities and schools.
7. Keep within predetermined restricted boundaries all direct information received in confidential meetings or obtained from confidential reports.
8. Actively initiate and arrange meetings in local school facilities of representatives of the Negro community, with or without invited school representatives, for the purpose of constructively exploring the educational problems and needs of the Negro community.
9. Attend those key meetings which are sponsored by representatives of the Black community that are open to your attendance.
10. Do not support, publicly or privately, those recommendations or programs submitted by a representative or representatives of the

Black community which you believe to be racist oriented in design and in intent.

11. Do not permit the school system to place you in the role of defending in the Negro community those policies, practices and programs of the school system which you believe to be unjust and indefensible.

12. Do not permit the school system to use you as its primary instrument to attack and discredit Negro leaders critical of the school system and its representatives, especially those critics who are the most vocal and vehement in their criticism of schools and educators.

13. Do not allow your professional and social responsibility to the school system or to the Black community to prevent your voicing opposition to educational policies, practices and programs established or proposed by either which you believe to be unsound or unrealistic.

8 | **Beware of the Administrator's Syndrome**

Robert T. McGee

Rare is the school administrator who has not been moved to some level of frustration in the past several months. Every social pressure and national concern—from Viet Nam and unemployment to what has been called the "rising militancy" of teacher organizations and parent demands for success of their children—face the educator not only in the morning, but, very likely, also when he goes to bed at night.

This frustration can be related, in part, to the experience and maturity level of the educator. If he is in his forties, he can recall periods of non-affluence or when social change was easier to cope with—at least it might *seem* so today. There is a standard built-in hazard of maturity and experience which centers around the temptation to refer to the "good old days." I propose that old answers may not be a realistic solution to today's problems. Wendell Johnson (*People In Quandaries*) long ago referred to the IFD Disease—"from Idealization, to Frustration, to Demoralization." All of us, but perhaps especially those of us in public sectors today, are susceptible to this disease. For the educator, be he in Podunk Center or Berkeley, it can mean the administrator's syndrome which has claimed so many honest and hard-working people. However, without being presumptuous enough to suggest all cause and all solution, it might be worthwhile to reflect about the nature of current administrative realities—especially as they relate to children.

First, although we live in a materialistic world, none but a fool would suggest that we alter this essential ingredient of modern society as we have come to build and know it. The living standard we have achieved has brought its own problems of personal satisfaction and adjustment. It brings us to the point of asking whether or not the idea about the dignity of labor and the "gift without the giver" is really out of style. Yet, is the responsibility for a job well-done and for honestly seeking to prove oneself any less essential today than it has been throughout history? Educators know the answer. Perhaps education is the last stronghold of the concept that one must finally earn his keep. No social legislation can guarantee anyone an education, let alone the right to that education. Our American Dream has always talked about rights for opportunities and protection against a denial of those opportunities, but no one can get from edu-

From *The Clearing House*, Vol. 41 (April 1967), pp. 494-496. Reprinted by permission of the publisher.

cation more than he is willing to give. Some people appear to be singularly reluctant to give very much. To presume that society and the schools are the variables which block this success (and sometimes they might be), rather than the student or his parents' attitudes and values, doesn't change reality.

Schoolmen who fail to stick to facts and to work to achieve a reduction of the teacher and material variable, and who pretend that student and parental commitment are secondary elements, are cheating themselves. Not many really do this, but it appears as though some educators permit themselves and their boards of education to fall into this trap. To regret the failure of students to succeed in education is honest, human, and professional; to accept full responsibility for such failure is naive and even dishonest. Philosophically, we cannot approve changing grades on the basis of outside pressure, but in practice we do it when we tacitly approve programs and procedures which permit the evasion of our commitment.

Second, discipline has far too long implied "keeping order." This is not very difficult to achieve. With no denigration of the military, drill sergeants are not known for their skill in the psychology of human relations, and yet they have discipline. Red tape alone can achieve this. Discipline ought to mean having achieved some standards and having proven one's sense of responsibility. We are not talking about academic prowess here. Bright students are often the most irresponsible, partly because they have never been taught a sense of grace and courtesy—*noblesse oblige* if you will. Our society is surfeited with this kind of selfish "intellectual." Sometimes we worry too much about the verbal student whose discourtesy, impudence, and wise-cracking we are determined to overcome by giving him "his hour" and letting him talk it out at the expense of other students from whom he ought to be learning—learning good manners and a respect for other people's opinions.

When we encourage students to criticize books they haven't read, leaders whose work and motivation they know nothing about, and standards which they have not been able to test, we do them a disservice. This is no plea for a conservative cloture of ideas and discussion; it is a plea for school-classroom guidance which encourages responsibility. Students ardently want this kind of guidance— often because they lack it at home and see little evidence of it in society in general. These are reasons for schools to do more, not less, to encourage responsibility. In a word, educators must be idealists to succeed; they must also be *realists*. This makes for a rare combination. We ought never to apologize for it.

A third area it not unrelated to the first two, for it concerns dealing with problems of staff—from recruitment through an adequate supervisory program. Operationally, there are few satisfactory definitions of the school administrator's role except in functional management terms. I suggest that before educators become either "negotiators" or "agents for the board," they are leaders who need some sense of commitment to standards and integrity. Overwhelmingly, the lags in teacher security and professionalism which have grown over the years are offset by the basic dedication and concern for children which teachers have in general. Good leadership and reasonable expectation by administrators ought to be the frame of reference for any kind of problem resulting from the "militancy" of teachers. The "happy family" concept of school operations may be a thing of the past (if it ever really existed!), but the art of teaching and the art of leadership have probably never really had a chance. We ought to be sure that we insist that this chance always be provided to serve as the springboard for all sound educative action.

Finally, the school administrator needs to stop apologizing for that which he knows and for skills he uses well. At the same time, he needs to listen carefully to the criticism and suggestions of his staff and his public. It is obvious that if any one of us knew all of the answers in this complex process of teaching and learning, no one school system would be large enough to hold him. What utter vanity for the educator to presume that he can expect 100 per cent success when no one would expect this in medicine, the law, or even in the space program! Self-pity never provides a suitable reward. Action preceded by thinking and commitment can be rewarding. Years ago in the heyday of radio when "Dr. I.Q." offered silver dollars for correct answers and candy bars for incorrect or no responses, I recall one lady's quick response as "I don't know the answer, but I'll take the candy bars." Perhaps alert administrators can take a lesson and remember that trying for the answer might be much more useful and rewarding than accepting the sweetly unsatisfying candied consolation.

None of these thoughts offers a panacea to the "IFD Disease" or what we might call the administrator's syndrome. The educator's job requires a level of frustration or at least disequilibrium; he ought to begin to worry if he feels too relaxed about the operation (and good ones do!). At the same time, self-pity is a poor substitute for analyzing the problems against a sense of personal standards and practical realities.

Rule from the Top | 9

Thomas Ford Hoult

I have just taken part in a dismaying meeting with a group of "West" Union High School System administrators ("West" being a pseudonym for the name of a large western city which, in terms of the apparent representativeness of its power structure and educational arrangements, could be almost any big city in the land). The only bright note is the hope that if the implications of the meeting become known to others, perhaps steps can be taken to alleviate similar conditions elsewhere.

The meeting was concerned with civil liberties—a "long-hair" case—and, throughout the discussion, the administrators appeared to lack even the foggiest notion of the meaning of civil liberties in a democratic society. Two of them went so far as to laugh when the totalitarianism of their system was mentioned.

After the meeting, I attended a party which included a number of friends who are high-school teachers. Noticing my down-in-the-dumps attitude, they pressed for details. After I told the story, one particularly fine math teacher consoled me with the disquieting observation, "Don't worry—only the worst ones become administrators."[1] This was a gross generalization, of course—and it wasn't even directed specifically at West—but it met no opposition from those at the party. The other teachers chimed in to agree that in their opinion it is quite reasonable to hypothesize that only the most authoritarian teachers are picked to be administrators. A few conspicuous exceptions were noted, but the teachers were unanimous in asserting that high-school and grade-school administrators, especially the former, are almost always selected from the ranks of those who believe that social control properly proceeds from "the top down," that the prime role of schools is to cultivate conformity, and that classroom decorum is more important than creativity. It was pointed out that athletic coaches, in particular, manifest the "proper" characteristics. Coaches generally have an unusually narrow educational experience that involves precious little concern with abstractions such as democracy and civil rights; they are trained to issue commands and to expect unquestioning obedience such as one would find in a traditional Prussian guard; and they frequently have a physique that intimidates the weak—all of which perhaps helps to

From *Changing Education*, Vol. 4 (Spring 1969), pp. 23-26. Reprinted by permission of the publisher.

1. Quoted statements are based on memory and therefore should not be interpreted as representing the exact words spoken by those quoted; the quotations do, however, represent the writer's understanding of the "spirit" of that which was said.

account for the otherwise inexplicable fact that they are so often appointed to administrative positions.

And then I recalled what happened at a school-board meeting I attended in a nearby suburb just a few months before. Representatives of the AFT local were there to ask, as they had asked countless times before, that the school-board members sit down with the union members—as equals—and come to some mutually agreeable conclusions. But the board remained adamant; the board president proclaimed that the board alone would make all decisions on salaries and working conditions. He then announced a substantial improvement in the salary schedule and appeared surprised when the union spokesmen denounced the new schedule as symptomatic of an outworn system involving rule-from-the-top.

But not all the teacher representatives were opposed to the traditional control system. The president of the local education association rose to thank the board for its "magnanimous" action and went on to say something like: "And when we are speaking of salary increases, let's not forget our wonderful administrators—they deserve more than anyone!" While the superintendent flushed, and members of the audience squirmed and hung their heads as if in shame, one person announced: "That's the most blatant bit of bootlicking I've ever observed." But—and this was the most disconcerting point of all—the union representatives then flatly predicted that the bootlicker would undoubtedly be made a school principal. "He would have all the qualifications the board wants," one teacher said. "He'd have a craven attitude toward those who have authority over him, and a callous disregard for his fellow workers. He'd be a natural for 'lower' administration."

At the time, I refused to believe it. As a university department chairman, I'm something of a school administrator myself, and I have not found that rational "higher" authority has any respect for subordinates who subject themselves needlessly to arbitrary rulings. But now I see that, so far as high-school systems are concerned, the union members were probably correct. The bootlicker type *does* seem to be a natural for administration in all too many secondary schools—or, at least this appears to be the case from the standpoint of those favoring a truly democratic society. Of course, if your fundamental value is authoritarianism, then you will see nothing wrong with making principals out of those who manifest licked-dog behavior when in the presence of their so-called betters; nor will you see anything amiss in the responses of the West Union administrators in our meeting about long hair.

PURELY PRIVATE BEHAVIOR

The meeting was called at the request of Stephen Ray (as I shall call him), executive secretary of the state branch of the American

Civil Liberties Union. Ray had received an appeal from a high-school lad who needed just one credit to graduate but who was not permitted to register in the summer session on the grounds that his hair "was too long" and, according to interpretations based on the established dress code, long hair is a disturbing influence in the classroom. On the grounds of principle, the boy refused to have his hair cut; in effect, he asserted that the right to life in a democratic society includes the right to be free of interference with purely private behavior which cannot be shown to injure others. The boy asked the help of one teacher, who then volunteered to solve the immediate problem by having the boy assist her so he could receive his needed credit without having to appear in class. When he was still not allowed to register, the boy followed the established appeal procedure. Merely having an appeal route would appear to safeguard individual rights—but the West procedure is so long and complicated that, like many such arrangements, it too often makes a mockery of rights. The process involves so many steps, appointments, interviews, etc., that it tends to make a moot case out of any given situation; it is such as to discourage all but the rare few who have mature convictions, dogged determination, and limitless time and energy.

Despite the complications and the pressure of time, our long-haired youngster was persistent enough to "exhaust administrative remedies" so far as they were available, given the limited period permitted for "late registration." After being denied redress to every level, the boy asked the ACLU to help him, and the meeting was arranged. Ray then asked me—as an ACLU board member—to join him, along with another university professor, two cooperating lawyers, and a university student. The school-system representatives included the assistant superintendent, the director of administrative services, the principal of one high school and the associate principal of another, and an athletic coach (!) newly appointed as social-studies coordinator. We—the ACLU group—were not told that our Friday meeting was being held the day *after* the last day when the boy would be permitted to register in any case, hence we did not know that in more senses than one we were gathered to talk into the wind.

'NEAT AND CONSERVATIVE'

The meeting opened with distribution of copies of the school-board's policy on student behavior and dress and with the related dress codes prevailing in the various high schools. All the codes called for boys to have *"neat* and *conservative"* haircuts.[2] Such codes and haircuts are needed, said the administrators, because people who *dress* poorly *act* accordingly, and the educational process is impeded.

2. Italics added.

When asked for some reasonable evidence—evidence beyond guesswork and gossip and "my experience"—that education is hampered when people dress their bodies and hair as they please, we were given nothing but hostile stares along with firm statements that we didn't know whereof we spoke. We were asked if we favored abolishing *all* rules and we responded, "No—when there is clear empirical evidence that a regulation really makes a substantial contribution to the proper functioning of the school, then it is sensible. All other regulations—especially those established by administrative fiat—should be abandoned as inappropriate in a democratic society."

But—said one of the administrators—with such a minimum of rules, what would you do about the pupil whose dress violated a legal statute? We answered, "Let those who violate the law suffer the penalties of law, with apprehension and punishment being administered by the police and the courts; where schools assume the role of the police and of judges, they run the risk of making it appear that teachers and stick-wielders are synonymous."

My university colleague pointed out that college administrators also used to assume that student dress must be regulated. Now, however, dress codes have been abandoned, or are ignored, in all but the most backward Podunk Normal schools. And still there are no university riots centering around miniskirts and boys with long hair. Even at Berkeley and Columbia, relatively few students appear in public without being clothed, cut, and combed in accordance with prevailing middle-class standards. Those who violate the standards constitute a small—and often scorned—minority.

'VAS YOU DER, CHARLIE?'

"But, have you ever taught in high school?" we were asked, and the implication was that, if we knew conditions "from the inside," we, too, would favor the existing rules. Not so, we rejoined—and we did not depend upon testimony from the one among us who *had* taught in high school. The proper answer to the "Vas you der, Charlie?" tactic is an old one: You do not have to eat a rotten egg to know something significant about its condition. One does not have to have syphilis to know that it is something to be avoided. One need not have been a resident of Germany to justify denouncing Hitler. And, similarly, it is possible to make cogent criticisms of school systems without being personally involved in them.

At one point in the meeting, I expressed concern about the "tone" of the various dress and behavior codes. Where, I asked, is there any acknowledgement of the importance of dissent? We're not here to encourage dissent, said an administrator, adding something to this effect: "If we let students express dissent, we'd lose our jobs tomorrow." The assistant superintendent interjected his resentment about the opinions expressed by the long-haired boy—the boy said he likes to challenge his teachers. "And what is wrong with that?" we asked. Teachers can't teach if they have to respond to challenges, said the assistant superintendent.

At another point, when we had, so to speak, driven the administrators into a logical corner from which there was no reasonable escape, the assistant superintendent trotted out the last refuge of the defenseless bureaucrat—namely: "Our job is to carry out the policies of the board; we cannot be held accountable for what the board decides." We said, "Your responsibility, then, is to educate the board; perhaps the board members are not aware of current trends and needs." The administrators' answer boiled down to: "Our job is to *obey* the board, not educate it." (Shades of Nuremberg!)

TOTALITARIANISM IS RAMPANT

Toward the end of what was all too clearly a useless get-together, I spoke of my deep concern with the implications of the meeting. "It seems to me," I said, "you men have no meaningful knowledge of the fact that this country was founded on dissent and challenge and difference, and that in social systems where dissent is forbidden or discouraged, those in control stand in constant danger of making frightful errors." I said it was apparent the West Union High School System was run in terms of totalitarian principles that would be appropriate in some societies but not in ours. In response to this charge, the principal grinned, almost as if he were thinking, "tough beans." "Your grin suggests," said one of my colleagues, "you don't think it matters that your system manifests many of the features one would expect in a prison." The grin faded and was replaced by the more usual hostile glare.

"I didn't realize our high schools were so totalitarian," the assistant superintendent observed in a very sarcastic tone of voice. "Are we unique in being totalitarian?" No, said one of the ACLU representatives—totalitarianism is rampant in the high schools of America and it is high time for a change at that level just as there was a previous change at the college level.

TWIN FEARS OF ADMINISTRATION

The chances of lessening the totalitarianism commonly found in high-school administration are hampered by the twin fears which appear to possess so many high-school administrators. One of the fears centers on the notion that if an administrator admits a particular rule is not justified, he may lose all control. The West administrators patently know that a boy's long hair, in and of itself, causes nothing significant; but they seem to view the hair rule as a symbol of the dominance they feel they can and should exercise. A related fear is the idea that anarchy will prevail if minutiae of behavior are not closely regulated—a fear which is based on the mistaken belief that human behavior is basically a function of technical law rather than of underlying cultural norms. It is important to note that for neither of these fears is there a scintilla of respectable empirical evidence.

But our group of administrators clearly felt that, since their minds were made up, it only confused the issue to speak of evidence. With every point we tried to make, we were rewarded with the glassy look of total resentment. Fundamental civil liberties, such as due process, free speech and free assembly, are inappropriate for students, the administrators implied. We got the impression that students should obey, not question; they should conform, not dissent; they should learn to manifest "conservatism!" With such attitudes apparently prevailing among those controlling the school system, it seemed appropriate for me not to resist the parting observation, as we left the meeting room, that the techniques being used in the West Union High School System are such as to maximize the chances that graduates will be the kind of meek conformists who provide the foundations needed for a dictatorship.

It is particularly disquieting that the administrator group apparently did not resent out charges about authoritarian procedures. They seemed mainly concerned that no one should interfere with their sacred rules! We concluded that they have a basic commitment to a hierarchical social system, hence do not even understand talk about the virtues of democratic processes and individual liberties. This worries me deeply. A nation eventually reflects that which predominates in its educational system. To the degree that the "spirit" of the West system prevails across the land, to that degree we must expect 1984 to arrive in a few short years. It is in the hopes that we may at least forestall the arrival of that date that this article has been prepared. Hopefully, "The West Story" will prompt thoughtful school boards and administrators to assess themselves and their policies in the light of meaningful democratic standards and to institute needed reform.

The Principal Must Be Replaced* | 10

Robert S. Thurman

It is widely recognized that rapid changes are occurring in American society. Many of these changes have important implications for education and are reflected in current educational innovations. These innovations, according to Sand, can be classified as practices designed to better utilize human talent, practices designed to better utilize time, and practices designed to better utilize technology.[1] There are three particular areas in which changes are most evident. These are in organizational patterns, in roles of teachers and other personnel, and in curricular content.

AREAS OF CHANGE

A variety of proposals have been developed and put into practice in an effort to provide an educational program geared to needs of individual learners and to use talents of teachers. These include the nongraded approach found more commonly at the lower elementary school level, though in some systems encompassing all elementary levels and, in a few, elementary and secondary; the middle school geared to the preadolescent learner; and the individualized approach attempting to allow each learner to move at his own rate and to a great degree in his own areas of interest.

The model of the classroom teacher as a person who stands before a group of learners dispensing knowledge is rapidly fading. Today classroom teachers make decisions on a level formerly reserved for administrative personnel. Frazier describes three models of the teacher which are emerging. These are the teacher as a specialist, as an executive, and as a professional in decision making.

As a specialist, the teacher serves as a member of a teaching team, as a resource aid to other staff members, and as a regular teacher. The teacher as an executive manages resources, serves as a team leader in cooperative teaching ventures, and coordinates teaching aides or auxiliaries. As a professional, the teacher is involved in

From *Educational Leadership*, Vol. 26, No. 8 (May 1969), pp. 778-783. Reprinted with permission of the Association for Supervision and Curriculum Development and the author. Copyright © 1969 by the Association for Supervision and Curriculum Development.

*Based on an idea developed by Jack Davidson, Superintendent, Oak Ridge, Tennessee; Francis Trusty, College of Education, University of Tennessee; Robert DeLozier, Greenville, Tennessee, and the author.

1 Ole Sand, "Basis for Decisions," In: *Role of Supervisor and Curriculum Director in a Climate of Change*. 1965 Yearbook (Washington, D.C.: Association for Supervision and Curriculum Development, 1965), pp. 45-46.

decision making about what is taught and how. This includes curriculum planning, innovation development, and experimentation.[2]

Expansion of knowledge is occurring at an unbelievable rate and has created pressure for education to reexamine the content of the schools. All content fields are undergoing scrutiny and major revisions have already been made in mathematics, science, English, and social studies.

CONTINUING EDUCATION

These changes create a variety of problems for teachers and for the professionals who work with teachers at the school system level. These major problems are: (a) how to help teachers develop skills and attitudes necessary for carrying out their emerging roles; (b) how to assist teachers in keeping pace with developments in content and in organizational innovations; and (c) how to help teachers in providing more effective learning situations for students.

Teachers have not found that continuing in-service education programs are geared to help them make continuous and substantial progress in learning new content, new roles, and new skills and the application of these learnings to their tasks as teachers. Several ways have been used at the university level for improving teacher effectiveness, such as Saturday classes, evening classes, summer programs, institutes, and conferences. None of these seems to have resulted in much change in participants. Several reasons are given for this lack of change but these stand out:

1. There is a lack of relevance between what is studied and what teachers need in their *own* situations.
2. Teachers do not believe they have adequate support from their administration and colleagues to institute change.

As Haubrich says, " . . . changes which can be recorded when the individual is out of his own organizational situation . . . do not have any long-term impact when the individual returns to the organizational setting. Change off the job has far less force than changes which occur *in situ.*"[3]

Continuing education programs at local school levels, according to Alice Miel,[4] apparently are not fully meeting the needs of teachers. The one factor which stands out is that there is little coordination between subject specialists, education specialists, and school person-

2. Alexander Frazier, "The New Elementary School Teacher," *The New Elementary School.* (Washington, D.C.: Association for Supervision and Curriculum Development, 1967), pp. 96-112.

3. Vernon Haubrich, "The Rhetoric and Reality of Educational Change," Mimeographed. Undated. P. 8.

4. Alice Miel, "New Patterns of In-Service Education of Elementary Teachers," *The New Elementary School* (Washington, D.C.: Association for Supervision and Curriculum Development, 1967).

nel in planning or conducting a continuing education program. All too frequently these programs resemble college classes with a professor lecturing to teachers, the only difference being that he comes to them instead of their coming to the university campus.

A factor which limits the effectiveness of classroom teachers in developing good learning situations for children or young people is the role expectation of the building principal. As pointed out in the 1960 ASCD Yearbook, *Leadership for Improving Instruction*, the principal's primary role is that of providing instructional leadership after which come his responsibilities for building management and public relations.[5] Stated more bluntly, the principal bears the responsibility for either assisting or permitting educational change. His support and expectations have more influence on whether a teacher changes than do colleagues or students.

Recognizing his responsibility for providing instructional leadership, the principal also must accept responsibility for staff and student personnel administration, administration of the school plant facilities, public relations, and school organization which involves scheduling, transportation, and cafeteria management. It is in these latter areas that the principal can find clearer courses of action to take and the results of action. In addition, in many instances, his preparation has dealt more with these managerial tasks than with providing leadership in instruction and curriculum development.

An examination of requirements for principals as described in university catalogs shows that programs in general include courses such as introduction to administration, school law, school plant, the principalship, finance, supervision, personnel problems plus some required study in a cognate area such as sociology, and some electives which can be but are not required to be in learning, human development, curriculum, or social foundations. As can be seen, the stress is on administrative procedures and technical knowledge. As expected, the principal operates within the framework he knows best.

NEW POSITIONS NEEDED

This is borne out when activities of principals are evaluated. Principals in elementary, junior high, and senior high schools were asked to keep a log of activities for ten days. Administrative and managerial activities such as supervision of bus transportation, rest rooms, and school plant; public relations; and similar duties far outnumbered supervision of or working with teachers in terms of improving the instructional program, teacher effectiveness, or learning situations for students.

5. "Educational Leaders in Action," In: *Leadership for Improving Instruction.* 1960 Yearbook (Washington, D.C.: Association for Supervision and Curriculum Development, 1960), pp. 110 ff.

Many superintendents and principals have recognized this problem and various attempts have been made to alter the situation. Vice-principals have been added, but too frequently their preparation has been similar to that of the principal—that of administering rather than helping teachers be more effective. In addition, when a vice-principal is appointed, one more rung is added to the administrative hierarchy and according to Griffith, the more hierarchical the structure, the less possibility of change.[6]

To alleviate this problem, it is proposed that two new positions be established, replacing the principal. These positions are a Coordinator of Learning and a Coordinator of Administrative Services.

COORDINATOR OF LEARNING

The position of Coordinator of Learning has two important facets. One, the Coordinator is freed from managerial tasks, thus enabling him to devote his energies and expertise to the task of improving the teaching-learning process. As this is a different role from that commonly associated with the principalship, the title of principal is replaced.

Two, the role and function of the Coordinator of Learning are closely related to those of teachers. This means a teacher can move into this position without having to enter a new preparatory program such as is required currently when a teacher prepares to be a principal. For the most part, programs for principals have little direct relation to classroom teaching-learning application. This new position, then, opens a new avenue for professional progression for career teachers who wish to remain identified with the instructional program but who have ability and interest in providing constructive leadership.

The work of the Coordinator of Learning is augmented through direct communication with the team leaders who represent teams of teachers planning and organizing the activities of groups of students. The team is composed of teachers, teacher aides, student teachers, paraprofessionals, and special resource personnel. The Coordinator of Learning has responsibility for the total instructional program within the school and he is responsible directly to the system-wide person in charge of learning and instruction. He can call on specialists from all walks of life, including available resources within the community and area and discipline specialists from the university level, as well as available personnel from state departments of education and other agencies.

He will not, however, be an "Administrator" of instructional programs but rather a facilitator who creates an atmosphere in which teachers can experiment and develop creative approaches to learn-

6. Quoted by Vernon Haubrich, *op. cit.*, p. 10.

ing. His will be an active effort to help teachers analyze problems and to consider alternatives to solving them; in short, he will serve as a learning counselor. Examples of his functions and responsibilities are shown in Figure 1.

COORDINATOR OF ADMINISTRATIVE SERVICES

The Coordinator of Administrative Services is charged with the functional aspects of the school operation, including such things as the work of secretaries, custodians, and other auxiliary personnel.

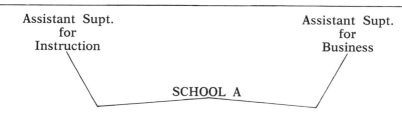

Coordinator of Learning

1. Is responsible for instructional leadership
2. Assists in planning continuing education program.
3. Assists in selecting teachers
4. Assists in relating program
   a. to objectives of school system
   b. to local community needs
5. Encourages innovation and experimentation on part of teachers
6. Meets with parents to discuss and describe program
7. Helps teachers develop more effective teaching-learning situation
8. Helps teachers deal with problems of pupil control and discipline
9. Aids teachers in effective use of instructional media and materials
10. Arranges for consultants to assist teachers
11. Works with other Coordinators of Learning, supervisors, and other staff members to relate program to the overall system program
12. Works with Coordinator of Administrative Services to provide smooth operation of lunchroom, secretarial services, use of resources, etc.

Coordinator of Administrative Services

1. Supervises non-instructional personnel such as secretaries, custodians, food service staff
2. Supervises transportation of students
3. Supervises buildings, grounds, and storage
4. Handles requisitions of supplies and materials
5. Maintains necessary records such as attendance of students and staff
6. Is responsible for fiscal operation of the school
7. Works with the public in community use of facilities
8. Works closely with the Coordinator of Learning in recommending needs to be included in school budgets to the person in charge of system-wide business matters
9. Can be approached by teachers directly without going through the Coordinator of Learning except for requisition of supplies and materials
10. Works with Coordinator of Learning to provide smooth operation of lunchroom, secretarial services, use of resources, etc.

Figure 1. Proposed Functions and Responsibilities

His task is to bring to bear those personnel and physical facilities necessary for supporting an adequate instructional program developed by the instructional staff. He handles the requisitions for supplies and materials, maintains necessary records, and is responsible for the fiscal operation of the school. Depending on the complexity and location of schools, the Coordinator of Administrative Services may be responsible for one or more schools. He reports to the system-wide person in charge of business operations for the school system. Examples of functions and responsibilities are shown in Figure 1.

The Coordinator of Learning will provide leadership for instructional improvement and be the final arbiter in the event a dispute arises concerning an instructional and a managerial matter. Since each person, however, has specific functions and each is responsible to a different head, coordination and cooperation between the two are essential.

RESULTS

Teachers can look forward to a more stimulating atmosphere in which they not only can talk about but can have immediate assistance in developing innovative programs. No longer will they have to wait for a curriculum specialist to come from the central office; one is at hand to provide assistance and guidance. Now they have a person in a leadership role at the building level whose primary responsibility is for and, more important, whose interest is in program development.

Teachers now can expect that all resources will be coordinated and available for the central purpose—that of providing a stimulating learning environment for children. This can be accomplished through the division of responsibilities so that each Coordinator can devote his energies and expertise to that which he knows best.

The position, Coordinator of Learning, opens an avenue for career development for both men and women which does not require extensive retraining. The position, Coordinator of Administrative Services, opens a new avenue for persons with a background in business administration and management. Needed also would be a broad knowledge of the function of schools in addition to specific knowledge of school law and finance as these pertain to the responsibilities of the Coordinator of Administrative Services.

The complexity of providing instructional leadership and carrying out the varied aspects of school management is such that no one individual can be expected to do everything in an adequate manner. It will avail little to develop innovative practices in curriculum unless similar advances are made in the instructional and managerial leadership areas.

part three

The PRINCIPAL
and INSTRUCTIONAL
LEADERSHIP

Curriculum
Leadership

III

Students have had it with the kind of curriculum that they perceive to be one of simonizing rather than humanizing their learning.

—OLD SAND

Of the many functions performed by the secondary school principal, probably the most significant is curriculum leadership. More than ever before, he is called upon to exercise leadership in the development of a curriculum which will meet the changing demands of students and society. He is charged with moving the students and the faculty through the constant swirl of curriculum change. The principal is held accountable for setting the stage for curriculum innovation and development.

"You ain't seen nothing yet." This quotation describes the theme of the article by Dwight W. Allen as he looks into the curriculum for the eighties. He challenges educators to design curricula that will enable our students to surpass us.

"How long can we afford to offer a 19th-century education to a 20th-century student who will spend a major portion of his adult life in the 21st century?" This is the question educators must deal with as they look to the future. Arthur P. Ludka reports on the progress of one state in examining the status of its education and interpreting future social forces into an emerging design for education.

Education for What Is Real! Edward C. Pino and Walter L. Armistead present a secondary school curriculum model designed to bridge the gap between the real world and the unreal world of the school. The model may well contribute to the development of a relevant curriculum.

Administrators will do well to consider the prospects of a relevant high school curriculum. Gerald L. Jensen presents key parts of a proposal to improve instructional programs in high school. This proposal describes a plan designed to show how the necessary improvement might be realized.

Staff involvement is the key to curriculum improvement. Richard G. Telfer predicts failure for the school administrator who neglects to involve faculty in curriculum development. He suggests "there is ample evidence to predict that teachers like to become involved in goal setting, decision making, and planning type activities."

The teacher is the essential person for curriculum innovation. Neil Amos assumes "that the direction and amount of curriculum change are directly and irrevocably dependent upon the teacher." Curriculum change is a human process.

Public schools are becoming involved more and more in educational research. Harold E. Turner encourages the principal to participate in educational research in order to keep his program up to date.

Curriculum for the 80's | 11

Dwight W. Allen

However bold and imaginative we may be in our preparations for the 1980's, the decade holds surprises which none of us can foresee. America is undergoing change at an incredible rate, yet American education still clings dearly to its traditional ways. Nineteenth-century curricula, classrooms, teaching staff use-patterns, and organizational structures still rule the roost.

In a world such as ours, such stagnation means that education will continue to fall further and further behind the changing times. If our traditional schools, classrooms, and teachers stay as they are, or change only moderately, they may well be buried within 20 years.

How must the curriculum change if it is not soon to be dead? First, it must stop being monolithic, as the traditional liberal arts curriculum now is. It must not make the assumption that it knows, for once and for all, the bits and pieces that students of all kinds must learn. It must not, in a word, teach geometry to all students, although it *might* teach geometry as one area of possible relevance among a wide range of alternatives. In a world of diversity and change, a curriculum that prescribes the same course for all students can have no relevance to their lives, to their individually divergent paths of growth, nor to society as a whole.

The curriculum of the future must no longer justify its existence by sheer tradition. The traditional social studies curriculum, which presumes to "start with the individual child" by studying first him, then his family, then his community, city, state, country, and world, has no basis in the world of the present, let alone the world of the future. In a society in which Viet Nam, race riots, and Apollo moon shots are closer to the minds and hearts of its children than the neighborhood fire station, reliance on an outmoded tradition that equates physical proximity with educational relevance can be only a hindrance.

Furthermore, the curriculum of the future must avoid the Puritanical assumptions that still guide the liberal arts curriculum. Until we rid ourselves of our 18th-century notions about hard work, until we learn that maximum achievement with minimal effort is more desirable than maximum achievement with maximum effort, until we stop punishing students into believing that learning is hard work, we will never be able to explore the range of curricular alternatives that our times require. Exploration of new teaching techniques (e.g., multimedia presentations), new skills to be taught (e.g.,

From *Scholastic Teacher* (January 1969), pp. 13, 16. Reprinted by permission from *Scholastic Teacher*, © 1969 by Scholastic Magazines, Inc.

skimming, reading chapter headings, etc.), and totally new curricula (e.g., aesthetics) hinges on relinquishing the Puritan attitude toward life that still holds sway in education.

Finally, the curriculum of the future must avoid the strong commitment to factual knowledge and rote learning that characterizes the liberal arts curriculum. The time for individuals to have to carry masses of knowledge around in their heads should have passed away with the Gutenberg Bible. The student of the future will need great skill in knowing what he needs to know, finding it, and using it.

In short, future curricula must succeed in presenting a wide range of alternatives to students, helping them learn what they find to be relevant and central to their future lives, capturing a sense of effortlessness and joy in the learning process, and focusing on a child's ability to find and use information creatively. These guidelines can lead to the design and implementation of a wide variety of curricular structures. One such possibility is what I would call a liberal science curriculum. This would urge that more factual knowledge be made *available* to students within a curriculum that focuses on developing creative individuality in gathering and using that knowledge.

Rather than starting with the traditional disciplinary triumvirate of the humanities, natural sciences, and social sciences, the liberal science curriculum would emphasize four areas that draw on all the major disciplines of mankind: communications, human relations, aesthetics, and technology.

The liberal science curriculum would focus on the ways in which human beings relate to, communicate with, and feel about themselves and others. It would begin with existing problems in human relations and communication, both in the world at large and the classroom itself. Disciplined knowledge, activities, and laboratory experiences would be designed and carried out as a means of helping students achieve a better understanding of themselves, how they communicate, how they feel, and how they relate to other people.

At the same time, the liberal science curriculum would face directly the growing problems of man and his relationship to his man-made world. As educators, we have all too often allowed our fear of technology to make us all the more susceptible to use by machines. As the world comes to rely more and more heavily on technology, we cannot continue to be used by our own inventions, seeking refuge through the liberal arts curriculum in the aesthetic glories of the past. The liberal science curriculum would confront the issues of technology, control, and aesthetics.

This curriculum would take a much broader and deeper approach to aesthetics than is currently the case and would make active use of technology for human ends. A technological society can become grossly ugly when its members have neither the aesthetic sensibilities nor the courage to use technology humanly. But the same society, when populated by an aesthetically sensitized citizenry, possesses the potential for producing and experiencing artistic delights on levels well beyond those attained by any of our ancestors.

The challenge of designing a curriculum for the future is one which we can no longer afford to lose by passive reliance on tradition. If we continue to do no more than bring students to the same level of humanity we have achieved, we are doing a poor job of preparing them for the world in which they will live.

Can we, as educators, design curricula that will enable our students to surpass us? If we are short on alternatives for our students, and even shorter on the courage to try drastically new approaches, can we expect them to create the momentous alternatives that will be necessary to keep American society alive? If we continue to be timid, we will continue to produce timid students for a world that demands boldness, and then we will lose the opportunity for making education relevant to the future.

12 │ Education for the Future

│ *Arthur P. Ludka*

Realizing that the child entering the public schools in the latter 1960's will complete his formal education in the 1980's, Colorado has participated in the Eight-State Designing Education for the Future (DEF) Project and given serious study to the implications that future changes in society have for education. Under the leadership of the Colorado Department of Education, 89 representatives from business, industry, politics, lay organizations, public schools, and institutions of higher learning have spent the past two years seeking to answer two basic questions: *Where should education be going?* and *How should it get there?*

Using various resources from the DEF project, study committees have examined the status of education in Colorado and attempted to interpret future social forces into an emerging design for education. To date, we in the Colorado Department of Education have released four monographs from this study of the educational program for the future. The first, *Issues Facing Education in Colorado*, attempts to answer the basic question of direction. *Educational Needs of Children, Youth, and Adults in Colorado* gives an overview of the elements necessary to insure optimal individual learning. *New Directions for School Staffing in Colorado* indicates an emerging design for the instructional process, with its related personnel needs. *Enhancing Tomorrow's Learning in Colorado Through Supporting Services* describes the interaction of school and community in support of the learner.

A CHANGE IN DIRECTION

These monographs contain explicit messages that signify an emerging change in direction for education.

One message ringing loud and clear relates to the nature of education, using the Latin meaning "to lead" or "draw out." In the teaching-learning process the emphasis is on the word *learning*, for it is the key to the development of human potential. The learning process proceeds from cradle to grave, with or without a formal education system. Man cannot escape learning from everything in his environment throughout his life. But it is equally true that man exercises a choice over what and how he learns. Student "tune-outs," "dropouts," and "don't cares" demonstrate this fact.

From *Scholastic Teacher* (January 1969), pp. 14-15. Reprinted by permission from *Scholastic Teacher*, © 1969 by Scholastic Magazines, Inc.

Therefore, the teacher must develop skill in directing learning. He must plan learning experiences relevant to the learner's individual achievement-oriented goals in three major life-related areas: (1) personal attitudes and behavioral traits, (2) basic skills, and (3) an understanding of basic concepts and processes within the social and natural environments. Our public schools should give the student an understanding of himself and others, as well as an understanding of society's elements, processes, values, and problems. They should also help him comprehend the nature and potential of society's various systems—economic, administrative, political, and social—and the scientific laws of the physical world. Further, students should come to grasp the physical and moral limits of what is possible, and the implications for humanity of what is technically feasible.

Another message of importance to the teacher concerns the concept that education is a human and humane enterprise and that a teacher gives of himself in the teaching process. Our best teachers will be those who have compassion for their fellow man and can deal with the problems of teaching. They will have warm hearts, deep understanding, and great patience in diagnosing problems and providing needed learning experiences.

Advances in educational technology will support the teacher's role as a director of learning. Telecommunication systems will give schools and homes access to real and simulated learning experiences, to instant information from information storage centers, to extended human resources, and to programmed material geared to individual learning needs. The equipment and material available to schools will foster a learning laboratory setting that will better meet the objectives of individual students.

The most important word describing the instructional staff of the future is "team." Certainly the present education system uses teamwork, but the future promises a new personnel structure effectively utilizing personnel with various levels of skill and preparation. Public schools will not be the province of the certified teacher alone. Other personnel will be used whenever needed and available. The interplay of full-time, part-time, and volunteer personnel should contribute to greater acceptance of the expanded role that education must assume to meet the challenge of the future.

Curricular building blocks for individual student growth will be (1) concept centered, emphasizing the structure of the fields of study rather than mere isolated facts, and (2) concerned with teaching individuals to conceptualize and to participate, rather than merely learning bits of information. Other curricula will provide opportunities for the student to put his ideas into action, to test concept against reality. Still others will provide a setting for focusing on the concerns and needs of the individual. Process and content will be regarded as inseparable aspects of learning.

GUIDELINES FOR THE EMERGING DESIGN

"Learning," then, becomes the name of the game rather than "instruction." The following concepts serve as guidelines for the emerging design for education developing in Colorado's study under the DEF project:

- Nothing is ever taught, it is learned.
- Some things are learned best by some students working independently, whereas other things are learned best through the mediating or facilitating influences of the teacher.
- The vast majority of youngsters are capable of learning; the variables are their rates of learning.
- The content of education (that which is learned) is always a means, never an end.
- Any subject matter can be learned, in at least some intellectually honest fashion, by any student at any stage of development.
- In order to be effective, learning must be relevant to the learner's perceived needs.

As we look to the future, we must deal with this question: *How long can we afford to offer a 19th-century education to a 20th-century student who will spend a major portion of his adult life in the 21st century?*

Toward a More Relevant and Human Secondary Curriculum

Edward C. Pino
Walter L. Armistead

"The day is coming," United Nations' Secretary-General U Thant recently said, when people everywhere will consider one or two years of work for the cause of development either in a foreign country or in a depressed area of his own country as a normal and basic part of one's education."

Education for What Is Real! This has been the hue and cry of parents, students, and educators the world over since the school form became a recognized social institution. It has not let up and indeed has even greater meaning to education today than ever before.

And Is It Any Wonder? Intellectual rebellion runs rampant around the world. Regardless of location, heritage, national purpose, or educational philosophy and pedagogy, institutions of higher learning—and now the secondary schools—are teeming from student agitation for a "more relevant" education.

Why? It is not the purpose of this discourse to analyze the numerous complexities of our way of life, many of which have attributed to the present disequilibrium. Certainly, everyone's "search for meaning" in today's life is made ever so much more complicated because of the tremendous scientific and social forces which test our values, challenge our "cool" and demand ever-increasing levels of performance. There is no easy explanation and, therefore, no easy answers. There are some notions, however, which when considered should cause us to reflect.

What's Right With Education? As in most things, there is good and bad in education. On the one hand, we should reassure ourselves that generally we are doing a darn good job of educating our youth. We can state quite categorically that by almost any measure this is so. Whether we compare the results of our testing programs, dinner table conversation, our economy, our race with space or with our own intellectual maturity at the same age, we cannot fail to feel generally comforted and reassured. Students today appear to be more alert, eager, honest, human, intellectually sophisticated, and mature than we who tutor and minister unto them were (and perhaps are) at the same age. The very restlessness about which we are now concerned is, in part, born of this higher level of intellectual questioning, objective analysis, and sensitivity for the welfare of others. These are pedagogical forms and human skills we have been striving to transmit to learners in better ways for years. Apparently, we have

From *The North Central Quarterly*, Vol. X LIII (Winter 1969), pp. 269-276. Reprinted by permission from the publisher and the authors.

succeeded beyond the humble expectations of educators and to the shock (and sometimes dismay) of the general public.

What's Wrong? We have come far but the quickening pace of change means we have much further to go just to catch up with other segments of our society. Our ability to reach the moon is not being matched by our ability to reach human beings. Our zeal to teach the new math is not matched by an equal desire to teach the new world. As a matter of fact, restructuring of almost every component of public education is desperately needed now. Facility, personnel, curriculum, instruction, management, and teacher education designs all need major overhaul. One imperative reason for this needed educational reform is that the American school as a social institution is very unreal.

What Is Real? The world is the only real frame of reference we humans know and, therefore, reality is the world itself. By comparison with today's world, the school is very unreal. If this appears to be too harsh a statement, please consider the following comparisons by way of example:

Learning in . . .

The Real World	**The Unreal World of the School**
• the world is the classroom	• the school is a box on a fixed site
• the environment includes the things of the world	• the classroom at best can only simulate the things of the world
• the teachers are all of the people—young and old, rich and poor, black and white, educated and noneducated	• the teachers are at best usually a largely artificial and stratified sampling of only some of the people
• the curriculum (content) is as of the moment—it is the new curriculum	• content is largely predestined, isolated, and compartmentalized
• children learn in a wide variety of multi-age groups	• children are grouped by subject and chronology
• learning experiences are direct and a part of living	• learning experiences are more abstract, sterile and programmed
• children can have privacy and independence in their learning experience	• children must pursue their learning experiences largely in groups
• children learn largely from one another	• children are taught to learn mostly from adults
• children pursue their interest and inclinations largely at their own pace	• children pursue learning paced by the groups and artificial schedules and time hurdles
• children assume a large responsibility of their own learning, discipline and custodianship	• schools are still largely custodial, highly regimented and with little responsibility passed along to the learner.
• performance is measured in terms of individual productivity.	• performance is normed and confined on a group basis
• apprenticeship training prepares the student for needed current skills	• vocational training is often for skills no longer in demand or in outdated techniques

We have created a very artificial gemini so incongruous with its twin as to be without the real appeal, value, and meaning school should have. For the college bound, we have trained for factual re-gurgitation instead of the enlarged responsibilities of an educated man. For the vocation bound, we have fallen far behind the rapidly changing technology with which the graduate must now cope and compete.

The point is that today's schools are out of phase with life as it is. The large problem is, however, that the more we rely on formal education for survival, the more it should be *in*—not out of phase with the surrounding society. The little red schoolhouse could have been more unreal and it would have made less difference because basic survival depended more on other things. Today, school matters. Increasingly and rapidly, survival is dependent upon the services of social institutions, including the school. We need look only to the family, church, and other institutions in a state of disequilibrium to recognize the problems which result when the purposes and practices of such institutions veer too far out of phase with reality.

It is the premise of this discourse then that the school is unreal in relationship to life today and that it must be made more congruent by becoming more life-like. The more a social institution becomes unreal and out-of-phase, the more unlikely it is that it will be replaced by a more meaningful response. The opposite must happen to our schools.

Apply this general premise to our specific curriculum and instructional practices. Too many artificial and unrelated experiences are presently scheduled in our secondary schools. Why, in most cases, is there no connection between American literature and American history even though both courses usually occur at the same level? In many instances, there doesn't even seem to be any communication between members of the social studies and English departments in the area of a literary and historical study. Mathematics is kept separate from the sciences. We find physics teachers teaching the math needed for their physics class because: "there is no assurance that the mathematics teacher has done an adequate job." We also find physical education and music divorced from other areas of our curriculum.

Time and time again students justifiably ask what connection to the real life of students can be found in our present curriculum and our present compartmentalization of the various disciplines. Students are concerned with such issues as race conflicts, authority, and urbanization. Shall they follow in search of material wealth above all else? Students reply that "life goes on outside of school; but in school we are protected." They have a wonderful opportunity to study Francis Bacon, the Indians, and Plymouth Rock, the true meaning of side-angle side, and the importance of learning how to take dictation, even though they probably will be using electronic equipment exclusively.

Our present instructional strategies are too time-consuming.
Long ago research confirmed that academic course preparation is
not the best indicator of success in higher education. Must we have
another Eight-Year Study to again point the way? Is failure in college currently more closely correlated with being unable to accept increasing and meaningful responsibility or to basic academic deficiencies? We waste time in our secondary schools while teachers
slow down for the slow, skip for the quick, and teach for the average.
Too few schools have individualized programs that allow the students to complete the required courses and begin to study those
things that the student believes are really relevant.

Student Responsibility. The area of student responsibility is being grossly ignored by most of our secondary schools for the simple
reason that responsibility is very difficult to teach. Professional educators find it difficult to stand by and watch the learning process ongoing. We have not yet educated our staff to help teach students as
well as subjects. Responsibility can only be taught by experimentation and counseling. The student begins experimenting in responsibility at some point on a continuum. Counseling is needed for the
inevitable problem of a student who does not grow in his ability to
accept responsibility. Will we continue to teach students responsibility as we learned it—by being in a situation where personal responsibility was not required but imposed, supervised, and controlled? Will we continue to increase the degree of student regimentation with each successive school year or prepare the student
for the freedom suddenly thrust upon him in college or the world of
work the day after graduation? Where in education do we find
schools prepared to make the task of learning to be responsible a
relevant and human experience for each student?

EDUCATION FOR WHAT IS REAL

How can this outmoded tradition and gap between the real
world and the unreal world of the school be overcome? A new curriculum is needed—a curriculum that tells it like it is—a curriculum
that looks ahead to tomorrow's problems instead of teaching merely
the antiquated facts of yesterday—a curriculum directly related to
life experiences.

The new curriculum must begin with worthy human aims. Some
of these aims will sound familiar; others indicate a new emphasis and
priority. They are listed below:

—To master sophisticated levels of impersonal relations and interaction based on deep convictions of the basic worth of all individuals;
—to prepare the student for the real world of work, study, service,
and recreation;

—to develop higher levels of creativity, critical thinking, and intellectual inquiry;

—to develop mastery of fundamental concepts, skills, and attitudes; and

—to insure a feeling of student satisfaction, success, and happiness with himself and his learning experiences while at the same time understanding that there are even greater intellectual heights to be conquered.

The articulation of these noble aims, however, is not enough. Most of us subscribe to goals like these and yet our programs don't always reflect them. Therefore, much greater specificity is needed. Educational objectives must lend themselves to implementation at the behavioral level. For example, many schools list an objective titled: "Preparing the Student for the World of Work," but the students receive only classroom instruction and never see the world of work until after graduation. To be relevant, these general aims must be translated into operational expectations from which man's worth can be evaluated in human behavioral terms. The following instructional objectives are presented with behavioral examples for purposes of illustration.

A. *To prepare a student for the world of life-long learning*: The student identifies personal goals; the student demonstrates knowledge of data collection tools (e.g. reading, listening and viewing); the student segments available time to gather information, classify, meditate, and plan future activities; the student utilizes agencies as sources (e.g. libraries, museums, zoos, corporations, schools, and governmental offices); the student classifies, analyzes (discriminates, and records information gathered (e.g. composition and typing ability).

B. *To prepare students for the world of work*: The student can financially support himself because he has saleable skill like apprentice level training in emerging fields such as data processing rather than in career fields which are fading from the employment scene.

C. *To prepare students to want to be of service to their fellowman*: When given the opportunity, the student responds in a positive manner (e.g. presents himself for projects, completes assigned tasks, organizes his time to be able to serve when called) and voices a willingness to become involved in activities for which there is no financial remuneration and which require a high level of commitment and giving of himself.

D. *To expose students to different kinds of socioeconomic, ethnic, and racial environments*: The student adjusts his standards of living and economic patterns to the group within which he lives; the student reacts in a positive manner to tasks assigned within ethnic communities (e.g. presents himself on time for work, completes tasks, organizes his time to complete required work); the student voices no discomfort in ethnic or racial relationships (e.g. Project Head Start and Vista) and volunteers to continue such relationships.

E. *To prepare students to make wise use of leisure time*: The student chooses those leisure time activities which are consistent with an expansion of his abilities; he uses a significant part of his "nonstructured" time to study and improve himself; he voices an understanding of the need and function of leisure time; he assigns worth to those leisure-time projects which are consistent with his personal goals.

F. *To prepare students to be able social beings*: The student voices no discomfort regarding human relationships in a social contest; the student attends social functions; the student has knowledge of and demonstrates acceptable, initiating, continuing, and concluding behavior and group discussion and conversation behavior. The student participates in social activities with same and opposite sex; individuals and groups.

GETTING STARTED!

To implement a more relevant education, a two-phase curriculum is suggested. This curriculum is not presented as the be-all and end-all in secondary education. In fact, we can see many weaknesses inherent therein. We do feel it is a step in the right direction, however, and worthy of consideration.

Phase I is considered the basic program. In the basic program a concentrated content is presented, mostly conventional in nature consisting of salient and the most relevant concepts, skills, and attitudes.

The basic program would be a familiar program to most parents and educators.

CONCEPTS such as those listed below should be implemented and integrated into our present curriculum and each discipline should develop many subconcepts for day-to-day teaching:

   —Peace is a necessary goal.
   —Space can be conquered.
   —The world is becoming smaller.
   —World overpopulation is a distinct possibility.

SKILLS would include such activities as:

   —I can read, write, speak, and listen effectively.
   —I can transport myself because I have a driver's license and competency in the automobile.
   —I possess a saleable skill.

ATTITUDES would be typified by the following:
—I understand the need for and the results of honest labor.
—I respect law and order.
—I want to be of service to my fellowman.
—I respect persons of every race, color, and creed.

Phase II is a four-stream program expected to be the normal part of the secondary experience of all students rather than experiences provided only to a few or to none. Stream A should be a *Work Experience;* Stream B, a *Service Experience;* Stream C, a *Teaching Experience;* and Stream D would be an *Exchange Experience.* Phase II should be considered as having as much value for young people attending secondary schools as the basic program heretofore noted.

Stream A should be *Work Experience.* It is herein argued that this ethic of our culture has continuing validity despite the increased amount of leisure time and that the responsibility of the school to teach this ethic is increasing as fewer work options are available to young people outside of the classroom. The goal should be to teach the dignity and enjoyment of work when the job is well done and the reward is commensurate with the effort expended. Students should receive this experience in the actual off-campus job environment. It is anticipated that the student should spend about the equivalent of one semester working at least half a day off campus and that he would receive monetary reward for this work. It should be the school's responsibility to arrange for relevant experiences as well as to supervise and evaluate the student's job performance cooperatively with the employer.

Stream B should be a *Service Experience.* The goals of this program suggest that one should do unto others as one would wish done unto him. There should be no salary of any kind and the service should be one where a student gives freely and unselfishly of his talents, time, and energy. The service experience should also be about a semester in length. During the experience, the students should spend two or three hours a day on various days of the week working with such activities as VISTA, Head Start, public libraries, museums, and zoos. They could assist at hospitals and other institutions requiring enthusiastic and hard-working personnel. In addition, various and vital community projects could be supported and augmented by students.

Stream C should be a *Teaching Experience.* The goals of this experience should be to convey the rewards of teaching others, to arrange instructional strategies for unmotivated learners, and to assist in the staffing of our schools. It should not involve salary of any kind. During this experience, students should spend about a semester assisting three days a week, for three hours, in their local or near-by elementary and middle public or private school classes as "teaching assistants." Their duties should be clerical, but also should include, on a regular basis, the instruction of students who are having difficulty because of the lack of opportunities for individualized instruction.

For example, in the area of science, the students may work as science assistants and be responsible for organizing experiments, acting as lab technicians and supervisors of open lab activities. In the area of math, they might act as tutors and as supervisors of mathematics open-lab space. In the areas of English, social studies, and foreign language, tutoring assistance might be given as well as assignment assistance for those students who have been absent. Supplemental assistance might also be provided for those students who require more personalized attention, and for the teacher in the performance of clerical, housekeeping, and para-professional duties.

Stream D should be an *Exchange Experience*. The students should in most cases have already completed their work, service, and teaching experiences. They should be ready to accept the rigors of living in an environment other than the one in which they were raised and to apply all of their prior learning on a full-time basis for at least the equivalent of one semester. During this stream of their experience they should live in a "community" different from their own and assist in as well as learn from the schools and students with whom they associate. The community might be another section in a metropolitan area, an Indian reservation or a partnership school overseas. The students should continue to serve, work, and teach as their previous training has now prepared them to do. The main objective of the exchange experience, however, should be to broaden and enrich their own background by day-to-day living in an area other than the one in which they were raised.

HOW IT WOULD WORK

This article cannot describe in detail how all of these experiences would be provided but we can outline a frame of reference by way of example. Let's consider Cherry Creek's project EPIC as illustrative of the kind of service experience we are talking about.

EPIC stands for Educational Participation In Communities. The EPIC idea came into being as the result of concern over the lack of student involvement in nonpaid service activities of our school community, a lack of exposure with environments different from their own, and a realization of the isolated nature of suburban living. As a result, students and staff members communicated their concern to parents and a joint steering committee was set up to formulate a service proposal for the Cherry Creek Schools.

EPIC is designed to increase student awareness and sensitivity to the rights and needs of other human beings; to develop student self-reliance, personal responsibility, and the skill to promote the growth of these abilities in other people; and to create student-parent-staff teams which feel a sense of obligation to be actively involved in service to their community and which gain mutual benefit and satisfaction from the joint effort.

The project is supervised by a steering committee. The EPIC Steering Committee is composed of one administrator, two faculty members, three parents, and three students. The PTA President, Head Boy, Head Girl, and the high school principal serve as ex-officio members. This committee receives, reviews, and helps process student, parent, and staff applications. It organizes orientation programs for students. It assists in forming the area teams, establishes general team guidelines, and receives reports and recommendations from the area teams at the completion of the working phase of the program.

Present areas of field service include:

1. Museum of Natural History (Cultural)
2. Arapahoe County Department of Public Welfare (Sociological)
3. Metropolitan Denver YWCA (Tutorial or Recreational)
4. Head Start (Educational)
5. Denver County Court Probation Services (Criminal Law)
6. Denver's Person-to-Person Program (Tutorial)

The students participating in the service areas are chosen through written applications sent to the EPIC Steering Committee. Participants form teams to work with each of the service areas involved. Each team is composed as follows: 4-12 students; two faculty members; and two parents. Teams are organized when information about additional service areas becomes available and when students indicate a desire to participate.

The time commitment for each group involved in the EPIC program is as follows:

—students—a maximum of six hours of school time per week
—staff—four ½ days or released time and two evenings per semester
—parents—six ½ days or evenings per semester

Students contract for field service with the agency to which he volunteers his time, talent, and energy. Students successfully completing a semester of participation in the EPIC program receive ½ credit in the elective area of the curriculum. Students are evaluated in accordance with how successfully they complete these contractual requirements.

Similar projects are also now underway to test the desirability and feasibility of the other streams. Exchange programs are being expanded with partnership schools in Denver, Mancos, Cortez (in the four-corner area of Colorado), and with the International School in Bangkok. Work experience programs are being extended to in-clude more students and our high school student assistants are now teaching, guiding, and helping their younger brothers and sisters in all of our lower and middle schools. Thus, we are attempting to sug-gest the kind of secondary school in which students may begin to be more human and relevant. It is not anticipated that all students should receive the same rewards for learning contracts in these four areas of curriculum. Compensation should vary in accordance with each student's unique requirements.

PROGRAM REQUIRES MAJOR CHANGES

To achieve the objectives of this kind of secondary school ex-perience, many changes are necessary. The conventional time sched-ule for each class must be modified to provide more flexibility and individualization. The campus boundaries must shift from the edge of the school property to include the whole community. The com-munity must become the classroom. Our schools must take to the road and our classrooms become mobile.

Responsibility must also shift to the learner with relevant ac-tivities and training scheduled early enough in the educational pro-gram so that by the time a student reaches his senior secondary school experiences he is prepared to handle this kind of increased academic freedom and responsibility. The Carnegie unit must be changed so that it no longer reflects the time basis for credit. Basic skills, concepts, values, and attitudes must be specified in behavioral terms so that both student and educator know when readiness for different experiences is achieved.

Teaching must be a cooperative effort by teams of adults in the community. The professional team must be expanded to include certificated teachers, counselors, and nonprofessional aids as well as employers, parents, volunteer workers, and other knowledgeable adults. Placement and pacing must become individualized.

Learning contracts must replace grading and promotion must be in relation to the achievement of meaningful academic hurdles and not merely the passage of time or the regurgitation of unrelated facts. Finally, colleges and the world of work must endorse the pro-gram sufficiently so the successful hurdling of experiences rather than grades and units of work are acceptable passports to further learning and employment.

The basic question is not if, but when; not what, but how; not for how many, but in what form. This then becomes our challenge.

Secondary school staffs must become creative and bold enough to try. Institutions of higher learning must adjust to public school experimentation. Accrediting associations must allow us to deviate from the conventional.

If American education is going to truly reflect secondary curriculum relevancy in the 1970's, we can no longer be satisfied with the six-period day, a restricted subject-oriented professional staff, and a curriculum designed between two covers of a book. We should expand our curriculum, our campus, and our professional team to the limits of our real communities and human ingenuity.

14 A Proposal for the Improvement of Instructional Programs in High School

Gerald L. Jensen

PREFACE

This paper contains key parts of a proposal to school administrators and teachers in Imperial County, California. The proposal is that a strong effort be made to change the instructional programs in the high schools in order that the schools may more effectively and efficiently meet their responsibilities to *all* students and the community.

It also contains key parts of a plan designed to show how the necessary improvement might be brought about.

WHY A THOROUGH OVERHAUL OF HIGH SCHOOL INSTRUCTIONAL PROGRAMS IS NECESSARY

Symptoms of Inadequacies in the Prevailing Instructional Programs

How would you rate a manufacturing establishment that had 30% rejects? How long could they stay in business? How would you rate a school system that had 30% rejects?

The number who graduated from Imperial County high schools in 1967 was only 70% of the number who were enrolled as freshmen in October 1963. Fourteen hundred forty four were enrolled as freshmen at that time; ten hundred thirteen graduated. This was a shrinkage of 431. Most of these were rejected by the school and most of them in turn rejected the school. Why?

An indefinite number of those who remained in school gave up and became indifferent to learning and thus, in effect, became dropouts. Perhaps typical of those who gave up and also many of those who dropped out was the experience of a young man who came to the writer for help. When asked when he dropped out of high school he replied, "I dropped out when I was in the 9th grade but I quit trying when I was in the fifth." Others bright enough to do well in high school also become indifferent to learning because they feel no need to learn or that the program of the school has no value to them. Why?

Special and remedial programs are the order of the day in present day education. We have special programs for the academically gifted, special programs for the mentally retarded, special programs

From *Journal of Secondary Education*, Vol. 44 (February 1969), pp. 86-95. Reprinted by permission of the publisher.

for the emotionally disturbed, and a number of others. A large portion of the programs under Title I of ESEA are remedial. Why? Why are so many remedial programs necessary? Some special programs will always be needed but why do we need so many?

Other symptoms of inadequacy in the prevailing instructional program include:

1. Hatred of school on the part of some students.
2. Under achievement—achievement below achievement potential.
3. Student unrest in high schools and colleges.

Factors Responsible for Instructional Inadequacies

Many factors are involved in producing the situations described in the preceding paragraphs. It may be heresy to say so, but many of the contributing factors are in the school itself. These include:

1. Schools do not make an adequate adjustment to individual differences in academic achievement potential and other factors which affect learning, such as motivation and handicapping conditions in the students' self and his environment.
2. There is insufficient opportunity for students to develop the qualities required for intelligent and responsible self direction.
3. There is an over emphasis on telling as a method of instruction.
4. There is inadequate effort to teach today for the changing world of the present and the future.
5. There is not enough of teaching by example and "learning to do by doing" in the teaching of democracy and citizenship.
6. Not enough attention is given to feelings and emotions. Instruction should include affective as well as cognitive aspects. The following quotation is illustrative of the situation which prevails in most schools:

   "Whatever educators may profess to the contrary, there is less urgency about teaching children compassion for their fellow man than about teaching them to read."[1]

**Widespread Failure to Make Adequate Adaptation
to Individual Differences in Ability to Learn**

Failure to make adequate adjustment to individual differences in ability to learn is one of the most serious weaknesses in our instructional system. Regarding this weakness Arthur Corey[2] states the following in an editorial in the March 1965 issue of the *Journal of the California Teachers Association*:

Recent events have dramatized the unbelievable inferior educational opportunities available to many American Negroes, but this ominous fact

1. This quotation is taken from a planning project report entitled *A Plan for Evaluating the Quality of Educational Programs in Pennsylvania,* submitted by Educational Testing Service to the Pennsylvania State Board of Education, June 1965.
2. Dr. Corey was executive secretary of the C.T.A. at the time. He has since retired.

should not blind us to other forms of educational discrimination which we cannot continue to ignore with impunity.

Beginning with his first day in school and continuing with increasing severity as he grows older, the child with limited academic competence faces grave discrimination. Not only in society at large, but in the school itself, the student's ability to handle abstract ideas is a pre-requisite to his recognition and progress.

After referring to what he calls our "mystical reverence for the academic," Corey states:

However, it now seems safe to assert that equating academic competence with success is sometimes a rationalization to defend existing educational programs which do not now and never did have any great value for many of our children.

The title of Mr. Corey's editorial was, "Discrimination Against Half of Our Children." But we also discriminate against the academically talented. We do this by failing to free them to learn up to their full achievement potentials, and by failing to adequately stimulate their creative talents, their powers to think, their powers to build realistic values and goals.

Adaptation to individual differences in ability to learn is a difficult problem for the range of differences is great. At the 14 year old or 9th grade level the grade equivalent of a 60 IQ is 3.4.[3] The grade equivalent of an IQ of 140 is 14.6. This is a range of more than 11 grade equivalents. The range becomes greater with each advancing year until at the 17 year level it is from a grade equivalent of 5.2 through 18.8 or a range of more than 13 grade equivalents. Should all be given the same learning tasks and textbooks?

School achievement is influenced by factors in addition to academic achievement potential as measured by intelligence tests. These also should be considered when designing the instructional system. They include the following:

1. Volitional or motivational factors such as level of aspiration, goals, purposes, understanding of the relationship between school achievement and personal goals and purposes, and motivational elements in the immediate situation.
2. Background factors such as habits, attitudes, skills, knowledge, language problems, and cultural background.
3. Physical factors, such as perceptual make-up, health, energy, presence or absence of handicapping defects, including neurological impairments.
4. Distracting influences such as bad home conditions, wrong friends, etc.
5. How the student pleases his teachers.

3. The figures here are based on the Binet IQ Scale.

Proposal for Action

IT IS PROPOSED HERE THAT THE HIGH SCHOOLS OF IM-
PERIAL COUNTY BEGIN MOVING *NOW* TO CORRECT THE
WEAKNESSES IN THE INSTRUCTIONAL SYSTEM THAT HAVE
BEEN POINTED OUT IN THE PRECEDING PARAGRAPHS.

ESSENTIAL FEATURES OF AN ADEQUATE INSTRUCTIONAL SYSTEM

Primary Characteristics

If the high school is to adequately fulfill its responsibilities,
both to its students and to the community in today's world, the instructional system must have the following characteristics:

1. Students work at their own achievement levels with instructional
   materials and learning tasks appropriate to these levels.
2. Students work at their own rates.
3. Progress is continuous, irregular perhaps, but without large gaps
   or breaks.
4. A high level of mastery is required before a student moves from
   one assignment, contract, or level to a higher one.
5. The teacher is:
   a. A director and motivator of learning activity
   b. A supplier of information not available or readily available in
      the instructional materials being used
   c. A stimulator, a skillful questioner, a guide to thinking
   d. A respecter, an encourager, a morale builder, a listener, a coun-
      selor
   e. Concerned about and is interested in every student, and shows
      it.
   The teacher's task is to make the learning activity, which he
   directs, of maximum value to each and every student.
6. Learning activity includes affective as well as cognitive elements.
7. Students are given much freedom of choice but held responsible
   for the consequences of their choices. Deliberate effort is made to
   give them opportunity to learn and to practice responsible behavior and to learn and exercise intelligent self-direction.
8. Subject matter is relevant to the present and probable future
   needs of students.
9. Flexibility and adaptability are characteristic of the instructional
   program with the best interests of the students being the guide
   to action.

Types of Teaching-Learning Activity

The instructional system should include the following teaching-
learning activity:

1. Large group activity—Teaching-learning activity that can be done
   as well in a large group as in a small group.

2. Small group activity—Teaching-learning activity which can be done only in a small group which students learn through thinking, interaction, and oral self-expression.
3. Individual study—Learning activity in which the student works at his own level and his own rate under the supervision of a teacher. In individual study the student may undertake projects of his own choosing in work that is above and beyond that to be done with basic instructional materials. Individual study includes independent study which requires unusual capacity for responsible self-direction.

*   *   *

In the following the writer attempts to illustrate briefly how these principles may be applied to improve the instructional system. Nothing that is suggested is entirely new. Most of it has been tried in the past and most of it is being tried at the present time in some of the high schools in California and other parts of the country. Much of it has already been tried with excellent results in the continuation high schools of Brawley and El Centro, and in Juvenile Hall. The validity and feasibility of what is being suggested has also been tested in practice by six teachers who have worked with the writer in the last two years.

GENERAL OBJECTIVES OF THE INSTRUCTIONAL PROGRAM

The Democratic Philosophy

The instructional system should rest upon and implement the democratic philosophy. This philosophy is succinctly expressed in the following paragraphs from *Pursuit of Excellence*:

There is no more searching or difficult problem for a free people than to identify, nurture, and wisely use its own talents. Indeed, on its ability to solve this problem rests, at least in part, its fate as a free people. For a free society cannot commandeer talent; it must be true to its own vision of individual liberty. And yet, at a time when we face problems of desperate gravity and complexity, an undiscovered talent, a wasted skill, a mis-applied ability, is a threat to the capacity of a free people to survive.

But there is another and deeper reason why a free nation must cultivate its own human potential: Such a task reflects the very purposes for which a free society exists. If our nation seeks to strengthen the opportunities for free men to develop their individual capacities and to inspire creative effort, our aim is as importantly that of widening and deepening the life purposes of our citizens as it is to add to the success of our national effort. A free society nurtures the individual not alone for the contribution he may make to the social effort, but also and primarily for the sake of the contribution he may make to his own realization and development.

Two sets of general objectives follow. Either one of them constitutes a good guide to instructional practice. The two together point out very well what the instructional program should accomplish.

The Goals Set Forth in the Pennsylvania Study[4]—Quality education should help every child acquire:

1. Understanding of himself and appreciation of his worthiness as a member of society.
2. Understanding and appreciation of persons belonging to social, cultural, and ethnic groups different from his own.
3. Mastery of the basic skills in the use of words and numbers.
4. A positive attitude toward school and toward the learning process.
5. Habits and attitudes associated with responsible citizenship.
6. Good health habits and an understanding of the conditions necessary for the maintenance of physical and emotional well being.
7. Creativity in one or more fields of endeavor.
8. Understanding of opportunities open to him for preparing himself for productive life which will enable him to take full advantage of these opportunities.
9. Understanding and appreciation of human achievement in the natural sciences, the social sciences, the humanities and arts.
10. Preparation for a world of rapid change and unforeseeable demands in which continuing education throughout his adult life should be a normal expectation.

Note the affective elements in this set of objectives.

Responsibilities of the School As Formulated by a Committee of the California Association of Secondary School Administrators

The schools' responsibilities as expressed by the CASSA Sub Committee on Curriculum Objectives[5] follows:

"Responsibility No. 1: To provide opportunity for understanding and appreciation of the need for individual flexibility in an atmosphere of change.

Responsibility No. 2: To develop in youth an attitude of inquiry; to teach the process of problem solving and decision making as distinguished from the storing of facts.

Responsibility No. 3: To continue training in the basic tools of learning.

---

4. Ibid.
5. From *Education Now for Tomorrows' World*, the 1968 report of a sub committee of the Curriculum Committee of the California Association of Secondary School Administration. Robert D. Morgans of Visalia was Chairman.

Responsibility No. 4: To develop a curriculum where the criteria for priorities is based upon relevance to contemporary and future needs of youth.

Responsibility No. 5: To prepare youth for a changing world of work.

Responsibility No. 6: To prepare youth for responsible, participating citizenship.

Responsibility No. 7: To provide preparation for productive use of leisure time.

Responsibility No. 8: To extend and emphasize the teaching of the fine arts.

Responsibility No. 9: To teach civilized human relations.

Responsibility No. 10: To build bridges to an understanding of all the peoples of the world.

Responsibility No. 11: To assist youth in developing moral and ethical guidelines.

Responsibility No. 12: To prepare youth to understand and deal constructively with psychological tensions.

Responsibility No. 13: To assist youth in developing ways of insuring individual privacy and worth in a world of increasing group activity and social supervision.

Responsibility No. 14: To provide opportunities for study and understanding of urban life and problems.

Responsibility No. 15: To develop an instructional program in school that fully utilizes information sources and agencies outside the classroom."

The two preceding statements of what the instructional system should accomplish, like all statements of general objectives, are of necessity comprehensive rather than specific. However, objectives that are formulated in the effort to implement the general objectives should be specific, measurable, attainable, and challenging.

CONTENT

General Considerations

Functions of content—Content has two principal functions in the learning process:

1. It provides information useful in living and problem solving in the present and in the future.
2. It serves as a vehicle in the development of the various controls of behavior which are sought as objectives—knowledge, habits, attitudes, ideals, appreciations, etc.

Content in relation to achievement level—Content must be appropriate to the achievement levels of the learners. Mastery of the content should be difficult enough to push and challenge the student but not difficult enough to frustrate and discourage him. According to information presented earlier, the lowest difficulty level of content should be at about 4th grade. There will be some whose achievement level will be below 4th grade, but these will probably be in classes for the mentally retarded or other special programs. However, if they must be in regular classes, they should be permitted to use instructional materials appropriate to their achievement levels whatever they are.

Selection of basic content—Selection of basic content should be primarily a process of selecting basic texts and other basic instructional material. Adaptation to the teacher and peculiarities in the local situation may be made by adding needed content, omitting the study of content that may be inappropriate, and by varying time and emphasis. Of course, if the teacher has the time and ability to write his own textbook, he should do so. The general rule should be—Don't make anything you can buy. Materials should be adapted to peculiarities of the situation when needed.

As basic materials are selected and adapted, this responsibility should guide action: "To develop a curriculum where the criteria for priorities is based upon relevance to contemporary and future needs of youth." The publication *Education Now for Tomorrow's World*[6] elaborates this responsibility as follows:

The educational needs of youth are becoming so great and time to learn is so short that problem areas of instruction must be selected that are relevant to the student's age level, maturity level, perception of the environment level, and personally critical in terms of immediacy of application. We can no longer afford to keep courses in the curriculum only out of respect to tradition. We must be willing to prune out offerings as a means of promoting vigorous growth of the total curriculum. New courses must be developed with full understanding that they will be eliminated later as their usefulness fades.

Some Ideas Pertaining to Materials of Instruction

Use of texts designed for use in the elementary school—Materials designed for the elementary school will be suggested for use by those whose achievement levels are within the elementary school range if suitable material designed especially for the high school age cannot be found. There are at least three reasons for this:

1. It is necessary to use these materials at these levels if students are to work at their own achievement levels.

6. Ibid.

2. At the present time it is impossible to find enough materials for the lower levels of achievement without using books designed for elementary school use.
3. Some of the books designed for elementary school use are very good and entirely appropriate for use in the high school. Many of the newer books at this level contain new facts and ideas.

There will be two principal objections to using materials in high school which were designed for use in the elementary school.

1. High school students will not accept them.
2. It would be an undesirable lowering of standards.

In answer to the first objection: It depends on a number of things including the following:

1. The teacher's attitude
2. The pictures
3. The presence or absence of materials designed to motivate young children.

This writer has found that the acceptance of elementary instructional material by high school students is not nearly as big a problem as most of us imagine. He has recently worked with a number of teachers using materials at 4th through 8th grade levels in 9th-10th grade classes. None of them had any problem in this respect.

If students are given freedom of choice and a high level of mastery is required, they will select the textbook and other instructional materials that are appropriate to their achievement levels.

In answer to the second objection: It is a matter of facing up to the facts that: 1. There exists among high school students a wide range of differences in ability to do school work. 2. In a normal distribution of high school students, half are below average with those in the lowest part of the range having achievement levels and academic achievement potentials comparable to average pupils in the 3rd and 4th grades. See page 102.

METHODS OF INSTRUCTION

General Statements Regarding Method

As new instructional programs are planned, it is wise to give full attention to method of instruction. It, more than any single factor, determines the effectiveness of instruction in attaining the objectives sought. Method is also important because it has a significant effect on teaching effort, teacher, and student morale, and other factors involved in the efficiency of instruction. The following paragraphs set forth some important elements in method.

Learning centered—The following paragraph quoted directly from *The Non-graded High School* by Frank Brown presents ideas that should have a controlling influence on method:

Although the student is responsible for getting his own education and moving ahead at his own pace, the non-graded high school is not student centered[7] but rather learning centered—learning subjects and learning-to-think centered. The teacher does not "give" students education, he helps the student get it. In classes the emphasis is on raising questions and on skillfully helping students to find answers for themselves. When a student does independent work, the teacher must know when to leave the student alone, when to help by raising good questions, and when to get out of the student's way.

Basic respect—The teacher must have basic respect for all students and be aware and considerate of them at all times.

Flexibility and adaptability—Method must be characterized by flexibility and adaptability.

Precept, example, experience—Teaching should be done by:

a. Precept
   This includes situations in which the student listens, reads, views films, etc.
b. Example
   If you expect to teach democracy, you teach in a democratic way in a democratic situation. If you expect to teach students how to think, you must show how it is done.
c. By experience
   You must utilize student experience and provide opportunity for experience from which the student may learn—understanding, judgement, skills.

Freedom of choice and accountability—Students should be given much freedom of choice but be held accountable for the consequences of their decisions. They should receive guidance in making the decisions. They should be given many opportunities to learn and practice intelligent self direction.

Types of Teaching-Learning Activity

Instructional programs should include the following teacher-learning activity:

1. Large group activity
2. Small group activity
3. Individual study

Large Group Activity—Large group activity may be defined as activity which can be carried on just as well in a large group as in a small group. This includes film lessons, lectures, demonstrations, oral reports by students, etc. Approximately one-fifth of the time should be devoted to this type of activity. Large group activity may be parallel to what is being studied in basic texts or it may be entirely supplementary. The film lesson and lecture will probably be

7. The school should be both learning centered and student centered.

the most commonly used large group activity. In addition to presenting useful content, film lessons and other large group activities may provide excellent starting points for individual study and small group activity. The large group may be an entire class or a combination of several classes.

Small Group Activity—Small group activity is defined as activity which requires a small group and cannot be done effectively in a large group situation. In small group activity, the learner increases insight and understanding through interaction with the teacher and other members of the group and by means of oral self-expression. In small group activity the teacher should indeed be a dictator of learning activity, a skillful questioner, a stimulator, and a guide to thinking. Small group activity provides opportunity for the student to enhance understanding, to learn the processes of discussing, to think, to form judgements, and to build values and moral guidelines. For best results the small group should be from 4 to 7. If larger than 7 the individuals in the group do not have full opportunity for interaction and self-expression. Small group activity should be approximately one-fifth of the time.

Individual Study—In individual study the student works at his own rate with instructional materials and learning tasks appropriate to his achievement level. He may work entirely at his own rate or he may move forward at the same rate as others in a small homogeneous group. He may also undertake projects of his own choosing in which he is responsible to the teacher but has much freedom of choice about how to carry out his project. Approximately sixty percent of the time should be devoted to individual study.

The time allotments suggested here have been suggested by Lloyd Trump. Of course, the time should vary according to need and other relevant factors. The use of instructional materials and learning tasks appropriate to achievement potentials will make it possible to allow more time for individual study than would be the case if all students used the same book and the same learning exercises.

EVALUATION

Establishing Beginning Level and Moving from One Level to the Next Higher Level

Establishing beginning level—In the operation of the instructional program being illustrated, it is necessary to establish a beginning level for each student.

This might be done as follows:

An initial beginning level, in terms of a grade equivalent, should be established for each student. The basis for this could be an intelligence test score, a general achievement test score, or a combination of both. Students are assigned to classes on the basis of this score.

The initial grade equivalent should be tested in each class each student takes. *The principal means of doing this is tryout performance.* This may be supplemented by standardized test scores, or any other valid means at hand.

The beginning level for each student should be that level at which he is able and willing to do what would be considered "A" or high "B" work at the level selected. Eighty-five percent might be considered a minimum on tests and other measures of achievement used in the course. Beginning level for a given student may vary from subject to subject. It is possible that the beginning level for a student may be different in all subjects.

Another way to do it would be as follows.

1. Prepare the students by a presentation and discussion of individual differences. Show respect for students regardless of achievement level.
2. Provide textbooks for the range represented by the class.
3. Allow students to select their own books with the understanding that they will have to do "A" or high "B" work at the level they select.
4. Allow two or three weeks to make the necessary adjustments. Move students up or down depending on performance, not arbitrarily but with conference and guidance.

Ascertaining beginning level should be very carefully done since much depends upon it. Two or four weeks should be sufficient time in which to do it, however. A student may be changed at any time his performance and welfare indicates that it should be done. All changes should be tentative pending evidence from performance.

Moving from one level to the next higher level—After the beginning level has been ascertained, the student works at this level until he finishes the requirements (both quantitative and qualitative) of the course in which he starts. Then, and only then, does he move to the next higher level. Thus, satisfactory completion of a course at one level is a prerequisite to enrolling at the next higher level.

Since the student works at his own rate he may complete a course and enroll in the next higher level at any time in the school year. If he does not complete a course in the school year, he starts where he left off when he returns to school. It is to be expected that students with high achievement potentials will finish typical high school courses in less than a year. These are the ones who will enroll in independent study courses. It may also be anticipated that students with low achievement potentials will take more than a year to complete a course even though the difficulty level is adjusted to their achievement potentials.

ADVANTAGES OF THE SYSTEM

The instructional system presented here would have the following advantages:

1. It does all the following better than the prevailing system of instruction:
   a. Adaptation to individual differences in ability to learn, in motivation, in background, in goals, in needs
   b. Adaptation to the psychological characteristics and developmental tasks of youth
   c. Application of what is known about the learning process
   d. Application and implementation of the democratic philosophy
   e. Education now for the changing world of the present and of the future.
2. It places responsibility for learning and rate of progress squarely on the student in a way that is understandable and motivating to him.
3. These advantages will result in:
   a. Less frustration on the part of both teachers and students
   b. Higher morale on the part of both teachers and students
   c. More effective and efficient learning
   d. Fewer discipline problems
   e. Citizens of the future more capable of responsible self-direction than if educated under the traditional instructional system.
4. Other practical advantages include the following:
   a. It can be fitted into traditional school organization or into the newer modes such as team teaching, flexible scheduling, etc.
   b. It need cost no more than conventional instructional programs.

Staff Involvement | 15
Key to Curriculum Improvement

Richard G. Telfer

Staff involvement is essential if curriculum improvement is to become a reality. The school administrator who fails to recognize this concept will in fact fail to provide the instructional program to meet the challenge of the changing social, political, and economic order of modern times. Daily, school leaders face problems for which they must find answers or provide solutions. These problems may include developing an inservice education program for their building, selecting new text materials, or charting the course of the social studies program.

The alert administrator realizes that, within his building or system, he has a wealth of resources—his staff members. The task then becomes one of involving the faculty in developing solutions for these problems. Some of the group will be willing to help regardless of the situation. Some will have no desire to participate, but have much to offer as resource persons. The challenge as seen by the administrator is: "How will I secure the help and cooperation of the entire staff on a project for which I have the basic responsibility?"

There are certain basic facts that the administrator either knows or should know about his staff. He should know their strengths and weaknesses in their subject field. He should know their ability to work cooperatively with other staff members. He should know their attitude toward participation in building or system projects. He should know the techniques necessary to stimulate action on the part of each member or groups of members.

The problem of involving the staff in curriculum improvement activities is made easier because of the fact that adults generally are attracted to groups or group activities. People like to have membership and obtain recognition in a group. This fact is easily observable if we just look around us at the many groups and organizations that exist in our society.

People become members of groups for many reasons. Verner and Newberry present evidence that people are joiners and like to participate in all types of activities, many for the purpose of improving a situation or their own proficiencies.[1] In observing schools where curriculum improvement is in evidence, one finds the action of groups. Throughout the country there is increased emphasis on the

From *The Clearing House*, Vol. 43 (May 1969), pp. 539-542. Reprinted by permission of the publisher.

1. Coolie Verner and John S. Newberry, Jr., "Nature of Adult Participitation," *Adult Education*, Vol. 8, No. 4 (Summer 1958), pp. 208-222.

concept of staff participation for curriculum study and improvement. Gibbons indicates the need for involving all persons affected by an educational change. He believes that all should work, study, and plan together if the change is to be understood and accepted.[2]

The extent to which such participation will be meaningful is largely dependent upon the degree to which the participants will contribute to the group and to what extent their individual needs are met or challenged.

Dodd discovered that men strive harder as they perceive better and that they perceive better the more they become involved in a situation.[3] This evidence gives strength to the need for allowing people to become involved in formulating plans or programs which will affect their work.

Many school administrators have found it advantageous to allow the staff to participate in decision making in an area such as curriculum improvement. The wise administrator does not give a directive to the staff regarding a pending curriculum study, but rather extends an invitation to them.

The instance to be cited is typical of many taking place throughout the country each year.

A newly appointed director of instruction of a district found resistance on the part of the faculty to accept materials that had been administratively developed. This was particularly true in the area of resource guides. A science guide had been developed in the "front office," without consideration of pupil or faculty needs, and had been issued with the statement, "This is to be followed to the letter." Needless to say no amount of coaxing could bring about its use.

Through observation of the problem it was evident that there was a need for assistance in the science area and that there were many teachers doing a fine job in certain science areas.

The following approach was attempted with productive results. A meeting of the faculty involved with the teaching of science was called. Coffee and rolls were served during the informal discussion period. Action began in a positive way. "During my visits to your classrooms I have noted, with interest, the many fine activities going on in the science areas. Some of you have indicated an interest in getting more usable ideas to help your pupils. All of you have said that the resource guide prepared two years ago does not meet your needs. What suggestions do you have for improving our science instruction?" Immediately several teachers suggested the formation of a curriculum committee for the study of the science problems. Within minutes a committee of volunteers was formed.

2. Charles Gibbons, "Improving the Climate for Creativity in Your Organizations," *Advanced Management Journal*, Vol. 29 (July 1964), pp. 43-49.
3. Stuart Dodd, "Conditions for Motivating Men," *Journal of Personality*, June 1957, pp. 489-594.

The result of this committee's work and study was a teacher developed resource guide which has been used extensively by the teachers. An improvement in science instruction was also in evidence as a result of teacher participation in the setting of goals for the program. Here the role of the director was not that of dominator but rather that of a stimulator and resource consultant. The responsibility for the total instructional program had not been relinquished; rather, by placing the task in the hands of the faculty, the director's work was made easier and the program was accepted.

The technique just presented is not unique for any one system but is used throughout the country by school systems where real action is desired. Faculty members are basically engaged in creative work and want to develop their own materials.

Research conducted by Roman further supports this concept. Roman found that professionals engaged in mentally creative work became more effective when the responsibility for goal setting was shifted to them from their superiors.[4]

Additional support for the concept of nonadministrative domination of meetings and activities is found in a study done by Blumberg and Amidon. Two types of faculty meetings were studied: principal centered and faculty centered. The results of the study indicated that teachers were more willing to participate in the teacher centered type of meeting and that they felt better about their work as a result of the participation.[5]

Unfortunately, all administrators have not realized the potential of the productive capacity of their faculties. Such administrators have been heard to say, "My staff just doesn't want to do anything with regard to participating in curriculum improvement activities." In an attempt to determine the validity of such a statement, a survey designed to determine the willingness of teachers to take part in planning staff meetings, setting course goals, and serving on curriculum study committees was given to 70 teachers enrolled in an education workshop at Wayne State University.

RESULTS OF THE SURVEY

Question I

As an educator do you welcome the opportunity to become involved in setting goals, serving on productive committees, and helping in planning meetings?

  Yes   91%   No   7%   Sometimes   2%

---

4. Daniel Roman, "Project Management Recognizes R & D Performance," *Academy of Management Journal*, Vol. 7 (March 1964) pp. 7-20.
5. A. Blumberg and E. Amidon, "Teacher Reaction to School Faculty Meetings," *Journal of Educational Research*, May-June 1963, pp. 466-470.

Question II

Does your principal give you an opportunity to participate or become involved in setting goals, planning meetings, and serving on committees?

Yes   70%   No   26%   Sometimes   4%

Of those who were not given a chance to participitate, 88% would have welcomed the opportunity, while 12% of the group didn't want to participate.

Though the sampling is limited, it does give an indication of how teachers feel about becoming involved in matters which will directly affect their work. Administrators such as the one quoted earlier should withhold comment regarding the willingness of their faculty to participate until they have evaluated their own values, objectives, and techniques. It would seem safe to say that teachers, if given proper opportunity, welcome the chance to become involved with goal setting, meeting planning, and committee membership.

In addition, each teacher surveyed was asked to rate certain professional competencies of school administrators.

COMPETENCY	ESSENTIAL	DESIRABLE	NOT NECESSARY
Ability to motivate others	70%	30%	—
Can delegate	63%	35%	2%
Can maintain leadership without dominating	71%	29%	—

It would seem reasonable to conclude that teacher interest in having administrators with these qualities is a further indication of their desire to participate in school affairs.

In attempting to determine effective techniques used by administrators for involving their faculties in curriculum improvement projects, some 20 representative administrators were questioned. The responses from these administrators most frequently mentioned included such activities as workshops, weekly staff meetings, round table conferences, problem solving situations, role playing, and even the suggestion box.

Each of the techniques suggested is basically designed to stimulate program improvement and teacher acceptance of a particular program. Administrators who use such techniques have recognized that there is little professional growth on the part of a faculty member who never receives recognition of his ideas or becomes a participant in curriculum improvement activity.

There seems to be adequate evidence to support the basic premise that people, and in this case teachers, like to become involved in goal setting, decision making, and planning type activities. The administrator who capitalizes on this fact by providing situations that allow his faculty to become involved in these processes has recognized the motivational technique that will stimulate his faculty to a productive end.

The Human Process Direction for Innovation? | 16

Neil Amos

Every individual, teacher and student alike, reflects upon some values and standards whereby he evaluates himself in context with other individuals and society. This is part of the human process, life-long in nature, which gives meaning and conceptualization to the quest for understanding and patterning of behavior.

An assumption of many educators and psychologists is that it is "human nature" to want to change one's behavior. What implications does this assumption hold for curriculum innovation?

First, administrators and supervisors must become more conscious of the nature of change and the activities within the whole organizational structure which either solicit or retard change—an assumption being made here that human behavior does not remain static. Social process among human beings evolves around a system or systems of conventional understandings basic to the well-being of one generation to another. In essence this is why compulsory education came into existence—to propagate more knowledgeable social citizens for the betterment of society. Where then should innovation in curriculum change be focused—upon the social beings within the organizational structure, teachers and students, or upon the often impersonalized school program?

TEACHERS AND INNOVATIONS

The nature of a teacher's role is that of dependency. This social concept is visualized when we see a teacher forced by the administrative structure to work with other teachers and many students in varied situations. Yet this structure opens the door for directional change. Where relationships among staff members, administrators, and students are positive and supporting, the necessary security for inward acceptance and need for change may take place with a resultant outwardly behavioral change following. If distrust, friction, or envy enter the innovation realm, negative results are quite possible.

SCHOOL HIERARCHY AND CHANGE

Just to change or innovate does not preclude quality. However, if the administration does not develop genuine attitude and involvement toward curriculum change, very little of much significance will

From *Contemporary Education*, Vol. 50 (November 1968), pp. 97-98. Reprinted by permission of the publisher and author.

probably occur. Therefore, administrative structures should serve as models for innovation, not as barriers which must be overcome before change takes place. Given this model direction, teachers in turn must be willing and capable of finalizing curriculum change.

TEACHERS: MODELS OF CURRICULUM CHANGE

The assumption here is that the direction and amount of curriculum change are directly and irrevocably dependent upon the teacher. After all, what the teacher does in the classroom is the final curriculum product for a school day, week, month, and year; thus, this whole humanizing aspect of the innovative process can only be evaluated around "how the teacher changes and behaves in the classroom."

In the absence of the needed time, or perhaps, effective ways of humanizing change, we often have a tendency to short-cut as well as possibly short-change effective innovations by failing to deal openly and honestly with the facts that schools are social institutions and their components—teachers and students—are social beings and should be dealt with accordingly.

THE PARADOX OF CHANGE

Two important factors have been discussed here which affect curriculum change. The first is the assumption that human beings want to change and that changing the curriculum requires changing teacher behavior. Second, and somewhat paradoxically, is that the role of the school requires the transmission of conventional and traditional understanding from one generation to another. However, this social institutional role too often reflects a detachment from the conscious and unconscious emotional social values of one's own culture. Thus, the student finds the curriculum impersonalized. Detachment from the human desire to learn and change sets in and a relatively unhappy social product may develop. This in turn, may present problems for classroom instruction which inhibit the desire on the part of the teacher to see and want to change due to the frustration of the present instructional program.

What seemingly must take place, in order for curriculum change to be a healthy and permanent event, is that the responsible curriculum administrators and innovators must take into consideration the fact that this is, in essence, a human process and must be personalized for positive results.

The Principal— | 17
Moving Toward Research

Harold E. Turner

Is the only respectable, justifiable research that performed at the University? Might it be conducted throughout the district as a whole? Are there other dimensions or levels which have the need for and which can support acceptable research? This writer says "yes." Not only can much adequate research take place at the local building level, but there is an increasing demand for such activity.

The sixties will very likely go down in educational history as the time of the great "research awakening." Increased sums of research money from a variety of sources have caught the attention of the profession. Most districts, even the smaller ones, have climbed on the bandwagon and have begun submitting all types of proposals for possible funding. This has become particularly true in respect to the various governmental titles. While austerity programs in Washington appear from time to time, the prospects are strong that research support will continue.

Such research activity, developing at the building and at the district level, has catapulted the principal into a new arena. While he has long been recognized as the educational leader of his school, seldom was he asked to be the researcher. With this change in emphasis the principal must take a creative, informed leadership role for research development. Unfortunately many administrators have little preparation, understanding, or regard for such activity. The principal who persists in this negative attitude toward educational research will most certainly find that he has been omitted from the "main stream" of innovative instructional activity.

Larger, better staffed districts often play the "grantsmanship" game using the central office personnel. When such is the case the building principal is often relegated to a secondary role at best, and seldom is looked to for research and innovation leadership without the expenditure of considerable effort and persistent initiative on his part. In the smaller districts with the limited central staff it is much easier for the principal to play an expanded role in this area. In fact, he will likely be expected to perform this function along with his usual administrative duties. Regardless of the size of his district the astute principal will seek opportunities to maintain his research leadership role.

From *Education*, Vol. 89 (February-March 1969), pp. 231-235. Reprinted by permission of The Bobbs-Merrill Company, Inc.

As a result of this emerging emphasis it becomes more important than ever before that the principal thoroughly understand the research process. The prudent administrator will assess his own research capabilities and attempt to strengthen any deficiencies he might recognize. The following are some suggestions which the busy principal might well consider as he moves into this broader theater of operations. Careful consideration of these items should strengthen his role as the instructional leader in his building and at the same time make him a more valuable member of the district team.

BEING FAMILIAR WITH LATEST RESEARCH

First, the principal must be a competent consumer of research. Should he be fortunate enough to work in a district maintaining a central research office, he can expect to receive from it some specialized support and assistance. Of more importance to him, however, will be the regular, systematic routine which he establishes to keep knowledgeable as he constantly searches for methods of improving his own situation. This can best be done by reading the reports of research studies being conducted throughout the country.

Elaborate procedures are now being developed to disseminate results much more quickly than ever before through the use of microfiche and various electronic techniques. Regional laboratories are springing up throughout the country with one of their stated goals that of rapid dissemination of research to the practitioner. Much effort and considerable money are being expended today from many sources to ensure prompt communication of present research. The principal should make use of this wonderful opportunity to quickly learn what is taking place throughout the profession. The knowledge thus acquired should provide him clues as to what changes he might consider for his building, what trends in education are developing around the country, what new truths are being discovered which might influence the teaching and learning process.

UNDERSTANDING STATISTICAL LANGUAGE OF RESEARCH

Second, to become a more effective consumer of research he must have a clear understanding of the statistical language of the researcher. As he analyzes the various studies reported, he should be competent to detect which study has been properly conducted and when there are obvious flaws in the procedures used, conclusions drawn, etc. If he expects to reap the maximum benefits from his investigation, the principal must be capable of comprehending these statistical reviews which are written in highly technical terms. He must be able to relate the significance of the research to his own situation. He must recognize the strengths and inadequacies of the original design, the procedures employed, and the results obtained. If he truly aspires for educational leadership, he will expect to perform this task himself rather than rely upon digests and analyses provided by others.

This means that the educational statistics course which has been considered an unpleasant hurdle to get over as quickly as possible in order to complete a degree requirement now takes on a new meaning and importance. Now an understanding of the basic statistical process actually has a purpose for the administrator. He must become an active user of this tool as never before. Principals who have little or no practical knowledge and who feel inadequate to work with statistical techniques should seek help either by enrolling in a formal course in educational research and statistics or obtain some self-study material.

KNOWING HOW TO PLAN RESEARCH DESIGNS

Third, it would appear to be extremely valuable for the principal to be capable of drafting a simple research design himself. Whether he expects to participate in a piece of action research, something more nearly resembling pure, theoretical research, or merely some type of proposed innovation, it is now more important than ever before that the principal have basic competencies in this area. This should not imply that he be as expert as the university researcher. There are less complicated research methods, especially those utilizing nonparametric statistics, which are more readily understood and which can be employed easily.

Too often in the past those activities which passed for research were very loosely prepared. As the level of sophistication increases, more attention must be given to the development of a sound design. If the principal is able to provide leadership in this area, regardless of the size of the central staff, he will be a much more valuable contributor to the efforts of the district. If he desires to submit an innovative proposal for consideration by a foundation or governmental agency, expertise in preparing the draft will greatly increase the likelihood of favorable consideration.

He should give careful consideration to the formulation of a series of pertinent and penetrating hypotheses which get at the basic problem under consideration. Carefully thought out and constructed hypotheses can well spell the difference between eventual success or failure.

A well-planned method of evaluation must be "plugged in" from the very inception of the project if it is to perform the necessary function intended for it. Too many otherwise good experimental programs have been scuttled for lack of adequate evaluation. While the judgment of the participants is interesting and of some importance, it is seldom sufficient as the sole criteria of success or failure.

Most foundations and governmental agencies will provide staff expertise to help refine proposals into finished drafts satisfactory to the funding agency. The original plan must be sufficiently structured to interest and satisfy the reviewing official. Often good ideas are lost when the original proposal is not carefully drawn.

LEARNING TO ACCEPT OR REJECT HYPOTHESES

Fourth, procedures must be detailed which collect necessary data and evidence to either accept or reject the original hypothesis. Too often in the past the educational researcher has felt a strong compulsion always to "succeed." He has not recognized, or the pressures of the profession have not permitted him to accept, the fact that all experimentation need not become a glowing success which in and of itself will revolutionize everything in sight. He must be aware that on occasion a given piece of research which fails may provide as much pertinent information toward an eventual satisfactory conclusion as apparent early success. Everyone recalls the many failures Edison experienced before eventually perfecting the electric light bulb. Certainly initial failure might be much more significant than a protestation of success which actually may not have occurred. As the principal begins to accept the research concept, he becomes less rigid and feels less threatened by possible failure. He then becomes free to seek the difficult answers and his endeavors will become increasingly meaningful to himself, his staff and his district.

MAINTAINING PERSONAL CONTACT

Fifth, it is imperative that sufficient personal contact be made between the principal-researcher and members of his staff. We are becoming increasingly aware that those individuals who elect to try something new do so because of, and only after, adequate personal contact. Furthermore, those individuals who command the respect of their peers serve a key role. As they give their approval to an innovation, or as they try a new practice, their actions tend to cause their peers to also accept and adopt the change. Certainly one objective which the principal has is to seek better solutions to educational problems and then attempt to implement whatever he can within his own program. This he cannot do by himself. He must have the active support of a portion of his staff.

The principal who recognizes these research findings will be more inclined to encourage action on the part of key staff members. At the same time he will be certain to include some of these key people as initial members of his research team so that diffusion of the eventual results of the research project can more easily be realized. Too often past research conducted by the university researcher never permeated to the classroom level, but remained buried within journals. This will not happen if staff members respected by their peers are active, willing participants with the principal.

LOCAL SOURCES OF SUPPORT

As the principal contemplates action based upon the above suggestions, he is aware of certain built-in support available to him. There are several local sources toward which he may turn for assistance in developing the research proposal.

(1) He needs the confidence and general backing of his superiors—the superintendent and the board of education. Knowledge that this support is available will greatly encourage continued effort on his part. Suspicion or fear that his proposal will be disapproved by his superiors will certainly limit or greatly curtail any creative work.

(2) The principal will need much assistance from the members of his staff. Sometimes he will be working directly with his total staff. Sometimes he will be concentrating on some aspect with only a few volunteers. He will do well, however, to regularly inform all staff members regardless of the number actually participating in the eventual project. He might, for example, bring the entire staff into his confidence at the very start, either to obtain original ideas or to get critical reactions to his initial suggestions. Whenever he finds it possible to do so, he should proceed with a general staff consensus serving as his overall guide. Certainly a minimum effort would include progress reports made to the entire staff as the project proceeds towards its eventual conclusion. Each staff member in the building should feel personally involved to the extent that he becomes committed to work toward a successful completion or that he feels no personal threat because of the unusual activity taking place around him but not directly involving him.

(3) Often the principal will find some person outside the school district able to perform a valuable planning service. Research offices have sprung up in state departments, regional and county offices. There usually is a university nearby containing possible resource persons with a wide variety of competencies. The principal will find his task considerably eased if he seeks out these potential "partners" in his research enterprise and obtains their advice *prior* to *starting* his project. Many otherwise excellent ideas fail because of poor initial research design. Much that has gone on in the past under the name of research turned out to be anything but scientific or defensible and often is forgotten almost as rapidly as it is completed.

SUMMARY

In summary, it has been pointed out that the building principal must become an active participant in educational research or he will find himself bypassed. Because of greatly increased research activity in the public schools, it has become more imperative than ever before that the principal be a knowledgeable student of research method. Increasingly he is finding himself preparing proposals and directing projects as he has never done before. He need not go it alone, however. A variety of resources are available to assist him in these endeavors, including members of the central office staff, the neighboring university and various governmental offices set up for this purpose. Carefully designed projects and wise use of staff, particularly key personnel regarded as leaders by their peers, will greatly assist him in reaching a successful conclusion to his project. Lastly, if education is to truly fulfill the promises of its potential, the principal must now develop his leadership potential for research as he has in the past taken care of other administrative functions.

Supervisory
Leadership   IV

The supervisory leadership role of the principal is one of marshaling resources—human and material. The leadership ability of the principal in this area greatly determines the quality of the educational program as well as the teaching-learning situation in his school. A configuration of responsibilities such as coordination of special service personnel and teacher-principal conferences are explored by the authors of articles in this chapter. Emphasis is on human involvement and development.

Principals must identify new leadership positions which will establish meaningful supervisory relationships in order to cope with the changing curriculum demands. Ben M. Harris pleads for "an experienced core of instructional generalists in high status positions with courage, authority, responsibility, and freedom for concern for the daily operation of the school."

A good supervisory program is dependent upon a high degree of agreement on the function of supervision. Everett L. Walden reports on a study designed to elicit the perceptions held by administrators and teachers concerning the supervisory process. Do you have a credibility gap in your supervisory program?

If they are to fulfill their responsibility to the disadvantaged, educators need to develop strategies for changing themselves, their colleagues, and their schools. Marcia R. Conlin and Martin Haberman discuss some of the fears and needs of teachers and supervisors who work with the disadvantaged.

Who knows how many qualified teachers have left the profession due to inadequate induction procedures. Douglas W. Hunt summarizes some of the outcomes of the NASSP teacher induction project. The results should stimulate principals to consider a teacher induction program in their school.

Microteaching is one of the most exciting developments of the past decade. Marjorie Gardner and Rolland Bartholomew describe the microteaching techniques for the education of science teachers. It is a medium for modifying teacher behavior. The emphasis is on self-analysis.

18 | New Leadership and New Responsibilities for Human Involvement

Ben M. Harris

The "in" word nowadays in education is *new*. Everything has to be new, bright, different, innovative. A decade ago the "in" word was *leadership*. A whole series of leadership studies in government and industry caught our fancy, and teachers, counselors, principals, and supervisors all lost their identity to become "leaders." A decade earlier the "in" word was *involvement* as a result of the group dynamics movement. We sought many silly and superficial ways to get people involved, even though we were able to adopt some worthwhile ideas.

Properly enough, I plucked these three "in" words from the several titles suggested to me for this guest editorial. I wanted to try to revive the big ideas represented by these terms—*new, leadership*, and *human involvement*. The fourth word of my title is *responsibility*, and it has never been an "in" word in supervision circles. My main thesis is that it should be!

U. S. education is often described as being in the throes of a revolution. We have new curricula, new people, new money, new forces, new agencies, new hardware, new militancy, new challenges, and a new breed of student all thrust upon the educational scene. A closed, tradition oriented, locally dominated institution may be rapidly becoming open, change oriented, and federally dominated. If so, it is indeed a revolution in the making!

Revolutions come in many forms. Some are violent; others are peaceful. Some relate directly to the changing needs of a society; others are abortive. Some produce only short periods of chaos and uncertainty; others produce lingering wounds of hatred and insecurity which seem never to heal. What kind of revolution will this one in education come to be? Who is responsible? Who will lead? What will the new developments be? Will human needs be well served?

These questions are still clearly unanswered in USA 1969. ASCD'ers can (and I think should) help answer these questions in ways that assure a productive revolution with a minimum of undesirable side effects.

From *Educational Leadership*, Vol. 26, No. 8 (May 1969), pp. 739-742. Reprinted with permission of the Association for Supervision and Curriculum Development and the author. Copyright © 1969 by the Association for Supervision and Curriculum Development.

RESPONSIBILITY FOR LEADERSHIP

The word *leadership* refers to showing the way and guiding the organization in definitive directions. New leadership is needed in this sense of the word. Two kinds are required:

1. Those in status positions must lead out with new boldness and find better ways of influencing the schools toward rationally planned, timed change.
2. New leadership positions must be created, staffed, and coordinated to facilitate the enormously complex job of leading instructional change.

Where instructional change is concerned there is no substitute for supervisors who know children, instruction, and how to work with people. Nearly every instructional innovation that has experienced any success has had supervisors closely connected with its implementation.

This is not an argument for more of the same. It is an argument for an experienced core of instructional generalists in high status positions with courage, authority, responsibility, and freedom from concern for the daily operation of the school. No combination of school principals, resource teachers, assistant principals, department chairmen, college professors, or curriculum committees will satisfactorily take their place.

The need for new leadership positions in education has been growing increasingly obvious with every passing year since Sputnik. Stimulating, creating, initiating, facilitating, controlling, and assessing revolutionary changes on many instructional fronts is not a job for principal and supervisor alone.

Technical support of many kinds is needed. Gradually we are seeing media, research, psychiatric, and computer specialists on the staffs of our schools. A nationwide movement to create regional educational service centers with staffs of instructional specialists is well under way. The reorganization of state departments of education is beginning to provide supervisory support to schools in master planning, curriculum development, and program evaluation. Research and development centers and regional laboratories are coming to recognize that supervision is their business in a real sense.

The big question in all of this concerns *coordination*. As disparate individuals and groups pursue worthy but uncoordinated goals and objectives, they tend to produce confusion; potentially significant developments fail to bloom. The general supervisor, regardless of title, must provide the leadership for unification of efforts on the part of these many new leaders.

RESPONSIBILITY FOR NEWNESS

We often doubt that anything is really new. But old or new, change has no intrinsic worth. Values and related criteria must be applied to every change to provide a basis for accepting, rejecting, or promoting it. Who shall provide the leadership for valuing proposed changes in instructional practice. We cannot continue to rely on trial and error approaches; the errors are too numerous.

We cannot leave the valuing process up to each individual teacher or school with neither guidance nor relief; the changes are too numerous and persistent. Surely we cannot allow responsibility for valuing changes to rest as it has in the past with proponents, pressure groups, and commercial interests!

The generalist in instruction must assume responsibilities for initiating, guiding, and coordinating rigorous evaluation procedures. This is not to suggest that supervisors' values must prevail. Quite to the contrary, the challenge to supervisors is to accept responsibility for seeing to it that every point of view is represented, that children's interests remain central, that critical questions are asked, that data are not only gathered but analyzed and interpreted.

Every new development which has a theoretically plausible base needs to be guaranteed ample opportunity for development and testing. Yet each must be subjected to critical analysis and the tests of consistency of values must be applied. *Only* those in key leadership positions with interests vested in quality instruction and in possession of broad-gauge supervisory competencies can assume such responsibilities.

RESPONSIBILITY FOR INVOLVEMENT

Like newness, *involvement* is not an end in itself, but a means to an end. As opportunities for improving education present themselves in increasingly complex forms, the problem of implementation looms large. Simple changes require little of those affected. When the textbook is revised or a new one is published, it matters little who is involved in the selection process. Good teachers rarely rely on textbooks, poor teachers memorize them, and it won't help or hurt the kids much either way. About the same thing can be said for many changes of the recent past.

Increasingly, however, we are flirting with changes in instruction which would profoundly affect teacher, child, parent, and society. When we contemplate the individualizing of instruction in any genuine sense, or providing for discovery learning, or confronting pupils with the real social issues, or cultivating autonomous, emotionally congruent persons, a new set of requirements for involvement emerges. When large, complex instructional changes are introduced, teacher behavior, pupil behavior, and parent behavior are all affected. These changes in behavior produce counter-currents which challenge and disrupt. Who is responsible for the involvement of all those likely to be affected by dramatic instructional change?

The kinds of changes mentioned here will, if well implemented, produce reverberations of great magnitude throughout the system. How naive we will be if we assume that revolutionary changes are greeted with open arms when they are "good for kids"! We are human beings and creatures of habit. Changes in the system create new problems, deny old satisfactions, demand new skills, and introduce uncertainties.

Involvement in many aspects of the change process can dampen such resistance. Involvement needs to be functional, however, not just an intellectual exercise or a form of tokenism. Involvement must cut across the subsystems to teachers, students, parents, and other people who are likely to be affected.

Who can assume responsible leadership for producing this more elaborate kind of involvement? Can the general supervisor, who specializes in working with people, who knows the larger complex of the system, who understands instruction and the behavioral consequences of major changes in program, provide such leadership?

Leadership has meaning only when it leads to desirable goals. Goal-seeking behavior implies change, seeking that which is different from what is. In education, and especially in instruction, goals are human and means are human. Hence, involvement of people as we lead is inescapable.

New leaders emerge to take up old and new challenges. Supervisors have their golden opportunities for productivity as the group with a long tradition of concern for instruction, change, and people. *Let no one suggest that the day of the generalist is past!*

19 | The Credibility Gap
     in Supervision

Everett L. Walden

The Credibility Gap, usually referring to the distance between fact and fiction, is not an exclusive property of big government alone. School systems have maintained credibility gaps for years. Autocratic administrators who run their schools under the guise of democratic procedures are as guilty of promoting credibility gaps as politicians. Boards of education who outwardly defend excellence in education, but who refuse to budget adequate funds to implement quality programs are also guilty of perpetuating credibility gaps.

The credibility gap in supervision exists, not by design, but for the simple reason that when teachers, administrators, and supervisors view the functions of supervision they each develop different perceptions. Current literature in this area recommends certain supervisory techniques and practices as being highly effective in improving the teaching-learning process. However, the improvement of this process is dependent upon teacher attitudes toward supervision. Although much has been written concerning supervision, it has not been emphasized that teachers and supervisors simply do not agree on what effective supervision is.

Most supervisors will agree that the function of supervision is to help teachers improve the teaching-learning process, but do their programs support their statements? Do teachers perceive supervision as a helping function? To answer these questions the writer conducted a study in five large Colorado high schools. Approximately 20 percent of the classroom teachers in each of these high schools were interviewed to determine their perceptions of the supervisory process. The principals of each school were also interviewed.

Both teachers and principals were asked to identify the purpose of supervision. All principals responded that the purpose of supervision was to help the teacher to do a better job.

Forty-five percent of the teachers agreed with the principals. In commenting, they used the word "help." These teachers perceived supervision to be a means of providing individual help.

However, 31 percent of the teachers viewed supervision as inspectoral in nature. Typical statements made by these teachers were: "I suppose supervision is an authoritarian approach to help or check on teacher shortcomings." "The purpose of supervision is to keep the teacher in line."

From *Colorado Education Review*, Vol. 2 (October 1968), p. 11. Reprinted by permission of the publisher and author.

The remaining 24 percent said the purpose of supervision was administrative. Statements common to this group were: "The purpose of supervision is to keep the teacher supplied with information and equipment, and to handle the paper work." "To handle functions teachers don't have time for."

These three categories—inspectoral, administrative, and helping —represent the perceptions of teachers concerning the *purpose* of supervision. They do not represent their perceptions of how the supervisory program was *actually* operating.

Since attitudes of teachers largely determine their acceptance of supervision and the ultimate success of the program, each teacher was asked to describe his feelings toward supervision. Over 30 percent of all teachers interviewed described their experiences with supervision in negative terms. The highest incidence of negative feelings was found in the group who initially defined the purpose of supervision as a helping function. The lowest incidence was found in the group who viewed the purpose of supervision as inspectoral.

These findings may appear incongruous, but closer study reveals a simple answer. When teachers find agreement between their expectations and the operation of the supervisory program they tend to react in a positive way.

In this study, those teachers who viewed the purpose of supervision as either inspectoral or administrative had a considerably smaller incidence of negative feelings. These teachers were experiencing a supervisory program which met their expectations. Over 50 percent of the teachers reporting negative feelings defined the purpose of supervision as a helping function. This high incidence of negative feelings suggests that this group did not see the supervisory program as meeting their expectations.

When teachers cannot agree on the purpose of supervision; when large percentages of teachers become negative toward supervision because it is not meeting their expectations; when supervisory personnel define supervision in one way and practice it in another, the result is a credibility gap.

20 | Supervising Teachers of the Disadvantaged

Marcia R. Conlin
Martin Haberman

Operationally, the disadvantaged are those whose teachers perceive them as disadvantaged. So we begin with occupational tunnel vision. The vernacular of pedagese derives from eviscerated concepts and results in near-miss approximations labeled "objectivity," so this circuitous definition does not reveal anything about the nature of these children. But it does focus on the most powerful determinant of children's achievement: their teachers' assessment of their potential. Methodology, curriculum, school organization and materials are all launched from this teacher perception.

How can supervisors help teachers surrender the distortions of these negative expectations? A beginning might be an injection of reality into what supervisors study, work on, and talk about.

The paucity of supervisory strategy is often attributed to the newness of our field; bogus cries are raised for a theory of supervision, more research and firmer value commitments. But what would such theory describe and predict? Which variables could be researched? And how might we strengthen our values? Finally, why would any of these exercises influence our daily practices of the social system of the school?

These "supposed" needs are merely smoke screens of a flight syndrome; the real problems are a little too real. For example, supervisors must develop coping behaviors and action strategies which are germane to urban schools serving the disadvantaged.

RELUCTANT TEACHERS

The supervisor's basic problem is like that of the Boy Scout helping reluctant little old ladies to cross streets when they would rather stay on corners. We Americans are socialized to believe we should be able to solve life problems independently. A welter of guilt results when we soon discover our need for friends, family, to borrow money, and to use hospitals. Overlay this fantasy-like moral prescription with a teacher education that portrays instructional prob-

From *Educational Leadership*, Vol. 24, No. 5 (February 1967), pp. 393-398. Reprinted with permission of the Association for Supervision and Curriculum Development and the author. Copyright © 1967 by the Association for Supervision and Curriculum Development.

lems as teacher or pupil faults, rather than as opportunities and we can see that an impossible role perception has been conveyed to teachers. As "normal" adult Americans, they do not want "help," and as teachers they cannot admit to needs.

As if this were not bad enough, the supervisor is perceived as someone who cannot "help" with reality problems. Just as the disadvantaged pupils perceive their teachers as powerless to help with any real problems (e.g., Can he get me a job? a decent place to live? police protection? a loving home? sexual gratification? equal opportunity?), so the supervisor is perceived as powerless to help with problems the teachers perceive as real. (Can he give me a smaller class? more supporting and psychological services? fewer emotionally disturbed pupils? effective methods and techniques for my instructional problems?)

TEACHERS' DISLIKE FOR CHILDREN

It is unpleasant, almost impolite, to mention our pretense that teachers like their pupils. Many do, but supervising others—particularly in schools serving the disadvantaged, who discriminate against poor youngsters of various ethnic backgrounds—is analogous to helping children learn subjects they hate. Without positive teacher regard, little beyond drill, rote, or mechanical teaching occurs. Youngsters might escape irreparable damage from the hands of a bigoted coach or bandmaster, but the positive regard of one's teacher is too powerful, too essential to their growth, to be completely washed out by even the most technical subject matter.

Teachers (certified in their states, tenured in their systems and paid-up members of professional associations) who dislike their youngsters have a natural reluctance to discuss their feelings, while we, their leaders, are often prejudiced and unaware ourselves. When this round robin of unawareness is revealed, we find we lack the know-how to change the behaviors from which prejudiced perceptions continue to develop.

The most grinding, debilitating aspect of their deprived subculture is its failure to offer these children any choices. When their teachers perceive their potential with equally negative expectations, their classroom experience concurs with and reinforces this demoralization. The positive regard of his teacher may be a deprived child's only hope.

Since the most powerful determinant of teacher effectiveness is his perception of pupils' potential growth, this effectiveness cannot help but be affected negatively by tendencies to stereotype, or to remain closed to the talents, divergencies and strengths of individuals of different backgrounds.

SUPERVISORS OF RESENTFUL WHITES

The status gap between teachers and supervisors is a real one; but teachers are often wiser about recognizing its validity than supervisors who attempt a strategy of co-worker, helpmate, team-member, colleague, etc. Overlaying these basic distinctions in role are age and sex differences; supervisors who are younger than teachers; women attempting to help men. These differences which deepen the natural gulf between them are compounded when we add the difficulties of Negroes who supervise whites.

Symptoms of the "racial problem" between Negro supervisors and white teachers usually occur in integrated or predominantly Negro schools—where one is most likely to find non-white supervisors. We find this constellation:

- Teachers who are fearful their supervisor will no longer back them up in situations involving corporal punishment of a Negro pupil
- Teachers who are reluctant to discuss their perceptions of "disadvantaged" problems because they do not want to appear prejudiced
- Teachers who over-react, love everyone, and have absolutely no problems
- Supervisors who become overly oriented to academic progress and avoid recognizing emotional problems of pupils. The remedial reading syndrome is a common phenomenon among supervisors bent on "proving" success
- Supervisors who solidify in the belief that only a Negro can understand the problems of educational disadvantagement—even a middle class Negro living in the suburbs
- Supervisors who become more concerned with their own advancement and play militant for the community and Uncle Tom for the system.

WHITE NEGRO TEACHERS

The interaction of mutual prejudice and fear between white teachers and Negro supervisors is understandable. After understanding, however, behavioral techniques are required to help supervisors who are struggling for an identity of their own to establish functional relationships. The problem is not unlike the fearful teacher forced to work with resentful, hostile youngsters at a time in life when self definition may be *his* greatest need.

One of the most difficult forms of pupil rejection occurs in schools serving urban Negroes. It is the lowest form of reverse prejudice which fails to recognize the wide range of abilities, attitudes and effectiveness amongst middle-class, well educated Negroes assigned as teachers in urban schools. Typical placement procedures which assign Negro teachers to schools serving the disadvantaged fail to recognize the personal needs and class level of different individuals. Many Negroes merely respond to the white "they all look alike to me" syndrome which lumps all Negroes together. As a result, some Negro teachers try to "prove" they are in no way related to or identified with these youngsters. Others respond with an intensified need to demonstrate masculinity, and they often try to dominate rather than relate to their pupils.

Many Negro colleges guide the least able into teaching; better students are advised to enter business, or the more prestigious professions in order to more influentially "represent" their group.

Although these problems all have causes which invariably derive from centuries of discrimination in which whites have brutalized Negroes, the fact remains that important problems are now at home roosting. Supervisors need courage to risk accusations of discrimination and reverse discrimination. More important, white leadership needs to open up all white schools to those Negro faculty members who work best with middle class students.

Most supervision is directed toward helping beginning teachers, although the evidence indicates that they do as well or better than experienced teachers. We assume (erroneously) that beginners are more amenable to change than experienced teachers. (This usually means "susceptible to directive influences." What are beginners changing from?) In reality much supervisory practice is the imposition of unwanted assistance, and beginners are less able to resist than the securely-tenured, more confident teachers. Another explanation is logistical; there isn't enought time to help all, and supervisory effort must be expended where it will do the most good. This is a dangerous rationalization, since most beginners work less than a year and merely pass through the profession, while the experienced "older" teacher with twenty years of experience is overlooked in spite of the fact that he may have another twenty to go.

CHANGING EXPERIENCED, "MODEL" TEACHERS

Unfortunately, many experienced teachers are perceived as having "connections" and as informal leaders in their schools and neighborhoods. Supervisors, particularly newly appointed ones, are reluctant to risk "rocking the boat" with such teachers under their egis. An experienced, informal teacher-leader has immeasurable power to control by merely threatening to request transfer. As a result, much supervision mollifies the strong and over-supervises the weak. In schools serving the disadvantaged, where turnover is high or requests for in-transfer infrequent, supervisors often practice the realistic but unprofessional philosophy of "leaving well enough alone." In reality, conservation of an inadequate status quo is preservation of failure.

The ignorant may become educated, the disaffected involved, and the prejudiced more open; but strategies to release the potentialities of the fearful teacher are as yet unexplored. We might begin with the recognition that many (perhaps most) supervisors, principals and teachers are fearful. But fear of what? The sources of fear may be in both the nature of the person who becomes a teacher and in the nature of a "disadvantaged" classroom where many pupils need to feel some power. Demonstrations of fear are natural responses to feelings of powerlessness.

FEARFUL TEACHERS

Do teachers fear change? Behind all the rationalizations (e.g., My principal won't let me. My fellow teachers will be upset. The children need structure.) is fear of the new, the unfamiliar, the unpredictable.

Do teachers fear expression of emotions—aggression, love, bursting joy? It is clear that schools are not the best settings for natural behavior. The current cardinal operating principle of American schools is "keep the lid on feelings." We were nearly run down on the sidewalk outside a junior high school recently by exuberant, naturally expressive adolescents whose apathetic, glazed-over responses in the classroom we had observed only five minutes earlier.

Fear of all three factors—supervisors, change, and emotions—are present to some degree. Also, these fears are all interrelated and derive from one basic fear: a fear of inadequacy. In their professional lives, teachers lack the ability to predict the multiplicity of problems with which they may be instantly and continuously confronted and they lack the more complete predictability present in other professional roles. They lack power.

To assume that fear is *not* a factor, or should not be, is unsound and unrealistic. By recognizing teachers' feelings of inadequacy, we can consider possible causes, and connect them with the teacher's perception of power. Since our own perceptions of fear and power are also involved, the problem is now more complex and emotionally charged. Power, personal and professional, is not given but taken. The usual discussion of how to *give* teachers more power is sterile; we need to identify situational elements and to structure conditions in which fearful teachers can learn to take power.

When teachers and supervisors independently arrive at the same objectives for changing themselves, we have an optimum condition for supervision. In practice, such convergence rarely occurs. Supervisors perceive their major raison d'etre as changing teachers' attitudes; teachers perceive their biggest problems as large classes, individual problem-students, and rigid curricula. Operationally then, supervision becomes a search for means to detour around teacher-perceived problems, and attempts to shift the locus of teacher concern from the children and the curriculum to themselves.

The democratic ethic, principles of learning and our own needs for approval prevent us from overtly imposing our ideas through directive supervision. Yet, we are powerless to deal with the structural and basic problems perceived by teachers—even when these perceptions may be accurate and we recognize that their perceptions must be the starting point for supervisory practice. The situation is not unlike the teacher who asks his class, "What are you interested in?" When they respond, "Girls, money, fame," he replies, "No, no. I mean like any of your after-school hobbies that might help me to relate your life experiences to the acid and base weights of the chemical elements."

Meanwhile, ask teachers to describe their basic concerns; they tell about classes that are too large to differentiate assignments, the need to cover prescribed material with children who cannot read, and the difficulty of managing a group situation with several emotionally disturbed youngsters. To which the supervisor replies, "No, no. I mean what are you doing that will help me to relate your problems to the workshop I offer Thursday afternoons of 'Creativity in Written Expression'!"

This article has raised issues and ignored canons. Our questions imply that what we have been doing is not good enough; yet no concrete suggestions have been made. (That's cynicism!) We have implied that opening up tough issues in urban schools may change supervisors personally and professionally, as well as teachers. (That's derogation!) One might infer that teachers and supervisors frequently perceive each others' services as somewhat less than useful; we need, first, to recognize that supervisory reality begins with teachers' perceptions—not supervisors' needs and interests. (That's insulting!)

Finally, the stress on disadvantagement has been underplayed; we believe that supervision, like teaching, is basically the same in all situations, but pupils in "disadvantaged" schools are less likely to learn in spite of their teachers, and their teachers are less likely to succeed without realistic help. (That's devious!) Right answers only result from the right questions: What are teachers' *real* problems? The right supervisory objectives will develop in the light of those needs.

21 | Teacher Induction
An Opportunity and a Responsibility

Douglas W. Hunt

The beginning teacher as we have come to know him during our three-year study has the heaviest work load of any member of your staff. Having been given a few months' warning of his assignment, sometimes armed with a sketchy curriculum guide that even the most experienced teacher seldom understands or follows, an assortment of textbooks (at least one of which will be changed before school begins), he embarks upon a full teaching schedule of five classes a day and a full complement of extra duties, each of which is entirely new to him. He has no experience to fall back on or upon which to base decisions, so that too often his planning is inappropriate and hours of preparation bear little fruit. Usually his senior colleagues have chosen the favorite courses and the ablest students, so the beginner quite often faces the more difficult classes of slow, often bored and belligerent students.

Much teaching done by beginners, therefore, is done under stress conditions. The reactions to stress, and the resulting defense mechanisms, are often inappropriate and sometimes crippling. If the beginner has pride and sets standards for himself, his work is never done—he can never know enough or plan enough, and he seldom has a feeling of completion or success. All too often the reality of his experience is devastating—nothing like what he had been led to expect during teacher training.

Common sense indicates that the beginning teacher needs assistance if he is to do a good job. We have got to stop kidding ourselves—teacher training institutions, however excellent, won't and can't prepare teachers for the full and immediate responsibilities they face the day they enter the classroom in September. Some of us recognize this, but thus far our attempts to bridge the gap between the theory of the teacher training institutions and the reality of the everyday classroom situation have been almost totally ineffective. Many of the principals with whom we have worked on the induction program for three years will tell you that orientation programs (however well intended) often do more harm than good. They bore the old-timer and confuse the beginner.

Once thus "oriented" the beginner typically is placed under the care of a department chairman, regardless of the chairman's interest in young teachers or ability to bring them along. In most schools, de-

From *NASSP Bulletin*, Vol. 52 (October 1968), pp. 130-135. Reprinted by permission of the National Association of Secondary School Principals. Copyright: 1968 by the National Association of Secondary School Principals.

partment chairmen have the responsibility for evaluation: this in itself often precludes the type of working relationship which we have found to be essential if true adjustment and learning are to take place. Our recent experience, however, convinces us that there are sound ways of inducting teachers, and that the school and its principal play a critical role in this stage of the new teacher's training.

Specifically, we have found that principals must give more careful consideration to the beginning teacher's assignment, basing it on his preparation and background, and not solely on traditional schedule "needs." We should limit the number of basic preparations with which beginners must cope to two whenever possible, and assign to the beginner the type or types of students that he is best qualified to teach. These will usually be the average groups for, after all, if the experienced teacher finds it difficult to challenge the top students and impossible to motivate and manage the slow ones, how can we expect the beginner to meet these challenges effectively.

But careful assignment is not enough. The beginner needs assistance in carrying out his assignment. Obviously the principal does not have the time nor is he able to provide this assistance, but he usually has on his staff several highly qualified experienced classroom teachers who, if given the *time* and the *authority*, could provide this support and guidance. We have found that such a cooperating teacher can usually work effectively with a group of from three to eight beginners providing they can all be brought together for a full period each school day. In effect, we propose a new specialist for the school staff—a person who, in addition to teaching classes of his own, teaches teachers and who, in this capacity, is responsible directly to the principal.

Lest you begin to think that induction is impossible for you, or too expensive, let me assure you that it is neither. The program that has evolved from our three years of experimentation with Mr. Conant's original proposal involves some released time, scheduling consideration, and talent. The talent is readily available in every good school. The released time and equipment should cost less than $2,000 per beginner (depending upon school schedules and salary schedules). When considered in terms of a year of teacher training, what we pay older staff members, and the improvement in instruction (which, after all, should be our primary concern), the cost is minimal.

But what is there in this program that has evolved from Mr. Conant's recommendations? Perhaps it can best be described in a time sequence that has four phases. But before I try to answer my question let me remind you what these recommendations were:

a. limited teaching responsibility for the new teacher
b. aid in gathering instructional materials

c. advice of experienced teachers whose own loads are reduced so that they can work with the new teacher in his own classroom

d. shifting to more experienced teachers those students who create problems beyond the ability of the novice to handle effectively

e. specialized instruction concerning the character of the community, the neighborhood, and the students he is likely to encounter.

Phase I: The Time Before School Starts. Induction should start the moment a new teacher is hired, and it should be considered a normal part of his first year load. Emphasis during the spring and summer is on helping the beginning teacher feel at home in his new (and probably first) job. The cooperating teacher might do the following:

- greet the beginner after the employment interview
- introduce him to his department head and other administrative personnel (The induction program supplements the normal department structure; it does not replace it.)
- take him on a tour of the school
- explain his assignment
- review texts and syllabi to be used
- review the teacher's manual
- discuss the nature of the community
- point out studies or references to similar environments

This kind of supportive activity can be continued over the summer by phone or letter and can do much to build up the beginner's self-confidence and, of prime importance, to give direction to his planning.

Phase II: Normal School Orientation or Special Beginning Teacher Orientation. Emphasis here has been on helping the new teacher understand his assignment and prepare for the first week of school. The cooperating teacher can supplement, or in many instances replace, the school's regular orientation program. This is not the time for speeches on theory but rather lots of practical assistance and advice. Activities have included familiarization with the building and special teaching resources. It is particularly advantageous for the cooperating teacher to attend any orientation meetings with the group and review the more important points with the beginners to see that they truly understand them. Explaining the school schedule, the attendance procedures, the record-keeping system, and the location and use of supplies; identifying administrators and supporting personnel (librarian, counselors, nurse, custodian); setting up classrooms; and reviewing opening-of-school procedures have proved to be especially helpful. The cooperating teacher has been encouraged to identify potential weaknesses and when possible to give special attention to individual needs of the various beginners.

Phase III: First Semester. At this time the regular daily group meetings begin, with emphasis on the practical arts of teaching. Groups and individuals, led by the cooperating teachers, have worked on lesson planning, organization of material and methods in terms of various ability groups, testing, grading, diverse teaching methods and techniques, supplementary material, homework, disciplinary techniques and school policy, guidance services, specialist services, parent-teacher groups, and community relations.

In addition to group discussions and individual conferences, activities have included observation of experienced teachers, visits to a materials or curriculum center, a tour of the community and a review of community services, seminars with specialists (reading teacher, guidance counselor, psychologist, community agent), common lesson planning, cooperative teaching, and training in the use of audio-visual materials. Let me again stress the word *practical* during this phase. During the first semester we are first concerned with survival and then getting on top of the job. Experience indicates that almost everything the group does should relate directly to what is going on in the classroom.

Phase IV: Starting About January. There will be a gradual shift from the practical daily concerns to a longer range, sometimes more theoretical, approach. Activities designed to help the beginner articulate and analyze his philosophy of education, his performance in the classroom, and his understanding of his students have included the following:

• case studies
• observation of his students in other classrooms
• demonstrations of various teaching techniques
• increased cooperative teaching
• analysis, through the use of video and sound tape, of teaching
• techniques and class participation.

These activities prompted discussions of teaching resources and methods, successful motivational techniques, learning theory, adolescent growth and development, and the slow learner. There are, of course, many other possibilities.

If this sounds like a continuation of teacher training, it is! But don't suggest that we should consider the beginners as students, for they desperately want to belong, to be accepted, to succeed as teachers. Nonetheless, as many of them have said and as the administrators now recognize, more constructive teacher *learning* can take place this first year on the job than in four years of teacher training, but for this to happen there must be structure and direction. It is indeed a continuation of teacher training, and it should be thought of as such by principals. Don't good teachers continue to learn and grow? As for a load on the school—yes, perhaps—but as one of our principals pointed out, "The people who really know

how to teach in my school are the ones who are doing it, not necessarily the 'experts' in a university miles away." It is an unreasonable
burden? We think not. In Richmond, where we worked with five
small experimental groups, every new high school teacher in all six
high schools is now participating in an induction similar to the one
which I have just described. In Detroit the experimental program
carried out in four schools has become a regular program involving
125 schools.

Teacher induction shouldn't be news. However, no other important profession is so careless about the induction of its new members. In most professions there is a carefully defined procedure used
to bring new members along—to induct them. A law firm would not
send its newest law school graduate to defend its toughest case right
after he reported for work. A medical doctor's internship and res-
idency might be too long, but at least the beginning doctor does go
out with more than a degree and six weeks of observation. So far
as I know, teaching is the only major profession in which the beginner is given full and immediate responsibility—the same or more
difficult assignment than the experienced worker has—and then he
is often criticized because he doesn't perform at the same level as
his experienced colleagues. The beginning teacher deserves better
and so do his students.

Microteaching: A Medium for Modifying Teacher Behavior 22

Marjorie Gardner
Rolland Bartholomew

What is microteaching? Is it anything like a mini-lab? Or semi-microanalysis? Is miniaturization moving in on science education? No, not really. Not in the usual sense, at least. Microteaching is an exciting new "small component" technique for the education of science teachers. Its usefulness is being demonstrated in both pre-service and inservice programs—particularly in programs that promote the inquiry approach to science teaching. Research with micro-teaching indicates that dramatic behavioral changes in teachers can be produced and sustained using this technique.[1]

Microteaching developed, at least in part, out of the frustrations of teacher trainers and education research specialists who met failure whenever they tried to identify effective teaching characteristics and behaviors and to train personnel accordingly. They always encountered the problem of too many variables in the global criteria and general approaches being tried. If such broad criteria do not prove manageable, one alternative is to follow procedures already demonstrably effective in the natural sciences (physics, chemistry, biology, etc.) and break down the problem to be studied into finer and finer parts which can then be studied and dealt with singly. Based on this reasoning, a group at Stanford University, under the direction of Dwight Allen, developed the technical skills approach and microteaching. They attempted to analyze teaching into well-defined components that could be practiced, taught, evaluated, and controlled. In science, this might be components such as (1) questioning, (2) establishing appropriate frames of reference, (3) setting a model, (4) controlling participation, (5) stimulating student involvement, (6) teacher listening, recognizing, and assessing of student nonverbal behavior, (7) providing reinforcement for student responses, (8) providing feedback, (9) achieving closure, etc.

Microteaching consists, then, of selecting a single component of teaching behavior for primary focus and providing the opportunity for a preservice or inservice teacher to teach a scaled-down lesson

From *The Science Teacher*, Vol. 36 (May 1969), pp. 45-47. Reprinted by permission of the publisher.

1. David B. Young, "The Modification of Teacher Behavior Using Audio-Video Taped Models in a Micro-Teaching Sequence," *Educational Leadership*, 26: 394-404; January 1969.

aimed at perfecting the selected skill. In this context, N. L. Gage defined microteaching as

. . . a scaled-down teaching experience. It is scaled down in terms of time because it lasts only five to ten minutes. It is scaled down in terms of class size because the trainee teaches a group of not more than five pupils. It is scaled down in terms of the task, since the trainee attempts to perform only one of the teaching skills in any single micro-teaching session. The sessions are recorded on video tape, and the trainee gets to see and hear himself immediately after the session. While he looks at and listens to himself, he receives criticism and suggestions from a supervisor trained to be both perceptive and tactful. Then, he re-teaches the same lesson to a new small group of pupils in an attempt to improve on his first performance on the specific teaching skill that is his concern in that session.[2]

David Young, who worked with Dwight Allen at Stanford, is extending the use of microteaching and the research associated with it in cooperation with the Science Teaching Center at the University of Maryland, among other groups. Dr. Young suggests that microteaching can be an important aid to an experienced teacher in preparing for his day-by-day teaching during the school year.

If a teacher wishes to try a new approach in a particular lesson, he ordinarily must wait until the following year to test alternatives to that lesson. In micro-teaching, the teacher can experiment with several alternatives with a limited number of students each time with the opportunity for immediate evaluation and additional trials. Following this limited application, the plan can then be presented to the classroom. In this way teachers may experiment with new methods and new content without the risk of defeating student learning and with much more satisfactory timing.

Many teachers have expressed a desire to study, develop, and refine teaching strategies in accordance with expanding demands on teaching. Micro-teaching provides this opportunity. For example, a teach–conference–re-teach sequence might focus on the verbal behavior of a teacher in a student centered small group discussion, or the inductive questioning technique in a student's self-discovery of a scientific principle. Then, logistically, micro-teaching is conducted outside a teacher's regular class schedule. Release time is often arranged by providing a substitute to cover classes for teachers while they are micro-teaching. A teacher can also participate in micro-teaching after school or at the secondary level during a planning period. It may be desirable to schedule a sequence when all the teachers in a department or team are available. Students are often provided by the Future Teachers Association or other student service organizations. It is also feasible to have eight to ten students come to

2. N. L. Gage, "An Analytical Approach to Research on Instructional Methods," *Phi Delta Kappan*, 49: 601-606; June 1968.

school on special in-service days or during a workshop in the summer months.[3]

Portable TV recording units are utilized in microteaching. Such units are self-contained with all of the components installed on a roll cart. The operation of a unit has been simplified to the point that a student can roll it into a classroom and prepare it for a recording in a few minutes. Since there are no hanging microphones, multiple cameras, and extra lights, the recording procedure is relatively unobtrusive in a classroom. A complete unit can be assembled for less than $2,000. Many school systems already have this equipment available.

Microteaching was utilized experimentally and very effectively in an Earth Science Curriculum Project leadership conference, funded by the National Science Foundation, and held at the University of Maryland last summer. For three weeks in July and August, 1968, a group of 33 scientists, science supervisors, and classroom teachers were deeply involved in a series of intensive experiences related to learning more about ESCP and the teaching of earth science. This experience included the anticipated content lectures, laboratory investigations, and field experiences. It also included an aspect unique to earth science education conferences, and relatively new to science education generally. This was the microteaching that became a closely interwoven component of the leadership conference. Let us be quite specific about the organization, procedures, and results of this model of microteaching.

The microteaching assignment was defined as a small learning unit (one concept or inquiry skill) to be used in teaching a small number of students (3-5) in a brief period of time (5 minutes). The first round of microteaching was organized to include four sequential experiences: the original *teach* (5 minutes), the *critique* (15 minutes), the *reteach* (5 minutes), and the *confirmation* (5 minutes). Each member of the conference was expected to plan and teach an investigative lesson that would involve all of the students. The teach and reteach sessions were video taped for playback during the critique and confirmation. The teachers were in teams comprised of a college professor of science, a science supervisor, and a junior high school teacher. The students were eighth- and ninth-grade youngsters from suburban areas and from the Upward Bound program. The design for microteaching was an experimental model. While one person was microteaching (for example, the college professor), another (the science supervisor) was operating the video

3. David B. Young, "The Analysis and Modification of Teaching Behavior Using Interaction Analysis, Micro-Teaching, and Video-Tape Feedback." Presented at the National Association of Secondary School Principals, 52nd Annual Convention, February 1968, Atlantic City, New Jersey.

equipment, and the third team member (the classroom teacher) was preparing to lead the critique by observing and taking notes on the "teach." Following a complete sequence, the roles were rotated so that each team member gained experience in (1) inquiry teaching of junior high students, (2) leading a critique of a teaching session, and (3) operating video-tape cameras and recorders. Each microteaching session was under the general direction of an experienced micro-teaching specialist, David Young or George Funaro, of the University of Maryland faculty.

After all of the 33 participants had been through the first micro-teaching experience, a second round was planned. Each team had the opportunity to develop either an instructional model or a micro-teaching model that could be video-taped to show to other educators in their geographical regions.

The evaluation of the microteaching experience indicated a high degree of interest and acceptance on the part of all participants. Although a statistical comparison of teaching differences between the teach and reteach sessions was not performed, most of the participants demonstrated significant observable differences in behavior. The supervision experience in the microteaching sequence promoted careful consideration of relevant teacher behaviors and concern for constructive modes of critiquing and making suggestions for improvement. The rotation of roles established a professional communication and a close rapport within each group.

The earliest use of microteaching was to train interns or preservice teachers. Our experience gives evidence that it is also an effective agent for change with experienced teachers. Relatively inexpensive and simple to use, the microteaching technique for training teachers to use the new inquiry and process approaches to science teaching has high potential for many local school systems and science teaching centers.

The Principal
and the Decision-
Making Process

V

chapter overview

Good administrators make few decisions. The fellow who makes a great many decisions is a poor administrator.

—Peter F. Drucker

More than ever before the secondary school principal is being called upon to demonstrate active leadership in the decision-making process in the establishment and attainment of educational goals. The configuration of forces reacting to change the traditional structures of our educational institutions calls for renewed dedication on the part of administrators to the implementation of democratic processes. There is a clarion call today for school administrators to broaden the base of involvement in the decision-making process. The articles in this chapter reflect the tenor of the time—involvement.

School administrators must be able to make meaningful decisions in their complex job. Peter F. Drucker suggests that Americans "look to the school as our central community function and as the agent of social and community change." Good principals make decisions which go beyond their school into the community and affect people. They are community leaders.

American educational institutions are in transition. Donald McNassor discusses the decision-making process during a revolutionary process. Educators and other interested persons are encouraged "to facilitate imaginative new forms of shared responsibility in the conduct of school."

Who are the Decision-Makers? Herbert M. Zimmerman identifies several "publics" which should be involved in the decision-making process. He cautions administrators, as did Peter F. Drucker, that real decisions take time.

Principals should provide the leadership in the establishment of an adequate democratic atmosphere in their schools. Ronald L. Abrell reviews the issue of democracy in our schools and offers suggestions for more democratic and competent administrative leadership.

The principal is the key to effective decentralization. Freeman H. Vaughn recognizes the critical position of the principal in breaking the central administrative stronghold. Decision-making has simply moved too far up a complicated line of authority to be meaningful in the neighborhoods.

Decision-Making and   23
the Effective Executive

Peter F. Drucker

Driving down here this morning, I thought back to the last oc-casion, four years ago, when I had the privilege of taking part in one of your meetings—in Chicago in 1964, I think it was—and about the things that have happened since in your area and in our school sys-tems. Of course, your Association has grown mightily and proudly, but that is not particularly important to the rest of us. Of the many things that have happened in education—particularly in secondary education—nothing would have been "news" to you four years ago. What has happened is, I think, that we, your constituents in the so-ciety around you, have become aware of how much rides on what you are doing.

Again, as so often throughout our history, we look to the school as our central community function and as the agent of social and community change. We have been doing this for 200 years. Ours is one country in the world—maybe Japan is another one—where the school is the central community organization. It is indeed the com-munity personified; sometimes I wonder whether we are not putting too much of a burden on it. The American people now realize that the school is expected to perform what 200 years of American history have been unable to do: to solve the fundamental spiritual problem of this country—the race problem. We are looking to the school essentially to atone for this old sin and to create racial harmony.

We are looking to the school to integrate tomorrow's world and our tradition. We call it "curriculum," and we talk about courses and so on. But that is really technical shorthand. We look to the school to break through and to give us the basic productivity of a knowledge society, to give us the educational basis of a so-ciety in which knowledge has become the central resource and capital.

You in the schools talk of a "methodology of teaching and learn-ing." For us on the outside there are much more fundamental ques-tions: How to generate knowledge with a minimum of cost and a maximum of effort? How, at the same time, to make the individual capable of using the fantastic array of mental skills and capacities we have now available?

From *NASSP Bulletin*, Vol. 52 (May 1968), pp. 24-39. Reprinted by permission of the National Association of Secondary School Principals. Copyright: 1968 by the Na-tional Association of Secondary School Principals.

SCHOOLS AND THE FUTURE

We are looking to the school to help the youngsters decide their future. Suddenly in one generation many people have been catapulted out of a world in which traditionally the number of career choices was incredibly small. When I was a child you could expect 99 percent of humanity to follow their fathers—even in the most affluent of the society of 1915. Primarily this meant, of course, tilling the land. Career choices were something very few people had to contemplate. Even for educated people, there were only the traditional professions: the teacher, the minister, the doctor, the lawyer, and maybe the engineer who was just coming in. That was all.

Today, career choices are unlimited. I listen a good deal to young people, and they are forever discussing the burden this puts on them. A central problem of the young is the embarrassment of choices at a time in their lives when they do not know enough to make choices, either about themselves or about the world.

The ablest boy of my generation was offered, when he graduated from Oxford, something that had never been offered to anybody in Oxford before—namely, a full fellowship at age 20, at the most prestigious college, as a mathematician. And his entire family—solid middle-class but not rich—descended on him in a body (this is 1930) and said: "You can't take it. You don't have an independent income. You know, you have to make a living," which was true. "There are only three jobs in England," they pointed out, "in which a man can make a living in mathematics: the senior professorships in Oxford, Cambridge, and London. Maybe you're good enough to get one— we don't know; we have our doubts. But even if you are very good, getting these prize plums is a matter of being at the right place at the right time when the right man dies; that's too chancy."

The point is not that the families are timid—families are always timid. The point is that the family was quite right. There were then no jobs for mathematicians. Now, you know, if a third-grader shows slightly better than usual proficiency in learning the multiplication table, IBM offers him a fellowship.

This change has happened very fast. I don't think we are aware of it unless we listen carefully to the young. It bothers them. They feel that they commit themselves. Yet we don't tell the young that one doesn't commit oneself, that at best jobs are experiments, and that the odds against anyone starting out where he belongs are astronomical. But we tell them that one takes a job and stays 35 years, and that just is not true. I doubt that there is anybody in this room who at age 25 knew what he wanted to be doing today, and expected to do it. One does not know enough about oneself until one is a good deal older.

THE REAL PROBLEMS

Altogether, American society now realizes that it looks to the school to settle the true, fundamental, real problems. These problems one cannot settle by spending money. These problems are not budget items. They require hard work, thinking, education, and risk.

Air pollution we know how to solve; it's going to be expensive —all right. But we do know how to solve it. We are going to fight over whether we want 90 percent or 95 percent purity of the air, because the last five percent will cost more than the first 90. But we will still fight over money. The basic problems that determine the structure, quality, and direction of society and community and person, however, are never budget items. And them we have again entrusted to the school.

You in the schools knew all this five years ago, but the rest of us are only now beginning to know it. The school administrator has not become more important, but we outside are beginning to realize his crucial importance. Because the administrator is the hinge on which our capacity to perform turns. Sure, the teacher in his or her classroom has an essential contribution to make. But the first interest of the teacher is and should be to make sure that little Susie learns her French irregular verbs. If the teacher can't do that, she isn't going to do anything else; and you know it.

The really good teacher is a master craftsman who is good because he never slights the detail. Whether he is building a house or a fence or tearing down a house, that does not really matter to the craftsman. But the administrator has to decide in advance what it is going to be. To be sure, the craftsman has a veto power, but he does not have a deciding power. It is the administrator who has to respond to the big challenges, and we have become aware of this. As a result, the administrators suddenly are very visible. This may be very uncomfortable for you ladies and gentlemen. But it's something you have no control over.

We in this country have begun to realize how much depends on this very small number of school administrators. You are a very large organization—35,000 members, and you probably have in this organization most of our secondary school administrators. But in a country of 200,000,000 people, 35,000 administrators is a very small number. The governor of this state or the president of the United States, when running for office, is not greatly worried about your vote. The bricklayers outnumber you about ten-to-one. But a great deal depends, individually and collectively, on you small guys. Commissioner Marburger [of the New Jersey State Department of Education] said here earlier that the secondary school principal is usually the most important man in the community. Perhaps you thought that this was just polite exaggeration. But believe me, he is right.

THE ADMINISTRATOR'S CONTRIBUTION

How important the secondary school administrator is you see whenever he has not performed. We all know a few communities where school administrators have let the community down. Not because they were stupid. Not because they were incompetent. Simply because they did not ask the question, "What is my contribution?" They were running the schools, and running them well. But they did not see that this is a part of the job.

One never gets paid for the important part of the job, for that can never be measured and can never be defined. But because these administrators did not ask, "What is my contribution?" these communities are in a mess for lack of leadership. Their school administrators are very good educators and did a good job in the schools. But they did not see themselves as community leaders. Nobody said to them what Dr. Marburger said to us this morning, "You are the most important man in the community." This is what all of us in this country have begun to realize, if only dimly.

I hope, let me say, that we will never realize this clearly; one realizes such things clearly only in case of failure. Things that work one does not analyze; one takes them for granted. I hope, therefore, that 10 years from now someone at a meeting like this will complain bitterly that the American public does not appreciate its school administrators. No greater compliment could be paid you than that we take for granted that you have done the job.

What does this mean in particular? Why did Dr. Tompkins choose Decision-Making as the topic for me? Why did I feel that it was appropriate? Mainly because what the situation calls for is for school principals to think through a few decisions and to think them through intelligently and with an understanding of how one makes a decision. Your job is not 100 percent decision-making. No administrator's, no executive's job is primarily decision-making. If you were to run a time-log on yourself, you would find that you spend almost no time on decisions. And I mean decisions; I don't mean dispositions.

If somebody comes to you and asks, "Should we have the picnic this year inside or outside?", that's not a decision. Very little depends on your answer; and, anyhow, a set of dice can do just as well as you. You know, on July 4 or the fourth of June, whenever it is, we might get rain and we might not; it depends on where you live. In Arizona, you have no problem. But you also know that if you guess wrong and start outdoors and then have to move it in, it is not going to be the end of the world either.

THE REAL DECISIONS

I am talking about making decisions that determine direction and fundamentals, that is, the real decisions. I am talking about it in full awareness of the complexity of your job. There is no more complex job. In any one area it may be a fairly simple job, compared with that of the fellow at NASA who has to get a space ship off on time. What makes your job so extraordinarily complex is that no other job has that diversity of publics: faculty and students and parents and community and school boards. You have more publics than anybody else. There are, moreover, overlapping publics rather than discrete publics. The businessman has got his union representatives here and his customers there and never the twain shall meet. They are separate. You deal with the same citizen in his capacity as a parent and a member of the community and a taxpayer and a school board member.

These very diverse and yet overlapping publics are, at the same time, only peripherally concerned with the school. Only the faculty really has a central interest in the school. For the others, the school is important only when something goes wrong. To the kids, school is terribly important. But the new girl on the block is—and should be—more important. After all, they do know: one fine day I'll be out of school. To them school is transitory, however important. For the 17-year-old in love, school is rightly not the most important thing. For the 17-year-old in rebellion against his or her parents, school is not the most important thing. It is even less central to the school's other publics.

This diversity of outside publics makes for a tremendously complex job. In a way you have only outside critics and not one ally. No one is really willing and able to see the school as central to him. And yet you have to make it central to the community. This I think is the challenge of your job, the excitement, and the difficulty.

Relations, in other words, are much more important to you than decisions. Yet, while decisions are not your main work, they are vital. Once you have made them, they determine the relationship.

I know that you do not accept the Hollywood model of the executive who constantly makes decisions. You know: he sits in an office a little larger than this hall, behind a desk a little larger than an aircraft carrier, grabs a telephone and hollers, "Get me Robertson." (Incidentally, nobody in Hollywood ever gets a wrong number.) Then he barks at Robertson, "Buy control of General Motors." And it's done. That only happens in Hollywood, no place else.

FEW AND FAR BETWEEN

Good administrators make few decisions. The fellow who makes a great many decisions is a poor administrator. There are always a lot of things to carry out, a lot of implementation action, some of it very tricky and involving a lot of judgment. For instance, there is the head of our math department, the best classroom teacher we have. But he is a problem: he is touchy; he always feels that math is not appreciated. Someone has got to be a little tactful with him, smear a lot of honey around his mouth before one can kick him in the shins, but one has to kick him in the shins eventually. Well, that's our daily work and we have to do a great deal of it day in and day out. But *decisions*, those one doesn't make very often.

People who make decisions all the time have not done their homework. They are doing the most dangerous thing in the world; they are depending on their own (or other people's) thinking of 20 years ago. They are depending on the world standing still. For one can only make decisions quickly if one does not have to understand what one is doing. If one has to understand, one has to go slow.

Understanding is very slow work. And so the people who make rapid-fire decisions—the Hollywood-type tycoons—always make wonderful decisions based on untested and usually invalid views of reality. They buy control of General Motors when what they should buy now is an electronics company. If you want to make decisions fast, you end up in the wrong business. If you want to end up in the right one, you had better spend a little time.

This is true of all important decisions. If you find you are making a lot of real decisions, the odds against your making the important ones right are astronomical. If you want to be right, make few decisions and spend a little time on each. What can one say about these right decisions on fundamentals?

There are two fundamental decisions of an administrator. He always has to live with their consequences.

First, there always are personnel decisions. Most of us in this room have learned that one makes personnel decisions with deliberate speed. Most of the problems I encounter in my consulting work result from unnecessary personnel mistakes. Those decisions were demonstrably wrong at the time they were being made. Yet they are being made—not out of stupidity or out of irresponsibility, but out of haste.

HASTE MAKES WASTE

A fast personnel decision is almost always the wrong decision. One always sees the visible first. Yet by definition there is no "right" personnel decision. The Good Lord did not create homeroom teachers, or gym teachers, or cost accountants, or even commissioners of education. The purposes for which the Good Lord created us are His purposes, not ours; and so nobody ever fits whatever job we have to fill. If we make a fast decision, we therefore always look for the least misfit. What we then get, inevitably, is mediocrity and not strength. We look for the man with the fewest rough edges. We do not look for the one who can produce. Yet the only thing that comes in universal supply is incompetence. Everything else one has to hunt for. And nothing causes more trouble than the man or woman who is "almost right."

Many years ago I met the Mother Superior of a hospital order. At age 21, she told me, when she had just got her bachelor's degree and was teaching her first junior high school class, she was made assistant to the administrator of a large hospital of the order. Then the Mother Administrator fell sick and three months later that older woman died. And there she was, age 22, running a 400-bed hospital. And I said, "Reverend Mother, what was the most difficult thing you had to learn when you suddenly became an administrator?" And she said, "That one cannot fire a nun."

This, believe me, is the wisest thing about administration I have ever heard, for one cannot fire anybody. One is stuck with them. Remember this and take time for personnel decisions. The obvious choice is usually a wrong one. One first wants to put in a man for the wrong reasons—one puts a man into a big job because he does not cause trouble for the boss. He does nothing. Of course, anybody can be pleasant to the boss by not doing anything.

When I was a minor-league academic administrator myself, I had to face up to the fact that my ablest department head and class-room teacher was absolutely unbearable in faculty meetings. That was of no consequence, that is not what people are being paid for. But I had no trouble in that department either with the faculty or with the students; the fellow was just wonderful with them. He was absolutely unbearable in the faculty meetings—aggressive, snide, and disagreeable.

Any good opera manager—and in a way we all are opera managers, we are all being paid to make stars effective—any good opera manager knows that it is his job to enable the prima donna to bring in results at the box office. And if this means that she makes a scene twice a day, well, that's what the manager gets paid for. This is his job—as long as she brings in the box office—on the one condition that when the playbill says "Tosca," she sings "Tosca."

Most of us know that we are stuck with our personnel decisions and so we take a little time, but we seldom take enough time. The great masters of personnel selection all know that one postpones the decision unless one has worked through it three or four times and still comes up with the same name at least twice in a row. Now one cannot always choose, but one can always think through the decision. And visibility, which usually underlies the fast decision, is almost the worst criterion for personnel decisions. It gets one to the man or woman who is usually in the most trouble.

I see it in business, I see it in government, in hospitals and in universities. In business that foreman gets promoted whom the works manager knows best. Why does he know him best? He is in his office every day because he is in trouble. There is Joe over there who knows his job perfectly—and there is no need for Joe to come in often. So when a promotion comes up, the works manager knows Jim—he sees him every day, he knows how he works—"Jim always does what I tell him." Yes, because you run his job for him. And so Jim gets the promotion.

This always happens when personnel decisions are being made fast.

LEADING, NOT SELLING

There is a second critical decision for the educational leader: the decision on his basic posture. This is crucial because of all these publics you have. You have to be flexible, and yet you have to take a stand. Above all, with the kind of decisions you face and the kind of publics you face, the attempt to "sell" a decision is hopeless. Anybody who thinks he can sell a decision fools himself. Decisions altogether cannot be sold. It's too late for this.

All you can do by trying to "sell" a decision is either to become a promoter and be totally unconvincing, or to alienate two out of five (that's all you need) of your constituents. I see it being tried every day. And "selling" a decision always ends in disaster. If you do not have public understanding of the issue before the action has to be taken, you are lost. If you have to sell—you might be able to get one bond issue through, but that's all. After that, you have used up your credit.

Yet we need understanding and acceptance of basic decisions on the school—on the content and methodology of learning and teaching, and on the guidance of young people to help them prepare for the difficult career choices ahead. Very often those are tougher decisions than the decisions on the money we need, the buildings we need, the personnel we will need. And you will only get the money, the buildings, and the personnel if you have understanding on these fundamental and highly controversial issues.

Therefore, you have to think through and face up to the issues. You have to say: What is my stand? You have to say: How do I get an understanding of what this is all about?

Selling not only comes too late. It also tries to get somebody to do something for you instead of enabling somebody to support you. And this latter one can only do by creating a little understanding of what the issue is all about.

In respect to crucial decisions, one has to ask: What are the truly important contributions which I, as the most important person in the community, have to contribute to this central, very complex, and vital institution that is in my keeping? What are the few things I can do? What new things should we be doing—things which are not just more of the same but which require new understanding, new attitudes and new action, and which yet have to build on yesterday? (One can't build on anything else—foundations are always historical.)

AIM FOR DISSENT

This already goes to the issue of the process of decision-making. There are hundreds of books written on decision-making. They always start out with two injunctions: first, get the facts; secondly, get agreement. But neither is what the effective decision-makers are doing. They do not start out with facts. They start out with opinion. They don't try to get agreement. They try to get dissent. When you look at them, you understand why. It is asinine to believe that people who have been 20 years in an area can start out looking for the facts. Of course, they all should have opinions.

I would take a very dim view of anybody in this room who, after 20 years plus in our school system, didn't have opinions on it. Where has he been? If he does not know anything, who does? Of course you have opinion. But that is not the main reason why one starts with opinion. I have yet to see anyone over 14 who cannot find the facts to support his opinion. One thing even the dumbest learns is the first law of statistics: Tell me what you want to prove, and I'll tell you where the facts are. Indeed, nobody in this room could operate for 10 minutes if he didn't know how to do that. So we all start out to look for the facts and to write the brief that supports our position.

But opinions we do understand. They are hypotheses. If you have been around long enough you are entitled to an opinion. In fact, you had better have an opinion. But what would reality have to look like for this to be a serious hypothesis? What would we have to find?

The decision-maker also needs dissent to understand what he is doing. The only way to find out what an issue is about are adversary proceedings. President Roosevelt was soundly criticized as a very poor administrator, but he made decisions that were highly effective. Whenever he had an important decision to make, he would say to one of his Cabinet members, "In strictest confidence I want you to work on this for me." No sooner had the man gone out of the door, however, than the President would pick up the telephone, call the man's closest political enemy, and say exactly the same thing to him on the same issue. In the end, then, he always got three people working on the same decision. This way Roosevelt made sure that he, the decision-maker, got every single relevant (and most of the irrelevant) positions fully represented and that he did not become the victim of the vested interests and limited visions of his associates.

This is not necessarily the best way of doing it. If you are the President of the United States and your subordinates cannot push you out of a job, it works. For anybody else, I would not recommend it. But it did the trick: Roosevelt made his decisions with a full understanding of what they were all about. Incidentally, when Roosevelt did not want to make a decision he swung into inaction with enormous fanfare and appointed a blue ribbon committee. This way he was absolutely sure that nothing would get done. No committee has ever finished its deliberation. One can always prolong the life of a committee without any resentment on their part.

But to make a decision and to take action, one has to have dissent. If need be, one creates it. One does not want fury, one does not want in-fighting. But one does want to make sure that opposing viewpoints are presented.

THE NEED FOR A "NO-MAN"

There is a nice story of a top management committee meeting of General Motors at which Alfred Sloan presided:

A young staff man made a brilliant presentation, and everybody was enthusiastic. Usually there was tremendous discussion in this committee, but that time everybody nodded in agreement. The old man said, "I take it, then, that you are all in favor of this?" "Yes, Mr. Sloan." "Then," said the old man, "I move that we table this for a month and give ourselves a chance to think." Next month it was turned down.

This tells you why one needs dissent. Otherwise one jumps for the plausible, for the thing that's nicely said, that's well presented, that uses all the "buzz words," that says what we want to hear.

One needs dissent, above all, because a decision without an alternative is not a decision. This is our problem in Viet Nam. I am not saying it was the wrong decision. I am afraid I would agree that it was the right one. But we had no alternative in that horror. And this is why we are in trouble. When the basic assumptions turn out to be wrong—and we are not in control of the universe—then one has to have an alternative.

May I again point to FDR. He was elected on a conservative platform, as some of us old-timers remember. There is no doubt that he believed in it. The Roosevelt of 1932 was not a "New Dealer" but a conservative, silk-stocking Democrat who believed in Recovery. But between election and Inauguration, the bottom fell out of our economy. We were no longer faced with an economic problem. The basic political cohesion of the country was in question. Recovery made no sense anymore. FDR had had a bunch of old-line progressives working in the back room on an alternative—though it wasn't *his* policy. He paid no attention to them during the campaign. But he had an alternative ready. And therefore he could swing into effective action the day he took the oath of office.

In international economics, however, Roosevelt had no alternative. All he had was the traditional economic policy of the Eastern liberal. Yet between election and Inauguration the bottom fell out there, too. Hitler came to power and so on. The traditional policy became absurd. Yet there was no alternative. So FDR had to start shooting from the hip. He hit all the wrong targets and did a lot of unnecessary damage. This is what happens to the most brilliant man if he does not have an alternative. Yet one does not even see alternatives unless one has dissent.

A few more words about the decision-making process. One learns to ask the question: Is a decision necessary? One does not make unnecessary decisions. Any important decision is a commitment, and any action is surgical. One makes the important ones and does not make the unnecessary ones.

One always asks: Is this a degenerative situation? Will it, left to itself, take care of itself or is it degenerative? One asks the question a good surgeon asks. If he sees the first trace of cancer, he'll operate—radically and fast. On the other hand, so many things can be lived with—they are not going to get better, they are not going to get worse. But the surgeon is not going to put a man with a weak heart on the operating table to take care of those things.

THE CHRONIC VS. THE ACCIDENTAL

Secondly, one asks: Is it a recurrent and chronic situation, or is it really and truly a nonrecurring one? If it is nonrecurring, one treats the symptoms, let me say. One does not try to come to grips with causes. Sometimes the situation can be remedied and it will go away if it is not degenerative and is pure accident. But in the recurring situations one never doctors the symptoms; one looks for causes.

Let me give you a very typical problem. It is not a school problem, though I know it is a problem some schools have been through. One of the worst problems is that of the successful business that started with virtually nothing and now has 30 or 40 million dollars of sales. Now it starts running into trouble. It is outrunning one-man management, but the founder is no longer very young and does not want to change—he usually doesn't know how. These are the businesses that get taken over or are liquidated, because they are too successful. This is clearly a recurrent situation. Yet that man who runs the business always tinkers with symptoms—production scheduling, and delivery, and quality control. He never comes to grips with his basic problem—that this can no longer be a one-man show but requires a management. As a result, he never solves his problems.

You cannot, in addition, make decisions as things come up. You have to anticipate. You therefore have to come to grips with the fundamental problem. Most of them are human problems.

A recurrent situation one fixes either by preventing it, which takes care of the basic problem, or one converts it into routine which the girl in the outer office can do. Most of the things we do as routine today were once problems that nobody knew how to handle. The definition of a routine is something that makes it possible for a donkey to do what it took genius to do yesterday. This is what the fire drill does. It is a routine in a situation which we all know to be recurrent. It isn't so long ago that we didn't know how to handle it. Fire drill is less than 100 years old, though it must have been a problem in school since we had the first school under a roof. There was a time—I can still remember it—when we thought this required "leadership." There was a time when people said, "This principal is a great man, he had a fire and he didn't lose anybody." Why, today we just have a fire drill and we know what to do and we don't believe that this requires anything but a routine.

These are the kinds of questions one asks in order to understand whether one should make a decision, and what kind of a decision.

The fundamental question on a decision is never what the right decision is. This only history can answer. The question is whether this is a decision about the *right matter*. Wrong decisions about the right matter may be beneficial, because we can change them fast and at least we understand what we are trying to do. But there is nothing worse than the right decision about the *wrong matter*. That we are not going to give up; we are going to stick to it. In our school system a lot of right decisions about the wrong matter have been made, and we all know it. These decisions misdirect people.

THE SCHOOL'S MANY PUBLICS

The school has a special problem. It has more interlocking and overlapping publics than anybody else. Yet it has few publics to whom the school is central. If your publics therefore do not understand what this is all about, you can't get anything. They aren't going to hold still very long. You can't educate them. They have to see what it is all about without a great deal of discussion. Therefore, if you don't think through what the right areas are, you can't operate.

I have sat in on enough school board meetings and enough PTA meetings to know that the administrator has exactly 28 seconds to get his point across. If he doesn't get the essential thing up front in the first half-minute, we are then going to spend the evening talking about the broom closet or the school band—and you all know it. Those 28 seconds are the attention span of your audience, particularly of middle-aged mothers. Middle-aged fathers are good for about half of that—about 14 seconds.

You have the same problem when you get up front before your students. If in the very first minute you say "this is it," you have them. They may be resentful, but at least they are focused where they should be. I know you can make a joke, but after that you've got a minute and then you are lost. They have so many other things they are concerned about—the history test that is coming up in the next period, and the football game, and the date, and the fight they had with their mother. If you want to get them, you have to get them fast.

This is not just rhetoric, this is true conceptually. You have to say what the right areas are. You have to take leadership or nothing can get done. You have to start out by telling us what the few contributions are which you can make in your position in the few years you have.

You have, I would say, more headaches than an administrator. But we all have to make the beds and sweep the floor, and sooner or later to start to pick up the garbage, even in New York City. The daily job always has to be done. One always has to wipe the noses of the runny-nosed kids—the chores are endless.

But the mark of a good executive, of a good school administrator, of a good manager of a business, or of a good head of a government agency is that he also has time and attention and thought for the basics, for the decision on his posture, for thinking through his unique contribution. He does not disappear in management. He keeps the routine to what routine is all about. Routines exist so that we don't have to worry about them. That is why we have routines. They free us so that we can use the mind the Good Lord gave us, the experience we acquire, the authority we have in the community, and the opportunity which this society now gives the school administrator, to make the decisions which go well beyond your high school or mine. These are the decisions that have to do with our people, with our spirit, with our values, and with our quality as a free people.

24 | Decision Making Process in a Revolution

Donald McNassor

It is a time of travail and tragedy, an age of transition when familiar values and institutions struggle for life. The leaves are falling in and out of season, law professor Paul Freund aptly observes. Dissatisfaction and suspicion, accompanied by a relish for violence and desire for instant reduction of life's frustrations are present in many segments of the population. The temper tantrum becomes a way of life. Paranoia is so inseparably mixed with rational complaints it is difficult to tell one from the other. "I demand" is commonplace language among minority people, professional groups including teachers, children and their parents, and people in public services. "I demand" is the language of threat and reprisal, of revolution, authoritarianism and paternalism in their worst form. But if we forget it also is the language of people who feel spiritually empty and absurd, we do so at the peril of repressing social regeneration.

Everyone searches restlessly and aggressively for a better way— black people. Chicano citizens, poor people, the American Indians, the frustrated, put-upon city dweller. Anxiety and resentment are seen especially in the young. Their temper is a good barometer of continuity and discontinuity in cultural change. They understandably rebel against the hypocrisies of morality, war and the law. But their resentment of social custom goes deeper; it is generalized, total, frequently irrational. Their chief target is the voice and experience of authority that has given them such a dangerous, materialistic world to live in. In their dreams in the night and their movements during the day, they cry out—The world is intolerable; I hate it!

Apparently it is one of the necessary ways of man-in-culture that each young generation must highlight the most self-defeating parts of the age. This generation is fulfilling its function with a vengeance. They are doing it in a strange mixture of healthy raw nerve and infantile, escapist behavior. Many are caught in a polarity between being committed to ancient values and a human fraternity and, in the case of the drug scene, being truants from life.

The ancient Chinese doom, "May you live in an age of transition," describes our plight well. But transitions, even those involving revolutionary change, can also herald intellectual and moral regeneration. It is hard to imagine that any blessings will come from episodes of violence and lawlessness whether they involve children,

From *Journal of Secondary Education*, Vol. 44 (October 1969), pp. 265-270. Reprinted by permission of the publisher.

school personnel, minority group members, or affluent white people who sound the alarm to defend the gates of the old city with stronger authoritarian controls than ever. The last thing we can stand in a world that is changing and that ought to change is mob rule to attain lofty ends.

Beneath the social unrest and the tragic breakdown in communication, I sense two healthy impulses that must not be repulsed or repressed by the leaders in education, government, and industry. Repression surely will lead to new cynicism in the young and to deeper cleavages among us. The first is a deep longing for a more generous humanity, new ideals to foster authenticity, honesty, and respect for oneself and for others. This is one active element sweeping our society and the world. It is intermixed with the violence and disruption.

The second impulse is for more authentic programmatic participation and responsibility. This one is clear enough. Its major expression is the desire for more power to change conditions that affect one's well-being. The demand for power and autonomy, as much as it presents dangers and arouses fear in all of us, at its center is the desire for more shared responsibility. We see it on every side. Black power and black identity. Brown people power. Student, youth power. Woman power. The road to reconciliation is to devise new forms of responsibility.

There is relevance in these observations for education at the local school as well as the county school level. In a period of revolutionary change, the schools usually get more than their fair share of blame. Modern man's efforts to improve his well-being always seem to start with changing the schools. Although a grossly simplistic idea, it is still a fact of life. The coming decade will be very traumatic for the schools. Many groups, including teachers, administrators, school board members, students, and different ethnic and social class groups will have divergent ideas about what schools should be and how they should be run.

Schools and colleges face agonizing issues that cannot be wished away or avoided. (1) The issue of relevance of some of our educational programs for living in this world or understanding it. This is the issue of the spiritual bankruptcy prevalent especially in secondary schools and colleges. It is a main issue the young are shouting about. (2) The issue of governance—the question of shared responsibility of teachers, administrators, board members, parents, and older students. (3) The issue of the significance of the educational experience for particular groups, the poor who contribute masses of dropouts, and minority groups. (4) The issue of decentralizing basic educational decisions to smaller units involving more direct forms of citizen participation. And finally (5) the issue of determining priorities, where to start making improvements and the question of who shall participate in setting the priorities.

Many things that we have been used to in more tranquil times clearly will no longer do. We have been used to educating all children alike in the specifics of the curriculum—the disadvantaged, the black, the brown, the poor, the intellectually talented; a common mold for all in all neighborhoods, more or less. There is a remarkable similarity among all schools just as there is among drugstores. We are not used to diversity in schools and colleges.

We have been used to concentrating power, in a massive way, in boards of education and boards of trustees without sufficient participation by other interested parties. Boards tend to be ruling bodies rather than bodies to promote rules.

We have been used to taking two to four years to study, then make changes in the curriculum and the day by day operation of schools. We have been used to faculties having responsibility to suggest improvements but with no real power to initiate them. In the elementary and secondary schools, teachers have had very little responsibility in educational innovation. They tend to see themselves as employees not as professional educators.

We have been used to filtering ideas for change from the top down—state, county, and local boards and administrators. Only a few educational ideas have come up the other way, through parents, teachers, and older students.

There are some principals of the decision-making process that can be applied to the current scene of revolutionary change. I am talking about decision-making during a cultural and educational revolution. There are no absolute principles of decision-making good for all time.

A fateful struggle for control is shaping up over basic educational policy decisions. The participants are clearly discernible: boards of education, administrators, many polarized citizen groups—including that silent majority of white working-class people who will soon awake to assert an identity, older students and teachers, and representatives of government. Each group has legitimate interests in what happens in the schools. Decision-making on basic questions must in some way involve responsible participation by all of these groups. The participation must not be in name only, politely listening to suggestions and complaints, then not doing anything about them. Here is the opportunity to regenerate democracy through shared power and responsibility. Up to this time, the groups with the greatest responsibility and voice have been government representatives, school boards and administrators. The groups with least sense of involvement and responsibility have been teachers, students and parents.

It will take great imagination and an intense willingness to change on the part of school boards and administrators in order to fashion new forms of shared responsibility for educational improvement. If we wonder whether it is going to be possible to break out of the worn paths, there is no other direction to go.

Involving older students in certain areas of educational policy should be easy for educators. Apparently it is not easy, for educators are exceedingly reluctant to involve students in anything except their social activities. It should be easy for administrators to share responsibility and power with teachers. But apparently it is not easy. The new industrial age has brought bureaucratic forms of governance desired by the rulers and the ruled alike, but for different reasons. It is not going to be easy to share responsibility for defining the issues and making decisions with the many voices of the community. But we must try to find ways of doing this better.

The greatest danger we face during the storm of divergent group perceptions of good schools is anarchy, nihilism, and separatism. All groups must proceed to share responsibility according to some rules and laws. The fashioning of these rules will have to be part of the decision-making process. By their nature, the rules or laws cannot accommodate "non-negotiable" demands.

I cannot foresee all the possible effective new ways of ushering in more shared responsibility, but I have some suggested directions. One is to place on teachers much heavier responsibility for curriculum evaluation and change. In these times we are overdue for some teacher task forces to identify weaknesses in the schools and to determine programs of innovation. Perhaps the local teachers' association should have major and serious responsibility here.

Second, the replacement of "public relations" personnel with people who are constantly in touch with different citizen groups, insuring that before new programs are implemented or old ones revised, the points of view and wishes of many groups are heard and given serious consideration. These individuals should not have strong allegiances to any organization. We have relied too much in the past on the noisy, emotion-filled Tuesday night Board of Education meeting as a forum for participation. By the time the meetings are held, the positions and ideas of all groups are polarized. Also, schools should make use of professional polling organizations to more quickly detect sentiment about educational issues in the community.

Third, the use of community, town hall forums of discussion, planned around known key issues and problems about which feeling runs high.

At some point in the decision-making process, where the voices of many groups are considered thoughtfully, a final umpire has to be used. I suggest that the umpire consist of a council of representative voices of all groups: citizens, teachers, boards, administrators, and secondary school students. Boards of education should have extraordinarily good reasons for not accepting the proposals of the umpire.

The third principle is to adopt procedures for telescoping the period for study, analysis, and program change. Usually it takes two or more years to conduct the dialogue, gather the facts and opinions, and make changes. During a time of social unrest and frustration, the process must somehow be telescoped into months or even weeks. For out of anger and fear there is the constant temptation to anarchy, disruption, and violence.

The fourth point has to do with minority groups. Boards should act quickly to involve such groups in the change process, *even if* they have not asked for a share of responsibility. What folly it is today for anyone to say as someone said to me recently, "There is no trouble in our community with Mexican-Americans. They are very peace-loving, quiet, and pleased with what our schools do for their children." I would give this person about two years or less before a storm hits his schools. We must not wait until storms blow.

Next, the process must be insured against administrator lethargy in making changes after recommended improvements are agreed upon. Many a study and proposal for change is concluded with nothing happening. School boards some day may have to hire a part-time community representative to insure efficient implementation of decisions mutually arrived at.

The principle of limited autonomy for any one group. "Shared responsibility" means just that. Perhaps we will have to redefine the areas in which different groups will have heavy responsibility: *curriculum* teachers, administrators, students, parents; *economics, finance, management, personnel*-school boards.

The principle of priority setting. This will be the most agonizing part of the process. Clearly today everybody wants something. Just as clearly everybody will not get everything he wants. I am referring to things more basic than salaries, such as a certain kind of education, values, happiness. Again we shall have to resort to the umpire, the council of final decision.

Bargaining, discussing in good faith is another one. Today most of us are talking but not listening. All of us will have to do a new kind of listening, the kind that opens up the mind to hear what that fellow feels and means—that fellow being black, or brown, teacher, student, or a person of ultra-conservative or ultra-liberal educational and political views. Part of our present tragedy is due to our hard of hearing condition. Much of the promise for better schools and for a more generous America depends on regeneration that can come from opening up the mind. We have a great deal to learn from youth, for they are feeling things we cannot feel and not all of what they feel by any means is morbid or unhealthy.

Then the matter of decentralizing decision-making. A long step was taken recently in the Los Angeles city schools. The board agreed to encourage a particular area to come forward with its own plan for a better curriculum and operational means. Much more decentralization, and greater divergency among schools in the content and means of education will do much to broaden the base of shared responsibility. The process does not have to result either in anarchy or poorer schools. The great danger to be guarded against in such a process is anarchy and the seizure of the neighborhood schools to promote new forms of bigotry and academic slovenliness.

I have not said all that needs to be said about decision-making process during a revolutionary period. The most important thing to say is that the county and local school boards and administrative staffs have no greater role today than to facilitate imaginative new forms of shared responsibility in the conduct of schools.

A very few years ago some of us may have regretted that we were not nearing retirement age. I, for one, was sorry I had to live through this transition of travail, unclear in its beginnings with no sight of an end. This feeling has changed in the last year or two. I would not now miss this chance to see if regeneration is possible if I could. Out of the agony something better might come if we don't resort to war and violence. In the midst of turmoil and desperation, a whole generation of children throughout the world arises to reaffirm non-materialistic values and to resist hypocrisy and frailty. Spring will come again in the unending cycles of the renewal of life. Storms that devastate also scatter seeds of renewal and regeneration in the human as well as in the natural world.

25 | The Community and the Schools
   | Who Are the Decision-Makers?

Herbert M. Zimmerman

Each year the temper of the times, educationally and in general, seems to set the theme of our convention sessions. One year Sputnik sent us all to sessions which dealt with the changing science curriculum; last year most of us flocked to any session dealing with the administrator as the middleman in teacher negotiations; and in 1969, in every type of local conference, and now here at NASSP, we deal with the many issues and unresolved questions which we as building principals confront in trying to respond sensitively to pressures from within the school and outside the school, all clamoring for a share in the making of decisions of all kinds.

Yet, I find myself hung-up on trying to define the terms in the title of today's session, for we need to proceed with some commonality of understanding, especially with the two words *community* and *decision*. The Unabridged Random House Dictionary lists seven definitions for *community*, and it wasn't until I had read down to number seven that I found the meaning most fitting our topic. You see, we aren't talking about the number one definition of "a community being a social group whose members reside in a specific locality and have a common cultural and historical heritage"— for in my own particular school, 15 percent of the student population comes from widely diverse parts of the city, diverse racially, historically, and economically. Nor are we able to use the number two definition of *community* as that of a "social group sharing common characteristics and interests as distinct in some respects from the larger city within which it exists"—no, this is hardly descriptive of my school community, which was at one time almost 100 percent Jewish but which now has a majority of white "greasers" and a minority of black students who come on permissive transfer. Even the black students reflect divergent perceptions and characteristics. It is only when we come down to the definition of *community* as "the public (or publics), as society in general" that we in the big cities might have found the right word. Only then does the statement, "We must consider the needs of the community," have general meaning for each of us—a kind of general welfare concept.

Defining *decision* or *decision-makers* is not quite so complex if we think of *decision*, not so much as a judgment with a definite finality, but as a process of "making a judgment" or "making up

From *NASSP Bulletin*, Vol. 53 (May 1969), pp. 169-175. Reprinted by permission of the National Association of Secondary School Principals. Copyright: 1969 by the National Association of Secondary School Principals.

one's mind"—the individual mind, or even the group's mind, or the community's consensus.

Another confusing aspect of this topic is that, when people speak about the decision-making aspect of community and its schools, there are often three words used interchangeably, but these three words do not mean the same thing at all—*control, involvement, participation.*

Control means money, and this is the most complex aspect of all. Control is analogous to the ownership of a baseball club, with all the responsibilities, accountability, and management functions: hiring, firing, raising revenues, and financing. *Involvement* is comparable to being a player for that ball club: being on the team, making the game go, feeling individual responsibility to the owners, being obligated to the team and to the controlling elements. *Participation* might be likened to a spectator who is *at* the game, but not *of* the game; he is an onlooker who, at the end of the game whether he is satisfied or not with what transpired, can leave and return another day, again merely as an interested on-looker. Just for the sake of argument, what I see as the answer to the question "Community and the Schools: Who are the Decision Makers?" can most meaningfully be *involvement.* I understand this to be a synthesis of owners, of management, and of players with mutual understandings of what is meant by accountability control, plus encouragement for and communication with those who remain on the participation level.

DECENTRALIZATION CONTROVERSY

This session could not possibly last long enough to analyze the whole decentralization controversy; you all know that there is not a current journal which is not focusing attention on the problem, with the New York headlines having been in the vanguard of the issue. One cannot think of the topic "Community and Its Schools" without consciously or unconsciously being reminded of the Brooklyn experiments. In many other cities, however, demands and/or plans for decentralizing are in various stages. It can readily be anticipated that wherever the issue is raised tensions are sure to follow, because guidelines, greatly needed, are not always being set. We all know the questions, but how to gird for action and answers is the hard part. I'm sure most of us would agree that thus far the "community decision-makers" debate can be characterized by an obvious lack of clarity. Specifics have become centers of contention; separate but interrelated issues have been lumped under the banner of these fashionable new words—decentralization, control, involvement, participation.

Who, then, is to clarify the issues? The local board of education, so far removed from whatever is one's idea of community? The smaller districts in a big city who themselves feel, and demonstratively so, that they are but one more hurdle in whatever communication could best serve the schools and the "community?" The local administrators—you and I—again caught in the bind between whatever local autonomy we think we may have and that of the whole administrative hierarchy? The teachers with their new agreements with boards of education, which we feel often circumvent the local school administration? The students? And we'd better not sell short this power block in 1969! (The journals all seem hard-pressed to decide which topic to feature—decentralization or student unrest.) The parents, with the long-time-in-coming "welcome mat"? The community agencies, which we recognize as important in involvement as the four walls of each schoolhouse have come tumbling down?

And if any, or all, or others of these concerned groups are to be considered as the decision-makers, then we must be asking three important questions related to the whole business of involvement: The first of these is whether educational effectiveness and educational options will be increased. Whether this whole involvement with local residents having a stake in the schools will lead to better education for their children (and there really can be no other goal than this) is still too new for either experience or research to evaluate. At the same time, it can be argued that our big city school systems (and I am not being professionally disloyal when I say this) have proven to be such failures that some new forms of structural experimentation are essential.

CREATING AN EXPERIMENTAL CLIMATE

Innovations of all kinds need to be fostered in each of our systems, whether with local funds, federal or state grants, or even on the informal no-cost level. The very fact that a total school system is amenable to change and re-evaluation as a result of creating an experimental climate could make possible significant educational reform. In our city, a number of new programs were initiated by a wide spectrum of individual schools, by official districts, by a group of inner-city principals who recognized a need for greater community involvement, by "mini-grant" projects, by Model Cities planning. In my own school, as an outgrowth of expressed concerns of students themselves, we have organized an advisory council comprised of representation of parents, faculty, and students. There is nothing particularly earthshaking or even new in this, but there is a new set of relationships emerging, and no longer is such a group just tolerated by the administration, but is welcomed as an integral part of the school's concerns.

The second question is concerned with the accountability of public education to the public, and it is in this area particularly that you and I probably feel most shaken in the "new regime." No one can deny that the big city educational bureaucracy in which most of us grew up, to which we returned in our professional capacities, and in which we now feel threatened, did, in fact, grow too distant. There is unquestionably a need for reconnecting the public to this bureaucracy. The narrow question again is: To which "public" should the bureaucracy be responsible? But the larger question is: How can or should public education in general become more accountable to the "public"? Shall we use the suburban school system as a model for parental and/or community involvement? City parents want the same control over their children's education that suburban parents seem to exercise. However, in the current eagerness to become decision-makers, one cannot tolerate the abolition of due process procedures or of state and local laws. The legislative road to reform may seem slow, but its processes do give opportunity for the wider community to have its voice heard.

LIMITS OF CONTROL

I have observed, in the members of my own local council, a growing awareness of the limits of power and control, because for the first time these people are sitting together with us, with open communication and resultant understandings. When this is the climate, there is a chance for understanding, regardless of the forms community involvement and decision-making take.

Certainly we can bear a re-evaluation of established definitions and credentials for "professional educators" and still keep our profession intact. If we become responsible to smaller geographic centers than has been traditional in big city districts, then we, as urban administrators, may one day play a role similar to that of suburban educators. That is, while the day-to-day operation of the school is in my hands, I might frequently have to justify my professional decisions to my public. Local principals' organizations as well as our national and state organizations should be in the forefront of some of the reshaping of our roles, not with the idea of downgrading our principalships, but rather in strengthening our roles as professional leaders.

The third important question of deep concern has to do with the consequences of new sets of intergroup relations. Opponents of decentralization or of community involvement with resultant decision-making cite the potential for institutionalizing the "neighborhood school" and racial separation at the expense of integration. In my own case, we tried to assure that the council was comprised of members who live within the designated school boundary lines as well as those whose children come from other areas of the city. This helps, we hope, to answer the argument of some neighborhood leaders that integration is an unachievable goal and should be sub-ordinated (if only temporarily) to the goals of more localized community identity and strength.

I must admit that integration seems a more difficult goal in 1969 than it did even a year ago, but I'm not ready to throw in the towel on that one. I do not accept the observation by some that without local control of local school boards, and the consequences for group solidarity, meaningful integration of minorities as equals cannot occur. I believe there are alternatives which avoid polarization, and in our city new options are possible. If only a portion of the system is decentralized, there are still opportunities for integration within a larger context, with such formalized programs as Wingspread, with informal articulation between schools, by innovations and experimentation by a combination of official districts, or again by informal working relationships between schools and between newly organized councils who wish sincerely to become involved. This is not an either-or argument. Government on any level should not institutionalize segregation, but since it has not been able to realize integration to the extent we would like to have it, there is need for a middle-ground position for the decision-makers, whoever they are.

James F. Redmond, the general superintendent of schools in Chicago, in his most recent report writes:

> In the Civic Center Plaza of Chicago stands a new structure, the Chicago Picasso. Through the skill of the artist, this sculpture, in reality rigid and unmoving, seems to be fluid and changing with a variety of forms. From one side, the viewer gets one impression; from another he gets an entirely different idea. Only as he views the sculpture from all sides does he begin to form a composite picture of the entire sculpture.
>
> Another structure is a large public school system. Here we have a structure which may seem rigid, but is, in reality, fluid, changing to meet the needs of the citizens and their children. In some cases, parts of the structure may be enlarged; other elements may be made smaller.

Who helps decide on the changing forms is the topic to which we have addressed ourselves today. Superintendent Redmond, all of us are asking, "How do you stir a city, board members, staff, citizens, students? How do you communicate so that each person becomes important in the solutions of the problems which the cynic says are insolvable?"

What I keep worrying about is how we are going to solve the basic problem of just living together, regardless of decision-making. We have all become interdependent as our society has grown more and more complex. If we don't learn to live and work together, we must certainly look forward to more and more problems. A large-scale effort must be made to bring to parents and citizens in general the understanding necessary to fulfill their roles so they may be partners in the task of decision-making. But this will come only through sincere dialogue, through the discussion and sharing of ideas and ideals. In the last analysis, this is a new day for meshing creative ideas cooperatively. Yet we are talking about human beings; thus, *all* of us will need to learn appropriate sensitivity through shared experience. This will be the most difficult task which faces us.

26 | More Democracy, Better Organization and Improved Administration for Our Schools

Ronald L. Abrell

The democratic faith in equality is the faith that each individual shall have the chance and opportunity to contribute whatever he is capable of.
                                                            —JOHN DEWEY

Professional educators in our schools seem to loquaciously champion such democratic ideals as the omnipotence of the individual, the inviolability of the right to dissent, the opportunity for each and all to participate in decision-making—the list could be extended indefinitely. Unfortunately such ideals, however well-intentioned the garrulity, appear to be pitifully and conspicuously absent to those who man and attend the typical schools of this nation. Not the least of those who feel the impact of undemocratic procedures are American school teachers! While it is ultimately the welfare of the student, nation, and world that suffers, this work centers upon the teacher as the recipient of injustice.

Let us begin with an examination of school organization and its failure to offer the classroom teacher an adequate voice in affairs that affect his teaching. For the most part, schools tend to be organized along lines of the model chosen by American business and government. The model selected by business and government, for whatever legitimate reasons, has been and continues to be the ideal bureaucratic framework proposed by Max Weber. A cursory glance at Weber's design suggests an organization based on such ideas as authority of a "monarch," impersonal social contacts, specialization, and *efficiency*-centeredness as opposed to person-centeredness.

Chris Argyris (1962) argues that current organizational plans (mainly production-directed) used by administrators are leading to human and organizational decadence. The fact that business, government, and in many cases education have sacrificed the worth and dignity of the person for the "cult of efficiency" is hardly in keeping with the democratic ethic. It seems clear that when one of the major objectives of public education is to promote democratic ideals, organizational structure must not only be created for efficiency but also (much more importantly), the opportunity for self-enhancement.

From *Michigan Journal of Secondary Education*, Vol. 10 (Winter 1969), pp. 39-45. Reprinted by permission of the publisher.

School organization is apparently conceived along rational lines and fails to take into account man's irrationality—such a plan does not allow for the employees' emotions. Again, Argyris has found that modern organization tends to set up a clear chain of command which in turn makes those on the lower end of such a hierarchy feel subordinate and dependent upon their superiors for rewards, punishment, direction, and employment. Such dependence, separation (many employees never see some of the hierarchy), and alienation plus the surrendering of independence to someone or some organization that one doesn't even see or know is scarcely providing for the individual growth that democracy champions.

In addition, the fact that modern organizations exercise control over what one produces, when he produces, and how he produces (school organization tends to tell the teacher what, when, and in some cases, how to teach—leading teachers "to fall into line with any workable mandate from downtown") reduces the employee to an infant-like existence. Such direction from above encourages conformity, organizational acceptance, confusion, and a reduction of creativity.

Modern organization is structured so that only a select few participate in decision-making. In the organization of the typical school, decisions of major importance tend to be made by the board of education, the superintendent, and/or the principal. In teacher-principal relationships there is considerable evidence to suggest that the latter is derelict in providing an adequate democratic atmosphere in many schools. In fact, school administrators are undemocratic in that they:

1. Fail, in large part, to allow the teacher the right to disagree.
2. Do not permit teachers the right to participate in decision-making. Teachers seem to participate, if at all, in: (a) the understanding of a set policy, (b) giving advice, and (c) carrying out the established policy.
3. Fail to provide for interpersonal relations between themselves and their teachers. *Administrative distance* tends to serve to discourage suggestions-making and the democratic process involved in the making of decisions.
4. Do not assure a fair way of evaluating their teachers. An overwhelming number of those who evaluate teachers are principals. They are not specially trained to do so, with the result being that "in many instances supervisory ratings are basically not efficiency rating, but compatibility ratings."

Corwin (1965) points out that Guba and Bidwell discovered that the ratings of effectiveness which principals gave to their teachers were a function of the degree to which the principal perceives that the teacher "lives-up" to his expectations of the teacher's role. In a society characterized by lock-step conformity the teacher who is different, who does not belong to the right groups, who does not attend the right meetings or do as he is expected, gives the impression of being incompetent.

As might be expected, such conditions are totally inadequate for professionals in a democracy. Some of the effects of an undemocratic organization and administration are as follows:

1. Encourages feelings of mistrust and confusion among teachers. Teachers are not certain of what to do or say, the result being that they do or say nothing for fear of angering someone or upsetting a traditional stolidness.
2. Fosters a reluctance to change. Superiors make all the decisions and subordinates are hesitant to make suggestions.
3. Precipitates an attitude of "if you can't beat 'em, join 'em." Males, in particular, strive for administrative positions when they are neither altogether desirous of nor competent for such positions.
4. Causes teacher apathy . . . teacher continues to teach in the undemocratic atmosphere for one reason or another, but his heart isn't really in it. Dewey wrote that when there is little power, there is likewise little sense of positive responsibility (1916).
5. Brings about a security-directed attitude and more recently, teachers are interested in making as much money as they can. One gets the feeling that the average teacher is becoming what Erich Fromm refers to as "market-oriented" (1957). Although many would hasten to deny it, teachers are learning to respect themselves in terms of the money they can command.
6. Initiates professionalization and unionizing on the part of teachers. In an effort to gain a stronger voice in those matters that affect not only their own welfare but also that of their students, teachers are increasingly (and disappointingly in some cases) turning to organizations that are not altogether dissimilar to the very types they attempt to escape.
7. Generates a fear of freedom among many teachers. Grambs speculates that some teachers need authoritarian rule (1950). This fear of or "escape from freedom" is undoubtedly the product of long-term conditioning; i.e., everyone is supposed to be afraid of the principal.
8. Causes anxiety that must be dealt with . . . unfortunately, it is dissipated in rather unhealthy ways all too frequently. Examples include keeping one's distance from administrative superiors, attempting to undermine the authority, adopting obsequiousness as a way of ingratiating one's self with the ruler, etc.

9. Transference of that which is undemocratic into the classroom. Many have speculated about a possible carry-over of administrative authoritarianism to classrooms.
10. Fosters the never-ending mass exodus of teachers that perennially plagues our schools. For some remarkably unbelievable statistics on the departure of teachers from the schools and some of their reasons for leaving, the reader is referred to *Life Magazine*, November 16, 1962. That The System stifles individuality and thrives on an "undemanding and noncompetitive" personality is in itself unthinkable, much less tolerable!

Assuming some of the above to be at least partially true, what can be done to ameliorate such sad conditions?

With regard to improving democratically inspired organizational effectiveness, we must decide on how much teacher-participation in decision-making is desirable. Currently ideas on this vary tremendously! National organizations should make a public declaration on this issue only after consultation with teacher representatives. Then the action must be suited to the word!

In addition, more effort must be made in recruiting top rate administrators, learning how to train them and get them into jobs where role performance will be most adequate. Certainly, a top priority in the recruiting and training of school administrators must be the selection of democratic-minded and humanistically oriented individuals. Also, the organization must develop within its personnel such traits as open-mindedness, flexibility, and adaptability if the organization is to function in an ever-changing environment.

Moreover, the organization must strive to provide for man's needs yet meet organizational demands. Both long and short-range effectiveness are enhanced when managerial strategy is designed to provide for the individual's: (a) basic survival needs, (b) social and interpersonal needs, (c) ego-involvement and self-esteem needs, (d) need for independence, and (e) self-actualization needs.[1] Argyris has shown that such provision for man's needs is not absolutely essential for efficiency, but both efficiency and individual psychological well-being improve where there is such provision.

Not only should the organization provide for participation of teachers in decision-making and the execution of such decisions by representative group action, but also it should attempt to promote more effective group action. This can be accomplished by: (a) encouraging the formation of groups within The System which tend to meet organizational needs as well as the needs of individual mem-

1. Edgar Schein, *Organizational Psychology* (Englewood Cliffs, N. J.: Prentice-Hall, Inc., 1965).

bers; and (b) attempting to reduce intergroup conflict and competition.

Finally, school organization must be conceived along lines that will guarantee an open system. Organization should be such that it maximize the opportunity for self-growth, possess a climate of person-centeredness, and provide for the utilization of humane approaches in helping to solve organizational and human problems.

At this time we may ask the question: What action may be taken to assure more democratic and competent administrative leadership? First of all, we must abandon the idea of increased graduate study as the *only* panacea for administrative shortcomings. Most of us would admit that this is one step in the right direction; however, it is not enough just to add up semester hours. Increased study may be more valuable if we change what we are trying to teach administrators. Education for the type of leadership we now need would include the following suggestions:

1. Emphasize the developing of a democratic-minded person rather than finding new ways of manipulating those of lesser rank for organizational ends.
2. Stress more humanism and less exploitation when dealing with subordinates. This would involve re-educating or unfreezing old and less human values.
3. Increase study of the behavioral sciences—particularly psychology, sociology, anthropology, group dynamics, etc. Administrators, as well as the rest of us, need a better understanding of the nature of man.
4. Emphasize that which lends itself to the development of administrators who possess *wisdom* rather than "administrative" expertise.[2] Admittedly, we need both; nevertheless, one fails to see how a narrow specialist can appreciate the many problems of his diverse subordinates. Here, more formal study, especially philosophy and the classics are recommended.
5. Educate for the growth of flexibility, creativity, imagination, reflection, introspection, empathy, and interpersonal competence.

In what type of setting might all this occur? In a human relations laboratory! Industry is already providing valuable training via these labs where executives share in arriving at creative solutions to simulated problems and are able to apply such solutions to real problems in real life.

While educational organization and administrators have been able to deny their beneficiaries sufficient democracy in the past, such is not the case today. The increasing militance of the American Negro, young teachers and their professional organizations, and

2. Harold Howe, II. "The Care and Feeding of Superintendents" in *American Education* by Paul Woodring and John Scanlon, eds. (New York: McGraw-Hill, 1964).

youth in general are crying out for all types of changes that will hopefully effectuate more adequately the pragmatic concept of democracy.

REFERENCES

1. Argyris, Chris. *Interpersonal Competence and Organizational Effectiveness.* Homewood, Illinois: Richard D. Irwin, Inc., 1962.
2. Bode, Boyd H. *Democracy as a Way of Life.* New York: The Macmillan Company, 1937.
3. Bradford, Gibb, and Benne, Kenneth D, eds. *T-Group Theory and Laboratory Method.* New York, London, and Sydney: John Wiley & Sons, Inc., 1964.
4. Brembeck, Cole. *Social Foundations of Education.* New York, London, and Sydney: John Wiley & Sons, Inc., 1966.
5. Corwin, Ronald. *A Sociology of Education.* New York: Appleton-Century-Crofts, 1965.
6. Dewey, John. *Democracy and Education.* New York: The Macmillan Company, 1916.
7. Dewey, John. "Democracy and Educational Administration." *School and Society,* 45 (April 1937), 457-462.
8. Fromm, Erich. *Escape from Freedom.* New York: Harper & Brothers, 1947.
9. Fromm, Erich. *Man for Himself.* New York: Holt, Rinehart and Winston, 1947.
10. Grambs, Jean. "Do Teachers Really Want Democratic Administrators?" *Nation's Schools,* 46 (November 1950), 40-41.
11. Grambs, Jean. *Schools, Scholars, and Society.* Englewood Cliffs, New Jersey: Prentice-Hall, Inc., 1965.
12. Howe, Harold II. "The Care and Feeding of Superintendents" in *American Education* by Paul Woodring and John Scanlon, eds. New York: McGraw-Hill, 1964.
13. Lee, Gordan. *Education and Democratic Ideals.* New York, Chicago, and Burlingame: Harcourt, Brace & World, Inc., 1965.
14. Melby, Ernest O. *The Education of Free Men.* Pittsburgh: University of Pittsburgh Press, 1965.
15. Padover, Saul *The Meaning of Democracy.* New York: Praeger, 1963.
16. Riesman, David. *Constraint and Variety in American Education.* Garden City, New York: Doubleday & Company, 1956.
17. Schein, Edgar. *Organizational Psychology.* Englewood Cliffs, New Jersey: Prentice-Hall, Inc., 1965.
18. Stiles, Lindley, et al. *Teacher Education in the United States.* New York: Ronald Press, 1960.
19. Whyte, William H., Jr. *The Organization Man.* New York: Simon & Schuster, 1956.

27 | Forget About Decentralizing If Your Principals Aren't Ready

Freeman H. Vaughn

Regardless of how many problems a school board thinks it can ease by decentralizing and "humanizing" its school district, chances are the effort will not succeed unless the district's principals have been carefully chosen and prepared for the move.

If the principals aren't ready, all the board is likely to create by moving to break the central administrative stranglehold is another thick layer of bureaucracy for the local schools to break through in order to function.

To work, decentralization must be a twofold effort: (1) Loosen the central grip, of course, in order to bring school authority and school clients closer together; (2) *Make sure the local authority is ready and able to deal effectively with local problems.*

The second idea is as crucial as the first.

If the neighborhood school principal isn't given the freedom and training to respond to community needs, no plan of decentralized authority will achieve much. Here's the same idea, stated more bluntly: Select, train, or retrain principals to deal directly with problems that used to be passed along to the central office—not many decentralization plans seem to recognize that necessity.

While it's easy to say that, it's not so simple to accomplish it. The administrative ability of principals, obviously, varies a great deal. One school may be running smoothly; another, in a similar neighborhood, may be the scene of near chaos. Often enough, the difference is the principal. Blame it on incompetence if you like, but it's just as likely to be a retreat into apathy by a potentially effective principal—one who had chafed and smarted too long from a lack of real authority and real training to carry out the leadership role specified for his job.

Most authorities seem to agree that a principal has four assignments: (1) manage the school; (2) select and train personnel; (3) improve the educational program as best he can; (4) work with the community.

The first task is what consumes the time of most principals— schedules, lunchrooms, maintenance, endless forms to fill out and send off to the central office.

From *American School Board Journal,* Vol. 156, No. 6 (December 1968), pp. 24-26. Reprinted by permission of the publisher. Copyright 1968 by American School Boards Association.

For improvement, take these four steps first:

• *Look at the man as a man.* The school board must see to it that its personnel policies pay at least as much attention to the applicant's personal qualities as a potential leader (not so easy, but make sure you have people on the staff who know how) as they do to test results and seniority considerations. Don't be afraid to insist that your administration recruit people from outside the system with a hope of importing, with them, some fresh ideas from time to time.

• *Make sure board policy calls for an effective and subjective in-service training program.* Regardless of how capable you think a man is, if you allow him to be assigned and forgotten, don't expect him to remain enthusiastic and capable of giving the intuitive, spontaneous kind of leadership that is supposed to make for a better local school operation. You'll need all of the resources that experts in psychology, sociology and management can muster. The program, to be effective, will have to include sensitivity training to the problems and reactions of the school's clientele, a hard interpretation of the sociological factors pertaining to the problems, techniques of dynamics in dealing with groups, public relations methods that work, and a continuing discussion of the changing social patterns in the system.

• *Give him some real authority.* If he can't make some on-the-spot decisions, the board ought to recognize that the whole idea of decentralizing is missed. Beyond that, he'll need some discretionary financial resources to implement experimental programs without the tedious process of gaining approval from downtown—a circumstance that now makes a good many principals wish they'd never asked in the first place. And, certainly, give him discretion to recruit and assign his faculty. Put him in charge of the total school program (don't, for example, place an evening program under somebody else's rule; the school in the urban neighborhood must be an institution with a coordinated day and night, year-round program, a real community center).

• *Diminish detail.* This is probably the most effective step you can take in helping your principal do his job. It's also the easiest. See to it that he has enough staff assistance to delegate the shop-keeping details that take up most of his day right now.

Let's suppose the school system has taken all four steps. What, then, does a school board, and its administrative agents, have a right to expect will happen?

Certainly, most of the troubles that plague urban school districts are the outgrowth of social problems that are frightening in their complexity. But, reduced to facts, they stem from dissatisfaction on the part of parents, students and teachers.

With no attempt to minimize the deep-rooted origins of the problems, isn't it reasonable to suggest that a principal with the right personal characteristics, careful training and sufficient time can do a great deal to diminish at least the outward manifestations of the dissatisfaction that exists?

It ought to be recognized by now that the principal is a part of the management team of the school system, but the fact that he represents the board of education in the neighborhood school should never preclude his exercising professional leadership. It should, in truth, enhance his role. Too often, right now, teachers look beyond the principal for decisions that should rightly be made at the neighborhood level. The idea of strengthening the principalship is to make it possible to reduce some of the tensions that are causing so much trouble in the local neighborhoods.

Myron Lieberman and Michael H. Moskow cited an example* of this in Canada, where "school boards have objected strenuously to having assistant superintendents, principals, and supervisors in the unit [bargaining] on just these very grounds. That is, these persons do not perform their duties effectively when the teachers they supervise negotiate conditions of employment for such administrative personnel."

More recently, Joe Mann, a member of the Burlington city board of education in North Carolina, and a member of the board of directors of the state school boards association, warned a negotiations conference that schools "must establish effective and reliable communications between teachers on one hand and the administration and school board on the other. . . . A school principal must be looked upon as a supervisor, and as a supervisor he must be considered a part of management. For it to be otherwise can result only in chaos." Through the principal must come the first-hand guidance for decisions to be made by the upper administration and the board of education.

Decentralization, according to Harold Howe, U. S. Commissioner of Education, "involves more than simply shifting bureaucrats around to different offices. It requires that the local administrator be given more leeway in tailoring his school to the character of the community, welcoming the contributions of parents and helping parents understand what kinds of contributions they can make. It calls not only for letting parents see how the school is run and explaining to them its policies and programs, but also converting the school into a community resource that offers adults instruction in a range of subjects, whether the activity be a benefit cake sale or a voter-registration drive. It means a school whose doors are open

*In their book: *"Collective Negotiations for Teachers"* (Rand McNally and Co., Chicago 1966).

nights, weekends, and summers. It means alliances between the school and community agencies of all kinds."

Achieving all of that requires a special kind of principal. Don't think for a moment, however, that just breaking up a large system into smaller units is going to solve all problems. It's hard to escape the conclusion that there is a strong feeling of alienation of the neighborhood school from the community that has grown up around it.

New York City is trying to change that feeling. Ronald Evans, principal of the famous Intermediate School 201 in Harlem, commenting upon the fact that the school was open during the city's teacher strike, told the New York *Times*: "Our first job was to stabilize the school, to get all the children to relax and to communicate to their parents that something new was happening here. This has now been done and we are ready to begin our work." The school and its 21-member board of parents, teachers and community representatives was a part of the experimental project for decentralization established by the New York board of education with assistance from the Ford Foundation.

One more word. Probably not everybody (not even all principals) will like, at least at first, the idea of recognizing the principal as the key to effective decentralization and of giving him the training and tools to carry it out. But if it's true that the local community is the very bulwark of a democratic society, then the local school administrator—the principal—must be the strongest that can be found.

VI

The Principal and Evaluation

chapter overview

Teachers have the right to teach unhampered by any demeaning, artificial, arbitrary, perfunctory, and superficial rating.

—Ava L. Parrott

The rapid expansion of the educational program in the United States in recent years has not been without criticism. The frustrations and fears of citizens throughout the country are constantly making headlines in newspapers and on radio and television. In unprecedented numbers American taxpayers are turning to the school for assistance in meeting the challenges of a troubled world. They are demanding a higher quality educational program for their boys and girls. This ultimatum for better ways of educating the nation's children has awakened a spirit of evaluation within the teaching profession. Articles in this chapter look at a traditional problem—the evaluation of teachers—and at a revolutionary approach for testing student achievement—national assessment.

It is vitally important that administrators understand the opinions held by teachers about teacher evaluations. Hazel Davis reports on responses by classroom teachers to a questionnaire study of evaluation in local school systems. The author suggests "that progress would seem to lie in the direction of the fullest participation of classroom teachers themselves in efforts to realize the benefits that seem possible in professional evaluation of teachers' services."

Historically, teachers have been reluctant to be evaluated. Stanley L. Clement raises several questions and attempts to answer some of them in an effort to justify the rating of teachers. His last question gets at the heart of the dilemma, "If we can't tell who the good teachers are, should teaching really be considered a profession?"

Evaluation of teachers is one way to improve the instructional program. John H. Hain and George J. Smith conducted a study to determine how principals rate teachers. They conclude that "as teachers become more militant and demanding, the area of evaluation will assume major proportions in education." Recommendations are offered to help the profession cope with the problem of evaluation.

What will be the principal's role in evaluation in the future? Dale Findley envisions a shifting of emphasis from the traditional role of the principal in evaluation to that of a leader in supervision to improve instruction.

In-service TV self-analysis appears to offer some solution to changing teacher behavior. Kenneth E. Shibata predicts the "emancipation of the teacher from the traditional routine."

National assessment has created considerable anxiety among school personnel. William A. Mehrens presents an up-to-date report on the national assessment program. He recommends active support of the assessment activities. Do you?

28 | What Teachers Say About Evaluation of Teachers

Hazel Davis

One of the early recorded statements of a classroom teacher about teacher evaluation was by Ava L. Parrott of New York City. In a paper read before the annual meeting of the NEA Department of Classroom Teachers in 1915, she demanded that teachers have the right to teach "unhampered by any demeaning, artificial, arbitrary, perfunctory, and superficial rating."

Ratings for teachers were already well established, however, and Miss Parrott's plea for their abolition was not heeded. The NEA Research Division found in one of its earliest studies, in 1922, that 55 percent of all urban systems were using teacher ratings. The practice declined to less than 40 percent of the systems, but in the past few years the downward trend was suddenly reversed. A 1962 study showed that teachers were being rated in 58 percent of all urban systems.

Although many individual teachers today might echo Miss Parrott's words of opprobrium, many others find positive values in current forms of teacher evaluation. One reason for some degree of acceptance may be at least a partial shift in practice and philosophy, along with the shift in labels from *rating* to *evaluation*.

In addition, the emphasis on quality in all aspects of education, the growing demand for greater autonomy in maintaining standards in the teaching profession, and the recurrent demand from the public for pay based on competence have contributed to a new interest in evaluation.

The chief element in evaluation in many school systems is still the assigning of a general rating or classifying judgment. The general rating sorts the teachers into several ranks or levels such as, "excellent," "very good," etc., or a series of symbols (e.g., A, B, C, D, E). Many aspects of the teacher's work may also be rated separately. The rating may be made and filed without consulting or informing the teacher concerned.

In other systems, however, evaluation is a cooperative process of analysis and discussion; the teacher is a responsible participant, and if a general rating is made, he knows about it.

The most commonly reported use made of written evaluations is in the improvement of instruction, but many questions have been raised as to whether evaluation is indeed contributing markedly to this objective.

From *NEA Journal*, Vol. 54 (February 1965), pp. 37-39. Reprinted by permission of the publisher and author.

Because of these various concerns, the NEA Research Division has conducted a questionnaire study of evaluation in local school systems. Of three questionnaires, one was addressed to classroom teachers; this article deals with some of their answers.

The teachers replying represented all but the very smallest public school systems. About 60 percent were beyond their third year in the system where then employed. About 80 percent had taught in the same system the year before.

Were the teachers given a written evaluation? One of the surprises was that so many teachers *did not know*. Of those who had taught the year before in the system where then employed, 44 percent knew that a written rating or evaluation of their work *had* been made, 35 percent knew that one *had not*, and 21 percent *did not know*.

Other data in the survey showed that a written evaluation actually had been made of most of the 21 percent who were unable to answer the question. Thus 1 in 5 of these teachers were in systems where written evaluations are so little discussed that their very existence is in doubt.

What were teachers told about their evaluations? Teachers who knew they had been evaluated in writing were asked whether they had been given a copy of the evaluation. Thirty-nine percent said they had, 28 percent had been shown a copy, and 28 percent had not seen it. Five percent did not answer.

Replying to a question on the type of evaluation used, not quite half the teachers said that it was a general rating of the classifying type, with a sequence such as "excellent, very good, good, fair, poor." Nearly a third received no general rating, but were rated on several different factors or were evaluated through the use of written statements. About 15 percent said they were classified merely as satisfactory or unsatisfactory. A remainder of 7 percent did not know what type of evaluation was used.

The teachers who had been evaluated according to a classifying sequence were asked whether or not they had been given the *highest* rating on the scale. A fifth were uncertain as to their ratings and a tenth left the question blank. Of the two-thirds making definite replies, 4 in 5 had indeed been given the highest rating.

What contacts with administrators precede an evaluation? Several questions dealt with these practices in the year then in process, which was a little more than half over when the inquiry was mailed in February 1963.

One item dealt with observations of classroom teaching; 27 percent of the teachers reported that their classroom work had not been observed by an administrator or supervisor for as long as five minutes even once during the preceding months up to February 1. Of teachers in their first three years of experience in the system, 19 percent had not been observed during the first semester. Those observed, however, included 40 percent who had received three or more supervisory visits. The median length of the most recent observation was twenty-two minutes. When teachers were asked whether the most recent observation had been helpful to them, nearly half said Yes.

When asked whether they had received the professional help and guidance they needed since the beginning of the current school year, nearly three-fourths of the teachers said Yes, but more than a fifth said No. More than a third of the teachers had not had a conference of as long as ten minutes with an administrator or supervisory officer regarding the teacher's work.

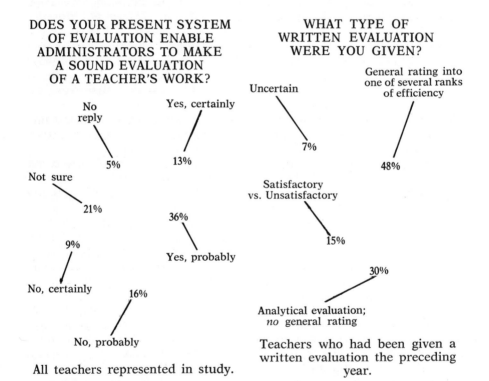

DOES YOUR PRESENT SYSTEM
OF EVALUATION ENABLE
ADMINISTRATORS TO MAKE
A SOUND EVALUATION
OF A TEACHER'S WORK?

No reply

Yes, certainly

5%   13%

Not sure

21%

36%

9%

Yes, probably

No, certainly   16%

No, probably

All teachers represented in study.

WHAT TYPE OF
WRITTEN EVALUATION
WERE YOU GIVEN?

General rating into
one of several ranks
of efficiency

Uncertain

7%

48%

Satisfactory
vs. Unsatisfactory

15%

30%

Analytical evaluation;
no general rating

Teachers who had been given a written evaluation the preceding year.

How valid are the ratings? Each teacher was asked, "Does your present system of evaluation enable administrators to make a sound evaluation of a teacher's work?" The check list for answering ranged from "Yes, certainly," to "No, certainly."

Nearly half of the teachers recorded either strong or modified confidence ("yes, certainly" or "yes, probably") in the plan of evaluation. The majority expressed doubt, left the question blank, or gave a negative opinion. All teachers in the study are represented in these replies. Many of them were in systems where no formal plan of evaluation exists. In every system, however, judgments are made on teacher re-employment, transfer, and recognition; there is always at least informal evaluation, and teachers can form an opinion about its apparent outcomes. Only 5 percent left the question blank.

Teachers who knew that written evaluations had been made indicated confidence in the evaluation system by higher percents than did other teachers, and made a smaller percent of "not sure" replies. However, there was practically no difference from other teachers in the percent indicating lack of confidence.

What were the results of the evaluations? Most of the questions were accompanied by check-list answers. One, however, had no check-list and allowed ample space to write a response. This question was, "What desirable outcomes from the program of teacher evaluation have you observed in your school system? Add other comments if you wish."

Fifty-one percent of the teachers in the study left the question blank, 30 percent reported desirable outcomes, 13 percent wrote None or a few words of similar meaning, and 7 percent reported undesirable outcomes (1 percent made both positive and negative replies).

Teachers who knew they had been evaluated in writing were also counted separately; 38 percent left the item blank, 39 percent reported desirable outcomes, 16 percent wrote None, and 7 percent reported undesirable outcomes.

Statements made by the greatest number of teachers reporting desirable outcomes were that evaluation stimulates the staff to do better work and that it develops teacher-administrator rapport.

Did size of school system make a difference in the teachers' replies? Teachers in large systems were more likely to have been given written evaluations than were teachers in small ones, but on several other questions, their replies were similar to those from teachers in smaller systems. For example, the percents reporting various numbers of observations and individual conferences were almost the same in large, medium, and small systems.

Did the school level taught or the sex of the teacher make a difference in the replies? Larger percents of elementary school than of high school teachers had been given written evaluations, had been observed while teaching, had had individual conferences with supervisory officials, and expressed confidence in the system of evaluation.

The replies of men and women in secondary schools were so similar that they were not reported separately. The number of men in the elementary school sample was too small to justify separate tabulation.

What are the implications of these replies from teachers? Interpretation depends on what part of each set of replies is considered. Possibly there is cause for satisfaction in that nearly half of the teachers expressed some degree of confidence in the soundness of the evaluations, and that nearly a third could report specific desirable outcomes. On the other hand, it seems a cause of concern, from the point of view of morale and of supervisory-administrative success, that more than half the teachers failed to express even limited confidence in the system and 70 percent failed to report desirable outcomes.

The distributions of replies on number and length of observations and on individual conferences show an extremely wide range of practice. Many teachers appear to be receiving with appreciation the professional counseling, cooperation, and stimulation which supervisory services are designed to provide. But a substantial minority of teachers, including many of those in a probationary

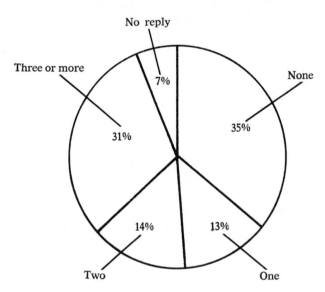

HOW MANY INDIVIDUAL
CONFERENCES OF TEN MINUTES
OR MORE DID YOU HAVE ABOUT
YOUR TEACHING WITH YOUR
PRINCIPAL OR OTHER OFFICIAL
OF YOUR SCHOOL SYSTEM IN THE
FIRST HALF OF THE SCHOOL YEAR?

No reply

Three or more

7%

None

31%

35%

14%

13%

Two

One

All teachers represented in study.

NEA Research Division

status, are being left to fend for themselves, and are being rated or evaluated on bases other than a firsthand observation of their teaching.

Most disturbing of the whole series of replies, it seems to this writer, were those showing that 21 percent of the teachers did not know whether or not written evaluations of their work had been made, and those showing that of the teachers who knew they had been evaluated in writing, 28 percent did not see the results. These two groups represent a third of the teachers replying.

Let it be granted that some of them might have made a guess that written evaluations were being made and that some not shown their ratings could have guessed what their ratings were; nevertheless, something in the situation and in the teachers' reaction to it produced these replies. The implication is that information had not been communicated to many teachers about a process that is of crucial individual importance to each teacher and of potential significance to continued improvement in the quality of instruction.

The Research Division's report shows that evaluation was under study in many school systems. In some places, local teachers associations are taking the initiative in proposing a cooperative approach to such a review. In the judgment of this writer, progress would seem to lie in the direction of the fullest participation of classroom teachers themselves in efforts to realize the benefits that seem possible in professional evaluation of teachers' services.

29 | # Why Is It?
Teachers Shun Evaluation

Stanley L. Clement

Why is it that teachers tend to be negative toward being rated, maintaining that the raters (administrators) would be too subjective in their evaluation? Isn't this a subjective evaluation in itself? Doesn't this imply that they can not only rate their administrators as excellent, good, fair, or poor, but they can also tell you specifically why? Or haven't you listened to discussions along this vein at the lunch table or in the teachers' room? Could it be that teachers' evaluation of ability rating is too subjective in itself?

Why is it that teachers will put faith in an administrator's judgment when hired and when put on tenure, yet feel that this same administrator is unable to evaluate them on the job? In the former case, the evidence is pretty much indirect, while on the job the administrator, being in close contact over an extended period of time, is in a far better position to evaluate.

In the former case also a new position is involved, and often a whole new career, but in the latter situation only an increase in pay. Note too that, while during the period of employment the administrator is unable to evaluate fairly, all of a sudden his ability in this direction is vastly improved as he is asked for a recommendation when the teacher seeks a new position.

Why is it that teachers work so hard for higher salaries, but do not use evaluation to indicate how this will improve education? How long will the public continue to allow the annual increases for more and more money when at the same time they are constantly hearing that teachers shouldn't do this and teachers shouldn't do that. The resulting implication is that teachers are getting more and more for doing less and less.

The desire to get one's money's worth tends to be strong in our American society. Why don't teachers capitalize on this desire not only by showing why improvement in working conditions should bring about better teaching but also by highlighting actual evaluated evidence that better education is really taking place because of it? If the public really feels it is getting more value from each additional dollar spent, the amount available would be more likely to be increased.

Why is it that teachers can mark students on a percentage basis with 101 categories, but they themselves cannot be rated on a simple four or five point scale? Many schools still use a percentage system,

From *The Clearing House*, Vol. 42 (April 1968), pp. 465-467. Reprinted by permission of the publisher.

and, where the school itself does not, many teachers still employ it. Often the distinction for awards or other classification has depended on a difference of only a fraction of a single percent for individual students.

Why is it that teachers feel that students should be penalized for being late or missing class work, but, when they themselves fail to meet obligations, it should be overlooked and not affect their evaluation? Have you ever kept track of teachers' reports and had to chase those who seldom meet the due date . . . yet be met with a disgruntled and belligerent attitude by these same teachers who would blast students if their work were late and subtract points from their grades because of it?

Why is it that teachers tend to complain about student absence and tardiness and the resulting extra makeup work when they in turn are absent from faculty meetings and professional conferences which really are a part of their jobs? Are they always on time and paying attention? Or haven't you noticed those who converse freely during the meeting and those (including the same ones) who think nothing of leaving right in the middle of the feature address or discussion? At least attendance and being on time could be easily evaluated.

Why is it that teachers encourage students to do extra reading and investigation outside class and recognize this in some way in their grade, when they themselves not only do comparatively little to improve their teaching but object violently if this fact counts to any extent in their evaluation? It would seem that each teacher would want to do a better job each year and would use study, professional conferences, workshops, travel, and other in-service means of achieving this end. Wouldn't they wish to have this effort recognized, rather than being treated in the same way as those who stay in the same rut year after year?

Why is it that teachers complain about lack of teaching materials, yet don't use much of what is available, or make little attempt to innovate or substitute? Use of materials would appear to be a fairly easy item to evaluate, especially when the teacher himself could be the one furnishing the evidence.

Why is it that teachers often rely almost entirely on one method of teaching, such as Q and A, yet feel that this should not be considered in evaluation? We still have some teachers who do little or no preparation since the last class period, and even have to ask the pupils where the class stopped the aimless oral reading of the day before. Again, teachers themselves could be the ones who should furnish evidence of the search for and the use of the best approach for the means of achieving each individual goal.

Why is it that teachers do not believe that administrators know who the good teachers are? Although jealousy often colors the situation, down inside everyone pretty much knows those whose teaching effectiveness is the best. Besides actual observation of teaching, this knowledge is acquired in many ways, including staff, student, or parent remarks, publicity related to special class achievements, and council or committee work.

Why is it that teachers want improved status and higher salaries but won't police their own ranks to weed out those people who don't deserve either and who are severely tarnishing the reputation of the profession as a whole by their unprofessional behavior? Let the lazy and incompetent be treated as they should be, and cries of discrimination and unfairness arise . . .   rather than thankfulness that some of those who are holding back improvement in the status of teachers have been eliminated. How can we justify more money if we can't indicate those who really deserve it?

Does the present theory about the importance of individual differences apply only to students? Are teachers to be considered all alike? Do we have inferior teachers? Should they be weeded out? Do we have outstanding teachers? Should they be recognized? Shall we discriminate against the most able by equating all? Should teachers be thought of as interchangeable units in an educational assembly line where the ablest and the weakest have the same students, teach the same subjects, use the same materials, receive the same pay, and progress at the same rate of salary schedule? Should an excellent teacher receive a lower salary than an inferior one because he hasn't taught as many years? Should salary increases depend largely on the passage of time?

Rating goes on anyway. Shall it be haphazard and discriminatory? Or should it be the joint, cooperatively planned and purposeful effort of all concerned? If we can't tell who the good teachers are, should teaching really be considered a profession?

How Principals Rate Teachers | 30

John H. Hain
George J. Smith

The principal's role in the evaluation of teachers is a vehicle which enables him to exercise leadership as the instructional director of his school. The judgments he makes concerning the effectiveness of each teacher contribute toward that teacher's professional growth. But if his judgments are unsound, they can also reduce a teacher's effectiveness as a guide to learning. Since principals mold the careers of a significant number of teachers, hopefully they exercise wise judgments and view their role as one of helping their teachers do a better job with students.

In late fall of 1966 the authors conducted a study of this important aspect of administration. A random sample of 336 elementary schools in New York State was selected. The schools were located in the largest cities of the state, small cities, central schools in rural areas and suburban schools; some were still blissfully unaware of current events in the world of education. Two hundred and sixty-seven elementary principals responded to questions about their supervisory practices. This represents an 80 percent return and justifies the use of these data to support some generalizations concerning current practices in the elementary schools of New York State.

STATISTICAL DATA

The size of the schools participating in this study is much larger than was expected—only three percent had an enrollment between 200 and 400 pupils. Twenty-eight percent were between 400-600 pupils, 36 percent had 600-800 students and 33 percent had enrollments over 800 students. There appears to be a trend toward ever bigger elementary schools, and it would seem that elementary schools are larger than the generally recommended size. The sheer size of the administrator's supervisory role appears to be unwieldy.

Unfortunately, the burdens of administration are not being shared as evidenced by the fact that 76 percent of the responding principals do not have administrative help. More than half of the principals reported that they alone are responsible for the evaluation of 30-50 teachers and 13 percent for more than 50 teachers.

From *American School Board Journal*, Vol. 155, No. 8 (February 1968), pp. 17-18. Reprinted by permission of the publisher. Copyright 1968 by National School Boards Association.

These responsibilities for evaluation and supervision of the increasing numbers of teachers can only lead to superficial help from the principal.

This problem is further highlighted when one examines the ratio of teachers to supervisor. Thirty percent have a ratio of 1-20 or less; 30 percent 1-30; 19 percent 1-40; 15 percent 1-50; and 6 percent 1 to more than 50 teachers. It is inconceivable that a principal can effectively supervise and evaluate, with any regularity, numbers such as the polled principals reported they had to help.

RATING FORMS

Two-thirds of the school districts provide principals with written procedures and standards to assist with the task of teacher evaluation. The tools of evaluation consist basically of "rating forms" where the evaluator checks or writes comments about various aspects of teaching. An analysis reveals that the majority of the rating forms consisted of lists of single words or phrases which sought to characterize distinguishing traits of teachers, and they contained no provision for the person being evaluated to see and sign the form. These unsigned forms tended to contribute toward that classic error of measurement known as the "halo effect" whereby the instrument becomes a vehicle for pseudo objectivity behind which the rater can place his initial biases concerning the teacher. And the instrument lends itself to the possibility of being used with little regard for the actual situation being observed and evaluated.

The evaluation forms which teachers were allowed to see and sign consisted mainly of descriptive or open-ended statements, and they tended to be constructed to serve as a focusing vehicle in a conference between the person doing the evaluation and the person evaluated. These signed forms are clearer and insure a greater opportunity to use the instrument to facilitate communication between teacher and administrator.

Principals feel their teachers are clearly aware of the school district's procedures and standards of supervision and evaluation. Seventy percent indicated that the teachers are aware of the standards. Only 13 percent said teachers did not know the basis of how their work is evaluated, while 15 percent indicated they did not know if the teachers were aware of the district policies. There is some possibility the principal is assuming an awareness for a generous number of his teachers concerning the way their work will be evaluated. After several years of contact with teachers taking graduate courses, the authors have found few who were aware of how their work was evaluated. This question could be clarified through additional investigation and research.

Less than half (41 percent) of the principals give prior notice of an impending supervisory visit. Fifty percent either do not give prior notice or do so on occasion. Many principals feel that notice will produce a "canned" lesson and does not reflect the day to day activities of the normal classroom. But "snoopervision" generally has proved futile, and greater professional competence on the part of the supervisor is needed. Since teachers will soon be demanding and winning the right to greater participation in educational enterprises, they may well be entitled to know when they will be visited and evaluated.

Principals tend to visit probationary teachers more often than tenure teachers, although 17 percent observe all teachers in the same manner. Fifty-six percent of the probationary teachers are observed at least once a month compared to 29 percent of the teachers with tenure.

The time spent in teacher observation varies from under ten minutes to all morning or all afternoon with 60 percent of the principals observing teachers from twenty to forty minutes. Twelve percent spend from ten to twenty minutes and 12 percent from forty-five to ninety minutes.

Formal observation is normally followed up with a conference between the principal and the teacher. Ninety-nine percent of our sample held a conference. Sixty-two percent of the principals provide a written report; however, 58 percent show or give a copy of the report to the teacher.

INFORMAL SUPERVISION

In addition to formal observation, principals consider other factors in evaluating teachers, factors almost as important as formal observation to the principal. Ninety-seven percent of the principals stated that they observe teachers during routine rounds of the building. Forty-three percent cited bus duty; 60 percent, playground duty; 50 percent, cafeteria duty; and 69 percent, while the teacher is moving the class from one teaching situation to another within the building. Surprisingly, two percent use the school intercom for supervision. Only a few teachers invite principals to visit their classroom. The principals would like teachers to invite them to see their class in action, but our sample disclosed that only 2 percent of the principals stated that their staff members issued such invitations.

Perhaps one reason for this unhappy situation is that teachers by and large view evaluation as an administrative prerogative and not as a joint effort. Cooperating principals were asked if they involved senior or mature teachers in decisions regarding the reappointment of teachers. Only 12 percent of the principals indicated that they utilize this type of consultation. Most of the principals appear to be satisfied with their teacher reappointment procedures. Eight percent thought their teachers were not in accord with plans for evaluating teacher effectiveness.

CONCLUSIONS AND RECOMMENDATIONS

As teachers become more militant and demanding, the area of evaluation will assume major proportions in education. To help the profession prepare for that day, the following intelligence is offered:

1. The ratio of supervisors to teachers should be reduced to enable the principal to engage in effective supervision. Today the average principal supervises between 30 and 50 teachers.
2. Observation should *always* be followed by a conference directed toward improvement of the teacher's professional competence.
3. There should be a written evaluation report, and the teacher should *always* receive and have an opportunity to react to this report.
4. Standards and procedures for supervision should be developed *jointly* by administrators and teachers. In far too many cases these procedures are the sole product of the administrators.
5. Principals should consult with senior teachers regarding reappointment. The old days of the principal with *his* teachers teaching in *his* school are being replaced by the principal and the teachers working together in *their* school.
6. Jointly agreed upon standards and procedures for evaluation should be published and available to teachers and, where necessary, explained to them. An explanation of evaluation procedures should be added to the orientation program for new staff and should be given periodically for the old staff. Most importantly, procedures should be reviewed and revised periodically—with teacher participation.

The Secondary Principal | 31
Evaluation and Supervision

Dale Findley

Research findings, according to Brain, indicate that teacher effectiveness cannot be adequately evaluated.[1] The literature also leads one to believe that principals have neither the time nor the talent to supervise effectively. Yet there are those who say they are able to evaluate teachers effectively. For the most part, what these individuals are evaluating can be termed "organizational compliance." That is, teachers are not evaluated on the basis of teacher effectiveness, but on how well they conform to administrative rules and regulations.

It is time to take a good look at evaluation and supervision to determine if principals should or should not play a role in these processes. Part of the problem stems from the fact that there has been no *real* distinction made between evaluation and supervision in practice; in theory, yes, but not in practice. Consequently, teachers have come to dislike supervision because it too often resembles evaluation. Evaluation implies that the principal and teacher are on opposite sides. Supervision on the other hand must be a cooperative effort to be effective. It would seem then that a principal could not effectively both evaluate and supervise.

Which then, if either, should the principal do?

One cannot help but wonder what effect teacher negotiation will have upon the role played by the principal in evaluation and supervision. Primarily, to this point in time, negotiations have dealt with salary and welfare benefits for teachers. It seems quite possible that the areas of evaluation and supervision are topics which teacher groups will be viewing as possible items of negotiation.

The increased training of present day teachers is another factor which will necessitate a change in the principal's role in supervision and evaluation. Today, many teachers have received as much formal education as principals. More male teachers are on the educational scene now than ever before. They may not tolerate conditions that women have been willing to accept.

At the present pace, the principal will shortly not even be the "keeper of the keys" because everyone will have his own. A plausible plan must be designed and strides must be made toward progress in the areas of supervision and evaluation.

From *Contemporary Education*, Vol. 39 (May 1968), pp. 276-277. Reprinted by permission of the publisher and author.
1. George Brain, "Evaluating Teacher Effectiveness," *NEA Journal* (February, 1965), pp. 35-36.

Many principals fear that they will soon be relegated to a subservient role to teachers as they view the present "militant" attitude of many teachers. However, perhaps for the first time, principals can truly become educational leaders. Schools can become truly democratic institutions. For the first time teachers will have true alternatives. The principal will be faced with decisions as to which of the alternatives posed by teachers he should choose. This will be a reverse role for many principals. Too often principals are their own source of alternatives and have not taken advantage of the talented staff they possess.

Yes, teachers probably will exhibit tendencies for "trained incapacities" in that they may view things with a limited perspective.[2] This provides all the more challenge for a principal. Today's teachers are full of enthusiasm and the desire to express themselves. Teachers want a larger hand in the task of education.

If teachers were allowed more of a chance to express themselves in their present position we might not find as many of them wanting other types of jobs. Increased salary benefits is often given as the reason for leaving the teaching field. This is a "handy" reason which most people will accept without much further explanation. There are deeper reasons involved with the fact that humans possess a drive which causes them to desire to become more independent and more responsible.[3]

The principal of the future then must become well trained in the area of human behavior—not human manipulation. Some administrators are imbued with the philosophy that those doing the hiring should also do the firing. As such they feel in order to fire they must be in charge of evaluation. The threat of being fired is not nearly as effective in making a better teacher as providing assistance through supervision. Evaluation implies the threat of being fired.

School systems need to employ better methods to screen teacher candidates before they are hired. Teacher training institutions should accept more responsibility in the identification and screening out of those persons who will not be good teachers. If these institutions are not able to identify unacceptable teachers, then can we expect to do a much better job in the field?

It just may be that teachers are more qualified to judge the effectiveness of a colleague than the principal. Teachers do need time to perform evaluation. Department heads with released time could be very effective in evaluation. Teachers and department heads would need some training in techniques of evaluation. Department

2. Robert K. Merton, "Limited Perspective of Staff Specialists," *Human Relations in Administration* by Robert Dubin (Englewood Cliffs, New Jersey: Prentice Hall, Inc., 1961), pp. 193-194.
3. Chris Argyris, *Personality and Organization* (New York: Harper and Row, Publishers, 1957), p. 50.

headships should not be permanent positions for any teacher. The position should rotate from time to time to prevent the person in the position from gaining the image of an administrator. The department head should retain some teaching duties also. These conditions are essential if department heads are to be effective in both evaluation and supervision. Department heads in conjunction with teams of teachers can provide recommendations to principals concerning their evaluations.

Research has shown that teachers often are evaluated on the basis of one or two five-minute classroom visits. The results of these evaluations are often not even shown to teachers.[4] Too often classroom visits for evaluation purposes have been carried out under the guise of supervision.

It is imperative that teachers know what is expected of them. Supervision carried out in a cooperative team atmosphere where expectations are known can produce effective teaching. Supervision does not imply that the teacher is always the factor that needs to be changed. Perhaps the environment needs to be changed also. The principal appears to be the logical team leader in supervision since he is the one person who has some control over the finances, equipment, and materials for his building.

The principal should be a member of the supervisory team along with the department heads and teachers. The team needs to work cooperatively toward improvement in a positive fashion. Teachers then are not forced to work in a negative atmosphere under the threat of being fired if improvement does not take place.

More effective teaching is being demanded. The process of evaluation has not provided the solutions sought. More time and effort should be expended on supervision and less on evaluation to develop better teachers. If principals are to supervise effectively then they must be given adequate time. This may mean the addition of good clerks, secretaries, automated devices, and assistant principals.

Teachers are increasingly striving to become professionals in the true sense of the word. They have reached the point where they desire and are capable of exercising control over themselves. Evaluation then more and more should become their prerogative.

No longer burdened with the evaluation process the principal can establish better rapport with his staff and, with adequate time provided, will be able to be an effective team leader in supervision.

4. Hazel Davis. "What Teachers Say About Evaluation of Teachers," *NEA Journal* (February, 1965), pp. 37-39.

32 | **Emancipating the Teacher**

| *Kenneth E. Shibata*

How can we free the teacher from certain unprofitable traditional approaches to teaching? In Educational Service Unit No. 6 (Milford, Nebr.) we tried instant-replay television. Some call it "mirror feedback"; we call it simply "seeing yourself in action."

In Educational Service Unit No. 6 (one of 19 intermediate districts created by the 1965 Nebraska Legislature to provide supplemental services to local school corporations), 96 teachers had television exposure during the second semester of the 1967-68 school year.

They didn't all like what they saw. Not at first anyway. But through a careful self-appraisal program the picture soon brightened.

The self-see video project allows teachers to see themselves and to analyze their performances. The purpose: to change teacher behavior for better results with students.

After viewing a demonstration video tape illustrating cognitive and affective objectives, teachers decide on their method and objectives. Next step: a live taping of their own in-class performance. Then comes the playback and data processing for follow-up evaluation.

Improvement comes once teachers become aware of course objectives and how to meet them. They can then do a better job of establishing their own objectives and meeting them. The instant replay tape dramatizes blank spots in the teacher's performance. As the gaps are filled, the behaviors that have limited the freedom of the teacher disappear and students begin to enlarge their responses and their interests.

The video plan's card-illustrated teaching methods help show why. They range from silence (and confusion) through techniques of lecture, questions and answers, demonstrations, direction, mastery, problem solving, clarification, and student inquiry.

Also included on the analysis card are verbal and non-verbal teacher expressions. Reflecting interaction with students, the appraisal scale begins with disapproval and continues through lack of response, lack of attention, routine, receptiveness, help, and support.

The 96 teachers in the K-12 pilot project were selected at random from a group of 175 volunteers from 26 schools. Four instructional areas were involved: language arts, social studies, math-science, and all other subjects. Elementary teachers were divided by grade level.

From *Phi Delta Kappan*, Vol. 50 (November 1968), p. 171. Reprinted by permission of the publisher and author.

As soon as the teacher's initial nervousness wore off, positive results were apparent. Awareness, understanding, and teaching effectiveness improved. Because of these positive results, we have determined to give all 900 teachers in our area an opportunity for in-service TV self-analysis on a voluntary basis this year.

Area administrators were enthusiastic and extremely cooperative from the start.

Emancipation of the teacher from the traditional routine has begun.

33 | National Assessment
An Up-To-Date Report

William A. Mehrens

By the time this article is published, 12 sampling units within the state of Michigan will have been selected for inclusion in the first year's national assessment. Approximately 30-35 Michigan school administrators will have already been asked or will soon be asked to cooperate in the assessment of the 17-year-old group. The impending assessment program is something, then, that at least some Michigan school school administrators can hardly ignore. While there has been considerable information published concerning the national assessment program, it cannot be assumed that all school administrators are intimately acquainted with it. In fact, as with all new projects, the dynamic and innovative nature of national assessment probably assures that few, if any school administrators are completely up to date. The purpose of this article is really twofold: (1) To present a brief review of the national assessment program—its goals, and its methodology, and (2) To discuss what types of cooperation the national assessment program will request from the schools in the sample, and what the implications of the program will be for those individual schools as well as for the nation.

NATIONAL ASSESSMENT: AN OVERVIEW

When the USOE was first established in 1867, one of the duties given the Commissioner was to determine the progress of education. In 1964, some 97 years after the USOE was established, it occurred to some educators that a determination of the progress of education had never been undertaken at the national level. To be sure, there is no dearth of information on what might be termed input parameters. The amount of money spent on education and how this amount continually increases is well documented. The number of school buildings and their average age are data which can be easily obtained. The average educational level of our teachers, and what percent of our schools have hot lunch programs and swimming pools are other examples of available input data. But educators should be primarily concerned with what students are learning rather than with what facilities are available. There simply are not adequate data available on what or how much students are learning. The Exploratory Committee on Assessing the Progress of Education (ECAPE) was formulated by the Carnegie Corporation in 1964 to develop an assessment

From *Michigan Journal of Secondary Education*, Vol. 10 (Summer 1969), pp. 10-18. Reprinted by permission of the publisher.

plan to obtain such outcome data. In July 1968, the plan ECAPE developed was turned over to the Committee on Assessing the Progress of Education (CAPE) for implementation.

The task CAPE has assumed, then, is to gather outcome data for the first time at the national level. The first assessment will provide dependable baseline information on where we stand in relation to certain educational objectives. Comparisons with measurements in the future will permit an estimate of the progress made in meeting these objectives. Naturally, data cannot be gathered on all the youth in our nation's schools. Even when one samples individuals, only a very small fraction of the learning that takes place in the schools can be assessed. Sampling of both students and subjects must be employed to make the task feasible.

SAMPLING OF SUBJECT MATTER

The sample of learnings that will be assessed has been categorized into ten areas: literature, science, social studies, writing, citizenship, music, mathematics, reading, art, and career and occupational development. (Three of these, citizenship, science, and writing, will be assessed during the first year.) No one suggests that only these ten areas of learning are important in our educational establishments. Foreign language and other areas could have been assessed. However, it was felt that these ten areas do represent subjects that the majority of our schools, regardless of size, region, or SES, are attempting to teach. Other areas will be added as the assessment program continues.

Objectives were developed by various contractors within each of the ten areas. These objectives had to meet three criteria:

1. The objectives had to be ones that schools were *currently* seeking to obtain,
2. The objectives had to be ones that scholars in the field considered worthwhile, and
3. Thoughtful lay citizens had to consider the objectives desirable for our nation's youth.

After the contractors had prepared objectives that met the first two criteria, CAPE asked eleven lay panels to review all the objectives, to suggest which objectives they felt were unnecessary, and to suggest those they felt were needed. Thus, all the objectives had eleven different independent reviews by lay people.

Once the objectives were accepted, exercises were developed. The same care went into this task as went into the development of the objectives. After the contractors had drafted the exercises, they underwent review by the CAPE staff and specialists in the subject matter areas. Exercises were rewritten or discarded as a result of these reviews. Special lay conferences were held to review exercises for potential offensiveness. Tryouts were conducted and exercises were revised in light of the tryout data. The final exercises to be used in the assessment were selected from the set which had survived all the previous reviews. Exercises were selected so as to result in a balance of easy, medium, and difficult tasks, as well as to provide a number of exercises for each objective.

SAMPLING OF INDIVIDUALS

Approximately 32,000 individuals will be assessed at each of the 9, 13, and 17-year-old age levels. The young adults (ages 26-35) sample will include about 24,000 individuals. For ages 9 and 13, only in-school sampling will be employed. Since only approximately 75% of 17 year olds are in school and about 75% of that sample will be obtained through the schools and the 25% of the 17 year olds who are out-of-school will be sampled using the same household frame sampling technique as will be used for the young adult sample.

The 32,000 students at each age in the in-school sample will come from approximately 600 different school buildings. Thus, on the average, there will be approximately 54 students selected from any one building. This number will obviously vary considerably from building to building depending on the number of appropriately aged students and the SES of the school.[1]

SAMPLING OF INDIVIDUALS BY EXERCISES

The assessment plan has been forced by its very size to sample both subject matter and individuals. In addition, the assessment will sample in a fashion such that no individual assessed in school will take more than 1/12 of the total set of exercises administered during that year. The students in a given school building would never take the whole set of exercises.

This sampling procedure was considered desirable for several reasons. The time limits for each of the three subject matter areas (citizenship, writing, and science) in the first year's assessment, are now set at approximately 180 minutes. (This varies slightly from age to age.) This means it takes about 540 (180 x 3) total minutes to administer the total set of exercises. Of course, it would have been possible to set up the sampling scheme so that one individual would take all the exercises, or at least all the exercises within one subject matter area. That way it would have been possible to obtain a score for a pupil. However, in the national assessment program pupil scores (or school scores) are of no interest. By dividing the exercises

---

1. These are only approximate figures since the actual buildings have not yet been selected at the time of this writing.

into 12 to 14 different packages, each of which takes about 45 minutes to administer, the assessment will be less disruptive to the school program, students will not become fatigued, and the data *will not be amenable to pupil or school comparisons.* This should relieve the anxieties of those critics who have felt the data would somehow be used for individual school or pupil comparisons.

REPORTING

If pupil scores are not to be obtained, what results will be obtained, and how will they be reported? The reporting will be by separate individual exercises. Approximately one-third of the exercises will be reported the first year. The remaining exercises will be used in future assessments so that change over time can be observed. Comparisons will be made, where relevant, across large reporting categories such as the four ages, four geographical regions, four types of communities, race, SES, and sex. For example, the following type of statement might be made:

> 90% of all 17-year-olds know the name of the Governor of their state but only 20% know the name of the Mayor of their city.

EFFECTS ON SCHOOLS

The above overview of national assessment is admittedly sketchy. More than four years of planning have gone into the program. All the decisions reached, and the justifications for those decisions, cannot be presented in this article. For more detail on the assessment program the reader should see *How Much Are Students Learning?* published by CAPE,[2] November, 1968. We will now turn to what may be of more concern to the readers. How much inconvenience will this program cause the schools which fall in the sample? What benefits and/or liabilities will result? Should schools cooperate?

In terms of time or inconvenience, the assessment plan will not noticeably affect the schools. A brief principals questionnaire will need to be completed, a list of students of appropriate age will need to be formulated, and either an attendance clerk or counselor will need to see to it that the students to be assessed (somewhere between 15 and 80) are sent to the appropriate room. The individual students will need to contribute approximately 45 minutes of their time. The examiner and all necessary materials will be supplied by CAPE.

What will the individual schools profit or suffer from cooperation? Nothing directly. No data will be reported on individual

2. 201A Huron Towers, 2222 Fuller Road, Ann Arbor, Michigan 48105.

school buildings or districts. Obviously no comparisons will be available for the superintendent, principal, teacher, school board member, or parent that can support changes in local education, for good or ill, on the basis of their *particular* school's cooperation or lack of cooperation.

If cooperation in the assessment admittedly causes at least a slight inconvenience and cooperation produces no direct benefits, why then, one might ask, should a school cooperate? The answer lies in the assumption that professional educators should be willing to assume a slight local inconvenience for the benefit of education in general. Accepting this assumption, it is only necessary to show that national assessment will benefit education.

With more than $40 billion in tax dollars being spent each year to support our educational system it is obvious that we are engaged in a giant enterprise. No one denies that our product is more important than that of any other enterprise. We continually make decisions which are sure to affect our product. Yet, we do not know nearly enough about the characteristics of our present product, or how changes in educational practice might affect it.

With the base-line data obtained from the first phase of the national assessment program educators will be able to make some decisions concerning allocation of resources. For example, *if* it is found that, say inner city youth or rural youth perform more poorly than youth from other community types, this might suggest that a greater proportion of our resources be funneled in that direction. The assessment of progress that is to take place every three years should give us some information as to the effectiveness of any reallocation. As another example, if it were found that students in general could not write as well as would be hoped, or did not have proper social attitudes, these findings might well trigger curriculum innovations to overcome such deficiencies.

Comparisons of the base-line data gathered during this first cycle with results obtained three years later can of course also be helpful (*not conclusive*) in evaluating various directions or changes in education *even though* the base data were not the precipitating factors in the educational change. For example, a new curriculum innovation in science could develop in the year following the assessment of science. Assuming that a common set of objectives existed from the first assessment to another made three years later, data would be available to help judge the efficacy of the new curriculum. The effectiveness of an increasing use of teaching machines, programmed instruction, or computer assisted instruction could all be judged, in part, by a comparison of data from one time to another.

It is well known that the dangers of national assessment have been debated. Bell (1965), Crosby (1966), and Hand (1965), to name a few, have all published articles in which the central theme is that national assessment will be followed by educational ruin. The greatest deluge of criticism came *prior* to the general availability of literature on the methodology of the national assessment program. While many former critics of national assessment have become advocates of the project, and others have moved to a neutral position, it is still apparent that there are vestibules harboring those who feel certain that the effects of national assessment will be more negative than positive. The arguments advanced most often revolve about the following three positions:

1. A national assessment program will stultify curriculum exploration and result in a national curriculum. (Some even suggest a centrally *controlled* curriculum would result.)
2. Teachers will teach for the test.
3. The assessment results will be used inappropriately as additional evidence to criticize the schools rather than as tools to improve them.

Regarding the first point, the intent of the assessment never has been to control curriculum or to curtail curricular exploration. It has been stressed repeatedly that only a sample of the total set of school objectives are being assessed, and that these objectives are ones the schools are *currently seeking to attain*. Further, the objectives will be reassessed continually in light of educational curriculum change so that as the schools' objectives change, so would the objectives assessed.

The accusation that teachers would teach for the test is particularly ill-founded. First of all, the only exercises teachers would know about would be those reported *after* the first assessment. Since these exercises would not be used in future assessments there would be no point in a teacher teaching for those particular exercises. Secondly, no individual pupil, teacher or school obtains a "test score."[3] Thus, even if a teacher were aware of the actual exercises to be used in future assessments there would be no incentive (pressure) for a teacher to teach these exercises. This is particularly true when one considers the extremely small probability of students from any given teacher's class showing up in the sample.

Parenthetically, teaching for a test is not necessarily bad. If a teacher has formulated a set of educational objectives for his own course it seems quite reasonable that he would teach toward these objectives. Then if he wished to evaluate his students' progress as learners and his success as a teacher it would seem reasonable that he assess whether or not the objectives he taught for had been obtained. In fact, if an instructor does not teach for his tests he must be testing for something that has not been taught. This does not seem to be worthwhile!

---

3. A typical package (test) that an examinee will take in year 01 will consist of exercises (questions) from all three areas (Citizenship, Science, Writing). A total score would be meaningless.

The third argument against national assessment is a very pessimistic (and hopefully *not* realistic) position. This author would tend to agree with those who suggest that what schools need is constructive advice (and support) rather than vituperative criticism. However, I would certainly not assume that data should be more helpful to the irresponsible critics than to the responsible professional educators who know that while there are many good aspects of our educational systems there are also some negative aspects. Surely one of the major reasons the public has been reluctant to support what educators are doing correctly and to provide funds so that educators can change or improve in those areas where it is warranted is because educators have been very remiss in providing outcome data to substantiate their positions.

It is anticipated that parts of the national assessment data will be interpreted as commendable and other parts as unfavorable to the schools. If indeed the schools are putting out a good product, the public should be told. If some aspects of the product need improvement, that data should also be made available.

I have taken the space to discuss three of the arguments set forth by anti-national assessment educators. The most discouraging aspect of many of the con arguments is that their general flavor suggests that gathering data on educational outcomes will likely produce more harm than good. Surely we are wise enough to use data correctly. To be sure, everything we do is potentially harmful, but not to assess because of some possible bad consequences is similar to not taking a tuberculosis test because it might show that one has TB.

It is certainly important to be aware of the potential harm of a national assessment program. The original planners of national assessment were cognizant of potential dangers and designed the study to minimize any potential misuses. Educational decisions must continually be made. Any empiricist would take the position that to make these decisions on less information than can be obtained is, indeed, poor administrative and educational practice. The national assessment program will provide valuable data. We should all look forward to receiving these data. In the meanwhile, we should actively support the assessment activities.

REFERENCES

Bell, Harry H., Federal "Exploration": First Step to Conquest, *Ohio Schools*, Dec., 1965, pp. 7-8.

Crosby, Muriel, "Curriculum Control? 'We Can Get It For You Wholesale'," *Educational Leadership*, Nov., 1966, pp. 119-123.

Hand, Harold C., "National Assessment Viewed as The Camel's Nose," *Phi Delta Kappan*, Sept., 1965, pp. 8-13.

part four

The PRINCIPAL
and PERSONNEL

The Principal
and the Staff

VII

chapter overview

The old shibboleth for the neophyte administrators, "organize, deputize, supervise," is as valid today as ever.

—Bertram H. Holland

Staff leadership is one of the major tasks of any school principal. The principal's efforts to secure the cooperation of people must be grounded in sound social and psychological principles. His effectiveness in personnel leadership is dependent upon his ability to cultivate the science of human relationship. He should devote his time, talents, and energy to aid and assist the classroom teacher in doing the job he was hired to do—"teach."

In most schools the principalship is no longer a one-man job. Bertram H. Holland sketches the design for developing a group of administrative assistants into a productive educational team. The failure on the part of the principal to organize and develop such a team could prevent him from creating a school relevant to the times.

The proper utilization of specialists in various service fields to reinforce the professional teaching staff is becoming a major challenge to school principals. Gordon P. Liddle and Donald G. Ferguson suggest ways in which these new services can be organized and directed most effectively.

Few positions in the history of American high schools have created as much debate as the position of department chairman. Yet, Paul R. Bingaman asks the reader to consider the department chairman "in the area of supervision and curriculum improvement in the comprehensive high school of today." As he says, "the discerning educator will sift through many ideas and choose those that are best for his particular situation."

The principal is responsible for setting the educational climate for creative teaching. Betty Jo Montag nominates the role of administrator as first, both in importance and magnitude, in developing the creative master teacher role. She recognizes the need for continued development of the teacher-administrator relationship to foster the conditions for spawning creative teaching.

Human resources are too precious to be used inefficiently. Dwight W. Allen recommends a plan—differentiated staffing—which puts teacher talent to work. He believes that the teaching profession has the talent and the willingness to use such a plan. Is it worth trying?

Teacher satisfaction is of utmost importance to the accomplishment of educational goals. Alexander M. Feldvebel reports on a study designed to examine a few of the conditioning factors in the school and teaching profession which may or may not contribute to teacher satisfaction. Principals need to be aware of these factors. The light of education is projected by the quality of teaching.

Paraprofessionals are rapidly becoming an important segment in the professional family. Frank P. Bazeli reflects on the organization and training of paraprofessionals. His analysis of the role of paraprofessionals in the schools suggests one pattern of differentiated staffing.

H. M. Louderback had an idea, "Why not hire a paraprofessional to help the science teacher do a professional job of science teaching by freeing him from tasks that could be performed by a person with a different training?" An imposing list of activities are carried out by the paraprofessional. This is only one example of the potential of paraprofessionals in the schools.

"You're Getting a Student Teacher!" Leonard E. Kraft recognizes the increased involvement of the public schools in the education of prospective teachers. He provides the principal with important guidelines for working with student teachers.

Effective staff communications are an essential element in the attainment of staff goals. Frank C. Mayer recognizes that effective staff communications are not easily achieved. He offers a few basic thoughts for administrators on methods of improving internal communications.

The challenge to provide the best possible channels of communications among members of a school faculty is an everyday affair for secondary school principals. Lloyd E. McCleary reports on a nationwide study of practices and problems relating to communications in large secondary schools.

The administrative tenure of a school administrator may very well hinge on his precepts for personnel administration. Laurence E. Ely implies that he is beyond the age to profit from the precepts distilled from his experience, but he is anxious to share them with "struggling schoolmen who have heretofore been denied the advancement to which their merits entitled them."

The Principal | 34
and His Administrative Team

Bertram H. Holland

It is axiomatic that the principal of the large high school needs administrative assistants. As the educational leader of the school, he must divest himself of as much routine detail as he can, else he becomes so bogged down with desk work that he cannot give attention to all the wide facets of the school. The more comprehensive the school, the greater is the diversity of items which must at one time or another receive consideration from the principal. The old shibboleth for the neophyte administrator, "organize, deputize, supervise," is as valid today as ever. Without adequate assistance, the principal will, in spite of himself, neglect some phase of his school.

Various formulas have been proposed for determining the number of administrative assistants required for the large high school. My personal rule of thumb is one full-time assistant for each 500 students enrolled or fraction thereof regardless of guidance or other ancillary personnel available in the school or in the system. The title given to these assistants is important only in its implications for the assistants' status in the local setting. In regard to status, the administrative assistants should be answerable only to the principal or in his absence to one of their number who is designated as acting head of the school.

Ordinarily if there are to be two or more assistants, then both sexes should be represented. They should be interested in school administration, aware of the scope of the school, sensitive to individual human needs, and resourceful in solving problems of human relations at both the adolescent and adult levels. A high reservoir of energy, as well as some formal course work in school administration and guidance, helps enormously.

The overworked principal may be compelled to resort to expedients to obtain added administrative help. An administrative intern can take some of the load from the principal in regard to certain definite aspects which are within the reach of the intern. Internships are temporary appointments, so a replacement must be secured at the end of a year. Otherwise the duties must be assigned to some other staff member, or they are resumed by the principal.

From *NASSP Bulletin*, Vol. 52 (November, 1968), pp. 56-65. Reprinted by permission of the National Association of Secondary School Principals. Copyright: 1968 by the National Association of Secondary School Principals.

AVAILABILITY A FACTOR

Part-time assistants are useful. However, two half-time assistants are not the equivalent of one full-time assistant, because they are not available when they are teaching or doing whatever occupies the rest of their time. And yet this arrangement may be better —if it has official sanction from the central office—than the principal's unofficially assigning administrative duties to staff members who must then be freed from other responsibilities in order to take on these particular duties.

It would be interesting to know how many administrative functions performed in schools across the country have been delegated by harried principals to willing teachers. Such tasks often are without place in the official table of organization, carry no monetary remuneration and may not even entail compensatory time. Usually the duties are specific, such as taking charge of the bookroom, issuing supplies, assigning lockers, or handling student accounts. Some may continue over the entire school year while others last only for a limited time as taking charge of the junior prom or graduation exercises. All are important to the life of the school and not only relieve the principal of certain administrative details but also give a sense of involvement in the organization as a whole to individual teachers, thus contributing to a better tone in the school.

DELEGATION OF ADMINISTRATIVE DUTIES

Assuming the optimum provision for administrative assistants, the delegation of their duties is the next consideration for the principal. Some duties are of a planning or advisory nature, such as the revision of existing procedures to improve results or the satisfaction therefrom. Others include the development of new procedures such as the introduction of data processing techniques.

Responsibility for routine procedures—such as fire drills, lunch period passing, and bus schedules—certainly should be delegated to an assistant. Much in the extracurricular area which has educational value may be delegated, including clubs and student government, but the principal ought to retain a definite personal relationship with the latter. The same is true of the administration of secretarial and custodial services and utilization of paraprofessional aides.

STUDENT DISCIPLINE

But by far the most likely area to be delegated to administrative assistants is the handling of student discipline. Over the years I have talked with assistant principals from many different schools and found that they spend a major part of their time in dealing with misconduct of students. They typically are least happy with this phase of their duties, particularly if they have no effective voice in improving the ways teachers handle problems of student behavior. The most important consideration gauging the reality of the assistant's part in effectively improving teachers' discipline tactics is whether that assistant has a definite role in evaluating teachers for retention or increment; if not, then he has no real influence on teachers' attitudes toward discipline.

JOB SATISFACTION

The degree of satisfaction which administrative assistants derive from their jobs depends not only on their status, both officially and in practice, but also on their relations with the principal. If the assistants are merely handed all the most disagreeable tasks routinely, with little help from the principal, then little job satisfaction is realized by them. On the other hand, if the principal is willing to involve himself in solving difficult problems, is available for consultation regarding problems *when needed* and solicits advice from his administrative assistants in the overall operation of the school, they are more willing to embrace significant components of the administrative package including student discipline. All members of the principal's administrative team need to attain a sense of the full sweep of the educational enterprise and to develop a feeling that they count as individuals in the success of the school.

The principal must be judicious in balancing his natural desire to outline in detail the duties he delegates to his administrative teammates with his wish to leave each as much latitude as possible to exercise professional judgment. However, the most explicit delineation of duties is needed when the principal has the benefit of more than one administrative assistant in order that each will know precisely the areas in which he will function. Such description of duties should be reduced to writing and given to each member of the team. In this way each one knows his own duties and those of his administrative colleagues as well. If there is but one administrative assistant, the problem is less acute because the principal and his assistant just divide up the duties; however, it is essential here that there be full understanding of who does what.

Any list of duties should stress *what* is to be done rather than *how*, for herein lies the opportunity for the assistant to employ his own initiative, imagination, and judgment. The wise principal holds his assistants accountable for results rather than methods, but each must realize that no administrator can ignore the impact of ill-considered tactics on the public, staff, and students.

DEVELOPING ADMINISTRATIVE TEAM WORK

The principal should hold his door open at all times for his assistants to try with him for size any new procedures they may have in mind. The most potentially valid innovation may fail dismally because of the way in which it is implemented. The principal ought to be able to detect flaws in a plan before his assistant falls on his face when introducing it. To encourage such consultation, the principal must give the highest priority to making himself available to his assistants when one of them wants to talk with him.

One of the best ways to develop administrative teamwork is to arrange frequent and regular meetings of the administrative staff with the principal. If such meetings are irregular they become infrequent and hence less effectual. They are especially valuable when a new assistant joins the staff. Not only do these serve as a valuable means of in-service training but also help to keep the principal informed about trends in types of problems which confront his assistants; otherwise, he may be less attuned to the pulse of the school.

Supervisors of instruction perform administrative functions to a degree and, hence, are a part of the administrative team. They, too, need to have their areas of responsibility defined, not so much as a ceiling but rather as a floor on which they work. They should be expected to assume some responsibility for the overall operation of the school, as well as for their particular phase of it. The principal should meet regularly with them as a group but probably not as frequently as with his full-time administrative assistants.

On occasion, he should schedule combined meetings of both groups. Conferences with department heads individually are necessary; in fact, most of the principal's time during the school day may profitably be spent with people: staff, students, parents, central office personnel, and community leaders individually or, less often, in groups. This usually means that he does his paper work in the evening.

A PROBLEM SHARED

Much of the time the principal listens. He lets people get things off their minds, for a problem shared is a burden lightened. Having listened, he responds. His reaction may be positive, negative, or qualified. Principals like to say "yes" whenever they can to encourage initiative. They often have to say "no," pointing out the disadvantages and suggesting alternatives wherever possible. The principal should not feel that he must immediately support or veto suggestions. If he needs to study an idea or seek advice of resource persons he should say so.

The principal should not be expected to produce all the new ideas in the school; if he tries to do so he will most certainly not develop a viable administrative team. He should be quick to recognize useful innovations and to give public credit to the persons suggesting them. Happy is the principal who creates conditions that put every member of the faculty on the team. At the same time he must culti-vate the idea that faculty suggestions must be reasonable and their implications thought through.

A corollary of this idea is the understanding that matters which could go to an assistant should be so referred. The principal cannot listen to all ideas or complaints and should encourage persons to pre-sent their suggestions or problems to another responsible person in the school, with the understanding that if not satisfied they may re-turn to the principal. The principal, already heavy laden with re-sponsibility, is torn between the temptation to send every appoint-ment seeker routinely to an assistant and the bone feeling that per-haps he ought to listen himself. One must train his impulses to tell him intuitively when to follow one course of action and when not to do so.

Face-to-face conferences and meetings are necessary, but much can be accomplished by telephone. The principal should be able to dial his assistants directly—and they him—no matter whether the locations of their offices are near or far. Written communications, also, save time and prevent misunderstandings. Staff members can-not—and should not—always be in their offices. Paper can some-times travel better than people and in several directions at once. The astute principal encourages this reciprocally.

RELATIONS OF ADMINISTRATIVE TEAM TO STAFF

The principal and his assistants need to review administrative procedures continually to make sure that these practices are the best that can be devised. Faculty committees are effective instruments for developing policies and modifying procedures. Committees are frequently maligned; nevertheless, the large school cannot operate efficiently without them.

One of the most useful aids which the writer has found for keep-ing his administrative team in touch with the faculty has been the Headmaster's Advisory Committee. It consists of one representative from each department in the school elected by the teachers of that department. The Committee elects its own chairman to serve for a year. Except for the Headmaster and one of his housemasters no administrative or supervisory personnel are allowed to become mem-bers.

The Advisory Committee meets once a month and considers sug-gestions or complaints which each member of the committee has solicited from his departmental colleagues. No holds are barred and the identity of the originator of any complaint is never revealed. No matter how insignificant the irritation, it is considered seriously by the Committee, which tries to assist the headmaster in coming up with a solution.

Over the years, a number of significant improvements have resulted from the constructive suggestions emanating from the Advisory Committee. Aside from this, it provides a way, without embarrassment to anyone, of cutting through red tape and gives a systematic means for the administrative team to communicate directly with teacher representatives about matters which concern the teachers.

PRACTICES FOR IMPROVING THE EFFECTIVENESS OF THE ADMINISTRATIVE TEAM

Many things can frustrate teachers in their desire to teach well. Probably the one which bothers teachers most is the uncooperative student who either disrupts the class by overt misbehavior or withdraws from participation in it. Most such problems are temporary in nature and respond usually to the teacher's efforts when aided by the resourcefulness of the administrative assistant responsible for the student. However, sometimes students have problems which do not respond readily to ordinary practices and require more thorough study and specialized treatment.

At Brookline High School a case clearinghouse has been organized to deal with just such acute or chronic problems which defy normal methods of solution. Under our House Plan each grade is a "house" and is administered by a housemaster who is responsible for all matters pertaining to students in his house, including discipline. (Each housemaster serves also as an assistant headmaster.) The housemaster may refer difficult cases to the Clearinghouse which meets every other week. The headmaster presides at the two-hour sessions which are attended by the chairman of the guidance department, school psychiatrist, school physician, school nurse, and adjustment counselors. Housemasters and guidance counselors present the case history with a brief sketch of what each has done to resolve the problem. Classroom teachers are invited to present problems and to give their observations.

The attendance officer, detached social workers, probation officer, welfare workers, and case workers from social agencies are asked to sit in from time to time when cases come up with which they are associated. The discussion of a case is continued until a course of action is agreed upon and someone present is designated with the responsibility of following through on it. All discussion is completely confidential.

CIVIL RIGHTS OF JUVENILES

Among the more sticky duties of an administrative team are those associated with the exclusion of students from school for misconduct. Not only are there statutes governing these disciplinary actions, but most school boards have local regulations within which the administrative officers of a school must function. Recent court decisions have defined more explicitly the civil rights of juveniles so that a principal needs to draw more than ever on the full resources of the school and school system to secure the exclusion even temporarily of students in those rare cases where no other recourse is compatible with the protection and control of the other members of the school. In such infrequent cases we have found the provision for a Board of Review to be useful. This procedure adopted by our school board has worked satisfactorily in a number of cases where the headmaster and his housemasters found their decisions challenged on legal grounds.

The Board of Review may be convened by the superintendent of schools at the request of the headmaster to review a case. In addition to the superintendent and headmaster it consists of the housemaster concerned, coordinator of pupil personnel services, school psychiatrist, and school physician. Other resource people may be called in, such as adjustment counselor, guidance counselor, attendance officer, juvenile police officer, or case worker of a social agency. The school board has given the Board of Review authority to exclude temporarily students who have broken laws or otherwise conducted themselves in a manner to besmirch the reputation of the school. The Board of Review also has authority to set conditions to be met by the student so excluded in order to be readmitted to the school. In serious cases, the Board of Review may recommend permanent expulsion to the school board but so far this ultimate step has not been necessary.

RELATIONS OF ADMINISTRATIVE TEAM TO CENTRAL OFFICE

As education becomes better adapted to the needs of all students, more specialists are needed. Usually they work out of the central office under the general direction of the superintendent or his assistants. The more personnel so assigned to the central office, the more complex becomes the task of the principal to relate himself and his administrative assistants to new developments. Several devices are useful in accommodating to this situation, among them:

1. Regularly scheduled meetings of the superintendent with all assistant superintendents, principals, directors, and supervisors of instruction.
2. Regularly scheduled meetings of the principal with his administrative assistants, department chairmen, and the directors of instruction assigned to his building.
3. Regularly scheduled conferences of the principal with individuals such as superintendent, coordinator of special services, guidance director, and certain supervisors or directors of instruction of departments having no department chairman in the school.

School systems differ in the way in which supervisory responsibility for subject areas is organized, but the principal must have some person in the building on whom he can rely for taking responsibility for all matters relating to each department. Otherwise the details of day to day operation will not be adequately handled. If the table of organization does not provide for a professional person to serve as head or chairman of each department, then the principal needs to designate someone as a head teacher and try to arrange the schedule of duties for this head teacher so that he has time to perform the duties delegated to him. It is not feasible to have a central office person discharge these duties because he cannot be sure that he can arrange his schedule to always be physically present in the building every time a crucial decision is needed.

With more specialists in the central office it is more likely in a large school system to find that more of the supervision of instruction is carried on by personnel based outside the school. Under such an arrangement the principal may be bypassed. In the press of performing their allotted tasks they tend to work directly with teachers. As central office personnel they do not attend faculty meetings, do not routinely read general notices from the principal or his administrative assistants to the faculty. Hence, the principal and his administrative team need to devise ways to involve central office personnel in the activities of the school at every appropriate opportunity.

LEADERSHIP

The goal of any plan to supply administrative assistants for the principal, to define their duties, develop teamwork, and organize ancillary services is ultimately to provide adequate leadership for the school. The key person in this organization is the principal who must fulfill the role of professional educational leader of the institution.

If the principal does not assume this function he will cease to be the navigator of the educational ship and become only its figurehead. As leader he seeks to influence rather than dominate, to be reasonable rather than directive, persuasive rather than autocratic. Events press in inexorably on the head of a school and will engulf him if he does not use his administrative team effectively so that he can find the time to observe, plan, organize, and to work with staff (hopefully also to get to know them) as well as students, parents, and central office in order to develop a vital school relevant to the times.

Leadership for Guidance and Personnel Services | 35

Gordon P. Liddle
Donald G. Ferguson

In placing your 1968 calendar on your desk, you close out what has been an astounding decade of progress in the development of guidance and other personnel services. The last ten years have been marked by vast changes in all phases of American educational programing. Historians fifty years hence may claim that the 1950's and 1960's were the period of greatest and most radical change ever experienced in the American educational system. One might speculate that the process of evaluating and reshaping, begun during our generation, will be continuous and will bring about reforms to characterize the American educational scene for generations to come.

Several developments which probably will last include the new emphasis on learning theories in curriculum development, the introduction of man-machine systems,[1] the improvement in teacher status and working conditions, and advancements in the equalization of educational opportunity. Perhaps more notable than any other change is the advent of federal support on a broad basis for educational programs.

Just ten years ago, guidance got its first major boost on a nationwide basis with the passage of the National Defense Education Act of 1958. This was followed shortly by the now-famous recommendation of James B. Conant that "there should be one full-time counselor (or guidance officer) for every 250 to 300 pupils in the high school."[2]

Developments came rapidly on the heels of those events. Although the secondary school generally has not yet achieved Conant's ratio, some districts have, and several states are approaching it on a state-wide basis.[3] Accrediting agencies, as well as the American Personnel and Guidance Association, are encouraging and in some instances mandating ratios comparable to Conant's.

From *NASSP Bulletin*, Vol. 52 (January 1968), pp. 1-10. Reprinted by permission of the National Association of Secondary School Principals. Copyright: 1968 by the National Association of Secondary School Principals.

1. John W. Loughary, *Man-Machine Systems in Education* (New York: Harper & Row, 1966).
2. James B. Conant, *The American High School Today* (New York: McGraw-Hill Book Co., 1959).
3. Although up-to-date summaries of ratios for state programs or individual districts are not available, some data for the states participating in NDEA programs can be obtained through the U. S. Office of Education.

BEFORE NDEA AND AFTER

Secondary school personnel services prior to this period were sketchy and informal and very halting in development. Many false starts marked their progress. Attempts in the early thirties to start programs, based largely on vocational education acts, were crippled by the economic depression. Subsequent attempts at major program development throughout the nation had to be put aside during the years of war.

A principal reflecting on years past could recall having one counselor on his staff, or perhaps a dean of students, and operating a program which included a few basic guidance services such as course selection and scheduling, orientation, records, and group testing. Today's program is a complicated system of services and involves highly trained and specialized personnel: counselors, psychologists, social workers, attendance counselors, and others. These specialists, particularly the most recently trained, bring new ways of providing better services and present a very real challenge to the principal in his attempt to provide leadership.

Since the next decade holds promise for continued growth and prosperity in the field, many educators are attempting to take stock and revise priorities. When change occurs there is often more to be done than we can get done, more need for money than there is money available, a greater need for personnel than there are specialists available, and more squeaky wheels than oil to quiet them.

By way of illustration, following are a few of the major pressures which are of concern to secondary school administrators:

- large pupil enrollments with greater heterogeneity than has ever previously characterized the student population
- pleas from teachers whose jobs have become increasingly difficult in the face of new technology and methodology, and who themselves daily face pressures from a more demanding student population
- demands of students, parents, and the community for a greater voice not only in the general conduct of the schools, but also in much of the day-by-day high school activity
- an instructional and extracurricular schedule which is so complicated and so demanding of skillful, systematic organization that it alone can keep an assistant fully occupied.

Today the principal—unlike the "loner," his counterpart of years past—is becoming the head man on an administrative team.

STAFFING PROBLEMS

One stubborn problem facing today's secondary school principal is that of integrating into the school's total program the various specialists and the services they provide. For example, the question arises: How does one retain the specialized value of social workers and psychologists and at the same time help them to "fit in"?

It has become generally accepted practice to surround the teacher with a variety of specialists, all of whom have facilitating of instruction as part of their job. Much of the work of the personnel services staff is geared to this end. It is commonly agreed that these specialists are of greatest value when dealing with problems for which skills peculiar to psychology and sociology are needed. This means that the preparation and background of these men and women should be quite different from those of a teacher. Perhaps even their attitudes toward children will differ, and yet they are expected to understand and be sensitive to the kinds of problems with which teachers need help.

Effective use of personnel specialists also requires that understanding come from both directions; that is, teachers must be helped to appreciate the special ways in which these personnel can be of benefit to them. Teachers need to be accepting of differences in perception which a modern counselor or psychologist might have with regard to a given youngster's problem. They need to be helped to recognize that, in the nature of things, the work schedules of these specialists will differ from those of teachers, that their ways of approaching their tasks and the techniques they use also differ, and that these differences are in large measure inherent in each specialist's value to the school.

SELECTING PERSONNEL WORKERS

Until recently, common practice was to select personnel workers from among classroom teachers, but only from those who had had several years of classroom experience. Consequently, to a large degree the basic competences of the personnel worker remained those of a teacher. Personnel workers now are typically coming through other preparation routes, as the desirability of their having specialized knowledge and skills is being recognized.

It has also been seen that the constant drawing from teacher ranks to fill positions in personnel services and administration has a negative effect on the teaching profession. One person recently commented somewhat in disgust that the clearest evidence of being a successful teacher seems to be getting out of the classroom and into counseling or administration.

For several reasons the entry pattern into pupil services work is moving away from a classroom-teacher base, even though this does tend to heighten the difficulty a principal may experience in integrating these specialists into the educational *team*. Complicating this is the fact that until recently some categories of pupil services specialists were rarely available in the secondary school. For ex-

ample, psychologists and social workers in the schools were formerly found almost exclusively at the elementary level but are now
increasingly employed in the secondary school.

As such specialists begin to appear in secondary schools, rarely
will they bring experience in the upper grades and seldom will the
principal have had experience in giving them leadership and in
coordinating their efforts. But now he must learn to do so. In his
article on "Team Action in Public Personnel," Bruce Shear notes the
various roles of the specialists and points to teaming as a way to
provide coordination.

UTILIZING STAFF MEMBERS

Another concern relating to integrating pupil services into the
secondary school is how to utilize the staff most effectively. How
does a principal give creative leadership in staffing the various pupil
services jobs to be done? There seems to be an endless battle to reduce the ratio of students to staff. This is not only a concern in the
pupil services area but obviously in the area of instruction as well.
The problem is a complicated one involving justification of a reduced ratio while striving to get the best education for the community's tax dollar.

Increasingly, school administrators are having to provide a
"balance-sheet" type of justification for their staffing requests,
rather than basing requests simply on value judgments. Principals
must be prepared to answer such questions as these: What evidence
exists that better programing will occur when student-staff ratios
are reduced? In what way would services differ and what advantages would accrue to the students and to the educational team
through more favorable pupil loads?

Some schools today, largely by virtue of federally supported
programs of ESEA Title I and Title III, have an opportunity to achieve
a ratio of one counselor to 100 students, along with, in some instances, full-time psychologists and social workers. This presents the
question of how to deal with the differences in services that can be
expected under such a favorable ratio.

In another article in this issue, John Fisher discusses new staffing patterns and arrangements where personnel trained below full
professional level (often called paraprofessionals) are employed for
a variety of assistance roles. This approach has merit on at least two
bases. First, such personnel—often indigenous to the community—
are able to perform some tasks which certificated school people find
difficult. They are able to communicate with members of the community, particularly minority groups, and can win acceptance denied to "professionals."

Another merit in the use of lay workers is that, if creatively employed and assigned, they represent less strain on the pupil-services

dollar than fully trained specialists. As the demand increases for highly skilled and competent people, the funding problem becomes more difficult; at the same time, many jobs within pupil services could be performed effectively by people who have less than full preparation. Some of these jobs are clerical or, as alluded to earlier, are jobs which must use local people if they are to be done effectively.[4]

IN-SERVICE TRAINING

A second area of concern to principals is in-service education and staff development. Lucy Wing discusses this in her article on "Staff Development Practices and Potentials." To give leadership in this area, the principal faces several perplexing questions: How does one justify the time and expense of providing additional preparation for people who are being paid a salary on the strength of their education? What staff development approaches are best? What evidence can one offer that various approaches pay off?

Few educators quarrel with the concept that for a school to function effectively there must be a continuing educational program for the staff. New teachers fresh out of the university generally require considerable seasoning and experience in order to become maximally effective, and those who have years of experience in the school business must be continuously stimulated and helped in upgrading their competencies. But consensus is lacking as to strategies and models for this in-service training.

One fact clear to us at IRCOPPS is that school districts we have visited because of their reputedly excellent pupil services were taking staff development responsibilities seriously. Although the kinds of programs and the activities emphasized vary from district to district, the leaders of these programs quote the same variables as critical to successful staff development. These variables include administrative support of staff ideas and planned, systematic, yet flexible in-service arrangements.

OUTSIDE CONSULTANTS

A combination of resources seems to offer the best approach to staff development, through the use of "in-building" and "in-system" personnel along with university and other consultants. Certainly on most staffs there are many who have good ideas and the ability to stimulate others if a proper atmosphere is provided and there is encouragement from the school administration. Often pupil services personnel are valuable resource people in the area of human

4. See *School Volunteers*, Administrative Leadership Service (Arlington, Va.: Educational Services Bureau, 1966).

growth and development, in measurement, and in the translation of learning and behavior theory into terms which make sense to other school personnel.

University and private resources can also be profitably included in a staff development system, particularly when they are carefully and cooperatively selected and where their participation fits into an ongoing program. They are, of course, less effective if they offer simply a transplant of some didactic course or a one-man show with little relevance to what concerns the staff. Additionally, results are better when there is institutional collaboration which pays off for the district and the university in mutual service and support.

One clear value in the recent federal support for education is that it is freeing school personnel from some of their daily duties in order to design and participate in such staff development activities. Staff members are investigating and experimenting in areas where the ideas might have long existed but where the financial support to try them out was not available.

PROGRAMS AND SERVICES

The principal must of course focus on programs and services, for these are what staffing and in-service development are for. Principals must constantly raise the questions: Are we properly responsive to the needs of students? Are we listening to them at all? Do our programs and services reflect a sensitive ear? Many program changes that have taken place appear to be responses to youngsters' speaking out, which seems to us to be a very hopeful sign.

Guidance services in the secondary school are moving from a limiting interest in vocational-educational guidance and scheduling and toward a complex of programs, services, and approaches. For example, a decade ago counseling was seen as a technique for providing educational guidance. Today it is more appropriately viewed as a service in itself. Today counseling objectives may relate to vocational-educational decisions, but they are likely to be much broader: self-concept development, building ego-strength, and making decisions with regard to a variety of life concerns.

Where yesterday's guidance worker was preoccupied with helping youngsters select courses and with arranging schedules for them, today's specialist spends more time developing relationships with students which focus on the student himself, rather than on his schedule sheet. This is the kind of relationship that one frequently hears students calling for, if he listens.

Not long ago, we interviewed some high school students who felt their counselors were spending most of the time with clerical chores related to scheduling and testing. These students did not really have a chance to talk with their counselor—"They are too busy to see us." These young people went so far as to suggest that students handle some of the clerical chores so that their counselors would be available to help in ways which the students thought were more important.

Few would deny the necessity of a well-organized scheduling system. However, one who is sensitive to the critical need in the schools for time to develop a personal relationship between students and faculty would take the foregoing sort of student criticism seriously. (A criticism, incidentally, which exists in more schools than one may think, even in some with apparently superior pupil personnel staffing.) Perhaps part of the problem lies in the counselor's not having shown the principal other ways in which his skills could be better employed. Another possibility is that too much of what is going on is done to protect the "system," to keep it running smoothly rather than to relate the programs of the high school to what youngsters need as optimum learning conditions.

THE SPECIALTY-ORIENTED STUDENT

A second program area where pupil services do make a difference and where leadership is necessary relates to noncollege-bound students—or, as they are described by Kenneth Hoyt in a subsequent article, the specialty-oriented student. To develop adequate educational programs for these youngsters has long challenged administrative leadership. It not only challenges the school's resources for programing but raises philosophical questions of the school's responsibility to produce a product that has relevance to the community's economic and manpower needs.

Many school heads and community leaders are bothered by the realization that while high school programs are heavily geared to the college-bound youngster, only a portion go on to college. And of those who do, many stay for only a short time, then return to the community and attempt to fit into the local occupational framework.

Recently one alarmed school administrator put the problem this way: About 75 percent of our youngsters are enrolled in a college preparatory course, but only about 25 percent of them go to college. Of those who are successful, few return to our community. Yet, those who complete the college preparatory curriculum but do not go to college, as well as those who do go but do not succeed and so return to the community, feel inadequately prepared to enter local industry and business.

Administrators are equally alarmed by the pressures to go to college exerted on students who either do not have the ability or do not have the interest, or perhaps lack both. Students lately have become increasingly vocal in their search for help in coping with these pressures.

Fred Hoffman in his article on "Personnel Services for Adults" discusses one Florida community's attempt to deal with some of these questions. He is concerned with trying to fulfill the school's obligation to youngsters who for one reason or another do not seem able to fit into the secondary program and who leave school early— dropouts or, as claimed by some, push-outs. That school system seems to take the position that schools have an obligation to help educate a youngster, even though his formal schooling is interrupted for one reason or another. And in this effort more than the content of instruction is involved.

MENTAL HEALTH WORK

Although schools are coming to accept—somewhat belatedly— responsibility for providing good mental health, the questions of how to approach mental health problems and how to provide developmental instruction have remained largely unanswered. Generally, though, school and community health workers have viewed the school's attempts as falling far short of the mark. For example, schools under present conditions are obviously unable to employ enough mental health specialists, such as counselors and social workers, to meet the most critical needs, not to speak of taking preventive measures.

A positive view of such criticism leads to the question of arrangement of the time and energy of personnel available to cope with the needs. In his article in this issue, Merville Shaw raises pertinent questions: Are there some ways in which counselors can work with groups rather than with individual youngsters, in order to reach more people? Are there certain kinds of objectives and outcomes which can be accomplished more effectively through group processes than through the traditional one-to-one relationship which mental health workers heretofore have almost exclusively espoused? Similarly, can the mental health worker appropriately spend all of his time working with pupils, despite evidence that such specialists currently employed in schools are not noticeably significant adults in the lives of children?

Counselors are generally seen as not having a strong influence on children's decision-making, and are not seen as models for development as often as other adults are. There are within a youngster's life people such as teachers and parents who occupy very significant positions; in some experimental programs, counselors are finding that working with these adults can pay greater dividends in changing students' behavior than will working directly with the students.

The areas discussed in this article where the principal is under pressure to provide leadership by no means exhaust the list; those selected are illustrative and ones with which readers of the NASSP BULLETIN no doubt will easily identify.

Certainly, problems and issues change with the passage of time, as do solutions, so the principal's role in and involvement with pupil services will change. But his responsibility for providing leadership, for setting priorities, for keeping abreast of needs for alteration and revision, and for providing a coordinated and integrated program will continue unabated.

36 | Consider Department Chairmen

Paul R. Bingaman

High school principals are missing a golden opportunity by failing to delegate considerable responsibility and authority to department chairmen in the area of supervision and curriculum improvement in the comprehensive high school of today.

As school districts increase in size—and most of them have as the result of legislated reorganization—the responsibilities of the high school principal proportionately increase. Administrative duties alone require most of the school day.

The most notable victim of this trend has been the opportunity for supervision of teachers and curriculum improvement by the high school principal. I would like to suggest an overview of the increasing possibilities for using the department chairmen as supervising and curriculum specialists in building a more effective school program.

Each school has individual peculiarities in its organizational structure making no two schools alike. However, it is hoped that from the ideas presented, each school district may devise ways to remold these ideas for useful application within the framework of its own school organization.

The literature is somewhat meager regarding the position of department chairmen. Some writers say the functions of the department chairman are administrative while others feel they are supervisory.

The department chairman probably functions best if *both* administrative and supervisory functions are assigned. All agree to his professional possibilities and charge they are not generally realized.

Some critics feel the position is outmoded and has ceased to function satisfactorily. The opposite view is to make this position that of a curriculum and supervisory specialist with full authority to develop his department.

The department chairman is unique in his three-fold responsibility for administration, supervision, and instructional functions. He must not only stimulate and initiate new ideas, but also sensitize his department to unrecognized needs, while still maintaining his primary role as a teacher.

From *Pennsylvania School Journal*, Vol. 118 (September 1969), pp. 27, 28, 57. Reprinted by permission of the publisher.

RELATIONSHIPS CONSIDERED

If the department chairman is to serve a useful function within the school, both the superintendent and the high school principal must consistently support this kind of organizational structure. The greater responsibility rests with the high school principal in that he must officially delegate authority to his department chairman.

The same relationship should exist between the principal and the department chairman as the principal hopes to have with the superintendent.

A master teacher with good interpersonal relations is obviously required for a department chairmanship. This person must hold prestige within the faculty and have the ability to lead his fellow teachers. Again, each school will have outlined its own qualifications for this position. Some schools advocate a rotation system with the chairman chosen by the faculty. In most cases he is recommended by the principal and then appointed permanently to the position by action of the school board.

The faculty within each department should be given an opportunity to rate their preference in the choice of a department chairman and the principal should consider this evaluation in making the selection. Choosing the teacher who, with pride and purpose, will strive to make his department the most outstanding in the area, much like a football coach, is really the basic qualification in filling the position.

SALARIES NOTED

What procedure should be used to determine the worth of a department chairman? Although it is more important to the school system to find the right person and outline his duties, to the person receiving the appointment, the remuneration is of primary concern. In the past, a common method of recognizing a superior teacher was to appoint him department chairman and pay him an additional salary.

According to a study made by Kenneth Easterday in selected schools in the mid-west, 6.3 percent received no extra salary, 50.6 percent received both extra pay and released time. Only extra pay was received by 15.2 percent and 22.8 percent were relieved of some teaching duties.

A department chairman must have assigned time to work in the department if he is to be the effective supervisor and innovator envisioned in this paper. He must also be given additional remuneration equal to the status of his position.

The basic problem is to first increase the status of the position by the attitude of the administration. The department chairman must also prove his worth by the department he develops. Hopefully, a just salary equal to his accomplishments will then be forthcoming.

One of the fairest salary plans for department chairmen is to add a fixed amount for each teacher under the chairman's jurisdiction plus a percentage of his base salary for the department chairmanship.

A teacher earning a salary of $8000 and serving as chairman of a department including 10 teachers might receive $25 per teacher plus 2 percent of the base salary or a total of 10 x $25 plus .02 x $8000 for a total salary of $8000 plus $250 plus $160 or $8410.

VARIED DUTIES

In 1959 the Public School System in Rochester, Minnesota, made a study of the duties of the department chairman which showed the following assignments, listed in frequency of mention:

1. Selection of textbooks with members of the department.
2. Regularly scheduled department meetings.
3. Building the course of studies.
4. Making annual requisitions for instructional materials.
5. Supervision of classes.
6. Assist in preparation of the budget.
7. Advise the new teachers.
8. Study methods of teaching.
9. Advise the principal.
10. Attend curriculum meetings.
11. Interview teacher candidates.
12. Attend coordination meetings with the junior-high school staff.
13. Direct the use of supplementary books.
14. Help in the assignment of classes to the teachers.
15. Coordinate the work of the teachers within the department.[1]

Since each school system operates individualistically, some of these duties can readily be enlarged while others may be diminished in scope. Each school should consider the advisability of using the department chairman both in a horizontal role within each grade and in a vertical role coordinating all grades, one through twelve. In most systems, the emphasis would fall within the secondary grades.

The chairman can be a valuable aid in coordinating the curriculum activities of each grade and reducing duplication of effort from one grade to the next. This is particularly true if several junior high schools operate within one school system.

1. Fred M. King and James Moon, "The Department Head in the Public Secondary School," *National Association of Secondary School Principals Bulletin*, 44:20-24, March 1960.

The same is true in preparing courses of study for each subject. This is of special importance when a school is preparing for a Middle States evaluation.

The department chairman may be assigned as a big brother (or sister) to new teachers beginning to teach within the school. In this manner the new teacher can be properly indoctrinated to the correct procedures and methods used by that school.

A plan that has met with considerable success is formation of an Advisory Council to the principal, composed of the department chairmen. At regular meetings the principal may check the pulse of his faculty on any problem, for faculty members are free to discuss their problems with department chairmen, either requesting advice or assistance to resolve their problems.

The principal may also use the Council as a curriculum council to innovate and update the curriculum within the school. Many other possibilities can be explored with this form of interaction.

Using the department chairman to interview new teaching candidates is an effective method of building staff morale. The department chairman may not only advise in assigning teachers to the master schedule, but at times can effectively write the class schedule for the department. This is especially helpful in such departments as physical education and business education.

There are certain fields in which a department chairman can be of particular assistance to the principal in supervision. An example of this is the foreign language department.

The department chairman with a knowledge of both the subject matter and modern methods in the use of the language laboratory can supervise the new or weak teacher more effectively than the principal. Working as a team, the two can readily improve instructional techniques within the department and at times even save a teacher who is not able to solve his or her problems alone.

CURRENT PRACTICES

In the study by Easterday, a majority of the schools reported chairmen in the following departments: (1) English, (2) science, (3) social science, (4) mathematics, (5) business education, and (6) foreign languages.

More than half the schools reported chairmen in the following areas: (1) industrial arts, (2) physical education, (3) home economics, (4) art, and (5) music. Other departments with chairmen reported were: (1) library, (2) vocational education, (3) guidance, and (4) agriculture.

Several larger school districts have established four or five larger divisions within the high school and then added subdivision chairmen. They serve on a school administrative council whose purpose is to determine school policy and originate studies for curricular improvement.

This plan does not seem to be so easily implemented as the plan described within this paper nor compatible with the organizational structure of most high schools today.

One of the most interesting features in the structure of our schools today is the variety of procedures used to reach the same goal. As one visits different schools, one will see many different ways of educating children. The discerning educator will sift through many ideas and choose those that are best for his particular situation.

Creativity or Mediocrity? 37
The Principal Sets the Climate

Betty Jo Montag

For the last 15-20 years there has been a great deal of educational discontent within the profession. This discontent has assumed many faces—the face of salaries vs. cost of living; the face of inadequate teacher preparation; the face of giving credentials to less than able individuals as teachers; the face of questioning all phases of education and educators; the face of public opinion about education; the face which mass media gives to education.

One of the questions that has been most posed is the pro and con of the "master teacher" concept. As with all philosophical questions, this one has both areas of strength and areas of weakness. Over and above the basic question of whether a master teacher program would facilitate better education, is the question of whether education is ready for creative teaching—or is content to wallow along in pre-established patterns of mediocrity. Although on first consideration master teachers and creativity in education may not seem related, further exploration of these two ideas will show many areas of overlap.

Perhaps both the master teacher and creative teaching should be defined before further discussion. A master teacher will be considered to be one who has had enough experience to be mature; has a sense of humor; is not only knowledgeable in subject matter, but whose intellectual curiosity fosters continued study; has a vital and enthusiastic approach with students; is flexible enough to not only try new methods but to handle students with a minimum of disciplinary problems; and is genuinely dedicated to the proposition that teaching is the greatest vocation in the world. Creative teaching will be defined in *exactly* the same way except for the addition of one thing—the actual production of new curriculum and teaching techniques. This may seem to overlap the fourth criteria of a master teacher. However, it does not necessarily, as a master teacher can be one who ably uses material developed by another, without actual creativity.

Thus defined, there *is* a great deal of correlation between the two. Therefore, the question to be explored is whether or not we as educators, and the public whom we serve, wish creative master teaching. Or perhaps we should ask, "can we provide this kind of education?"

From *Journal of Secondary Education*, Vol. 44 (February 1969), pp. 65-68. Reprinted by permission of the publisher.

Historically, educators have often created a timid, horn-rimmed glasses, severe bun, long faced stereotype. This is no longer a valid prototype. More really sharp individuals are entering the teaching profession than ever before! No longer is the old saw that "if you can't do anything else, teach" true! It would be utopian to suggest that all individuals currently enrolled in teacher training are potentially creative master teachers. *But,* a greater proportion than ever before are! Much of the educational training across the country has been updated from the "mickey mouse" reputation it has had. Many teacher training institutions now require more hours in subject matter than in education courses per se. Along with a more realistic approach to salaries in most parts of the country is the increased awareness of teachers in community and civic endeavors and therefore a much more vital image of teaching is emerging. So more and more potentially fine teachers are showing interest in the vocation.

What of the individuals who have taught for many years? Are we all old fuddy duddies ready for the scrap heap? Emphatically not! Innumerable seasoned teachers have been and continue to be creative master teachers. Many have worked over the years under heavy handicaps to develop into this kind of teacher. It is much easier today to be a creative teacher than it was twenty years ago. Today many, many "gimmicks" are available commercially at relatively low cost to implement illustrative materials. Also, most school districts are more financially able to augment creative education than they have been heretofore. Leafing through any catalogue of school supplies would make our colleagues of fifty years ago gape in wonder. Walking through any modern educational plant would also create such wonder. So, *it is* easier today to be a creative master teacher than it was in the first half of the 20th century. The question remains, then, of whether or not educators and the public want to nurture this aspect of education, and if so, how to best implement its progress.

If a poll were taken, one would hope that the first part of the proposed question would receive a resounding yes! All indications are that both educators and parents *do* wish the best possible teachers, facilities and equipment. The caliber of new schools, innovation of TV, mass curriculum work, citizens committees, along with increased positive coverage in mass media, etc., show this interest. What then are the criteria for developing the creative master teacher role in the maximum number of individuals with the potential for this role?

First, both in importance and magnitude, is the role of *administration.* If the total chain of administrative command is not dedicated to this concept no amount of interest by teachers or public will allow development of creative master teachers. Specifically, there are several areas of administrative responsibility. Concurrently are the criteria for teachers:

1. In the individual school, the principal must have several characteristics and attitudes. It is no longer possible for one individual to be "up on" all subject matter changes, be a financial genius and a building and furnishing expert. Therefore, his greatest challenge is to provide the attitudes that will best serve the interests of his staff. This involves both the staff as individuals and the welfare of the staff as a whole. The first necessitates a positive encouragement for creative teaching. Enthusiasm is catching. If a teacher approaches a principal with a new idea and is told "Let's wait and see how it works out in Timbuctu," creativity is stifled. If on the other hand the administrator is encouraging and takes the time to help the teacher work the "bugs" out of the plan, creativity is served. Not only that, but the rapport between administration and staff is strengthened! The principal must use discretion in allowing new ideas to be tried. He must, also, firmly, but kindly, be able to reject ideas. The teachers involved must be willing to work *with* the principal on these areas and not just feel they are working *for* him.

   The second important attribute for a creative environment is praise and recognition. A principal really interested in creative teaching will be as generous with praise as he is ready to criticize. This awareness of excellence in the classroom should involve definite and specific reports to higher administration and the board of education. Outstanding work might even be presented to the local press. Too often creativity withers aborning for lack of a few words of praise and encouragement.

   Last, a suggestion that may cause some negative response. That is, that the principal should be more severe with poor or mediocre teaching. This necessitates a strong district policy on teacher competence. But in the past it has too often been the role of both principal and superintendent to be "good guys" and appear not to see sloppy and inadequate teaching. If this is not done it can very drastically affect whether or not those teachers who can, will become creative master teachers. Being human, it is almost impossible to develop creative teaching when you are getting the same salary, same evaluations and same recognition as the individual who is a page turning, textbook reading, lazy sluggard!

2. Second is the responsibility of the superintendent and board of education. Most of this responsibility revolves around finances. Creative master teaching *is* more expensive than mediocrity! If both we and the public wish it to be fostered, it must be paid for. A constructive attitude toward the cost of innovation is essential. Along with the responsibility for financing creative master teach-

ing is the need for these people to be aware of what is being done in the classroom. Communication (or lack of it), probably presents the biggest bugaboo in education. Informing top administration and the governing board of creative master teaching in a large district is often neglected. This is where the vital role of the principal is seen. He *must* see that the work of his creative teachers is presented to the superintendent and board. For outstanding creativity, it is essential for the superintendent and board to recognize excellence. It is rarely possible to do this in any material way, but a letter of commendation can often mean as much or more than money.

Lastly, districts must look to innovations in its own philosophies that will motivate creative master teaching. Some specific areas that should be considered are: professional recognition of creative teaching; commitment to the need for paraprofessionals; salary increments for extensive creativity (writing a book; developing a syllabus; evolving a complete series of illustrative material; etc.); willingness to grant sabbatical leaves to those willing to take them; organization of *meaningful* inservice training; well paid summer workshops; release time for creativity; and willingness to foster excellence in any reasonable way.

3. What is the teacher's role? This is so self-evident that it is probably not necessary to reiterate. Actually, the definition originally given of a creative master teacher covers most of the criteria.

There are a few additional professional attitudes that will aid the creative climate. One of these involves the role of the teacher in supervising practice teachers and/or beginning teachers. While principals often neglect to chastise peers doing a mediocre job, we often are too soft hearted in evaluating student teachers. How often have you said to a colleague, "I really shouldn't have given him a good grade in student teaching, but he was a nice guy." We *do not* need "good guys" in teaching—we need good teachers! This is our responsibility. Until we are willing and able to police our own ranks, we will not have a climate for creative master teaching!

The other attitude change involves the teacher-administrator relationship. Too often in the past the teaching staff and administration were so widely separated in philosophy that there was actually undeclared war. Sometimes this is inevitable. A strong staff and a weak administrator (or vice versa) are bound to be at swords points. But this does not happen very often anymore, even though the distrustful attitudes generated by dictator principals and/or mutinous teachers still persist. Today we must eliminate the idea that administration is the bully looking for errors to pick on and criticize. Also, administration must eliminate the stereotype of the Cro-Magnon character of teachers!

Nothing new has been said, really. But it seems a good point in time to reconsider the needs and aims of excellence in education. Creativity and master teaching are well within the capacity of most individuals in education. Much of it is being thwarted, however, by a climate that is just slightly less than adequate. It is as foolish to waste creative teaching as it is to allow inefficiency in industry!

38 | Differentiated Staffing
Putting Teacher Talent to Work

Dwight W. Allen

Considering all the talk in education today about meeting the individual needs of students, attention to individual differences among teachers is long overdue. Common sense tells us that the needs of the student unlucky enough to sit out the year in a math class taught by an incompetent teacher are not being met, to say nothing of the needs of the teacher, who may be highly competent to plan a new algebra course or who may be a master at small group instruction. Neither the student, the teacher, nor education is served by staffing patterns that allow this kind of thing to happen. It happens because we staff schools as though differences in teacher ability don't exist or don't matter if they do.

Under these illogical circumstances, endurance becomes the only logical criterion for rewarding teachers, and so we reward them with tenure and a pay scale based on longevity. In staffing schools we ignore the educational needs of most students, and the professional aspects of teaching.

If the case seems overstated, it is because the waste that results can scarcely be overstated. A great many of the most talented teachers are quitting or accepting promotions away from students and into administration to get more status or more money, or simply to find some outlet for their talent and enthusiasm. More students than we would like to admit are failing or dropping out because fate (certainly not planning) has unwittingly placed in the classroom next door the teacher who might have encouraged them to continue school. Good money follows bad as more teachers are hired to make up for the inefficient use of teaching talent hidden but on hand.

Innovation that does not fit the interchangeable-parts pattern of teacher assignment now used dies stillborn, whatever its potential. The malady is obvious and the list of symptoms are threatening to compound the waste.

If the way we staff public schools doesn't make sense and is so terribly wasteful, why don't we abandon it? I suggest we do just that, fully aware that the journey from the certainty of the cure will be at times perilous and never easy. To me, and I hope to most thinking educators, the certainty of the disease should be motivation enough.

From *Pennsylvania School Journal*, Vol. 118 (December 1969), pp. 100-102, 144. Reprinted by permission of the publisher.

A FOUR-LEVEL STRUCTURE

Fundamental to the differentiated teaching staff I propose is a four-level structure within which both the levels and the kinds of teaching responsibility can be assigned and rewarded in keeping with identified educational functions and professional needs. Under the plan (which I have no reason to believe offers the ultimate answer to all the problems just described), teachers at the top two levels of responsibility would be hired on a 12-month contract and those at the bottom two levels on the same 10-month contract and under the same tenure rules as teachers are hired now.

Senior staff members, for purposes of illustration called *Professors* and *Senior Teachers*, would represent no more and usually less than 25 percent of the total staff and could not hold tenure in these positions other than that for which their annual performance qualified them. They might hold tenure, however, at the two lower levels, labeled here as *Staff Teachers* and *Associate Teachers*.

Despite what the labels might imply, I am not suggesting a new bureaucracy or a hierarchy that gives recognition to an elite. I am suggesting a structure based on levels of responsibility in a teaching organization that takes its overall shape from what needs to be done educationally, now and in the future, in a given school, from what teachers are available and best qualified to be responsible for the tasks identified.

This, of course, presupposes a differentiation of tasks far beyond what the interchangeable-parts pattern has so far allowed. Considering the number of practical educational innovations now standing in the wings waiting for such an opening, this "new tasks" dimension should not surprise anyone.

Taking educational policy making out of the hands of the administrative hierarchy and sharing it among the most talented teachers is just one major objective of the differentiated staff concept. In this as in other respects it has no educational precedent, a fact worth noting by those who think it will be easy.

Professors and Senior Teachers, as members of a school cabinet chaired by the principal (also a Professor), would seek full authority from the school board and the superintendent to formulate new educational policy; to make decisions as to what educational functions should be served, how they should be served, and by whom they should be carried out; and in general to govern the school as an autonomous body. This does not mean the cabinet would not seek outside help. On the contrary, it would seek and get the kind of help in introducing constructive change that schools have been cut off from up to now.

I do not know, in specific terms, what the Professor at the top of a salary range rising to $18,000 per year would be doing that would make him worth that much more than an Associate Teacher at the top of a salary range rising to $7,500. I do not know because no one in the profession has implemented such a proposal. To find out we must look past failures in education full in the face and open the system wide enough to admit solutions that get to the root of the problem. I foresee incompetents approaching that high figure on the basis of longevity alone, and we can point to talented teachers easily worth $18,000 a year who left teaching long before coming close to $7,500. Investigations have established that a salary range of $5,800 to $18,000 could be accommodated within typical existing school budgets. In terms of educational returns, we are already paying more for less.

ROLES AND FUNCTIONS

The fact is that I do not want to know, in specific terms and *a priori*, what the Professor, Senior Teacher, Staff Teacher, and Associate Teacher will do. If I said the Professor would have a PhD, would be responsible for shaping the curriculum, researching new instructional techniques, and investigating new modes of learning, I might well be right in fact but wrong by omission. The same might be true if I said that the Senior Teacher would often be a department head, hold a master's degree, and be responsible for making the concepts and goals of the curriculum explicit for a given course or grade level.

The Staff Teacher then would be the most likely person to translate curriculum units and goals into highly teachable lesson plans and, along with Associate Teachers, to assume the major responsibility for carrying them out. I say major responsibility, because in the differentiated staff, no teacher at any level should be entirely cut off from teaching responsibility.

In a general sense, the foregoing examples describe teaching responsibilities at the various levels as I perceive them. More important, however, they imply the framework within which educational tasks will be identified and assigned. *A priori* job descriptions for the Professor, Senior Teacher, Staff Teacher and Associate Teacher could easily obviate the purpose of the differentiation is a dynamic principle to be applied over a period of time to roles within each level of responsibility and to specific functions within individual teaching roles.

When the occasion and his particular skills demand it, a Professor might spend some time on remedial work with a small group that might normally be handled by a Staff or Associate Teacher. An Associate Teacher with special knowledge or otherwise obtainable skill might be the principal lecturer in some in-service training program for senior staff. It is by such exceptions rather than by rules that the differentiated staff concept would prove itself valid.

ESSENTIALS OF DIFFERENTIATED STAFFING

Although the differentiated staff structure might be arranged on a number of basic patterns other than the four levels suggested here, three conditions are essential:

—A minimum of three differentiated staff teaching levels, each having a different salary range.

—A maximum salary at the top teaching category that is at least double the maximum at the lowest.

—Substantial direct teaching responsibility for all teachers at all salary levels, including those in the top brackets.

Simply inventing responsibility levels, writing job descriptions, and assigning teachers arbitrarily will not work because that is essentially what we are doing now. The differentiated staff concept calls for innovation and reorganization of the basic structure of our schools, with full participation in such reorganization by the teaching staff. Ideally, the state or private organizations should provide incentive funds to defray any initial implementation costs that might occur in revising instructional materials, facilities, and equipment.

NONTEACHING ASSIGNMENTS

Any proposal to employ teaching talent where it will do the most good must recognize that much of it is now being wasted at the ditto machine, monitoring the lunchroom, taking roll, and doing other jobs for which professional ability and salary are unnecessary. In addition, persons with technical skills common in industry but new to education are becoming increasingly essential to school teaching staffs. Both economy and necessity recommend that the differentiated school staff include an expanded nonteaching category of classified personnel to handle clerical functions.

Within this nonteaching category, as in the professional category, assignments should match responsibility with talent and competence. In the absence of a teacher, a bright clerical assistant familiar with the program and acting as a substitute would be more likely to sustain class progress in a course that a substitute teacher brought in from the outside. A technician's proposal in a school cabinet meeting could conceivably change the direction of a failing audiovisual program to one of success.

THE ACCEPTABILITY PROBLEM

Despite the plentiful examples of resistance to change, I contend that teachers will willingly innovate and experiment in a context in which responsibility does not exceed competence and in which com-

petence is mobilized and rewarded. So far, innovation has tended
to come from outside—usually brought in by some expert—and ap-
pended as a trial balloon, easily cut loose when it doesn't work by
itself or whenever it becomes a nuisance.

Where there has been an enlightened administration and teaching staff dedicated to improving the quality of education in the
school and looking for a way to do it, innovation has brought remarkable results. When it has failed under these circumstances, it
has been a failure qualified by a wholehearted attempt. The fact
that such attempts have been made and the examples of outstanding success should persuade us all that, throughout the public school
system, both the talent and the willingness to use it do exist. Experience with implementing flexible scheduling convinces me that,
within the differentiated staff, such talent would be many times more
viable.

I expect that teachers worn by years of mediocrity to fit smooth
and tight in the existing interchangeable pattern will resist being
jarred loose from a comfortable staff structure. It is possible that
there will be some initial expense in securing cooperation, or at least
compliance, from old guard elements by grandfather rights where
the incentives of the differentiated system seem threatening. If so,
it will be a cheap price to pay for liberalizing existing talent and for a
staffing system that attracts and retains the most qualified professionals. I do not believe hostility to a staffing pattern based on professional opportunity and just reward could be sustained for long.

I do not presume that the differentiated staff is the answer to
all the problems in education today or even to all those implied by
the potential advantages listed. I do say that existing staff and salary
patterns create a context in which the most pressing problems are
very difficult if not impossible to attack. The differentiated staff
structure, open-ended to functions identified and to identifying new
functions, brings educational decision making and problem solving
back to the point of contact between pupil and teacher, where all
education ultimately must find its meaning.

Teacher Satisfaction as a Function of Conditioning Factors in the School and Profession

39

Alexander M. Feldvebel

Job satisfaction is a rather global concept involving attitudes which people hold toward their work or toward factors associated with their work. The concept is not precise, and although it carries a lot of identical freight with such expressions as morale and esprit, we are not clear about the differences between these terms. The task of differentiating and explicating these concepts is outside of the scope of this paper. In spite of this objection, we will use these terms interchangeably and treat them as symbols of positive attitudes which individuals hold toward their work.

What is more, we must also be cautious about our assumptions concerning the sources of attitudes contributing to what we shall describe as job satisfaction. In a study conducted in industry, Brayfield and Crockett have warned against treating worker satisfaction as a global concept.[1] They have pointed out that most workers function in a number of social systems within and outside of the job situation. They also point out that conditions of the work performance on the job are seldom a means to satisfying relationships in all of these social systems. Differences in the orientation toward these various social systems and differences in the motivational structures of individuals accounts for a great deal of variability in job performance and job satisfaction within a work system that extends comparable, if not identical, work conditions to all its members.

It is one of our purposes here to examine a few of these conditioning factors in the school and teaching profession and to point out that motivational systems outside of, or ancillary to this job can be as potent in influencing individual attitudes as those inside of the system.

In addition to factors causing variability, there are those factors accounting for a commonality in experiences and the consequent common conditioning effect on attitudes. Some of these negative conditioning factors are so prevalent in the circumstances associated with teaching that one is inclined to consider them as almost indigenous to the profession. It is the position of this paper that although these pervasive factors are potent, their effects can be minimized and offset by imaginative personnel practices and policies.

From *The Clearing House*, Vol. 43 (September 1968), pp. 44-48. Reprinted by permission of the publisher.

1. Arthur H. Brayfield and Walter H. Crockett, "Employee Attitudes and Employee Performance," *Psychological Bulletin*, Vol. 52, 1955, pp. 396-424.

SEX, STATUS, AND JOB SATISFACTION IN TEACHING

Historically, the teaching profession in the United States has been a low status occupation. Josh Billings' 19th Century portrayal of "The Distrikt Skoolmaster" has been an image that has persisted throughout much of the history of education in the United States and has been softened only somewhat in recent times. As Billings relates, the "skoolmaster" is a man looked upon "with mixt pheelings of pitty and respekt." Josh also points out, "pitty and respekt, as a general mixtur, don't mix well." The present surge of teacher militancy is undoubtedly having a marked effect upon the remnants of the Billings' image of the schoolteacher.

Nevertheless, this heritage of low status has a marked conditioning effect upon those entering the profession and especially upon male teachers. The traditional male role as breadwinner has been embroidered with additional motives growing out of our middle class orientation to the achievement and success ethic. Status and success are closely identified with a number of job characteristics, but pre-eminent among them is the factor of monetary remuneration. Low salary standards are, as a rule, related to low status. In our society the successful man is the man who earns a high income. Another low status factor in teaching is the preoccupation with children which has been traditionally viewed as the work of women.

A study of school climate in a large midwest suburban high school[2] supports the hypothesis that differences in levels of esprit among faculty members are associated with differences in sex. Esprit was here defined as satisfaction derived from social and personal interactions in the school and was one subtest of an instrument intended to measure social climate in a school.

Lower male percepts of esprit in the school are probably further encouraged by the special control function which men are required to play in most school settings. Extra supervisory assignments in the school cafeteria, detention room, hall corridors, school bus, etc., are usually the domain of the male faculty member.

This finding leads to further speculation about differences between sexes in the profession. The greater need of the male for status in the occupation appears to be reflected, in part, in the distribution of sexes at the various grade levels of the school. Lowest status is associated with the youngest children at the lowest grade levels. This maldistribution is most evident at the primary school level for one extreme and at the college or university level at the other extreme. Here the ultimate in status is achieved when a professor has opted himself out of virtually all necessity to be associated with students and spends his time instead in the euphoria of research.

2. "Articulation Study," Unpublished Report of a Study of School Climates Conducted in 1965-66 at Bloom Township High School, Chicago Heights, Illinois.

The content of instruction appears to be another factor associated with status. The more esoteric the content of instruction, the more prestige associated with the position. Once again, differences in the grade level of instruction are associated with prestige and the consequent maldistribution of sexes.

What are the implications of these observations? Social attitudes can be offset in part by internal motivational systems. Administrators have an obligation to devise other avenues for the achievement of status within the school and for providing means of achieving intrinsic satisfaction from teaching. A school climate which recognizes and rewards innovativeness and experimentation, a mileau which encourages the development of the teacher's personal characteristics as opposed to the standardization of the teaching role, and the encouragement of profession-wide interests and activities on the part of teachers are examples of interventions which can maximize internal satisfaction within the teaching profession.

ROLE EXPECTATION, SOCIALIZATION, AND DEPERSONALIZATION OF TEACHER-PUPIL RELATIONSHIPS

In research reported by Dan Lortie[3] there is a hypothesis that teachers pass through three distinct stages. Stage one is characterized as a struggle to survive in coping with the day-to-day demands. Stage two is described as a period of experimentation in which the teacher is most likely to innovate and exercise creative energies in his work. The third and final stage is seen as a period of crystallization in which the teacher settles into a stable pattern of routines and practices. Resistance to change is a hallmark of this last stage.

Once again, the school study reported earlier has provided additional evidence to support a finding arrived at independently by another author. In this study, pupils perceive significantly greater supportiveness among those teachers who differ from their colleagues primarily on the basis of amount of teaching experience.

We are inclined to agree that the beginning teacher in any school system must fight a battle for survival. A particularly important skirmish is the matter of coming to terms with the pupils over the respective roles of dominance and subordination.[4] This is a very unstable relationship, particularly for the new teacher, and it depends more upon the amount of prestige and personal ascendency that the teacher is able to establish than upon school sanctions and authority

---

3. Dan C. Lortie, "Teacher Socialization—The Robinson Crusoe Model," *The Real World of the Beginning Teacher*, Report of the Nineteenth National TEPS Conference, Hotel Commodore, New York City, 1965.

4. Arthur L. Stinchcombe, *Rebellion in a High School* (Chicago: Quadrangle Books, Inc., 1964). Stinchcombe's study points up very poignantly the extent of the current rebellion against the traditional doctrine of adolescent inferiority.

that may be brought to bear. This is a period of experimentation in which the teacher is developing his self-image and testing out any models that he may strive to emulate. At this stage the teacher is most concerned about teacher-pupil rapport and makes unusual efforts to be "liked" by his pupils.

The new teacher fights this battle between authority and rapport and over a period of time develops personal adaptations and a style to assure his ascendency. An important factor in this development is the process of socialization experienced through colleague relationships. Sanctions for the ascendency of the teacher in his classroom relationships come not only from the administration but also from fellow teachers to the extent that his status with fellow teachers and the administration frequently hinges upon his capacity to establish this ascendency over his pupils. More often than not, the advice and council received urges a relationship with pupils that is formal, impersonal, and marked by social distance. It is no wonder that the pupil sees such a teacher as restrictive rather than supportive.

A teacher in responding to administrative and community requirements for discipline and control tends to see this as a primary function of the teacher. His role, in *loco parentis,* is even sanctioned by the courts. The teacher who has mastered this role tends to place his relationship with students on a depersonalized level. Along with this, there may come a certain depersonalization of the teacher. The teacher learns from his colleagues that he must maintain this social distance and depersonalization in order to carry out his control role as expected.

The teacher spends the vast majority of his time in interaction with students; it is highly unlikely that the kind of relationship described here will produce many satisfying personal experiences and it will minimize the personal influence that teachers may have upon pupils. It is suggested that precisely here is where the potential for satisfaction from pupil relationships is greatest.

One of the obvious implications is that programs of instructional supervision must take into much greater account the complexity and subtlety of the authority-rapport problem of the classroom teachers. There must be more satisfying ways of managing and directing pupil behavior than through a rigid formalization of relationships. It is suspected that a great many matters which are treated as behavior problems are in fact instructional problems. To treat these issues as behavior problems may resolve them in the short run, but they will reoccur for continual confrontation in the long run. Perceptive supervision must lay emphasis upon those instructional shortcomings which may be the source of behavior problems.

It must also be stressed that, although the teacher's role in the classroom is one which requires direction and control of pupil behavior, there is a wide choice of modes of control open to the teacher. The modes of command and punishment are styles which, if used to the exclusion of other forms of more personal influence, are sterile and self-defeating techniques in pupil relationships.

THE STEREOTYPE SYNDROME

In Lortie's research[5] it is reported that after five years of teaching experience the teacher tends to become more conservative and resistant to change. He attributes this to the "moss of psychological investment" that the teacher has in the particular style or mode of teaching which he has developed. In the study of school climates there is an indication that pupils perceive instruction by the more experienced teacher as more "task oriented" and more "routine" whereas the younger teacher is seen as more "stimulating." These perceptions are supported by the teacher's own perceptions of the classroom climate.

As we have already suggested, the teacher in his early years of experience has not yet established a firm professional self-concept. The whole experience of teaching must be described as experimental at this stage. The teacher is experimenting with subject matter, with his teaching methods, and in his relationships with pupils. In addition, he is closer in age and outlook to his students. All of this introduces variability into his job and his outlook toward the job.

There is, however, the risk in teaching, as in any other profession requiring a habitual response to recurring social situations, to respond in stereotyped ways. The development of specialization and a proficiency along a particular line may be responsible for a loss in general adaptability and a deepening of certain grooves. As we have indicated, the experienced teacher sooner or later develops his self-concept as a teacher and more likely than not he resolves the problems of student relationships on the side of authority, dignity, and social distance. Intercourse with students is limited to "business" and relationships tend to be characterized by a shutting off of any student behavior which threatens this equilibrium.

In addition, the experienced teacher may come to look upon his task as a continuously recurring demand to "drill" his students. The zest of exploration and experimentation may have lost its glow and the teacher may become cynical by what is sometimes described as the "drag of the adolescent mind."

It is clear that these kinds of attitudes do not develop in all experienced teachers nor are we prepared to say what proportion of them can be described by this process. The answer to this problem lies perhaps in a closer look at the experienced teacher for whom teaching is a continuous experiment requiring continuous adaptation and renewal of outlook.

5. *Op. cit.*

We are inclined to believe that the process of team teaching, at its best, carries with it an inherent tendency to bring out the dynamic and self-renewing aspect of teaching. There is a built-in requirement of continuous professional dialogue with colleagues and an incentive to teach well not only for the sake of students but almost as much for the fellow teachers who are also observers. Once again, an incentive or a motivational system ancillary to the classroom can have a significant bearing on job performance and job satisfaction.

In summary, we can see that teacher satisfaction is subject to conditioning by factors inside and outside of the profession. To understand these various motivational systems and the effect that they have upon teacher attitudes is a first step in devising policies and in developing an organizational climate which will minimize negative effects and maximize positive tendencies.

The whole question of how job satisfaction may be related to job performance is another problem. We will not attempt to explore this question, although there exists an unexamined assumption that higher teacher satisfaction will be reflected in improved job performance. Whether or not this is true, it would seem that the encouragement of positive work attitudes and the feeling of personal well-being associated with this is an end worthwhile in itself. The school administrator must recognize that the ideographic goals and purposes of individuals in the organization are his legitimate concern even though they cannot be demonstrably related to the furtherance of organization goals.

Organization and Training of Paraprofessionals | 40

Frank P. Bazeli

Recent advances in the professional status of teachers and startling adaptations of technical procedures to education have prompted leaders in the field to abandon stereotyped concepts of school staffing patterns and teacher roles. New organizations, which include a support staff of paraprofessionals in every school, are now proposed.[1]

To be sure, most schools today operate substantially as they did 30 years ago. Teachers remain locked in a role hierarchy which is not quite professional in status and largely sub-professional in nature. The routine activities required of them every school day seldom permit more than limited attention and energy being spent upon the diagnosis of pupil learning progress and in the development of sound teaching strategies. This situation will not continue for long.

Within the next generation, large urban and suburban schools will change over to administrative operations utilizing advanced systems procedures and sophisticated computer and data bank hardware. New sets of interrelationships are evolving, in which the professional faculty will no longer be clearly subordinate to the administrative staff. School administration will become a support and service function. Master teachers with at least six years of professional preparation will be largely self-disciplined. They will be strongly represented in policy decisions and will have relative freedom to initiate and carry through applications of the latest research in education. Newly graduated teachers will intern in learning centers under the direction of the master teachers, and with the support of paraprofessional technicians and sub-professionals.

Other professionally directed services provided in large, progressive schools will include a counseling and test center, a media production and distribution department, and an information retrieval center (the old library). Each of these service centers will employ various types of paraprofessional specialists and sub-professional personnel.

From *The Clearing House*, Vol. 44 (December 1969), pp. 206-209. Reprinted by permission of the publisher.

1. Wayne Newlin, "It Can be Done: Teacher Aides Can Make a Difference in Illinois," *Illinois Education*, Vol. 30, No. 5 (January, 1968), pp. 213-216.

Roy A. Edelfelt, "Staffing for the Changing Pattern of Organization for Instruction and Learning," *Virginia Journal of Education*, Vol. 62 (September, 1968), pp. 15-17.

National Commission on Teacher Education and Professional Standards, NEA, "Auxiliary School Personnel," Reprinted in *National Elementary Principal*, Vol. 46 (May, 1967), pp. 6-12.

THE SUB-PROFESSIONAL STAFF

While still in the initial stages of institutionalization, it is fairly clear that the support staff will include a hierarchy of positions with at least two major divisions: the paraprofessional specialists with from two to four years of advanced preparation, and sub-professional personnel with limited training. This hierarchy of job levels will provide opportunities for advancement and specialization after suitable preparation and experience to those individuals who seek it.

The sub-professional staff will assume, in general, two types of service functions: monitorial control of pupil activities outside of the learning centers, and clerical help for the teaching faculty and the professional personnel in the service centers. While no distinct titles have been given to individuals performing these duties, for the purpose of differentiation they might be called "staff aides" and "clerical aides."

The roles of the staff aides will include those pupil control tasks now taking up so much of teacher time. Under the direction of administrators and teachers the staff aides will monitor pupil traffic where necessary in corridors, the cafeteria, at assemblies and other gatherings, on field trips, and outdoors. In addition, their usefulness will range into any activity which may be enhanced by the experience and understanding of an adult. In effect the staff aides will provide the professional faculty with a pool of adult resources highly useful in many facets of the school program and operation.

The clerical aides will relieve the faculty of the second most burdensome set of sub-professional duties, which consume so large a part of the school day. Assigned to instructional teams, and employed in the service centers, the clerical aides will be responsible for essential organizational routines, record keeping, typing, filing, duplicating, inventory control, and other duties which facilitate the smooth operation of the school. This will allow the faculty to address itself more fully to pressing professional problems.[2]

RECRUITMENT, SELECTION, AND TRAINING

The recruitment of sub-professional aides ought to be confined, where possible, to applicants living within the school community. This is important especially within the inner city of large urban districts. Aside from the accrual of economic benefits and job opportunities, substantial numbers of individuals, working as full- or part-time employees in the neighborhood school, open up a communications channel of great mutual value.

In the community the aides will constitute a cadre knowledgeable about the operation and organization of the school. Through

2. Julia H. Hill, "Expanding Teaching Time and Talents," *School and Community*, Vol. 55 (October, 1968), pp. 24-25.

informal contacts the aides could make known to parents effective ways to interact with the school, aid their children in the education process, and alleviate the fear and suspicion often blocking meaningful relationships. Locally recruited aides would benefit the school through their ability to interpret community sentiments and needs, identify and help contact indigenous leaders, interpret to the professional staff the substance of unfamiliar sub-cultural mores motivating pupil behavior, and influence to a considerable extent the curriculum offerings and teaching strategies in the school.[3]

In effect the recruitment of local residents for sub-professional aide positions in the school will dispel to some degree the situation which frequently occurs in which the school is seen as an outpost of an alien, dominant society within the sub-culture of the neighborhood. The school will more truly belong to the community which it serves.

Because the staff and clerical aide roles do not require a great deal of specialized training, the selection criterion in education might be set at about the high school completion level, signified by a diploma or its equivalent. Special talents, skills, experience and maturity should be weighed more heavily than formal credits, at least at the entrance stage. Some attention ought to be paid to the applicants' ability to articulate, to assume responsibility, and to evidence of freedom from serious physical and mental health problems.

Pre-service training of sub-professional personnel will probably remain the responsibility of the school system. It is important that the district develop an organized, carefully planned program in which all new employees should be paid and required to attend prior to taking up duties at individual schools. While each program will reflect the special needs of the system, a pre-service training period might take three weeks, probably held just prior to the opening of school, and cover the following general areas of concern:

1. An orientation to the organization of the school district and to the operational structure of individual schools, with attention to educational processes and programs.
2. An examination of the roles of the subprofessional staff in the school organization, their work relationships with other personnel, and conditions of employment, promotion, and retention. Eventually, these conditions will be negotiated in union contracts.
3. An overview of child growth and development, with special attention to the problems of children as they strive for emotional, intellectual, and social maturity. Policy concerning treatment of pupils must be carefully spelled out.

3. Barry A. Passett and Glenn M. Parker, "The Poor Bring Adult Education to the Ghetto," *Adult Leadership*, Vol. 16 (March, 1968), pp. 326-328+.

In-service programs may be planned and conducted on the individual school level. These programs should reflect the peculiar needs of the school, its staff, and the community which it serves. Sub-professional aides should be given every opportunity for personal development leading to increased pay and promotion.

THE PARAPROFESSIONAL STAFF

The advancement of professionalism in education is in large measure due to adaptations of cybernetic technology to learning processes. With the introduction of teaching machines, talking typewriters, economical video-tape production and playback equipment, computer programming within individual schools or through tie-in devices, the conversion of libraries into sophisticated information retrieval centers which utilize data bank equipment and micro-film material, and the establishment of learning laboratories with individual programs through console controlled equipment, there is now arising an accelerated demand for specialists trained in educational technology.

Teachers will use technologists to facilitate production of programs, retrieve information for classroom presentations, and create the technical capabilities necessary for individual pupil progression. Further, technologists and cyberneticians will make it possible to establish rapid and efficient administrative procedures on a school and district wide basis. Finally, trained specialists will perform the routines of testing and reporting evaluations of pupil progress, freeing counselors and teachers to function in their professional capacities.

A second category of paraprofessionals will provide direct assistance to teachers in carrying through the specifics of professional activities. Instructional aides under the supervision of teachers will tutor individual or small groups of pupils in specific skill development, work with them on research projects, demonstrate specific operations and experiments in classrooms, laboratories, and shops, and, in fact, perform many duties now considered professional in nature.[4]

RECRUITMENT, SELECTION, AND TRAINING

Recruitment of educational technologists and instructional aides will likely parallel practices current in filling teaching positions. For

4. Dwight W. Allen and Donald DeLay, "Stanford's Computer System Gives Scheduling Freedom to 26 Districts," *Nations Schools*, Vol. 77, No. 3 (March, 1966), pp. 124-125.
Lamont Jensen, "The Instructional Aide in the Open Biology Laboratory," *The American Biology Teacher*, Vol. 29 (December, 1967), pp. 748-749.

the present and near future, graduates of junior colleges and private technical schools will comprise the bulk of applicants. As schools become even more technically and professionally oriented, more advanced programs will probably be established at four-year colleges and universities. This will be true especially for instructional aides. Eventually, as much preparation will be required for advanced level instructional aides as is now demanded of entrance level teachers.

An associate degree in educational technology or instruction will probably become the standard criterion for the selection of applicants for some time to come. Junior colleges have an opportunity to create programs and establish themselves as prime suppliers of specialists for these positions. Due to the demands of business, programs for the preparation of computer programmers and systems analysts are well established in most community colleges and many are presently initiating preparation sequences for specialists in education. In addition to courses in general education and major fields, most teacher aide sequences require courses in "Introduction to Education," and "Educational Psychology." An excellent program would include a methods course with a related practicum or internship under the guidance of cooperating professional staff and college supervisors in local schools.

It is expected that many capable educational specialists, through the encouragement of enlightened school systems, will continue their education until they achieve professional status.

PERSONALIZED INSTRUCTION

The adaptation of cybernetics to school operation and the incorporation of support staffs of paraprofessionals will make it possible for children to be freed from the mass education methods, which waste so much human potential in traditional schools. While there is a real danger that the computer age may result in a dehumanized education process, this need not and should not happen. The use of a differentiated staff will allow teachers to spend most of their time in close, personal and professional contact with their pupils on an individual and small group basis. This intimate attention will enable children to progress at their own speed with the elimination of grade failure. The replacement of regimented class session by more flexible learning center activities will allow for greater personal interaction between pupils. This will promote social and emotional growth and provide many more opportunities for the exercise of leadership and self-discipline.

Frustrations permeate the learning process. The personalized attention of a differentiated staff can prevent these frustrations from becoming permanent blocks to pupil progress. Instead, learning defeats may be turned into valuable lessons in creative problem solving and skill development.

41 | Nonprofessional Aides in Science
The Paraprofessional Smooths
Teachers' Days

H. M. Louderback

The idea that the science teacher can single-handedly be the "do
all and know all" in the teaching of science is almost as archaic
as to imagine a physician doing heart transplant operations by himself. Along with team teaching, where the plan is to use talents of
individual teachers in a common effort, there is a new school staff
member called a paraprofessional. He is the technician whose special role frees the teacher to be a professional.

Almost every science teacher has used the laboratory assistant
at some time to help in the setting up of an experiment. In England,
secondary schools employ a technician to prepare solutions, unpack
and store supplies, and do the household tasks of science teaching.
A letter received last summer from a language teacher in England
whose daughter was soon to go up to the university, asked if we
could find her work as a technician for a year in an American school.
All of this finally catalyzed an idea. Why not hire a paraprofessional
to help the science teacher do a professional job of science teaching by freeing him from tasks that could be performed by a person
with a different training?

We secured approval for this project from the principal of Joel
E. Ferris High School and set out to find the man. Different ideas
were to use a college student, a person who had recently retired from
an organization with a science orientation, or a person who had retired from science teaching. Finally we obtained a man who had
worked as a machinist for Raytheon. He was retired and wanted
something to do. This gentleman is 70 years old, has all kinds of
"savvy" about practical matters, and has made the job of teaching
in our high school a great deal more pleasant as he has gone quietly
about the job of repairing balances, fixing microscopes, checking in
supplies, distributing materials to science teachers, and helping
other departments of the school. Recently I asked Mr. Campbell to
list some of the things he has done in his 70-hour month at Ferris.
This is what he said:

The paraprofessional is assigned to a department to be of service in
any job that comes up. He can be of great assistance to the individual
teacher as well as an asset to the department. There are certain duties
that can be performed by this assistant to relieve the teacher who is al-

From the *Science Teacher*, Vol. 31 (January 1969), pp. 58-59. Reprinted by permission
of the publisher.

ready pressed for time. There are many time-consuming jobs, not altogether in the teacher's line of duty, that can be taken care of by the paraprofessional.

Below are some activities the paraprofessional has carried out.

1. Numbering and cataloging science equipment
2. Repairing equipment
3. Building shelves and cabinets where students can deposit their daily assignments
4. Making visual aids
5. Recording the loan of equipment such as movie projectors, film-strip previewers, etc.
6. Cataloging science department books
7. Picking up and delivering mail and science periodicals
8. Posting notices and items of interest concerning science on bulletin boards
9. Hand printing master class schedules and preparing folders for convenience in handling
10. Hand printing material for the ozalid transparencies needed for large group presentations
11. Sitting in for teachers who need to be out of their classrooms for a few minutes
12. Cutting stencils
13. Numbering (painted numbers) and cataloging balances, meters, peg boards, microscopes, etc.
14. Painting peg boards for the IPS program
15. Repairing equipment such as recording timers, ammeters, balances, and microscope lights
16. Printing characters on blank typewriter keys
17. Building student paper deposit boxes with 5-6-24 sections
18. Making a dissecting instrument storage rack designed by a biology teacher
19. Making a rotating calendar of events for the dean of students
20. Repairing and setting glass in a large aquarium
21. Rebuilding wire seed package rack for displaying paperback books
22. Making a wooden molecular model of DNA
23. Making and setting dividers in material drawers of the chemistry stock room to increase storage
24. Making cubes of different sizes for visual study

When we first employed Mr. Campbell, we discussed possible "feast or famine" aspects of the job. Our fears were groundless, because there has always been more than he can do. Some present projects include: staining slides, making plant presses, making a drying rack, and rebuilding some cast-off refrigerators into incubators.

The job the paraprofessional does at Ferris makes life as a science teacher pleasanter and freer from frustrations than it used to be, but there is another benefit, too. It is important for some retired people to have something to do and to have a feeling of being useful. At Ferris hiring a nonprofessional aide has been a two-way street. We need our paraprofessional, and our paraprofessional needs us.

"You're Getting a | 42
Student Teacher!"

Leonard E. Kraft

"You're getting a student teacher," the caller from the super-intendent's office told the principal. "He'll be there Monday morning."

One might hypothesize that in this case the superintendent thought the principal was willing to work with student teachers and could do so effectively. But there is a great danger that under this procedure, student teaching in the public schools will be a hit-and-miss affair.

Why should school principals be interested in the education of student teachers? There are a number of reasons. For one thing, the role of the university laboratory school has changed from directing student teaching experiences to research, experimentation, and innovation. This leaves the public schools with a larger role in preparing future teachers. Also, a vast number of educators feel that student teachers are likely to have a more natural teaching situation in the public school. The outlook is that more and more school systems will be cooperating with colleges and universities in providing opportunity for student teaching, and it is important that this be done well. For these and other reasons, the public schools—and their principals—are very much involved in the education of teachers.

What are some of the important guidelines a principal might keep in mind if he receives a message from the superintendent's office saying, "You are getting a student teacher"?

BEFORE THE STUDENT TEACHER ARRIVES

1. Establish a current file of teachers qualified and willing to work with student teachers. A cooperating teacher should possess:

   A demonstrated ability to plan and organize his classroom

   A sense of security and a friendly and honest manner in his associations with children, faculty members, and parents

   An enthusiasm for his work

   A professional attitude toward his responsibilities with student teachers

From *The National Elementary Principal*, Vol. 45 (January 1966), pp. 17-18. Copyright: 1966, Department of Elementary School Principals, National Education Association, all rights reserved. Reprinted by permission of the publisher.

The willingness to permit student teachers the freedom to suggest and carry out ideas which they have developed thoughtfully

The capacity to be tolerant of the student teacher's mistakes

Better than average ability as a teacher

A desire to work with young people.

2. Assemble all pertinent information about the student teacher. Additional information may be requested when the student arrives.
3. Match the student teacher in terms of his qualifications, interests, and needs with the most appropriate qualified teacher. Often this may be done in cooperation with the superintendent's office or preparing institution.
4. Inform the staff of the assignment, including the student's name and college, where he will live, duration of assignment, etc. Notify the local newspaper and insert an article in the school newspaper.
5. Explain to the faculty their role with the student teacher.
6. Explain to other school personnel their role with the student.
7. Send the student a letter of welcome and an invitation to visit the school prior to his first day on the job.

WHEN THE STUDENT TEACHER ARRIVES

1. Give the student teacher, when he arrives, a general orientation to the school district, the local school (both program and facilities), and the community. If possible, introduce the student teacher in a general faculty meeting.
2. Describe the role of the student teacher, as you see it, in your school.
3. Provide the student with a copy of all necessary literature pertaining to the school and the school district. Policies and procedures, curriculum guides, and similar information are vital if the student teacher is to function properly.
4. Inform the student teacher that a file will be maintained on his performance while in your building and that he may add any information which might be of importance.

DURING THE STUDENT TEACHING

1. Treat the student teacher as nearly as possible in the same manner as the regular faculty. Provide an opportunity for the student to participate in all school functions.
2. Provide opportunity for the student teacher to visit with you at times, in addition to regularly scheduled conferences. At these meetings, you may discuss such things as the role of the classroom teacher; curriculum development; the role of professional

associations; the role of school administrators; and what you look for in interviewing a prospective teacher.

3. Make an effort to see the student teacher "in action" in various situations—in the classroom, in the teachers' lounge, on the playground.
4. Keep records of all observations.
5. Consult regularly with the cooperating teacher about the student teacher's progress and assist the cooperating teacher in providing the student with useful experiences.
6. Assist in the final evaluation of the student teacher, if called upon.
7. Provide opportunity for the student teacher to evaluate his experience in your school.
8. Evaluate the cooperating teacher's ability to work with a student teacher.

AFTER THE STUDENT TEACHER LEAVES

1. Maintain in the permanent file a copy of all information pertaining to the student teacher, including assignment, experiences, and evaluations by the university supervisor, cooperating teacher, and yourself. These records will aid you in recruiting good teachers; assist other employers who wish information about certain individuals; and assist you in the evaluation of your role in student teaching.
2. Consult with the preparing institution in an effort to assess and improve the way in which your school works with student teachers.

43 | Internal Communications

Frank C. Mayer

The effectiveness of a school administrator is governed to a large degree by his public relations skill and know-how. The stronger he is in public relations, the stronger he can be as an administrator. This is especially true today because of the community ferment and criticism which prevail in school districts. The administrator must have his staff and community "with him" if educational progress is to be made. The effective administrator must give priority of time and energy for effective communications and public relations.

BASIC THOUGHTS ON INTERNAL COMMUNICATIONS

Internal communication will always exist in every school whether school officials like it or not; whether officials are aware of it or not. The internal lines of communications will always be active and lively. In the absence of planned internal communication, the unplanned circuit will be haphazard, disorganized, and riddled with misinformation. Untempered sources will originate with teachers, custodians, secretaries—much of which will be inaccurate and prejudiced.

Communications can be classified as: (1) *one way*, (2) *feedback*, and (3) *two way*. The term *one way* refers to the public relations efforts or products which travel just one way—to staff members; no information is returned. Examples of one way media are newsletters and speeches.

The term *feedback* refers to the staff reaction to communications—the thoughts, opinions, reactions, and evaluations. Feedback occurs, for example, at a meeting of the Superintendent's Advisory Committee when members inform him of certain staff problems.

Two way media provide direct information to the audience and allow for a return reaction or flow of information. A teacher evaluation conference with a building principal in which information flows from both parties is an example of a two way process.

One way communication media are most often found in school-staff information programs—board reports, newsletters, news bulletins. They are most common because they are easy to produce, we are most familiar with them, and feel comfortable with them. There should be a balance, however, between one way, feedback, and two way efforts.

From the *Clearing House*, Vol. 44 (January 1970), pp. 290-295. Reprinted by permission of the publisher.

A Proper Foundation

The internal public relations program must have a proper foundation:

1. The board of education must insist on strong public relations; it must back this demand up with an adopted policy on school-community relations.
2. The central office staff, building principals, and staff must be public relations oriented and knowledgeable.
3. The educational program must be strong. An often used cliché among public relations personnel is "operate a good school program and you have the cornerstone of a good public relations program." When the program is riddled with deficiencies, time and energy is usurped in maintaining the program and in "plugging the holes."

A True Picture

A well balanced internal communication program must mirror a true picture of the school system—it must present accomplishments as well as problems and failures. It is tempting for the administration to present only the "positive picture" and "the beautiful" and to keep hidden the problems and unpleasantries. For example, if school buses arrive chronically behind schedule during the beginning of the school year, the administrator must air the problem with the staff and seek suggestions. If the achievement test scores drop over the previous year, the problem must be discussed with the staff and solutions sought. Shortcomings cannot be swept under the carpet! In today's society, criticism and dissent are a basic part of the American fabric and they will be an expected reaction from a communications program which presents the whole school story.

A Human Touch

To be effective, the communications program must have a "human touch." Communication can be cold and lifeless if a certain amount of human involvement isn't included. Face-to-face, person-to-person contact is a most effective two-way communication technique. Person-to-person contacts do not allow for reaching large numbers of the staff and are time consuming. There must be a balance, however, between the printed lifeless media and the personal face-to-face contact. The administrator must occasionally get away from his cobwebbed office to be with the troops. He should make a personal visit to the kitchen to talk with the ladies; he should talk with bus drivers and mechanics; he should visit in the teachers' lounge. A superintendent should periodically tour each school building with the principal at his side. The administrator's image must appear occasionally before members of his staff; he must be viable and visible. This provides the human touch needed for public relations and communications.

Warmth in Communications

Busy administrators must guard against writing notes or memos which are too formal, stiff, or cold. For example, a superintendent may have the school secretary relay a message to the music teacher, "Call the superintendent's office." It would be a warmer message, however, if the relayed message were, "The superintendent would like you to call his office to arrange for an ensemble request." A short, curt message from the superintendent may cause a worrisome teacher to think, "What did I do now? Is there something wrong?" The message with a human touch is worthy of the extra effort involved.

The Non-Certified Staff

The non-certified employees are the most neglected personnel in the field of school public relations. Too often the superintendent forgets about these school personnel and their part in the public relations program. He often neglects the highly important people who take or delete his phone calls, greet his visitors, and play host to the public. He must be reminded that the citizen's first impression of school often results from the efforts of the nonteaching staff. The appearance of the buildings and grounds, the way a visitor is greeted by the secretary are first impressions and lasting ones.

An Open Door Policy

The superintendent and his administrators must always maintain an "open door" policy and should always be willing to talk with staff members. Although staff grievances must first be presented to the immediate supervisor, if satisfaction is not received, they must be heard by the superintendent.

THE BELL STUDY

A study of supervisory-employee relations was conducted by the Illinois Bell Telephone Company to determine the effectiveness of face-to-face internal communications. The study, which parallels principal-teacher relationships, indicated that one-half or more of the employees would like to have more information from their supervisor and up to one-third felt that supervisors never discuss non-job-related subjects. Almost one-fourth indicated that they had no chance to ask questions of their superiors!

As businesses and schools become larger and more complex in operation, too many supervisors and principals have lost a part of the art of staff communication.

Bell employees gave the highest ratings for communications which involve (1) small group meetings, and (2) face-to-face talk with the supervisor.

Merton Knapp, assistant vice-president for Bell public relations, states, "We have found ourselves in the business persuading supervisors that it's to their own self-interest to talk to their people. We have found ourselves having to sell at all levels of management the idea not only that the company can afford the considerable time it takes for two-way discussion, but that the company cannot really afford not to take the time."

The most important responsibility of the building principal is to be the educational leader of his building. The additional demands for reports, evaluations, conferences, and administrative meetings require time and energy of the principal. To budget sufficient time for informal discussion and talk with the staff becomes a herculean task. The contemporary principal, however, must be well organized; he must decide on the priorities for his time and energy and must know how to budget his time. These many tasks and responsibilities become an impossibility for the "disorganized" building principal.

"ONE WAY" TECHNIQUES

Printed Communications

Printed school publications are the most widely used instruments to communicate with staff members. Teachers and noncertified personnel, however, are overwhelmed with printed materials in their school mailbox and in their homes. School personnel are very discriminate in what they read. Therefore, printed staff communications must be:

1. BRIEF
2. appealing in appearance and tone
3. balanced in appearance and content
4. laid out conducive to quick readability
5. properly distributed and timed

To illustrate point #5 we distribute a weekly staff newsletter, *The Monday Report*. Although it arrives at the buildings on Monday afternoon, occasionally a derelict secretary fails to distribute the publication until Tuesday. Some of the effectiveness is lost.

The Staff Newsletter

The staff newsletter keeps the staff informed—teachers, cooks, custodians, bus drivers, and secretaries. The newsletter should appear weekly; it must be brief (one or two pages), and written in a crisp, interesting syle.

A monthly staff newsletter, although making a contribution to the school public relations effort, is not able to present news which

is as fresh or current as a weekly publication and the more volumi-
nous the publication is, the fewer the people who will read it.

The Board of Education Summary

A summary of the board of education meeting should be available in each school building when the staff arrives for work the next
morning. The report can be placed on the teachers' bulletin board
or a copy placed in each staff mail box.

A Central Office staff member can prepare the summary as the
meeting progresses. A secretary can report early the following day to
prepare copies of the summary. A building secretary, principal, or
teacher who lives close to the central office can pick up the report
on the way to work.

A board report will help spike rumors which inevitably occur
following a board meeting. In the absence of a report, a verbal
inaccurate, grapevine version will be disseminated among staff
members.

Flash Report—An Immediate Announcement

Occasionally, a superintendent wishes to communicate an immediate message to his staff. A special form should be available for
this purpose. News of a levy passage or approval of a salary adjustment might justify such a special effort. A unique letterhead designed
for a news release allows quick identification of a special message.

Board Agendas

Board agendas should be made available to the staff prior to the
board session—at least a day or two before. Copies can be posted in
convenient locations such as office and lounge bulletin boards. The
teachers association building representative and principal should
receive a copy. The posting of agendas in advance helps keep the
staff informed and, more importantly, indicates to them that the administration operates in the open and doesn't seek to hide anything.

Principals' Report to the Board of Education

Each building principal should be asked to make a monthly, one
page report for the Board of Education on what has been happening
in his building. These reports, which are assembled and attached to
the monthly board agenda, serve several purposes:

1. they keep the board and superintendent informed about what is
   going on in the buildings;
2. they enable the principals to know what is occurring in other
   buildings, and, more importantly, the reports give them additional
   ideas for their own buildings;
3. they "prod" the do-nothing principal; he is easily identified when
   his monthly board reports are sterile and barren.

Special Recognition for Outstanding Work

A special certificate can be designed to recognize staff members who served beyond the call of duty during the school year. The certificate, signed by the superintendent, expresses appreciation for work contributed for such assignments as chairman of a committee; leading a special task force; keeping school buses in good running condition.

Use of Questionnaire Techniques

A superintendent requested that his principals evaluate staff morale. Some principals solicited feedback information through conferences with small groups of his staff; others talked individually with each faculty member. Another principal developed a questionnaire to obtain more objective information. The teachers completed the surveys anonymously and returned them to him for appraisal.

An evaluation of the district's "new teacher orientation program" can provide information for improving future orientations. Feedback information can be obtained by placing several beginning teachers on the orientation committee which plans the program. Additional evaluation can be obtained by sending a questionnaire to each new teacher. Included with the survey form should be a stamped return envelope, because some teachers hesitate returning a questionnaire through the school office for fear that the principal or secretary would identify the teacher with the returned questionnaire.

The "exit questionnaire" is another valuable source of staff information. Resigned employees, certified and noncertified, should be mailed an exit questionnaire shortly after they leave the district. A stamped, return envelope should be included. The questionnaire allows the ex-employee to evaluate the supervision, supplies, staff morale, program, and to make constructive criticisms.

Closed Circuit Television

Closed circuit television is being used increasingly for staff communication. Rather than have an entire school-wide faculty meeting, a superintendent can address his teachers via television as they remain in their home school.

Schools in Southwestern Ohio are using television for an in-service program on Negro history. The program originates weekly from Miami University (Oxford, Ohio) and is placed on tape. Principals schedule teachers to view the tapes at times which best suit them.

"TWO WAY" TECHNIQUES

The Superintendent's Advisory Committee

The Superintendent's Advisory Committee, composed of elected teacher representatives, can return valuable information to the superintendent. The committee can also serve a valuable function by disseminating information to the staff. Noncertified members can serve on the committee or they can meet as a separate group with the superintendent or business manager. The volume of feedback information will depend on how the group is permitted to function. The superintendent can dominate the committee and thereby throttle a great deal of feedback, or he can allow participants ample time for expression, thereby expediting the flow. Members must be able to express themselves freely without fear. They must be assured that there will be no retaliation; they serve with "diplomatic immunity." If the superintendent is not able to foster a "free flowing atmosphere," only candy-coated platitudes will be expressed by the representative.

The Advisory Committee sessions can help the administrator discover what is "bugging" staff members in sufficient time to keep problems from building up into major issues. The meetings can serve as a catharsis for pent up feelings and resentments held by staff members.

To reduce rumors, results should be summarized and a copy provided for each staff member a day or two following the meeting.

The Principals' Advisory Committee

The principal can obtain improved communications with his staff by also having an Advisory Committee. Members should be "elected" staff members and should meet with him periodically, as once a month. The principal should seek the advice of his committee when important decisions are to be made; he should encourage feedback from his representatives on school problems and staff concerns.

Teachers at Board Meetings

A representative from the Teachers' Association should be present at each board meeting. The representative indicates that the teachers are interested; he can carry information to the staff; he will be available as a source of information. Educational topics are often presented for the board by members of the staff on topics related to the educational program such as "the teaching of reading" or "elementary libraries."

Such teacher presentations:

1. help build understanding between the board of education and teachers;
2. keep the board better informed about the educational program;
3. expose or acquaint board members with outstanding teachers;
4. give the opportunity for teacher recognition.

The Public Relations Committee

A school public relations committee can be most useful. The public relations committee, for example, which advises me, is made al Staff* 271

up of teachers, classified personnel, students, parents, a representative of the press, and a representative of the radio. The first project of the committee was to evaluate the effectiveness of the staff newsletter and the Superintendent's Advisory Summary. Each staff representative is also charged with the responsibility for encouraging maximum news reporting for his building.

The Curriculum Council

A district-wide Curriculum Council enables the staff to work together and builds staff confidence since the administration is allowing teachers to guide curriculum improvements.

A district Curriculum Council should begin in the individual school. A Curriculum Committee should be elected from that school to study building curriculum problems. A teacher from this committee should be selected for the district Curriculum Council. Members of the Curriculum Council should be given released time for their meetings; the Council should have a budget. Although the superintendent would review the recommendations of the Council and has the right to veto, this power should rarely, if ever, be used. Recommendations of the Council should be implemented as quickly as possible.

Service Awards

Staff members should be recognized for long service. Business and industry honor their personnel for years of service. Schools, too must show recognition for staff members. A banquet provides a nice setting for such recognition. Staff members should receive a certificate or small gift for 10, 15, 20, 25 years of service. Local business and industry will often contribute money for such recognition banquets.

EVALUATION OF THE PROGRAM

The internal communications program must be evaluated. A questionnaire, distributed to staff members, can be used for such an evaluation. An outside team of public relations experts can be asked to evaluate the program. Such a team can be made up of public relations personnel borrowed from industry. Public relations consulting firms are available. Such evaluations identify ineffective techniques so that they can be discarded and provide a source of additional suggestions for an improved communications program.

CONCLUSION

Effective staff communications are not easily attained; developing effective internal communications is one of the most difficult school assignments. Although the school administrator may work diligently to strengthen communications, the network occasionally breaks down and he receives the brunt of criticism for poor communications. He must use an array of communications instruments and media, some of which will be successful; others will fail and have to be discarded. No stone can be left unturned in the search for better communications. The greater the effectiveness of the program, the greater can be the staff support for the school program and the administrators.

Communications in | 44
Large Secondary Schools |

Lloyd E. McCleary |

Communication is one of the chief concerns of secondary school principals, and they recognize that effective communication is a key to their success as administrators. These are conclusions to be drawn from the facts and comments provided by about a thousand principals of large high schools who participated in a nationwide study sponsored by the National Association of Secondary School Principals on practices and problems relating to intraschool communication. The present paper contains some of the data developed by the study supplemented by my comments as director of it.

For all that communications have been given attention in professional discussions for many years, actually very little of a factual sort was known about communication procedures and policies as they exist in large high schools. To provide more substance on which to base further discussion of communications problems, NASSP's Committee on the Larger Secondary School undertook the investigation reported here.

It was decided at the outset to use as the research population those secondary schools that enrolled more than 1,000 students and in which the principals were members of NASSP. More than 5,000 schools were available, as determined by these criteria. (Like most criteria used for selecting a research population, these are somewhat arbitrary; but they appeared to the investigators not to be unreasonable, and no unusual bias seemed inherent in their application.) The questionnaire by which the information was gathered was sent to every fourth name on the list turned out by the computer, a total of 1,240 principals. With usable responses from 80 percent of these men and women—969 individuals—there is every reason to believe that the data as summarized give a reliable picture of conditions as they exist in the schools.

FOCUS OF THE STUDY

The study aimed to obtain information about methods and media of communication, characteristics of communications systems in operation, principals' perceptions of needs and priorities for improvement, and some evaluation of the effectiveness of various practices. These elements of the study are reported in some detail.

From *NASSP Bulletin*, Vol. 52 (February 1968), pp. 48-61. Reprinted by permission of the National Association of Secondary School Principals. Copyright: 1968 by the National Association of Secondary School Principals.

In addition, the questionnaire was designed so as to test certain hypotheses relating to differences between types of schools and of communities, sizes of schools, and geographic location. Some of these findings are also presented.

An outline of the questionnaire follows to indicate the kind of data that were gathered.

GENERAL INFORMATION: School Enrollment, Grade Pattern, Type;
Community Population and Type

Part   I. Methods of Communication
    A. Means of facilitating communication among staff

Face-to-face	Frequency	Extent of principal's responsibility
Printed	Frequency	Extent of principal's responsibility
Visual-electronic	Frequency	Extent of principal's responsibility

    B. Means of communicating: principal and staff

| Face-to-face | Frequency | Rating of value |
| Written | Frequency | Rating of value |

Part II. Characteristics of Communications (checklist of conditions that characterize communications as judged by the principal)

Part III. Priorities for Improvement; Greatest Needs; Communications Best Utilized.

In addition to supplying the general information requested about school and community, each principal responded to 101 objective items, 10 items that permitted listing additional media or practices, and three open-ended questions. More than 75 percent of the responding principals made additional entries and more than 65 percent took the time to write one or more full paragraphs for each open-ended question.

Findings of the Study

Basic to the effective functioning of a professional staff are the means available and used to exchange ideas, share understandings, and negotiate differences. The principal is central to all these activities: He not only is largely responsible for planning and supporting the structure by which these kinds of interchange take place; he also sets the tone (and perhaps the unwritten rules) regarding what can be dealt with and how and with whom. One of the concerns of this study, therefore, was to discover the kind and frequency of opportunities for face-to-face communication and the extent of the principal's responsibility for or participation in these opportunities. Table 1 summarizes practices in the 969 schools in the study sample.

The methods most frequently reported by principals for bringing the entire staff or significant parts of it together in face-to-face situations are listed in the table in order of the relative frequency with which they are seemingly used with some regularity; that is, monthly or more often. General faculty meetings, department meetings, principal's cabinet meetings, and meetings of department chairmen lead all other types of gatherings by a significant margin. Of these four, as might be expected, the principal assumes the least direct role in department meetings.

TABLE 1

FREQUENCY OF USE OF VARIOUS FACE-TO-FACE COMMUNICATIONS PRACTICES IN LARGE HIGH SCHOOLS AND NATURE OF THE PRINCIPAL'S RESPONSIBILITY FOR EACH

METHODS AND MEDIA	FREQUENCY				PRINCIPAL'S RESPONSIBILITY			
	DAILY OR WKLY.	1 OR 2 PER MONTH	LESS THAN MTHLY.	NOT AT ALL	CON- DUCTS	DIRECT SUPER- VISION	GEN'L SUPER- VISION	NO RE- SPONSE
General faculty mtg.	6.6*	68.8	23.4	.1	67.0	25.0	5.4	2.5
Department meetings	5.7	66.3	24.6	1.1	4.0	8.1	81.2	6.4
Principal's cabinet	26.1	29.7	12.7	22.9	49.1	12.4	5.1	33.2
Dept. chairmen mtg.	9.6	45.7	28.8	9.8	35.8	19.8	23.8	20.4
Teacher teams mtg.	18.8	8.8	17.6	54.5	1.0	4.5	38.4	56.0
Standing committees	1.3	18.5	49.3	21.2	5.2	12.8	48.7	33.5
Ad hoc committees	2.0	6.2	34.7	28.8	4.2	11.7	26.7	57.3
T-group, "self-assess-ment" groups	1.1	2.5	20.2	55.5	3.2	4.4	16.8	75.8
All other groups	5.7	11.2	1.3	3.4	6.1	6.2	11.6	

* All percentages are based on the *total* sample.

In addition to the procedures specified in Table 1, a scattering of other practices were noted by 18 percent of the schools, but they were so varied that they could not be readily detailed in the table.

Although the responding principals checked only a relatively few methods of communicating with individual staff members in face-to-face settings, all of these few were being used by a large percentage of the principals. Further, these methods were highly valued by the administrators, as is clear from the data in Table 2. Written comments, reported in a later section of this paper, portrayed a strong desire to increase these activities and to make more effective use of them in obtaining staff members' views about problems and conditions and in obtaining a better understanding of their interests and coming to know them better as persons.

Individual, face-to-face communications represent the most perplexing dilemma for the principal of the large school. Repeatedly, respondents reported the frustration of too little time to confer adequately with individual staff members. Several of them listed entries from their appointment books and desk calendars to illustrate the numbers of individuals they were attempting to see during the work day. Some said they set aside Saturday mornings at certain times of the year to confer with individual staff members.

TABLE 2

EXTENT OF USE BY PRINCIPAL OF VARIOUS INDIVIDUAL FACE-TO-FACE
COMMUNICATION PRACTICES AND VALUE PLACED ON THESE PRACTICES BY
ADMINISTRATORS USING THEM

COMMUNICATION WITH INDIVIDUAL STAFF MEMBERS	FREQUENCY			PRINCIPALS' VALUE RATINGS*		
	REGU- LARLY	RARELY	NEVER	VERY HELP- FUL	HELP- FUL	LITTLE HELP
Classroom visits	84.1†	11.7	3.9	56.2	41.4	2.4
Individual conferences	82.8	9.2	7.9	75.4	23.5	1.1
Small group meetings	74.6	18.1	7.1	51.3	47.0	1.7
Social functions —lunch, coffee, etc.	57.1	35.4	7.2	34.8	47.1	18.1
Systematic interviews	45.9	32.6	21.2	40.2	37.6	22.2
Others	9.5	1.1				

* Value ratings are based on responses from principals making some use of practice.
† All percentages are based on the total sample.

More than 100 principals wrote that their schools had grown so large that they could no longer maintain an "open door" for staff members. Apparently, by training and disposition principals expect to relate directly with staff members and students; and they feel that school size has definitely limited their opportunities to maintain the kind of individual relationships which they prize highly.

WRITTEN COMMUNICATIONS

Table 3 lists the written communications most often cited by principals, arranged in descending order of frequency. Although the daily or weekly bulletin to the staff leads the list, it should be noted that in their comments principals expressed dissatisfaction with this means of communication far more frequently than with any other type in any category.

Writing can be of particular value in communicating information and directions, but it often is of limited value in communicating

TABLE 3

PERCENTAGES OF SCHOOLS USING VARIOUS FORMS OF WRITTEN COMMUNICATION AND EXTENT OF PRINCIPAL'S INVOLVEMENT

PRINTED MEDIA	FREQUENCY				PRINCIPAL'S RESPONSIBILITY			
	DAILY OR WKLY.	1 OR 2 PER MONTH	LESS THAN MTHLY.	NOT AT ALL	PRE-PARES	DIRECT SUPER-VISION	GEN'L SUPER-VISION	NO RE-SPONSE
Regular bulletins	68.7*	8.4	6.1	16.8	31.4	26.1	24.8	18.7
Special bulletins and announcements	45.7	30.1	17.5	11.2	45.8	31.4	9.1	14.4
Staff handbook or manual	8.1	2.3	66.7	22.4	28.3	31.8	18.7	21.2
Staff newsletter	5.1	9.9	11.3	73.4	.5	3.2	19.9	77.4
Reports of work groups	3.9	64.1	25.0	6.7				
Polls of staff opinion	2.9	35.5	48.4	12.5				
Surveys of practices	5.1	32.9	42.4	18.8				
Other printed media	6.0	5.1	6.1					

* All percentages are based on the *total* sample.

or in changing attitudes, opinions, and beliefs. Principals cited as most effective the use of written media to reinforce announced decisions, to follow up discussions, and to disseminate results of studies and deliberations. Apparently principals who use written media effectively attempt to link them to other forms of communication and do not rely upon the written word alone to communicate changes in procedures or new ideas that run counter to current practices.

VISUAL-ELECTRONIC COMMUNICATION

A primary interest in studying communications in the large secondary school was to learn the extent to which visual-electronic media are utilized to overcome the problems caused by size and complexity of operation in such a school. The results of the survey were disappointing in terms of the effectiveness of visual-electronic media.

TABLE 4

FREQUENCY OF USE OF VARIOUS VISUAL-ELECTRONIC COMMUNICATIONS MEDIA AND THE NATURE OF THE PRINCIPAL'S INVOLVEMENT WITH THESE MEDIA

VISUAL-ELECTRONIC MEDIA	FREQUENCY				PRINCIPAL'S RESPONSIBILITY			
	DAILY OR WKLY.	1 OR 2 PER MONTH	LESS THAN MTHLY.	NOT AT ALL	CONDUCTS	DIRECT SUPERVISION	GEN'L SUPERVISION	NO RESPONSE
Intercom or P.A. system	74.0*	2.6	2.6	20.4	18.1	21.9	32.6	27.4
Conference telephone	16.2	2.3	4.5	76.9	6.5	4.9	10.0	78.6
Overhead projector in meetings	4.2	12.7	59.8	23.3	10.8	10.9	43.9	34.4
Slide projector in meetings	3.6	10.2	53.1	44.1	7.9	9.5	40.1	42.5
School-made tapes, voice	5.0	4.9	24.5	65.3	2.1	3.0	25.9	69.0
School-made video tapes, kinescopes	2.7	1.8	6.2	88.9	.5	.5	8.9	90.1
Closed circuit TV	4.9	.7	1.7	91.8	1.1	1.1	6.4	91.4
School radio	4.5	.8	1.1	93.5	1.2	2.6	25.6	90.6
All other	1.8	.6	2.0					

* All percentages are based on the *total* sample.

Seventy-four percent of the respondents reported that they use public address or intercom systems to communicate with staff on a daily or weekly basis; next most frequently used was the conference telephone. No more than five percent of the respondents reported the use of any other type of visual-electronic media as frequently as weekly. These data are given in Table 4.

Since a total of only 4.4 percent of the schools used any visual-electronic equipment other than the eight kinds specified in Table 4, it appears that newer media of communications are little used. But these newer media do have possibilities worth consideration by schools in which more traditional means of communication are overburdened. These new media can transmit information rapidly and accurately, and some can even facilitate person-to-person contacts.

CHARACTERISTICS OF COMMUNICATION PRACTICES

Each of the participating principals was also asked to respond to a list of questions which asked about the use of some one communications practice or policy. The kinds of responses that were possible are shown in this illustration:

Are school policies, rules, and regulations recorded and made readily available to staff, parents, and students?	YES	YES, WITH EXCEPTIONS	USUALLY NOT	No	CANNOT ANSWER

Principals typically rated conditions in their schools favorably. The six questions which most frequently received negative responses and the percentages of principals who checked "usually not" or "no" are as follows:

	USUALLY NOT OR NO (PERCENT)
1. Are checks made to see that communications are received and understood?	21.8
2. Are routes of appeal defined in event of disagreement or conflict between staff members and superiors?	19.7
3. Is the staff surveyed in a systematic way for opinions and suggestions relative to problems and issues?	19.4
4. Are communication channels specified in the written materials of the school?	15.2
5. Do staff members complain of the volume of communications?	12.5
6. Do staff members voluntarily report breakdowns in communications?	11.4

When comparisons are made of teachers' responses to similar questions as reported from other studies, and principals' responses as gathered in this investigation, characteristically principals rate conditions more favorably than do teachers. Therefore, indications of inadequate communication such as the foregoing six items point up deserve serious analysis.

Principals ought especially to consider the circumstances indicated by the responses to the first four of the foregoing items. One of the most common observations concerning ineffective administration is that there is a lack of follow-up on directives, announcements, and administrative decisions (Question 1). The next three items—relating to routes of appeal, solicitation of staff opinion, and specified channels of communication—also reflect common dissatisfactions of teachers.

A list of questions like the ones used in this study, asked of a school's teachers by the principal, could initiate a self-study that would lead to significantly improved communication in that school.

NEEDS, PRIORITIES, AND BEST USES

More than 600 of the principals responded to each of three open-ended questions with one or more paragraphs of comment. The principal was asked to identify (1) what he needed most to improve his school, (2) whether time, resources, or help had first priority in improving communications in his school, and (3) what communications were presently best utilized in his school.

Content analysis was employed to provide a substantive listing and frequency count for each of the open-ended questions. As a group, the responses to these three questions reflected a high degree of sensitivity to communications processes in the administration of schools and to the responsibility for facilitating communications.

The greatest needs for improvement indicated by the comments of respondents centered upon the relationship of the principal and the staff. Most frequently reported was the need for time and help to increase personal contacts with staff, to work with new teachers, and to involve staff with planning and decision-making. Next most frequently reported was the desire to consult with staff in order to obtain feedback about the quality of teaching, problems of teacher-pupil and parent relations, and the interests teachers had in professional improvement.

Two other responses followed well behind those but were widely commented upon: (1)use of electronic media to expedite routine messages and information handling and (2) value of expert help to systematize and improve the quality of communications.

Reflecting the needs they saw as greatest, principals gave the highest priority in improving communications to freeing teachers and department chairmen for group work within the school day and to increasing the informal, direct contact of the principal with teachers in order to exchange ideas, discuss problems, and share experiences. Judged next in order of importance were introducing parents and resource people into the school and improving the quality of department and faculty meetings through better planning and concentration upon improved instruction.

Among the communications methods best utilized at present, principals listed in this order: individual conferences, small-group planning meetings, faculty meetings, personal contacts, daily or weekly bulletins, and intercom systems.

DIFFERENCES AMONG TYPES OF SCHOOLS

Several hypotheses were tested statistically. These related to differences expected among categories of schools. Of the sample, 95.3 percent were public schools, 2.6 percent were parochial schools, and 2.1 percent were independent schools. The statistics which follow concern the kinds of schools and types of communities included in the sample.

KIND OF SCHOOL

ENROLLMENT	PERCENT	GRADE LEVELS	PERCENT
Under 999	8.2	6-8, 7-8	1.0
1,000-1,499	43.2	7-9	16.1
1,500-1,999	27.3	9-12	31.8
Above 2,000	21.1	10-12, 11-12	34.6
		Other	16.4

NATURE OF COMMUNITY

POPULATION	PERCENT		PERCENT
Under 10,000	9.8	City with	
10,000-49,999	42.9	rural area	30.0
50,000-199,999	25.2	City outside metro-	
Above 200,000	21.9	politan area	14.7
		Suburban	30.3
		City, metropolitan	
		center	24.9

A detailed account of the design and statistical treatments will not be undertaken in this article; however, a discussion of certain of the findings are pertinent.

No significant differences were found between categories of schools based upon size of enrollments. An initial error in listing the schools to be used resulted in introducing into the sample about 80 schools smaller than the criterion. Unintentionally, this made possible some unplanned comparisons. The only items in which these smaller schools differed from those schools classified as large was in their having intercom public address systems, and closed circuit TV less often. In all other respects the small schools could not be differentiated from the large ones.

This leads one to wonder whether large schools do indeed have problems quite different from those of smaller schools. Put another way, the question can be raised as to whether principals of large schools are still attempting to administer large schools as though they were small ones.

Schools in metropolitan centers (cities above 200,000) differed from "suburban" schools and from schools "outside of metropolitan areas" in the extent to which they used visual-electronic media but did not differ in use of face-to-face or written methods, as had been hypothesized. Further, no significant differences existed among these categories of schools in the frequency with which principals wrote about the need for direct contacts with staff.

These findings might lead to the conclusions that suburban schools are choosing to move into fuller use of electronic-visual media (and have the means to do so); and that principals of large schools in metropolitan areas value and try to develop direct, face-to-face staff relationships as much as do principals of large schools elsewhere. The myth that secondary schools in large cities are less personal is *not* supported by responses of principals from these schools.

Comments on the Findings

The objective data reported in the tables are open to interpretation by the reader. The nature of the sample and rate of return lend considerable confidence that these data present an accurate picture of the present status of communication conditions and practices in the large secondary school. Then, the question arises as to whether principals of large schools should seek to change this picture in any particular fashion.

Should an effort be made to increase the opportunities for bringing staff together? If so, which methods would be most useful and for what purposes? Should the principal increase his individual contacts with staff? If so, how is he to do this under the conditions of size and complexity of the organization he heads? Would the increased use of visual-electronic media facilitate communications? Perhaps principals can make use of these data against which to measure practice in their own schools.

SUGGESTIONS TO PRINCIPALS

Do not fall into the trap of readily blaming problems or the inability to solve problems on a failure in communications. Communications is not a cure-all. The principal might consider communications as (1) a system or network for obtaining and transmitting information and (2) a process for sharing understanding, diagnosing, deciding, and monitoring (or controlling) activity according to decisions made.

Thinking of communications as a network or system for obtaining and transmitting information relative to the operation of the school might mean arranging for such devices as bulletins, a public address system, individual conferences, group meetings, and the like, and training staff to use them. Individuals in the school organization, including the principal, then expect these devices to be available and used when required. The administrator's task is to see that communication devices are sufficient to link together the individuals in the school organization, that the individuals who are to use them understand and anticipate their use, and that the devices are adequate for the purposes they are meant to serve and the "load" of messages they are expected to carry.

The principal also needs to view communications as a process. In this regard, he might think of key administrative functions as a means of examining how he uses communications. Seven axioms which apply are described in the following paragraphs.

DIAGNOSIS

The principal is constantly engaged in diagnostic activity. Whenever he uses questioning or investigating devices such as an interview, questionnaire, and so on to gain information, he is using communications. In the communications system, he is the receiver. For example, he may raise the following kinds of questions: Does the curriculum need revision? Would a self-study lead to improved instruction? Can teachers be involved so they will be motivated to improve?

Any judgments he might reach imply courses of action; and in the process of making judgments the principal uses information-getting devices to reduce uncertainty (omitting the possibility that he may decide *a priori* to make decisions off-the-cuff).

Since time and circumstances never permit getting all the information needed to understand a problem and its conditions, the principal must decide which communications devices to employ.

1. *The principal needs to take into account the nature of his uncertainty as well as the value of the communication devices.* Some communications devices provide little gain in information even though they are valid—if the principal already knows how certain teachers feel, he gains little by interviewing them even though the interview per se is a valuable information-getting device.

2. *The principal must judge the communications devices he wishes to use on the basis of the fidelity required.* He may wish to inquire into many facets of a problem. As he proceeds he might conclude that a particular facet is not important and ignore it; he may remain uncertain about it; or he may decide that it is very important. If he has a range of communications devices at his disposal, he can fix on one facet of a problem and probe for maximum information; *or* he can try to get information about many aspects of a problem and accept less certain information.

Communications devices are either "wide-band" or "narrowband"—the principal can get fidelity only at the sacrifice of coverage and vice versa. This leads to a third axiom:

3. *The principal should incorporate both wide-band and narrowband devices into his communications system.* Responses to the study questionnaire lead to the inference that principals tend to base their communications networks on wide-band devices and pay little attention to narrow-band devices that give maximum information on specific questions.

DECISION-MAKING

The band-width and fidelity concepts help to make decisions more rational. One principal may want concrete facts and quick decisions. He decides upon the aspects of a problem he feels to be important; he narrows the field rapidly, obtains accurate information about relatively few things, and reaches a decision. Another principal may wish to consult widely, seek alternatives, delay decisions as long as possible, and attempt to get committees to judge the information obtained. Each, of course, is gambling, which does make administration exciting at times. But in any event,

4. *Principals should be conscious of the approach they are taking and make use of appropriate communications devices for decision making—narrow-band devices for fidelity, wide-band devices for coverage.*

5. *As the principal makes use of communications devices in his decisions, he should make judgments about the accuracy of information they are providing.* Irreversible, terminal decisions should be avoided when the information is incomplete or fallible. This is particularly true when the principal is making decisions about people, and most of his decisions affect people directly and indirectly. The degree of finality of a decision should be proportional to the accuracy of information upon which it is based. Whenever the accuracy of information is in doubt decisions should be cast in as tentative a fashion as possible, monitored, and corrections made as more information becomes available.

CONTROL

Administration, in one sense, is a formalized way of controlling organizational activity to achieve purposes that have been rationally decided.

6. *The principal needs to have a fully functioning communications system that provides continuous, accurate feedback.* Each procedure and process of the school's operation should be monitored so that decisions can be adjusted. Perhaps the greatest shortcoming in school administration occurs in this communications activity.

7. *The principal will need to decide what his communication system is to be sensitive to and how sensitive it shall be.* He can then build in new devices that insure coverage and fidelity, accurate and continuous feedback, and means of determining the accuracy of information he is using.

The foregoing seven principles will be useful to the principal in understanding how he is communicating and may help him to diagnose any communications problems he has. Hopefully, the study reported here and this brief examination of communication concepts will provide insights and useful measures of current practice.

45 | The Principal

A Machiavellian Guide for School Administrators

Laurence E. Ely

I have long pondered the lives of both eminent and obscure schoolmen. Years of study of these men would, I believed, disclose distinctions which might prevent other aspiring administrators from living out their professional lives unheeded and poorly paid.

It is a sad fact that what I have taken so many years to learn has come to me in age and too late to be of use to me. It is my hope that by making the results of my observations available, other schoolmen may not have to learn so many painful lessons from personal experience and thus can shorten the climb to success.

Although the precepts distilled from my experience are especially helpful to struggling schoolmen who have heretofore been denied the advancement to which their merits entitled them, they should be heeded by all those who are ambitious to rise in any profession or enterprise.

Among the challenges to the school administrator none is more pervasive or crucial to his success than personnel administration. For this reason I have formulated certain precepts whose efficacy in manipulating persons has been apparent to experienced and perspicacious men since man became a member of the tribe.

Should a favorable reception be accorded by initial effort to be of service to school administrators I will be encouraged to expand the *Handbook* to deal with such problems as curriculum development, school public relations, innovative projects, and attracting federal funds.

PRECEPTS FOR PERSONNEL ADMINISTRATION

Three phases of the school administrator's work require a cool head and systematically applied principles of personnel administration. These are: establishment of the administrator's status and building faculty good will, the inauguration of change, and the execution of the administrator's plans.

From *The Clearing House*, Vol. 43 (May 1969), pp. 519-522. Reprinted by permission of the publisher.

The heavy debt I owe to Machiavelli's *The Prince* is obvious. Niccolo Machiavelli, *The Prince and the Discourses* (The Ricci translation as revised by E. R. P. Vincent) (London: Oxford University Press, 1950).

Establishment of the Administrator's Status
and Building Faculty Good Will

1. Do not attack the faculty as a whole. If you do not they will be generally contented; thus you will only have to deal with the ambitions and envy of the few.

2. Like administrators in all well-ordered schools, you must strive not to drive the officers of the boards of education, department chairmen, curriculum coordinators, supervisors, etc. to desperation and you must try to satisfy the teaching staff and keep them contented.

3. Dwell at length and publicly on the merits of newly appointed staff members. This demonstrates your discernment and tends to inspire loyalty in the newcomers.

4. Nothing so surely secures to you the esteem of the staff as some remarkable action or saying dictated by your regard for their good, showing you to be magnanimous, liberal, and just. Another unfailing means for gaining their esteem is the launching of great enterprises.

5. You will be wise to keep the staff and student body occupied at convenient occasions of the year with festivities, popular causes, appearances on campus of discreetly radical personalities, and other celebrations; and as every school has its different departments, classes, clubs, athletic teams, fraternities, professional organizations, committees, etc., you ought to pay attention to all these groups, mingle with them from time to time, and give them an example of your interest and approachableness.

6. Let yourself be seen as often as practicable with celebrities of the community, being careful that this association is limited, as far as may be, to those who have gained the good will of the local citizens. However, it is not imprudent to share a rostrum or panel with a leader of the current, even if questionable, new movement.

7. Encourage staff members, on occasions propitious to your purposes, to mistake personal and departmental advancement and status for the welfare of students and the school. They will need very little stimulation from you as most of them cannot, in any case, avoid this mistake. Having made it, their energies and attention are somewhat diverted from you and they will value you for having encouraged them.

8. In disciplining a staff member, the entire action should be taken in one step, so that being less tasted, it will give less offense. However, benefits should be accorded little by little so that they may be the better enjoyed.

9. To threaten is more dangerous than actual disciplinary action. Therefore, you should guard against indulging in menacing statements and acts. For you bind your staff to you by benefits, or make sure of them in some other way. Never reduce them to the

alternatives of either having to defeat you or to be defeated by you.

10. It is advisable at times to feign folly and this is sufficiently done by praising, speaking, seeing, and doing things contrary to your own way of thinking but in order to please those whose support you require.

11. If your program prevails, you will be judged honorable and will be praised by almost everyone. Success, even of a bad program, will draw the admiration of many. The vulgar are always taken by appearances and the issue of the event, and the few who are not vulgar are isolated.

12. You may acquire esteem in any project; in success, as already noted, it follows as a matter of course; in failure it may also be acquired, either by showing that you were not at fault, or by promptly concluding some other project that neutralizes the effect of the failure.

13. As a wise school administrator, you will find it advisable from time to time to astutely foment some opposition, so that by suppressing it you will augment your official status and thus assure later successes.

Inauguration of Change

1. If you desire to reform some aspect of the school program (for example, the curriculum) and wish to have the changes accepted, you must at least retain the semblance of the old forms; so that it may seem to most of the staff that there has been no change in the institution. For most of the faculty are satisfied with appearances, as though they were realities, and are often more influenced by the things that seem than the things that are.

2. When about to make a move that may stir serious opposition, see that the leaders commit themselves to you on the issue privately and individually before you act. Weaker potential opponents, fearing to defy you face-to-face, generally capitulate and so are removed from the opposition. Others are forced, in advance, to expose themselves as your antagonists.

3. Of those who opposed you at the beginning of your administration, seek out the ones who are in need of your support to maintain their position and status, for these can easily be won over. They are the more compelled to support you as they know they must by their deeds cancel the bad opinion you previously had of them. Thus, you will always derive greater help from them than those who, feeling greater security because they always supported you, neglect your interests.

4. Do not hesitate to seek counsel but discourage absolutely all attempts to give you advice if you have not asked for it. Nevertheless, the formality of open lines of communication should be maintained.

5. If you feel that you must conspire to achieve your purposes, remember that whoever conspires cannot act alone and cannot find sympathetic ears except among those who are discontented; as soon as you have disclosed your intention to a malcontent, you give him the means of satisfying his own ends; for by revealing your intention, he can hope to assume his place among the more favored and loyal staff members. His gain is certain if he exposes you, but his position is full of danger and his gain doubtful if he conspires with you.

Execution of Plans

1. Consult most often those of whose opinion you already feel sure and who are most likely to support your position. It should be possible, in this manner, to muster what can be made to appear overwhelming support for any course that seems desirable to you.
2. Maneuver the strongest of the opponents and probable opponents of your plans into positions in which their self-interest will force them to oppose each other. The rivalry among them will call for little encouragement from you, as it is aroused inevitably by their ambition and by their competition for status, power, and funds. Thus their resistance to your plans is reduced or eliminated.
3. Do not afford your associates in the execution of your confidential plans any time to betray you. Confide your projects to them the moment of their execution and not sooner.
4. When the loyalty of your staff is in question, remember that there is no better indication of a man's character and loyalty than the company he keeps; for it is impossible that there should not be some similarity of character and habits between him and his associates.
5. You may talk freely with one man about everything. Unless he has committed himself in writing, the "yes" of one man is as good as the "no" of another. Therefore, you must guard most carefully against writing, for nothing will convict you quicker than your written word.
6. Beware of bringing others to power, for whoever is the cause of another's coming to power may himself be ruined. For power results from craft or force and both of these are suspect to the one who is raised to power.
7. Beware of the single-minded. When a man commits his energies and professional fortunes to one focus, as when he becomes a specialist, he takes leave of perspective and rationality. However, though he is perverse, his infirmity renders his behavior transparent and predictable and subject to manipulation.
8. Your projects may well be defeated when they become the subjects of professional meetings before you have prepared a proper

setting. Therefore, assure their favorable consideration by judicious frequenting, with the right people, of the fairways, the
lanes, the bridge tables, and the cocktail parties. The proposals
of an affable and sociable companion who is also a good host
are rarely rebuffed.

9. Time and energy, like other assets, are limited. None should be
   expended on an opponent who is without power of influence. At
   worst he is an annoyance that can be safely ignored.

10. When some program which you have sponsored is to be "evalu-
    ated," be sure that those charged with judging it identify their
    own success with that of the program. A fair and favorable
    evaluation can thus be assured.

11. Opposition is as much aroused by good works as by evil, and
    therefore if you wish to maintain your administration you will
    often be forced to carry out programs which you do not consider
    to be good. For when those parties, whether legislators, pro-
    fessional associations, commissioners of education, school board
    members, parents' associations, department chairmen, or faculty
    organizations (whichever it is that you consider necessary to you
    for keeping your position) are corrupt, you must follow their
    humor and satisfy them, for in that case good works will be
    against your interests.

*   *   *

The schoolman is obliged to know well how to act both as a fox
and a lion, for the lion cannot protect himself from traps and the
fox cannot protect himself from wolves. He must, therefore, be a fox
to recognize trickery and a lion to frighten the powerful. A prudent
schoolman ought not to keep faith when by so doing it would be
against his interest and the welfare of the school, and when the reasons which made him bind himself no longer exist. If men were all
good, this would be a bad precept. But they are bad, and would not
keep their faith with him, so he is not bound to keep faith with them.

The Principal
and Professional
Negotiations   VIII

The impact of professional negotiations on the quality of education is not yet known. One point is clear, however, negotiations will be a fact of life for educators for some time to come. Through the efforts of school boards, teachers, and administrators several workable patterns for negotiations were established in the decade of the sixties. Collective negotiations in the decade of the seventies could determine the fate of the secondary school principalship. Negotiations may propel the principalship into becoming a major force in the improvement of education or into a museum piece in the Education Hall of Fame.

"There is still time to outgrow the more petulant concepts of negotiation and to move toward more mature concepts of negotiation and to move toward more mature concepts of shared professional responsibilities." This statement expresses the position of the American Association of School Administrators toward professional negotiation in 1966. Time is running out.

Professional negotiations are not likely to promote the health, welfare, and spirits of the friendly, local building principal. Nevertheless, Lorraine W. Addelston maintains that the principal must be present in the negotiations of the educational authorities with the community representatives. She specifies four categories in which the principal should have a significant part.

The impact of negotiations is causing school boards to review and redefine the role of the principal. Joseph H. Cronin foresees two possibilities for the principalship as an outgrowth of negotiations: (1) it veers sharply to turn toward "instructional leadership" or (2) it hurtles further onward toward the role of building manager. The latter role is a dead-end street.

School principals throughout the country are striving to find their role in teacher-school board negotiations. Edward Keller reports on the activities of administrators in one state who organized to negotiate. He believes that principal organizations can negotiate to achieve their desired goals and to secure professional and personal rights.

Professional negotiations are creating new frontiers in education. David A. Singer describes the developmental pattern of professional negotiations and projects the growth of the movement. Through this new concept in human relations he envisions the improvement of the professional position of teachers in the South and the quality of education.

Negotiations are, in part, an outgrowth of teacher militancy. Reed H. Hagen identifies several causes which apparently contribute to teacher militancy and defines the role of the principal to meet this challenge.

School Administrators View Professional Negotiation | 46

American Association of School Administrators

Professional negotiation may be defined as a process by which teachers and other professional employees exert formal and deliberate influence upon school board policy. Properly viewed, professional negotiation is an orderly step in the steady evolution of democratic school administration, which has been in the process of development throughout this century at least. The slowness of this evolution may have had much to do with the rather sudden burst of demands of school staffs for fuller participation in the formulation of school policies—a demand that has been generally referred to as teacher militancy.

Doubtless this demand—sudden, sustained, and often stated in belligerent terms—came as a surprise to some superintendents and school boards, for the simple reason that many, if not most, believed that they had for years been pursuing enlightened, progressive personnel procedures. Superintendents and school boards felt that to consult with the professional staffs, to talk with them and listen to them, constituted democratic and satisfactory procedures in staff relations.

In some places, however, policy formulation was unilateral and frequently quite arbitrary. In such places, staffs were not consulted; they were told. Too little dependence was placed upon the competence and creativity of the individual teacher or of teacher organizations. It was thought that precise administrative procedures with creativity and direction flowing through proper channels was the epitome of efficiency.

Although boards and administrators have worked intensively and sincerely during the past decade to democratize school administration and increase staff participation in policy formulation, the pace has still been too slow for the flow of the times. School staffs working through their organization spokesmen have been moving faster in their concepts of what creative participation in the educational enterprise means, and they have begun demanding a real part in the process. They have begun demanding a change in the hierarchical machinery and the development of a horizontal concept of educational authority.

From *NEA Journal*, Vol. 56 (January 1967), pp. 23-25. Reprinted by permission of the publisher and author.

Doubtless this reordering would have come in time. But again the flow of the times has been too fast; the upsurge of the expectations of people, including teachers, has been too great.

So the "days that were" in school staff relationships are fast fading, giving way to formalized guarantees of staff participation in policy making, the planning of formal give-and-take negotiation, and provisions for appeal in cases of impasse.

To be sure, the old order remains here and there, accompanied by tenacious clinging to the status quo. Such outmoded concepts of administration, however, are rapidly being swept away in the flowing tide of social reform engulfing society and the schools.

In 1963, the Executive Committee and staff of the American Association of School Administrators developed and published a lengthy policy statement entitled *Roles, Responsibilities, Relationships of the School Board, Superintendent, and Staff*. It contains a section which sets forth the beliefs of school superintendents concerning the development of personnel policies. The section bears restatement in the context of professional negotiation:

We believe that teachers, school administrators, and school boards must together seek pathways yet uncharted in the area of personnel policies and practices.

We believe that the superintendent has a responsibility to see that opportunities are provided for staff members—teachers, supervisors, principals, and specialists—to play appropriate roles in developing personnel policies and in maintaining professional working conditions.

We believe that the superintendent has a responsibility to assist staff members—in ways satisfactory to them—in studying welfare problems, in developing proposals pertaining to staff welfare, and in presenting them to the school board for consideration and action.

We believe that shared responsibility in policy development is a professional concept. It assumes a commonality of goals and interests among teachers, school boards, and administrators; and it assumes that service to children is the paramount consideration and that welfare provisions for teachers are means to that end.

We believe that the right to discuss pros and cons and to participate in developing a program does not imply the right to make decisions. Although consensus should always be patiently sought and will often prevail between staff and school board, the board must retain its responsibility and legal right to make decisions.

We believe that no matter how generous and benevolent arbitrary decisions may be, they have a debilitating effect. When people are involved, they not only assume responsibility for making decisions work, but each performs at a higher level of productivity.

We believe that failure to find appropriate and acceptable means of involving staff members—teachers, principals, and supervisors—in developing policy that directly affects them will lead to divisiveness, tension, and conflict that will impair the schools and adversely affect the education of children.

We believe that there is no one best procedure for sharing responsibility for policy development. School board members, administrators, and classroom teachers must develop policies and practices appropriate to local conditions, rather than adopt those established elsewhere.

We believe that if boards of education fail to make reasonable welfare provisions for all staff members and fail to provide machinery through which grievances can be given appropriate consideration, their respective state legislatures are likely to establish appeal procedures.

We believe that there is an intrinsic value in local decision making which is worth preserving to the maximum extent consistent with the obligations of citizenship in the state and nation.

In its 1965 resolution entitled "Staff Relations," AASA said this:

We believe that teachers, school boards, and administrators are all committed to the advancement of public education and that the goals and interests of these groups are highly interrelated. We believe strongly that the development of school policies and programs and the solution of school problems can best be accomplished by these groups working in harmony and with respect for the roles of each. We believe that effective policy development involves important contributions by each group.

We believe that evaluation in staff relations is to be welcomed. We commend careful study and the development of principles that should govern these relations and define the responsibilities of the various groups while maintaining the integrity of each. We believe that shared responsibility for policy and program development is a professional concept requiring a unique professional approach. We maintain that the superintendent of schools has a unique responsibility to provide leadership in these matters.

It is apparent that the development of personnel policies in the sixties calls for far different, and certainly more formalized, procedures than heretofore have existed in most school systems throughout the nation.

The wishes of the professional staff on negotiation procedures and on the content of agreements will frequently prevail. It is essential, however, that the superintendent of schools be deeply and actively involved in the development of policies which affect the staff and the school system's operation.

Concerning the superintendent's specific role in negotiation, two extreme positions are often voiced: (a) that he be completely bypassed and have no place in the negotiation process, and (b) that he be the chief negotiator representing only the board of education in all of its dealings with the staff.

AASA does not believe that either of these positions will contribute to the long-term good of the school district or its educational program.

The superintendent should play a significant role in professional negotiation, his basic obligation being to the welfare of the pupils and to leadership in the formulation of sound educational policy.

He should be an independent third party in the negotiation process. He should review each proposal in light of its effect upon students and work closely with both the board and the staff representatives in an attempt to reach agreement in the best interests of the educational program. His position as leader of the staff and executive of the board requires this.

The superintendent, or his representative, must carry this role into formal negotiation where, in most cases, with legal advice, he will continue to serve as interpreter in difficult communications between the board and the staff.

In school systems where such a position exists, he may delegate the actual negotiation to an associate or assistant superintendent or a director of personnel acting under his direct supervision. In smaller school systems where the superintendent performs all of the functions of a central office staff, he inevitably will have to assume this role himself. In no instance should responsibility for negotiation be delegated outside the profession.

Obviously, the superintendent cannot be represented in negotiations by the local association, whether or not he is a member. Likewise, his position of independence would be undermined were he to vote in any election to determine the negotiating organization.

Patterns of negotiation inevitably vary, depending upon the size of the district, the wishes of the staff, and former relationships and modes of operation. Regardless of the pattern, however, the superintendent under no circumstances should be bypassed. Somehow, the negotiation process must recognize the uniqueness of education and the uniqueness of the superintendent's role. Anything which weakens the effectiveness of his position in the district will ultimately weaken the schools as well.

New patterns of staff relationships require many changes in local school administration; old, established traditions and processes no longer suffice. It avails little to debate the desirability of these changes in relationships or to bemoan either their existence or their speed. Changes are here, and their pace will quicken rather than abate in the years ahead.

New processes and new insights into the nature and means of policy formulation are needed, not only to upgrade the professional status of teachers but also to improve the conditions under which they work, thus enhancing the quality of education. As personnel policies and administrative processes are revised and improved, much will depend upon the wisdom, care, patience, forbearance, and sound judgment of the individuals and groups of individuals involved in this professional evolution.

It is the firm belief of AASA that problems are better prevented than solved and that satisfactory negotiation procedures are best developed in a climate of goodwill before the need for them becomes acute. It is believed that the superintendent of schools, if he is to continue in his position of educational leadership, must assume responsibility for initiating and guiding changes in patterns of staff relationships.

Written negotiation agreements which carefully delineate the roles and responsibilities of the superintendent, the board, teachers, administrative and supervisory staff, and professional organizations are essential to the smooth and efficient operation of the schools. Whether at the local level or through state legislation, it is imperative that the voice of the superintendent be heard with respect to the most desirable type of agreement or legislation.

There is still time to outgrow the more petulant concepts of negotiation and to move toward more mature concepts of shared professional responsibilities.

The superintendent must contribute his professional judgment, experience, and understanding to the development of appropriate new procedures of staff negotiation. The challenge has been given; professional negotiation is the best means by which it can be met.

47 | # The Principal's Stake in Professional Negotiations

Lorraine W. Addelston

Negotiations in which the principal has a significant stake have fallen into at least four categories. In each case, the negotiations have resulted in an erosion of the principal's authority without any corresponding decrease in responsibility. In fact, accountability has been forcibly increased while power has been forcibly decreased.

The four areas of negotiations are:

1. Negotiations with pupils and/or their parents as representatives of those pupils concerning what we might call the working conditions of the pupils;
2. Negotiations with the community or the so-called and sometimes self-styled community representatives;
3. Negotiations with teachers and other staff members, e.g., paraprofessionals;
4. Negotiations with the supervisory staff including the principal himself and his superintendent.

Let us examine each of these categories and let us see how efforts to yield to the pressure and the demands of each of these groups have resulted in erosion of the principal's authority.

PUPILS AND/OR THEIR PARENTS

In this connection when I say "parents" I am indicating adults, sometimes *in loco parentis*, who speak for the individual child, usually a disruptive child. I would consider the American Civil Liberties Union, for example, *in loco parentis* in this connection.

Sometimes the demands of the pupils involve curriculum and school program. We have experienced, for example, great demands for black studies for black students. If the school head yields to these demands and negotiates with the representatives of the black students, he finds himself caught between two or more student groups in a power struggle. Each act of negotiation leads to additional acts of negotiation. Each attempt to placate a group of students erodes the authority of the school head. Indeed, decisions made in response to pressure set precedents which decrease the role of the school head's professional judgment.

From *NASSP Bulletin*, Vol. 53 (May 1969), pp. 181-190. Reprinted by permission of the National Association of Secondary School Principals. Copyright: 1969 by the National Association of Secondary School Principals.

At the convention of the American Association of School Administrators held in Atlantic City, I was privileged to hear Professor Frankle of Columbia University talking about this type of disruption at the collegiate level. He made a very important point which I think too many of us overlook, i.e., that all students need the curriculum which has been colloquially called Black Studies. It is wrong to provide it merely for black students. If a curriculum is good and necessary, as this one is, for maintaining the American way of life, then it is necessary, if not more necessary, for the white students than for the black students. The principal's stake in negotiations with one group of students concerning curriculum content and student program is therefore very great. His school may inadvertently go downhill, under pressure, because the principal has negotiated away his responsibility and authority in curricular design.

Students and parents have challenged the principal's authority in matters of dress and discipline. The superintendent of schools in New York City, in negotiating with parents and pupils, announced recently that girls might come to school wearing slacks. But he neglected to define the word, slacks. The result was that, with unparalleled immediacy, girls arrived in school in shorts, culottes, jump suits, and pajamas. Some of these variations on the word slacks had never occurred to the superintendent, his social milieux being out of contact with the culture of the pupils who extended his permission. When the superintendent of schools, negotiating with pupils and their adult representatives *in loco parentis*, gave away the right of the principal to enforce reasonable dress regulations, he negotiated away the control the principal had over the disciplinary tone of his school. The principal's stake in these negotiations was large.

If a principal is, as he is certain to be, held responsible for the safety of the girls in his building, then he must necessarily be able to exercise a modicum of control over the clothing worn by the girls in that building.

Indeed, in this case, the superintendent negotiated away some of his own authority. A committee of heads of supervisory associations met with the superintendent of schools and asked him with some unusual impertinence, "When the warm weather arrives, will you permit the girls to wear bikinis?"

If pupils are to be permitted to alter the requirements for diplomas, if pupils and pressuring parents are to be permitted to decide which teachers are to remain on a staff and which are to be let go, the principal will become less than a clerk in the school.

COMMUNITY

In all of the discussions concerning decentralization and community control, it has become increasingly apparent that activists in the community wish to take from the principal, indeed, from the district superintendent, aspects of his authority while making him more and more accountable to the community for what the community considers his failure to produce. The community's spokesmen, frequently self-styled, frequently non-residents but rather peripatetic community spokesmen who wander from place to place creating dissension and polarization, start rumors and create chaos. They create a situation in which the superintendent is completely beholden to them for his job. In New York City, after generations of tenured superintendents with security, we now have annual contracts for superintendents. This negotiation with the community on the part of the city fathers and the city board of education and this negotiation with the district superintendent must necessarily result in altered working conditions for the principal. The principal will appear increasingly to be in competition with his district superintendent. The principal who wishes to become a superintendent will find it necessary to attack the district superintendent's position mercilessly; and conversely, in order to maintain his position as district superintendent and in order to secure successive renewals of contract, field superintendents will find it necessary to exert their superiority and authority over the principals in their district. In negotiations which involve the community, the principal's enlightened self-interest must result in his constant vigilance. The job he saves may be his own.

The job he saves may, indeed, be his own; it may even be the job of a student intern he has sought to train effectively. I learned while at the AASA convention in Atlantic City that Los Angeles has managed to beat New York City in negotiations to reduce requirements for supervisory licenses for deprived applicants. If you are a black American or a Mexican American in Los Angeles, you do not have to take the same examination for certification as principal as a white American. In New York City there are many and varied efforts under way to accomplish the same thing. In these negotiations every principal and every candidate for the principalship has a tremendous stake. In New York City we now have sizeable lists of fit and meritorious and duly licensed principals for elementary schools and for junior high schools. These people are serving in lesser capacities in the school system and are awaiting appointment from those lists. Several of them have served as interns in our school systems in order to be readied for their future appointment.

I have had four such interns in the last two years; my fourth intern is at work in my school now during my absence. None of these interns is Black, Puerto Rican, or Mexican. All of them are white Americans representing three different religious groups and both sexes. If the negotiations of the special interest community groups with the Board of Education and the Legislature result in preferential treatment for black and Puerto Rican candidates in New York City, none of these four meritorious and qualified people will ever be appointed. It would seem to me that the stake of the principal in the negotiations currently under way between pressure groups in the community and duly constituted local boards and legislatures is a tremendous stake indeed.

As professional people, we have an additional stake in these negotiations. As the qualifications for the positions of responsibility in our school system are reduced, the importance of the position must necessarily be reduced also. The qualifications and authority cannot be eroded without resultant loss of status, significance, and respected leadership.

We are not doing our profession any good if we yield to negotiations to reduce qualifications, no matter how necessary it may be socially to admit representatives of deprived groups into our midst. If children are not being properly educated now, as the current rumor goes, why should we expect that they would be better educated if the heads of schools were less well qualified? There must be alternative methods of securing minority group representatives in the positions of leadership in our profession which would not carry with them the necessary decrease in status, significance and skill; let us find them.

Principals have a stake in maintaining access to our profession without regard to race, creed, color, sex, or previous condition of servitude.

In the negotiations with the community, where the governmental representative—be it the local school board or the legislature —has permitted the erosion or the threatened erosion of supervisory status, a polarization of groups has developed. Militant community representatives have hurled "accountability" at the professionals' soft underbelly and then charged that professional inadequacy has caused the polarization.

Polarization has resulted from the agitation for immediate decentralization and immediate shift of control and immediate licensing of minority group representatives without regard to previous conditions of eligibility. In the negotiation of the educational authorities with the community representatives, the principals, whose stake is tremendous, must be represented.

As a final statement on the principal's stake in negotiation with community and community sub-groups, may I quote the first paragraph of the minority report of the Board of Education of the City of New York relative to decentralization?

As you may know, the Board of Education of New York City has been packed by our Mayor whose anxiety is reflected by the pressure on the legislature for immediate decentralization. His anxiety is furthermore reflected in his successive efforts to rid our school system of its Board of Examiners and its merit system. In this way he hopes to make speedily possible the entrance into the system of minority group representatives, qualified or not.

Three stalwart members of the Board of Education, who were members before it was packed by the Mayor, wrote their own minority report which is entitled "A Moderate Approach to School Change." It begins:

New York City is in a state of crisis—a crisis brought about by and focused on the issue of school decentralization. While many New Yorkers have supported a decentralization plan as the remedy for bigness and bureaucracy, they have had second thoughts in recent months as violence, dissension and race hatred have emerged from the controversy. The cure is proving to be worse than the disease.

Surely the principal's stake in the negotiations which have brought this crisis about in a huge school system cannot be measured. His entire professional life is at stake in this seething cauldron brought about by hasty negotiations.

TEACHERS AND OTHER STAFF MEMBERS

In this area I am confident that the principal's stake will be more readily discerned.

Contracts have been coming to the desks of principals in New York City, for example, with great frequency. Indeed, it would appear that an entire desk drawer is required to file those contracts, which include the following:

- contract with the United Federation of Teachers
- contract with the secretarial staff
- contract with the custodial staff
- contract with school aides
- contract with paraprofessionals
- contract with the lunchroom workers.

Each time the teachers gained a right in their contract which affected their assignment or their program, that negotiated right affected the working conditions of the principal.

The current contract with the United Federation of Teachers, for example, includes an item which says that only 35 percent of teachers with official classes shall be given administrative assignments. On the surface, that doesn't appear to alter the principal's working conditions. The fact is that it has altered them considerably.

A faculty departmental conference, for example, is defined as an administrative period. Because of this item it is impossible to schedule into the school program a joint period for all teachers in the mathematics department, so that they may meet together for a weekly conference. Unless all math teachers were without official classes, or were defined as making up the greatest percentage of the 35 percent eligible for administrative periods, their program cannot include conference time. The principal's supervisory activity was curtailed by the negotiations which resulted in the 35 percent contract item. In addition, this item impinges upon the principal's personal time; it is necessary for him to schedule conferences after school. These after school conferences are furthermore limited by the number of in-service and other courses teachers may be required to take as well as by the fact that many teachers have or claim to have afternoon jobs to supplement their incomes.

Another result of this 35 percent limitation is the limit on hall patrols, yard patrols, and locker room duty assignments. If only 35 percent of the homeroom teachers may be given such safety assignments then, to quote many experienced principals in New York City, our school halls and staircases and yards are not safe.

School aides also have their union and their contract. One of the most interesting results of their contract grew out of benefits they managed to secure in negotiation which affect the principal's authority and responsibility. During the recent school strike, when almost none of the aides worked, principals hoped that time might accrue toward assignment at the end of the school year. We do not receive an allotment of specific positions for school aides; instead, we receive a grand total number of hours to be consumed as the principal sees fit during the course of the school year. Once headquarters negotiated with the aides, however, and paid them for the time they did not work during the long school strike in the Fall, a part of the bank of time was used up, and we look forward to the month of June with no aide time left for us. Obviously, when this was negotiated, the principals had a stake in the results. They were not, however, consulted in the course of the negotiations. They were merely informed that they would not have the total amount of time available to them during this school year.

The principal is caught between the contract with the teachers, where the aides are specifically noted as relieving the teachers of duties which teachers find onerous, and the contract with the aides which has specifically secured for them pay and time credited for times when they did not work. The net result is that the principal will have to lose his own time in debating the inequities with the teachers at the end of the school year.

The impact of negotiations with teachers and others upon the working conditions of the head of the school is revealed in the contract demands of the Council of Supervisory Associations. The discontent and erosion of authority of the principal are revealed in supervisors' negotiations for themselves.

THE SUPERVISORY STAFF

The contract which the supervisors hope to secure is being negotiated with the Board of Education and the Superintendent of Schools by the Council of Supervisory Associations of the Public

Schools of New York City. The following items are selected from the demands which are submitted for the purpose of negotiating a written agreement.

Until this time the supervisors had felt that an oral agreement was all that was necessary; recent events have proven the folly of our ways. We know now that, unless guarantees are written down and notarized, there are no guarantees.

The High School Principals Association of New York City listed ten items for negotiation; these included the following:

1. "Principals should be consulted on any contemplated changes in policy or administration that involved their responsibilities before such changes are put into effect."
2. "Supervisors should have the right to file a grievance against school UFT chapters in situations where there is patent harassment of the principals."
3. "In administering the policy on rotation of teachers in various assignments, stronger weight should be given to the principal's judgment in determining who is qualified. . . ." Note that this item reflects the rotation items in the contract with the teachers; such items have certainly eroded the principal's authority while he remained increasingly accountable for the educational results.
4. "Principals should have the right to some control as to who is transferred to their school." This item also reflects on a transfer right item in the teachers' contract which makes it possible for them to be transferred into a school without prior knowledge or interview with the principal.

The Junior High School Principals Association of New York City submitted these additional items for inclusion in the negotiations:

1. A transfer policy geared to seniority of service. This reflects the results of community negotiation because, in the demands for decentralization, the transfer policy previously negotiated with the Board was completely abrogated.
2. An appointment policy which will not place new people before displaced veterans. This item also reflects the insecurity of the supervisors under conditions of decentralization and community control.

Another item—a step by step planned program of reasonable, viable decentralization—indicates the emotional stress endured by supervisors under the chaotic conditions resulting from the negotiations between our Board of Education and the community activist groups.

And now, in closing, I would like to read what I consider to be pertinent items from the demands which have been submitted by CSA. These are dated December 6, 1968, and they will give you an insight into the stake of the supervisory staff in negotiation. Some of them are amazing in their frankness and what they reveal concerning the chaos in our school system.

For example, "All tenured supervisory personnel shall retain their salary and rank should their duties or assignments be changed or abolished." How insecure can a large city school system make its experienced supervisory staff feel?

Another one: "It shall be the policy of the Board to fill all the supervisory vacancies with licensed personnel."

Next item: "The District Superintendent shall consult with all principals concerning the assignment of every teaching position to their school before May 1 of the current year to ensure proper coverage for all purposes."

Again this is an indication of an unstable relationship between the District Superintendent and his principals.

The next one is a very interesting one.

An administrative aide shall be assigned to every elementary school for the purpose of relieving chairmen, assistant principals, and administrative assistants from such duties as inventory of materials, distribution of books, preparation of reports, and similar duties.

In other words, if teachers have aides, so should supervisors have aides.

This is another very interesting item:

Messenger services shall be provided through the office of the District Superintendent to pick up from and deliver to the school such items as checks, testing material, reports, and other pick-ups or deliveries that might be required.

This item stems from the fact that the teacher's contract no longer permits a principal to send a teacher out to pick up materials. The net result—the principal or the assistant principal goes himself.

And, finally, I would like to close with the preamble to these demands for our supervisors' contract:

Appointments to all supervisory positions up to and including the rank of high school principal should be made on the basis of merit as determined by the Board of Examiners. The factor of race, color, sex, religion, or national origin must not enter into such appointment.

48 | **School Boards and Principals—
Before and After Negotiations**

Joseph H. Cronin

The school principalship in America approaches a cloverleaf.[1]
Either it veers sharply to turn towards "instructional leadership"
or it hurtles further onward toward the role of building manager.
In the latter role, the principalship will "waste away" to that of
master technician whose presence by teachers will simply be tolerated as the man in charge of keys, custodians, and kids in trouble.
Indeed, more than a few principals have finished this journey. Let
us call them "caretakers," for theirs is the function of caring about
all the little things that take place in a school building. The big issues
are left to the teachers, or left unsolved.

The spread of collective negotiations in education now requires
school boards and superintendents to reappraise the web of relationships with principals. Negotiated agreements now lay out with increasing specificity the prerogatives of teachers vis-a-vis principals
and spell out exactly the ways in which teachers can move beyond the
school level to secure satisfaction of grievances. The New York City
or Chicago principal, for example, finds in the contract 20 pages of
detailed regulations concerning what he can and cannot ask a teacher
to do. If he does it anyway, the contract specifies exactly how a
teacher can reach for and secure proper remedies for this mistreatment.

So low is the estimate of principals in some quarters that the
proposal to elect principals from the tenured members of school
faculty now receives serious consideration. This choice at the cloverleaf is not yet clearly marked, but traffic along it may increase
shortly.

Those who will shape the new life of principals may wish to explore briefly the current predicament faced by principals. Three
questions can be raised:

1. What has become of the principalship, and why?
2. What happens to the principal because of collective negotiations?
3. What mechanisms could strengthen the principal's potential in
   shaping school policy?

From *Phi Delta Kappan*, Vol. 59 (November 1967), pp. 123-127. Reprinted by permission of the publisher and author.
1. The "cloverleaf" in an age of freeways replaces the rather dated "crossroads."
Mauritz Johnson of Syracuse University developed this analogy several years ago at
a meeting of the NASSP.

These questions are raised neither to console incumbents of the principalship nor to confound their superiors with academic explanations. Rather, an analysis of some of the reasons for the current shape of leadership at the school level must precede acceptance of fairly drastic remedies. Without careful analysis, well-meaning administrators or school board members might tinker contentedly with token changes. They might miss the main point—that the principalship in its present form even prior to collective negotiations had become emaciated.

THE PRINCIPALSHIP IN THE PAST

The Harvard Center for Field Studies recently completed a survey of a metropolitan school system of 6,500 pupils.[2] The staff carefully reviewed the Rules and Regulations of the school system. A broad policy statement regulating the work of school principals offered these expectations:

1. Principals shall have general supervision at all times of the pupils, personnel, grounds, buildings, and appurtenances in their schools. They shall be held responsible for the neatness and cleanliness of the premises.
2. They shall see to the enforcement of the rules and regulations of the committee and strictly carry out the directions of the superintendent.
3. They shall make such rules, not inconsistent with these regulations and the superintendent's directions, for the guidance of teachers or for the discipline of the pupils as may in their opinion be necessary for the successful conduct of the school.
4. They shall see that the school registers are properly kept.
5. They shall have control of the janitorial staff of their respective buildings and shall report promptly any neglect of duty.
6. Any defects in equipment that cannot be immediately remedied by the staff or facilities at hand shall be reported in writing to the assistant superintendent.
7. They shall report promptly to the superintendent any case where extra hours put in by the custodian, caused by the school building being open for public use, interfere with his services to the school or upkeep of the building.
8. Doors in all elementary and junior high schools shall be locked from the outside during the school hours, but no bolt or lock shall be so used in any school to prevent the opening of doors from the inside.
9. In cases of truancy in their respective buildings they shall cause the supervisor of attendance to investigate and report thereon without unnecessary delay.

2. *Watertown: The Education of Its Children* (Cambridge, Mass.: Center for Field Studies, Harvard Graduate School of Education, 1967).

Principals were also given the authority to suspend students for bad conduct, the responsibility for requisitioning textbooks (and seeing that they were properly labeled), and the duty to submit end-of-year inventories of books and equipment.[3]

These expectations may be summarized as follows: building supervisor, rule enforcer, chief disciplinarian, head keeper of attendance registers, czar over custodians, inspector of door locks, and tabulator of books.

What was more alarming than the low level of leadership functions expected was the discovery that these so accurately described what a principal of a school actually did. They did exactly what they were expected to do. No one really complained about that. If there were problems—of communication, curriculum planning, teacher orientation, staff evaluation, and program coordination (and there were all of these)—then no one saw the connection between these and the job description of principals. As a consequence, high school teachers were named as part-time "coordinators" to try to exert some leadership at least in their subject areas.

Principals all over the country have been allowed to drown in a sea of paperwork and related administrivia. Principals in most school systems must sign all requisitions, payroll sheets, attendance registers, and many documents pertaining to student transfers.

Central school offices everywhere require periodic inventories of equipment on hand and evaluations of instructors on hand, especially the newer ones. (The inventories can be delegated; the evaluations must be done personally.) Principals must prepare statements about all manner of situations—the custodian dismissed for shiftlessness, the teacher selected for an N.D.E.A. institute, and the assistant principal bucking for promotion. Even the student tapped for participation in the county science fair can't go without the principal's "endorsement." Many of the new federal programs require extra reports from the school building level. But the paperwork generated by Public Law 874, aid to federally impacted areas, taxes the ingenuity of principals who may not rest in peace until every parent has admitted or denied working on a federal contract or living on federal property. The retrieval of these simple forms from family units will someday tax the ingenuity of operations researchers who have never met parents who protest conformity or "invasion of privacy" by mutilating their 874 forms. With such clutter is the life-space of a principal too often filled.

Paperwork aside, the level of teacher preparation in some states has caught up to that of principals, while the curriculum itself has

3. *Rules of the School Committee and Regulations for the Public Schools of Watertown, Massachusetts,* revised November 11, 1953, pp. 5, 6. The rules also require of the superintendent that he call on principals for help in interviewing prospective teachers and appraise teacher performance.

surpassed their limited capacity to supervise its efficacy. Instructional leadership, in other words, no longer resides so clearly in a front-office expert with a master's degree. Most of the teachers have, or are getting, that degree, and they know more about the "new math," the "new science," or audio-lingual methods than he does. The principal as a teacher of teachers no longer has much to teach newcomers other than the unfinished business of classroom control techniques.[4]

Elementary school staffs have been strengthened by the addition of subject matter specialists and traveling supervisors of art, music, and physical education and more recently in counseling, testing, foreign language perhaps, and remedial reading. Not only are these teachers hired and assigned centrally, but the principal may no longer have much to say about teachers assigned to his building.

The combination of parental pressures for "equality" and economic necessity has served to generate standard formulae for allocating money for texts, new programs, equipment, and library books. Every school gets the same amount of money per pupil per function. A principal, to get some unique equipment or program, must still get the P.T.A. to sell cookies, show films, or sponsor a fair or potluck supper. To put his school ahead he finds a way to subvert the standard of "equal education for all."

Teachers now trained to cultivate "divergent thinking" and to stress initiative and risk-taking behavior surprisingly enough are themselves thinking divergently and taking some risks—in bypassing the school administration and voicing "demands" directly to local boards of education. Teachers realize they must wrestle for power with those who seem to hold it, the boards of education. If decisions are really made at the top, then men in the middle are left simply to carry out those decisions made collaboratively by teachers who won legislative authority to negotiate with boards. Current teacher strategy may diverge from textbook platitudes about "chain of command" but does not diverge from realistic thinking about the locus of power. Boards, not principals, have kept most of it in their own hands.

In short, principals have lost ground as experts on the total curriculum and no longer can expect deference as the best-educated man in the building. He signs more forms but makes fewer decisions about allocating resources or acquiring staff than ever before. He still organizes the program to some extent, but others write the curriculum, while specialists whisk in and out to render the more technical services and solve the more serious problems.

4. For several of these observations I am indebted to Frank W. Lutz, who with Joseph Azzarelli edited *Struggle for Power in Education* (New York: The Center for Applied Research in Education, Inc., 1966). His subsequent manuscript on grievance procedures, rules and the principalship was of great value in understanding current problems.

PRINCIPALS AND NEGOTIATIONS

It is not yet true that principals are "odd men out" in the bargaining process between teachers and boards. Principals here and in
Canada sometimes head up the negotiating team for the teachers
with great flair and skill.[5] A few superintendents are making sure
that principals sit with the director of personnel on the school board
negotiating team. Other principals have been left out, at least for
the moment.

A year ago administrators worried about the rulings of state
labor boards on whether teachers and supervisory staff could remain represented in the same negotiating unit. To drive administrators out of the unit (a long-time union objective) seemed to drive a
wedge between teachers and administrators needlessly. But separate
"bargaining units" have not meant that an association splinters into
pieces. Separate units merely safeguard the right of the teachers to be
represented by teachers for purposes of arguing the case for other
than supervisory personnel. Furthermore, some administrators have
successfully followed the teacher units in gaining hefty increases
maintaining previous ratios. Actually, the evidence to date on losses
and gains is inconclusive. In Massachusetts the old partnership has
not been punctured in many places. But in Michigan the superintendents have already pulled out of the Michigan Education Association in response to the bloody battles waged this past year, and principals may follow them out of the teacher group.[6] Should conflict
and tensions mount as high in other states, then expect DESP
and NASSP,* and quite logically ASCD and the AASA, to move out
of the NEA building to form new alliances, possibly with the tech-
nologically more sophisticated American Management Association.

The more significant, if not as dramatic, consequence of teacher
negotiations (when principals have been on neither team) include
contract provisions for teacher transfer, notice of promotions, and
school scheduling which administratively cannot work. Superintendents in several states have commented on how useful the testimony of principals can be in shaping workable provisions no matter
which team includes a principal.

Wildman at the Cubberley Conference at Stanford reported a
similar finding, that "the initial practical impact of a negotiated
agreement falls most heavily on the local school principal. If repre-

5. Myron Lieberman and Michael Moskow, *Collective Negotiations for Teachers: An
Approach to School Administrators* (Chicago: Rand McNally, 1966).
6. *Education Negotiations Service* (Washington, D.C.: Educational Service Bureau,
Inc., February 15, 1967, and June 1, 1967).
*The initials stand for elementary and secondary school principal groups now affili-
ated with the National Education Association, which also houses the organizations of
supervisors and other school administrators.

sentatives of this group have not had a voice in the drafting and bargaining of the contract, resentment and disaffection often follow."[7]

A critical question then is, "On whose team will the principal play?" First, it becomes increasingly clear that the superintendent of schools speaks primarily for the school board and community around the bargaining table. Teachers insist on the right to choose their own spokesman, and rarely will this person be the superintendent. Teachers are willing to relieve superintendents of the need to represent simultaneously both the staff and the school board and the children. Furthermore, the school board hires a superintendent to serve as a major consultant across-the-board in matters financial and pedagogical; his expertise is ordinarily indispensable to the board, nor can he deny it to the board. Principals provide vital components of that expertise. They know well the variations between schools and the difference between the problems teachers encounter and the problems teachers create. That knowledge must be shared with the school board's other administrators. Only in bargaining for their own salaries and related conditions of employment should principals form a separate pro-tem alliance with other supervisory and administrators.[8]

If principals are left out of the negotiations process, it is because: (1) they have neither been invited nor have they volunteered for service on the bargaining team, and (2) they have not insisted on their right to assist with school boards' preparations for negotiations.

What is meant by the latter? Why, clearly school boards could prepare for negotiations, although by no means have many to date shown recognition of this need. Nor is it enough simply to prepare the board's own demands, e.g., for more teaching hours per day or an in-service course every other summer. The board's preparations must include an assessment of the present conditions of work to determine what inefficiencies and obstacles to teacher productivity now exist. This task requires time and expertise that board members lack. Therefore, through the superintendent, principals should be asked to meet as a group and identify problems in the way teacher time, talent, and other resources are used. For one, the demands of the teacher group can then be anticipated in advance. Then also, the board can decide what programs and changes in conditions it wants to finance. The negotiations process ideally provides an opportunity for school boards to describe to teachers face-to-face the kind of improvements in teacher performance sought by the community. Not

7. Wesley Wildman, "What Prompts Greater Teacher Militancy," *The American School Board Journal*, March, 1967, p. 32.

8. This position differs but slightly while expanding upon an analysis and the prophetic guidelines developed by Benjamin Epstein, *The Principal's Role in Collective Negotiations Between Teachers and School Boards* (Washington, D.C.: National Association of Secondary School Principals, 1965).

to prepare for such inspiring communications means that a board, and administrative staff, forfeits a splendid opportunity to call for an upgrading of services to children.

Much of the above comes under the heading "preparing for negotiations." But the experts disagree on what issues are negotiable and what issues are simply "discussable." Both American Federation of Teachers and National Education Association officials feel that everything a school system does could be negotiable. Board members cringe at the thought of losing prerogatives.

Actually, teacher leaders simply want to establish the right of teachers to be consulted and respectfully heard on questions of educational policy. The more sophisticated teacher group spokesmen will admit it would be ludicrous to "negotiate" textbook selection, courses of study, teacher recruitment procedures, student evaluation systems, and other unwieldy and intricate "educational questions." Certainly "negotiations," especially at budget time, provide a less than hardy vehicle for a long, careful look at, for example, what educational technology can do for both children and adults in school. Alternative vehicles for teacher participation in the decision-making process are needed.

Last year some of these other vehicles for communication grew out of the attempts to force boards to agree to discuss educational issues with teachers. Such questions as the adequacy of the curriculum or the methods of selecting textbooks were referred to "study committees" rather than kept in to clog the agenda of negotiating teams. The most spectacular decision was the one made in Quincy, where the teachers and school committee agreed to set up an Educational Development Committee.[9] The scope is very broad and includes review of all proposals concerning "curriculum, teaching methods, aids and materials, educational facilities," new construction, and any other program carried on or proposed. Members of this committee shall include six appointees from the association and six appointed by the school committee. Teacher appointees include a principal; the school committee appointees come from the community at large.

Not only can principals help the board and superintendent prepare for negotiations; they might also clamor for representation on such study groups as will examine cooperatively and clinically some of the more fundamental and not-so-easily negotiated concerns of professional staffs.

To dramatize the need to involve principals more closely in such basic policy and program deliberation, the Center for Field Studies recently recommended to a school system the following bodies:

9. Contract: School Committee—City of Quincy and Quincy Teachers Association, effective March 1, 1967, pp. 8, 9. See also the Professional Conditions Committee, similarly composed, which will consider questions of class size, teacher aide ratios, and other matters.

1. The Superintendent's Cabinet—to provide principals the chance to shape major programs along with the assistant superintendents and other system-wide directors.
2. The Personnel Council—to provide principals and elected teacher representatives from each school and program area a chance to shape the personnel recruitment, selection, and in-service training procedures to be administered by the assistant superintendent.
3. The School Curriculum Councils—to provide each school with a joint committee of teachers-principal-community spokesmen to shape curriculum decisions at the school level. School study groups would forward ideas to a system-wide group on which employers and other citizens would sit with educators.
4. The Budget Planning Council—to provide a year-round forum for principals working with an assistant superintendent to weigh and evaluate various claims for budgetary increases and to begin to apply cost-benefit analyses to alternative programs.[10]

Some of these "councils" could be merged. But the point is that both quality and quantity discussions of educational programs and process are all too rare and have too often been absent. As Robert Anderson put it, the missing ingredient in education is criticism— of teaching, of each other's work, and of current modes of operation.[11] Principals and teachers need not fewer meetings but rather more sessions in which programs and proposals receive more thorough consideration.

A very creative proposal is that of Charles Benson, who has urged that principals and staffs be encouraged to submit proposals to the board, through a central screening committee, so that local needs might be met through imaginative program variations.[12] The absence of such encouragement feeds the fires of discontent of parent and community groups who want more control over the curriculum and a chance to replace unsympathetic principals. It is not enough to ask principals and staffs to have ideas or to expect that a principal listen to the voices of school clients; the board has an obligation to review the current expectations held of principals and to redefine the role before, or as a consequence of, negotiations.

10. *Watertown: The Education of Its Children, op. cit.,* pp. 58, 59.
11. Robert H. Anderson, *Teaching in a World of Change* (New York: Harcourt, Brace & World, Inc., 1966).
12. Charles S. Benson, *The Cheerful Prospect* (Boston: Houghton Mifflin, 1965). Presumably staffs would be allowed to respond to the special needs and aspirations of minority groups. The board would encourage innovation and departures from the standard curriculum by letting principals build different alternatives into school budgets.

Principals Wonder

49 | # What Is Our Role?

Edward Keller

School principals throughout Michigan are voicing concern about their role in teacher-school board negotiations as well as their role in administrator-school board negotiations. Some principals have decided their only role is that of serving management in teacher-board negotiations. Others find themselves so confused they are refusing to take any part in negotiations.

What has led to this situation?

There are certainly many reasons that school principals have given, including the following:

"The law doesn't give us the right to negotiate."

"How can we organize and negotiate? We don't have tenure."

"Organizing would jeopardize our relationship with our board of education."

"Our superintendent told us not to join the MEA."

"We are part of the management team. Our superintendent will take care of us."

"The board just rescinded our salary policy. What can we do?"

"The board thinks we should consider the extra four weeks of work as a privilege to be fulfilled without pay."

"What can we do?"

What can be done? What role is appropriate for principals to take?

First, let us look at the principal's role as a part of management. Under this concept, all employees of a controlling board who serve in administrative or supervisory roles are deemed to be on a "team," pulling together for the good of all.

In its most restrictive form, this concept requires administrators at all strata of the line-staff relationship to speak with one voice, all policies to be interpreted and implemented identically, no disagreement be allowed to exist within the "team," and the "captain" or chief executive alone to represent the team before its employers. Such a concept also implies that the team will jointly develop policies regarding its own salary and working conditions. This team also adopts an adversary role to the teacher unit at the bargaining table and in the implementation of the contract.

From *Michigan Education Journal*, Vol. 46 (October 1968), pp. 16-19. Reprinted by permission of the publisher.

Another form of the management team concept is referred to by Dr. Lester Anderson of the University of Michigan. In this approach, all members of the management team review teacher contract proposals and make recommendations as to acceptance, rejection, or revision. Top management, rather than middle management, participates in direct negotiation with teacher unit representatives. Middle management serves in an advisory and consultant capacity only. This, as Dr. Anderson puts it, is the executive function of the middle management administrator—the principal and supervisor. The principal, therefore, advises the superintendent and/or board of education as to the merits of the teachers' proposals but leaves direct negotiations responsibility where it belongs—in the hands of the board of education and/or its chief administrative officer, the superintendent.

Principals have a legislative function also, Dr. Anderson says, and should organize, develop recommendations, and present these for school board action. Principals have as much right as any other school employee to influence decisions concerning their salaries and working conditions. With effective, enlightened school boards and positive leadership from superintendents, this may be accomplished within the concept defined as the management team.

Within the concept, principals may organize such committees as an economic policies committee, a communicating committee, or an administrator council to investigate, study, and make recommendations to the superintendent on administrator salaries and/or working conditions. The success of these committees will depend on the thoroughness of their preparations as well as the attitude of the superintendent and board of education.

If recommendations are thoroughly prepared and if the superintendent and board of education believe in the management team concept, then principals stand an excellent chance of success. If, however, recommendations are not supported by evidence or if the board of education and superintendent do not fully endorse the management team approach, then the principals' voice will not be heard. Under these circumstances, other approaches must be instituted—if the principals are to be heard.

One approach is by administrators in a school district organizing themselves into an administrator unit. The purposes of such a unit, in addition to improving education and the well-being of its members, is to negotiate with respect to wages, hours, and terms and conditions of employment.

After forming such an organization, electing officers, and appointing committees, particularly the negotiation committee, it is appropriate to inform the superintendent and the board of education that such an organization exists and is prepared to negotiate on behalf of its members. Should a negative response be received or should no positive negotiation take place under this rather informal approach, the administrator unit should formally request the board of education to recognize the unit as representing administrators in the school district.

This stipulation should include recognition of this unit's right to negotiate wages, hours, and terms and conditions of employment for the administrators in the school system. With this stipulation, the administrator unit is authorized to proceed with negotiating a master agreement.

Another way for an administrator unit to achieve recognition is to petition the State Labor Mediation Board (LMB) to conduct an election to certify the unit as the legitimate bargaining agent for the administrators. This route to recognition does not depend upon board of education approval.

Whether by stipulation or by certification through the election process, recognition of a negotiating agent makes it mandatory for the board of education to agree to the negotiating of a master agreement.

In the event of difficulties in negotiations created by either party, the services of the LMB are available. If there is evidence of little progress in negotiations or failure by the board of education to negotiate in good faith, the administrator unit, as the agent of a group of public employees, may seek mediation and other assistance from the LMB. The appropriate petition may be filed with the LMB when a minimum of 51 per cent of the members of the unit indicate that they want mediation help.

The LMB usually determines if a petition has a sufficient number of signatures by comparing it with the unit's membership list or with the school district's roster of administrators.

Throughout all the processes of recognition and negotiations, the services of the Michigan Education Association are available to administrator units.

Negotiations merely establish in contractual language what were formerly included in personnel policies. In many school systems, due to the advent of Public Act 379 and the ensuing ratification of teacher-school board agreements, which are essentially teacher personnel policies that have been formally negotiated by teachers and school boards, there has been growing concern that administrators, particularly the school principal, are somehow left out. The obvious remedy is to make it possible for principals to participate actively in influencing policy and in developing, securing, and implementing administrator personnel policies as well as being responsible for the implementation of teacher personnel policies.

Joseph H. Cronin, director of Harvard University's Collective Negotiations Institute, states it as follows:

> The school board hires a superintendent to serve as a major consultant across the board in matters financial and pedagogical. His expertise is ordinarily indispensable to the board, nor can he deny it to the board. Principals provide vital components of that expertise. They know

well the variations between schools and the difference between the problems teachers encounter and the problems teachers create. That knowledge must be shared with the school board's other administrators. Only in bargaining for their own salaries and related conditions of employment should principals form a separate alliance with other supervisors and administrators.

Separate bargaining units have not meant that an association splinters into pieces. Separate units merely safeguard the right of teachers to be represented by teachers for purposes of arguing the case for other than supervisory personnel. Furthermore, some administrators have successfully followed the teacher units in gaining hefty increases maintaining previous ratios.

There are many approaches to the achievement of principals' goals in a school system. Under a management team concept, they might be very well represented by the superintendent and well treated by the board of education. There may be opportunities under a management team concept to review teacher proposals and to make recommendations to the board of education negotiating team regarding them. There might also be opportunity under this concept to organize administrator committees to develop recommendations on salaries and working conditions for presentation as proposals to the superintendent of schools.

Should this concept not function, several other approaches are available. The informal approach may continue in negotiations with the superintendent or perhaps with the board of education. Organization of a fully functioning unit of administrators is important here and in future developments in negotiations of a more formal variety. Should the informal process not be successful, then more formal processes are available such as: (1) Seeking mediation of the present dispute with assistance from the LMB, using the available petition process; (2) Seeking recognition by stipulation of the board of education; (3) Seeking a recognition election by petitioning the LMB.

Principals must not vacillate. To achieve their desired goals, to secure professional and personal rights, their direction is clear. *Principals must organize locally and must negotiate.* The vehicle to be used and the speed of the venture must be determined by the competence, attitudes, and understanding of all parties involved; principals, chief executives, and boards of education.

Relationships among all members of the administrative staff in a school district and their board of education should be characterized by mutual respect, shared decision-making, and cooperative support. Unfortunately, however, this is not always true. When principals find these relationships are not reciprocated by the board of education or, in some cases, by the chief school executives, then they must unite and negotiate collectively, utilizing their full legal and professional rights.

In each school district, principals must ask themselves:

—What is my current status with the board of education? With the superintendent?

—What influence do I have on school policy decisions?

—What influence do I have in determining my own salary and working conditions?

—What rights do I have to equate with my many responsibilities?

Answers to these and other questions will help each principal to determine the type of organization and negotiation procedure to utilize. The Michigan Education Association is ready, willing, and able to assist principals and other school administrators in achieving their rightful voice in their professional future.

What are you waiting for?

New Frontiers | 50
for Professional Negotiations

David A. Singer, Jr.

A predictable, developmental pattern is evident as school districts proceed into the professional negotiations process—a practice whereby teacher groups organize and bargain collectively with school board representatives, relative to matters that are of universal concern within the local school district. The purpose of this article is to provide insight into this developmental pattern for public school administrators in the large block of states yet untouched by negotiations.

Professional negotiations, a comparatively recent force in the affairs of public education, are paramount considerations in the school districts of the vast metroplex extending from the New England states, across the Northern states, and through the Midwest. This new concept in human relations, involvement, and leadership in education is moving slowly toward the Southern states.

It is no accident of geography that professional negotiations in public education had their inception in the North. Negotiation procedures between labor and management are a way of life in the industrial areas. They are reasonably well-understood and accepted. Their results are evident in an economically substantial labor force and in a dynamic economy. Even though there is a vast chasm between the motivations and procedures of labor negotiations and professional negotiations, it was inevitable that the teaching profession in the industrial states turn to collective action in its efforts to enhance its position in an affluent society. The success of labor organizations served as a motivating force for teacher groups.

When the process of professional negotiations was in its infancy in the North, it was viewed variously by members of the profession. Many teachers saw release from arduous hours in the classroom, some anticipated involvement in the affairs of the school district, and all envisioned higher pay and increased fringe benefits. These are but a sampling of their dreams of a new and professional future.

Administrators, on the other hand, anticipated different results stemming from professional negotiations. To some, the entire concept was a grim spectre that threatened to destroy the autonomy; to others, it was an adversary to be beaten into submission. Still others saw in professional negotiations the strength of a united teaching profession.

From *School and Society*, Vol. 97 (October 1969), pp. 370-372. Reprinted by permission of the publisher.

In the industrial areas, the early efforts of organized local affiliates of the National Education Association to mobilize for negotiations were characterized by the activities of two distinct groups of teachers. The majority wanted significant change. They were concerned with the conduct of school district affairs, and sought honest involvement in matters affecting their activities. They did not want to negotiate the curriculum, they merely wanted to negotiate the right to be involved in curriculum development. As is so often the case with people of foresight and good will, these professionals did not make their position known—they remained silent.

Other teachers were quite profuse in their pronouncements about what they considered professional treatment: "I work from eight to three and I want pay for anything beyond that"; "If I'm going to work on that curriculum committee you'll just have to provide release time"; "I don't want to hear about it. As far as I'm concerned, it's teachers against administrators."

Fortunately, this outspoken group made more noise than they made impact. They often held positions of leadership in the local professional organizations through the early phase of professional negotiations when economic factors were the primary focus. When the demanding tasks of involvement in the change process began to become evident, these "vocal leaders" were significant in their absence.

The progress made under professional negotiations has been beneficial to teachers and administrators as professional groups. The excesses that might have resulted from the bargaining of the teacher professional organizations have been absent for the most part. In most cases, administrators have bargained in good faith with the teacher negotiating units. There is still a notable lack of trust between teachers and administrators, but this is to be expected when two groups first attempt to work together.

Professional negotiations are leading the teaching profession toward the good life from an economic standpoint. However, a much more significant aspect of the good life resides in the involvement in curriculum decisions that teachers have realized as a result of negotiations. The militant teachers who were so vociferous during the first phase of negotiations have suffered from the backlash of involvement. They were interested only in more money. They got what they wanted and they also got the resultant hard work they did not want. Many others did not anticipate the significance of their new role in the profession, but have accepted it enthusiastically. Some expected to become engaged in curriculum planning and are making the most of it, to the benefit of students, the community, public education, and a very large corps of skeptical administrators. This absorption in curriculum work has led teachers to long hours of meaningful group curriculum planning—without overtime and with some release time. Involvement has driven teachers to a critical reappraisal of the conduct and competencies of their colleagues, and has forced them to the realization that their goals are consonant with the goals of their administrators who are, after all, still interested in schools and students and teachers.

In short, many teachers have found it necessary to become professional in the true sense of the word, and they find that they enjoy the significant involvement, interest, and commitment that their professional behavior has made possible.

Public school administrators in the South currently are adopting one of two views of professional negotiations. One group, by far the largest, avoids discussing the matter because of a total absence of understanding of the impact that professional negotiations inevitably will have on education in the South. The negotiations process does not respect state lines. Another smaller group views negotiations in the same manner that their colleagues in the North viewed them in 1963. A predictable and perhaps necessary scene once more is being enacted. However, Southern public school administrators, if they dare, may be recipient of the knowledge of those who already have experienced the negotiations syndrome.

The Southern school administrator, anticipating the inevitability of professional negotiations, can expect a rather clearcut two-phase developmental pattern. Economic considerations appear to be paramount in the planning of all negotiating units. Higher salaries and increased fringe benefits are likely to constitute the primary focus during the first two years of the negotiating process in any school district. Certainly, these considerations will continue indefinitely as matters of concern. Much to the surprise of many administrators, and to the delight of those who are forward-looking, teacher interest will transcend these monetary concerns after the initial economic thrust. Teachers are concerned about students. They want to be involved in the conduct of the educational enterprise. They want to assist in the formation of the policies and procedures that so vitally affect their professional existence. And, most importantly, they want a voice in the development of curriculum, the real business of schools.

This interest in the development of curriculum, the second phase of the developmental pattern, is a signal of maturity in the teaching profession. It is a testimonial urging renewed faith in teachers. More important, it is definite indication that the individual school district can benefit from professional negotiations. These benefits ultimately transfer to students and finally to the greater community. There is no question about it—the negotiations process costs a great deal more money. Citizens in the industrial areas have discovered that one gets what he pays for. They also have discovered that, prior to negotiations, they had been paying for second best and that was what they had been getting. Hopefully, negotiations and the resultant process will be accepted by Southern school administrators soon. The benefits which will accrue are needed.

Negotiations have not been successful in all school districts. In some cases, teachers have failed to conduct themselves in the best interest of their profession. In one school district in a large metropolitan area, the teacher organization demanded the right to exercise final judgment in matters pertaining to teacher dismissal. They withheld contracts and pursued their cause to the very last days prior to the opening of school in September. The local organization leadership, while anxious to serve as a court of last resort relative to teacher dismissal, was unwilling to participate in the construction of an evaluative procedure.

In this same school district, and in numerous others in the same metropolitan area, there has been a tendency for the local professional organization to protect the incompetent or maladjusted teacher. This protection, in the form of job security, often has existed even after the leadership of the organization privately recognized the fact that the teacher in question should not remain in the profession. One specific example of this kind of behavior involved a tenure teacher in a large elementary school. The teacher, plagued by a long history of alcoholism, paddled 14 of his students. This act, coupled with many similar examples of poor judgment, all carefully documented, led to a request for his resignation. Association leadership, while privately recognizing the fact that he should not remain in the classroom, mediated his case. They protected the teacher, but not the students with whom he will come into contact in the future. Surely, there were many other factors attendant to this particular case, but the primary issue is clear. The teacher organization failed to police its own ranks. This is a common problem.

There are other examples of teacher abuse. Since the advent of the master contract and its explicit pronouncements relative to the length of the teacher day, administrative units have experienced some difficulty involving the total teaching staff in the process of curriculum development. Some teachers refuse to recognize the fact that meaningful curriculum work requires an expenditure of time above and beyond the hours prescribed in the master contract.

Teachers have bargained for necessary leaves for personal business and illness, based on the assurance that leave would not be taken unless it was absolutely necessary. Teachers in some school districts have abused the leave provisions in their contract agreements.

The examples cited above would lead the casual observer to conclude that teacher groups want to take, but not to give. However, this generalization does not apply to all professional organizations. While teacher organizations have been guilty of some excesses, school districts, represented by their school boards and their administrative groups, also have failed to act in good faith in some cases.

School districts have found that monetary resources can be concealed relatively easily from teacher groups. Medium and large school districts, at times, have concealed funds in "padded accounts" such as teaching supplies and contingency. This type of action represents bargaining in bad faith that reaches the point of blatancy.

A rather frequent practice among school administrators has been to demand that teachers give unstintingly of their own time. Prior to the entrance of the young married male teacher into the profession, teachers were not inclined to protest these demands. Now, in the day of the master agreement, most teachers realize that true professional conduct includes voluntary service beyond the hours prescribed by the contract. However, they also refuse to allow administrative groups to exploit their desire to build the profession. This new trend in teacher behavior is becoming evident, at times painfully, to school district administrative leadership.

These cases, while regrettable and illustrative of poor judgment on the part of teacher organizations and school districts, are not the rule, but the exception. Professional educators, teachers and administrators, are recognizing a high degree of competency within their own ranks. The mutual respect that is generated by this recognition of competency has resulted in exciting new programs in many school districts. Through professional negotiations, teachers have become interested in curriculum development, have become involved in the change process, and are committed to the outcome of their endeavors.

Professional negotiations, when conducted by men of good will who similarly revere a dynamic profession dedicated to the education of students, can be a powerful instrument toward aiding American education. They can improve the professional position of teachers in the South and can be instrumental in an expanded and enriched school program featuring involved teachers.

51	Teacher Militancy and the Role of the Principal

Reed H. Hagen

A few years ago it was relatively easy to find guidelines that out-lined the responsibilities of the principal. Today, this is virtually impossible because changes in society in recent years have brought about uncertainties in establishing clear educational objectives and administrative functions. The principal's job has traditionally been one of administration and management, supervision of instruction, and the development of good community relations. At present, the principal is looked upon not as a teacher of teachers, but more as a manager and strategist.

Much of this change has been brought about through the in-creasing unrest and newly developed militancy of teachers. In 1964, the *New York Times* reported:

> There is mounting evidence that teachers are no longer content to rule only the classroom to which they are assigned. They want a hand in the assignment and a voice in the policy that controls their professional lives.[1]

A recent article in the *Saturday Review* attributes the militancy to the fact that teachers feel alienated from the school and com-munity. The alienation is due in part to "the growing impersonality of the school as it has become larger and more highly structured" and because teachers seldom live in the community where they teach.

Further alienation is caused by the unrealistic demands being made upon the schools today. Teachers are asked to assume a variety of responsibilities from investigating the intricacies of sex educa-tion to teaching the evils of alcohol. While being asked to assume the additional responsibilities, teachers have been disappointed by the failure of the public adequately to support education so that class size can be reduced and lunch free duty hours can be implemented. Teachers have been repeatedly frustrated by school boards who have neglected to listen to demands for adequate salaries and added fringe benefits.

THE NEW TEACHER

A new breed of teachers is entering the teaching profession. They are better educated, less dedicated, and more pragmatic than their

From *Pennsylvania School Journal*, Vol. 117 (January 1969), pp. 315, 338. Reprinted by permission of the publisher.
1. *New York Times*, January 16, 1964.

predecessors. They are more confident of their own ability, are reluctant to assume nonprofessional responsibilities, and have little patience with the inadequacies of facilities and administrative support.

The authors conclude:

The forces that have contributed to teacher alienation, and consequently, to militancy, almost certainly are going to increase rather than diminish in the years ahead. And the virus of change is already spreading from its point of origin in the city to the suburbs and beyond. We can expect that as the forces reducing job satisfaction for many teachers increase, the demands for higher salaries will become more intense. And each time the teachers win one more bitterly fought contest for higher pay and improved working conditions, their sense of group solidarity will be increased—and their feeling of alienation from the community will grow.

Any realistic appraisal of teacher militancy today seems to indicate that we have seen only the beginning.[2]

How does the increase in teacher militancy affect the role of the principal? A principal finds himself trying to make workable the terms of a contract which in most cases he has had no part in designing. He must not look upon this phenomenon as a threat to authority and abdicate his responsibility as an educational leader. Rather, he must, despite the necessity to share some measure of his authority, find ways through this power which he shares, skillfully to mold together all facets of his staff to develop effectively an efficient and worthwhile educational program. He must ask himself, "How do I adjust the role of myself and others in the administration to the new process so that I maintain fully effective avenues for the exercise of professional and administrative leadership which it is my obligation to provide?"[3]

THE PRINCIPAL CHANGES

The principal must understand that today's schools and teachers are changing and change with them. He must have an administrative style that fosters innovation and experimentation among the teaching staff. The principal must feel comfortable in a setting of change wherein new ideas are tried, new curriculum materials are used, and teachers have freedom to experiment.

A principal must continually mediate between two dimensions of administration—structure and individual. On one hand he has to define carefully the policy of the organization's objectives and on

2. James Cass and Max Birnbaum, "Why Teachers are Militant," *Saturday Review*, January 20, 1968, p. 56.
3. Wesley A. Wildman, "Implications of Teacher Bargaining for School Administration." *Phi Delta Kappan* Vol. XLVI, No. 4, December 1964, p. 155.

the other hand he has to realize that he must use the talents of all people who will contribute to the fulfillment of the goals toward which the group is working.

Traditionally the principal has been responsible for the supervision of teachers. However, as the knowledge explosion continues and the specialization of school personnel increases, the principal finds it increasingly difficult to be sufficiently knowledgeable to evaluate teachers in their areas of proficiency effectively.

It is also evident that teachers are less tolerant of the authority of the principalship and more sensitive to the authority of specialists in their own field. Thus, the principal is forced to leave the supervision of teachers to the specialists and has to concentrate on the difficult and demanding task of coordinating the work of many specialists.

It is increasingly pertinent for the principal to know, through exposure to such disciplines as sociology, social anthropology, psychology, and social psychology how the pupils and communities he serves have come to be what they are. The principal has to understand group dynamics, perception, communication, human relations, motivation, and morals. He has to study the likely results of various administrative organizational structures, procedures, and decisions, and has to design a total school program to meet specific objectives in specific settings.

THE CHILD

The principal must remember that the welfare of the child is the main objective of an educational program. Communication between administrators and teachers must be maintained. The principal must develop a rapport with teachers based not upon regulations and authority but upon cooperation and the mutual concern for the education of children. Teacher-principal conflict is tragic because it stifles the initiative and creativity of teachers and administrators resulting in a deterioration of quality education.

The principal can be an effective agent for change and progress within the framework of a contract negotiated between teachers and the board of education, but he must be able to exercise his leadership by taking the unique human material parts of a school and community and skillfully blending them into a cohesive whole which operates for the welfare of a specific group of pupils in a specific locality at a specific juncture in time.

This is the challenge of the principal.

part five

The PRINCIPAL
The STUDENT
and The COMMUNITY

The Principal
and the Student

IX

chapter overview

It was the best of times, it was the worst of times.

—CHARLES DICKENS

The role of today's secondary principal is precarious. He finds himself the centerpiece on the table of student action. Student activism is a potentially constructive force. Through the principal's leadership can come responsible protest, accompanied by responsible reaction. Administrators are challenged to channel the great thrust of student involvement to the attainment of a relevant educational program. Failure to recognize this crisis in our public schools as a catalyst for long overdue change is to court the possible destruction of public education in America.

Schools of the seventies will be confronted with threats of more trouble from protesting students. Abby Chapkis reflects the current mood of high school students and the response of renowned educators to the crisis. Like the little red schoolhouse, "school" as we now know it will disappear.

Student rebellion is a growing concern on college and high school campuses today. Sociologists have long held that education is a social system. Using this as a base of operations, Jack R. Frymier discusses some of the critical points in the system which may be causing the rebellion.

School board members are being called upon to take an earnest hard look at their schools. From various reports by authoritative groups, Gregory R. Anrig distilled six suggestions for school boards to consider in meeting the challenge of high school protesters. "School boards need to change the ways in which they select and train those who take the critical job of high school principal" is one of these suggestions.

Educators can better understand today's youth by listening to what he has to say. Mary Kathryn Patterson enunciates some of the dreams and some of the concerns of her peers. In a few paragraphs she is able to bridge the "generation gap."

329

Principals are caught in the middle of the debate on student constitutional rights. William E. Griffiths pleads for bold and imaginative leadership on the part of all professional educators, especially secondary school principals, to strike a balance between the rights of the individual student and the demands of the institution.

Personalizing the high school program is possible in a large high school. Robert R. Ford invites the reader "to use our experiences as a springboard toward additional questing for his own school in a matter that requires concerted effort on the part of the faculty and the student body." He does not offer a panacea for personalizing the high school program, but he does offer helpful hints.

How free should the high school press be? This is the question posed by Elizabeth Einsiedler in an attempt to assist high school press staff and their advisers during the critical period of student discontent. By using examples, she shows it is not necessary for a high school press to go underground in order to reflect student opinions.

Administrators are frequently accused of reacting rather than acting. Glenn C. Atkyns creates "Bill," the fictional school principal, to dramatize the dilemma faced by many school administrators today and to recommend appropriate policy to effectively deal with problems related to sex. Data provided from a study by the author assist "Bill" in overcoming his predicament.

Is sex education a school responsibility? Considerable attention is being given to this question by educators, parents, church groups, civic organizations, and various governmental agencies. The condensation of a speech by Eleanore Braun Luckey, entitled "Responsibility for the Issues Involved in Sex Education," provides some assistance to administrators pondering the role of the school in sex education.

Boards of education throughout the country have given approval to the inclusion of sexual information in the program. Frank Battaglia reports on how one school meets the challenge of sex. The experience gained by the program in his school is worthy of review.

The use of drugs by students is one of the most serious challenges facing secondary school principals. Few, if any, of our high schools are free of the growing drug problem. Phyllis C. Barrins discusses the problem and suggests possible avenues of approach to curb the problem. Her closing remarks are the words of Donald B. Louria, "If you want to cure the drug problem, the name of the game is commitment."

"Schools have no choice but to take the initiative in developing new programs and approaches in dealing with drug use and its attendant problems." Sheldon L. Winston describes the operation of a drug counseling workshop devised to help those students who violated narcotic laws on campus but who were not considered hard-core users or sellers. However, the author recognizes that the drug counseling workshop is a "controlled moderate response to a particular law violation."

"A Schoolman's Guide to Illicit Drugs" should be placed in the hands of every teacher and administrator in your school district. Information in the guide may help nip serious problems in the bud.

52 | Relevance or Revolt

Abby Chapkis

"It's relevance or revolt . . . and when it comes to revolt, you haven't seen anything yet."

These are not the words of a Berkeley or Columbia student extremist. They come from Angie, a 16-year-old product of America's public schools.

Angie is not angry about dress regulations in her school, though her counterparts in at least 25 states have disrupted classes because of such regulations.

Nor does her wrath center around discipline, the cause of outbreaks in more than 28 junior and senior high schools across the country.

Angie is angry about the quality of education she is receiving. She wants change. Now.

And she is not alone.

Angie's threat, directed at 42 superintendents meeting this summer at Teachers College, Columbia University, follows a rash of active protests this past year by high school and junior high school students across the nation—black and white—who disrupted schools in suburbs and rural areas as well as in cities, and who threaten even greater waves of protest this fall.

The superintendents, chilled by surveys, including one by the National Education Association that showed three out of five principals reporting some form of active protest in their schools, were attending the 28th annual Superintendents Work Conference when Angie and several of her classmates delivered their blistering indictments of American society and its public schools.

"This land of fruit and plenty is a farce!"

"I'm tired of adapting to schools; let the schools adapt to me!"

"From a lousy elementary education, I was led like a lamb into the slaughterhouse known as the American high school. . . ."

The superintendents, from 35 states, heard about "the man"; "the greasers"; the closed-society nature of high schools resulting from ability grouping practices, from socioeconomic status, from the presence of city ghettos and of "white ghettos" caused by the lack of open housing in the suburbs.

They heard about students who were regarded by themselves and others as second class citizens. They heard about marking systems which convinced students by the end of elementary school that they didn't have it and wouldn't make it!

From *Ohio Schools*, Vol. 47 (September 1969), pp. 22-24. Reprinted by permission from publisher and author, Copyright 1969 by the Ohio Education Association.

They listened somberly as students told them about racism in the corridors, classrooms, and offices; teachers who like neither their jobs nor their students; Mickey Mouse Student Councils.

Some students mixed open pleas with their diatribes. A 22-year-old former Radcliffe College co-ed, who as a high school student ran away from home and became addicted to drugs, told the conference that less money should be spent on formal drug education programs in the schools and more on teachers who can communicate with their students.

"Schools have as much responsibility as parents in helping kids grow up to be healthy, happy, loving people," said the girl, who identified herself as Marge. "It's time for schools to change from cold machines to 'caring' institutions."

And repeatedly during the two-week conference in New York City the supervisors were warned—not only by the students but also by harassed college presidents, by union leaders, by statesmen, and by economists, psychologists and sociologists—to expect violent student disruptions unless schools are reorganized to give students more power, reduce racial tension, introduce new courses, and change teaching methods.

Angie's challenge was to be reinforced by "experts" several times during the conference.

Dean Robert J. Schaefer of Teachers College and Alan Westin, professor of public law at Columbia, told the superintendents that the use of unilateral power by school administrators and faculty could not curb the student movement. The unrest, they said, is not due to trivial incidents but to deep-seated dissatisfaction with the quality of American life.

Both educators advocated a complete restructuring of the secondary school systems, the involvement of students in school problems and curriculums and the abandonment of the traditional authoritarian methods of instruction and discipline.

Said Professor Westin: "There is no technique for turning off student protests. You can station policemen every few feet in the school corridors and it won't have any effect."

This is so, Westin said, because students' grievances are directed against a society they deem capable of great technological triumphs but incapable of solving its racial, social, and economic problems. In the opinion of these students, high school and junior high school teaching methods and curriculums, like those in the colleges, have little relevance to the realities of American life, the two educators said.

"And who is to argue," concluded Dean Schaefer, "that young students are not wholly right when they observe the chaos which we have wrought?"

Whether students are right or wrong, dupes or perceptive dissenters, one thing seems clear: the unrest and turmoil which the nation's colleges and universities have experienced has been, and is likely to be, repeated in some fashion in most secondary schools across the nation.

The questions facing educators, parents, and citizens alike are "Why?" and "What can we do about it?"

To understand why there is unrest among today's youth, it is first necessary to understand the use and significance of "power" in education.

This is the lesson Dan W. Dodson, professor of education at New York University, sought to teach the school superintendents meeting at Teachers College.

It was a lesson alluded to many times during the two-week conference as speakers and participants grappled with the meaning of "student power," "teaching power," "community power," and "black and brown power" and the impact of these types of power on the schools.

According to Dodson, a sociologist and director of NYU's Center for Human Relations, schools have been found wanting in the eyes of youth because the values and standards which the schools seek to perpetuate and extend are relevant mainly for the dominant power holders of American society—the white middle class.

Conflict erupts, observed Dodson, when the middle class mythologies, rituals and practices are imposed on the powerless—comprised mainly of the poor and the black and brown minority groups in this country.

A child who is a member of a powerless group in the community cannot grow up without some traumatic damage to his perception of himself, caused by his identification with this group whose power has been compromised.

These youth have responded to their lack of potency in one of two ways, according to the New York sociologist.

The first is to resign to apathy.

"The apathy of the slums, the problems of teaching the children in such neighborhoods, is mute testimony to this pervasive sense of powerlessness" which fills their lives, he said.

The other reaction to this powerlessness is what Dodson called a "siphoning off" process. Here, he said, the establishment gets the brightest of the powerless youth, "gets them to participate, gets them to believe in the mythologies of the American Dream that all will be rewarded according to their initiatives and their ability, makes them ashamed of their heritage, alienates them in their sentiments and sympathies from the group of which they are a part and, when they are finally sandpapered sufficiently to meet the specifications of the power arrangement, they are transmuted into 'ideal Americans.'"

When this occurs, Dodson said, they lose their identity as members of their minority group and are absorbed within the dominant group.

"This is what is often referred to by those who have come through this process, when they tell other powerless groups that they must also 'earn their place.'"

Dodson reminded his audience that such a notion keeps alive the canard that the limitations of such powerless groups are the limitations of the human potential, not those of the system.

The education professor also pointed out that a major cause of unrest has been the racial tension that has resulted from the black—and more recently the brown—students' "struggle with identity."

"Heretofore, these students have responded to powerlessness with apathy," he said, noting that most realized the rewards of public schools were not for them, hence they dropped out.

"With the emergence of militancy," Dodson continued, "a new wind is blowing. These erstwhile powerless are now beginning to see through the mythologies and the rationalizations of the establishment and are gaining a new perception of themselves."

Dodson told his audience of educators that they will have missed the point of history if they "see these manifestations of a growing effort to shake off apathy and acquire power as merely disruptions —as sand in the gears of bureaucracy."

Educators must understand, he said, that the alternative to this kind of upthrust is continued apathy.

"Power must be taken; it cannot be given," stressed Dodson. "These youths and their parents must respect themselves before they can expect anyone else to respect them. They cannot respect themselves so long as they live in compromise and impotence."

Turning to an examination of the types of disruptions that are only incidentally related to race, Dodson pointed out that many white students are not buying the mythologies of the dominant society.

"They see the values of the upwardly mobile, middle class as fundamentally phony," he said, "and they are attacking a value system which sacrifices growth and development goals of education to status goals of families."

One student participant, summarizing what she feels America's restless students are saying, put it another way:

I am a human being. See me. Hear me. Please help me to find out who I am. Help me to discover what life is all about. Soon.

Listening to the plea of today's students and recognizing their desires is only half the battle. The bigger problem is finding those changes needed to cope with the growing student dissatisfaction.

One change needed, according to Harold B. Gores, director of the Educational Facilities Laboratory of the Ford Foundation, is the environment of the school—not just from the physical standpoint but from the emotional and social viewpoints as well.

The New York educator pointed out that schools—particularly the junior and senior high schools—have been designed with a rigidity and sterileness more appropriate for prisons than for places of learning. Thus, many still have desks screwed to the floors, set in neat rows, located in small square rooms divided one from the other by floor-to-ceiling walls. These classrooms, usually painted a "washable" grey or brown, contain functional overhead fluorescent lighting, controlled only by the teacher, whose desk is also rigidly fixed— by "bolts of distrust"—to the classroom front.

Gores would like to see, at the very least, expansion of the newer trend in building schools without interior walls or with flexible ones. He would like to see classrooms that provide students with the dignity and comfort of living room or denlike furniture and furnishings, including wall-to-wall carpeting, lamps students can turn on or off at will, and cushions and comfortable chairs they can move.

"It is no wonder," he said, "that students confined to ceramic containers wear buttons reading: "I am a human being; do not fold, bend or mutilate."

The educator counseled the superintendent to seek the advice of students when planning new facilities—and to trust their answers.

At the same time he praised the "school without walls" concept such as the experimental Parkway School in Philadelphia—a school without a site, whose "classrooms" are the museums, libraries, business institutions, and government offices of the city. "It is a school that permits students to do the kind of creative, independent study they are rightfully seeking," said Gores.

Another change that must come is a curriculum that is more relevant to the lives of students.

"Students have had it with the kind of curriculum that they perceive to be one of simonizing rather than humanizing their learning," says Ole Sand, director of NEA's Schools for the seventies publications program.

In an article he prepared for the September issue of *Today's Education,* Sand pointed out that students seem to be asking for more "existential" learning—learning from their own living. And they want a curriculum that confronts the facts of war, racism, riots, and urban decay, and helps students find answers to these societal ills as well as to the urgent perennial questions of:

Who am I? Where am I going?

There was also a feeling among conference spokesmen that technology must begin to be used more skillfully to change the teacher from a foreman on a school assembly line to the prober, the diagnostician, the catalytic agent who spurs students to want to learn.

Though today's student activist decries the indifferent, computerized education he feels he receives, it may well be the computer and other products of modern technology that humanize the schools.

According to Sand, the teacher of the seventies will spend hundreds of hours in planning and programming instructional materials for the computer, preparing educational television programs or recording tapes and records.

"School" as we now know it will disappear. A student may not arrive at the school building until noon because he has been studying with instructional television at home. Or he may go to a community center (maybe a converted storefront) where there are computers to teach him how to read or spell or figure.

"But he will still need—and receive more of—the teacher's guidance," stresses Sand, "not the kind of teacher who has to be an all-purpose walking-talking oracle all day every day to 25 or 35 youngsters, but a clinical specialist who can diagnose his students' private personal needs and strengths."

"And even with computers available at a score of other locations, the student will come to school—not for its information so much as for its argument," says the NEA staff member. "The discussion with his fellows and a wise teacher in the pit can determine whether he turns out to be educated rather than just smart."

Will these changes produce the "relevance" and "humaneness" in education that students are demanding?

Not in themselves, perhaps, but both Gores and Sand feel that such changes can produce an environment, a curriculum, and a style of teaching that make no compromise with truth or significance.

53 | Why Students Rebel

Jack R. Frymier

Student protests are not new. Confrontation on a widespread scale, though, is fairly recent. Why is this so? Why are students protesting, anyway? Descriptions are in the news almost every day. Analyses and explanations, however, are more difficult to come by. This paper is an attempt to set forth one explanation of why young people are striking back at the institutions which are supposedly designed to serve their educational needs.

Educational institutions are social systems. Every social system is a human undertaking aimed at furthering or realizing human goals. Because people are involved, problems always arise. Human ventures are subject to human frailties simply because people are not perfect.

WHAT ARE THE OPTIONS?

When a problem area comes into focus, what options are available to those who are involved? Five avenues of thought or action seem possible.

When a person or group of persons in an educational situation feel oppressed, denied, or restrained, the "problem" comes into view. Whatever the nature of the problem, the first option available to the individual who feels slighted or wronged is to request a change. He can go to "the powers that be" and complain, and thus attempt to persuade them to bring about change. If those who feel wronged or constrained are successful in their efforts to persuade the professor to change the grade or the chairman to grant the raise or the college to expand the program, then the problem is solved.

If he is unsuccessful in his efforts to persuade, then the person with the complaint can "go over the head" of the immediate authority and complain to those "above." That is, if the student cannot convince the professor to change his grade, he can request the department chairman to bring pressure to bear in hopes of getting the professor to change his mind. If the professor cannot convince his departmental chairman to grant a financial raise, he can appeal to the dean or even further up the academic "chain of command." If members of the Black Student Union cannot get the history department to offer a series of courses in "black history," they can go

From *Educational Leadership*, Vol. 27, No. 4 (January 1970), pp. 346-350. Reprinted with permission of the Association for Supervision and Curriculum Development and the author. Copyright 1970 by the Association for Supervision and Curriculum Development.

to the faculty senate or the academic vice president of the institution which is involved. Employing the traditional concept of administrative appeal, those who feel oppressed or denied can ask persons in positions of authority "over" those who refuse to bring about the change to use their superior "power" to "force" the others to change. Recycling the original request back through the entire authority chain, then, is the second option open to any person with a problem such as those that have been described.

If these efforts to persuade fail, what happens then? What options are available to persons who have been unsuccessful in their efforts to persuade "the powers that be" to change? Three choices seem evident: give in, get out, or revolt. To the person who feels that he has a legitimate concern, none of these alternatives is seen as a "positive" or "desirable" choice at all.

As long as "the powers that be"—be they instructors, administrators, janitors, secretaries, or counselors—are *reasonable* men, the system functions reasonably well. That is, if those who are in a position to give grades, grant raises, open closed courses, offer new courses, or whatnot are thoughtful, sensitive, honest, considerate men, then most problems can usually be "talked through" to a satisfactory solution. Through the give-and-take of dialogue and informal negotiations, persons who have honest differences of opinion can usually work out their problems in a mutually acceptable way. But if the person "in charge" (of the course of the department or the program) is a rigid, insensitive, inflexible, dogmatic human being, then the problem remains and may even be enlarged.

Back to the options which remain. If the original effort to *persuade* the individual in a position of authority to change is unsuccessful, and if recycling the persuasive effort through *appeal* further up the administrative line also fails, then the *give in, get out,* or *revolt* options confront the individual who feels that he has been wronged or constrained in a very direct way.

"Give in! Knuckle under! Do as you are told!" This choice is clearly available, and many persons in educational institutions accept this alternative as the lesser of evils. Because it requires submission on the part of the person who feels that he has been wronged, resentment and frustration generally accompany this option, if it is pursued.

"Get out! Withdraw! Leave!" This is another possibility which becomes evident if the persuasive efforts have failed. The individual may leave—physically or psychologically—and many admonitions along that line are sure to come his way. "If you don't like it here, why don't you leave?" "Either do as the authorities say, or get out and stay out!" The choice is exceptionally clear and some persons leave. Others "drop out" psychologically; they become apathetic, but stay. Such persons forego the hardships of the moment for the diploma and what it seems to assure, but their self-respect and their integrity have been destroyed. "If you can't beat them, join them," they are apt to say.

Some students, however, revolt. Unwilling to accept the fact that their efforts to persuade have come to no avail, they will not give in or get out, so the only option left is to strike back and out and down. "The system must be changed," they say, but most people do not seem to know just what they mean.

Violence, rebellion, and destruction are terrible extremes. One can attempt to explain away such actions on the basis of an "international conspiracy" or a "wild group of young nihilists," but there is a more fundamental and even simpler explanation. The system is rigid. The *system is not capable of rational, deliberate change.* The system must be changed.

There is absolutely no doubt that some Marxists and some anarchists are participating in revolutionary efforts on college campuses and high school campuses today. That much is certain. One only has to walk through college bookstores, read underground newspapers, or listen to certain protesters to recognize the fact that some persons are espousing the Marxist-Leninist or Mao Tse-tung propaganda line. Such persons are very easy to find. Like all persons advocating the ideology of a closed society, the propositions which they advance and the monologue which they maintain are never their own. One can even predict what their next words will be, they hew so closely to the party line.

Such self-styled revolutionaries are dangerous on a campus or anywhere, not because they advocate a Communist or anarchist philosophy, but because they are articulate automatons who seem to but actually do not think. Such "true believers" are always dangerous, precisely because they are irrationally convinced of the justness of their cause.

But there are not many of these "hard core" revolutionaries on any campus or in any place where there is unrest in the United States today. The basic reason for the militancy is inherent in the fact that the system as a system is not capable of systematic, intelligent, compassionate change; thus the cry that "the system must be changed." To say it another way, *the system must be changed so that the system can cope with change.*[1]

To charge that the system is not theoretically capable of change, though, is a serious charge. Is that statement true? I think it is.

---

1. These ideas are developed more fully in: Jack R. Frymier, *Fostering Educational Change* (Columbus, Ohio: Charles E. Merrill Publishing Company, 1969).

CHANGE IN A SOCIAL SYSTEM

Education is a social system. Those social systems which have integrity—that is, those which are whole and concerned with truth—are characterized in particular ways which might be thought of as "democratic" or "effective" or both. There is a deliberate *distribution of authority according to function,* in other words, and a way of working which ensures that truth will out and the best answer will prevail. Educational systems are not characterized in either of these ways.

Planning, implementing, and evaluating are the primary functions which any social system must accomplish if it is to realize the human objectives which it seeks to attain. Those social systems which have integrity and are fully functioning are characterized by the fact that each of the functions outlined above is accomplished by a different group which has authority. Further, the evaluative function is that point at which both continuity and change can be assured.

At times some systems work better than others, that much is sure, and at times any system functions more effectively or less effectively than it did before. Even so, the evaluative function is the key. Perhaps a closer look at the system as a functioning whole will show why this is so.

The planning, conceptualizing, thinking-through policy-making phase of education is typically accomplished by the governing board. It is here that general directions and broad policies for the system are described. In government this is where the laws are made. In industry this is where the decision to produce a particular product or service is made. Every social system has a planning, direction-setting, conceptualizing function which must be performed.

The accomplishing, implementing, doing phase of the educational system is a function which the professionals perform. Converting policies into programs and concepts into organizational and methodological procedures, the professional staff of any educational system operationalizes the plans which the governing board sets forth. In government this function is accomplished by the executive branch. In industry the policies established by the board of directors are converted into products or services to be sold by management and workers. Cars are manufactured. Coal is mined. Food is sold.

THE EVALUATIVE FUNCTION

The evaluative function in education represents a system void. There is no formally established group with influence which accomplishes the assessing role. In government the evaluative function is accomplished by the judiciary. The courts weigh and consider and judge. "Are the laws which the legislature made constitutional?" "Are the actions of the executive branch appropriate and legal in a constitutional way?" In industry the buying public evaluates the product or service when it goes on sale. "Is it made well?" "Will it do what I want it to do?" "Should I buy it—yes or no?"

Those social systems which are fully functioning use evaluative data as corrective feedback to improve. When evaluations occur, new information is generated which did not exist before. If the buying public refuses to buy a particular product or service (in other words, if their evaluation results in negative action), what they do is create new knowledge which tells those who planned or those who produced that something about their efforts went wrong. Perhaps the idea (for example, the plans to produce a car with certain characteristics, with certain dimensions, in a given price range, etc.) was inappropriate or wrong, or perhaps it was not operationalized in a satisfactory way (for example, the seams were not welded adequately, the motor did not run efficiently, etc.), or both. On the other hand, if the evaluations are positive and the people buy, that also creates new knowledge that did not exist before (for example, the price range is right, the production line is doing a superb assembly job, the motor functions powerfully in a very efficient way), and the system uses the feedback as a basis for keeping the operation satisfactorily and effectively under way.

The evaluative function, then, is the precise point at which new information is made available to enable the system to maintain its operation or to improve. Those social systems which are both durable and responsive—self-perpetuating, but with the capacity to change—reflect three different but related factors when the evaluative function is accomplished: *generation of new information, evaluation by a group with authority of its own, and a criterion against which to judge which is both accepted and clear.* When these factors are in evidence, then the evaluative function has the theoretical power to enable the system both to continue and to change.

The existence of the judiciary as a separate branch of the government, for example, illustrates the existence of an evaluative group. When the courts make decisions, they create new information which did not exist before. These decisions also have power. The rest of the system, in other words, pays attention to the feedback. Because there is a Constitution which clarifies the purposes and which has been ratified, the reality of an articulated and accepted criterion is also involved. In economics the same thing is true. One group plans. Another produces. And the buying public judges the plans and the product or service in an evaluative way. Furthermore, the judgments of the buying public have power. The producers and the planners have to pay attention to what the buyers say. And the criterion of profit is both conspicuous and accepted by all parties involved.

In education the system is otherwise. There is neither a formal nor an informal group which functions as a part of the system to accomplish the evaluative role. There is no "third party" which is "objective" and which has authority to whom those who feel constrained or denied can turn. They can only go back up the same "legal line" which created the circumstances out of which the problem grew in the first place. Further, when evaluations are made, there is no insistence within the system that they be utilized. New data may become available as a result of evaluative efforts, but there are no clearly stated objectives which either have been ratified or are so widely understood as to have impact. Therefore, when evaluations do take place, they may be attended to or they may be completely ignored. It is in this sense that the educational system as presently conceived is largely incapable of self renewal and rational change.

CHANGING THE SYSTEM

What might be done? Several things might be attempted, but the system must certainly be changed. Changing the people has been often advocated. Changing the system is another thing. Unless the system itself is changed, it will not be capable of thoughtful, deliberate educational change.

What is needed, of course, is some kind of evaluative mechanism which is sufficiently sensitive to the problems and concerns of those who are involved that it will be in a position to respond. However, this group must have adequate authority of its own. It dare not be a part of the hierarchy, and there must be a deliberate effort to distribute authority according to function rather than to consolidate authority. The "top-down" concept must be changed.

One cannot portray our concept of government in a "top-down" way. The legislative, the executive, and the judicial are separate and equal branches of the government. It is possible to show a line and staff arrangement of each of the three branches separately, but one branch of government cannot be described as "above" the others in a hierarchical way. Each has a function and an authority of its own.

In education, though, the policy makers and implementers are typically thought of and described in linear ways: governing boards are at the "top" and those who implement are "below." There is no separate group which has authority in the evaluative realm, either. That conceptual void has to be filled with a newly devised group, and that group must be granted the authority to accomplish the evaluative role.

Some universities have inaugurated the ombudsman idea, for example, as an effort to fill that theoretical void. Others have attempted to involve students more extensively in the formal decision-making structure of the university in order to assure them that their voice and their concerns would be heard. Such steps will not solve the problem, though they are definitely appropriate directions in which to go.

Expanding involvement is very important, but guaranteeing participation is no assurance that the evaluative function will be adequately performed. Likewise, the ombudsman idea is most certainly sound, but in those countries where the ombudsman functions most effectively,[2] there already exists a fully-developed judicial system which accomplishes the basic evaluative role. Presuming that the ombudsman can satisfactorily perform all of the basic evaluative functions plus the "extra" evaluative refinements which he traditionally accomplishes is probably not reasonable. This is not meant to suggest that the ombudsman idea is not an important one—it is. Yet we dare not expect one man to accomplish on an "extra" basis (usually in addition to certain other duties) that which probably ought to be attended to by a group of persons working full-time in an evaluative way.

The basic issue, of course, is the governance structure of the educational system. Can it be satisfactorily accomplished "top-down"? Will it work effectively if evaluations are accomplished by the same persons who have responsibilities for policy making and implementing roles? I think not. The system must be changed.

Young people all over the world have been sending the adult community messages in many ways. Their ideas are not all sound. Their behavior is certainly not always appropriate or defensible at all. And the fact that some persons flout the law, destroy property, and violate the integrity of other persons is certainly not to be condoned. Such behavior is unacceptable and must be dealt with in legal but humane ways.

Even so, the complaints are real. The system is rigid. It is not capable of rational, deliberate change. "Good" men in the system can do a lot to make the system function reasonably well, but any system which requires "good men" to make it go is also a system which will allow a scalawag or an autocrat to wreak havoc and behave in arbitrary, obstinate ways. That is the system we have today, and that system must be changed. We must devise evaluative mechanisms which are sufficiently sensitive but fully responsive to the dynamic state of education. We must agree upon the purposes of education, and see to it that assessments and judgments are made according to those terms of purpose.

Schools do not exist to serve taxpayers' needs. Neither do they exist to serve administrators' or teachers' needs. Schools exist to

2. Walter Gellhorn, *Ombudsman and Others in Nine Countries* (Cambridge, Massachusetts: Harvard University Press, 1967).

help young people learn. Students are rebelling, but many of their complaints are unquestionably real.

Those who work in education have a problem. Since problems are their stock-in-trade, it seems reasonable to expect that they should apply the power of intelligence to the business of solving this particular problem. Let's hope they will. Repressive tendencies abound. We do not need educational institutions which are less free, but rather those which are more free. Progress always starts with criticism. Many persons are complaining now. "The system must be changed," they say. The governance structure of the educational system is one place to begin.

54 | Those High School Protestors Can Boards Put Up With Much More?

Gregory R. Anrig

Any other society at any other time would find teenagers like ours fully productive members of the community—earning a living and raising a family.

Yet in an age when students are brighter than ever before, better educated and more concerned about a contributing role in society, we continue to treat them as young children rather than as young adults.

Do we wonder, then, why student unrest in high schools is on the rise?

The college protestors still get most of the attention, but the fact is there already have been more incidents of student unrest in the *high schools* than in the colleges. The situation is likely to get worse in the future.

The facts are enough to cause considerable worry for school boards. In just the four months between last November 10 and March 10, for example, more than 340 student protests took place in high schools in 38 states and the District of Columbia. According to a study conducted by the National Association of Secondary School Principals, three out of five high school principals have experienced active protests of one kind or another in their schools. In large urban areas, it is three out of four.

The potential for disturbances in high schools is impressive. There are, after all, no more than 1,600 four-year colleges and universities in the country. But there are *twenty-six thousand* high schools with two and a half times the enrollment of the colleges. Certainly, school board members and administrators don't need to be reminded more than once that these younger high school students are potentially more volatile than their college counterparts. Nor will I dwell upon the identification of the local community with its high school and the vulnerability of these schools to community pressures of all kinds. While the press and television are not yet focusing prime attention on high school unrest, school boards must share the concern that alternatives to violence and repression must be found and put into effect before the situation in the high schools becomes explosive.

In an effort to find such alternatives, Robert H. Finch, shortly after his appointment as Secretary of Health, Education and Welfare,

From *American School Board Journal* (October 1969), pp. 20-24. Reprinted by permission of the publisher. Copyright 1969 by National School Board Association.

organized a number of study groups to analyze key social issues and recommend to him what HEW's position should be for the future. Each group was urged to involve the private sector as well as other agencies of government. It was my privilege to lead a study of student unrest in our colleges and secondary schools.

In a sharp departure from traditional government planning, members of the study group have since crossed the country meeting privately with school officials and community representatives in the hope that sharing our findings will help school boards deal more effectively with the issues of unrest in their own communities.

Student disorders, we found, are increasing in rural and suburban areas as well as in the cities. For the first time, school personnel and board members in places like Jonesboro, Ga., and Kingsville, Tex., and Lowell, Mass., are experiencing the kinds of tensions and pressures that urban board members and educators have learned to face as a matter of routine.

We have discovered a great deal of similarity in the surface and basic issues underlying unrest both on the college campus and in the high school. Both typically are concerned with dehumanization of institutional life, inequities in our society, educational irrelevance, and racial and cultural discrimination.

But there the similarity ends. The difference: College disorders tend to be planned, structured, deliberate acts of protest. High school disorders usually are more precipitous, spontaneous and riot-like, touched off by such incidents as the election of cheerleaders all of one race, suspension of a student, or a scuffle between two students. High school disorders also are more often marked by student-to-student conflict and therefore are more physically dangerous than college disorders.

The 341 high school incidents that took place during those four months of the last school year fall into five general categories. Most often the incidents involved racial issues. Other categories of disturbances in order of frequency were political protests, resentment of dress regulations, objections to disciplinary actions, and educational policy issues. Many disturbances involve two or, in some instances, more of these general categories.

As on the college campus, black protests in the high schools are distinct and different from those of white students. While some of the more radical white students totally reject our social system and its values, black students more often than not are protesting to get a greater "piece of the action" within the existing framework. Black protests are for recognition, respect, greater power, and the right of self-awareness—all within the society, albeit a greatly changed society. Minority protests are not limited to black students alone; similar issues have been raised by Mexican-American and Puerto Rican students in many high schools.

Our findings convince us that it is a mistake to assume that *root causes* of disorders—in the high schools or the colleges—are a few disgruntled agitators from inside or outside the school. As one administrator frankly admitted to us, an agitator can be effective only where widespread discontent exists.

It is important to recognize that demonstrators and their sympathizers usually comprise a significant number of the total enrollment in a school. Increasingly this group includes some of our brightest and most socially concerned students—the ones we always took pleasure in honoring at graduation ceremonies.

A report prepared for us attempted to analyze teacher and student views on high school disorders in a small sample of troubled schools. Teachers and students identified four causes as most often contributing to the disruption in their schools: (1) interracial tensions among students, (2) outside agitators and the mass media, (3) permissive upbringing of children and normal adolescent rebelliousness, and (4) student disrespect for teachers. Black students additionally stress the generation gap and teacher discrimination. When teachers in the study were asked what school changes they would most like to see, the most popular answer was "tighter discipline" followed by "changes in the curriculum" and "better caliber of administrators."

When they were asked who should influence school policies, teachers in the study strongly desired (1) reducing the influence of superintendents, (2) increasing the influence of principals and teachers, and (3) maintaining the current level of influence of students. Students uniformly favored increasing the influence of persons low in the current school hierarchy—themselves and teachers—but they differed predictably from teachers on how they would share this new influence. Although students in general did not advocate much greater parental control, black students did. This may reflect their reaction to the fact that most school authorities they see are white.

It is unquestionably true that high school and college disorders reflect societal ills outside of the school, and yet we found strong feeling that there would still be disorders even if problems like Viet Nam were solved tomorrow. *Students also are protesting basic institutional weaknesses in our educational systems at all levels.* In many ways, students are vocally and sometimes violently expressing their impatience with the slow pace of educational change in today's fast changing society. In this context, they are joining you—school board members and administrators who have been working hard in your communities to improve education. While we may be offended by some of their techniques, we ought to recognize that *many student demands are sound and legitimate demands for educational improvement.*

It is essential as well that we recognize that youngsters employ the techniques they do because they have lost hope that change will result without such confrontations.

Some observers believe student disputes should be mediated on the model of labor-management bargaining. We found little support for this concept by those actually experiencing disorders. Many of the disorders are viewed by the students involved as dealing with "gut" issues such as justice and equity, for which there can be no compromise. Many school board members and administrators believe the disorders go to the very existence of their institutions and the laws under which they operate. The result is a "nonnegotiables" barrier on both sides, further complicated by the formlessness of student protest, and lack of continuous spokesmen. In short, mediation requires bargaining, and bargaining assumes there are two identifiable sides that are willing to deal with each other on an equal basis. Very few, if any, student protests present this kind of order.

What can school boards do—indeed, what *must* they do—to ensure that constructive educational change, for the better, results from the current unrest?

Change, it has been pointed out before, is most likely to occur when those involved finally recognize that what exists is not doing the required job. In that sense, today's student unrest is a significant opportunity once boardmen get over the shock of its accompanying rhetoric and emotional heat. It took Sputnik, a small Russian satellite, to shake taxpayers and educators across the country into upgrading educational opportunities for intellectually gifted children in the 1950s. Perhaps student disorders can have a similar impact towards improving opportunities for *all* students and making our schools more attuned to the realities of the world our students face.

It is in this context that I urge school board members and administrators to think more in terms of educational change than in terms of repression and control when considering student unrest. *Suppression may temporarily solve disorder but it does not cure unrest.* No one wants violence and destruction. We all advocate judicious use of all available legal resources to protect persons and property. I am urging that school boards not limit themselves to the issue of order and discipline when dealing with today's student unrest.

It is in that context that I would like to return to the overriding question: How can boards and administrators work for a constructive result from student unrest? Here are six suggestions:

- All school districts should follow the lead of those urban districts that are encouraging increased involvement and are sharing real

power with teachers, students and parents. As any board of education member will admit, no one can be entirely ready to accept decision-making responsibilities in education. You learn as you go
with the help of others. We must be willing to share this opportunity and make our schools more public in the truest sense.

- School boards must find alternatives to the "tight ship" syndrome
  that characterizes the regimented life a student faces, especially
  in our high schools, where even the need to go to the washroom requires a public declaration in class and a brightly colored plaque
  visible enroute.

- School boards must open up new and broader communication with
  their patrons and clients—the students in our schools. Our schools,
  our economy and our homes seem to be prolonging childhood for
  a serious generation of young people who want to be a part of the
  action. These youngsters need more respect. Certainly while we
  may debate what is "negotiable," we likely would agree that *student* views on policies and practices that directly affect *students* at
  least are "discussable." We need to listen to youngsters in the fullest sense and *to judge the merit of the views—not the age or appearance of the speaker.*

- School boards need to seek greater relevance in learning—relevance to the world of work, and relevance to the community with
  which the student identifies himself. Most school-sponsored work
  experiences, as we know, begin *after* the student is eligible to drop
  out of school—often too late for him to recognize that learning is
  relevant to earning a living. Too frequently school job training is
  outmoded and outclassed by training resources outside of school
  that might better be used. We urge social conformity on young
  people but provide little opportunity for social participation. Why
  not have store front schools? Why *not* use high school students
  from the ghetto to work with elementary school children or with
  adult illiterates? Why *not* move the school experience out of the
  classroom and into the social service centers of the community?
  Many of our urban districts already can point to exciting projects
  that spark enthusiasm and learning. But these projects continue
  to experience the fate of too many before them—great ideas that
  never become part of all school operations.

- School boards need to change the ways in which they select and
  train those who take the critical job of high school principal.
  Should seniority, certification requirements, and examination
  scores prevail over sensitivity and imagination? I think not.
  Boards must bring pressure to bear upon schools of education to
  recruit more effectively, educate more effectively, and screen more
  effectively those who enter the education profession. The reservoir
  of talent available to school districts must be enlarged and en-
  livened and enlightened.

- Finally, school board members and all the rest of us who have some power in this business of education must be more willing to look at ourselves critically, to judge our own actions and reactions regarding those who confront and trouble us, and be willing to change our attitudes towards others who are claiming what they see—often quite accurately—as their rights.

55 | In Search of New Answers

Mary Kathryn Patterson

We hope to become the leaders of tomorrow's world. We realize, however, that in order to really contribute to the progress of humanity we must first attempt to understand the people and the problems of the world. But even before we can do this, we must understand ourselves. We must recognize our own strengths and weaknesses. Only with this foundation can each of us realize our own unique possibilities. We hope our education has given us this basis for understanding ourselves.

In high school we tried to determine our strong points as well as our weaknesses. We also discovered some of the things we like to do —the things we have a talent for doing. This is a good beginning.

But it is only a beginning. You have seen us strive to attain this beginning. You have seen us go through all sorts of growing pains, and I'm sure many of you have wondered whether you would make it from one day to the next when we rebelled against what you thought was best for us. But we really weren't trying to be difficult—we were only trying to express ourselves. This rebellion was a way of proving to ourselves that we were grown and had minds of our own. This rebellion was our way of convincing ourselves that we were capable, self-reliant and responsible.

We could not always take your advice and still be proud of our accomplishments. But we have learned a lot about how to express ourselves during these years in school. Many different teachers have taught us how to observe, how to think, and how to say what we think.

We have found that it is not good enough just to repeat what we have been told. The problems of today's world need new answers, and unless we think and feel things for ourselves and then express our thoughts and feelings there will be no new solutions to these problems.

We want to be able to believe in our ideas and principles enough to stand up for them even when others disagree. It is easy to be agreeable and to go along with the ideas of others. It requires no effort. But it takes strength and courage to stand up for our convictions when they set us apart from the crowd. High school students are often criticized for being non-conformists, when we are really only trying to express our individuality.

From *North Carolina Education*, Vol. 36 (September 1969), p. 17. Reprinted by permission of the publisher.

In order to develop strong traits of character we must learn to stand by our convictions in the face of criticism.

In our process of maturing we have, at times, felt restrained by parents, teachers, regulations, and requirements. Out attitudes toward these restraints may have often led you to believe that we rejected your principles. But we did not do so. We were only trying to develop our own principles. Perhaps we were sometimes unconsciously testing *you* to see if *you* would really stand by *your* convictions. For it was the people who stood by their beliefs whom we came to respect and to wish to imitate.

Our new urges and interests are trying to find a useful channel. A revolt may be a new and useful idea trying to come out. We are aware that at times our rebellion against discipline and authority may seem completely undesirable to parents and teachers. We hope you will believe that at least sometimes something good may be trying to come out.

We want you to listen to our ideas and be receptive to those which are good. We hope you will listen honestly and be open to new thoughts. If so, you can help us to evaluate our new ideas. This is the kind of help you can give us now.

I believe each person has a unique set of talents and capabilities and only in developing them can he find the most satisfaction in living. The world needs new ideas and fresh solutions to old problems. New problems must be recognized and new solutions provided. We have been born into an environment which favors independent thought and development. This new climate is ideal for self-expression.

We are ready to try expressing the best ideas we have. We hope to lead lives that will contribute in some way to human progress.

56 | Student Constitutional Rights
The Role of the Principal

William E. Griffiths

"You can't do that to me, it's against the law!" "I'll sue you!"
"You are taking away my constitutional rights!" There are probably
few secondary school principals who have not heard some variation of the foregoing from pupils or parents in recent years. And
in all likelihood such confrontations will increase rather than
diminish.

We have entered a new era of individual rights and the chances
are great that the secondary school will be increasingly affected.
Beatle-type hair cuts, distinctive dress, the wearing of slogan buttons,
and the donning of black armbands may be but the forerunners of
things to come as adolescents seek new ways to express their freedom. The new bounds established for freedom of speech, religion,
and press; the revolution in pretrial criminal procedure; the revamp-
ing of juvenile court processes to accord the young accused rights
formerly reserved for adults; the ferment of the college campus—all
will most certainly have influence on high schools.

While the underlying stimuli and relative merits of those "new
freedoms" will probably be debated for some time, the secondary
school principal is unable to postpone involvement until the final
answers are given. The principal has a precarious role to play in
helping his institution adapt to the dynamics of society, since as an
institution the secondary school properly reflects social change.

A SPOT IN THE MIDDLE

In the area of student rights the principal is the man in the
middle, a spot with which he is all too familiar. He is caught in
the crossfire of multiple pressure groups asserting divergent, inconsistent, incompatible, and sometimes nebulous demands. To reconcile the pressure from teachers to terminate the attendance of the
nonconforming student and the demand from the civil libertarians to
accord nonconformity a priority in the value system would require
the patience of Job combined with the wisdom of Solomon. Similarly, to reconcile the rights of the individual students with the mores
of the school community is no mean task. Add to this the admonition
of administrative superordinates and school boards to refrain from
"rocking the boat" and we find the secondary principal in an awk-

From *NASSP Bulletin*, Vol. 52 (September 1968), pp. 30-37. Reprinted by permission
of the National Association of Secondary School Principals. Copyright: 1968 by the
National Association of Secondary School Principals.

ward stance at best in the crosscurrents of legality, morality, and vested interest.

What can be done to strike a balance between the rights of the individual student and the demands of the institution? The answer lies in bold and imaginative leadership on the part of all professional educators, but especially of those in a position closest to the heart of the problem, the secondary school principals. The handwriting is on the wall; public school students will be protected in their constitutional rights. This has become clear in federal court decisions which will be discussed in a moment and which afford sound guidelines for administrative action. Educators now face the dilemma of seizing the initiative or of permitting the decision to be made for them by the courts, the "collective conscience" of the country.

It should be noted that educators stood by for decades, perhaps reluctantly, while the religious freedom of students guaranteed by the First Amendment was impinged upon. Likewise, no great clamor was heard from the profession to reduce educational inequalities caused by racial segregation. In each instance the judiciary was called upon to decide an issue in education which the professionals were reluctant to recognize or unwilling to admit. There are indications that the matter of "student rights" is far from settled by the judiciary. Significant constitutional issues are yet to be resolved, but the trend is clear. Educational leadership wisely exercised can avoid the necessity for conforming later to judicial decree.

INSTANCES OF JUDICIAL ACTION

Before making suggestions for administrative action it might be well to examine several court cases concerned with student rights. A decision involving a " Beatle" haircut was rendered by the Supreme Judicial Court of Massachusetts in 1965.[1] George Leonard, Jr., a senior at Attleboro High School, appeared at school on opening day wearing a long hairdo. Two days later he was sent home by his principal and told not to return without a haircut. A letter followed advising that dress regulations did not allow extreme haircuts. Subsequently, at a hearing before the school committee, the principal's action was upheld. At all times the student was well-behaved, conscientious, and properly dressed. He earned substantial sums of money as a musical performer, and he and his parents had gone to considerable expense in furtherance of his musical education. The Court upheld the theory that a school committee can make all reasonable rules and regulations for the discipline and management of the public schools and can expel a child for sufficient cause.

To the contention that the rule was unreasonable and arbitrary, the Court stated that there is a presumption in favor of school com-

1. Leonard v. Attleboro, 349 Mass. 704, 212 N.E. (2d) 468 (1965).

mittees that rules are made after mature deliberation and for the welfare of the community. "[We] need only perceive some rational basis for the rule requiring acceptable haircuts to sustain its validity" the Court said, and then found a rational basis in the possibility that "departures from accepted customs in the manner of haircuts could result in the distraction of other pupils." The Court also refused to accept the argument that the hair style was a private matter, touching upon the student while at home and under the jurisdiction of his parents and that the school rule reached too broadly into the domain of private life and parental responsibility. " . . . [the] domain of family privacy must give way insofar as a regulation reasonably calculated to maintain school discipline may affect it," the Court asserted.

Perhaps more significant than the rather sweeping ratification of school committee authority was the Court's rejection of the constitutional issues raised. Counsel for the student had included in his brief that "freedom of mind and of expression is part of the basic guaranty of the First Amendment." The Court dismissed this with the comment, "The constitutional points suggested in the plaintiff's brief require no discussion."

Will the decision of the Massachusetts court pass the test of time? It is doubtful. Viewed in the context of a dynamic society, that decision seems to ignore a burning constitutional issue. In allotting such priority to school committee authority, the Court appears to fall into a trap in which it was ensnared before. Prior to the Supreme Court mandate on religious freedom,[2] for example, it was common for state courts in public school-religion cases to disregard constitutional issues raised and base decisions on school board authority. Thus in Massachusetts a court (in 1866) saw fit to declare it within the sphere of school committee authority to require attendance of a public school pupil at a religious ceremony against the wishes of the pupil and her parents and further to prescribe the mode of posture during such devotions.[3]

CHANGING VIEWS ON SCHOOL AUTHORITY

It is also interesting to note that the same Massachusetts court which today permits committees to exclude students from school for nonconforming hair styles was a pioneer in upholding racial segregation in the public schools.[4] In this decision the Court held as a valid exercise of school committee authority the enforcement of a

2. Engel v. Vitale, 370 U.S. 421, 82 Sup. Ct. 1261, 8 L. Ed. (2d) 601 (1962); School District of Abington Township v. Schempp, 374 U.S. 203, 83 Sup. Ct. 1560, 10 L. Ed. (2d) 844 (1963).
3. Spiller v. Woburn, 12 Allen (94 Mass.) 127 (1866).
4. Roberts v. The City of Boston, 5 Cush. (59 Mass.) 198 (1849).

regulation requiring that white and Negro elementary school pupils be educated in separate schools. It may be significant that the decision hinges upon the broad interpretation of school committee authority in both decisions.

In each of the two preceding instances—religious freedom and racial segregation—the veritably limitless authority of the school committee to invade the rights of pupils gave way in time to a legal philosophy which protected the rights of students while acknowledging the authority of school committees. Can this middle road be found by educators without the intercession of the courts?

The issue of how far a school board can go in enforcing regulations which infringe upon students' freedom of speech and which are anticipatory in that they are promulgated and enforced prior to any disturbing effect upon the school was the subject of a recent Federal District Court decision.[5] The case originated in an action taken against the enforcement of regulations prohibiting the wearing of black armbands by pupils. In December 1955, it came to the attention of school authorities in Des Moines, Iowa, that pupils intended to wear black armbands to school for the purpose of protesting the Viet Nam war. A regulation prohibiting such wearing was promulgated and students who violated it were sent home. They returned after the Christmas holiday without wearing them.

To the question whether the enforcement of the rule deprived the pupils of constitutional rights the court answered in the negative. Wearing of armbands is a symbolic act which falls within the free speech clause of the First Amendment, the Court found, but pointed out that the freedom is not absolute, that abridgement of free speech must be considered in relation to the intent of the regulation and the abridgement that actually occurs.

Affirming the right of school authorities to enact regulations which anticipate *future possible* school disturbances, the Court said that school officials are to be given wide discretion and if " . . . under the circumstances a disturbance in school discipline is reasonably to be anticipated, actions which are reasonably calculated to prevent such a disruption must be upheld by the Court." In view of the vehement debate over the war and such protests as draft card burnings the Court found the rule reasonable. "In this instance, however, it is the disciplined atmosphere of the classroom, not the plaintiff's right to wear armbands on school premises, which is entitled to protection of the law."

In my opinion, granting power to school authorities to enforce regulations which impinge upon students' freedom of speech where school officials reasonably anticipate disruption of the school may be carrying the "clear and present danger" doctrine too far.

5. Tinker v. Des Moines Independent Community School District, 258 Fed. Supp. 971 (1966).

RECENT JUDICIAL GUIDELINES

Perhaps the most useful guidelines for action can be extracted from two companion cases recently decided by the U. S. Court of Appeals. In the two cases the cause of action involved similar circumstances, arose in the same judicial district, and were decided by the same court at the same time. These decisions have become known as the "freedom-button cases" and should be known and appreciated by all secondary principals.

The first case originated in Philadelphia, Mississippi,[6] when pupils sought an injunction to restrain school officials from enforcing a rule prohibiting students from wearing freedom buttons at school. The buttons were disc-type pins one and one-half inches in diameter inscribed "One Man One Vote" around the perimeter and "SNCC" in the center. The pupils claimed infringement of free speech rights under the First and Fourteenth Amendments.

The Court of Appeals stated that the Constitution protects the free speech of school children against unreasonable rules and regulations imposed by school authorities. The liberty of expression so guaranteed, however, can be abridged if legitimate state interest necessitates an invasion of free speech. The test of school rules is one of reasonableness, the Court added, and regulations are reasonable if they are essential to maintain order and discipline even if they do invade students' rights to freedom of speech and association. Applying that test, the Court found the Philadelphia, Mississippi, school regulation arbitrary, unreasonable, and an unnecessary infringement on the students' protected rights of free speech.

Evidence in that case showed that the student body expressed only a "mild curiosity" over the presence of from 30 to 40 pupils wearing buttons. In fact, the principal testified that the pupils were expelled for disobeying a regulation, not for creating a disturbance or disrupting the school. In the absence of disturbance and interference with educational activity the principal had exceeded his authority in enforcing the rule, the Court said, and continued:

. . . [School] officials cannot ignore expressions of feeling with which they do not wish to contend. They cannot infringe on their students' right to free and unrestricted expression as guaranteed to them under the First Amendment of the Constitution, where the exercise of such rights in the school buildings and schoolrooms do not materially and substantially interfere with the requirements of appropriate discipline in the operation of the school.

In the second decision the same court reached the opposite conclusion. The facts were similar in most respects except that in the second case students wearing buttons were creating a disturbance by talking in the corridors when they were supposed to be in class.

6. Burnside v. Byars, 363 F. (2d) 744 (1966).

Also, some students took the liberty of pinning buttons on fellow students although they were unasked for. Such activity, the Court found, "created a state of confusion, disrupted class instruction, and resulted in a general breakdown of orderly discipline."[7] In upholding the enforcement of the rule under the circumstances the court pointed out that: "In each case [courts] must ask whether the gravity of the 'evil,' discounted by its improbability, justifies such invasion of free speech or is necessary to avoid the danger."

LOOKING AHEAD

What are the implications of the foregoing judicial decisions for secondary school administration? First of all it should be stressed that the court opinions are not a substitute for administrative creativity and instructional effectiveness. While it is imperative that the administrator have a knowledge of the limits of administrative and board authority, if the educative process has been effective the number of "showdowns" should be few. The principal should be sure of his ground by knowing and understanding the law of his state. To avoid being forced into an indefensible position he should also be aware of school board rules, regulations, and attitudes on sensitive areas.

The resources of the classroom and guidance department must, of course, be tapped to assist in preventing such problems. Personal counseling might enable pupils to perceive their behavior for what it is. Perhaps social studies classes could study the original or abridgements of actual court decisions on individual rights and thereby acquire an appreciation for both sides of such controversies.

When educational efforts fail, as no doubt they will in some cases, then the "freedom button" cases afford the best and fairest guide to administrative action. In those cases, it will be remembered, the doctrine of actual interference or disruption was employed by the Court. By this standard the school authorities are not permitted to impinge on the freedom of students unless student behavior substantially and materially interferes with the discipline and good order of the school.

In all equity and justice, it is not enough that a segment of society—be it teachers, school board members, or administrators—disapproves of elements of pupil behavior or dress. Nor is it sufficient that school authorities think that the pupil if unrestrained will create some future disorder. Adhering to the standard thus far set by the judiciary will retain for educators the power of decision-making in this highly sensitive area, will avoid much needless litigation, and, most important of all, will protect the rights of students as American citizens.

7. Blackwell v. Issaquence County Board of Education, 363 F. (2d) 749 (1966).

57 | **Personalizing Student Life and Student Activities**

Robert R. Ford

Personalization of the high school program has been a long-term concern of educators as high schools have tended to increase in size. The growth in maximum enrollment has been a phenomenon wherever the availability of school sites is at a premium whether it be in the inner city or a suburban area of high real estate values.

The latter situation pertains to West High School which is one of four high schools in the Torrance Unified School District located close to the ocean in southwest Los Angeles County. This four year high school serves a middle-class suburban community. It opened in 1962 with a thousand students; present enrollment is 2,300, and it is master planned for an enrollment of 3,200.

The following article is a result of a discussion among the administrators of West High School to review present practices for personalizing student life with particular emphasis on student activities. We do not proffer a panacea for the ills of impersonality in the large school. Rather, the reader is invited to use our experiences as a springboard toward additional questing for his own school in a matter that requires concerted effort on the part of the faculty and of the student body.

When freshmen enter high school in Torrance, they come from the security of community K-8 schools. At West High School they meet freshmen from eight feeder schools and might or might not have contact with friends from their former schools. Personalizing or individualizing a student's experience so that he does not feel like a bent punch card becomes both an immediate and long-range task.

ARTICULATION

Individualization of student life at West High for incoming eighth graders starts in the spring prior to registration. Principals of the eight feeder K-8 schools share at a luncheon meeting hosted by the high school opinions and ideas on changes in curriculum and registration. When the need arises, departments host their counterparts from the elementary schools to adjust scope and sequence of

From *NASSP Bulletin*, (November 1968), pp. 76-82. Reprinted by permission of the National Association of Secondary School Principals. Copyright: 1968 by the National Association of Secondary School Principals.

the curriculum. Counselors visit the feeder schools to confer with eighth grade teachers and to explain registration procedures and materials to students. Counselors are accompanied by representatives from the music and athletic departments who explain special try-out enrollment procedures. Parents are invited to the high school for an evening meeting where counselors speak to them in small groups to provide information similar to that received by their students. Providing registration information to both parents and students promotes home discussion and involves parents in the decisions of their student. Parents are taken on a tour of the school. This is followed by a reception where they have an opportunity to meet the staff and other parents.

Parents and students are invited to meet with a high school counselor during the summer months to discuss student achievement and goals, and to finalize the selection of courses for the fall semester. Students are encouraged to give direction to their high school career by developing a tentative four-year program which, of course, may be modified as interests and abilities develop.

ORIENTATION

Freshmen are invited to school the day before classes begin for an orientation program. The principal welcomes the class, and officers of the student body are introduced. In class groups, freshmen are provided with a West High School identification card, a copy of their class schedule, the student handbook, and their book locker combination. Teachers assist students who are unable to operate locker combinations. Members of the student service group, the Chieftains, help alleviate the "butterflies in the stomach" feeling by taking freshmen on a guided tour to locate their classrooms. At the conclusion of the program, cokes and cookies are provided by the student body and freshmen are encouraged to make new friends among the students of the several feeder schools.

PROGRAM SELECTION

Academically talented students are given an opportunity to become acquainted with the high school by enrolling in a limited choice of summer school subjects at the end of the seventh and eighth grades. During their eighth grade, academically talented students may study one course at the high school, choosing algebra, earth science, or a foreign language. Fifty percent of the student body elect to individualize their instructional programs by enrolling in summer school courses. A few enroll to raise a grade. Others take courses offered only in summer school or enroll for courses which they cannot fit into their schedule during the school year. A further opportunity exists for students with a *C* or better average to individualize their programs by enrolling for seven instead of the usual six subjects.

INDEPENDENT STUDY

Independent study is an accommodation to a student's desire to focus his interest. Students as individuals or in small groups may be released from class to develop a special report or a unit of the course in which they are particularly interested. Those who are interested in longer-term independent study may receive credit for directing their own learning from a course outline, or developing a special project under the guidance of a faculty sponsor. Special project reports are bound and added to the library collection. Students in independent study have, for example, composed music, written up research on holograms, the Mormons in San Bernardino, the nature of a sophisticated mathematics formula, and composed books of poetry and stories. Some recent independent study project titles have been: "Julius Caesar: Patriot, Statesman, or Opportunist Dictator?", "The Ruby Laser," "The Presidential Role and the Proposal and Direction of Legislation," "Nationalism and Communism in China," "Compulsory Arbitration," "India's Religion," "A Study of the English Novel Since 1900," "Observations on Eugene O'Neill," and "Was Reconstruction Radical?"

MERIT PROGRAM

A merit program augments the independent study program. Students who have demonstrated the ability to direct their activities without supervision may apply for admission to the merit program. A merit student is provided an identification card to be presented to the teacher when he would like to be excused from a class. With the approval of the teacher, the student may be excused to visit the library, a laboratory, a shop, or another class in pursuit of a special interest.

LABORATORIES

The use of laboratories suggests the accommodation of individual needs. Science and language laboratories are open before and after school, as well as during regular class periods. The shorthand laboratory enables the teacher to provide dictation simultaneously at four different speeds and allows students to receive taped dictation from business executives. Experience has indicated that this laboratory has significantly increased proficiency and reduced the shorthand drop-out rate. Students are more proficient in one year than they used to be in two.

All ninth grade students are provided a reading laboratory experience for five weeks. They receive developmental reading instruction, and problems are diagnosed for instruction as needed on an individual basis. A mathematics laboratory has been established for students who have a history of difficulty in comprehending mathematical concepts.

ADVANCED PLACEMENT OR VOCATIONAL TRAINING

Qualified seniors may choose to individualize their program by enrolling for a course at El Camino College. Students with an interest in vocational preparation may select from the courses of six shops. A maximum twenty credits are available to those who choose to earn while they learn with on-the-job training. Courses planned which will provide added individualization of student programs are nursing skills, business occupation skills, chef's training, and plastics. Students may elect to augment their program with instruction at the Southern California Regional Occupational Center. The Center is a cooperative venture of seven school districts to provide the greatest possible scope in the development of saleable, vocational skills.

ACTIVITIES ADVISER

The services of a full-time activities adviser are of increasing importance in a large high school, because he deals most directly with students in matters affecting school spirit and morale. It is through the efforts of his office that students have an opportunity to broaden their interests, deliberate on ways of accomplishing goals, and learn techniques for dealing with other people. Students presently are interested in more than athletics, assemblies, clubs, and dances. Today's students need the guidance of an effective activities adviser in their quest for individual expression, involvement with the operation of their school, and concern for the well-being of their fellowmen.

STUDENT GOVERNMENT

Individualization of student life, through the presentation of challenge and opportunity, is no more explicit than in the current atmosphere of student body elections. Students seem to be interested more in a candidate's proposals for improvement of the organization and welfare of the school, or his suggestion of worthy projects, rather than in campaign promises of more social activities for the student body. The structure of student government provides meaningful individualization. During orientation, social science classes serve as a medium for dissemination of information about campus life and after orientation as sounding boards for opinion and as represented groups in student government. Opinions expressed in social science classes and carried to the house of representatives may result in a bill acted upon by student council or a proposition of a student body election. As an example: considerable involvement preceded an election when the student body voted to lower the grade point average required to run for student office.

MEANINGFUL ACTIVITIES

Students have demonstrated their interest in school and community operation by participation in administrator-teacher day and junior citizens' day. As the titles suggest, students become involved with the operation of the several school offices; some prepare lesson plans under the direction of teachers and actually teach classes. This experience has developed an interest in a teaching career for several students. Junior citizens observe the problems confronting their adult counterparts in municipal government and attend a meeting of the city council. Establishment of a Youth Advisory Council with representation from each high school has been an outgrowth of this activity.

Student interest in their fellowmen has provided two opportunities for creative participation. A principal of a school in Nepal visited West High as a guest of the United States Government. Upon learning of the meager equipment at his school, students raised funds for the purchase of a microscope which was sent to Nepal. A framed expression of gratitude was delivered by a member of the Peace Corps, returning to California.

Last Christmas, students desired to be involved in a project of more lasting effect than, and in addition to, donation of canned food to families in need. They elected to earn money individually to contribute 500 toys to a Head Start center. A bus load of students delivered the toys to the children at the center.

SATURDAY SEMINARS

Enlarging horizons and developing self-realization were accommodated this spring at a series of Saturday morning seminars involving such programs as a trip to the computer research facility. As a result of this visit one of the students is now carrying on correspondence about computers with a member of the corporation. At another Saturday program individual interaction between pairs of black, white, and brown students led to enthusiastic participation for an hour beyond the allotted time.

STAFF-STUDENT RELATIONS

The adults of a school, through display of a warm and accepting attitude, help students regard school as a place where they belong. Creating a sense of identification is individualization in its most meaningful form. Regard for students is expressed in many forms: eye contact and a smile extended to a number of students while crossing the campus, a faculty talent show to portray the "human side" of people past thirty, and the increased understanding by teachers who participated in a sensitivity group with the school psychologist.

Personalization was the concern of many during student deliberation of dress regulations. Concurrence was reached on regulations which permit expression of personality within the framework of "good taste."

A similar opportunity was recently presented when need for an editorial policy regarding the student newspaper became evident. When students pitted their desired "freedom of the press" against their responsibility for the well-being of their school, they were not found wanting.

Individualization of student life through involvement provides opportunity for great strides toward mature concerns. Once a month before school the principal meets with students to learn of their concerns and answer questions. The year started with questions such as, "Why don't we have a senior square at our school?" and has progressed to, "What additional programs would assist the student body in developing better communication among people of different color?" The foregoing considerations have resulted in plans to extend personalization of student life and activities by:

- Extending the opportunity for independent study to students of average academic ability;
- Experimenting with the merit program to provide for greater student self-direction;
- Involving students to a greater degree on faculty committees;
- Charging Student Council and the Associated Student Body to continue and extend their school and community service;
- Developing additional elective courses to meet the growing variation of student interests;
- Working toward development of course outlines and materials at varying levels of complexity to make success available to all students;
- Providing additional vocational information by increasing the number of speakers from business and industry who visit the campus throughout the school year to give information to interested students;
- Engaging in a project to reaffirm an appreciation for our American heritage;

- Extending the activities of the student exchange club to include exchange with other parts of the United States as well as foreign countries;
- Establishing a student body account toward the funding of a project in another country.

How Free Should the | 58
High School Press Be?

Elizabeth Einsiedler

While the country is still reeling from the shock of protest and riot on the college campus, the "revolution" is spreading to the secondary schools. In high schools all over the country, student discontent is a painful fact of life—independent high school unions, chapters of Students for a Democratic Society, and underground newspapers proliferate. The last are a source of particular consternation, for there is something very final and damning about criticizing in print, with or without four-letter words, the institutions of our society and the forces that run them.

Estimates of the number of underground high school papers vary, but one thing is certain: No high school is completely safe from the "threat" that one might spring up. So many are already rolling off presses and mimeo machines in all parts of the country that a student-run press service, the High School Independent Press Service (HIPS), has been set up in New York City to feed them copy.

Many of these papers convey teen-agers' outrage at what's happening in the world. Stories about Vietnam, the draft, law and order, and poverty reflect this concern. Others concentrate on their own school—its curriculum, staff, and extracurricular program. The copy varies from prose—"We must wipe out this school of death. We must wipe out those teachers of death, we must wipe out this education of death."—to poetry—"Conformist football heroes/Plastic teeny boppers/Faces affluent with lies./Living in a pizza world,/Pray for your saddle shoes/And your narrow minds./When you open your eyes/You will find/Individuality is rare here."

By and large, the student writers of the underground press are the children of the affluent. Many are highly intelligent. For example, a sizable portion of the staff of the *New York High School Free Press* attend the highly selective Bronx High School of Science. They're sophisticated and aware of the paradoxes of life in general —and school in particular. Last fall, a student wrote in the *New York High School Free Press*: " . . . Oh, we're trained for participating in the 'democratic process'—we have our student governments— they can legislate about basketball games and other such meaningful topics. Don't mention the curriculum—THEY'LL tell us what to learn. Oh, we can express our complaints in the school newspaper—but the principal says what gets printed. . . ."

From *NEA Journal*, Vol. 58 (September 1969), pp. 52-54, 85. Reprinted by permission of publisher and author.

At about the same time this young man was lashing out in New York City about paradoxes in our way of life, a student at Montgomery Blair High School in Silver Spring, Maryland, attacked the same subject from a different angle in a column titled "Doublethink." He discussed what he defines as our nation's "ability to accept conflicting ideals and practices at the same time without question." Writing about the Democratic convention in Chicago, he said, "There, politicians in power who proudly proclaim their opposition to communism were forced to openly illustrate some of their own techniques of staying in control: dissenters who had joined The System were handled with blatant parliamentary manipulation: those who had not, with tear gas, mace, and nightsticks."

Both of these young men were concerned about what they consider paradoxes in American life; both were highly critical of some aspects of the "Establishment"; both turned to the written word to express themselves. But the difference in their dissent is that the staff member of the *New York High School Free Press* went underground to vent his anger, while the Montgomery Blair student's comment was printed in *Silver Chips*, the official student paper at his high school.

Chips, an eight-page semimonthly, is not strikingly different from other official school newspapers put out by staffs that are allowed freedom of the press. In other high schools—where students have imagination and administrators remain cool under criticism—papers carry stories about such topics as drug addiction, dropouts, Vietnam, and censorship in a school's own library.

And in many respects *Silver Chips* is not too different from school papers that are rigidly censored. Much of what appears in *Chips* is typical high school fare. Last school year, for example, various issues of the paper gave front-page coverage to the basketball team's winning of the state championship title, the student production of *Teahouse of the August Moon*, and the new course offerings in the curriculum. Features ranged from profiles of Blair's two foreign-exchange students to a story on the night school ("Blair Parents Moonlight as Pupils") to an article about the school's favorite pizza-maker—who also happens to be an English teacher and coach.

The editorial page and in-depth coverage of some subjects are not typical of the average high school paper, however. Last school year, *Chips* featured a series of articles on the causes and prevention of vandalism and took a comprehensive look at counseling services at Blair, which included three articles on the problems of the counselors from their point of view, plus a poll representing student opinion, and an editorial and cartoon on the subject. In the editorial, the editors advised, "Blair needs young, tuned-in counselors that are receptive to students and their ideas. Too many of our counselors now are turning off too many of Blair's best (and most troubled) students."

The editorial page often crackles with critical comment, and criticism doesn't end with teachers and administrators; the editors also point out their grievances about the student government and the student body in general. Even the staff of *Chips* is fair game. In the Letters to the Editor column, one senior criticized the column on "Doublethink." He said that the writer "with his 'expertise' in such matters, managed to attack the United States in situation after situation. . . . If [these] opinions . . . are not objectionable to you, certainly the printing of them in a school publication should be."

What makes *Chips* so unusual is the way its staff, its adviser, and the principal of Montgomery Blair cooperate in its publication. Yet, it's hard to analyze the way it all jells, for as one former *Chips* editor commented, "Everything about the whole operation is very informal."

Of utmost importance, it would seem, is the fact that William Brennan, the principal, and Dorothy Settle, the *Chips* adviser, respect the students and share a commitment to the philosophy that young men and women develop into responsible adults when they are given the freedom to grow. Their feelings come across without fanfare or sermons—and the students get and appreciate the message. In their final editorial, the 1967-68 *Chips* editors heralded Dr. Brennan and Mrs. Settle as "pioneers in a school system just emerging from academic and extracurricular conservatism."

Dr. Brennan reads the paper for the first time when it's distributed to the rest of the school population. He doesn't censor copy; yet once in 1967 the administration confiscated all the available copies of one issue of the paper. The teacher serving as adviser at that time found some material in it objectionable; he hadn't seen all the articles before the paper went to press. Dr. Brennan took the action he did because he felt that one of the stories was damaging to a Blair student. *Chips* staffers strongly objected to the action and some resigned, but according to a local paper, many of the student journalists felt "the incident was due in part to growing pains as the role of a student newspaper changes."

Mrs. Settle deplores external censorship of any kind. She does approve of self-censorship, however, and tries to develop this quality in *Chips* staffers. She says that this is her most difficult task, for it may mean hours of discussion with a reporter who has a "juicy" story ready for print. At such a time, pub-office conversation turns from deadlines and story outlines to the ethics of responsible journalism.

Mrs. Settle reads what the staff writes, not so much for content, but for the way it is written. All the copy goes through the editors, who correct most of the errors in grammar or construction. In addition to working with the editors at the school, she spends a lot of time with them at the printer's. (Putting the paper to bed at the

printer's each issue means that every other week *Chips* staffers spend
almost all of Sunday as well as Monday evening—and sometimes
Tuesday night—at the the printer's.)

In her role as adviser of the paper, Mrs. Settle has met with
some faculty criticism, "I'm used to faculty comment," she says, "because we have 125 members of the faculty, some ultraconservatives,
some middle-of-the-roaders, and some liberals. This means that no
matter what comes out in *Chips*, some faculty members are going to
disapprove. Some really want to see a school newspaper like the
kind they're used to—the high school papers of the thirties and
forties that were really company papers."

As Mrs. Settle sees it, *Silver Chips*, a student newspaper, cannot
be "legitimately criticized for expressing student opinion." At the
same time, she believes faculty opinion has a place in the paper in the
Letters to the Editor column.

Because Dr. Brennan and Mrs. Settle grant free expression to the
staff of the paper, *Chips* reflects the attitudes and viewpoints of the
staff and the student body at Blair. Naturally, therefore, the paper's
personality changes somewhat from year to year. In its "High School
Newspaper Pacesetters" series, *Graphics / Communications* featured
the 1967-68 *Silver Chips* as a "hard-hitting, uncompromising, crusad-
ing, in-depth paper." That year, the paper reflected the special concerns of a staff that wanted to speak out on drugs, dropouts, race
relations. But the 1968-69 *Chips* gave less attention to such controversial subjects because the staff felt the paper had already covered
these areas.

Despite many differences in specifics *Chips* has been a liberal
paper over the past few years. This seems to pose no problems, however, for those staff members who do not count themselves among
the ultraliberals. As one such staffer explained, anytime *Chips*
printed something he objected to, he would feel free to write a letter
to the editor, and the staff would print it.

An incident last year demonstrates how principal, adviser, and
staff react in a difficult situation. Just before midterm exams,
Chips ran an editorial on that subject which began, "Oh, Christ, not
again. Whip out the No-Doze, 5 sharpened pencils. . . ." Two
weeks later an apology appeared on that same page: "The editorial
staff of *Silver Chips* wishes to apologize to any of its readers offended by the language used in the examination editorial. . . ."

The story behind the editorial was that it had been written off
the cuff at the printer's and that Mrs. Settle didn't see it until it was
in print. She felt let down by the staff, who, she was certain, knew
that this type of comment would be offensive to some people. And it
was. Dr. Brennan received a number of calls from members of the
community who felt that profanity was not in "keeping with a school
newspaper." This information was relayed to the staff.

The editor-in-chief accepted responsibility for the editorial, because although she hadn't written it, she had let it go through. After being told about the complaints, members of the staff asked Mrs. Settle whether she wished them to print an apology. She replied, "It isn't a matter of what I want. You were the ones who put it in; now you must decide what action—if any—you're going to take about it."

The apology appeared. As one staffer said, "It was our responsibility to do something. *Silver Chips* doesn't only serve the school, it goes to other areas in the country, and we have to think of that aspect." Mrs. Settle summed up the experience: "I think the staff learned a lesson—that they couldn't just write for themselves, that they couldn't just be a little in-group. It made them aware that the paper is public property."

Sometimes *Chips* staffers are startled to find out how free they are. One of them made this comment about freedom of the press at Blair. "I think I was rather naïve. I went to a journalism conference thinking that all papers had as much freedom as we have, but I found out that every single paper that was represented in my study group was censored except ours. Every article in those papers had to be okayed; it might be cut by the adviser or its contents changed so that the writing is the censor's, not the reporter's. I was shocked to learn this."

Some students believe that the reason why Montgomery Blair hasn't had an underground paper thus far lies in the fact that students have the right to express themselves in the official school publication. One reporter believes that "the people who might have the incentive and the ability to publish an underground paper might already be on the *Chips* staff.

And he may be right. But Mrs. Settle acknowledges that an underground paper could spring up tomorrow at Blair. So does Dr. Brennan. The only thing they can be sure of is that the reason for the underground paper won't be a repressive censorship policy on the part of Blair High School's newspaper adviser or administrators.

59 | # The Administrator and His Problems Related to Sex

Glenn C. Atkyns

"Birth Control Pills Given to Teenagers"[1] screamed the sub-headline of the *Big City Chronicle.* Bill groaned inwardly as he read that a hospital in a neighboring city was experimenting with the distribution of "the pill" to sexually active girls in a program aimed at the "extremely large number of pregnancies and live births among girls 16 and under." As the principal of a new Regional Secondary School in a recently organized district, he had been asked by the Board of Education to draw up a suggested policy statement for Board study, dealing with married students, pregnant students, and student mothers. He wondered whether that headlined story would add to or subtract from his future problems. But he had a problem to face now—that policy statement—in a new district that had not demonstrated a clearcut viewpoint on the subject involved.

The rumor was that the district had a pregnant junior high student—the policy was needed! There were more young marriages these days, more pregnancies at an early age. The age of puberty had been dropping at a rate of about four months each decade since the turn of the century. In the United States the average age of first marriage for men had dropped one and a half years since 1940; for women, one year. These facts helped to explain why things were different than when Bill had been in secondary school, but they offered no solution.

Bill habitually wrote a "plan of action" when time permitted; he started one now. He had previously discovered, when presenting material to the Board, that the members usually wanted to know what the experience of other school districts had been, particularly the larger ones because they had "more" of a problem, and thus more experience in coping with it. Bill was not just a follower; he had ideas of his own. He had a real commitment to helping "all the youth," though he recognized that you could not necessarily help them all in the same way.

Policy-making is complex; sometimes unexpected events contribute to policy formation. A nearby city had a minority group that had more births among school-age youth than the average for the community. One of these days, thought Bill, someone might ask whether restrictions on the education of teen-age mothers was not really, in disguise, discrimination against a minority group. To Bill,

From *The Clearing House*, Vol. 42 (February 1968), pp. 372-375. Reprinted by permission of the publisher.
1. This headline and story appeared in a metropolitan newspaper, April 1967.

the more important question was whether refusing to educate school-age mothers wouldn't merely perpetuate present problems into the next generation. The rate of marriage failure among those who marry young is disproportionately high. Could this rate of failure be reduced with educational help and guidance?

But Bill's present task was to know what other districts were doing! He wrote: "How permissive are the attendance practices of the large school districts for married students, pregnant students, and student mothers? Are there regional differences? What are the data on smaller districts? Are trends discernible? What kind of classes are held for these particular types of students? Are the classes 'separate'? Is instruction offered in maternity and child care?"

He paused a moment. The curriculum of his new school did not include sex education; perhaps it should. He wrote, "What per cent of the districts have sex education programs? Do they continue such programs?" He had never heard of one being abandoned. But then *new* programs are always announced; *unsuccessful* programs are eliminated without fanfare.

The next afternoon at the State University library he found most of the needed data in a recent national study of school districts with over 100,000 population.[2] Eighty-three per cent of the nation's 153 major districts were represented in the study, which also presented regional data. It reported that in a scant majority of the districts (53 to 57 per cent) the decision-making was done in accord with "written policy" rather than "practice." Three per cent of the districts had formulated neither a policy nor a practice concerning a particular student situation—for example, prohibition of attendance at school of unmarried mothers. The districts comprising the three per cent varied from situation to situation. The remaining districts (40 to 44 per cent) had a definite "practice," rather than a "written policy." In most administrative matters, Bill favored "written policy" over "practice," believing that people should know where they stand. Also, Bill believed that if a policy was not in line with the best thinking of the community, people could let the Board members know their feelings before a crisis arose.

Bill learned from the national study of policies and practices related to school attendance of married students, student mothers, and pregnant students, that large school districts were adopting a more liberal policy since 1940.

Bill found the information for his region reassuring; at least his personal "feelings" were not too different from the policy or

2. The data and Tables I and II are based on an unpublished study by the author at the University of Connecticut, Storrs, Connecticut, May 1967. The study was conducted by questionnaires sent to the superintendent of schools of the nation's large school districts with population over 100,000.

practice of the big cities in his area. There were regional variations, he noted. The West Coast was the most permissive and the Southeast the most restrictive. None of the reporting districts in the Southwest, West Coast, or the Mountain States forbade attendance to married students or to student mothers, married or unmarried. The treatment of pregnant students was more restrictive. Bill abstracted a small chart from the study to summarize these practices for the Board.

For small school districts, data in the study were incomplete. He did find one study of all the Connecticut school districts, however, which revealed that small districts were more conservative than the large districts in the national study.[3] The small districts in Connecticut, however, were less conservative than the large districts in the Southeast. More important to Bill, the small districts showed the

TABLE I

PER CENT* OF SCHOOL DISTRICTS DENYING ATTENDANCE TO STUDENTS

	1966	1960	1955	1950	1945	1940
Married male	3	9	14	14	17	17
Married female	4	10	14	16	18	20
Married mother	5	13	16	18	25	25
Unmarried mother	8	15	20	21	28	30
Married pregnant	38	49	54	54	58	59
Unmarried pregnant	44	56	63	64	68	70

* Per cent rounded-off to nearest whole number.
NOTE: The number of districts replying to a particular question varied. Of those reporting, 97 per cent indicated practice or policy on a particular question in 1966. On the other hand, only 58 per cent to 71 per cent (depending on the question) of the school districts identified their 1940 situation. The per cent in Table I is the per cent of those who know the 1940 situation and report it. Many did not know the 1940 situation because "practice" frequently does not leave a readily visible record. Nevertheless, even on the basis of a small number reporting, the changes from 17 per cent to 3 per cent, from 70 per cent to 44 per cent, are so large that there can be little doubt regarding a major change. The change is consistent in each five-year period and there is a larger number of districts reporting each successive five-year period.

same sharp trend in practice toward retaining more of these students in school as was true of the large districts. Court decisions in cases affecting married students, student mothers, and pregnant students, Bill learned from another report, likewise were increasingly concerned with retaining these students in school. Bill thought of the students who were going on to post-secondary education. The

3. The information for Connecticut schools is based on an unpublished study by the author, May 1967. Data were received from 120 superintendents of schools, which is 100 per cent of the superintendents in Connecticut who had secondary education units.

study reported that 64 per cent of the 1966 graduates of public high schools in Connecticut had continued their education in post-secondary schools. Teen-age married students and teen-age parents need economic competence for adult life as much as other youths. But what kind of education, where and how presented—the answers to these were more obscure.

Virtually no school districts in the national study reviewed by Bill reported "separate classes only" as their solution to the problems of married students, student mothers, and pregnant students. Only 4 districts had "separate classes only" for married students or student mothers, and only 12 districts had this practice for unmarried pregnant students. In general, school districts which allowed married students or student mothers to attend school at all, allowed them to attend any class much like other students.

"Homebound instruction only," on the other hand, is provided by 15 per cent and 25 per cent of the districts to married and unmarried pregnant students, respectively. Some school districts provide homebound instruction for the pregnant students, and other types of instruction as well. Only two districts provide homebound instruction in child and maternity care for the unmarried pregnant student. Twenty-three districts had a special class in maternity and child care and closely related subjects.

Bill noticed that 54 of the nation's large school districts made use of the adult evening school for one or another of these groups of

TABLE II

PER CENT OF DISTRICTS, BY REGION, PROHIBITING ATTENDANCE IN 1966

	NORTH-EAST	SOUTH-EAST	MID-WEST	SOUTH-WEST	NORTH-CENTRAL	MOUN-TAIN	WEST COAST
Married pregnant	32	59	38	59	31	50	6
Unmarried pregnant	27	68	38	75	38	50	6

students. Twenty-six districts explicitly allowed attendance of these students in the adult evening school "only," although the specific practice varied widely among these schools. One district, for example, forbade any type instruction for married boys, but allowed "adult evening school only" for the other five groups of students. The number of districts applying this practice or policy to each of the six group students in the study was as follows: married male, 10; married female, 11; married mother, 13; unmarried mother, 8; married pregnant, 19; unmarried pregnant, 18.

There was a wealth of information regarding sex education classes which Bill found in the professional journals at the University. In the national study from which he had obtained his historical data, Bill noted that approximately half of the large city districts reported having sex education classes, though it bothered him a little that 14 per cent of the large districts that had experience with sex education classes had abandoned them. He wondered why.

When Bill left the library he knew the basic policy he wished to recommend for the Board's consideration: permit attendance by married students, student mothers, and pregnant students, thus providing instruction for all groups of students though not necessarily in the same way. About the types of classes and programs he was still uncertain. He had jotted down a list of new things to consider, once a basic policy decision was reached:

Should some guidance counselor have special competence to work with married students? Should married students and student mothers attend school dances, or was the nature of these as socializing events such that they should not? Hold school office? Play in the band (it carries course credit)? Be allowed to participate in varsity athletics?

The entire idea of giving sanction—almost encouragement—to early marriage Bill knew had to be faced by the Board and the community—and the evidence for success of early marriages was hardly favorable. A little ruefully he mused to himself that the problem was not getting any simpler.

Sex Education | 60
A School Responsibility?

Eleanore Braun Luckey

As recently as two years ago, the question was being asked: Is it appropriate for the school to concern itself about education for family living—especially that part of family living that includes sex? Since then the U. S. Office of Education has indicated it will give financial support to such programs. Several state departments of education have made well-defined and well-defended statements of policy favoring sex education in the schools. Boards of Education all over the United States have nodded assent if not demanded programs of education that include sexual information. Teachers are putting their heads together to create some kind of program in sex education. A need for such a program seems to have been well established; let us move directly to four areas on which we can focus our comments.

1. What are the objectives of such education? What is its purpose?
2. How do we best reach these objectives?
3. When do we reach them?
4. Who is to offer the guidance—who is to teach?

If we are to begin with objectives, we ask ourselves

1. What are we educating for?
2. What are we hoping to produce?
3. What kind of behavior?
4. What kind of person?

This brings us to the core of one of the most difficult problems of sexual *values*. A broad continuum of values is represented within our contemporary American society at one end by what might be called total sexual freedom and at the other by extremely restricted use of sex for reproduction only. Between these two extremes, there is a tremendous variance in attitudes and practice.

For many reasons we hold different values—our education, our religion, our socio-economic group, our ethnic background, our family background, *plus* the individual experience of each of us.

Nevertheless, our culture has exerted some rather strong and *predominating* influences that in some way or another have touched *most* of us who live in this society. We come out of a long history of restrictive puritanical attitudes that have surrounded sex with

From *Virginia Journal of Education*, Vol. 61 (January 1968), pp. 11-14. Reprinted by permission of the publisher.

silence and sinfulness. At the same time our competitive capitalistic society has discovered the *selling* power of sex, and our whole world is simply crammed full of sexual stimuli. Essentially we live in a world where sex is over-glamorized, over-valued, and held up to be extremely desirable; and at the same time we have enforced by punishment all kinds of restrictive attitudes and have been kept in ignorance by taboos that do not permit us to talk about sex openly and intelligently. As a matter of fact, we have been so restricted in speaking about sexual matters, that we have inadequate vocabularies, and because we think in language, we are handicapped in thinking about sex because we do not have the words with which we can comfortably think about it.

Given this setting, what specific goals might we expect to establish in a sex education program? Education is supposed to modify or effect behavior. What modification do we want? What behavior are we eager to bring about? Most of us can say that we would like our children to have adequate information about the physiology of sex—about the reproductive system, the genitals, their own bodies, and the bodies of the opposite sex.

Yet, we seem to be extremely fearful of giving youngsters full and accurate information. We avoid discussing masturbation except in the vaguest terms. We do not talk of petting. We do not consider the topic of contraceptives and their effectiveness a part of sexual instruction in the high school. We tell them very little about coitus, and even avoid discussing venereal disease. We have acted on the belief that if we gave young people information with regard to sex, they would want to put their knowledge into practice. So we've tended to give them partial information and hoped it would be enough to satisfy.

A second objective that we frequently say we are striving for is to create the "right" or "wholesome" attitudes toward sex; yet we live in a society that is obviously confused about a proper attitude toward what sex is—or even whether there exists *a* right attitude. Our concern here is with the social group as much as the individual in it. In other words our goals—like all social goals are to provide information and whatever else is necessary for individuals to live satisfying, fulfilling lives—sexually but in the context of our *society*.

Because individuals do live in groups, we do have to consider the welfare of the group. For example, our society has not yet provided a very adequate way of caring for children born out of wedlock, and so it is desirable for us to avoid these kinds of births. Thus one of the goals of sex education would be to reduce illegitimate births. Another social concern is venereal disease. No satisfactory way of avoiding infection has yet been found. Homosexual practices are of social concern because reproduction of the species requires a heterosexual pair. However, all three of these major problems are likely to find solutions before too long.

We cannot deny that our goals are ambiguous and confusing and certainly that they are changing. In a society that is changing so rapidly, it is inevitable that social attitudes will change. What is immoral in today's society may be quite moral in tomorrow's. And what is right for us in our society today may be quite wrong for a generation that is yet to come.

We must think not about educating for sex but for use of self. We must help individuals grow into a selfhood and a maturity that permits them to relate in a caring, responsible way to other human beings.

In many ways the very term "sex education" misleads us. We want to produce not only a sexually fulfilled individual, but one who accepts and values his total self—who understands himself, his behavior and standards; one who has the integrity to defend his values. We want to foster individuals who can live in freedom and who choose their freedoms keeping in mind their neighbor's freedom. There is no sexuality that is separate from personality. And whenever we attempt to deal with it in this way, we set a trap for ourselves by dealing with sex out of context. Sexual behavior is a part of a total pattern of behavior. Sexual mores are part of a total social pattern.

In our present concern to educate, we must be careful not to embark on a program which is likely further to emphasize and isolate the sexual factor from the total self or from a total society. Our more basic concern is education for *interpersonal relationships*, and our goal is the mature individual able to feel genuinely concerned for the welfare of others, eager to and capable of establishing an intimate and permanent relationship with others, and desirous of creating and rearing children. If we can achieve this goal, sexual behavior takes care of itself.

Given such an objective, let us now move to tackle the questions *how, when,* and *by whom.*

The *how* can be answered fairly simply. Sexual matters need to be dealt with always in context of some total picture, whatever that picture is. By that I mean sexuality is a normal part of personality and sexual behavior a normal part of life. If we dealt with sexual matters as they present themselves to the child from earliest infancy in an open and frank way, there would be no problem of sex education at all, except in unusual cases. This implies, of course, the answer to our question *when.*

There is only one logical answer to the question *when* and that is, at the time the child is curious about it. And this will vary from child to child and will be dependent on his intellectual ability and his drive to explore as well as the situations he is exposed to.

And because there is not likely to be in normal circumstances any one set of persons around when children are curious, the question *by whom* all but answers itself. For it requires that all of us may be at some time in a position to give a younger person information, to convey attitudes, and, in general, do some explaining.

We are a part of the society that has been afraid to educate or to discuss the sexual use of self, and now we have come to a period where we are afraid not to educate for this kind of use. Yet we are awkward and uncomfortable because we have never been able to incorporate it into our own personalities.

The kind of education, that we are attempting in the schools at this point, is a type of emergency measure. What we would really like would be the kind of education I have described, but since this isn't possible for us, we will do the best we can to make a positive step in that direction. The realization of a system that provides for the acceptance of and an incorporation of sexual factors of self into a gradual total picture of personality development will have to come from our children and grandchildren and great-grandchildren. It will take a long time, but we can be optimistic in that our current struggle for openness is a beginning to a better way of dealing with sexual matters than we have had before.

The central focus of sex education right now must be on us, the adult generation, more than on our children. It is our own viewpoint, until we are able to deal with sex openly and frankly and are able to answer many of the questions that up to now we have refused to even phrase.

I am a marriage counselor and perhaps see more of the confusion that is experienced with sex than most people do, yet what I see is not an unusual cross section. And it is not only infidelity and adultery that give evidence of confusion, for fidelity that exists because of fear or lack of thought also represents uncertainty.

We cannot deal with premarital sexual behavior until we deal with the total cultural attitude toward sex. We need to consider the morality and immorality of sexual relationships *in* marriage as well as *out* of marriage. We need to consider the commercial use of sex that is flaunted every day on TV and in advertisements of stripped, lovely nude females that are pictured on billboards, in magazines, practically every place we want to sell anything.

It seems incongruous that we should launch extensive sex education programs in the schools without launching equally as vigorous education for adults who are past the years of schooling. In the same way it seems incongruous to expect children to be able to deal with sex openly, honestly, and frankly when we ourselves cannot deal with it in this way. And we do suffer from those kinds of handicaps.

It is not only the school that needs to define its role, the home must define its role too, for, indeed, the home has by far the more crucial role. Sexual attitudes are formed very early and are well set before a youngster comes into even a preschool situation. The church too, must define its part. If the church is to advocate certain specific values, such as premarital chastity, fidelity in marriage, monogany, and no divorce then the church must be willing to assume its responsibility and speak out loud and clear. It must do what a public school in a democratic society cannot—which is to take a value position and defend it. As it stands now TV, car movies, and *Playboy* magazine are probably the most effective sex educators in our society.

EFFECT—GOOD OR BAD

The school has the advantage of reaching practically all children of all social classes and religious inclinations. If what we do is good, the effect will be widespread—so will it be, if it is *not* good!

I would like to see every teacher in the school system, from preschool through high school, able to deal openly and frankly with any kind of sexual problem that presents itself. I am aware that teachers and nurses cannot be expected to have all knowledge at their finger tips, but they can exhibit a willingness to seek answers and to demonstrate an openness in their attitude.

Social science courses offer opportunities to deal with today's social problems which include sex; and certainly our health classes offer an opportunity to deal with menstruation and reproduction and venereal disease. Our Home Economics classes in child development and finally relationships probably offer the best opportunity for full discussion on dating, courtship, marriage, and how sex is a part of these. I see these as natural occasions to deal with matters that are sexual and except in unusual situations they are opportunities lost primarily because teachers are not taught how to use them, and are themselves unsure and uncomfortable in trying it. As an attempt to overcome this kind of inadequacy, we are currently creating courses or units which we are injecting into the junior high and the high school, concerned more specifically with that we call family relationships.

Regardless of where or how sexual information is given, the effectiveness of it will be dependent primarily upon the individual—the *teacher*—who gives it. This points the finger very squarely, at our universities and colleges which prepare our teachers and at our state departments of education which set up standards and certification requirements for courses and for teachers. It also places a responsibility on school systems themselves, developing in-service training not only for teachers of family relationships but for teachers of music, literature, social studies, science, and health. It means helping *all* teachers develop an open, frank, honest attitude toward sex and helping them to have at hand the necessary information about sex. It may even mean helping teachers solve some of their own problems before they are ready to help students with theirs. The best way to do this is through sensitivity group training under trained leadership.

I am aware that there are problems that stand in the way of the schools providing complete and open sex information even after that goal has been established; for example, the receptivity of the community to such a program. Fortunately, most parents are grateful for a helping hand. There is hardly a visible minority protest in most communities.

PARENTS NEED HELP

Solutions will depend on the specific problem, on the community and on the context in which the problem developed. However, I would like to see the school administration help shoulder the responsibility of developing programs to help parents and adults face their own attitudes and values toward sex as well as being concerned about developing programs within the schools. Parents *need* help and I would like to see the school provide that help. They need to know what they really mean when they speak of "normal development of sexuality" in their children. I would like to see the school sponsor small group meetings under expert professional leadership where parents could discuss their own fears, their own attitudes and could be permitted to define more clearly what they really want for their child in terms of his sexual development and his sexual behavior. And in all cases the school needs to count the community *in* from the beginning of its planning.

In summary, I see the school's function at this point in our history as serving a kind of emergency first-aid measure. We have become aware that we ourselves are not very clear about sexual values and sexual behavior and their meaning. We live in a culture and a time when the sexual has been distorted out of context, honesty and frankness will help. The school ideally would deal with sexual information wherever and whenever it came up and in *all* classes. Until we have teachers who can do this, we will probably continue to have special classes centering on family and interpersonal relationships where sex is considered a normal part of self and a way of relating to others. I have urged that the school define its responsibility as being not only to its children but to parents, and that the school insist on adequately trained teachers. In whatever way it can, if the school helps us to define our goals more clearly and more adequately, we will have come a long way toward answering the simpler questions of how, when, and by whom.

How One School Meets | 61
the Challenge of Sex

Frank Battaglia

What is homosexual?
Can pregnancy occur without the sexual act?
What is masturbation?

These are but a few of the questions submitted by students enrolled in the Health Education Class at Miami Springs Senior High School at the request of a team of teachers engaged in the task of planning a sex education course. While the young people of today are seemingly more "knowing," their doubts, misunderstandings, and naivete are clearly expressed in their queries.

Viewing education in human sexuality as a vital part of the educational process for all youth, a tentative program was broadly conceived to cover:

—Physiological Aspects
—Social Attitudes and Values
—Individual Freedom and Responsibility

In the desire to establish a reality-oriented sex education program which would objectively provide knowledge, insight and values to aid the young person in solving his individual problems, the teachers sought assistance from many sources. High schools and colleges with established courses provided valuable information. Requests for resource materials went out to various social agencies, churches and publishing companies. Turning to the local community, the teacher contacted professionals from several fields to seek their advice and assistance in developing the program.

Many hours were spent in reviewing the students' questions, previewing films, evaluating available literature a priori to any decisions regarding the content of the course. A sex education course which meets the needs of the questioning teen cannot be merely a "telling" process nor can it be textbook oriented. It must be inquiry centered. Greater student involvement through honest dialogue and a variety of activities was a major concern of the planning team. To achieve this goal the following activities were included in the program:

—In-Depth Discussions—conducted by teachers and counselors for small groups with an interest in a special topic.

From *Florida Education*, Vol. 47 (September 1969), pp. 11-12. Reprinted by permission of the publisher.

—Socio-Dramas and Films—depicting real-life problems of young people. Such films as Phoebe, The Game, Worth Waiting For, and How Much Affection.
—Interviews—conducted by students with representatives of community agencies.
—Panels—discussions of various points of view.
—Lecture-Discussions—with physicians, clergymen, judges, and psychiatrists.
—Parent Night—parent reaction to teen sexuality.

Since participation was to be voluntary, letters of introduction were sent to parents requesting permission for their son or daughter to enroll in the course. Parents were also extended an open invitation to attend any or all of the class sessions. Involvement of parents from the outset was a crucial factor in the subsequent success of the program.

Six weeks was allotted for the program. A variety of teaching methods were employed. Large group instruction centered on significant films and lectures from community resource people. Guidance counselors conducted small group discussions as a means of feedback and further questioning from students. Reading lists and student projects provided outlets for students to function independently. Inasmuch as the emphasis of the program was on demonstrated student "need" much flexibility was important to the success of the program. Individuals were given options throughout the duration of the program.

Two types of arrangements are made for guest speakers.

Small groups—two speakers are secured to make presentations on the same topic at different hours of the day.
Large groups—a single presentation is made to all of the students involved in the sex education program. Students are excused from regularly scheduled classes by presenting a special permission card.

Continuous evaluation is an essential part of any good instructional program. As the course progressed the team of teachers sought informal student reaction through written comments. Adjustments were made in the program on the basis of student comments and criticisms.

Having been successful in bringing the home, the church, and the school together to develop a sex education program, the staff turned to parents, professional people and students for final evaluations. Their comments might very well serve to encourage you who are giving consideration to developing such a program.

—"Helps you to better understand what you have been taught at home."

—"The program offers the student clear, straight-forward facts and well reasoned ideas."

—"For once, I could discuss sex as an adult with another adult."

—"No one told us it was 'right' or 'wrong' but I know I am responsible for what I decide."

The result not only indicated the importance of thorough planning in introducing controversial topics into the curriculum, but further showed that when the major parties involved in the instruction participate in the planning and implementation then you practically insure the success of the program from the outset. Reasonable questions from community members, students and fellow teachers were handled openly and honestly. In all cases the participants viewed the program as *their* program and not the program of the teachers alone. Thus, they were responsible for its success or lack of success.

As a direct result of this pilot program in sex education, the local administration saw fit to make this curricular innovation a permanent part of the health education curriculum. Of course, changes will be made to improve the program, but an already firm base has been established for curriculum change.

62 | Drug Abuse—The Newest and Most
Dangerous Challenge to School Boards

Phyllis C. Barrins

Put your finger almost *anywhere* on a map of the United States
and chances are it will point to a community where more and more
school children are using drugs of all kinds, and beginning at younger
and younger ages.

Probably even your own school district. And, distasteful as the
task may seem, your board likely will soon find itself being called
upon to work directly with parents and other community agencies
to curb the growing drug problem.

Before school boards can begin to play a role in controlling drug
use and abuse—before they can impart information to students on
dangers of drug taking or alert parents to current trends in drug
abuse—they must understand what the drug problems are, and how
widespread drug abuse among school children has become in this
country.

Let your board's education and the case for children's education
in drugs start here.

Use of narcotics and drugs has spread from slums to middle
class neighborhoods, from high schools down to junior high schools
and, in too many cases, into elementary schools—a fact that has
led certain drug specialists to advocate mandatory drug education in
the early grades. Pushing of marijuana cigarets on school play-
grounds, for example, compelled Dr. Dominick Lacovara of Fort
Worth's National Institute of Mental Health addict treatment center
to begin his public school drug lectures in the fourth and fifth grades
instead of at the junior high level.

That is none too early, either, judging from increasing instances
of glue sniffing, gasoline sniffing and spray can inhalation among
the very young around the country—difficult for parents to accept,
indeed, but none too early nevertheless. Not having faced drug use
or abuse as children, today's school board members, administrators
and parents often cannot comprehend how any child, let alone their
own, could become involved with drugs or need to be educated
about drug hazards as early as the fourth grade.

While the true addict unconsciously seeks to destroy himself,
according to Dr. Lacovara, youngsters who sniff glue or smoke grass
(marijuana, pot, hemp, maryjane) are more likely to do it for kicks
or out of curiosity or to follow the crowd, pooh-poohing possible

From *American School Board Journal* (October 1969), pp. 15-18. Reprinted by permission of the publisher. Copyright 1969 by National School Boards Association.

harmful effects in the process. All too often a shocked family and a shocked community find out about a local drug problem too late, when a youngster's first experiment with stimulants, depressants or hallucinogens backfires—and becomes his last.

Certainly it is better to head off would-be drug experimenters than to have to rehabilitate them after they have become addicts or, sometimes, psychotics. Since drug addiction is an ailment cured only with the full cooperation of its victim, rehabilitation remains slow and frustrating, in spite of the growing body of research into drug use and various ways to cure addicts.

Even certain manufacturers have recognized the importance of education campaigns and are spending large sums of money to reduce misuse of their products. The Toilet Goods Association provides an example. The object of its drug campaign is the danger to be found in common household aerosol sprays, particularly freon 12, the highly concentrated propellant in most aerosol cans. When sprayed into plastic bags and sniffed by youngsters, just one whiff of freon produces a tingly sensation, lightheadedness, perhaps mild hallucinations. Second and third whiffs freeze the esophagus and congest the lungs, causing almost immediate suffocation—so immediate that summoning help is useless.

Two or three dizzying gulps from a plastic bag of aerosol spray, and a child is dead.

Is it any wonder that the Federal Trade Commission ordered that all aerosol cans carry warnings about the possibility of injury or death from inhalation of the spray? Yet even these printed warnings won't be heeded unless children are educated to believe that the label means what it says.

Other lethal inhalants used by young people today include everything from mouthwash to mineral oil, gasoline to glue, dry cleaner fluid to just plain air. Yes, even the air we breathe, if gulped quickly and hard enough, can make anyone violently wild and irrational. But the chemical substances have the capacity to kill within minutes when inhaled vigorously. Or to cause irreparable brain damage. Brain tissue, unlike fingernails and skin, does not replenish itself; medical science knows no means to restore a damaged or dead area of the brain.

While abuse of inhalants prevails in some parts of the country, other areas find pills to be their number one drug problem. A school board in a southwestern town was horrified at the discovery that its youngsters were regularly throwing "fruit salad" parties—something like the old-fashioned pot luck suppers to which everyone brought something, with this big difference: Each youngster reaches into the medicine cabinet at home for his contribution to the "salad"—a handful of mom's or pop's pills. Once the pills are pooled at the party, each youth gets and gulps his share of the colorful mixture's combined total. Everything from heart medicine to cathartics, diet controls to aspirin, sleepers to tranquilizers—no one knows for sure what he's got, except that it's an even handful.

Sick? You bet, and in more ways than one. At the very least, a few violent allergic reactions can be expected from participation in a bash like that. Other possible side effects run the gamut of physical and mental ills, without any guarantee against death.

Still other youngsters get their kicks from the warm glow of injected substances, and in some areas of the country, almost anything suffices as the substance. A mixture of boiled down peanut butter and milk was what youth in one northwestern town were injecting— huge globules of fat directly into their veins, without any regard for feverish efforts of physicians to prevent the formation of life-threatening fatty embolisms in the veins of older persons. [On a drug documentary televised recently in Chicago, a Los Angeles physician told of youngsters injecting Accent food flavor enhancer and drinking diluted Murine eyewash and Ban deodorant in efforts to get high.]

In several school districts youngsters were found to be injecting boiled down sleeping medications, tranquilizers, and various alcoholic beverages, some ten times as potent when injected directly into the bloodstream as the suggested oral dosage. The kick is immediate. To understand just how immediate, recall the hangover you might have from taking one sleeping pill, then imagine what that hangover would be like if the drug had been taken more directly via intravenous needle.

The common denominator among drug users of all ages is ages-old marijuana, weakest of all stimulants or hallucinogenic drugs. With marijuana, the user feels he can control his high; by smoking a certain number of cigarets (joints), he can remain high for the length of a party. By periodically munching a few bites of marijuana salad or sipping marijuana tea, he can retain a glow almost indefinitely. All at a fraction of the cost of a bottle of whiskey. This fact, coupled with the marijuana user's ability to control effects of the drug usually better than he can handle alcohol, leads many youths to remark to adults, "You had your booze; how come I can't have my pot?"

Here is one good reason: The African Black variety of marijuana is now finding its way into the United States. It is an addictive strain of the plant (unlike our native marijuana) that can cause withdrawal symptoms similar to those caused by withdrawal from heroin. Marijuana grows wild in all parts of the world; its potency, which varies from climate to climate, is attributed mainly to amounts of sunlight. But the soil in which the African Black variety grows is thought to account for its particular potency.

Although our high school and college youngsters seem to have little trouble finding new hallucinogens, popularity of at least one established drug is waning. Use of LSD, the test tube drug, is on the downswing, mainly because evidence of related chromosome damage and of takers who haven't returned from their trips has had a sobering effect on would-be users. In the meantime, however, LSD's more dangerous big brother, STP (also a test tube drug), has been rising steadily in popularity.

Among the latest of the mind-expanding drugs appealing to young people is the amphetamine compound Methedrine or Desoxyn (speed), which produces a quick euphoric flush when swallowed or injected. With continued injections of methamphetamine, users stay awake for days, eat little food, then often slip into a temporary coma following withdrawal of the drug.

Even of you're pretty sure none of these drugs abound in your district or community, don't sit back and breathe a sigh of relief. The child of the age of Aquarius is not necessarily doomed to face stark reality; he is, instead, likely to find other substances to help him cop out against today's uptight society.

And he need not search beyond the spice cupboard in mom's kitchen. Chewing nutmeg, for example, will bring a heady glow, and no doubt other misused spices can be even more numbing. The list of house, garden, farm, and desert plants that may be sniffed, chewed, smoked, or cooked by anybody hoping to get high is inexhaustible. Even the morning glory now stands accused of being a potent and dangerous hallucinogen, capable like overdoses of LSD of causing flashbacks, where psychotic-like effects of the drug keep coming back at intervals for up to a year or more.

The facts speak for themselves—and for an incumbency on the part of school boards to arm youngsters early in life with knowledge of drugs. Although the federal government currently is considering a new bill to control drug use and abuse, only education will save the life or the healthy brain of a child tempted to experiment with drugs. If properly educated in drug dangers, most youngsters ("follower" personalities excepted) will react with reason when that temptation arises.

How does a school board find out how widespread the drug problem is in its community? By seeking out those persons who usually have the most contact with youngsters in any kind of trouble—physicians, clergymen, policemen, family counselors, local health department officials, teachers. Some areas have crime control groups whose members volunteer their services to help teachers and parents recognize the symptoms of drug taking. Other areas have police or health juvenile officials who counsel youth after episodes of drug abuse or before an anticipated invasion of drugs. Still other areas have drug abuse committees formed by physicians or city officials.

Don't wait for these people to invite your board to join their fight against drugs. Often they won't. They need more than moral support. Show the interest and concern of your board by asking how you can contribute best to curbing drug influence in your own school district. The answer probably will be by establishing some kind of districtwide education program for both students and parents.

Beyond getting in touch with local agencies, continue to expand your own knowledge of drugs and drug education, beginning with basic understanding of the Narcotic Addict Rehabilitation Act of 1966, inadequate as it may be. (Inequalities in drug laws have been the inevitable result of the boom in narcotic use during the past ten years and of the lack of knowledge about new test tube hallucinogens.) In spite of their inadequacy, current drug laws must be scrutinized by anyone wishing not only to carry on an intelligent discussion of narcotics with youngsters but to help curb the drug problem as well.

Then proceed to read as much of the available material on drugs as your board can acquire. Also ascertain whether nearby colleges and universities are making any significant approach to the problem of drug education. Many are. Colleges in Arizona, California, Colorado, Georgia, Massachusetts, Tennessee and West Virginia even offer traveling programs for education of junior and senior high school students in those states.

A program sponsored by the college of pharmacy at Tucson's University of Arizona is a good example. There, senior Robert A. Frazier, chairman of his school's student committee on drug abuse education, heads a group of student volunteers who travel across the state giving free drug lectures to any junior or senior high school on request.

Lecturers wear no suit coats or ties, insist upon being introduced on a first-name basis, and speak informally. They gear their talks to each audience, answering student questions frankly and without preaching. The approach is strictly student-to-student, with no holds barred (except lecturers won't discuss drug laws).

During the first five months of 1969 alone, University of Arizona pharmacy students spoke before 10,000 youngsters throughout the state. They neither ask nor want pay for this service but have submitted proposals to their college for travel funds to further their work. When asked his opinion on what a school board could do about drugs, Frazier replied, "School boards could pay expenses to cover programs like ours."

Or, in the words of Dr. Donald B. Louria, president of the New York State Council on Drug Addiction, "If you want to cure the drug problem, the name of the game is commitment."

Drug Counseling | 63
A Workshop with a Purpose

Sheldon L. Winston

When the drug abuse age burst upon school districts, secondary schools were ill-equipped to react to the avalanche of new disciplinary problems engendered by drug use. The usual student behavior codes were poorly designed to deal with the numerous campus narcotic violations.

Very early in this period the South San Francisco Unified School District enunciated a very specific policy to deal with obvious cases of selling illegal drugs or marijuana on campus. The trustees required that any student caught selling marijuana or illegal drugs on school grounds, with the action corroborated by a police report, was to be referred to them with a recommendation for expulsion. The students involved were not just experimenters nor were they selling narcotics as a lark. The trustees took decisive action in these cases and all students so recommended have been expelled by the board.

In the past two years, however, the district has been faced with a new dilemma. The problem is not unique to school districts but it is to South San Francisco. Secondary students have become involved in an increasing number of relatively minor on-campus narcotic violations. They have been apprehended for such actions as selling one or two marijuana cigarettes or smoking "pot" on a field trip. These young secondary students were not addicts nor were they hardened delinquents. They were experimenters, youngsters acting on an impulse of the moment or on the verge of entering the drug "culture."

Doubts arose as to whether expulsion was any solution for these students. Moving the student to another school or meting out a brief suspension offered little hope of causing attitude changes. Was there a different approach that could be taken with these students?

Obviously the school district as a public agency was obligated to respond to these narcotic violations. The district's response, though, would be designed to impress upon the student the gravity of the situation, as well as offering help to the troubled youngster and parent. It would also give the administrator a new approach to use in coping with minor narcotic violations.

With the unanimous approval of the Board of Trustees, a drug counseling workshop was quickly developed and implemented. The workshop encompasses a number of techniques to help those stu-

From *The Clearing House*, Vol. 44 (December 1969), pp. 227-228. Reprinted by permission of the publisher.

dents who have violated narcotic laws on campus but are not considered hard-core users or sellers.

1. Students who have been named in a police report as a drug user and have admitted the use or possession of drugs on campus to school and police officials are required to attend this workshop.
2. At least one parent is to accompany the student to this series of meetings. Should the student or parent refuse to attend, the student is recommended to the Board of Trustees for expulsion.
3. The workshop is conducted once a week for two hours for four weeks or a total of eight hours. The workshop is started when it is necessary for three or four students to attend.
4. The workshop is held in the evening at a site centrally located to the district's secondary schools. It is a location, such as the community library, that minimizes the possibility of any embarrassment to the student or parent.
5. The series of meetings are led by a qualified staff member or psychologist. This individual is reimbursed at the prevailing district adult school rate.
6. The time devoted to this workshop is brief, but it does attempt to explore the following areas:
   a. the pharmological aspects of illegal drugs,
   b. the meanings and dangers of drug abuse,
   c. personal observations and views of relevant guest speakers,
   d. the feelings and attitudes of the parent and child toward each other.

During the initial year, the emphasis in each workshop has drifted toward the relationship and interaction of the child and parent. With only six to eight individuals in the workshop, the instructor is able to explore, even though briefly, some of the difficulties that have arisen between the parent and child. It has brought parents to the point of inquiring about the availability of help offered by other community agencies. The instructor is then in a position to offer aid and information at the time it is being requested.

Obviously this drug counseling workshop cannot be considered the definitive word in handling minor cases of narcotic violations. There is one salient point, however, to keep in mind about this approach. It is a school sponsored and controlled attempt to help young students who have fallen into a particularly difficult situation. It is a controlled moderate response to a particular law violation. Schools have no choice but to take the initiative in developing new programs and approaches in dealing with drug use and its attendant problems. The drug counseling workshop gives the South San Francisco Unified School District a new and different resource to utilize in dealing with student narcotic violations.

A Schoolman's Guide | 64
to Illicit Drugs

James E. Doherty

HALLUCINOGENS

SLANG NAMES: LSD, Acid, Cubes, Big D, DMT.

WHAT THEY ARE: LSD derives its name from the colorless, odorless substance of which it is made—lysergic acid diethylamide. It comes from the semi-synthetic derivative of the ergot fungus of rye, a black substance that grows on the grain. The easiest way to produce it involves a basic parent substance, several hours of laboratory time and relatively uncomplicated equipment. Other hallucinogens are DMT (dimethyltryptamine), an extremely powerful drug similar to LSD; mescaline, a chemical taken from the peyote cactus; and psilocybin, which is synthesized from Mexican mushrooms.

HOW TAKEN: Orally, as tablets or capsules. However, the properties of hallucinogenic drugs are such that they can be disguised as various powders or liquids commonly encountered on the person or in the household. Saturated sugar cubes are often used, but authorities have also found LSD on chewing gum, hard candy, crackers, vitamin pills, aspirin—even on blotting paper and postage stamps. As little as 100 micrograms of LSD can produce hallucinations lasting for hours.

PRIMARY EFFECT: Users experience distortion and intensification of sensory perception, along with lessened ability to discriminate between fact and fantasy. The mental effects are quite unpredictable but may include illusions, panic, psychotic or antisocial behavior and, sometimes, impulses toward violence and self-destruction. Persons on LSD "trips" often speak of seeing sounds, tasting colors, smelling noises, and so on.

HOW SPOTTED: There may be no outward signs of drug intoxication. However, 20 to 45 minutes after taking LSD, the user may become extremely emotional, shifting moods frequently and laughing or crying uncontrollably. He may be unresponsive to his environment and meaningful communication may be difficult. One tip-off: there is a very noticeable dilation of the pupils and dark glasses are often worn, even at night.

DANGERS: The threat of violence—either by or against the user—always accompanies the use of hallucinogenic drugs. Serious mental changes, psychotic manifestations, nervous breakdowns and suicidal tendencies can also result. Medical evidence has been advanced to show that LSD induces chromosome breakdowns, which, in turn, may lead to physical or mental abnormalities in chronic users or their offspring. This claim was strengthened recently with the first authenticated report of a deformed baby being born to a girl who took LSD while pregnant.

MARIJUANA

SLANG NAMES: Pot, Grass, Tea, Weed, Acapulco Gold, Joints, Sticks, Reefers, Roaches, Mary Jane, Muggles, Mooters, Gage, Indian Hay, Loco Weed, Mu, Giggle-smoke, Mohasky, Hashish.

WHAT IT IS: Marijuana is the dried flowering or fruiting top of the hemp plant, *cannabis sativa.* It looks and smells like dried oregano. The plant grows wild in many parts of the United States and is easily cultivated by persons who want to maintain their own source of supply.

HOW TAKEN: Almost always smoked in cigarettes or pipes. However, occasionally it is made into candy and chewed, sniffed in powder form, mixed with honey for drinking and even mixed with butter and spread on bread. Cigarettes are hand rolled, thinner than commercial cigarettes and twisted on both ends. Tip-off to a pipe used for marijuana: a fine screen, stuck half-way down the bowl.

PRIMARY EFFECT: Users report a wide variety of reactions. Some become "high" after only a small dose. Others become depressed and withdrawn. Still others will feel virtually no effects. The most common reactions are a feeling of elation, exaggerated sensory perceptions and a distortion of the ability to measure time and space.

HOW SPOTTED: Users may appear mildly intoxicated, stare off into space and look glassy-eyed. They sometimes pass into semi-consciousness or drift into sleep.

DANGERS: Because of the exhilaration which results from the use of marijuana, users may lose restraint and act in a manner dangerous to themselves and/or to others. The distortion of the ability to measure time and space—i.e., a rapidly approaching car seems to be moving slowly—increases the dangers of accidents. Although marijuana is not physically addictive, it can produce a psychological dependence on the part of the user. Not the least of its dangers, of course, is that it appears to serve as a "gateway" to far more serious drugs. It has been estimated (this statement is steadfastly disputed by most social or "weekend" marijuana smokers) that more than 90% of all heroin addicts "graduated" from marijuana.

DELIRIANTS

WHAT THEY ARE: Airplane glue, Gasoline, Lighter fluid, Paint thinner, Freon and similar commercial products. Although the deliriants cannot be classified as either "drugs" or "narcotics," they are nevertheless a prime cause of addiction among youngsters.

How TAKEN: Sniffed or inhaled—sometimes directly from the container, sometimes from a paper bag.

PRIMARY EFFECT: Reactions vary, according to the particular deliriant used and the amount inhaled. Generally, however, deliriants produce a "high" similar to that produced by alcohol. Users can experience hallucinations and extreme mental confusion.

How SPOTTED: Users appear highly intoxicated and are often surly and belligerent. Users frequently suffer nausea and then "pass out."

DANGERS: The deliriants can cause serious and permanent damage to many parts of the body. Glue sniffing, for example, can cause injury to the brain, heart, liver, kidneys and bone marrow. The inhaling of Freon—a product used to chill cocktail glasses and for refrigeration—can, and has, killed youngsters by freezing their larynx and respiratory system. There is still another danger: the use of deliriants can become the first step towards the use of pills, LSD and the "hard" narcotics, such as heroin.

AMPHETAMINES

SLANG NAMES: Speed, Pep pills, Dexies, Ups, Bennies, Drivers, Crossroads, Footballs, Co-pilots, Hearts, Crystal.

WHAT THEY ARE: Amphetamines are stimulants, prescribed by physicians chiefly to reduce appetite in obese patients and to relieve minor cases of mental depression. They are often taken by truck drivers, college students "cramming" for exams and others who wish to stay awake for long periods of time.

How TAKEN: Orally, as a tablet or capsule, or intravenously.

PRIMARY EFFECT: Normal doses produce wakefulness, increased alertness and initiative and a great deal of activity. Large doses— such as might be received by the body through injection—produce exaggerated feelings of confidence, power and well being. Amphetamines can also act as a powerful aphrodisiac and can give the user an immediate rush of pleasurable feelings. Habitual users often take amphetamines continuously for three or four days, eating nothing, "on the go" constantly . . . until they black out from exhaustion.

How SPOTTED: Heavy users may exhibit restlessness or nervousness, with tremor of hands, dilated pupils, dryness of mouth and excessive perspiration. They may be talkative and have delusions and hallucinations. Smaller doses will produce an almost abnormal cheerfulness and unusual increase in activity; however, if usage is heavy and prolonged, the user may exhibit symptoms that closely resemble paranoid schizophrenia.

DANGERS: "Speed kills" is a slogan that teenagers themselves have tacked onto methedrine and it can generally be applied to all other amphetamines, as well. While the drugs are not physically addictive, users can be "hooked" emotionally and psychologically. Since the body builds up a tolerance to amphetamines, usage is often a one-way street—toward heavier and more frequent doses. The dangers are threefold:

• Users are inclined to be violent, particularly if and when they enter a paranoic stage.
• Users are highly susceptible to such ailments as pneumonia, malnutrition and exhaustion, as a result of going without food and sleep for prolonged periods of time.
• Users can develop high blood pressure, abnormal heart rhythms, heart attacks and permanent brain damage.

BARBITURATES

SLANG NAMES: Downs, Barbs, Redbirds, Yellowjackets, Blue heavens, Goofballs.

WHAT THEY ARE: Barbiturates are sedatives, prescribed in small doses to induce sleep or relieve tension. There are some 1,500 types of barbiturates available, but all are legally restricted to prescription use only.

HOW TAKEN: Orally as a tablet or capsule.

PRIMARY EFFECT: Small amounts make the user relaxed, sociable and good humored. Heavy doses cause sluggishness and depression. The user may slump into a deep sleep or coma, depending on how much of the drug he has taken.

HOW SPOTTED: Look for the barbiturate addict—from 10 to 20 pills a day—to exhibit the common symptoms of drunkenness. Speech becomes slurred and indistinct. There is a loss of physical coordination, which may be accompanied by mental and emotional instability. Many barbiturate addicts display a quarrelsome disposition and a hair-trigger temper. Many, also, carry tell-tale burns on their fingers—caused by cigarettes that have burned down unnoticed, because the pain was blocked out.

DANGERS: The abuse of barbiturates carries with it numerous risks. First, barbiturates are physically addictive and withdrawal is both painful and dangerous—even more so than withdrawal from heroin. Serious accidents can occur, since the warning signals of pain are effectively dulled. Overdosage is common, because the user may forget how much of the drug he has already taken—barbiturates are frequently the cause of intentional and accidental suicides. Finally, barbiturates, when taken with alcohol, can lead directly to coma and death.

CODEINE

SLANG NAME: Schoolboy

WHAT IT IS: Codeine is the weakest derivative of opium and is less addictive than heroin or morphine. It is frequently prescribed to ease mild pain and is often found in cough medicines.

HOW TAKEN: Drunk in cough medicine, taken in tablet form or diluted with wine or water.

PRIMARY EFFECT: Perception dulls, attention strays and the user becomes unaware of his surroundings. Overdoses, taken by young children, may produce convulsions.

HOW SPOTTED: Users may be dazed or act mildly intoxicated.

DANGERS: Codeine is frequently the beginning of addiction for teenagers. (If it is regularly consumed in cough medicines that have a high alcoholic content, the user can become an alcoholic as well as an addict. If this happens, and the alcoholic user "progresses" from codeine to barbiturates, the combination of alcohol and depressants may kill him.) Withdrawal from codeine is less difficult than with other drugs.

HEROIN

SLANG NAMES: H, Horse, Hard Stuff, White Stuff, Junk, Smack.

WHAT IT IS: Heroin is diacetylmorphine, a synthetic alkaloid formed from morphine. It is a white, off-white or brown crystalline powder.

HOW TAKEN: Usually cooked into a solution and then injected into the vein. It can be sniffed, however, and this is frequently the first step on the road to heroin addiction.

PRIMARY EFFECT: A few seconds after injection, the addict's face flushes, his pupils constrict and he feels a tingling sensation, particularly in the abdomen. The tingling soon gives way to a feeling that "everything is fine": as the addict expresses it, he is "fixed." Later, he may go "on the nod," drifting into somnolence, waking up, drifting off again, and all the while indulging in daydreams. The effects of the drug wear off in three or four hours.

HOW SPOTTED: Users are dazed and often begin to "goof" (stare into space dreamily) or "nod" (drift into sleep—even when in a semi-upright position). If deprived of the narcotic, addicts will develop symptoms closely resembling those of severe influenza—chills, sweating, watering eyes and running nose, a restless tossing whether asleep or awake. Other clues: constricted pupils, white needle scars or reddish scabs on arms and thighs, and the presence of small glassine paper bags (used to package heroin) and of a hypodermic needle, a syringe and/or a burned bottle cap (used to inject and cook the narcotic).

DANGERS: Judgment, self-control and attention rapidly deteriorate and the user can become a mental degenerate. Loss of weight and appetite are common. Overdoses can cause convulsions and death, while withdrawal is both painful and dangerous. Addicts usually resort to crime to support their habit.

COCAINE

SLANG NAMES: C, Coke, Snow, The leaf.

WHAT IT IS: Cocaine is an alkaloid made from the leaves of the coca plant. It is a white, fluffy powder that resembles crystalline snow. Occasionally, it is made into a pill.

HOW TAKEN: Although cocaine can be taken orally, addicts usually sniff it or inject it into their veins (sometimes in combination with heroin).

PRIMARY EFFECT: An almost immediate feeling of exhilaration and well-being, accompanied by a quickened pulse, an acceleration of circulation and a remarkable overconfidence in one's capacities and physical strength. Extremely large doses can produce hallucinations and feelings of persecution.

HOW SPOTTED: Users become alert and seem perceptive. Their physical reactions are sharp. As the dose is increased, reactions become very acute and then subside as depression sets in. Users may pant, have dilated pupils, rise in temperature and loss of sense of time.

DANGERS: Vertigo and mental confusion are often present. Large doses can cause depression and nervous exhaustion lasting for many days—even convulsions and death, due to a paralysis of the respiratory center. Addicts can develop dangerous hallucinations and may assault people who are "persecuting" him. Although cocaine addicts do not suffer physically from withdrawal, treatment is nevertheless difficult, because users are less conscious of their condition and have less desire to be cured than do heroin addicts.

The Principal
and
the Disadvantaged   X

chapter overview

Schools, instead of working with and educating the disad-
vantaged, merely mirror the world they have learned to reject.

—ALLAN C. ORNSTEIN

In recent years it has become fashionable for school systems to extol their efforts in teaching the disadvantaged. The commitment of federal, state, and local funds to the development of educational programs for the disadvantaged during the period 1965-1970 has no equal in the history of American education. However, these efforts have hardly scratched the surface in the improvement of the quality of education for the disadvantaged. Besides pointing up some of the pitfalls encountered in this gigantic endeavor, the articles in this chapter provide vital assistance to educators in meeting their responsibility to the disadvantaged.

American schools have not been responsive to the educational needs of the disadvantaged. Allan C. Ornstein pleads with teachers and administrators to recognize the differences in values and conflicts between cultures without viewing one as right or better. It is his belief that educators "should not try to reshape the disadvantaged child, but accept and clarify his values and improve him within the scheme of his own values." He recognizes the need to convince the taxpayer of the economic value in reaching the disadvantaged.

All too often neither the teachers nor the administrators are prepared for the shifting of school boundaries. Stanley D. Ivie experienced the plight of a middle-class school attempting to cope with students with lower-class values. He offers advice to administrators in their efforts to cope with the problem.

A primary task in teaching disadvantaged youth is focusing on ameliorating traits or problems characteristic of the disadvantaged. Virgil A. Clift suggests a curriculum strategy for teaching the disadvantaged. The strategy is based upon knowing the expected characteristics of culturally disadvantaged youth.

Why ghetto school teachers fail should be of concern to all Americans, especially those in the teaching profession. Allan C. Ornstein describes the conditions which attribute to the ghetto teacher failure. He is convinced of the need to create a more positive image of the ghetto school teacher.

Children of wealthy parents can be disadvantaged. James A. Meyer cautions educators to examine seriously their educational programs to see if they are relevant for the economically advantaged youth. Students in suburbia, too, are calling for help.

Let's Start Reaching the Disadvantaged | 65

Allan C. Ornstein

Schools, instead of working with and educating the disadvantaged, merely mirror the world they have learned to reject. Generally geared to the aims and ambitions of middle-class culture, schools berate and reject those who do not want to be fitted into their mold. The disadvantaged do not value such a culture; they reject it because it rejects them. Children who grow up in poverty, embittered by rejection because of color, refuse to accept the possibility of joining and succeeding in the middle-class for themselves. They realize that the middle-class will allow as a part of its world only the few who are really exceptional. They learn to protect themselves by minimizing their activities outside their ghetto. They learn to distrust even those who arrive with good words and encouragement—say, teachers. They do not depend on the middle-class world; they either exploit it as much as possible through welfare, or reject it by dropping out of school and displaying and defending their values. They have themselves to depend on; they have faith only in their group.

Teachers, middle-class themselves, find it rewarding to work with those whose values are like theirs. When they encounter the disadvantaged child, whose values and life style are different, they judge him in terms of their own middle-class standards. Further, they often perceive him in terms of the absence of a culture, rather than the presence of a different set of standards and culture. (Many observers—Gans, Harrington, Lewis, Riessman, to name a few—have postulated the existence of a culture of deprivation with a system of life very much its own.) They try to change him and encourage him to succeed only on their terms. In effect, this means teachers are given the task of convincing the child that his values are wrong. To win their favor and to receive the rewards of school that come with middle-class conformity, the child must give up his individuality and style of life. For example, he must change his habits, speech, dress, and behavior, and this much sacrifice is hardly worth the effort and cannot justify the loss of personal identity. Thus, the teachers are seen as a threat, as foreigners who are at best condescending caretakers, who lack understanding and want to make him into one of them. Then, if they fail with him, and they usually do, they blame him for not caring.

By applying labels to groups—a source of comfort rooted in the work of behavioral and social scientists— and so being able to group

From *Kappa Delta Pi Record,* Vol. 4 (February 1968), pp. 67-71. Reprinted by permission of the publisher.

many children as "disadvantaged," teachers come to see the children in terms of group characteristics rather than individual characteristics. In turn, a stereotyped "deprivation theory" is fostered: these children are unteachable because they come from deprived homes and neighborhoods. The result of such thinking is what is commonly called the self-fulfilling prophecy; that is, children who are considered uneducable invariably become just that. Teachers, then, misinterpret their own difficulties and blame their students for what is really the failure of themselves and the school. Also, they gradually shift their function from teaching to custodial care and discipline.

The clash between the culture of the disadvantaged and the middle-class is reflected in terms of "us" and "them." The school represents the outside world. It hampers the children in expressing their values. Henceforth, out of frustration they occasionally turn to violent forms of rebellion in school, just as their society turns to violent protest in the streets. But most of the time, the children, as well as their society, merely withdraw into their own group, and make their own laws so no teacher, no outsider, can tell them what to do.

Just as the school intimidates its disadvantaged children, it threatens their society. The school is built around the desire to siphon off the "bright ones," which, in turn, alienates them from and changes their group loyalty to a desire for individual success, concurrently making them ashamed of their culture and heritage and absorbing them into the "ideal," middle-class world. Those who are absorbed usually move out of and reject the group, and even their families, and adopt new ideas; they rarely, if ever, return to the old neighborhood to supply leadership. For these reasons, mobility into the middle-class is opposed, especially within the Negro ghetto since it is synonymous with the white world. The climb from poverty to the middle-class is an individual venture which is accompanied by unexpected isolation and hostility from the group.

How do we reach the disadvantaged? Despite all the material written about them, it seems we are going nowhere fast. Relying on compensatory education, although this has gained nationwide acceptance, without changing the basic middle-class philosophy of the schools, is wasteful in terms of money, time, and energy. The meager effects of these programs, although billions of dollars have already been funded, seem to indicate that money alone is not enough, and the taxpayer may soon become disgusted. These programs, although they have the nicest objectives, are staffed by moonlighting teachers and other middle-class professionals whose attitudes and values are the reasons the schools have failed in the first place.

True, compensatory education and "special services" are needed, as shown below, but the beginning of the solution is to do away with the self-righteous middle-class standards of the school. They are effective with middle-class children and in fact reinforce what they learn at home; however the standards do more harm than good with the disadvantaged. The school must accept the disadvantaged on their own terms and work to achieve its goals by serving as an ego-supporting and meaningful institution. It must encourage diversity and teach the disadvantaged to become their best possible selves by utilizing their own culture, not by trying to change it.

Students behave according to what they perceive to be their role. If they are expected to be stupid, subservient, or inferior, they will behave accordingly but will ultimately rebel. The school must bury these stereotypes. Students should be encouraged to take the initiative and influence their own school activities, rather than remain passive. Instead of the school authorities dictating what students can do, the students should have the opportunity to organize, take action, and govern their own behavior and fortunes in school.

To start, a student government might be organized. In an ideal student government, everyone has the right to vote, hold office, and voice his own opinions. No one is isolated or rejected. There are no middle-class restrictions put on students who do not conform to middle-class standards. Each class elects its own officers and representatives. The formal governmental structure is organized as a pyramid, with class councils at the bottom, grade councils in the middle, and a school council at the apex.

Ideas for improving the school, raising money, determining the class curriculum, operating school clubs and activities, even judging behavior offenses of their peers, become the function of the different councils. Hall, cafeteria, and auditorium monitors are also chosen by the councils, not the teachers, with different ranks so students can recognize and strive for different levels of responsibility.

Major decisions reached by the lower councils are channeled upward to the school council. If the school council is also in agreement, it goes to the principal and/or teacher group for approval. If the decision is rejected, the reasons are explained, and there is opportunity for the students to make revisions for approval. Thus, the students are given responsibility for making and enforcing decisions, with the cooperative effort of the principal and teachers—thereby generating a feeling of partnership and mutual trust. The students govern themselves by their own values. They help shape policy and take an active role in solving school problems, proving to themselves that they are not helpless and that by effectively organizing and operating under democratic procedure, they can preserve their values and life styles, even enhance them. They learn policies and methods they can concurrently use to make gains through their neighborhood poverty programs. Their school organization and their new power seem to serve as a springboard for learning about local social and political issues in the classroom. Hopefully, this new learning will encourage the students to become future leaders. It will offer them a way of improving their environment and status without selling out or moving away from their family and friends.

The home is a major source of the child's ego ability to learn, life style, and culture. Special efforts are needed to gain support of the parents and improve the school's image. The school must make parents active observers of and participants in the learning process of their children, as teachers aids, tutorial helpers, community liaison workers, etc. The school needs to arrange for special meetings and discussions on child development problems, and ways in which they can assist with homework and reinforce school learning at home. Parents should be taught how to use the local public library, and to encourage their children to use it with them. They should be given periodically a list of programs on television and places of interest that have educational value.

A variety of open-house, all-year-round adult educational programs, leisure-time activities, and field trips need to be organized. Amateur nights and parent-children sport and game nights need to be offered, too. Evening concerts, dance groups, and musical performances in school can bring cultural activities into the neighborhood and, coupled with the other parent activities, can enhance the school as the center of community recreation.

The school should arrange for classes to help cope with the special problems of the city, involving all community services: health, housing, employment, legal, psychological, etc. For example, the parents may live near a health clinic, but not know what it is for or how to use it. They may live near an employment agency, but be confused by its forms and red tape. They may be without heat in the winter, but be unknowledgeable to do anything about it. The school could arrange for a lawyer to visit the adult center to give advice and answer questions.

The school needs to enter into relationships with local businessmen and other community resources—churches, local press, etc. Successful residents of the neighborhood, preferably those whose success has depended on education, need to be hired as part-time members of the staff, showing that learning is desirable and attainable. Community agencies and poverty programs should be invited in to work with and support compensatory and remedial programs. Such programs, staffed and supported by these groups, are likely to have greater impact than programs administered and staffed solely by teachers, and professionals and local officials, all of whom represent the middle-class world and are viewed with suspicion.

If the neighborhood lacks a poverty program, the school must use its resources to organize one. Most likely it already does, and the school must join in, work with, and become a part of it, in effect, a part of the neighborhood movement; otherwise, it will be left out and lose even more status within the home and neighborhood.

Closely allied with the poverty programs are the Negro protests which will continue to grow in both intensity and depth. Already, it is difficult to find a magazine or newspaper without an article on civil rights and the black-white conflict. How can we not teach about this movement in class? Here is the chance for the school to teach the Negro to determine his own destiny, rather than being a helpless pawn with a hopeless future. Here is the chance for students to voice their own opinions and be exposed to all sides and make their own decisions. Here is the chance for the school to have real meaning for the disadvantaged.

Actually, the civil rights movement does not offer new values or challenge our way of life, but demands that old values and ideas be realized. To be sure, teaching about the civil rights movement is a lesson in liberty and citizenship. It is a movement toward, not against, the mainstream of American culture. Teaching about the civil rights movement should improve the self-image of the Negro and produce positive attitudinal changes toward school and society.

In this connection, teachers should refuse to use racially biased materials or textbooks. Teachers' unions must use pressure tactics to bring about reform and provide orientation sessions for new teachers. They must insist that school libraries be stocked with accurate, fair material. Students must be taught to exercise initiative where biased materials are used. They must be encouraged to bring to class material printed by civil rights and black power groups to substitute, or at least supplement, the regular materials. They need to learn about black heroes and Afro-American history and culture. They need to understand what color and race mean. They need to recognize that there are more colored people than white people in the world. They need to recognize their potential power, not only in the world but locally, as more Negroes migrate to the city. They need to examine and compare the basic principles of the K.K.K., John Birch Society, N.A.A.C.P., Black Muslims, and other black power groups. They need to read not only Anderson, Carver, and King, but also Baldwin, Brown, and Malcolm X, even if discussion makes the white teacher feel uncomfortable or guilty. They need to investigate the reasons for the riots. They need to learn how to take socially acceptable grass-roots action in solving their own local problems, to become involved with learning and participate in doing something about what they are learning. They need to organize demonstrations, sit-ins, marches—to engage in real-life experiences. This method is the best way to integrate reality with learning, the civil rights movement with the school. This is the way to get students excited, to make school make sense—concurrently, to develop students' intrinsic motivation—making the task of education much easier. Of course there is danger, but there is more danger if we ignore what is happening outside the classroom, and Negro youth develop their own, unguided strategy. The race riots testify to this fact. In short, school must teach not only democratic values and basic economic skills, but also pride in one's race and culture, and social and political skills needed to cope with life outside the school.

It does little good to belabor the teacher for possessing middle-class values. Instead, teachers need to recognize the differences in values and conflicts between the cultures, without viewing one as right or better. They should not try to reshape the disadvantaged child, but accept and clarify his values and improve him within the scheme of his own values. Indeed, I am not asking teachers to change their values, but to maintain their own system of values and at the same time be at least sympathetic toward, to respect, even enhance the child's values to reach him. I am saying, too, that all children, and especially the disadvantaged, need to be respected; they need to exercise their own values and develop their own thinking in context with their life style and culture.

Teachers need to present a fair, purposeful, relaxed, but at the same time structured classroom atmosphere. Classes should be organized around small groups of students working together. The work the students do should be more on a problem-solving, discovery basis, with students learning from each other, rather than on a teacher-directed lesson. There should be opportunities for small groups to work at home and plan panel and committee reports. This training will serve as a prelude to helping them organize and plan grass-roots action and neighborhood activities. Although this type of creative teaching is needed for all students, it needs emphasis with the disadvantaged, since teachers are often reluctant to experiment with these children. Teachers must stop regarding the disadvantaged as discipline problems or apathetic learners, and thinking that the fostering of creative teaching will lead to the loss of classroom control. On the contrary, it should increase control through added rapport and interest in the lesson.

If teachers are to accomplish all these things, and note that no extra money is needed, means their own self-images and ego-strengths need to be positively reinforced. Wholesale and generalized criticism of teachers of the disadvantaged is unjust and must stop; it does injustice to the many competent and concerned teachers. These teachers are working harder and under extremely more difficult conditions than any others. They are working to overcome problems which are primarily the result of the operation of the school system and other institutions within our middle-class society. While the hostility and frustration of parents and neighborhood, coupled with criticism by professors of education, are understandable, their attacks drive good teachers out and disillusion new teachers who are about to be assigned. T-groups, although usually unstructured, should be organized during teacher-administrative periods in context with the mutual examination of teachers' attitudes, values, and strategies. Teachers need to observe each other, clarify their problems and gripes, and organize within the school so action can be taken. Students', parents', and teachers' groups should publicly recognize effective teachers. This way, a better teacher-student-parent relationship could develop, and teachers would be accepted and admired, becoming influential objects of emulation.

Although segregated schools are legally and morally wrong, and for these reasons should be abolished, there is no evidence—only commentary—to show that in integrated schools Negro children improve their attitudes toward learning, suffer from less feelings of rejection, work harder or do better in their learning; in fact, the opposite may be true. We are asking the schools to accept a child from a low-income home and different culture, who lacks experience, background, and motivation to learn as effectively as middle-class, white children—a child who probably received an inferior education, who is therefore performing several years below grade level. He is to be put in a class with middle-class children who are performing on or above grade level. Do we expect white children, even from liberal families, to feel there is really no difference between themselves and the slow, often rebellious Negro students? Will the Negro children, even though they have integrated, feel equal to their white classmates who appear smarter, cleaner, and better dressed? Can teachers individualize instruction in a class of thirty or thirty-five, when the students' range of ability might vary as much as five or six grades? If students are grouped according to present ability, most Negro students will be internally segregated in the slower classes. Will the Negro students stay after school for tutorial work and leave for home in the dark? And will Negro parents cooperate with the school if they and their children have to travel outside the ghetto? In short, we must no longer pursue the idea that quality education can only be achieved by integrated education.

Nothing is safer these days than denouncing segregated schools. But sad experience indicates that desegregation is very far from being accomplished, or that it is feasible. American schools remain just as segregated as they were, despite all the court orders that have been issued since 1954, discussions, proposals, threats from the Federal government to cut off aid, and other attempts to enforce compliance with these court orders.

Integrated education is not going to happen, not on any mass scale. Population trends show it is rapidly becoming unfeasible to integrate the city schools. In addition, white parents, both southern and northern, do not want to send their children to an integrated school. School integration in the South has proceeded at a snail's pace, and proceedings have not commenced against any school district for failure to comply with the provisions of a plan accepted by the Office of Education. School integration in the North leads many white families to send their children to private schools or to take flight to the suburbs. Even some ardent advocates of civil rights fear the quality of education that their children get will be lowered as a result of integration.

There is something bigoted, even racist, about saying that Negro children can learn better if they sit next to white, middle-class children. Improvement comes not because they are mixing with whites but because the white schools are often superior to their ghetto counterparts in "special services" and facilities. This is what makes the difference, not integration per se—but any proposal to provide ghetto schools with "special services" is usually construed as a revision of the old doctrine of "separate but equal."

Negro children have the same potential as anyone else, but their poverty and deprivation handicaps them. If we are realistic, the great majority of them will continue to be educated exclusively in segregated schools. The problem of educating the Negro child, then, must come from within the school. The key to overcome their handicaps is not so much by integration—although this has legal and moral implications— but by providing enough "special services" to create a superior ghetto school. New York City's Demonstration School Project in 1957 and now its More Effective Schools indicate that when segregated schools have enough "special services," Negro children are able to overcome their poverty and deprivation and perform on or above grade level. The Demonstration Project had excellent results, at a cost of about $200 extra per child. When the City tried to get the same results with 64,000 students at ¼ the extra cost, in Higher Horizons, it failed. MES cost about $400 extra per child, and there is pressure to cut funds. Similarly, the money provided for Head Start's enrichment program has shown positive results. However, when the children make their way through the primary grades and the school attempts to maintain the progress of Head Start by operating a regular classroom situation at a much lower cost per child, the children fall behind.

Obviously, "special services" and compensatory education cost money. Just as white families are unwilling to send their children to an integrated school, taxpayers are unwilling to provide enough money even for good ghetto schools. But while integration of the schools is an emotional conflict which cannot really be resolved by legal or mandate tactics, providing enough money for superior ghetto schools can be resolved, and just by such pressure. It is not that the taxpayer cannot afford it, but that he doesn't want to improve the lives of others if it means not having three televisions and two cars. The taxpayer must be made to realize that for every dollar he saves on education, he will have to spend almost twenty on social ills, as exemplified by welfare, crime, delinquency, and race riots.

'Lower Class Values | 66
in Middle Class Schools'

Stanley D. Ivie

Until recently, I was teaching at a public high school. During the three years I was there, the school underwent a drastic change. Because of the completion of a new high school in the vicinity and the subsequent shifting of school boundaries, the population served by my school underwent a rapid transition. One year the students were predominantly Caucasian and middle class; the following year they were overwhelmingly Negro and lower class. For the bewildered faculty, "disadvantaged youth" ceased to be an abstract term and became a day-to-day reality. The school, with its middle class teachers and its middle class set of values, was not prepared to cope with large numbers of lower class students. The traditional orientation of the school toward general education and college preparation held no meaning for its new clientele. Neither the teachers nor the administration was prepared for the siege that followed.

It is no hallowed secret that the urban Negro population makes up the largest single block of poverty in our society, and it is no mere accident of history that Negro students compose the largest single segment of culturally "disadvantaged youth." The plight of the Negro is the result of historical forces over which he has had little or no control. From slavery, through segregation, and into de facto segregation, his position has been the one ascribed to him by our society—a position of subservience and second class citizenship. The seeds of present day poverty were first sown in the cotton fields of the South, but they are now being reaped in the urban sprawl of the North. The problem of the Negro, like the problem of poverty, is not regional but national in character. It is a truism of history that we are now suffering from the effects of choices made in the past, the choices of slavery and segregation. In the school, as in the larger society, the errors of history linger on.

Let me make it clear at the beginning that the generalizations I have to make about Negro students do not apply to everyone who happens to have a dark skin. For I have known many Negro students who were quite middle class in their style of living. The effects of poverty upon human values are the results of class and not the results of race *per se*. The subcultural values of the Negro are learned habitual attitudes, and they are functional within the conditions of poverty. In fact, lower class Caucasians in our society demonstrate

From *Arizona Teacher*, Vol. 56 (January 1968), pp. 10-11. Reprinted by permission of the publisher and author.

value patterns similar to those shown by lower class Negroes. Values are derived from one's social experience and not from one's biological endowment. The color of a man's skin does not determine his behavior; that is, it does not determine his behavior unless his society attaches a specific status and role to those having a dark skin.

Since the days of slavery, the Negro family has been very loosely organized. On the plantation the buying and selling of slaves discouraged the development of any family ties. Slavery discouraged the Negro male from asserting a positive role of leadership in the family. His role was to be docile and submissive. Under the plantation system, the Negro woman fared far better in terms of status than did her male counterpart. Consequently the Negro family has become a rather loosely organized matriarchal structure. In fact, many maternal grandmothers exercise extensive power in the raising and supervising of children. Because our society has very often undercut the power of the Negro male to provide his family with even a modest living, the Negro female has often had to assert herself as the "bread-winner" for the family. This has increased the power and prestige of the female over the male. Also, it has been more lucrative for the Negro woman to be accepted either as a servant or as a welfare recipient. Since our society has placed economic power in the hands of the Negro woman, it is little wonder that her status and self-esteem are greater than those of the Negro man. The Negro woman has become the source of security and authority within the family.

The matriarchal Negro family provides more suitable models for girls than it does for boys. Girls learn to identify more readily than do boys. In school, girls are better adjusted and more responsive; they are less hostile toward teachers. They show a greater capacity for cooperation and acceptance of authority. They have learned to accept themselves because they have been able to draw a certain amount of status and self-esteem from their mothers. The story of the Negro boy, however, is quite another matter. He has had the psychological problem of finding suitable models to identify with. He has not been able to identify with and draw self-esteem from a father figure because in many cases there has not been a father figure available, and when one was available usually the father figure did not have any self-esteem to spare. The Negro boy is inclined to be hostile toward authority in general and the teacher's authority in particular. This attitude of defiance sets up a barrier to learning. It is as though he were daring you to teach him—to make him learn.

Negro children do not receive the close parental supervision that middle class American children take as a matter of course. Quite frequently, they are left on their own to shift for themselves. Consequently, the models with whom they tend to identify are not those of the adult society, but those provided by older adolescents. In the rough-and-tumble world of adolescent society, physical prowess is an absolute necessity. For physical power "gets you what you want." Fighting is an important means of gaining status, even among girls. To the middle class school, fighting is tabu. Fighting poses a threat to social cooperation. Yet, by forbidding fighting, the school has cut off one channel by which Negro adolescents select their leadership. In this light, perhaps the school should consider the policy of supervised fighting. A boxing ring might prove to be a fruitful way of channeling off destructive emotions.

Coming from a background that values physical prowess, it is only natural that Negro students have asserted themselves in sports more than in academic pursuits. Besides, the line between sports and status is far clearer and more immediate than the line between academic achievement and future success. Also, the door of opportunity has been open longer to Negroes in the world of sports than it has been in the world of intellect. Although the door to higher education has now opened wide for the Negro, the change has come about so fast in recent years that many find themselves unprepared to take advantage of the new opportunities. Education was for so long a blind alley which led nowhere that it is little wonder that the Negro developed an attitude of indifference toward it. This indifference is one of the foremost problems that teachers must face in working with "disadvantaged youth."

But the largest single problem is discipline. When I speak of discipline I am not referring to trivial problems such as chewing gum and talking out of turn (although these can become major problems when they are multiplied by the power of thirty-five students). What I am referring to is "hard core" discipline: problems such as insubordination, swearing at or threatening the teacher, and even occasionally "taking a poke" at the teacher. This is what I mean by "hard core" discipline. It is this kind of discipline which really disrupts learning in the classroom, and it is this kind of discipline which the administration and the public in general would sooner ignore.

"Hard core" discipline destroys the intellectual climate necessary for learning. It makes effective teaching virtually impossible. It threatens the position of the teacher, and a threatened teacher can have little sympathy for his protagonists. What the teacher desires is security and social distance. As mutual hostility displaces understanding, all effective learning comes to a halt. Faced with a classroom full of belligerent and indifferent students, what a teacher desires is strong administrative backing. The administration should be concerned with the crucial questions in education. It should be prepared to back the teacher all the way. What is not needed in this situation is an administration that is preoccupied with trying to win a popularity contest by pleasing the students and the board of education. Given a school in a "culturally deprived" area, the administration will have to make many unpopular decisions; it cannot afford to vacillate. The board of education should make a point of picking only the most secure and professionally minded administrators for these schools.

American culture relies very heavily upon the internalized conscience—self-criticism growing out of guilt feelings—as a primary mechanism for social control. The school uses this cultural pattern as a means of controlling its students. Unfortunately, lower class Negro students do not have a highly internalized control system. To Negro students, authority is external to the "self." As one Negro student of mine put it, "Anything is all right if you can get away with it." The teacher, like the policeman, is a representative of the white society; he is an authoritative figure; he is "The Man." Because of the low level of self-control among Negro students, classroom control rests in the hands of the teacher. Students can be expected to do only what the teacher demands. If the teacher will permit it, they are quite content to sleep the day away. (I am not talking about one or two students dozing for a few minutes; I am talking about most of the class sleeping for most of the hour.) The effort the teacher makes to keep them awake is a superlative one. Given this kind of disciplinary setting, the shortest route to pedagogical suicide is to divide the class up into little groups and to expect the students to carry out a collective enterprise. The little group method of instruction assumes a safe margin of self-control, of ability to cooperate, and a native interest in the subject. Negro students score low in all of these traits. What is demanded by this kind of setting is a teacher with a forceful personality. For if he is not in control of his class, no one else will be.

Negro students are very vocal. They tend to talk at full volume. It is not uncommon to see a group of Negro girls formed in a circle, all of them talking at once; no one listens, everyone talks. The voice is a symbol of physical prowess. Dominance and recognition are obtained by being boisterous. In the classroom the teacher can expect a maximum amount of noise; he will have to exert an overt effort to make it otherwise. The power of the teacher's voice indicates his degree of dominance to the class. Negro students expect a robust voice from a teacher who is firmly in control of his class. A weak voice means a weak teacher, and the students will take it from there. If a teacher wishes to maintain the respect of his class, he must always speak with authority and assurance. His voice is his only instrument of control. And if he should ever lose this control, he is lost.

In the past, white America created the image of the "good" Negro. He was to fit the prototype of "Uncle Tom." "Uncle Tom" was safe; he was subservient to whites; he "knew his place." In recent years, this image has been swept aside. In fact, groups such as the Black Muslims would turn the tables entirely. They would make black synonymous with good and white the essence of evil. The image which the Negro has of himself is currently in a state of flux.

The only positive thing that one can say about it is that this time the Negro is determined to create it for himself. Images are important for education. For men tend to behave in a way consistent with their self-image. In the classroom, for example, the concept of imagery can be demonstrated in projective tests and art work. Negro children do not wish to accept themselves as they really are. When I had them draw a self-portrait, the sketch almost invariably turned out to look more Caucasian than Negro. And when they were asked to write a short essay telling me about the person they sketched, they immediately set up a wall of resistance. Negro students do not like to talk about their social plight. They do not like to think about their social environment. They do not like to think of themselves as being members of the lower class. They do not want to take a critical look at their own self-image.

Whatever the new Negro image is to be, the school can play a vital role in helping to shape it. For the school is in a position whereby it can and should provide models for Negro students to imitate. The school can and should provide bright, masculine Negro teachers for its students to identify with. And at all costs, the school should avoid the error of employing teachers who are reminiscent of the "Uncle Tom" type.

To the Anglo-Saxon middle class, the Negro sense of humor often seems to be sadistic. War films, for example, showing death and destruction, are often the objects of uproarious laughter, and scenes of poverty are found to be extremely humorous. Students who fail or make glaring mistakes are often made the objects of ridicule and laughter. Given this sense of humor, the wise teacher is one who learns to roll with the puns. He should not try to fight it. Rather, he should capitalize upon this humor as a means of control. And in so doing, he will have captured an act which his students respect and understand. For humor, whatever its source, is a refreshing thing in any school.

Schools that serve a population which contains a large number of lower-class Negro students should not rely very heavily upon standardized test scores either for placement or for counseling purposes. For these tests, either I.Q. or achievement, assume the student is motivated and is trying his best to make a good score. In testing disadvantaged students, this is very seldom the case. Because a timed, standard test is a tedious and boring task, students are inclined to skip hard questions or just take a random guess at everything or go to sleep and forget about it altogether. Test scores arrived at under such conditions cannot possibly be valid. Yet statistical averages do not take these factors into consideration. Under these kinds of conditions, no one should be surprised that the intelligence scores for Negroes are lower than those for whites. If standardized tests must be given, they should be individual rather than group tests, and every score should be taken with a grain of salt.

In the past, the mixing of the races, Caucasian and Negro, only went in one direction. The relationship was between the white male and the Negro female. The reverse relationship was a cultural tabu. The whole drama of miscegenation has its counterpart in our integrated schools. Presently the amount of interracial dating that takes place in an integrated school is far less than one might expect. Most students tend to identify with and date within their racial group. Where there is a crossing over of the "color line," however, the pattern tends to run in one direction; that is, the relationship is between the Negro boy and the Caucasian girl. I can only infer the reasons for this particular pattern. First, there seems to be an element of excitement in breaking an old and cherished cultural tabu. Second, the girl seems to receive more affection and consideration from the Negro male than she has been used to. Third, there seems to be that very elusive element that is present in all heterosexual contact, namely, choice.

Given the problem of trying to turn lower class Negro students into middle class citizens (if this is really what we are trying to do, and I believe that it is because I have not seen any other goal), what can the schools do? In all honesty I must reply: far less than most educators are willing to admit. For any significant change in either administration, curriculum or teaching personnel is bound to cost a lot of money. To provide the kind of program designed to change lower class students into middle class citizens will cost far more than the most expensive of college preparatory programs. No small token of anti-poverty money is nearly enough to do the job, and until the public is willing to "foot the bill" to provide a really comprehensive program, we shall continue to have a conflict within our schools—a conflict stemming from the clash of values—a clash of values between the middle class school and the lower class students it serves.

Curriculum Strategy Based on the Personality Characteristics of Disadvantaged Youth | 67

Virgil A. Clift

Listed below are characteristics one may expect to find among disadvantaged youth. Certainly no one individual would be expected to be characterized by all of these traits. It is true, however, that teachers who are working with typical classes where a large number of disadvantaged youth are enrolled will be able to identify many students who can be characterized by traits listed here.

In a very real sense, the traits listed represent disabilities, handicaps, or disadvantages which the individual has that make it very difficult, and almost always impossible, for him to function in school up to an acceptable level. Unless the teacher is able to ameliorate these problems, teaching does not produce desired results. All of the love the teacher may have for poor children, all of the respect she may be able to muster for minority children, all of the "hip" language she may use with children, and all of the other similar tricks and devices she may employ, are of no avail. Instead, the successful teacher of the disadvantaged must be a clinician who can help young people deal with traits or factors we know to be limiting the ability of these children to learn.

This being true, the daily teaching act, class period after class period, must focus on ameliorating traits or problems characteristic of the disadvantaged. Social studies, language arts, and all other areas of study must be organized and presented, in terms of content and method, so as to help students deal realistically with special characteristics peculiar to their personalities.

Characteristics presented here represent what the individual is like as a person. The next step is to spell out objectives in each area or course the student pursues in school, grade by grade. These objectives must be specific, definitive and relate directly to helping the student solve or ameliorate personal problems.[1]

The traits or problems presented in this paper have been grouped under three headings: (1) factors of personality, (2) factors of cognitive function, and (3) factors in relation to educational values.

From *The Journal of Negro Education*, Vol. 38 (Spring 1969), pp. 94-105. Reprinted by permission of the publisher and author.

1. See: Benjamine S. Bloom, *et al.*, *Taxonomy of Educational Objectives*, (New York: David McKay Co., Inc, 1956); Robert F. Mager, *Preparing Educational Objectives* (Palo Alto: Fearon Publishers, 1962).

It is often the case that subject matter in one field can be used more effectively than that from other fields to help students overcome certain of their specific problems. The task confronting the teacher is to select objectives which help students deal with their personal problems and at the same time help them to acquire essential knowledge. For example, the *Diary of Anne Frank, The Life of George Washington Carver,* or the *Life of Hans Christian Anderson* may do much more to help the youngster with a deeply ingrained negative self-image than some things currently being required. On the other hand, if we know the disadvantaged youngster tends to be more present-oriented and less aware of past-present sequences, we should try to modify our approach to teaching history and refrain from a total emphasis on chronological order which might remove the student 2,000 years from the present, when in reality, he may not be able to place events of five years ago in their proper relationship with those of five months ago. All of this is to emphasize that after objectives have been formulated, the next step is to select meaningful subject matter to achieve the objectives.

In the process just described there are three steps:

1. Become acquainted with the traits or problems which characterize the disadvantaged child. Be able to recognize these in students.[2]
2. State objectives for the course, subject area, and daily lessons which give greatest promise of relating directly to individual characteristics and to essential knowledge to be learned in a course or subject.
3. Organize the subject, course, and daily lesson in a way that will make possible the achievement of the objectives.

For years educators have emphasized that we must "start where the students are." Characteristics of disadvantaged youth listed in this paper represent "where" these students are. It is the established consensus among teachers that all teaching must be related to objectives. Yet it is precisely in this area that all education is vulnerable because too often objectives are woefully inadequate, and sometimes meaningless.

Hopefully, one of the benefits which seems certain to come from our efforts to educate the disadvantaged will be more articulate statements of objectives. Another benefit will be a more systematic selection of subject matter to achieve educational objectives for individuals who bring to the learning situation different backgrounds of experience.

Educators often write about disadvantaged youth and their education as if there is something strange, mysterious and baffling about them. It will be helpful to remember that the disadvantaged are hu-

2. The major part of this paper is devoted to this step in the detailed enumeration of traits under the caption Expected Characteristics of Culturally Disadvantaged Youth.

man beings, responding as any other human beings would respond, had they been exposed to the environment and forces the disadvantaged have. We come now to the traits which characterize disadvantaged youth.

EXPECTED CHARACTERISTICS OF CULTURALLY DISADVANTAGED YOUTH[3]

A. Factors of Personality.

1. He may exhibit negative feelings about his personal worth.
2. As a result of prolonged feelings of negative self-esteem, he may come to feel self-hatred and a rejection of his own ethnic, racial, national, or family group, but not his peer group.
3. Boys from certain disadvantaged groups (Negroes in particular) may suffer from role confusion and be completely unsure of their worth as a result of living in a matriarchal society.
4. He may suffer from the disorganizing impact of mobility, transiency, and similar factors which are caused by the fact that he is of minority status.
5. He may have absorbed some of the mental and emotional problems which are more commonly found in his family and peer-group than in the population as a whole.
6. He may feel frightened as a result of early emotional or physical abandonment by his parents.
7. Since the peer group exerts much greater influence on him at a much earlier age than in middle-class surroundings, he may reflect their values almost completely and have no sense of relating to an adult world.
8. He may have unrealistically high levels of *expressed* academic and vocational aspirations, which are an attempt to bolster his flagging self-esteem.
9. He will usually show, however, *low* levels of aspiration when concrete action is needed. This is very often a result of negative feelings toward himself and repeated attempts that have ended in failure.
10. His need for immediate financial independence because of early desatellization from his parents may make him emotionally unable to consider any form of education or training that will make him temporarily unable to be self-supporting. He may be emotionally unable to accept the idea of receiving money from his parents during the time that would be necessary for him to finish school.

3. Characteristics listed here were derived from related research, the behavioral sciences, and studies in connection with *Project APEX* at New York University.

11. He may exhibit an even greater fear of the unknown than is normal for children of his age group. He may respond to any new situation negatively.

12. He may show signs of an authoritarian personality which has been absorbed from his parents. This personality complex includes the need to dominate or be dominated, a tendency to view people as "in-groups" and "out-groups," relative resistance to change, or belief in a supernatural power which will eventually regulate the problems which the child faces. An authoritarian person is apt to be more ethocentric and prejudiced than others are.

13. Having grown up in an authoritarian home, in many cases, the child may seek an authoritarian leader in school. At the same time, he will evidence an underlying hostility toward authority of any kind, which will create ambivalent feelings and reactions.

14. He may show anxiety at having to work with two systems of values. The fact that in his culture certain actions or ways of living are accepted, but are rejected by the world of the school, may lead to confusion and hostility toward one or both of the systems of values.

15. He may respond primarily with anxiety to any threatening situation and may attempt to solve problems by repeated withdrawal.

16. He may indicate reactions of lethargy, apathy, and submission in any situation which he does not feel capable of mastering. These are usually suppressed feelings of aggression.

17. His massive anxiety and confusion may result in his being unable to maintain one kind of activity or reaction, and periods of submission (suppressed hostility) may alternate with periods of strong aggression and hostility.

18. He may show his feelings of resentment and hostility toward the rejecting majority group (the white middle class, in general).

19. If he feels unable to show his hostility, he may turn to reaction formation, where he will seemingly adopt the ideals and values of the majority culture, to the exclusion of other members of his own group.

20. His feelings of anxiety and sense of failure may lead him to withdraw from competition in the larger American scene, especially in relation to any activities that characterize the middle class.

21. He may show self-deprecatory reactions in any situation.

22. He may be prone to delinquent behavior because of family disorganization.

23. He may evidence feelings of shame about his family background which makes it more difficult for him to relate to others.

24. He may have deep-seated anxiety about achievement in any domain.

25. He may exhibit a complete lack of ego-involvement in school, and thus he may be a target for easy failure. This is due partly to the fact that the school, as he knows it, is completely incapable of meeting his emotional needs or helping him with his problems.

26. He may have built up a "fight for what is mine" psychology.

27. He may be rude and uncouth.

28. He sometimes shows little restraint and has few inhibitions.

29. He may be keenly sensitive to insult.

30. His major goals may seem to be "to grow up and get by."

31. He may be unconsciously bent toward self-destruction.

32. Companionship in the gang may be sought to make up for elements missing in the family structure.

33. He may have a sense of values that is not only different from that of the middle class, but that may be beyond the comprehension of middle-class observers.

34. He may show no fear of personal injury, may have been encouraged to fight and not to be intimidated by police or others. In fact, he may have learned that this is the only thing that works with the slum landlord, the slum merchant, the dishonest bill collector, and the crooked cop.

35. He may have enjoyed so little attention and affection that he responds quite differently from the middle-class child when praised for success in school. He may have never experienced success and the gratifying feelings of success and security. He may be expected to respond differently from his middle-class counterpart for whom these have become a way of life.

36. He may be extremely bitter and justifiably so.

37. He may have a general feeling of being "hemmed-in" and as a result may crave excitement.

38. He frequently knows that he has been stereotyped as "dumb," "ignorant" or "worthless" and is hurt internally as a result.

39. He may be loud and boisterous due in part to life style, or as a means of attracting attention, or because of lack of self-restraint, or because he is excited due to anxiety, etc.

40. He may "giggle," exhibit loud laughter, and find humor in things that may not be the least bit funny to middle-class children who have enjoyed an entirely different background of experience.

41. He may have learned to make heavy use of survival skills needed for protection in the slum streets and in the gang. He may not know that the middle-class system expects a different kind of behavior.

42. The successful disadvantaged child may experience considerable trauma because he operates in terms of survival skills when in the slum environment, and in terms of accepting social skills of the middle class when in school. The successful disadvantaged child must operate in two very different worlds at the same time

and thus develops two distinct personalities. As a result, he may on occasions be characterized as schizophrenic or may become disgusted or traumatized by all the hypocrisy and act out in various ways.

43. He may cope with authority figures by maintaining appropriate social distance, and by interacting with these figures on the basis of the formalized role rather than as persons.

44. He may feel himself the object of derision and disparagement and unworthy of succorance, affection, praise, etc., and may for that reason reject efforts of teachers and counselors to offer helpful encouragement or praise.

B. Factors of Cognitive Function.

1. Even if high levels of perceptual sensitization and discrimination are present, these skills tend to be developed better in physical behavior than in visual, and better in visual behavior than in aural.

2. They tend to lack any high degree of dependence on verbal and written language for cognitive cues.

3. Many disadvantaged youth have not adopted receptive and expressive modes traditional to and necessary for success in school.

4. Their time-orientation varies from that expected for school. It is less consistent with reality.

5. They are characteristically *slower* than middle-class children in cognitive function.

6. They do not have good powers of concentration.

7. They are not generally persistent in problem-solving tasks.

8. They characteristically score low in recognition of perceptual similarities.

9. They tend to ignore difficult problems with a "so what" attitude.

10. They depend more on external than internal control of things.

11. They tend to have a more passive approach to problem-solving tasks.

12. Culturally deprived children have a restricted variety of stimuli to foster development of cognitive processes.

13. The particular stimuli they receive are less systematic, less sequenced. They are, therefore, less useful to growth and activation of cognitive potential.

14. They are limited by both the "formal" and "contentual" aspects of cognitive development. ("Formal" aspects are those operations or behaviors by which stimuli are perceived. They have poorly developed auditory, visual, tactile aspects. "Contentual" aspects mean the actual content of knowledge and comprehension.)

15. They lack in environmental information.

16. They have a poor general and environmental orientation.
17. Their concepts of comparability and relativity are not appropriately developed for their age level.
18. They lack ability to use adults as sources of information for satisfying curiosity.
19. They lack an ability to sustain attention.
20. They are farther away from their maturational ceiling as a result of experimental poverty. Therefore, they have poorer performance on I.Q. tests, and the tests tend to be poor indicators of their basic abilities.
21. They generally have not developed a concept of expectation of reward for accumulation of knowledge, task completion, or delaying gratification.
22. They have difficulty in seeing themselves in the past or in a different context.
23. Evidence indicates that they tend to be more present-oriented and less aware of past-present sequences.
24. They have difficulty working with time limitations.
25. They tend to have difficulty in handling items related to time judgments.
26. They are poor in judging figure-ground relationships.
27. Their spatial organization of the visual field may be impaired.
28. They may have memory disorders. Adults generally link past and present for children by calling to mind prior shared experiences. In lower-class homes they generally neglect to do this.
29. A combination of constriction in use of language and in shared activity with adults results in much less stimulation of early memory function.
30. The assignments that they receive at home tend to be motoric, short in time-span, and more likely to relate to very concrete objects. This is not attuned to school demands.
31. They usually experience a minimum of non-instructional conversation at home.
32. The lower-class home is not a verbally-oriented home. They, therefore, have little opportunity to hear concepts verbalized.
33. The ability to formulate questions is essential to data gathering in formulation of concepts of the world. Questions are not encouraged in their environment and are not responded to; therefore, this function does not mature.
34. They lack *training* in listening to a variety of verbal materials.
35. They lack an opportunity to observe high quality adult language use.
36. They learn inattention to sound, and "tune out" sounds; thus much of the talk they hear becomes "noise."
37. Lower-class children tend to differ from middle-class children in the definitions of common nouns. They give largely functional definitions. This is prominent at every age level.

38. One of the major differences between culturally deprived and non-culturally deprived children, is that the culturally deprived have a slower increase in the use of formal (generic) responses and tend to use a high proportion of functional responses.
39. They are handicapped in anticipatory language skills, i.e., the correct anticipation of sequence of language and thought made possible by knowledge of context and syntactical regularities of a language.
40. They are most probably maturationally ready for more complex language functioning than they have achieved.
41. Speech sequences in lower-class homes tend to be temporarily very limited and poorly structured syntactically.
42. They may have a deficit in language development in subject continuity.
43. They have more expressive language ability than generally emerges in the classroom.
44. They are at a disadvantage when precise and somewhat abstract language is required for the solution of a problem.
45. It is possible that the absence of well-structured routine and activity in the home is reflected in difficulty in structuring language.
46. Their language development often lags behind their perceptual development.
47. The deprived child may not have the following types of information: his name, address, city, rudimentary concept of number relationships, differences between near and far, high and low, etc.
48. They have a tendency to concrete rather than symbolic approaches to problem solving.
49. They lack training in experimenting with identifying objects and having corrective feedback.
50. Their reading abilities are affected by poor auditory and visual discrimination.
51. Their general level of responsiveness is dulled.
52. They often have difficulty with the verb form "to be."
53. Often they have difficulty with subject and verb agreement.
54. They tend to use action verbs.
55. Usually they have difficulty in defining, comparing, judging, generalizing, etc.
56. They may have difficulty with auditory sequential memory.
57. A different perceptual disposition may be carried over into verbal expression, memory, concept formation, learning and problem solving.
58. There is a high level of undetected mental insufficiency among disadvantaged youth due to poor pre-natal care and environmental influences.

59. The thought process is more often inductive rather than deductive.
60. There is often little or no understanding of rewards that are not tangible or situations that are not "felt."
61. The home situation is ideal for disadvantaged youth to learn inattention. There is a minimum of constructive conversation and a maximum of non-instructional conversation directed toward the child, and most of it is in the background of confusion. Results: poor auditory discrimination, a skill very important to reading.
62. They have great difficulty in organizing response tempo to meet time limitations imposed by teachers. Middle-class teachers organize days by allowing certain amounts of time for each activity. The teacher may not realize that her view of time as life's governor may not be shared by all segments of society.
63. In disadvantaged homes, there is no setting of tasks for children, observing their performance, and rewarding of their completion in some way—nor is there disapproval if they do not perform properly or when they leave something unfinished. Much classroom organization is based on the assumption that children anticipate rewards for performance and will respond in these terms to tasks which are set for them.
64. The disadvantaged youth is not accustomed to using adults as a source for information, correction, reality testing as in problem solving, and for absorption of new knowledge. They have difficulty in relating to the teacher, therefore.
65. They are not prepared to question, or to demand clarification.
66. They do not come to school with verbal fluency which serves as a foundation for reading skills, and conceptual verbal activity. They have difficulty communicating with teachers.
67. They quickly lose interest in school if unsuccessful. This is due to weak ego development which they bring to school.
68. They have less deep-seated anxiety with respect to internalized needs for academic achievement and vocational prestige than middle-class children.
69. They may exhibit retarded academic growth as a result of actually having received poorer instruction and less instruction than other students. Slum schools have greater teacher turnover, more inexperienced teachers. This is also due to geographic mobility of low-income families.
70. They place greater stress on such values as money and tend to prefer agricultural, mechanical, domestic service, and clerical pursuits.
71. They make lower vocational interest scores in the literacy, esthetic, persuasive, scientific, and business areas than do middle-class adolescents.

72. They learn inattention in the pre-school environment, and their level of responsiveness diminishes steadily. This is disastrous for structural learning situations in school.

C. Factors in Relation to Educational Values.

1. There is no or very little interest in reading which is so valued by school. Reading is not valued or considered necessary in their environment.
2. They have not learned or been encouraged to concentrate, to persist in their studies, to have a long attention span. Teachers, therefore, often tend to term them stupid.
3. They have no feeling that economic position can be improved through effort and sacrifice.
4. They have no pressure to maintain a reputation for honesty, responsibility, and respectability.
5. They often do not focus on individual advancement, self-denial, and competent performance which leads to esteem for formal education, rationality, controlled and respectable behavior, hard work, all of which are values of middle class parents, schools, and children.
6. They have no severe standards against aggression. Control of behavior is seen to have little relevance to social success or job maintenance.
7. They often recognize that they are not considered as "good" as middle class students who have been taught to control anger, inhibit direct aggression, etc., but they do not know why they are not considered as "good" as middle class students.
8. Cultural values which impinge upon them in school are meaningless.
9. Facts of a changing economy (decrease in menial or manual jobs) seem remote and external to them.
10. They display hostility to teachers and school administrators because they represent authority figures. They are often hostile toward any authority figures that they know have imposed constraints and administered punishments.
11. They lack an understanding of middle class teachers' mode of operation: kindness is misinterpreted as weakness; results in a disorientation as to how they should act.
12. They are used to unsupervised play, little parental influence, etc. Therefore, they are rebellious to the restrictiveness of school regulations.
13. They do not try to please teachers as a result of short term dependence on parents. They are not used to striving for parental approval.
14. They feel conflicts between personal interests, e.g., earning money, being with friends, wandering around, etc., and the goals and time demands of school.

15. They are often used to a mother who maintains considerable social and emotional distance from her children. They feel threatened when a teacher does not maintain this distance.
16. They are used to a mother who desires unquestioned domination over them with suppressive forms of control. Thus they often do not understand the coaxing atmosphere of school and school officials.
17. They have fear and suspicion of school. This stems from the general feeling of their segment of society: disengagement, nonintegration, mistrust with respect to major institutions of the large society.
18. They have little desire to work for far-distant goals of a college education, etc., when they know most of it is impossible. Result: lack of motivation.
19. They have even greater hostility toward school because their values and segment of society are threatened by school. They are aware of negative opinions the school has of them and their families. They know society looks down on "unmarried mothers," families on welfare, etc.
20. They are limited in terms of experience and gross knowledge as compared with middle class students due to a restricted environment. The result in school is failure after failure, increased sense of inferiority, and a more negative self-image. Their solution is to drop out.
21. Their status among their family and friends is not dependent on academic achievement, and academic achievement often has the opposite effect.
22. They come from an environment that does not provide examples and models of social skills and work habits essential for success in school. The home does not teach initiative, creativity, and self-reliance—qualities which are rewarded at school.
23. Their cognitive style is not geared to academic work. Failure is practically guaranteed.
24. Misunderstanding and alienation are often inevitable because initiation into sex comes early for disadvantaged youth. School officials consider them "immoral" for such things.
25. When a school population is composed entirely of a single ethnic group, or ethnically mixed, but culturally disadvantaged group, there are often not enough academically successful students to form a strong sub-group to withstand pressures of street gangs.
26. When the school population is mixed, a slum child is often barred from social membership in the group of academically successful students, and may find the risk of identifying with its values too great.
27. They are generally unfamiliar with tools confronted in school due to scarcity of objects of all types, but especially of books, toys, puzzles, pencils, and scribbling paper, in their homes.

28. They and their parents have no or little knowledge of the opportunities available in the middle and upper employment classifications. They have no way of learning incidentally or otherwise the basic skills, life style, and prerequisites for moving up the socioeconomic ladder.
29. Parents and relatives most times feel it unbelievable that the child has potential or ability to raise above their own status in life; therefore, they tend to reinforce whatever apathy already exists.
30. They seldom if ever gain status and recognition from peers for academic attainment and success.
31. Higher education, technical education, etc., are thought to be prohibitive because of costs and ability to succeed.
32. They have little appreciation for beauty in art, music, drama, etc., and have generally become accustomed to a disorganized, cluttered personal environment.
33. They treasure items of immediate need and access to them.
34. They may have warped personalities and personality problems which stem from an inhospitable environment and make it impossible for them to function in a school environment.
35. The kinds of rewards the school gives have no meaning for them. They may feel just as well off without them.
36. They may conceive of their school and teachers of being of little worth or much less worth than other schools and other teachers (especially if they are segregated Negro schools or schools in depressed areas.)
37. They often gain status among peers and in the community if they are disobedient and defy school regulations and school authority.
38. The life style, language and values of the educated person are so different from that of the disadvantaged child that he feels completely out of place with a person who is so different from him. It seems impossible and inconceivable that the teacher could have anything in common with him or really care for him.
39. They often have little pride in the American heritage and do not feel in any way related to it.
40. American heroes, traditions, institutions, etc., provide little inspiration. They see no way of emulating any of the great or even moderately successful men of the present or past.
41. They have usually had no help in evaluating their own potential ability and aptitude. They often have no realistic yardstick with which to measure their own personal resources.
42. They may show little respect for school property and even be destructive of it.
43. What appears to be faulty and poor judgment may be the result of woefully inadequate experience and a lack of information or facts on which to make valid judgments.

44. They may express fantasy on many levels.
45. They often tend to confuse kindness on the part of the teacher with weakness.
46. They may be prone to prejudices and "scapegoating."
47. Social-psychological obstacles may confront them due to the unreality of the text book world when it is put along side their own world.
48. School often interferes with present gratification in terms of peer status, earning power, and independence. It is often a place where they must return day after day to failure and to social situations where they are relegated to the lowest possible status.
49. They may revolt against school regulations and society by becoming delinquent which often helps them to become a member of the "in-group" and protects them against isolation in their real world.
50. Excessive success in school may be fraught with dangers from their peer group.
51. A tight social group is often developed among friends and provides security and solidarity. Their behavior, speech patterns, and values conflict with those of the school and thus the school is rejected.
52. The social systems operating in the school reject them and they have no techniques of becoming a part of any "in-group" that values academic achievement.
53. They see too much evidence and can point to too many examples that convince them that teachers and counselors dislike them, have no confidence in their ability to succeed, and do not respect their worth as individuals.

68 | # Why Ghetto School Teachers Fail

Allan C. Ornstein

We have the peculiar notion that we are doing good as long as we spend large sums of money. We believe that the problem of educating the disadvantaged can be solved by simply dispensing money to provide compensatory education, which we hope will guarantee "quality education" and "equality of opportunity" for the disadvantaged. Yet, despite our huge outlay of money we are not making significant gains; the problem is snowballing into a vicious, stubborn cycle. In effect, we have vaulted madly off in all directions and have adopted a saturation approach—with the hope that some programs will work—which blinds us with false hopes and makes it difficult to find the best way of solving the problem.

My purpose here is to come to grips with the problem and suggest why we are failing. I am governed by a major assumption as to the reason for the problem and the stage that it has now reached. None of the compensatory programs has come up with a substitute for good teaching. No amount of money is adequate if teachers are doing an inadequate job. New schools, smaller classes, integrated textbooks, etc., are meaningless if teachers are indifferent. In short, it profits us little to spend billions of dollars on compensatory education and then place the students under ineffective teachers.

The idea that teachers are failing to reach and teach the disadvantaged is not new, but I suggest that we explore the reasons, in turn, so that we become aware that everything we are attempting is superficial and merely a waste of time, energy, and money. The teachers are the victims of an intolerable system, which causes them to become angry, frustrated, and finally indifferent.

Teacher-training institutions do an appalling job of preparing teachers. Those who are assigned to "good" schools usually manage to get by, since their students have the ability and intrinsic motivation to behave well and learn on their own. However, whenever teachers are assigned to work with the disadvantaged, poor teaching becomes obvious, because these students depend on good teaching. That a limited number of ghetto-school teachers do succeed and maintain their faith in themselves and in their students may be attributed to their unusual personality, that despite their poor training allows them to gain experience and effectively teach the disadvantaged.

The trouble with teacher training is that courses consist merely of descriptions, recommendations, anecdotes, and success stories,

From *Kappa Delta Pi Record,* Vol. 4 (April 1968), pp. 99-101. Reprinted by permission of the publisher.

which are nothing more than opinion, but often taken as gospel. Readings consist of wonderful, glowing reports and advice, but fail to demonstrate how or why the advice works. Indeed, the advice is at best a "gimmick," a dead-end approach. What is suggested for or works with one teacher does not necessarily work with another, even with the same group of students. The best advice, in fact, can sometimes do the most harm.

Eager, but unprepared, the ghetto-school teacher is usually doomed to failure. The disadvantaged are astute appraisers and knowing manipulators of their environment; they easily see through "gimmicks." They know what will upset teachers, often better than the teachers know; they readily sense what they can or cannot do with a particular teacher. They realize that threats are ineffectual and that the teacher's authority is limited. In this connection, they usually assess the teacher as a person before they become interested in him as a teacher. A negative assessment—which is common, because of the conflict of values and life styles between the teacher and students—can provoke a dramatic incident, or it can be drawn out into a series of minor clashes. In either case, the students proceed to capitalize on the teacher's weaknesses, then ridicule and abuse him as a person, for example, derogating his personality and physical appearance. Once having demolished the teacher's self-respect and authority, they readily express indignation and contempt toward him, and all their hostility and their resentment of authority are directed at him.

Disadvantaged students at the junior-high-school level are generally the most difficult to deal with. By then, many are rebellious and too retarded in the basic skills to learn in a regular classroom. Many are strong enough to be a physical threat or sophisticated enough to probe a teacher's weaknesses. On the other hand, they lack self-control and are not mature enough to reason with or old enough to be legally suspended if they really cause trouble.

The outcome is that the teacher soon tends to see his students as adversaries. Each day leaves him emotionally and physically exhausted. Anxiety overwhelms him, too, as he becomes aware that almost anything can happen. He is confronted by a bored and hostile class, a group of thirty or thirty-five students he can no longer control. He sees no tangible results of hard work and feels no sense of accomplishment. For his own mental health and disposition, then, the teacher is forced to learn not to care. His apathy protects him; it is his defense; it is his way of coping with the meaninglessness or the possible danger of his situation. That the students are not learning is no longer his major concern. Weekends and holidays become more important; he needs to rest, recuperate, and regain his strength and rationality. Sometimes he cannot wait, and becomes "ill" a day or two before the weekend. Sometimes he does not finish the term; often he does not return for the next term.

The teacher turns to his supervisors for help, but quickly learns that he must solve his own problems. His supervisors rarely have the time to provide assistance on more than an emergency basis. Often the supervisors are suffering from many of the same problems as the teacher, for example, lack of training and experience. Many are un-willingly appointed to the school; and like teachers, they are anx-iously awaiting their transfer to a better school. The only difference is that they can shut their office doors, which they often do, thereby divorcing themselves from the teacher's problems.

Of course, some supervisors are concerned and eager to provide assistance. Nonetheless, they often become inspectors. They work under the assumption that the teachers are not teaching and students are not learning—which is almost always true under the existing situ-ation—and therefore must be coerced and controlled. However, the unanticipated consequences of this teacher-supervisory relationship increases the teachers' indifference, and reinforces minimum ac-ceptable teaching performance which in turn becomes maximum standards. Minimum performance convinces the supervisors that their assumptions are correct, and they proceed to check more closely on the teachers and treat them as subordinates. The relation-ship worsens and the teachers soon realize they must battle students and supervisors.

If the teacher is a substitute, his colleagues advise him not to re-turn in September, to leave before he becomes regularly appointed. If he is already regularly appointed, he learns to "mark time" until he is allowed to transfer to a better school. Even if the teacher is regularly appointed, if he is young enough not to be trapped by a pension or a deferment from the Army, he may be so depressed that he leaves the system or the profession entirely.

The point is that most regularly certified ghetto-school teachers are trapped by the school system. In order to reduce the turnover of teachers, many urban schools require five or more years of service before a teacher can even first request a transfer. What happens dur-ing the interim? The longer the teacher has to wait to be transferred from a school he wants no part of, the more meaningless teaching be-comes and the more cynical he becomes. Involvement, commitment, dedication, the joy of teaching, and the rest of the splendid jargon become cliches.

Who suffers more—the teacher or student—is questionable. Both are victims and victimize each other; both are the prisoners of the school system; both have dropped out in fact if not in name from the learning process; both often drive each other out of the school. As for the teacher, one hundred eighty days a year he faces a living death—a feeling of hopelessness and despair—perhaps the bleakest existence any person can experience. Instead of teaching, he finds he must face a long-drawn-out humiliation, a state of helplessness and hopelessness, when the worst may be still to come in which the only certainty is there is no solution in sight to his predicament.

Prisoners adopt an air of dull-wittedness, of cooperative and willing incompetence. Subject peoples act much more incompetent and indifferent than they are, by declaring their minds free from their enslaved state. Ghetto-school teachers are subject people. Their schools are a kind of jail sentence, and "torture" is not too strong a word to describe some of the things that they have experienced in the classroom. Is this not a partial explanation of the incompetence and indifference that teachers often display in ghetto schools?

The hypocrisy of the system—compounded by its bureaucracy, inertia, pettiness, and total disregard for teachers—reinforces the teachers' indifference for teaching. The system operates by syphoning the teachers' energy and enthusiasm; it operates by first coercing teachers into and then prohibiting their escape from an almost impossible teaching situation, and therefore meaningless existence.

While the teachers are being assaulted, the system produces glowing reports. Pilot programs always seem to work, especially if evaluated by their directors. Instead of consulting their teachers, the system calls upon "experts" from local universities, governmental agencies, and foundations to reexamine, and reorientate. (*The Bundy Report* is the latest example whereby an outside group of "experts," whose total teaching experience adds up to zero, is attempting to tell the teachers how they should teach and how their schools should be organized.) The belief is that teachers are rank-and-file workers with no legitimate right to define policy. Directions and decisions are passed on to teachers with no concern for them and no avenue of communication open to them, except by disrupting the system and striking. The entire system is organized to keep teachers in a second-class position, with no ego-involvement in curriculum development, no participation in policy, and no means of sharing credit given to the schools. Their supervisors, instruments of the system, run roughshod over them, because supposedly, that is "the way things get done in the system." Similarly, the supervisors decide almost everything and take whatever praise may come, but poor achievement is looked upon as an inadequacy of the teachers.

Having to fend against students, supervisors and the system, the teachers are confronted by a group of angry parents and condescending educators, who have taken to the task—of course, only with the best intentions—to vent their criticism of ghetto-school teachers. Although their criticisms are understandable, they are wholesale and generalized and overlook the reasons for poor teaching, and therefore, they have done grave injustices. Their harsh tone and constant criticism add to the problem of recruiting teachers, discourage competent and concerned teachers from remaining, and harden the already widespread feelings of indifference and futility, as well as reinforce poor teaching morale and performance.

The attackers are either too emotional or too remote from the actual classroom situation to understand the teachers' plight. They fail to recognize that these teachers were once working harder than any others in the profession, but because of impossible conditions and lack of adequate support were forced to retreat from teaching. They fail to comprehend that ghetto-school teachers would rather teach and fulfill their professional commitments. They fail to appreciate that these teachers are overwhelmed by despair and need assistance, not criticism. They fail to realize that they have abandoned and further alienated the teachers.

In particular, the professors of education, who trained these teachers and now criticize them, would do well to accept the "challenge" they talk about and apply for teaching licenses and teach. There are many vacancies in ghetto schools, and there is much need for good teachers. One reason is that professors have failed miserably in training their clientele.

To be sure, it would be interesting to see if the professors really know what they are talking about, or if they could do any better than the teachers. I dare them. At least, they ought to go into the classroom to "find out what it is really like" to teach the disadvantaged, and experience what the teachers experience. Again, I dare them. Instead of patronizing the teachers, criticizing them for negative attitudes and ineffectiveness, and berating them for failing to understand and appreciate what they have done for them, the professors should apologize for failing to do their jobs, that is, training teachers.

At the time of this writing, the proposal for decentralizing the New York City schools, and having a local ethnic group run the schools and choose the teachers and curriculum, is hotly contested. But what effect will this have on teaching morale and performance? Parents and educators urge teachers to maintain their dedication and behave as professionals while simultaneously undermining their independence which is an essential ingredient of professional morale and status. Certainly, pride and power for the ghetto community would be beneficial, but the lack of pride and power for the teachers is detrimental.

Why can't we have parents and teachers working together and sharing pride and power? Why can't parents and teachers, black, white, or purple stop distributing blame and sit on the same side of the fence? If parents alone fill the power structure of the schools or share it only with unwieldy, entrenched bureaucrats, the teachers, once again, will feel abandoned and remain indifferent, reviving only when their contract expires and they can pursue their own self-interests.

On a large scale, it is impractical to talk about screening teachers for their attitudes or professional suitability to teach the disadvantaged when there are not enough teachers who are willing to work with such students. If a change is what we really want, let's stop attacking the teachers and start giving them support and a voice in running the school, for improving the education of the disadvantaged all boils down to what the teachers do.

Suburbia | 69

A Wasteland of Disadvantaged Youth
and Negligent Schools?

James A. Meyer

The time has come to include our suburbias in any comprehensive assessment of the strengths and weaknesses of American education. At least among the vast middle classes, suburban life has long
been thought of as ideal and suburban educational systems as exem-
plary; but there is mounting evidence that even by conventional
standards such is not the case. One need look no further than the
suburban youth—products of our co-called utopias—to suspect that
suburban societies and their educational institutions have been over-
rated and underproductive.

Indeed, suburban youth can no longer be taken for granted. How
can they be, considering today's frightening world of aimless youth?
The average suburban teen-ager is often pictured as either consumed
with self pity or alienated into withdrawal from society. He is said to
know it all, to be intelligent and amoral, well-mannered yet merciless,
cynical in a young-old way, and oh so sophisticated. Some suburban
youngsters are in flight from their own lives; others are deeply worried about what the future holds for them; and some are in revolt
against their parents' suburban values.

At first glance most of our suburban youth share a common
background of comfortable homes, loving parents, "good schools,"
high intelligence, excellent health, and almost unlimited opportunities for self-development. They have almost all the advantages that
many of their mothers and fathers growing up during the Great Depression and World War II were denied. Yet many of today's middle-
class suburban youngsters exhibit disturbing character qualities—
sexual libertarianism, vehement rejection of adult authority, and a
widespread disposition to experiment with drugs.[1]

Is the older generation really at fault? Or is this rebelling suburban generation the product of an overpermissive educational system? Are modern suburbia and its so-called cultural attributes a
myth? Do the hypocrisy and callousness of suburban living really
distort the values of modern youth? Unfortunately, it does seem that

From *Phi Delta Kappan*, Vol. 50 (June 1969), pp. 575-578. Reprinted by permission of
the publisher and author.
1. Yet Kenneth Kensiton in *Notes on Committed Youth* (New York: Harcourt, Brace
and World, 1968) asserts that these young radicals are unusually "healthy" youth who
have solved their psychological problems to a higher degree than most and have
achieved "an unusual degree of psychological integration." With respect to drug use,
read "Scarsdale Seeks To Curb Use of Drugs," *New York Times*, January 27, 1969,
and "Cause Shown," *American School Board Journal*, February, 1969, p. 5.

the tremendous reservoir of young, creative talent located in suburbia is not being cultivated in a manner essential to effective growth
of democratic ideals; and there are now some real doubts emerging
about the kinds of leadership suburban youth might someday contribute to our society.

SUBURBAN DEPRIVATION

Our nation's suburbias are evidently becoming so segregated that
children can grow up without genuine contact with others of different racial, religious, or social backgrounds. The result is a growing
provincialism in spite of ease of travel and communication. Suburbia's children are living and learning in a land of distorted values
and faulty perceptions. They have only the slightest notion of others;
they judge them on the basis of suburban standards (such as "cleanliness" and "niceness"), generalize about groups on the basis of the
few they might have known, and think in stereotypes. In short, they
usually have little association with or knowledge of people who differ
in appearance or attitudes.

Dan Dodson, director of the Center for Human Relations and
Community Studies at New York University, addressing himself to
the problems facing youngsters living in suburban societies, declared: "In the suburbs a significant hardship on youngsters is their
essential uselessness. They are 'kept' people well into their teens and
often longer. There is little a youth can do to contribute to his family's well-being except to make top grades. But this contribution
can go to a limited number only."[2]

Dodson further claims that there is considerable evidence that
life in the suburbs is harder on boys than on girls. One reason is that
the fathers are away from home so much of the time that their sons
have only a vaguely conceptualized father-figure with which to identify.

Similarly, the values, attitudes, and behavior of older generation
suburbanites are often exposed by the mass media as superficial and
empty. For example, youthful critics of the middle-class suburban society vividly illustrated their rejection of suburbanite values in their
acceptance of *The Graduate*, a film which devastatingly portrays the
affluent, banal, swimming pool-and-corner-bar suburban set as seen
through the eyes of its youthful "hero." The chief reason this film
became such a social phenomenon is, perhaps, the forlorn manner in
which the protagonist copes with the phoniness of a materially comfortable contemporary society. It says something about the meaning-

2. Dan Dodson, "Are We Segregating Our Children?" *Parents Magazine*, September,
1963.

lessness of affluent life which distorts youthful aims and ambitions. It dramatizes the generation gap, portraying a youth almost paralyzed by the rapacious hedonism of his suburbanite parents.

Some authorities suggest that this alienation of the suburban child from "others" is a recent phenomenon stemming from the unique structure of suburban life. Discussing this idea, Goldman[3] uses the words *sidewalk* and *station wagon* as keys to understanding:

The sidewalk [once] symbolized the avenue of communication between one child and another. In many areas this has vanished. . . . Sidewalks are no longer built . . . in some suburban housing developments. The response to the disappearing sidewalk is the mother-driven station wagon. Instead of relying upon informal mingling of children, the image of the station wagon implies a planned, structured mingling of children: the Boy Scout meeting at 7:30, the Little League game at 4:00, the music lesson at 5:00, etc. What is gained by structuring common activities for children may be lost by some of the concomitant results—the loss of spontaneity when games and recreation must be carefully scheduled and supervised, the early creation of the "organization man," etc. The increased number of nursery schools is part of the same response to the deprivation of young children.

Other critics of contemporary suburban life have asserted that parents in suburbia pamper and spoil their children to such an extent that the children grow up without any real parental supervision. Halleck has declared that "some parents in suburbia have, through painstaking efforts to avoid creating neuroses in their children, abdicated their responsibility to teach and discipline their children. In so doing they have reared a generation of spoiled, greedy youth who are unable to tolerate the slightest frustration without showing an angry or infantile response."[4]

On the other hand, many critics put the blame for youthful unrest in suburbia on the way the children are overprotected and parentally dominated. This goes beyond an overabundance of material things. Rather, it consists of parental hovering and a reluctance to let their youngsters assume self-responsibility and self-direction. Perhaps some suburban parents fear their children will make mistakes and embarrass them. In any case, from an early age many suburban children are given little opportunity to use their own resources and make appropriate decisions.

Obviously, both extremes are unhealthy and undoubtedly contribute greatly to the restlessness and antisocial behavior patterns of rebelling suburban youth.

3. Louis Goldman, "Varieties of Alienation and Educational Responses," *Teachers College Record*, January, 1968, pp. 331-44; Charles H. Harrison, "In the Suburbs," *Education News*, September, 1968, pp. 15, 19.
4. S. L. Halleck, "Hypothesis of Student Unrest," *Phi Delta Kappan*, September, 1968, pp. 2-9.

Of one thing we are sure, and that is that parental influence over suburban youth has deteriorated markedly; and children are cheated and deprived of experiences essential for effective development of wholesome ideals and attitudes. Unless more authentic human values are developed within our suburbias, the suburbian style of life will significantly contribute to the further deprivation of suburban youth. While little can be done about the attitudes and values inherited from parents, the schools still have the opportunity to reach these restless youth and redirect their energies. But first the challenge must be recognized.

SCHOOLS SHARE THE BLAME

"Suburban children are underprivileged. . . . There is little in their education, formal or otherwise, to familiarize them with the rich diversity of American life." This judgment by Alice Miel in *The Shortchanged Children of Suburbia*[5] grew out of a series of research studies designed to explore life in suburbia and to determine what is being taught about human differences in our schools. Her findings were alarming and resulted in a sharp indictment of the suburban school for failure to do something about preparing suburban children for a healthy, wholesome life in our society.

The results of this study indicate that:

- The typical suburban elementary school student's life is almost totally insulated and circumscribed.
- Suburban youngsters learn, individually, to be bigoted and hypocritical about racial, religious, economic, and ethnic differences at an early age.
- Group prejudices, too, take root early—and go deep.
- Materialism, selfishness, misplaced aggression, fake values, and anxiety top the list of common characteristics.

Yet many educators today are neither adequately trained nor perceptive enough to cope with the problems experienced by adolescents growing up in our affluent suburbs, and these inadequacies of staff hamper efforts to provide compensatory treatment.

For example, on the basis of some recent career pattern studies, it is now estimated that about 85 out of every 100 secondary school

5. Alice Miel and Edwin Kieste, *The Shortchanged Children of Suburbia.* (New York: Institute of Human Relations Press, American Jewish Committee, 1967). It is interesting to contrast Miel's publication with the University of Chicago's recent study, *The Quality of Inequality: Urban and Suburban Public Schools* (Chicago: The University of Chicago Center for Public Study, 1968), the authors of which seem to feel that suburban schools are successful by any measure and provide the efforts necessary to offset deficiencies of environment. In all fairness, however, this title is misleading, for the book primarily examines the problems of urban education and only indirectly addresses itself to the defects of suburban schooling.

teachers in our suburban schools are from family backgrounds that differ markedly from those of the majority of the students in their classrooms. These teachers are said to undergo an emotional trauma when teaching suburban pupils. Problems of adaptation and adjustment are many. Faced with an "affluence" and "sophistication" (as doubtful as it may be) that they themselves might never have experienced, teachers in suburbia often expect and accept different standards of behavior. It stands to reason that by condoning these unique standards of behavior, teachers must bear some responsibility for the distorted values and attitudes as well as the antisocial behavior patterns often displayed by suburban youth.

Not only are some suburban educators not emotionally equipped to teach suburban youth—they may not be intellectually equipped either. "Many secondary school teachers have lower I.Q.'s than those of the suburban children they teach." This is what S. Alan Cohen of Yeshiva University said about suburban educators when he suggested that:

These teachers are unable to challenge their better students because they are afraid to. Many teachers are terrorized by the intellectual precocity of middle-class children. As a result, they cling tenaciously to rigid, lockstep pedagogies and mediocre materials to hold down the natural flow of intellectual curiosity.[6]

In asserting that suburban middle-class schools are not providing as good an education as they should, critic Cohen cites the growing evidence of educational inadequacy—the irrelevancy of curriculum content and the poor pedagogy—and concludes that superior test performances of children from "Scarsdales" tend to reflect the enriched verbal home environments rather than the school's educational program. "As a result," says Cohen, "the weak content and pedagogy in the middle-class schools are good enough, or perhaps more accurately, not bad enough to ruin these children."

Disappointingly enough, there are reports that school guidance counselors also experience difficulties when counseling in suburban schools. College counseling, for example, is theoretically only part of the total guidance function in secondary education. But in suburbia, college counseling becomes a major item of responsibility, and the counselor must become a master at it. Indeed, in the wealthy suburbs, where the citizenry have the money and desperately want to send their children to good colleges, they generally perceive counseling in "college" terms. Ivan Faust,[7] a suburban counselor, has written that:

6. Alan Cohen, "Local Control and the Cultural Deprivation Fallacy," *Phi Delta Kappan*, January, 1969, pp. 255-59.
7. Irvin Faust, "Guidance Counseling in Suburbia," *Teachers College Record*, February, 1968, pp. 449-458.

The trouble with most college-oriented communities and the coun-selors they hire is that college placement rather than welfare of students proves the guidance program; it becomes the total force rather than the natural result of a developmental counseling experience. . . . What-ever else arises is subordinate. He's awash in the suburban synodrome that says it's worse not to get into college than to flunk out. And it's worse not to get into a particular college, or colleges, for collecting accep-tances is part of the game.

Suburban youths themselves have become progressively more sensitive to the lack of substance and meaning in the curriculum of their schools and are voicing strong concerns over the lack of rele-vancy. Many suburban youngsters, for example, are now said to be articulate, irreverent, humorless, and relentless in their contempt for what they honestly view as the meaninglessness of suburban educa-tion. They turn to one another when shaping beliefs or seeking ad-vice, for they have learned to distrust both their parents and their teachers.

For some time now, the attentions and interests of most edu-cators have been directed toward the educational problems relative to urban conditions of life. Recently, however, some concern has been given to shortcomings in rural education. But only little con-cern has been shown toward the possible needs of suburban youth, and the thought of any possible weakness in the education of sub-urbia's children has been virtually nonexistent. But the cultural cir-cumstances of the suburbs are alive with challenges to the schools. Without compensatory approaches in the educational program, the suburban schools will fall far short of achieving the high purposes they are expected to achieve.

COMPENSATORY PROGRAMS

Occasionally school officials and boards of education in affluent suburban communities are perceptive enough to grasp the defects of contemporary suburban life and commit themselves to some form of action. There have been some noteworthy attempts to revitalize the suburban curriculum and bring meaning and substance to in-struction. One major illustration of this is the growing tendency among suburban schools to emphasize a human relations approach to instruction in the classroom.

Indeed, human relations programs hold promise for the future of suburban youngsters. Without instruction relative to the human environment in the suburban schools, many suburban youngsters will grow up with little chance for wholesome personal development. But setbacks do occur. In one well-known Buffalo suburban com-munity—Williamsville, New York—the board of education backed away from a regional Title III project which would have sent a corps of teachers into its schools to improve instruction in human relations. The reason? A band of more than 100 citizens opposed the program, claiming "it would interfere with parents' lessons in human relations."[8] A sad day for Williamsville.

There are other programs suburban educators might seriously consider introducing in their schools if they would wish to see their students overcome the restrictive aspects of suburban life. Examples include:

- Instruction about different groups and cultures which could help eliminate prejudices and misconceptions about others. Personal experiences with children of other groups can show a disadvantaged suburban youth directly, immediately, and concretely that not all members of a different group are "stupid, dirty, or dishonest." Suburban youths need supplementary reality experiences to make it possible for them to "see" society as it really is so that they may develop the empathy and compassion essential for the development of wholesome values and attitudes.

- More social, interscholastic, and subject-matter club activities in order to involve students in meaningful intergroup situations. Service clubs and school-community organizations serve as a very useful vehicle in relating the schooling process to community needs while restoring a sense of personal worth for our troubled suburban youth.

- Suburban schools should actively assist in fostering a return of the "family unit" by encouraging child-parent attendance at school functions. Rather than tolerate parental isolation, the suburban schools must assist in creating a climate conducive to close family ties through school-centered activities, attempting primarily to entice fathers to share in these school events with their children.

- The schools of suburbia must expand the counseling staff at both the secondary and elementary levels. Individual and group counseling is imperative—especially in the elementary grades when attitudes are still malleable. After-school counseling with parents also seems essential, in view of the alarming increase in family conflicts occurring within the suburban communities.

- A major factor—perhaps the most important one—in providing suburban youth with direction and eliminating youthful prejudices is that of teacher attitudes.[9] Suburban educators must teach suburban youth with warmth, respect, and understanding. This, however, can only follow self-examination and insightful knowledge of the problems and pressures experienced by suburban youth. The

8. "Suspect Negroes of Being Human," *Education News*, September 9, 1968.
9. *See Report of the National Advisory Council on the Education of Disadvantaged Children* (Washington, D.C.: Government Printing Office, January 31, 1967).

attitudes of teachers about themselves and their relationships with
and responsibilities to the suburban disadvantaged must first be
clarified through in-service programs. Suburban teachers must
develop a more comprehensive understanding of the nature of
suburban life and its inherent defects.

• The schools should involve students more deeply in the task of
teaching and curriculum construction, thereby serving two purposes: (1) determining just what aspects of the curriculum are
indeed relevant from the student's point of view, and (2) improving the sense of worth of the student through responsible participation in the educational process. Why not have students contribute their views through previewing of audio or visual materials;
through examination of textbooks, library books, and other resource materials; through assisting in the instruction of slower or
retarded children; through assuming leadership responsibilities in
discussion groups and seminars? Why not delegate to the students
more responsibility in designing school codes of conduct; supervision of study, library, or lunch areas; and enforcement of school
discipline? Much could be gained—both by the schools and the
students.

The defects of suburban society and the misconceptions brought
by suburban students to the schools remain serious obstacles in the
path of social progress. If the people of the suburbs—including suburbia's educators—would have their children grow up to respect all
men and to seek for others the same scope of opportunity available
to themselves, it is imperative that the suburban schools help develop
the understandings and attitudes essential for constructive citizenship. Otherwise, the American Dream becomes the American Tragedy, and alienation and isolation become even more a way of life
for youth trapped in their suburban environment.

The Principal
and Integration

XI

The cause of integration in education is inseparable from the cause of education.

—BENJAMIN SOLOMON

The principal has a responsibility to exercise leadership in moving the integration process into the realm of reality. Desegregation is simply physical placement of children. After the school board has made the decision to desegregate, the principal is the key local change agent in integrating the school. The tempo and quality of the integration process in a particular school is, in large measure, a product of the principal's personal beliefs concerning the value of the individual and human life and his desire to fully develop the potentiality of every student.

What can be done to achieve the goals of desegregation? In order to overcome the problems of integration, Shirley H. Schell suggests we acknowledge certain facts. She also recognizes the need to develop ways of identifying teachers and administrators who can work effectively in integrated schools.

Many myths and gaps are blocking the solution to the problem of school integration. Neil V. Sullivan identifies some of these myths and gaps and reviews the actions taken by one school system to achieve integration. He believes the schools will have great difficulty in bridging "the gap between expectations and possibilities."

Desegregated schools do not automatically provide an integrated educative experience for the students. Conrad F. Toepfer, Jr., considers five main points for integrating educational experiences in desegregated schools. This approach requires a new philosophical commitment by a large percentage of the teachers and administrators in our schools today.

The isolation of Negro students in desegregated schools is a real problem. Morrill M. Hall and Harold W. Gentry conducted a study in which they examined a number of factors that may be related to

441

the social isolation of Negro students in formerly all-white secondary schools. The discussion of their findings should be of interest to principals faced with this problem.

Can school parks help urban schools in the integration process? John H. Fischer recognizes that the school park is no panacea. However, it is his belief that the school park concept, or something like it, must become a reality to provide the necessary setting for the "indispensable means to a decent and productive life."

The Spirit of the Law | 70

Shirley H. Schell

• The next day all hell broke loose. Man, when they threw that teacher through the window, I cut out for home. I covered those twenty-six blocks in nothing flat.

• Well, it's like every day is just something I got to get through. They'd like me to quit, but I ain't gonna give 'em the satisfaction.

• Well, it's all right, I guess, but we're just kinda there. We ain't really a part of the school. I know it's supposed to be better, but mostly we wish we had our own school back.

• I have four Negro children in my first grade class this year. I know I should treat them the same as I do the white children, but I just can't. Somehow I just can't.

Each of these statements was made by a person in a desegregated school, three students and one teacher. The first statement was made by a white boy as he described the near-riot which occurred in his high school following the assassination of Martin Luther King, Jr. He attends a desegregated school, which now has about an equal number of black and white students, in a small city on the Atlantic seaboard.

As the number of black students has increased, the problems of desegregation have become more acute. The black students are becoming militant in their demands for greater recognition, for teachers who can relate to them, and for more opportunities to participate in school activities. The turnover of faculty and administration has become a serious problem. This school is typical of a great number of urban high schools which have undergone dramatic changes as black families have moved into residential areas abandoned by whites in their exodus to the suburbs.

The second statement was made by a black girl who is one of about a dozen black students attending an affluent suburban high school, typical of many which are "integrated" by a handful of black students whose great misfortune is to live in an otherwise upper-middle-class suburb. This school has no black teachers, and there is no effort made to meet the individual needs of the few black students. The typical student in this school drives his own car, probably carries more pocket money than his teachers, and displays little awareness of, or concern for, the problems of his society. This girl

From *Educational Leadership*, Vol. 26, No. 2 (November 1968), pp. 122-125. Reprinted with permission of the Association for Supervision and Curriculum Development and the author. Copyright © 1968 by the Association for Supervision and Curriculum Development.

444

The Principal, The Student, The Community

described to me the gauntlet she must run daily as she passes from class to class. "Nigger" is probably the kindest of the epithets she is called. She reported that she had complained to the principal and vice-principal, but nothing was ever done to help her. "You can't do nothing to those rich kids," she said. "The teachers are all afraid of them."

The third statement was made by a black student in a rural high school only recently desegregated because of consolidation. His attitude was one of resignation and acceptance of the fact that he and the other black students were getting short shrift. He had wanted to take a leadership role in the student government organization, as he had done in his segregated school, but had found that positions of leadership were going exclusively to white students. Perhaps he will not always be resigned. Perhaps other black students will not be as willing as he has been to accept the status quo.

The last statement was made by a first-grade teacher in a newly integrated school in the Middle-West. She described how the little children would crowd eagerly around her for attention and affection. In spite of her intellectual acceptance of desegregation, she found herself unable to give the same attention and affection to the little black children that she gave generously to the whites.

FAILURE OF DESEGREGATION

These examples illustrate as no statistics can some of the attitudes and problems which are causing black parents to feel that desegregation is not the answer to the educational problems of their children. In a recent article in the *New York Times Magazine*, Robert S. Browne[1] discussed the case for two Americas and pointed out that the failure of school desegregation is a factor in the Black Nationalist movement and in the demands of black parents for local control of their schools.

If white Americans are sincerely interested in searching out the causes for the obvious failure of school desegregation, we do not have far to look. We have been so busy finding ways to implement the letter of the law that we have given little thought to the spirit of the law. Indeed, a great deal of effort has gone into devising ways to subvert the spirit of the law while fulfilling the letter. Bussing, pairing, redistricting, consolidation, and many other strategies have been tried to achieve desegregation.

With some notable exceptions, these arrangements have failed because little real effort has been made to change attitudes in the white communities. For example, in practically every case the em-

1. Robert S. Browne, "The Case for Two Americas—One Black, One White," *The New York Times Magazine,* August 11, 1968.

phasis of the much disputed bussing has been on getting the black child to a white school so that he might be made a little more like the white child. Little has been done to help the white child believe that he also would gain something from the experience. White America simply does not believe it has anything to gain from integration.

If "separate but equal" schools are inherently bad, then "integrated" schools ought to have some positive benefits for *all* students, white as well as black. Nevertheless, the focus in integration has been exclusively on the advantages to be gained by the black children. It is hard not to conclude that it was presumed the white children would gain nothing from the new experience. Perhaps this is the key to the failure. It has been too one-sided. White society has said to the black student that the purpose of integration is to help him become more like the white students.

The emphasis of integration should have been to provide the black student with a better opportunity to discover himself and realize his own potential. Perhaps the white child should have understood that integration would have some advantages for him, too—opportunities to know people different from himself, to learn from them and to share his own experiences. Despite many fine declarations to the contrary, the emphasis in American education has long been on making all students as nearly like one another as possible. The failure of desegregation is just one more example of the failure of American education. We cannot make black students like white students, any more than we can make all white children copies of one another.

PROBLEMS OF INTEGRATION

There are now two possible courses of action. We can acknowledge desegregation as a dismal failure, accept the thinking of an increasing number of black parents that quality education can exist in *de facto* segregated schools, and work to make the ghetto schools as good as, or hopefully better than, the best of our suburban schools. Or we can attempt to fulfill the *spirit* of the law and work to achieve true integration. To do the latter requires that we acknowledge certain facts.

First, it is a fact that every certified teacher is not qualified to teach the economically and educationally deprived. Only when an effort is made to remove those teachers who are psychologically unable to relate to these children and replace them with teachers who can, will any real progress be made. It may be that many teachers, both black and white, can be enabled to do such teaching by extensive sensitivity training. Yet few, if any, teachers are helped to teach the "disadvantaged" by attending a summer seminar or an in-service program in which the focus is on understanding the disadvantaged child or the presentation of new teaching methods or gadgets.

The problem that needs to be dealt with is not the "needs of the child" or "understanding the inner-city culture." The problem, the real problem, is the teacher's ability to accept and respond to these students as human beings with the same basic needs as his own and with unique personalities which can enrich his teaching experience. If he cannot do this, he cannot teach these students, and his presence in the classroom does harm to all the children, black and white.

Before any real progress is made, we must devise ways of determining which teachers and administrators can be effective in integrated schools and give them all the support they need. An administrator who supports a track system, and is not disturbed by the fact that most of the black students in his school are in either the basic education track or some kind of vocational track, will never provide effective leadership for an integrated school.

A principal who advises a teacher desperately trying to be effective in an overcrowded, desegregated classroom that the black students cannot learn much anyway and he should just talk with them is not psychologically suited to foster integration. The teacher who cannot respond emotionally to what he acknowledges intellectually will cripple the capacity of all his students to respond to each other.

It is also a fact that the black children have a great deal to contribute to the educational environment. We must acknowledge this and build on their contributions. There is much discussion now about the "self-actualized"[2] person. Carl Rogers and Abraham Maslow have identified some of the characteristics of such persons as spontaneity, joy, and awareness.[3] In working with many students from economically deprived backgrounds in the Upward Bound Program, I have been impressed by the fact that it is these very qualities which keep these young people going in the face of overwhelming obstacles.

One of the most reassuring anecdotes I have ever heard is an experience related by one of our Upward Bound students. She described in hilarious detail her 30-block journey to school on a morning when the sidewalks and streets were coated with ice and the buses were out on strike. In spite of economic hardship, personal family tragedy, indifferent and hostile teachers, this girl is still able to find much that is wonderful and much that is funny. She is able to relate to others and to share their problems. If her school environment had valued these qualities, she could have made a significant contribution.

2. Jane Howard, "Inhibitions Thrown to the Winds," *Life* 65 (2); July 12, 1968.
3. Abraham H. Maslow, *Toward a Psychology of Being* (New York: D. Van Nostrand Company, Inc., 1962).

Another of our Upward Bound students, when I questioned him about what he had found most valuable in the program, answered that he had learned that he could learn. He should have been enabled to discover this in his school. How many are there who, like him, will not make this discovery in school? Can our society afford to lose their contributions?

We have not achieved integrated schools. To integrate means to make a whole by putting together the parts. Resegregation of desegregated schools? Merely to desegregate, if by that we mean only to place the two races together in one facility, is at best a dubious goal.

We must decide what we want. If we want integrated schools, we must find ways of implementing the spirit of the law. If we merely want to desegregate, then we ought to acknowledge that the idea is doomed to failure, abandon it, and give our support to those black parents who are demanding quality schools, segregated or otherwise.

71 | Myths and Gaps in School Integration

Neil V. Sullivan

A rabbit was crossing the highway at night. He stopped suddenly to stare into the headlights of an onrushing car. Frozen with terror, he stood immobile as the car bore down on him. This modern fable applies forcefully to American education. Like the rabbit, our educators and boards of education are paralyzed by indecision as they face the onrushing problem of school integration. They wish it would go away. Some would like to take a backward leap to the "safety" of preintegration days by "upgrading" segregated schools. Some would simply like to play dead and hope the problem would miss them entirely.

The truth is that integration of education must be faced and faced now. Leaders, whether political or academic, who do not face up to integration will be run over as surely as the frightened rabbit.

If any Americans are under the illusion that integration is well under way in the United States, they need only read the first paragraph of the U. S. Office of Education's illuminating "Equality of Educational Opportunity" (the Coleman Report) summary. "White children are most segregated. . . . Almost 80 percent of all white pupils in 1st grade and 12th grade attend schools that are from 90 to 100 percent white."

This report was compiled 11 years after the U. S. Supreme Court's desegregation decision of 1954, and in the three years since the report the percentages have changed alarmingly little.

To solve the integration problem, we must understand it—particularly the emotion-charged myths about it that block a solution.

No one can ignore the fact that a large number of Americans are hostile to integration. Many have very real fears about racially balanced schools, but most of these fears are based on a few deeply rooted half-truths. I have run into all of the myths since becoming superintendent of the Berkeley, California, Unified School District, where we are actively committed to integrating our schools.

A myth is, for our purposes, a widely held belief that contains only a grain of truth.

One of the most persistent myths is that school integration will cause academic achievement to suffer. Those who voice this myth mean that the child in a "privileged" environment (the Caucasion

From *NEA Journal*, Vol. 57 (September 1968), pp. 38-41. Reprinted by permission of the publisher and author.

child) will suffer socially and academically if his school becomes racially integrated. But according to the Coleman Report:

> . . . if a white pupil from a home that is strongly and effectively supportive of education is put in a school where most pupils do not come from such homes, his achievement will be little different than if he were in a school composed of others like himself. But if a minority pupil from a home without much educational strength is put with schoolmates with strong educational backgrounds, his achievement is likely to increase.

Even more startling, this massive survey found that the student body was the most important single in-school factor in improving the academic achievement of minority group children. To my surprise, and I'm sure to the surprise of Dr. Coleman and most educators, the mixing factor was more important to raising academic achievement levels of disadvantaged pupils than were good teachers (although these were the second most important), equipment, texts, buildings, or other related factors.

I do not mean to imply that racial and "class" integration will automatically insure academic excellence in a school. Academic excellence has always needed educational leadership, and, in the last analysis, a combination of many factors, especially high-quality teachers. But even the Caucasian child in an unintegrated school suffers from his segregation. As far as can be determined from incomplete surveys, segregation of the white child is a disadvantage to that child.

One of the most difficult myths to combat is that violence in the schools will drastically increase if they are integrated. Despite the lack of conclusive studies on this subject, my own experiences in Berkeley—we are just across the Bay from San Francisco and its Hunter's Point ghetto, where rioting occurred in 1966—would indicate that race-based violence in our school is amazingly low.

In 1964, we in Berkeley completed the integration of our junior high schools and in the process created an unusual one-year school, called West Campus, for all of Berkeley's ninth graders. Garfield Junior High had been virtually an all-white privileged school; Willard had been fairly well balanced, and Burbank (which became West Campus) was almost entirely Negro.

Naturally, we were apprehensive about the move. Teachers frankly were afraid academic levels would collapse. (Some of them, too, believe in myths!) Many prophesied wholesale violence. The Berkeley Teachers Association, however, strongly supported both the concept of integration and the courageous board members who voted to implement it.

The first year of complete integration at Garfield was tense, but the way the students worked to make it work was wonderful. At West Campus, also, everyone was determined to make the unusual one-year school work—and they did, beautifully. The second year we had the normal problems expected with first-year high school students, but they were not integration problems, not racial violence.

In the 1967-68 school year, there were racial incidents at one of our junior high schools on the heels of Martin Luther King's assassination, which was a more than symbolic, ultimate act of white racism. It triggered long-standing student resentment against a tracking system which seemed to guarantee segregated classes within the desegregated school. It also reflected some staff insensitivity to the needs of a mixed student body. The immediate racial incidents were met by quick emergency action to keep the peace on campus and in the classroom. Students, parents, and teachers of the various races immediately became deeply involved in improving the whole school scene, and this involvement has continued.

The truth is that disillusionment, hostility, hopelessness, and violence by young people are on the rise everywhere—even in all-white schools and communities where race is not at issue. There is very real confusion about fights between members of different races. Some undoubtedly have racial animosity at their base, but do most of them? Is our habit of attributing racial trouble instantly to any fighting between boys of different races responsible for the persistence of the "violence myth"?

The greatest outbursts of racial violence occur where no steps have been taken toward integration or when those taken are so timid, so obviously phony, that the minority race believes the token integration step was taken to prove total integration would not work. If such a thing were done to whites, they, too, would be fighting mad.

Those who repeat the "violence myth" ignore the fact that it is the Negro who has been on the receiving end of most interracial violence down through American history. The myth-sayers appear unconcerned about violence done to the Negro, except as it disturbs the surface calm of our society. However, no matter which side mounts the racial attack, both white and black are the losers. The cure lies in breaking down the ghetto barriers in education, housing, and employment. Then the violence will cease.

Another myth concerns the "great exodus." This one usually comes up at a board of education meeting, phrased this way: "School integration will be followed by a mass exodus of Caucasians from the community. Again we are faced with an observable element of truth. White families do move away as ghetto conditions advance. Some of the easily alarmed ones flee to all-white suburbs or rural areas at the first sign of an "alien" element in the schools. The flight to the suburbs is well-documented. But is it a "race flight"?

It is in some instances. But I suggest it might also be called a "smog flight" or a "congestion flight." Some families fly from high taxes and deteriorating city services—only to discover that taxes can be higher in suburbs and services even less satisfactory. Many move out of the dense city simply so their children can see grass growing, sit in the shade of a tree, hear a real, live bird sing.

Recent Berkeley experience was an instructive one with regard to the "great exodus." We were warned that the city would become a ghost town overnight, that it would soon be all-Negro if we proceeded with integration. The City Council even established a committee to study ways a racially mixed Berkeley could face the years ahead without becoming a ghetto.

Before the committee went to work, we knew that there had been a gradual decline in white enrollment in the schools, a decline that had already tapered off. Some presumed that this reflected the movement of white families away from a system they feared would soon be integrated.

In the fall of 1966, with our efforts to implement racial balance a year along, we took a racial census of students in Berkeley schools. The census showed that, not only had the decline in Caucasian enrollment stopped, it had been reversed. Both the number and the proportion of Caucasian students attending Berkeley schools had increased. The 1967 fall census indicated another slight gain in the number of Caucasians in our student population. For Berkeley, the flight to the suburbs was a myth.

A myth attractive to Negroes and whites alike is that compensatory education, by itself, can solve the problems of racial discrimination and poor education for disadvantaged children, eliminating the need for integration of schools.

What is meant by compensatory education? It means pouring money and teachers into poor ghetto schools. The theory is that by smothering these schools in educational goodies—psychologists, researchers, counselors, top-quality teachers, better school buildings, cafeterias—we can put all-Negro schools on a par with all-white schools of the best quality. This, the story goes, will make it unnecessary to worry about integration because children of all races will have equal educational opportunities everywhere.

There are individual instances of spectacular success when bright ghetto youngsters are given substantial amounts of special help, but there is no real evidence that the mass of minority children can benefit by this technique.

The Coleman Report and a report of the U. S. Commission on Civil Rights both indicate that one of the most important ingredients in education—hope—is not provided by compensatory techniques. Hope for a better future, hope to become an accepted member of society, hope for an end to discrimination—none of these is satisfied by compensatory education.

Involuntary segregation, no matter how benevolent, is rejection. Segregation is the classic symbol of society's centuries-long tradition of discrimination, and it says unequivocally to black people and other minorities, "You are inferior."

Thus, compensatory education, which does have some very valuable features, can never, in my opinion, be a substitute for integration. Many black children who are kept segregated develop a "What's the use?" attitude. Even if their equipment is improved and they get better teachers and special attention, they have no yardstick by which to measure the improvement in relation to what the "other" or white children are receiving. They cannot be convinced that they are not getting scraps from the table.

Compensatory education can be very useful in helping to make up for the deprivation ghetto children have suffered, but it must be used in conjunction with—not instead of—integration. Then it will show spectacular results.

Many Americans still cling to another myth—that integration is not a problem of the schools. Integration, the argument runs, must start with housing: Minorities now have the right to buy houses and rent apartments anywhere. This does not mean, though, that all segments of the population will be mixed together and that schools will be automatically integrated.

However, when ways of integrating housing are discussed, potent real estate groups and frantic property owners insist that this can only be accomplished when the employment sector has been thoroughly integrated. They say that when the Negro and the other minorities get better jobs, they will have the money to upgrade their ghettos or, presumably, to buy better property.

The discussion with employers and unions on integrating jobs brings out the contention that until Negroes and other minorities have had more education, they cannot hope to get or hold better jobs, etc., etc., and around and around.

The fact is that segregation is a problem in all of these areas and solutions must be found in all of them. We educators are under no illusion that desegregation of education alone will solve the problem completely. Solutions must come also in housing and employment, and ultimately in all phases of society. But it is essential that the educational sector not hang back waiting for integration to begin somewhere else first. Education must not be afraid to assume leadership.

I do not delude myself that the myths will soon be completely destroyed or even that the hostility of many white Americans to integration can be entirely overcome. But we will have to live with the myths and with the hostility, and get on with the job of integration. There is no choice. Events are forcing us to act.

Even an all-white community with all-white schools must face up to the race problem. The children in such a "protected" town bump into the problem on TV, in the press, in comic books. Even if they are not asked to discuss it or confront it in their narrow little world, they bump into it whenever they move out of their cocoon. Will they be equipped to deal with the problem intelligently?

Compelling as the case for school integration is, simply mixing students in classrooms is not enough. Some very real gaps have to be closed to make integration work. Yet since desegregation cannot wait, we must integrate and work to close the gaps at the same time.

To professional educators, the most obvious gap is the academic achievement gap—or chasm. Historically, this gap is easily explained. In many areas of the United States, Negroes were deliberately kept uneducated.

When it could no longer be denied that black people were human beings and even could learn to read, write, and manipulate figures, the U. S. Supreme Court came up with its famous "separate but equal" school facilities ruling. Since then, facilities for Negroes have certainly been separate but never equal.

It was not just that equipment was unequal, but that many teachers in ghetto schools were inexperienced and poorly trained. They were not poor in courage, certainly, but many of them had little more than a high school education, and that from inferior segregated schools. Thus, even those Negro children who did thirst for knowledge and who did do their best to get something out of school were cheated. The gap between their education and that of the whites was enormous, and still is.

Beyond the educational gap there is, in many instances, a cultural gap. The very institution of segregation has forced many minorities—but particularly the Negro—into the role of lowest-class citizens. Unemployment is high, so blacks have to live in cramped, unsafe quarters. Food for their tables is inadequate, and food for their minds is even more deficient.

As a baby and preschool youngster, the ghetto child often did not have any practice at naming things and has difficulty doing so when he finally gets to school. For him, the classroom is a new world where the symbols are all different. In a school outside the ghetto, he runs into children who are quite at home in the world of symbols. Quickly falling behind, he becomes discouraged and is frequently rebellious or apathetic.

The "behavior gap" is related to the cultural gap. If a child's home life places no emphasis on consideration for others, then his behavior is going to be a problem in school. But children are sensitive creatures and, when properly handled, soon learn to follow the socially acceptable behavior of their peers. In a thoroughly integrated school, behavior patterns depend on what the school tolerates—just as they do in all-white schools. The behavior gap depends for its solution primarily on teachers and administrators who know when to be firm and when to be yielding, and are always fair.

As Americans should know by now, merely to put children of all races in one school does not mean integration. You can have complete segregation within the school if Negroes speak only to Negroes in the schoolyard and whites to whites. I have seen it happen. Thus the "friendship gap" must also be closed in the schools.

This is not nearly as difficult as we originally supposed. The solution is to capture the children's interest. West Campus School in Berkeley does it with literally hundreds of clubs and activities. An art club, a science club, a hiking club—you name it and West Campus probably has it. Mutuality of interests quickly transcends race. Friendships develop. The de facto segregation pattern in the schoolyard begins to disintegrate.

A gap that the schools will have great difficulty bridging is the gap between expectations and possibilities. When the black child comes out of the ghetto, he is promised freedom, justice, and equality, and he may get them in school, where be becomes an educated man. In the larger community, he collides with brutal reality. The job he is educated to take may not be open to a Negro. His school years of integration are over, and now his expectation of an integrated life as a fully accepted American citizen is blasted.

This last gap is still a matter of education, but it is not one that educators alone can bridge. It has to be a community effort and a national effort. We can exercise the myths and close the gaps if we will, but we must get about the job now and with vigor.

Integration | 72
A Curriculur Concern |

Conrad F. Toepfer, Jr.

Problems of racial integration in public schools continue to command increasing attention in professional education writings. Attempts to ameliorate and eliminate racial imbalance in the schools are literally legion. Unfortunately, most of these plans provide only for desegregation of racially imbalanced schools, and, in themselves, cause no effective integration of educational experience for students in newly desegregated schools. In many instances, however, it has been erroneously assumed that desegregation efforts automatically provide an integrated educative experience for the students involved.

The main points to be considered here are:

1. Integration of information and learners is invariably a curriculum planning process;
2. Desegregation of racially imbalanced schools cannot be considered in itself as causing racial integration in schools;
3. Integration of learning for Negro students in racially balanced schools must be achieved through curriculum planning to communicate their experimental background with that of the white, middle-class orientation;
4. Failure to follow up desegregation with curricular integration will present a critical problem; and
5. Resources and means are available to begin organizing integration programs.

CURRICULUM PLANNING FOR INTEGRATION

Prior to the problems of racial balance, integration had important meaning for curriculum planning. Krug states the following:

Although the subject organization is the usual and to some people the inevitable pattern for classroom studies, it has been criticized. Those who do so contend that it results in the splitting up of human knowledge and skill into arbitrary segments and that the student who pursues it comes out with piecemeal education. Such criticisms have led to efforts to modify subject organization along the lines of "broad fields." The term "integration" is somewhat used to describe these efforts, although there

From *Educational Leadership*, Vol. 26, No. 3 (December 1968), pp. 285-288. Reprinted with permission of the Association for Supervision and Curriculum Development and the author. Copyright © 1968 by the Association for Supervision and Curriculum Development.

are those who contend that true integration takes place in the learner rather than in the reorganization of content.[1]

The concept of subject matter correlation [2,3] suggests that integration of learning within learners best evolves when the organization of subject matter helps learners see the relevance of subject materials to each other and in relationship to their own environment. The development to homogeneous grouping and "track" programs for specific ability levels has required, on paper at least, the planning of special curricula for these diverse groups, including organization of subject matter, graded instructional materials, and differentiated instructional techniques. Wide gaps among groups of intellectually superior children, slow learners, and special class groups have long posed problems to curricular integration in the instructional program. Where efforts have succeeded, teachers have invariably organized programs to provide students from wide ability ranges the opportunity to compete and achieve individually. Thus an integration of learning has been achieved and for a range of students with widely varying backgrounds and capabilities.[4]

DESEGREGATION AND INTEGRATION

It is suggested here that integration as a curriculum planning procedure can likewise meet the needs of racial and social class integration in public schools today. There are differences between the situations described in the foregoing section and needs for racial integration in schools but these should properly be recognized as differences of degree and not of kind. Some planned improved educational experience must be developed as a second step after desegregation. This integration process must design curricular programs and opportunities for experiences which communicate to the cultural and experiential backgrounds of all students in that school. Failure to achieve this second step will cause impoverished students to once more be exposed to instructional programs as meaningless as those formerly experienced in segregated schools.

My own son attends an elementary school into which Negro children are bussed to combat *de facto* racial segregation. When the program began in September 1965, the Negro children would gather

1. Edward Krug, *Curriculum Planning*. Revised Edition. (New York: Harper & Brothers, 1957), p. 103.

2. Harold Alberty, *Reorganizing the High School Curriculum*. Third Edition. (New York: The Macmillan Company, 1962), pp. 204-30.

3. Roland Faunce and Nelson Bossing, *Developing the Core Curriculum*. Second Edition. (Englewood Cliffs, N. J.: Prentice-Hall, Inc., 1958).

4. Nelson Henry, editor. *The Integration of Educational Experiences*, Part III, The Fifty-seventh Yearbook of the National Society for the Study of Education (Chicago: University of Chicago Press, 1958).

as a separate group in the school playground despite their age range from kindergarten through eighth grade. Through the autumn this condition changed with increasing evidences of white and Negro children playing together. By the end of the school year there was almost complete *social integration* through personal friendships. It has become common to see Negro and white children in "arm-around-each-other" buddy friendships. However, there has been no attempt to develop integrating curricular programs upon this base of social integration. Yet, many educators feel that total integration has thus been achieved. They have failed to see that development of new curriculum programs in this encouraging social climate could build *educational integration* upon the foundation of desegregation and correction of racial imbalance.

CURRICULUM PLANNING FOR RACIAL INTEGRATION

If curriculum planning is to be successful in effecting educational integration, it must identify the basic problem which plagued education in segregated schools. The learner in that setting was isolated from the white, middle-class values and background upon which the curriculum was built. Because this isolation made the curriculum remote and meaningless, impoverished children, both black and white, had extreme difficulty in achieving the desired ends of learning in the curriculum. Research has revealed that compensatory education designed to help students in segregated schools with heavy racial and social class imbalance is largely ineffective.[5,6]

Planning integrating curricular programs requires a philosophical commitment. Such efforts must eventually develop teacher skills and perceptions through in-service education programs and must create instructional materials which will teach skills in terms of the environmental experiences of Negro and other impoverished children.

The end goals of educational programs for the impoverished will be much the same as programs in middle class environments. However, the jump from beginning to end in the environment of poverty is far too broad for the majority of learners to comprehend and accept. The end objectives are so far removed from the learner's experience and so abstract from his own environment that he rejects them because of their remoteness and because he cannot see how he can ever achieve them. To counteract this, new sets of vital and immediate objectives, objectives which are so concrete that you "can taste them" must be developed to

5. Kenneth B. Clark, *Dark Ghetto* (New York: Harper & Row, Publishers, Inc., 1965).
6. A. Harry Passow, *Education in Depressed Areas* (New York: Teachers College Press, Columbia University, 1965).

provide a continuum for the learner to reach toward the end objectives of a better life for himself.[7]

Failure to work at this problem has resulted in curriculum voids such as the following:

The poverty-stricken child needs to learn to read but not initially to read about a middle-class world in which he cannot even fantasy himself. His own environmental needs to read are critically important to the point of life and death but are typically not noticed by the school. This child needs to learn to read and understand the meaning of "danger" and "poison" on cans of rat poison, "pure" and "safe" on other containers. Other things to be read and understood include signs on condemned buildings with words and expressions like "condemned," "under razing," "structure not safe," "symptoms of rabies are"; but the reading materials used in class talk about a boy, a girl and their dog and their environment in all-Caucasian suburbia.[8]

Unless such approaches develop, the gains in learning for former ghetto school children will be limited to mere social acculturation through their associations with a predominance of white, middle-class classmates.

DILEMMA OF DESEGREGATION WITHOUT CURRICULAR INTEGRATION

In racially imbalanced schools, the Negro student was exposed to a curriculum with learning situations geared to white, middle-class race experience. While such experiences were often non-intelligible and rejected, the Negro student still had the security of his own culture. In schools where integrating curricular programs do not develop upon the correction of racial imbalance, he will still be as isolated from the curriculum as he was in ghetto schools. In the desegregated setting, however, the majority of his classmates will understand the white, middle-class orientation of the curriculum because *they* are white. This may well provide the Negro student with increased cultural insecurity.

Thus, curricular isolation of students will continue in racially desegregated schools but now with the pernicious danger of mistaking racial desegregation for racial integration. If the curriculum in desegregated schools is not planned to integrate the life experience of both Negro and white students, supporters of racial segregation who preach Negro inferiority may falsely seem correct. Continua-

7. Dorothy Rosenbaum and Conrad Toepfer, Jr. *Curriculum Planning and School Psychology: The Coordinated Approach* (Buffalo, New York: Hertillon Press, 1966), p. 136.
8. *Ibid.*, p. 137.

tion of desegregation-only programs could facilitate such a catastrophic misconclusion.

RESOURCES AND MEANS TO SOLVE THE PROBLEM

Organization of both preservice and graduate teacher education sequences to develop teacher awareness as well as planning and teaching skills must be a primary step. Likewise, needs for in-service programs which focus on similar teacher skills in actual school settings rate high priority. Despite cuts in federal government support, federal monies still offer promising resources to underwrite such beginning efforts.

In theory and practice, curriculum planning offers succinct means for actualizing effective integration programs in schools. Such efforts must identify and organize appropriate instructional objectives, content, materials, methods, and evaluating devices for improved learning experiences to follow the correction of racial imbalance. Two recent innovations seem to hold broad promise for integrating curricular patterns. The nongraded school offers a flexibility which could well accommodate the wide ranges of student background and ability in desegregated schools in designing improved learning experiences. The importance of individualizing instruction for all students recommends the computer-based resource unit concept[9] as a succinct means to integrate educational experiences in desegregated schools. Curriculum planning in desegregated schools must interrelate the facets of classroom experience, special services, and cocurricular activities in creating a new and vital all-school program which will facilitate curricular integration in its most specific applications.

The five points considered herein point to this single need and fact. Whatever is developed for those students in racially desegregated classrooms *must* be definitively different from present and existing curricular problems. To provide students more of that which was a meaningless failure in racially imbalanced schools will be tragically myopic. Furthermore, it will candidly indicate that the problem of racial integration in schools has either not been recognized and defined or that we do not know how, or care, to deal with it effectively!

9. Robert S. Harnack, "Resource Units and the Computer," *The High School Journal* 51(3): 126-31; December 1967.

73 | ## Isolation of Negro Students
in Integrated Public Schools

Morrill M. Hall
Harold W. Gentry

In a recent report the United States Commission on Civil Rights clearly documented the persistent problem of racial isolation in the public schools.[1] Isolation, as presented in the Commission Report, is merely another way of saying that the public schools, some thirteen years after the Brown decision, are in many instances still segregated by race. Some of the more fundamental causes of racial isolation, as stated by the Commission, are: disparity in income between the white and Negro races, discriminatory practices in housing leading to residential segregation, the flight of white citizens to the suburbs, the traditional practice of basing school enrollment on residence in attendance zones and the unwillingness of some school officials to take effective steps to relieve the problem.[2]

Racial isolation as defined above is a serious and continuing problem. A related problem, and one that seems to have received little attention, is the isolation of Negro students who attend integrated public schools. The problem is placed in focus by the following statement:

> Student activities and social affairs are a vital part of the total school program. In the desegregated schools of the border states, white students and Negro students are on the same teams and in the same music groups; they take gym classes together, eat in the same lunchrooms, and attend the same dances. They are generally polite and considerate. They speak to each other in the halls and accept each other as classmates. Their relationships, however, end at this point. They do not accept each other socially and there are very few cases where white and Negro students become close friends.[3]

According to another author, the results of school integration point to an apparent tendency for both white and Negro students to segregate themselves at the college level as well as in elementary and secondary schools. The author suggests ". . . . that voluntary group segregation does not necessarily decrease even though minor-

From *The Journal of Negro Education*, Vol. 38 (Spring 1969), pp. 156-161. Reprinted by permission of the publisher and authors.

1. United States Commission on Civil Rights, *Racial Isolation in the Public Schools*, Vol. I (Washington, D.C.: Government Printing Office, 1967).
2. *Ibid.*, pp. 70-71.
3. Herbert W. Wey, "Desegregation and Integration," *Phi Delta Kappan*, XLVII, (May 1966), 513-14.

ity group students are consistent members of the school population."[4]

THE PROBLEM

The general purpose of this study was to examine a number of factors which may be related to the social isolation of Negro students in formerly all-white secondary schools.

Specifically, the study sought to answer the following questions: (1) To what extent do Negro students participate in extra-curricular activities? (2) If Negro students do not participate in extra-curricular activities, why do they not do so? (3) How frequently are Negro students invited by white students to participate in school activities? (4) How frequently do Negro students return to the school they formerly attended for the purpose of taking part in social activities? (5) How often do the parents or guardians of Negro students attend functions sponsored by the school? (6) Do the "best friends" of Negro students attend the school in which the students are enrolled? (7) Do the variables of sex, grade level and years in attendance condition the responses of Negro students to the questions posed above?

PROCEDURES

In May of 1967 a selected sample of Negro students in integrated secondary schools was asked to respond to a questionnaire which requested information relative to major questions posed by the study. The students were attending sixteen secondary schools in eight different school districts in a southeastern state. The school districts ranged in size from the fifth largest to one of the smallest in the state. All of the districts had integrated their secondary schools at least three years prior to the time the questionnaire was administered.

All of the secondary schools attended by the sample students were accredited by the regional accrediting agency and all offered a number of school activities, ranging from athletics to clubs having national affiliation. The largest school enrolled approximately 2,000 students and the smallest some 350 students.

The questionnaires were administered in a group setting in each school by a person selected by the superintendent of the school district. In an attempt to secure an honest and objective response to the questionnaire, the students were given an option as to whether they wished to participate in the study. To insure anonymity, no identification was requested on the questionnaire. The question-

4. Robert Lee Green, "After School Integration—What?", *Personnel and Guidance Journal*, XLVII, (March, 1966), 705.

naires were returned to the investigators by the individual responsible for their administration. A total of 377 students returned completed questionnaires. However, one or two students failed to check isolated items. Thus, the total is not the same in every case.

RESULTS

One concern of the study was to determine the frequency of participation by Negro students in extra-curricular activities in the integrated school. As shown in Table I, approximately 60 per cent of the total sample of Negro students reported that they participated in activities of this nature. When sex was considered in the analysis, a somewhat different picture emerged, as 71.67 per cent of the male students reported taking part in extra-curricular activities as compared with approximately 49 per cent of the female students.

Further examination of the data showed an apparent relationship between participation in extra-curricular activities and the grade level of the student. With the exception of the tenth grade, the percentage of participation in extra-curricular activities increased with each successively higher grade level. The same pattern was also true as related to years in attendance. While 58.30 per cent of the students in the first year of attendance reported participation in extra-curricular activities, the percentage had moved to 71 per cent in the third year and to 100 per cent in the fourth year.

Examination of data related to the reasons given for not participating in extra-curricular activities showed that the most frequent reason given was "do not have time" and the second most frequent was "belief that I am not wanted." When considered by sex of the student, the most frequent response for males was "do not have time" and for the female student, "belief that I am not wanted." There was an apparent relationship between the grade level of the student and the two most frequent reasons given for not participating in extra-curricular activities. Those responding to "do not have time" increased from 20.69 per cent in the eighth grade to 62.50 per cent in the twelfth grade, with an increase being shown at each successively higher grade level. Those students responding "belief that I am not wanted" decreased from 58.62 per cent at the eighth grade to 25.00 per cent in the twelfth grade, with a decrease being shown at each successively higher grade level.

Another concern of the study was the frequency with which white students invited Negro students to participate in school activities. Analysis of these data showed that 53 per cent of the Negro students had never been invited by white students to participate in school activities, while 11 per cent were frequently invited to do so. Again, there was an apparent relationship between the sex of the students and the responses. Approximately 66 per cent of the female students responded that they had never been invited by white students to participate in school activities as compared with 39 per cent of the male students. Also 44 per cent of the male students reported they had occasionally been invited to participate in school activities by white students as compared with 27.41 per cent of female students.

The grade level at which the student was enrolled and the number of years he had been in attendance at the school both appeared to be related to the student's responses to this question. Thus, the percentage of students indicating a "never" response decreased at each succeeding higher grade level and also decreased as the number of years in attendance increased. Likewise, the percentage of Negro students who were occasionally invited to participate in school activities tended to increase at the higher grade levels and with an increase in the number of years in attendance.

The next question was concerned with whether Negro students returned to the school they formerly attended for the purpose of taking part in social activities. Examination of these data showed that over 57 per cent of all of the Negro students returned at some time to their former school to participate in social activities.

Further examination of the data revealed that female students returned to their former school more frequently to participate in social activities than did male students. Approximately 29 per cent of the female students indicated they frequently returned to their former school for such purposes as compared with 21.67 per cent of the male students. Further, some 33 per cent of the female students indicated they occasionally followed this practice as compared with 31.67 per cent of the male students. There was no consistent pattern of responses evident when this question was considered in terms of grade level or years in attendance in the present school.

Data relative to the question of how often parents and guardians of Negro students attended functions sponsored by the school showed that approximately 17 per cent of the parents or guardians frequently attended school sponsored activities. Forty-eight per cent indicated that their parents occasionally attended school functions, while 35 per cent reported that their parents never participated in activities of this nature.

When sex was considered as a variable, the results showed that 19.80 per cent of the female students, as compared with 13.89 per cent of the male students, reported that their parents frequently attended functions sponsored by the school. On the other hand, 36.55 per cent of the female students reported that their parents never attended school functions as compared with 33.33 per cent of the male students.

The grade level at which the student was enrolled apparently had some relationship to the participation of parents in functions sponsored by the school. For example, the percentage of parents who never attended school functions decreased from the eighth to the twelfth grade. Furthermore, there was a general tendency for the percentage of parents who occasionally or frequently attended school functions to increase at the higher grade levels.

There was also an apparent relationship between the number of years students had been in the school and the extent of attendance by their parents at school functions. This relationship is most clearly shown by the fact that 45.17 per cent of the students in their first year at the school reported their parents never attended school functions; while only 14.71 per cent of second-year students gave this response. Of possibly more significance, no student who had been in attendance for more than two years reported a "never" response to this question.

The final question considered in the study was concerned with whether or not the best friends of the respondents attended the same school. Sixty-two per cent responded in the affirmative. Fifty-five per cent of the female students gave an affirmative response as compared with 69.44 per cent of the male students.

There was no consistent pattern between the grade level of the students and their response to this question. However, after the first year there was an increase in the percentage of affirmative responses as the number of years in attendance at the school increased.

DISCUSSION

It seems to be apparent from the results of the study that some isolation of Negro students existed in integrated schools. On the other hand, the general pattern of responses indicated that isolation was reduced as the length of time Negro and white students were in school together was increased. For example, the analyses of data showed that as the years in attendance at the integrated school increased, there was more frequent participation by Negro students in extra-curricular activities, more frequent attendance by their parents at school functions, and an increasing frequency in invitations from white students to participate in school activities.

An exception to this general pattern was the frequency with which Negro students returned to their former school to participate in social activities. Unlike the trend indicated above, the length of attendance in integrated schools did not appear to be related to the pattern of student participation in social activities.

This exception suggests that there is a tendency for the wall of separation between Negro and white students to break down in activities such as school organizations, clubs and athletics which are more formally organized and for the wall to remain in such informal, social activities as school dances, and parties. Failing to find outlets for social activities in the integrated school, the Negro students com-

TABLE I

Responses (in Per Cents) of Negro Students to Questions Related to the Social Isolation of Negro Students in Selected Integrated Secondary Schools, May 1967

RESPONSES	ALL STUDENTS	SEX		GRADE LEVEL					YEARS IN ATTENDANCE			
		M	F	8	9	10	11	12	1	2	3	4
Question: Do you participate in extra-curricular activities at school?												
Yes	60	72	49	49	59	56	65	79	58	61	71	100
No	40	28	51	52	41	44	35	21	42	39	29	0
Question: If your answer to Question 4 is "No," why do you not participate in extra-curricular activities?												
1*	44	59	36	21	36	51	58	62	44	43	33	
2*	16	16	17	21	15	18	13	12	14	22	33	
3*	40	25	47	59	49	31	29	25	42	35	33	
Question: How often have you been invited by white students to participate in school activities?												
Frequently	11	17	7	8	14	9	13	14	11	10	21	100
Occasionally	35	44	27	25	27	32	49	48	30	49	43	
Never	53	39	66	67	59	58	38	38	59	41	36	
Question: Do you return to the school you formerly attended for the purpose of taking part in social activities?												
Frequently	25	22	28	24	34	20	24	24	26	24	14	50
Occasionally	32	32	0	33	30	22	37	40	24	35	21	50
Never	42	47	38	46	44	43	35	52	42	41	64	0
Question: How often have your parents or guardian attended functions sponsored by the school?												
Frequently	17	14	20	18	15	16	18	21	14	23	21	50
Occasionally	48	53	44	38	41	47	59	59	41	63	79	50
Never	35	33	37	44	44	37	23	21	45	15	0	0
Question: Does your best friend among students of your age attend this school?												
Yes	62	69	55	67	67	59	58	62	62	59	86	100
No	38	31	45	33	33	41	42	38	38	41	14	0

1* Do not have time.
2* Have no interest in available activities.
3* Belief that I am not wanted.

(Other response choices were provided but none were checked by respondents).

465

pensate by returning to their former school to participate in these activities. Such an analysis would appear to be supported by Wey's contention, cited above, that white and Negro students accept each other as classmates but do not accept each other socially.

The study further indicated a relationship between sex and the isolation of Negro students in the integrated school. There was rather strong evidence that male students had made a better adjustment (or had been more fully accepted in the integrated school than had female students). The reasons for this are by no means clear. A plausible suggestion is that males in general are more amenable to the socialization process. This explanation may be especially true when relationships between the races are considered in the shadow of centuries of segregation. In segregated communities, the restrictions placed upon the behavior of females, by the traditions, mores and customs of the community, were probably more severe than those placed upon males. As a result, females may find it more difficult to accept or be accepted by members of another race. They are in essence more "locked-in" by their previous experiences and expectations than are male students. A more practical explanation may lie in the fact that athletics, particularly football and track, provide more opportunities for participation by the male Negro student.

Another factor which may have contributed to the differing responses by sex was the fact that a larger percentage of male Negro students reported that their best friend attended the integrated school. It may be that the presence of a friend in a new setting serves to encourage the student to become more involved in the activities provided by the school.

School Parks for Equal Opportunities | 74

John H. Fischer

Of all the plans that have been put forward for integrating urban schools the boldest is the school park. This is a scheme under which several thousand ghetto children and a larger number from middle-class white neighborhoods would be assembled in a group of schools sharing a single campus. Placing two or more schools on one site is not a new idea, but two other aspects of the school park are novel. It would be the largest educational institution ever established below the collegiate level and the first planned explicitly to cultivate racial integration as an element of good education.

A small community might house its entire school system in one such complex. A large city with one or more large ghettos would require several. In the most imaginative and difficult form of the proposal a central city and its neighboring suburban districts would jointly sponsor a ring of metropolitan school parks on the periphery of the city.[1]

The characteristic features of the school park—comprehensive coverage and unprecedented size—are its main advantages and at the same time the chief targets of its critics. Is the park a defensible modern version of the common school, perhaps the only form in which that traditionally American institution can be maintained in an urban society? Or is it a monstrous device that can lead only to the mass mistreatment of children? Whatever else it is or may in time turn out to be, it is neither a modest proposal nor a panacea.

Since even one such project would require substantial commitment of policy and money, it is obvious that the validity of the concept should be closely examined and the costs and potential benefits associated with it carefully appraised.

The purpose of this paper is to assist that process by considering the relevance of the school park to present problems in urban education and by analyzing, although in a necessarily limited way, its potentiality.

THE PROBLEM

Twelve years of effort, some ingeniously pro forma and some laboriously genuine, have proved that desegregating schools—to say

From *The Journal of Negro Education*, Vol. 37 (Summer 1968), pp. 301-309. Reprinted by permission of the publisher and author.

1. Thomas B. Pettigrew, "School Desegregation in Urban America," unpublished paper prepared for NAACP Legal Conference on School Desegregation, October 1966, pp. 25-33.

nothing of integrating them—is much more difficult than it first appeared. Attendance area boundaries have been redrawn; new schools have been built in border areas; parents have been permitted, even encouraged, to choose more desirable schools for their children; pupils from crowded slum schools have been bussed to outlying schools; Negro and white schools have been paired and their student bodies merged; but in few cases have the results been wholly satisfactory. Despite some initial success and a few stable solutions, the consequences, for the most part have proved disappointing. Steady increases in urban Negro population, continuing shifts in the racial character of neighborhoods, actual or supposed decline in student achievement, unhappiness over cultural differences and unpleasant personal relations have combined to produce new problems faster than old ones could be solved.[2]

Underlying the whole situation are basic facts that have too seldom been given the attention they merit. Some of these facts bear on the behavior of individuals. Few parents of either race, for example, are willing to accept inconvenience or to make new adjustments in family routines if the only discernible result is to improve the opportunities of other people's children. A still smaller minority will actually forego advantages to which their children have become accustomed merely to benefit other children. Most parents, liberal or conservative, hesitate to accept any substantial change in school procedures unless they are convinced that their own children will have a better than even chance of profiting from them. While prejudice and bigotry are not to be minimized as obstacles to racial integration, resistance attributed to them is often due rather to the reluctance of parents to risk a reduction in their own children's opportunities.

.   .   .   .

The controversy over what constitutes viable racial balance in schools or neighborhoods remains unsettled, for the data ʹ﹍﹍ from complete. There is abundant evidence, however, that mi̶ dle-class families, Negro or white, will choose schools enrolli̶n̶ ma- jority of Negro children if any alternative is available. Additional complications arise from social class and cultural relationships. Although borderline sites or school pairing on the periphery of a ghetto may produce temporary racial desegregation, these devices rarely bring together children of different social classes. As a consequence, the predictable antagonisms between lower class white and Negro groups increase the school's burden or adjustment problems and diminish the benefits of cultural interchange.

.   .   .   .

2. Jeanette Hopkins, "Self Portrait of School Desegregation in Northern Cities," unpublished paper prepared for NAACP Legal Conference, October 1966, pp. 1-3.

The moral and legal grounds for desegregating schools are clear and well-established. The factual evidence that integration can improve the effectiveness of education is steadily accumulating.[3] For the purposes of this paper there is no need to review either. But it will be useful to examine what is now known about the conditions that must be met if schools are to be well integrated and effective.

The first requirement is that the proportion of each race in the school be acceptable and educationally beneficial to both groups.[4] This means that the proportion of white students must be high enough to keep them and, more importantly, their parents from feeling overwhelmed and to assure the Negro student the advantage of a genuinely integrated environment. On the other hand, the number of Negro students must be large enough to prevent their becoming an odd and isolated minority in a nominally desegregated school. Their percentage should enable them to appear as a matter of course in all phases of school life. No Negro student should have to "represent his race" in any different sense than his white classmates represent theirs.

Many efforts have been made to define a racially balanced school, but no "balance," however logical it may be statistically, is likely to remain stable and workable if it results in either a majority of Negroes, or so few that they are individually conspicuous. This suggests in practice a Negro component ranging from a minimum of 15 to 20 per cent to a maximum of 40 to 45 per cent.

School districts with small Negro minorities, even though they may be concentrated in ghettos, can ordinarily devise plans to meet these conditions without large scale changes in the character of their school systems. Central cities with sizeable ghettos and smaller cities with larger proportions of Negroes will usually be required to make substantial changes in order to attain integrated schools.

But even when such acceptable racial proportions have been established, an effectively integrated school can be maintained only if a second condition is met: The school must respond to the educational needs of all its students better than the schools they might otherwise attend. The school must possess the capacity, the physical facilities, the staff strength, the leadership, and the flexibility required not only to offer a wide range of programs and services, but also adapt them to the special circumstances of individual students.

THE PARK AS A POSSIBLE SOLUTION

In school districts where redistricting, pairing, open enrollment, and bussing offer little hope of producing lasting integration and high

3. James S. Coleman, *Equality of Educational Opportunity* (Washington, D. C.: U. S. Department of Health, Education, and Welfare, 1966), p. 332.
4. Pettigrew, *op. cit.*, p. 17.

quality school programs, the school park may well offer a satisfactory solution. School parks (called also educational parks, plazas, or centers) have been proposed in a number of communities and are being planned in several. The schemes so far advanced fall into several categories. The simplest, which is appropriate for a small or medium-sized town, assembles on a single campus all the schools and all the students of an entire community. As a result the racial character of a particular neighborhood no longer determines the character of any one school. All the children of the community come to the central campus where they can be assigned to schools and classes according to whatever criteria will produce the greatest educational benefits. The School Board of East Orange, N. J., has recently announced a 15-year construction program to consolidate its school system of some 10,000 pupils in such an educational plaza.[5]

Another variant of the park is a similarly comprehensive organization serving one section of a large city as the single park might serve an entire smaller town. Where this plan is adopted the capacity of the park must be so calculated that its attendance area will be sufficiently large and diversified to yield a racially balanced student body for the foreseeable future. Merely to assemble two or three elementary units, a junior high school and a senior high school would in many cities produce no more integration than constructing the same buildings on the customary separate sites.

Less comprehensive schemes can also be called school parks. One, applicable to smaller communities, would center all school facilities for a single level of education—e.g., all elementary schools, or middle schools, or high schools, on a single site. Single-level complexes serving less than a whole community are also possible in large cities. . . .

A fourth, and the most comprehensive, type of park would require a number of changes in school planning and administration. This is the metropolitan school park designed to meet the increasingly serious problems posed by the growing Negro population of the central cities and the almost wholly white suburbs that surround them. The proposal, briefly stated, is to ring the city with school parks that would enroll the full range of pupils from the kindergarten to the high school and possibly including a community college. Each park would be placed in a "neutral" area near the periphery of the city. Each attendance area would approximate a segment of the metropolitan circle with its apex at the center of the city and its base in the suburbs. Since many students would arrive by school bus or public carrier, each site would be adjacent to a main transport route.[6]

5. "Desegregation. Ten Blueprints for Action," *School Management*, X (October 1966), 103-105.
6. Pettigrew, *op. cit.*, pp. 25-33.

The potentialities of school parks in general can be explored by projecting what might be done in such a metropolitan center. We can begin with certain assumptions about size and character. In order to encompass an attendance area large enough to assure for the long term an enrollment more than 50 per cent white and still include a significant number of Negro students from the inner-city ghetto, the typical park, in most metropolitan areas, would require a total student body (kindergarten to Grade 12) of not less than 15,000. It would thus provide all the school facilities for a part of the metropolitan area with a total population of 80,000 to 120,000. The exact optimum size of a particular park might be as high as 30,000, depending upon the density of urban and suburban population, the prevalence of nonpublic schools, the pattern of industrial, business, and residential zoning, the character of the housing, and the availability of transport.

The site, ideally, would consist of 50 to 100 acres but a workable park could be designed on a much smaller area or, under suitable circumstances, deep within the central city by using high-rise structures.[7] Within these buildings individual school units of varying sizes would be dispersed horizontally and vertically. On a more generous plot each unit could be housed separately, with suitable provision for communication through tunnels or covered passages.

The sheer size of the establishment would present obvious opportunities to economize through centralized functions and facilities, but the hazards of overcentralization are formidable. To proceed too quickly or too far down that path would be to sacrifice many of the park's most valuable opportunities for better education.

Because of its size the park would make possible degrees of specialization, concentration, and flexibility that are obtainable only at exorbitant cost in smaller schools. A center enrolling 16,000 students in a kindergarten 4-4-4 organization, with 1,000-1,300 pupils at each grade level, could efficiently support and staff not only a wide variety of programs for children at every ordinary level or ability, but also highly specialized offerings for those with unusual talents or handicaps.

Such an institution could operate its own closed circuit television system more effectively, and with lower cable costs than a community-wide system, and with greater attention to the individual teacher's requirements. A central bank of films and tapes could be available for transmission to any classroom, and the whole system controlled by a dialing mechanism that would enable every teacher to "order" at any time whatever item he wished his class to see.

7. Harold B. Gores, "Education Park; Physical and Fiscal Aspects," in Milton Jacobsen (ed.), *An Explanation of the Educational Park Concept* (New York: New York Board of Education, 1964), pp. 2-7.

The pupil population would be large enough to justify full-time staffs of specialists and the necessary physical facilities to furnish medical, psychological, and counseling services at a level of quality that is now rarely possible. Food service could be provided through central kitchens, short distance delivery, and decentralized dining rooms for the separate schools.

The most important educational consequences of the park's unprecedented size would be the real opportunities it would offer for organizing teachers, auxiliary staff, and students. In the hypothetical K-4-4-4 park of 16,000, for example, there would be about 5,000 pupils each in the primary and middle school age groups, or enough at each level for 10 separate schools of 500 pupils.

Each primary or middle school of that size could be housed in its own building, or its own section of a larger structure with its own faculty of perhaps 25. Such a unit, directed by its own principal, with its own complement of master teachers, "regular" teachers, interns, assistants, and volunteers, would be the school "home" of each of its pupils for the 3, 4, or 5 years he would spend in it before moving on to the next level of the park. A permanent organization of children and adults of that size employing flexible grouping procedures would make possible working relationships far superior to those now found in most schools. Moreover, since a child whose family moved from one home to another within the large area served by the park would not be required to change schools, one of the principal present handicaps to effective learning in the city schools would be largely eliminated.

While not every school within the park could offer every specialized curriculum or service, such facilities would be provided in as many units as necessary and children assigned to them temporarily or permanently. Each child and each teacher would "belong" to his own unit, but access to others would be readily possible at any time.

The presence on a campus of all school levels and a wide range of administrative and auxiliary services would present the professional staff with opportunities for personal development and advancement which no single school now affords. The ease of communication, for example, among the guidance specialists or mathematics teachers would exceed anything now possible. It would become feasible to organize for each subject or professional specialty a department in which teachers in all parts of the park could hold memberships, in much the way that a university department includes professors from a number of colleges.

For the first time, a field unit could justify its own research and development branch, a thing not only unheard of but almost unimaginable in most schools today. With such help "in residence" the faculty of the park could participate in studies of teaching problems and conduct experiments that now are wholly impracticable for even the most competent teachers.

Much would depend, of course, on the imagination with which the park was organized and administered and how its policies were formed. Since the metropolitan park, by definition, would serve both a central city and one or more suburban districts, its very establishment would be impossible without new forms of intergovernmental cooperation. At least two local school boards would have to share authority, staffs, and funds. The State educational authority and perhaps the legislature would be required to sanction the scheme and might have to authorize it in advance. Public opinion and political interests would be deeply involved as would the industrial and real estate establishments of the sponsoring communities.

The planning of a metropolitan park would have to be viewed as a concern not merely of school people, parents, and legislative or executive officials. It would have to be approached from the outset as a fundamental problem in metropolitan planning. Its dependence on quantitative projections of population and housing data is obvious, but equally important is its relation to the character of the housing, occupancy policies, and ethnic concentrations. To build a park only to have it engulfed in a few years by an enlarged ghetto would be a sorry waste of both money and opportunity. No good purpose, educational or social, would be served by creating what might become a huge segregated school enclave. A school park can be undertaken responsibly only as part of a comprehensive metropolitan development plan. Where such planning is not feasible, the establishment of a metropolitan school park would be a questionable venture.

It may be reasonable in some circumstances to project a park within the limits of a single school district. Where the analysis of population trends and projected development justify a single district park, the intergovernmental problems disappear, but agreements within the municipal structure will still be important and may be quite difficult to negotiate. The need for comprehensive community planning to assure the future viability of the park is certainly no less necessary within the city than in the metropolitan area.

Once the park is authorized, the question of operating responsibility must be addressed. In a sense that no individual school or geographic subdivision possibly can, the school park permits decentralized policy development and administration. Because of the natural coherence of the park's components and their relative separation from the rest of the district—or districts—to which it is related, the park might very well be organized as a largely self-contained system. The argument for placing the park under a board with considerable autonomy is strong whether it is a metropolitan institution or a one-city enterprise. For the first time it could thus become possible for the citizens in a section of a large community to have a direct, effective voice in the affairs of the school serving their area. . . .

Citizen participation would have to occur at points other than the board, however. If the park is to be strongly related to its communities, and integrated in fact as well as in principal, parents and other citizens would have to be involved, formally and informally, in many of its activities. These might range from parent-teacher conferences to service on major curriculum advisory groups. They could include routine volunteer chores and service as special consultants or part-time teachers. The specific possibilities are unlimited but the tone of the relationships will critically affect the park's success.

. . . .

Obtaining the necessary cooperation to build a metropolitan park will not be easy but the financial problems will be equally severe. A park accommodating 16,000 pupils can be expected to cost in the neighborhood of $50 million. The financial pressures on cities and suburban districts make it clear that Federal support on a very large scale will be required if school parks are to be built. But it is precisely the possibility of Federal funds that could provide the incentive to bring the suburbs and the central city together.

While categorical support through Federal funds will continue to be needed, effective leverage on the massive problems of urban education, including, particularly, integration, can be obtained only through broadly focused programs of general aid, with special attention given to new construction. Little can be done toward equalizing opportunities without a sizeable program of school building expansion and replacement. Such aid, moreover, must be available for both the neglected child and the relatively advantaged.

If much of this new assistance were expressly channeled into creating metropolitan parks, on a formula of 90 per cent Federal and 10 per cent State and local funding, it would envision equalized, integrated schools of high quality in most cities within a period of 10 to 15 years.

Would such a program mean abandoning usable existing school buildings? Not at all, since most districts desperately need more space for their present and predictable enrollment, to say nothing of the other uses that school systems and other government agencies could readily find for buildings that might be relinquished. The impending expansion of nursery school programs and adult education are only two of the more obvious alternate uses for in-city structures.

Is the school park an all-or-nothing question? Is it necessary to abandon all existing programs before the benefits of the park can be tested? Short of full commitment, there are steps that can be taken in the direction of establishing parks and to achieve some of their values. The "educational complex" put forward in the Allen Report for New York City is one such step. As described in that report, the complex is a group of two to five primary schools and one or two middle schools near enough to each other to form a cooperating cluster and serving sufficiently diversified neighborhoods to promote good biracial contact.

An educational complex should be administered by a *senior administrator*, who should be given authority and autonomy to develop a program which meets appropriate citywide standards but is also directly relevant to the needs of the locality. Primary schools within the complex should share among themselves facilities, faculties, and special staff, and should be coordinated to encourage frequent association among students and parents from the several units. Within the education complex teachers will be better able to help children from diverse ethnic backgrounds to become acquainted with one another. Parent-teacher and parent-school relations should be built on the bases of both the individual school and the complex. The children—and their parents—will thus gain the dual benefits of a school close to home and of membership in a larger, more diverse educational and social community. The concept of the educational complex arises in part from the view that the means of education and much of their control should be centered locally.

Although it may not be possible to desegregate all primary schools, ultimately most of them should be integrated educationally. This will aid the better preparation of students for life and study in the middle school; it will more nearly equalize resources; and it will give the staff in the primary schools new opportunities for innovation and originality in their work.[8]

Experimental projects on a limited scale might also be set up between city and suburban districts to deal with common problems. The Hartford and Irondequoit projects transporting Negro students to suburban schools are examples of what can be done.

Additional efforts could include exchanging staff members; involving students, particularly at the secondary level, in joint curricular or extracurricular activities; setting up "miniature school parks" during the summer in schools on the city-suburban border; conducting work sessions in which board and staff members from metropolitan school systems examine population changes, common curriculum problems, and opportunities for joint action.

Establishing school parks would mean a substantial shift in educational policy. In addition, as has been pointed out, the metropolitan park would require concerted action among governmental units. New forms of State and Federal financial support and sharply increased appropriations would be essential. . . . Parents and

8. State Education Commission's Advisory Committee on Human Relations and Community Tensions, *Desegregating the Public Schools of New York City* (New York: New York State Department of Education, 1964), p. 18.

other citizens, school leaders, public officials and legislators will be justified in asking for persuasive factual and logical support for such radical proposals.

The response must be that critically important educational, social, and economic needs of a large part of urban America are not being met by our present policies and practices and that there is no reason to think that they will be met by minor adjustments of the present arrangements. The evidence is irresistible that the consequences of racial segregation are so costly and so damaging to all our people that they should no longer be tolerated. Through bitter experience we are learning that the isolation of any race is demeaning when it is deliberate and that it is counterproductive in human and economic terms, no matter how it is caused or explained. The elimination of this debilitating and degrading aspect of American life must now be ranked among the most important and urgent goals of our society. The task cannot be done without concerted action among many forces and agencies. Participation by private agencies and by government at every level will be needed. But central to every other effort will be the influence and the power of the public schools. Those schools, which have served the nation so well in achieving other high purposes, can serve equally well in performing their part of this new undertaking—if the magnitude of the task is fully appreciated and action undertaken on a scale appropriate to a major national purpose.

The steps that have heretofore been taken to cope with segregation have been of no more than tactical dimensions. Most of them have been relatively minor adaptations and accommodations requiring minimal changes in the status quo. It should by now be clear that we cannot integrate our schools or assure all our children access to the best education unless we accept these twin goals as prime strategic objectives.

. . . .

Establishing rings of school parks about each of our segregated central cities would, to be sure, require decisions to invest large sums of money in these projects. The prior and more important commitment, however, must be to the purpose to which the money will be dedicated: effective quality of educational opportunity at a new high level for millions of our young people.

The school park is no panacea. In itself it will guarantee no more than a setting for new accomplishment. But the setting is essential. If we fail to provide it or to invent an equally promising alternative, we shall continue to deny a high proportion of our citizens the indispensible means to a decent and productive life.

The Principal
and
the Community XII

chapter overview

The governance, the politics, of the public schools is acquiring a new image as the society moves rapidly toward the twenty-first century. Emerging community participation patterns are challenging the traditional foundations of the educational system. These participation patterns are seeking ways for their schools to become more relevant. The teaching profession, too, is painfully assessing its responsibilities as it works with the community to provide the highest quality education. This surge of community involvement is creating new demands upon school administrators. Articles in this chapter have been selected to assist the principal in this golden era of community participation in school affairs.

Over the years educators have assumed the lion's share of determining a quality education program. Ernest O. Melby reflects on the rising impatience of the public for a "piece of the action." He believes that "if through community involvement we can mobilize the vast resources for education now found in every community, we can open a new era in educational achievement and new levels of democratic living for our society."

School-community relations historically have functioned at the surface level. Charles V. Willie recognizes new perspectives in school-community relations. It is his thesis that school-community relations are a dimension of community power relations. School administrators need to know the people of power.

Confrontations with pressure groups is not a new phenomenon for school administrators, but its intensity has increased during the past few years. Myron Lieberman encourages school administrators to learn new skills in the field of non-employee negotiations. He recommends taking the initiative to avoid excessive and unproductive negotiations with community groups. This can be achieved by developing a positive program for constantly involving responsible groups in considering issues that concern them.

477

	Decentralization
75	and Community Control
	Threat or Challenge?

Ernest O. Melby

The insistent and often strident demands for community control of education constitute an interesting commentary on the current effectiveness of both educational administrators and theorists in the field of administration as far as the improvement of education is concerned. Throughout most of the history of educational administration, both groups have seen themselves actively engaged in the task of persuading the public to adopt better educational programs, and of training and inspiring teachers to a higher level of professional performance. The easy assumption has been that both theorists and practitioners in the area of administration had a larger view of education with higher standards than either the teachers or the public. Now the public, out of patience with what it believes to be ineffective education, demands a share of the control at the local level, while the teachers through collective bargaining are becoming involved in types of decision-making previously seen as the prerogative of administrators and boards of education.

Professors of administration with their programs for preparation of administrators, also confront new problems. The phenomena of the city—poverty—racial conflicts, have given the content of courses in administration low priority if not irrelevance. The city school administrator thus has no place to go for help. To make matters worse, the university students of administration are so involved in abstraction, and so far removed from the urban maelstrom, they are not very helpful. Their characteristic response has been to withdraw still further into abstraction, to draw models and theorize about decision-making and simulated experiences. The result is that professors keep busy with studies that fill the shelves with an ever more complex and technical verbiage less and less understood by the practicing administrator, to say nothing of the layman.

The professor can, of course, withdraw to his theory but the administrator has no such avenue of escape. Daily he has to face dissident board members, hostile minority groups, student unrest and violence. Underlying all of this is the growing conviction on the part of many community people that present education is not only ineffective, but controlled by the wrong people. Students want something to say about their education. Teachers are really getting

From *The Community School and Its Administration*, Vol. VIII, No. 3 (November 1969). Reprinted by permission of the publisher.

a significant role in decision-making through collective bargaining and the public—the community—now demands control of the education being given their children.

What do teachers demand? Usually teacher welfare. What do students demand? Often self- or group-centered proposals that take little account of anyone else's problems. There is a reason. Bureaucracy is increasing in nearly every aspect of society. When the individual finds that bureaucracy and organizational rigidity have closed the door to his own fullest development, he moves in highly individual and often selfish directions. Similarly, administrators make decisions and generally plan their work so as to reduce the "heat" on themselves. Thus, they become self-protective bureaucrats rather than public spirited problem-solvers. Interestingly enough the result is more and not less "heat." In general the outcome of all this is a noncommitted profession. Where we should be leading the public and the profession we spend our time putting out fires.

In our total political and community life our educational administrators are not the only ones in trouble. The demand for more participation in government and community affairs is not limited to the field of education. The most powerful recent entrant into the community control scene has been the poverty programs with their community action programs. Such projects were designed on the assumption that the individual community decides how best to attack poverty in its midst. Even though mistakes have been made, no matter how one feels about the success of the programs, the people have had a taste of participation. Their attitudes have changed. They want a share in shaping their own community lives. An especially striking situation prevails in New York City. It is here that the demand for community control has been most insistent. The motivations are not always desire for educational change, but constitute power plays by some ethnic group leaders.

What New York's black militants really want, what they are competing with one another for, is not the overthrow of the white 'establishment' but sovereignty over the black populace. And this the whites are, in the end, likely to be only too willing to grant them.

This is what lies behind the whole 'decentralization' issue in New York and that is why the related topic of 'community control' is so crucial. The question of depriving white ethnic groups of their present positions—as teachers, sanitationmen, policemen, firemen, construction workers, etc.—for the presumed benefit of blacks is inflammatory, as it is intended to be. But that is not the ultimate meaning of this controversy. (The blacks are already moving into these jobs in a massive way, and in some cases now are 'represented' beyond their proportion of the population.) What is ultimate is—well, to see that, let us assume that 'community control' has been effected, and then let us imagine what New York City is like. There will be black communities having control over their own services, over all the jobs in the area, over their own local budget, over housing, etc. Next to them, there will be white communities with comparable powers. And now let us ask: how does a man move from one to the other? The answer is short and easy; he won't be able to. And this, precisely, is what the militant black nationalists are after.

A shifting power base makes power hungry men anxious and insecure. And it is for this reason that the black nationalists have, with great political acumen, raised the matter of 'community control.' They want to *freeze* the neighborhoods of New York. They want to prevent middle class or working class blacks from moving to the white areas, elsewhere in the city or in the suburbs. Their aim is *apartheid*, because only in *apartheid* can they ensure their rule. Nor do they care about the economic and social consequences. The poorer, the more ignorant, the more isolated the black communities are, the better the chances for black nationalist leaders to play upon their grievances and to stimulate their fantasies.

Lower and middle income whites in or near the gray areas who live in fear and resentment of Negroes and the ghetto, would like nothing better than to have the power to keep Negroes out and to maintain 'their' neighborhoods. Thus, the great diversity of New York's population and the inevitable tensions among its groups lend decentralization an almost universal appeal; to each group and neighborhood it promises power, status, territorial integrity, and an immunity from threatening others.[1]

It is clear that in speaking of the community's role in administration the dangerous word is not community but *control*. In New York the issue is *ethnic*. In other situations the issue can be a different one but it may still be disruptive, it can still fragment our society. If we are to build a great education we must have community involvement, but it should not be complete local control.

There may, of course, be some administrators and students of administration who believe that this is a passing fad and that we will someday get back to Cubberly-Strayer-Englehardt assumptions. No one who has been close to the life of the modern urban complex can easily accept such a view. A much better guess is that present trends will continue and become more dominant. Also, that both practitioners and theorists face the task of rewriting our books, and in the process develop a new theory calling for greatly modified practices. The old administration is obsolete. The unhappiness of some of our administrators comes in no small part because they are trying to function in the classical manner in a situation which is no longer classic.

We in the university do not like this. Like many, I have been continually critical of the old assumptions, but believed that by changes here and there we could become effective. I no longer hold to such a naive view. The age of innocence is over. Painful as the ad-

---

1. Irving Kristol, "Who Knows New York," *The Public Interest.* Summer Issue, 1969. The entire issue is of interest to those engaged in urban education.

mission may be to us, the old administration, the old roles, the old preparation, the old theory, are all dead or dying.

I am fully aware that I will win no popularity contest with this statement. At the same time, we are making it harder for ourselves by being defensive. We should not be too apologetic. We have little to be ashamed of. The old administration did great things for American education. For its day, like the Model-T Ford, it performed pretty well. But like the Model-T it is obsolete. It has been made obsolete by social change and scientific-technological development. And in administration, as was the case with the Model-T, minor annual improvements will not help. They merely waste time we should be using in designing and implementing the needed new model. It is, therefore, my thesis that we should undertake, without delay, the building of a new administrative concept, with new assumptions, new roles for public, administrators, boards, teachers and students.

If we, as university faculty members, wish to have a role in developing the new administration, the first thing we must do is to leave the campus, the library, the faculty meeting, and get into the community, into the schools, the social agencies, the city government. It is not enough to be a casual observer. We need to stay, face the problems and help work on solutions. This will call for great humility on our part. We will begin as learners, a new role for university professors. We see ourselves as the experts, those who tell others what to do. We are no longer competent to play such a role.

In the past, universities have seen communities primarily as laboratories in which they could do research—research in which the university professor's interest determined what was under study rather than the need or interest of the school system. Actually, we have not been concerned with what we as university people could do for the community, our interest has been in what the community could do for us. My impression is that schools and communities have had their fill of such studies. Now the problems in the community are so urgent, so vitally related to the survival of effective education, that local readers have no immediate use for the university specialist unless he is willing to work on the problems deemed of higher priority by the community and its leadership personnel.

We thus need to work out new attitudes on the part of both specialists and school administrators. We also need changed assumptions concerning internship as an element in the preparation of administrative personnel. No longer is the intern merely observing the practitioner in order to learn how to be an administrator. To do so would only tend to perpetuate obsolete practices. On the contrary, the intern comes into the community to study the problems which need attention, and in the process join local personnel in developing new assumptions and more appropriate practices. In short, the professor and the student see themselves as learners, trying to solve the community problem. Here we can create a new relationship between the university and the community, a relationship that will give forward thrust to community education and relevance to university study.

In order to give some sense of reality to our discussion let us take a concrete example: the problem of providing equal educational opportunities for all our children. By now we know that with all our talk of equal opportunity, the reality is that for a large proportion of our children this equality has little meaning, especially for the poor, the black and other minority groups, though these are not the only sufferers. Were we to begin by studying the problem of inequality of opportunity in a metropolitan area we would discover first-hand that the present total structure, instructional, administrative, and organizational makes equality of opportunity impossible of achievement. For example, with a fixed teacher-pupil ratio, slow learning children have little chance. If they are to have a chance the policy controlling allocation of instructional resources must be changed. We, as participants, could help work out the changes. We would see, also, that the school alone cannot solve the problem. Parents must be involved, but how? Housing should change, but what is the relation of education to housing? We would work with housing agencies.

We would find that in certain schools there is a drive for experimental approaches but the central bureaucracy frowns on them. Can we free the principal and the school? If so, how do we shape the new relationships? If each school is free to meet the problems of its own community and schools as a result vary greatly, what is the role of central supervision? What is the new role of the superintendent? Internal decentralization is a must, but how is it to be accomplished?

What decisions should be made by professional people and what decisions by the lay people? Where should lay involvement be decision-making and where advisory? How should professional personnel react to lay opinion about matters of professional knowledge and skill?

As we give heed to the present demand on the part of the public for greater involvement, we should take a look at the effect of decades of professional control of education. Has our educational system lost its basic mission of education and become a giant selection agency for our society? What has been the effect of the whole testing movement. Has it, as many believe, whittled down the image of man? Has it made cognitive learning a god and overlooked the arts and man's relatedness to his fellowmen? Has it sought excessive objectivity in a realm which must have many subjective elements if man is to be man in the fullest sense of the word? Have we in the university, immersed in specialization, overlooked the wholeness of human personality and human society? Has our emphasis on quantification caused us to lose sight of the unique human personality?

There are countless other questions, but the answers to very few of them can be found in books. More than that, unless we are involved in community education we are not likely even to ask the right questions. Beyond the stimulating, broadening impact of the total urban complex we need the help of present administrative personnel. As university specialists we tend to downgrade such personnel, even in some instances viewing their present practices as damaging to our students—teaching them to do what they should not do. . . . While this may be true in some instances, the fact is we cannot get along without present administrators in the task of building new concepts. These people may not know all we know (or think we know), but they do know from firsthand experience what we do not know. Moreover, we are in the current position of weakness, in part because for decades we have celebrated theory and relegated practices to lower priority. There is no assurance that if the superintendents of schools in the 100 largest metropolitan areas were replaced by a selected 100 professors of educational administration, education would be advanced.

It is not, however, my purpose to detract from the competence of either university specialists or administrative practitioners. Too often we look for personal failure when things go wrong. Instead of examining our concepts and assumptions we blame persons. How many fine people must we damage before we see that it is the whole system that is obsolete? To get new roles and behaviors we need the two groups working together in the community setting, this last because what professors say on campus may be quite different from what they would do if they had the real problems to face. When we face the problems together we both grow.

What do we expect of our prospective administrators in such critical areas as equality of educational opportunity and racial attitudes? Are we and our students ready to give our professional lives to the task of building one America?; of giving our full rights of citizenship and cultural-human equality to the black man? Will we and our students stand up and be counted on the issues?

Working together in the community does not mean less study and reading. The fact is, the administrative fraternity in America, both professional and administrative, has the vast backlog of reading and study in anthropology, sociology, political science, urban renewal, municipal government, and philosophy. The need for such study seems far more urgent to you when you work in the inner-city than when you are teaching a class on campus.

Something might be said about the selection of an urban complex in which to work. Often we look for demonstration schools, schools so excellent they are models for our students. We shall not find many such schools, and perhaps just as well. Here school board and administrative staff attitudes toward experimentation are more important than present excellence, and willingness to change more vital than a generous budget. Working relationships should be carefully and clearly defined. There should be no hierarchy or expertise but the responsibility and authority of local boards and their personnel should be recognized.

The undertaking coming under the head of "decentralization and community control" is highly complex. Some recent experiences indicate that American education and its administration are both in danger of foundering on the shoals of the problems created by ill-considered, and piece-meal efforts in the area of community involvement. It is possible that such efforts may delay or disrupt constructive community involvement in education. They might lead to patterns of organization which defeat community involvement. We need to make a careful survey of the situation we confront. The first thing we will see is that what we now have is not working. Children are being deprived of opportunity, parents are frustrated and militant teachers are baffled and feeling hopeless. It is becoming crystal clear that the problem cannot be solved within the schoolhouse, by the professionals and the public officials who now hold the legal responsibility. Even die-hard supporters of professionally controlled education must now admit that we cannot succeed by educating the children alone. We must educate the entire community.

The moment we set out to educate the entire community we are in a new ball game. We now can no longer be separated into two groups, teachers and pupils, we will in a real sense all be teachers and all be students. Some will teach as a life work, others will teach merely to learn (teaching being the best way to learn), or at least learn in the process of teaching. The administrative problems now become more complex, with the result that the old separation of planning and performance concepts break down. Control by status personnel now must be exercised with the greatest care lest it limit the freedom of all to learn. Where in the past we have too often asked *who* is right, we must now ask *what* is right. We need to learn how to listen, how to understand.

I believe we have something to learn from the ecologists. For example, Richard E. Farson suggests that instead of trying so hard to change people we should try changing the total environment in such ways that the environment stimulates behavioral changes. He further suggests that:

Instead of looking to a professional elite for the solution to any social problem, look to the greatest resource available—the very population that has the problem. Many of us tend to have a low opinion of people, those wretched masses who don't understand, don't know what they need or want, who continually make mistakes and foul up their lives, requiring those of us who are professionally trained to come in and correct the situation. But that is not the way it really works. The fact is that some drug addicts are much better able to cure addiction in each other than are psychiatrists; some convicts can run better rehabilitation programs for convicts than do correctional officers; many students tend to learn more from each other than from many professors; some patients in mental hospitals are better for each other than is the staff. Thousands of self-help organizations are doing a good job, perhaps a better job at problem-solving than is the profession that is identified with that problem. People who have the problems often have a better understanding of their situation and what must be done to change it. What professionals have to do is learn to cooperate with that resource, to design the conditions which evoke that intelligence.[2] In this way, society can be truly self-determining and self-renewing. The special beauty of this formulation is that it fits the democratic goal of enabling the people to make a society for themselves. Mankind can rely on people as a resource for much more than is possible to imagine. It is really quite difficult to find the ceiling of what people can do for themselves and each other, given the opportunity.[3]

The paragraph I have just quoted, sets forth a philosophical premise for a successful program of total community education. Such a program must rest on faith in people and their capacity to learn. Administration in such a program must design the conditions which grow intelligence and proceed by cooperating with all the community resources. Present preparation for administrators helps them deal with the people they control, but their success in total community education depends more on their ability to deal effectively with the people they do not control than those they do control. The tools of the past administration are legalism, rules and regulation, line and staff authority. This same administration is short on inspiration, on freedom of action and too often frowns on innovation. It is short on faith in people. Here the testing movement based on an earlier psychology has laid the foundation for a low estimate of human potential. Fortunately, modern psychology supports more generous estimates of human potential.

Community involvement cannot be merely attached to our present obsolete administrative structure. To do this can lead to disfunctional conditions for education with frustration of all concerned. We need a new theory and practice of administration designed for total community education, an education in which all the people of the community are involved. Such education mandates community involvement in educational policy determination, educational leadership, and day to day educational programs. Complete community control of education could mean a narrow provincial, even racist education for some communities. Such a development would surely be a threat to true democratic education.

2. Richard E. Farson "How Could Anything That Feels So Bad Be So Good," *The Saturday Review*, September 6, 1969. pp. 20.
3. *Op. cit.*

In some areas further centralization is in process and to be desired. We need, for example, to give the federal government a larger share in defining equality of educational opportunity and in the support of education necessary to give economic substance to the goals of equal opportunity we set. The same is true of the states and their role.

The task of designing a concept of educational administration attuned to the needs of education in our time should not be viewed as a mere technical exercise. The project must be undertaken with a full realization of how far our society has already gone toward what John Gardner calls the beehive model, how restrictive many of our gigantic institutions of industry, government and education have become, and how isolated and helpless large numbers of our people have become. The administration we design and work out in practice must so energize the profession and the people of the nation, that we will together build an education that will give our people greater commitment to our historic values. Only in this way can we bring the individual human being greater justice, deeper sense of brotherhood, equality of opportunity, sense of his own as well as of other's dignity and worth with larger feelings of social responsibility. Seen in the light of such an educational goal for our nation, community involvement, rather than being viewed as a threat should be seen as a great challenge. In fact, if through community involvement we can mobilize the vast resources for education now found in every community, we can open a new era in educational achievement and new levels of democratic living for our society.

New Perspectives | 76
in School-Community Relations

Charles V. Willie

There is an association between the school and the community. For example, James B. Conant said ". . . a caste system finds its clearest manifestation in an educational system."[1] A. B. Hollingshead discussed the manifestation of a class system in an educational system in his book, *Elmtown's Youth*. He said, ". . . upper class control tends to result in the manipulation of institutional functions in the interests of individuals and families who have wealth, prestige, and power. . . . Such manipulation . . . is justified always . . . as being in the interest of 'all the people'. . . . The acceptance of this view by the rank and file . . . will seriously hinder the development of any effective program designed to reorient the schools. . . ."[2] Thus, any discussion of school-community relations that is significant and meaningful is a discussion of community power relations.

In the past, this has not been the focus of analyses of school-community relations, mainly because many educators have insisted that the school is primarily concerned with the transmission of culture and should not become an instrument of social reform. As pointed out by David Goslin, ". . . public education in the United States has traditionally been organized on a local basis with . . . relatively little interference from political or other influences outside the community."[3] In recent years, more and more groups have recognized that the local values and traditions which schools have transmitted to children are the values and traditions of some of the people—the dominant people of power—and not the values and traditions of all of the people. This becomes an increasingly important issue if the assertion by John Seeley and his coauthors be true that ". . . the regulative ideology of the North American culture is now transmitted by way of the school more than by way of any religious or other institution."[4] This means that the schools often are

From *The Journal of Negro Education*, Vol. 37 (Summer 1968), pp. 220-226. Reprinted by permission of the publisher and author.

1. James B. Conant, *Slums and Suburbs* (New York: McGraw-Hill Book Co., 1961), pp. 11-12.
2. A. B. Hollingshead, *Elmtown's Youth* (New York: John Wiley and Sons, Inc., 1949), p. 452.
3. David A. Goslin, *The School in Contemporary Society* (Chicago: Scott Foresman and Company, 1965), p. 15.
4. John R. Seeley *et al.*, *Crestwood Heights* (New York: Basic Books, 1956), p. 227.

used as an instrument for maintaining the status quo, which serves the dominant people of power. The schools have not operated beyond the reach of political influence as is often asserted. Subdominants now wish the schools to serve their interests in social reform. Harmonizing these conflicting interests is the major task in school-community relations confronting the Educational Establishment in local communities throughout the nation.

The "token integration" of public schools in Dallas, Texas, is an example of how school-community relations are power relations in which issues other than the teaching of children are involved. An influential member of the Dallas Citizen Council (which consists of the most powerful and wealthy businessmen in that city) came before that group and told what had happened in other cities, especially pointing out how much business had suffered when there were sit-ins and other forms of demonstrations for school integration. Warren Leslie quoted one member of the Council as saying, "It was not an argument over whether Negroes should be integrated or not. It was simply a matter of dollars and cents." The group was convinced that Dallas should not experience any disruptions such as those which occurred elsewhere which might affect the business climate. So, two members of the Council were assigned the responsibility of bringing about integration in the public school system, since all legal steps at preventing it had failed. The two members of the Council worked long and hard with Negro leadership and with white people. Leslie has described their activity as "a massive job of infecting a total community with belief in an idea repugnant to it." And the outcome: "The integration so far achieved in Dallas has taken place without unpleasantness."[5]

It should go without saying that if the dominant power interests in the community brought about integration in the public schools in the present, they had a great deal to do with maintaining segregation and inequality in education in the past. Clearly, the power of dominant decision-makers in the community has been used in a different way today with reference to schools and education. Yet, their efforts to formally desegregate the schools have been a self-interest approach which tends to confirm the Hollingshead observation noted above. Moreover, dominants still tend to move at a slow pace in innovating and not as quickly as subdominants might wish.

These facts are often overlooked by analysts and administrators who attempt to deal with school-community problems as educational issues only, as if public school education were independent of community power relations. One social scientist has said that "the desirability of doing away with racially segregated schools is only partly an educational issue." He has further stated that "the question of

5. Warren Leslie, *Dallas Public and Private* (New York: Avon Books, 1964), pp. 57-58.

how best to improve the quality of Negro education is one which, at least *theoretically*, is subject to objective discussion based on what we know about learning processes and educational techniques, the subculture of the Negro, and prevailing local conditions."[6] (Italics added) As I have stated elsewhere, ". . . we have several decades of empirical evidence that the doctrine of 'separate but equal' does not work. It can not work. The reason for separating the races in the first place is to accord them differential treatment. Anyone who ignores this fact is whistling in the dark."[7] Negro education and Negro segregation and Negro discrimination are all rolled up together, making it impossible to deal with one without dealing with the others.

A report of the United States Commission on Civil Rights summarized the findings for the Madison Area Project in Syracuse, New York, which emphasized new and different ways of learning within the context of racially segregated schools:

The Madison Area Project was conducted in two elementary schools and one junior high school, each of which had a Negro enrollment exceeding 80 per cent. Approximately 2,000 children participated in the program each year. It lasted nearly three years and cost $207,150 a year, or about $100 more per pupil than the normal allotment in the Syracuse schools— about twice the expenditure involved in the Higher Horizons Program.

When Syracuse school officials evaluated the junior high school segment of the Madison Area Project, they found results similar to those in the Higher Horizons study. The relative academic standing of students in the Madison Junior High School and students in other junior high schools before and after the project was compared. The special cultural and educational programs aimed at raising the achievements of Negro students had no apparent effect.[8]

After reviewing the Madison Area Project in Syracuse and other similarly racially segregated compensatory educational programs throughout the nation, the Civil Rights Commission concluded that "none of the programs appear to have raised significantly the achievement of participating pupils, as a group, within the period evaluated. . . ."[9]

Theoretically, it may be possible to separate the educational problems of disadvantaged children, including methods and techniques of teaching them, from issues of segregation and discrimination in the community; but I doubt if this can be done pragmatically. Thus, issues of what and how to teach children are at once com-

6. Goslin, *op. cit.*, p. 17.
7. Charles V. Willie, "Deprivation and Alienation: A Compounded Situation' in Daniel Schreiber (ed), *Profile of the School Dropout* (New York: Vantage Books), p. 174.
8. A Report of the U. S. Commission on Civil Rights, *Racial Isolation in the Public Schools* (Washington: U. S. Government Printing Office, 1967), p. 128.
9. *Ibid*, p. 138.

mingled with issues of where, when and under what conditions children are taught. Certainly the setting and the environmental conditions of schooling are a function of community power relations. Thus, it is naive to state, as did one city superintendent of schools, that "he [is] in the education business and should not become involved in attempts to correct the consequences of voluntary segregated housing."[10] The naivete is compounded by attempting to separate education from the power forces in the community in which it takes place and by asserting that housing segregation in America is voluntary.

How, then, should the school relate to the community in developing a program of quality education for all children, and especially children of disadvantaged circumstances. The Report of the National Advisory Commission on Civil Disorders had this to say about community-school relations:

Teachers of the poor rarely live in the community where they work and sometimes have little sympathy for the life style of their students. Moreover, the growth and complexity of the administration of large urban school systems has compromised the accountability of the local schools to the communities which they serve, and reduced the ability of parents to influence decisions affecting the education of their children. Ghetto schools often appear to be unresponsive to the community, communication has broken down, and parents are distrustful of officials responsible for formulating educational policy.

The consequences for the education of students attending these schools are serious. Parental hostility to the schools is reflected in the attitudes of their children. Since the needs and concerns of the ghetto community are rarely reflected in educational policy formulated on a citywide basis, the schools are often seen by ghetto youth as being irrelevant. . . .

In the schools, as in the large society, the isolation of ghetto residents from the policy-making institutions of local government is adding to the polarization of the community and depriving the system of its self-rectifying potential.[11]

On the basis of discussion thus far, one might say that the school has always related and been responsive to the community, but not to all segments of the community.

The position and role of the school superintendent are most important in implementing change in the school system, as found in several communities studied by Nelson Polsby and Robin Williams.[12]

10. Conant, *op. cit.*, p. 30.

11. *Report of the National Advisory Commission on Civil Disorders* (New York: Bantam Books, 1968), pp. 436-437.

12. Nelson W. Polsby, *Community Power and Political Theory* (New Haven: Yale University Press, 1963), p. 77. Robin M. Williams, Jr. and Margaret W. Ryan (eds.), *Schools in Transition* (Chapel Hill: University of North Carolina Press, 1954).

However, most school administrators tend to follow the customs of the community at large. As pointed out by Robin Williams and Margaret Ryan, in their commissioned studies of school desegregation in border states between North and South in the U. S. A., ". . . the legal framework within which an integrated school system could develop was available for many years before the local mores and customs changed to permit such a move."[13] The authors are quick to point out, however, that superintendents can become community leaders and contribute to community change rather than waiting to be directed to move in one way or another. Specifically, they discuss the need for ". . . firm policies advanced by the superintendent of schools and his staff . . ." as one way of contributing to change. "The evidence seems clear," they concluded, "that cooperative planning which recognizes established feelings can reduce actual discrimination long before it is possible to remove deep-rooted prejudice."[14]

Most superintendents are not likely to give innovative leadership. One can understand their reluctance to give this kind of leadership for change and social reform when they are given the following kind of advice in textbooks for courses in Educational Sociology. Read these words and the simplistic notions of community power and leadership which they convey:

> Every community has a power system. . . . Power refers to the ability or authority to dominate or to compel action. There are people or groups in every community who make important decisions and have the ability to enforce them. This is an inevitable community social process, for without power, and therefore control, it would be impossible to have social order. . . . One cannot understand a community until he is able to locate the sources of power. . . . Decisions affecting the entire community may be made under informal circumstances at a poker game, luncheon, or party. . . . School people need to know the sources of power and need to have the support of the dominant power groups in the community if the school program is to function smoothly.[15]

It is because school administrators have been responsive only to dominants in the power structure that school-community relations are at a low ebb and that subdominants are now shaking the foundations of the social order and the ground on which the schools have stood.

Indeed, there are dominants in the power structure of all communities. But there are subdominants, too. They also have power.

13. Williams and Ryan, *op. cit.*, p. 48.
14. *Ibid*, p. 48.
15. Wilbur B. Brookover, *A Sociology of Education* (New York: American Book Company, 1955), pp. 378-79.

After analyzing the history of a hospital construction controversy in Syracuse, New York, I made the following observation:

> Popular conceptions of the community power structure have resulted in our identifying industrialists, financiers, and merchants as people of power. However, our analysis reveals that they comprise only one category of the power system—the dominant category—which is inefficient without the subdominant category. So we must recognize the veto power of the subdominants. They, too, are the right people and must be recruited and brought along in effective community organization.[16]

Dominants, of course, have the power to implement and veto community programs. Veto power is not exclusive dominant power, however. This kind of power is found among subdominants, too. Because subdominants use their veto power less frequently, its presence is often forgotten. Thus, school superintendents and other public officials are surprised when their plans run aground due to veto actions of subdominants.

Because it is unanticipated and comes from an unexpected source, the veto power of subdominants is considered to be disruptive by some school administrators and Board of Education members. Yet there is a creative push in the activities of subdominants. School boards throughout the nation are agonizing over new and different approaches to quality education, mainly because of the fuss about desegregation which subdominants have raised. In Syracuse, New York, for example, the Board of Education refused to recognize race as a variable in establishing school boundaries as late as 1962.

This means that the Syracuse Board, ostensibly in its effort to be "color blind," did nothing to reverse the increasing number of racially imbalanced public schools. After the central office of the Syracuse City School District was picketed by the Congress of Racial Equality, a school boycott was organized by a coalition of several community groups, and the State Commissioner of Education directed all school districts in New York State to study the extent of racial imbalance in local public schools and report to him what districts planned to do about their findings, the Syracuse City School District accepted race as a legitimate variable to include along with several other variables of the school and community population when drawing and redrawing the boundaries of neighborhood schools.[17] It is only because of this disrupting or veto action by subdominants in the community that Syracuse now has become one

16. Charles V. Willie, "A Success Story of Community Action," *Nursing Outlook*, IX (January 1961), 20.
17. Robert LaPorte, Jr., Jerome Beker, and Charles V. Willie, "The Education of Public Educational Policy: School Desegregation in a Northern City," *Urban Education*, II (No. 3), 153-154.

of the more active school districts in New York State searching for solutions to inequality in public education and ways to improve the quality of education which all students receive.

It is doubtful that members of the Syracuse Board of Education and school boards throughout the nation would have taken these new initiatives on their own, had there been no pressure from below, from community subdominants. This, in effect, is what the Commissioner of Education of the State of New York told the U. S. Civil Rights Commission at a public hearing in Rochester, New York. He said, "I think Negroes in their demonstrations, in their peaceful demonstrations, have done more than any other segment of our society to push us to the point where we have now gone. I would urge that they . . . continue to make known to the American people that there are deprivations."[18]

The creative impulse resulting from subdominant action in the decision-making process has been recognized by others, such as Dan W. Dodson. He points to the value of all sectors of the community participating in educational decision-making, not only for the school system, but also for the sense of significance such participation may engender among the disadvantaged. In an article about new forces in educational decision-making, Dodson said:

We had better realize that the smallest power among us can create disruption enough to block the whole . . . .

. . . New forces are emerging that are going to require our boards of education and superintendents of schools to move into new approaches to the issue of decision making. If children are not going to get hurt in this process, we are going to have to develop new skill with which to approach this conflict of interest. People must honestly come to face each other and honestly say that we have differences and ask how we can reconcile and compromise and how do we work them out to some sort of viable solution.

From this process will come a new sense of education. . . . All the community will feel involved in the dynamics of the decision-making process and a new sense of worth will emerge.

This may be threatening to some who feel that their status is jeopardized. . . .[19]

And so the successful school superintendent now must do more than play golf with the community business and governmental influentials. He must also come to know the subdominants. This may

18. U. S. Civil Rights Commission, "Testimony of Dr. James E. Allen, Jr., Commissioner of Education, State of New York," *Hearing Before the United States Commission on Civil Rights in Rochester, New York*, September 16-17, 1966, (Washington: U. S. Government Printing Office, 1967), p. 207.

19. Dan W. Dodson, "New Forces Operating in Educational Decision Making," in Meyer Weinberg (ed), *Integrated Education, a Reader* (Beverly Hills: The Glencoe Press, 1968), p. 21.

require eating chitterlings and corn pone with the poor as well as recreating with the rich, if he is to synthesize the disparate interest groups in the community into a phalanx of support for a creative public policy designed to achieve quality education for all.

The Syracuse, New York experience is sufficient evidence that the involvement of subdominants in the decision-making process can be beneficial. As a result of the fuss about *de facto* segregation in Syracuse, the City School District has developed a plan for campus elementary schools which, if implemented, not only will foster racial integration but will also contribute to quality education for all children.[20]

When school-community relations are viewed from the perspective of community power relations, then the many current attempts to decentralize the decision-making apparatus of large school systems can be understood better. In general, it is asserted that a decentralized authority would be more responsive to neighborhood communities and local districts and would therefore improve the quality of education. This may or may not be so. But one thing is certain; decentralized educational authorities would give subdominants greater power in the decision-making process, particularly if decentralized district school boards have power to hire and discharge personnel. *Theoretically*, the issue of centralized versus decentralized authority could be debated from the point of view of administrative and management efficiency. Pragmatically, however, the debate cannot be so limited because of the history of past exclusions of subdominants from the central decision-making authority. Thus, communities now must deal with a complex policy situation pertaining to the centralization or decentralization of public educational administration that is commingled with the issue of community power distribution between dominants and subdominants. The two issues cannot be separated.

Thus, school-community relations are indeed a dimension of community power relations and should be approached with this perspective. Dominants and subdominants are people of power. The school must learn to do business with both.

20. Syracuse City School District, *The Campus Plan* (A Report on a Feasibility Study for Elementary School Construction in Syracuse, New York), Syracuse: Syracuse Campus Site Planning Center, 1967, pp. 2-4.

Negotiating with Pressure Groups | 77

Myron Lieberman

In many districts, school administration has—within the short span of just a few years—become almost synonymous with "confrontation management."

First, there was an unsettling upsurge in teacher militancy, culminating in teacher-school board negotiations. Then, other employee groups began to press for collective negotiations. Administrators were literally forced into annual or biannual confrontations on terms and conditions of employment.

But civil rights groups also began to demand curriculum and personnel changes, and their successes have contributed to the formation of other community pressure groups, all concerned with issues that have little or nothing to do with the actual conditions of employment.

Today the school administrator suddenly finds himself faced with a bewildering collection of demands—for more liberal rules of dress or conduct, for opportunities to protest the war in Vietnam, for curriculum change, for (and against) integration, for just about anything that catches popular support at the moment. Such demands may be made by students, by parents, or by community groups. They are often accompanied by threats of demonstrations, boycotts, or other forms of protest and persuasion.

Because these growing demands frequently lead to "negotiations," it may be helpful to clarify some of the similarities and differences between non-employee negotiations and those involving teachers and school boards.

WHO IS THE SPOKESMAN?

In negotiating with teachers, there is usually no problem determining who represents them. The procedures for designating teacher representatives are often regulated by statute. Where they are not, procedures for settling representation are well established.

It is relatively easy to determine who represents students, too—at least, on a given issue.

But deciding who represents parents, or a neighborhood, or a black community, can be extremely difficult. Dealing with persons who do not really represent the group they claim to represent can escalate problems. At the same time, refusing to deal with persons who are the *de facto* leaders of parents or a community can be equally troublesome. The problem is exacerbated by the fact that most school controversies flush out a considerable number of self-styled community leaders or representatives.

In my own community, I recently witnessed a dramatic illustration of this problem. A group of black students had damaged some school property after one of their "demands" was refused. Subsequently, a group of parents, alleging to represent all parents, presented several demands to the administration, including amnesty for the students. The basis for their claim to represent all parents was simply that the local paper had carried an advance announcement of the meeting at which their demands were formulated. However, the announcement did not state the purpose of the meeting or indicate that it was open to all parents. The local press subsequently gave wide publicity to their demands—but raised no critical questions concerning the representative status of the leaders. As a result, the administration felt forced to negotiate with a group that really did not represent more than a handful of parents. In fact, many parents who had never heard of the group resented its claim to represent them.

WHO'S ACCOUNTABLE?

The absence of a feasible representational system for parents or community groups leads to another basic difficulty in "negotiating" with such groups, which is their inherent lack of accountability. It is easy for students, parents, or community groups to demand certain changes in the curriculum or in school operations. Unfortunately, these same groups are not really accountable for the consequences of their demands.

For example, suppose students demand certain courses or changes in grading policy. Suppose, further, that the changes are made and have undesirable consequences in practice. The students who originally demanded the changes are not likely to be around when the consequences can be adequately evaluated. Even if they are, it is extremely difficult, if not impossible, to hold them accountable for advocating policies which turn out to be undesirable. The school administrator is likely to be held accountable for undesirable outcomes, regardless of who initially requested them.

This being the case, administrators must be cautious in sharing their decision-making power with individuals or groups who are practically immune from any responsibility for the consequences. In fact, such immunity is one reason why administrators are often confronted by unrealistic, even irresponsible demands. It is easy to make such demands when the other fellow has to suffer if they don't work out.

Note the difference, on this issue, between teacher-school board negotiations and negotiations with students, parents or community groups. The teacher negotiators are either teachers themselves or full-time representatives of teachers. Their own level of compensation, or even their jobs, are likely to depend upon the effectiveness of their negotiations. Furthermore, they must live with the administration after negotiations are concluded. As a result, there are built-in restraints on their negotiating behavior—restraints that do not apply to non-employment negotiations. Teacher negotiations are increasingly regulated by statute and governmental agencies which prohibit unfair practices, whereas "negotiations" with community groups are more prone to irrational or unethical behavior which makes it difficult to reach agreement.

Not long ago, I attended a meeting where a group of black parents made six demands on a high school principal. The demands included: increased employment of black teachers, introduction of black history, amnesty for black students who had damaged school property, and no restitution for property damage resulting from a recent outbreak of vandalism. The demands were made with a newspaper reporter present, and the school administration was given until three o'clock the next day to accept the demands, which were labeled "non-negotiable," Obviously, such behavior at teacher board negotiations would constitute an unfair labor practice.

WHAT'S GOOD FOR THE GOOSE . . .

The scope of non-employment negotiations is also much different from negotiations over terms and conditions of employment. In fact, non-job negotiations frequently deal with curriculum, admissions, and other matters of educational policy. Many school administrators—including some in higher education—are courting trouble on this point. In teacher negotiations, they typically assert that educational policies are not negotiable. Inconsistently, they then negotiate such policies with groups who carry no legal responsibility for the outcomes. In my opinion, this is an additional reason why administrators should avoid the term "negotiations" in referring to discussions of this nature.

At City College of New York (CCNY), the administration "negotiated" an admissions policy that would have permitted half the incoming freshmen to be admitted without meeting the normal admission requirements. The agreement was later rejected by the faculty, but even that is not the crucial point. What is crucial is that the entire sequence of events tended to legitimatize the notion that the administration should negotiate on admissions policies with community groups.

But let's face it: Negotiations with community groups are essentially *political* accommodations. And as such, they do have important similarities with teacher board negotiations.

For example, in both situations, the parties need to save face and avoid the appearance of capitulation. In one school system with which I am familiar, the superintendent agreed to certain proposals made by a community group. The newspaper story referred to the superintendent's "capitulation" to the pressure groups. The story was unfair, but it illustrates a point. The administration must appear flexible and responsive—but it seriously risks public support if it seems to give in too easily to pressure groups.

Here, as with teacher-board negotiations, it may be crucial to have the parties keep talking during a crisis.

It is also desirable to observe certain amenities in dealing with community groups. Even when it is necessary to disagree with them very vigorously, a special effort should be made to avoid personal affront. They will often seem acutely sensitive to one who is accustomed to the rough-and-tumble of negotiations over conditions of employment.

FAMILIAR STRAINS

In general, most of the techniques of negotiating with teachers are to some degree applicable to negotiations, "confrontations," or "consultations" with other groups. It is significant that the American Arbitration Assn. (AAA), which plays such a prominent role in mediation in employment relations, has recently established a mediating service in the area of community relations. Some of the AAA's most experienced labor and commercial arbitrators are now active in community relations.

True, "negotiating" with a community group over a pupil transportation policy, for example, or a policy on student dress, does call for knowledge about those specific subjects. In employment negotiations, what other districts are doing—especially nearby districts —is very important and this is also true with respect to other types of controversies. If all other nearby school districts bus elementary pupils one mile or more from the nearest school, it will be easier for the administrator to carry out such a policy in his district. The herd instinct is not confined to employment relations, as any experienced administrator knows. Thus, the technique of citing what others do has broad application.

But be careful: As in teacher negotiations, the experienced administrator will avoid citing practices in other districts that increase, rather than decrease, his vulnerability.

The big problem, again, is that negotiations outside the employment context are so unstructured. In employment negotiations, there are certain constraints on the parties. These constraints do not eliminate all inexperienced and unsophisticated negotiators, or all the crackpots and irresponsibles. But they do have a healthy tendency in this direction.

In teacher negotiations, for example, the administration spokesmen will recognize the political needs of their adversaries. Thus, they will usually try to help the teacher representatives look good—to the teachers. By the same token, the administration negotiators will usually expect certain kinds of help from teacher-representatives,

In negotiating with community groups, however, the administration is more likely to be confronted by spokesmen who are ignorant or heedless of the long-range consequences of a particular tactic.

TAKE THE INITIATIVE

Experience in negotiating with non-employee groups is limited. But already, it is clear that the best way to avoid excessive and unproductive negotiations with community groups is to have a positive program for constantly involving *responsible* groups in considering issues that concern them. By taking the initiative here, with both student and community groups, the administration has a better chance to structure their involvement in a satisfactory way. The administration also stands a better chance of avoiding the kind of emergency, *ad hoc* negotiations that have been so disastrous to school boards that have been unprepared for negotiations with teachers.

part six

The PRINCIPAL and EDUCATIONAL TECHNOLOGY

Educational
Technology

chapter overview

The word *technology* is derived from the Greek word meaning "systematic treatment." It is defined as (1) the science or study of the practical, and (2) the science of the application of knowledge to practical purposes (applied science). Technology in education is not a recent phenomenon, nor is it a panacea for all educational ills. Without exception, all of our modern technological developments in education are discussed in terms of their limitations and advantages. The articles in this chapter focus on some of the crucial issues and the role of technology in our schools. The implication for the secondary school principal is quite obvious—tune in or be tuned out.

Technology is more than tools. Indeed, Edgar Dale views technology as a process. He envisions technology assisting educators in the attainment of stated objectives.

Rest at ease! Technology is not going to replace the administrator. Richard G. Nibeck projects the role of machine and computer —assisted instruction in the 1970s. It is his feeling that the role of the classroom teacher will be significantly changed by the employment of modern technology in education.

What is a media center? Robert C. Gerletti considers the question in his article. His discussion of the question suggests patterns of organization for the improvement of instruction through school plant planning.

One of the most discussed innovations in education today is modulate, or flexible, scheduling. Nelson L. Haggerson is convinced of the value of flexible scheduling in individualizing the instructional program. His article also recognizes the need for computer help in the preparation and operation of a flexible schedule.

Educators are constantly reminded of the knowledge explosion and its implications. Norton F. Kristy looks at the future of educational technology. He foresees a "convergence between three forces —computer technology, information systems, and changing educational requirements and practices."

503

78 | Technology Is More Than Tools

Edgar Dale

How systematic should a curriculum be? How can we avoid ritualistic, barren formalism on the one hand, and careless, ineffective, unplanned opportunism on the other? The question has long concerned teachers and supervisors. Indeed, major educational reforms have often aimed to correct the extremes of excessive systematization or a vague and diffuse opportunism.

This issue arises when we discuss educational technology, the use of programed instruction, language laboratories, or new, highly systematic approaches to the teaching of mathematics, biology, physics, and chemistry. Do some of these courses eliminate local curriculum planning, transform the teacher into a mechanical maid to a teaching aid? Will increased systematization discourage innovation, make teachers less creative?

We shall waste time in aimless experimenting and acrimonious debate unless we answer some of these questions by more precise planning of the behavioral outcomes of education. What do we expect our graduates to do, or be?

In any systematic program of educational development we must know two things—first, the broad and the specific goals of instruction insofar as they can be predicted, and second, the experiences which learners need to undergo to master the stated objectives. Included here, of course, will be the varied instructional materials, e.g., radio, recordings, programed materials, filmstrips, photographs, charts, graphs, maps, and study trips. We need, therefore, a taxonomic approach such as those by Benjamin Bloom, *Taxonomy of Educational Objectives;* Nolan C. Kearney, *Elementary School Objectives;* and Will French, *Behavioral Goals of General Education in High School.*

A shortcoming of current instruction is that it has confined itself chiefly to informational goals involving imitative reaction, rote learning. We have given limited attention to creative interaction—anlysis, synthesis and application of principles. Sometimes stated goals are so general that no content can be derived from them. Or they may indeed be so specific that the principles they illustrate are not made clear.

This excessively general approach is illustrated by the colleges which say that their chief aim is to develop the thinking man. Yet a

From *Educational Leadership*, Vol. 21, No. 3 (December 1963), pp. 161-166. Reprinted with permission of the Association for Supervision and Curriculum Development and the author. Copyright 1963 by the Association for Supervision and Curriculum Development.

study of their curricula shows that they do not have a carefully planned, continuing program to reach this objective. This is disclosed by the heavy emphasis on rote learning in *all* examinations in college or professional school. Dressel and Mayhew in *General Education: Explorations in Evaluation* (American Council on Education, 1954), say that humanities courses, for example, "were restricted to knowledge of fact with some incidental attention paid to intellectual manipulation of that content. . . ."

PREDICTING FUTURE NEEDS

To develop a systematic approach to teaching and learning we must be able to predict the future needs of students. How well can this be done? Certain phases of reading have a highly predictable content. We can predict with 100 percent accuracy that the letters of of the alphabet will all be used every day. We can be certain some 3,000 predictable words will always make up 95 percent of easy reading and 70 percent of hard reading. We can predict that all pupils will need certain reading-study skills. Similar predictions can be made in arithmetic and other subject-matter fields.

We can also predict that all students will need certain abilities and attitudes in problem solving, critical reading, critical thinking. We can plan for these competencies although they are not routine skills.

However, since we cannot predict all the key problems an individual will face we must systematically help him become a problem-framer and problem-solver. We can systematically plan for this and use technology to present open-ended problems, to develop skills in the framing of hypothesis making and the like. To systematize, therefore, is not necessarily to mechanize. We can carefully plan for creativity, for thinking responses. We can then turn to technology for certain kinds of help.

Just what is a technology anyway? A primitive man who had no tools at all would be living in a non-technological world. But let us suppose that he extends his arm by means of a hammer. He is now developing a technology—a system. Later he may learn to move objects by means other than brute strength. He may learn to store food by preservation and later by domesticating animals. He masters ways of using a microscope, an extension of the eye. He develops a megaphone or a public address system or recordings, extensions of the mouth. He produces systems of transportation, an extension of his legs. He has produced systems for finding out about the world in ways impossible with the natural senses. And technology plays an important part in these systems.

Just as the biological researcher uses an electronic microscope, so, too, there are technological tools for teaching and learning. Obviously we need devices to store and retrieve information to aid the professor and the student. And so we study our libraries and try to invent better ways for storing, retrieving, correlating information. We develop increasingly complex abstracting systems in the sciences and we use modern electronic processing methods in so doing. We Xerox materials so that the student does not take an hour to copy something that he can get in a minute. We store and retrieve information by video tape, by film, by tape or disc recordings.

Inexpensive paperbacks enable us to revolutionize many present ways of teaching. The student can own his book, write in it, keep it because it has no value at second-hand book stores. But without technology, without mass production, that paperback book would not be possible.

TECHNOLOGY IS PROCESS

But technology is more than tools. It is basically a process by which tools are integrated into a system. Indeed, such a system is needed to produce the tools.

Will this technology "mechanize" education, dehumanize relations between teacher and pupil?

Let us look at some examples of systematized approaches using the best of modern technology and see what we approve or disapprove. Some believe that carefully planned systems will result in a stereotyped, sterile and unchanging teaching and learning process. Not so. We cannot operate without some system, but we must constantly experiment with already developed systems to improve them, to reorganize them.

One example of a systematically programed study was carried on by Paul R. Wendt and Grosvenor Rust of Southern Illinois University and reported in the *Journal of Educational Research* (Vol. 55, No. 9, June-July 1962). The study dealt with teaching library techniques to college freshmen. First of all, they programed by a branching technique and used 2x2 slides in a random access projector. They tried to maximize transfer to the actual situation in the library by means not only of pictorial frames but through performance frames where the students were required to do something.

But these experimenters did not stop after they had developed a systematic method for learning library skills. Next they studied the possibility of using a lecturer to present the materials ordinarily presented in the programed, branching slide material and tested it against a lecture group which had access to all of the slides but presented them in a linear fashion. They also had a bright group who had no program at all.

They found that the lecturer with the carefully prepared slides which had been developed for the program achieved as good results as the programed section. Further, students who were in the top group, the A students, did as well without instruction as the others did with instruction. Obviously they may have had instruction before.

So how does a teacher respond to a proposed system? He does not blindly accept it. He tests it, he retests it, he checks it. And he sees that some students go into the system and others remain outside of it and participate in a subsystem. By the way, it was found that this systematic approach to library guidance enabled the freshmen in six weeks to reach a standard that comparable samples of freshmen, sophomores, juniors and seniors did not ordinarily reach until the end of the sophomore year. Further, there was much greater spread among the ones who picked up the techniques as contrasted with those taking the systematic freshman program.

We can, therefore, make provision within a system for branching, for individualized approaches. For example, sixth and eighth grade pupils in Columbus, Ohio, are participating in a system of programed vocabulary development which a colleague and I developed. Do all children need this year-long program? Yes and no. As improved systems of vocabulary development are provided in the earlier grades some children reaching the 8th grade may not need this specialized guidance and could omit it from their program.

To those who are rightly concerned about over-systematization may I say that much high school and collegiate education is already over-systematized in the sense that it does not provide varied approaches to fit individual need. The 30 percent of high school dropouts is one proof of this weakness.

THE LIBRARY AS A TEACHING-LEARNING SYSTEM

What we need in all fields is a curriculum plan whereby certain broad systematic approaches are made, where there is a freedom to move back and forth from individual to group approaches and where specialized, highly systematic materials aid those pupils who either lag behind or want to get ahead. To reach this goal requires a systematic use of all tools of instruction—in short, an educational technology.

So within a broadly planned system, whether it is a curriculum for spelling in the 6th grade or the mathematics curriculum for 12th grade, there can be highly systematized material. Some material can be loosely programed, some very closely and meticulously programed. If children in a particular grade are misspelling the possessive *its* by putting in an apostrophe or if they are misspelling *to*, *too* and *two*, we can develop a systematic program to eliminate these errors. The issue is not total-system versus no-system, but rather the degree of required systematization.

Another example of the development of a systematic approach to learning is found in better integration of the library into the total learning process. Indeed, if we are aiming to develop the person who has learned how to learn and has developed a taste for learning, we require a quite different kind of library.

The prototype of this library or library function has been developing in the audio-visual field. A long time ago public schools, notably in Los Angeles, Oakland and St. Louis, were seeing the key role that differentiated learning materials could play in effective education. Courses of study listed varied materials to be used in developing major concepts. Book libraries in turn began moving in this direction through major projects of the American Library Association. Film and filmstrip collections were added to their regular collections of material.

Far-seeing librarians realized that ideas were communicated also by means other than books. So modern libraries include recordings, filmstrips, varied pictorial materials, and films in their collections. It is significant that a number of years ago the *Saturday Review of Literature* changed its name to the *Saturday Review* and began including articles and comments on films, television and recordings.

A LEARNING CENTER CONCEPT

A later stage in the growth of the integrated, systematic approach to learning which includes the library is exemplified by a program in Shaker Heights, Ohio. Two elementary schools are experimenting with the teaching of study skills making use of school libraries that have shifted to the learning center concept. A technician has been employed to produce materials for overhead projectors, and basic presentations of varied types of study skills are made to groups of 75 to 100 children.

All major types of learning materials are indexed in the library so that if a child needs material on Africa he finds all the varying types in the learning center. He can view films and filmstrips. Facilities are available also for individual and group listening to recordings. All materials are related to a central purpose, the mastery of important study skills.

What will technology do to the role of the teacher? Why is he sometimes reluctant or afraid to use these new media? I do not think it is because he fears the equipment itself. Indeed, new equipment is increasingly easier to operate and the average teacher is managing more complex technology at home than he operates at school. Thus, the teacher fears a diminished role.

Certainly some technology will replace the teacher, as did the textbook—a technological product. But since most textbooks were not self-teaching, the teacher became a translator of complex prose. However, as explanations of subject matter in books or programed materials are sharply improved, become more self-teaching, where does this leave the teacher? Certainly he should not teach what can be taught as well or better by films, recordings, television, programed materials, etc.

The task of the teacher is to do the complicated, artful things that preplanned materials cannot do. The professional teacher will help students plan their work and their lives more effectively, see that they engage in thoughtful, creative interaction as contrasted with the rote learning of imitative reaction. The teacher will become a diagnostician and prescriber for the remedying of weaknesses, and the fortifying of strengths. He will help students correlate, refine, integrate, and interrelate experiences relevant to important learning goals.

THE INDEPENDENT LEARNER

The teacher will give up some of his or her correcting activities. Indeed the occupational disease of many teachers is a penchant for correcting. The teacher of English, for example, is too often a custodian of a correctional institute. We found in some of our work with programed materials in vocabulary that the teacher felt at a loss when he was not correcting the self-correcting items.

The teacher's significant role is to develop the independent learner. For example, we teach children to read because we want them to be on their own in reading, figure out words for themselves, consult dictionaries and encyclopedias. The teacher must prize the independence of the child and realize that his success lies in changing the child's dependent role to an independent role. We can use our personal relationships to help youngsters become more mature, not to make them more dependent.

The teacher will then take a more integrative role, help youngsters systematize their knowledge. Too often the subjects taught are all down a single subject track, without interconnection, interaction, interweaving. The teacher sees that these interrelationships occur and this is a difficult and complicated task.

In summary, we have no choice as to whether we use advanced technology. The choice is whether we use it intelligently to achieve the objectives we want or use it unintelligently. I see no particular merit in the approach which Frederick Raubinger made about two years ago when he said: "Well, I simply cannot tell the public of New Jersey that the keys to Utopia are at hand; that the team teaching plan, the dual progress plan, the lay reader plan, are the simple answers to better schools."

Who said it was a simple answer? Who said it was Utopia? I too have lived through a dozen plans—the Morrison Plan, the Gary Plan, the Winnetka Plan, the Dalton Plan, the platoon plan, etc. My answer is, "So what?" I lived through the Morrison Plan and learned a lot from it. I was a part of the Winnetka Plan and learned a lot from it. I lived with and through progressive education and learned a lot from it.

To suggest that these plans do not prove to be utopian evades the basic issue. There will be more and more plans. All of these earlier plans left a residue. Naturally those who were in favor of them were enthusiastic and sometimes overstated their case. "What else?" But was there not a case? Did not these programs and plans have powerful effects on the schools?

I suggest that we not look with jaundiced eye on new plans or innovations, but rather examine them hopefully, knowing full well that they will have inadequacies. But these inadequacies can be detected and changed. Let us not reject them till they are tried. The obligation of the professional person is not to adopt a new method. It is to explore the proposal, to investigate it, to experiment with it, to apply educational theory and sound logic to it. Does it help the student toward increased maturity in thinking through his own problems? Does it set up the conditions under which he can become more sensitive, a more compassionate person? Does it enable the teacher to work at a higher level of instruction than at present?

What mechanizes a mechanized education? Not the machine I assure you. If this were the criterion, every writer would have used a pointed stick. He could not use such machines as the fountain pen, the typewriter, the dictaphone, or a tape recorder. The real issue is: Does technology enable us to do what is really important?

It is true that communication machines or devices may help people become more alike. But we must be alike before we can be different, otherwise there will be no communication. We are trying to make our students more alike in the sense that we want them to share common concepts in citizenship, mathematics, physics, whatever the field may be. We are being educated when we are being made enough alike so that we can communicate so that we can be different. And we can be creatively alike as well as creatively different. But technology also helps people be different.

All of us in some degree have a nostalgic feeling for a return to a state of nature, a lost state of innocence. But this fancy cannot be indulged very fully in the kind of world we live in. A few may rebel against the use of television or motion pictures or the jet airplane or the automobile or the freeway, but our rebellion is a limited one.

Our responsibility is a simple one. It is to state our objectives clearly and then to use all the means there are to achieve these objectives. The child born today will live half of his life in the 21st century. An 18th or 19th century approach to problems simply will not do. Furthermore, since the one basic thing we can predict about the future is that it is unpredictable, young people must learn how to become independent learners. To do this requires all the brains that we have and all the brains that we can borrow. To do less is to cheat children of their birthright of present and future growth.

Technology—The Challenge to Make It Your Own | 79

Richard G. Nibeck

The technological promise of the 1970's is both exciting and overwhelming. Articles in popular magazines continue to hint at wonderful things that will change our schools. These range from programmed textbooks, through tutorial tapes, to that mystical wonder of our age, the computer.

The articles not only suggest a future, machine-dominated classroom that does marvels for students, they also imply that the teaching function may be transferred from the teacher to the machine. The vision of wires and boxes cause many to shudder and some to say, "Not to *my* students you won't."

It is unfortunate that our society is so machine conscious and that the machine tends to be the popular image of technological progress. Technology does not mean machine any more than the presence of a school building means that learning occurs inside. True enough, the machine is usually part of a technological system but that's not the whole story. What the machine does, how it does it, to whom it does it and who decides what it does are important questions too often left unstated in popular articles on the future of educational technology.

A somewhat oversimplification of the basic elements of a learning environment would suggest that it consists of three basic elements: a learner, information to be learned and a means to display the information to be acted upon. The word "information," as used here, includes facts; concepts and processes. Although all three elements have a complex interrelation and are inseparable in any real learning situation, it is helpful to separate them for discussion. For the purposes of this article, let's concentrate only on the third element—the means to display information.

To display information means more than a simple display or presentation of facts. As used here, the concept implies to display, to motivate, to perceive and to have a logical order of events or activities designed to bring about desired results. It also implies a means of evaluating the success of achieving the desired results or goals.

In any given teaching situation today, all of these steps are accomplished by a variety of methods. The traditional teaching-learning configuration would find the teacher presenting information either verbally or through printed materials. The teacher would have created a setting in which students were motivated toward the materials, as well as having selected materials which would stimulate student attention. She would have in mind a presentational strategy for the sequence of events based on concepts of learning theory. And she would have some means to evaluate the student's progress in order to determine the success of the teaching effort. In most cases, it is difficult to order these events in time since they usually occur simultaneously, or nearly so.

MEDIATED TEACHERS

In the classical school setting, the teacher herself performs all of these functions. In today's schools, however, some of the various elements just described are more frequently being performed by someone other than the immediate teacher. It is important to note that "immediate teacher" refers to the teacher being physically present in the classroom at the time of instruction. When a textbook is used to display information, then the author of the book can be referred to as the "mediated teacher." So also is the individual who has prepared a programmed text or a teaching film. Although he is not present in the classroom, he performs the function of teacher through the selected media.

Mediated teaching—i.e., the use of textbook, television, film, etc. —is fairly common in most classrooms today. The next 10 years in education will see even more of an emphasis by teachers on the use of mediated instruction for the bulk of classroom time.

The immediate teacher, it is predicted, will concentrate her efforts on the management of elements within the learner's environment so that they best serve the interests of the student. Mediated teachers, on the other hand, will handle routine instruction through combinations of both simple and complex technological systems. Whether or not these mediated teachers are machines is not very important. What these devices and materials can do and how we can use them for the student's betterment is our concern.

The following are some of the systems which will probably be found in some form in most of our schools in the 1970's.

TEXTBOOKS

The *textbook* is the simplest display machine now used in the classroom. It is basically an information storage and retrieval system which has built-in, logical sequencing of information. It is motivational through its style of writing and the use of attractive illustrations and often has evaluation instruments in the form of printed, self-administered tests at the end of each unit of information.

Although the textbook will remain for many generations as the fundamental storage device, it is very inefficient by today's standards. It is, however, inexpensive when compared to other storage systems, and will probably remain so for some time to come. Future developments will probably include more paperbacks and loose-leaf books as well as hard-copy printouts of selections or abstracts of books that have been stored in computer systems.

Programmed textbooks are better than regular texts in displaying information in two particular ways:

The first is that the sequence of presented information has been scientifically developed by having the content tested on students before it is printed. The readability and comprehensibility is, therefore, guaranteed, provided the book is later used with students having similar skills to those of the test population.

The second advantage in a programmed text is that the evaluation of progress is an integral part of the reading effort. The prepared text is a series of presentations and questions incorporated into the same paragraphs in order to evaluate each step of advancement in the student's progress through the book. The student knows immediately of his own progress by this system.

The mediated teacher (author) may elect to present content in somewhat larger steps and then provide a means for a student to obtain supplemental instruction should his self-evaluation prove that he hasn't understood a concept. This system, called branch programming allows many students to move more rapidly if their reading comprehension permits.

The traditional book and the programmed book are both usually limited, because content is printed with only infrequent use of visual and no auditory reinforcement, unless the immediate teacher steps in. For these reasons, they work well for the student whose learning style preference is for written materials, but not as well for students showing preferences for visual or auditory presentations. Examples of such text would be the popular *English 2600* and *English 3200* by Harcourt, Brace & World found in many schools throughout the nation and *Algebra* by Central Scientific Co.

The advantage of non-book machine systems is that they can give a greater variety of choices in both display channel options and styles of presentation. To list the variety of these devices would fill hundreds of pages, but a few examples are presented to serve as hints of what exists today and what we can expect in the future. They are clustered in groups according to similarities.

Audio-tutorial devices impart basic information to the student through pre-recorded presentations. Frequently, these pre-recorded lessons are supplemented by printed student worksheets or instruction manuals. Sometimes filmstrips or 2 x 2 slides are used; and in the case of the Bell & Howell Language Master printed words and symbols on cards provide a visual display capability. The author of audio-tutorial materials programs the sequencing of information and the time interval of student responses by experimentation and field testing. The materials may use printed or oral tests to evaluate the progress of the student. These systems are usually designed for small group and individual student use, but the materials themselves are produced for mass audiences.

The basic machine in this system is the reel-to-reel or cassette tape recorder. Some manufacturers use recorded discs. The main features of the method are that the child has the materials in hand and can plug them into a machine when he is ready to use them. What materials to use and in what sequence is controlled in the classroom. The materials themselves may be made by the individual teacher, a department and school district, or they may be purchased commercially from such companies as 3M, Imperial Tapes, Rheem Califone, SRA and Charles Merrill.

The more complex machines have student response buttons to help the child evaluate his progress, in addition to having a selection of audio and visual presentation channels. Some machines are designed for large group use even though students have push buttons for their individual response. Some examples of machines with student response buttons are Columbia Broadcasting System's AVS-10 and Borg Warner's System 80.

Commercially sold programs include audio tape and coordinated books such as those from Doubleday (Prime-O-Tec), Random House and Charles Merrill. Examples of programs having audio-visual components which include student response capability are Educational Developmental Laboratories' Aud-X and Hoffman Industries' Mark IV. Representative of the complex group presentation system, including student group responder, is the Raytheon 600 Media Master.

Mass presentational materials are also common today, but will undoubtedly be used more extensively in the future. These would include educational films and television. Such systems tend to be self-motivating through a richness of presented material not easily duplicated in the average classroom. They are also programmed in the sense that there is a sequence of the presentation of content. They seldom have built-in evaluation and responders, unless they are parts of a more sophisticated system such as a driver training simulator.

Film is usually more flexible than television since it can be used by the class as a whole, as well as by individuals. It can also be used when the teacher or student desires. Television has the advantage of a high probability of more up-to-date content. It may also be used by groups if recorded on video tape for replay.

Present advances in smaller motion storage devices such as 8-mm film, CBS's electronic video recording (EVR) and the new RCA hologram will lead to a lower unit cost for materials and greater usability in the form of cartridge loading machines. The unit cost for 15 minutes of material in 8-mm is $18, EVR will cost $8 and holograms are expected to be about $2. This should put large collections into the individual school.

Just as exciting as cost reductions are the newer presentational techniques of available films. Encyclopedia Britannica Corporation's single science concept short films are an example, as are the Bailey Film Associates' with alternate endings. Many producers are making available open ended materials so that the student formulates his own conclusions.

Remote access system and *electronic classrooms* can be found in most sections of the country today and it would seem that more will be used in the 1970's. Basically, there are audio-tutorial systems but some have television display. The popular designation "dial retrieval" describes the system's function.

Individual students, or an entire class at a teaching station, can use a telephone-type distribution system to dial for and use a piece of instructional material stored in some central location. The characteristics of the learning system are the same as those of audio-tutorial except that availability of material is dictated by the electronic switching circuits and the number of students using the system. The students do not have the materials in hand.

The advantages are largely that fewer duplicates of the original material are needed and that students cannot damage materials. It is also easy to update content in the system simply by changing the master. This system allows the student to call from his home telephone and receive his lessons without reporting to school.

In those institutions which use audio-tutorial methods, the machine systems usually carry the burden of dissemination of basic information. Then the immediate teacher analyzes student progress and prescribes the next step in the learning sequence. In this way she can alter the learning experiences according to individual student needs. But since little learning material is commercially available, some schools are producing their own materials. Chester Electronics, Continuous Progress Education, DuKane, Multimedia Learning Systems (a division of AV Electronics) and Ampex are representative manufacturers of this equipment.

Computers and their application to instruction represent the most recent experimentation with machines serving the classroom. The mystique that has arisen around the computer as a master "mind" is an unfortunate happenstance. Fundamentally, a computer is as simple as the common flashlight with its on-off switch. To compute a solution to a problem, it turns on and off according to a prescribed set of rules known as a program.

The computer is an information storage and management machine. Its value lies in the quantities of information it can store and the speed with which it can handle this information. The extent of application to learning problems is limited only by the mediated teacher's ability to program the device properly.

Computer assisted instruction (CAI) is creating the most excitement in any consideration of the future of computers in schools. Simply stated, CAI uses a computer to turn pages in a programmed textbook. A teacher-author writes a sequence of learning activities just as he would in preparing a book, but instead of printing on paper the program is stored in the computer memory. Also stored are instructions for the computer to take certain actions when the student responds in a prescribed way.

The learning materials are presented to the student by a typewriter printout, on a television tube as words or pictures, or in a combination of these, including prerecorded audio messages, slides and film. The student responds by use of a typewriter or possibly a light pin directed at the picture to give his answers to the materials presented.

Computer prescribed instruction (CPI) is another subject of considerable experimentation. In CPI, the computer is programmed by a teacher-programmer to grade a student's test, compare the student's work with past performance records and then to prescribe a new learning activity.

The task performed by the computer is similar to that undertaken by any good teacher, but it has the advantage of holding hundreds of student records in its memory at one time and can sort out the appropriate information within a few seconds. This action is limited only by the imagination of the teacher programmer in selecting varieties of learning experiences and in predicting which experience is best to overcome the errors made by the student on his test.

For example, if student A did very well on lesson 42 and his past record indicated he consistently did well, the teacher-programmer's instructions might be to skip lesson 43, which is largely redundant, and go on to 44. Student B, however, was only fair and his past records indicate that he performs best with written material, so his printed instruction suggests a chapter in a book covering lesson 43. Another student may have the same results, but his past records indicate he learns best from visual and oral instruction, so a sound filmstrip on the substance of lesson 43 is recommended.

Computer managed instruction (CMI) is sometimes thought of as the same thing as CPI, but it is more accurately a combination of CAI and CPI. Only experimental programs now exist which can use computers to evaluate student progress and on the basis of the evaluation put together and present to the student a sequence of learning activities best geared to his style of learning.

In all the systems described so far, the student uses prepared materials designed for any student to use and only the sequence is controlled. Since it is mediated instruction (the teacher recorded in some form) and since the student uses the material himself it is properly called mediated self-instruction and not individualized instruction as is popularly supposed.

CMI, on the other hand, has promise of being truly individualized instruction in that the system tailors learning experiences which are best suited to the learner according to his unique learning characteristics. Not all students learn the same thing in the same way, obviously. Proponents of CMI systems think that the next decade will see certain parts of the curriculum handled by such a system.

Where will the teacher fit into this maze of machine environments? There is no doubt that the role of the classroom teacher will change significantly, as have all other roles when technology influences a human activity.

The use of x-ray machines, laboratory procedures, artificial body organs, computer comparisons of patient symptoms and the increase in specialties like nurses and laboratory technicians have not created a decreased need for doctors. The same can be predicted for the teacher.

In the schools of the 1970's, we should see machines handling the rote dissemination of basic content with the teacher directing most of her efforts toward the use of this content and the production of new ideas. Most important, however, will be that the teacher is freed from routine tasks so that her efforts can be directed toward the development of human communication and understanding among her students.

80 | What Is a Media Center?

Robert C. Gerletti

A media center is many things. It is called a learning resource center, learning materials center, educational media center, educational resource center, educational services center, educational communication center, instructional technology center, a library, an audiovisual center, or an educational materials center. As Humpty Dumpty has said, "Words can mean whatever we choose them to mean, neither more nor less."

Therefore a media center is whatever we choose it to be. At the present time it has many forms. The form it takes is based on an idea, a concept, a philosophy held by a person or persons in a school district.

What seems to differentiate one center from another besides the name that is given to it?

When you visit various centers you are interested in what really goes on in the center. This is when you find out what the differences are in various centers.

The key question seems to be, "What do learners do in the centers and how do they get there?" There are at least four reasons why learners are in centers:

- They are in the center on their free time browsing to obtain information in which they are interested.
- They are there to prepare an individual or small group report. They have been sent there by their teacher or they are in there on their own accord.
- They are there to sample interest centers established as a result of needs expressed by teachers or students or principals or coordinating teachers.
- They are there as an integral part of courses of study in which they are engaged. The student in this case is actually programmed by design into the center for information, to learn a skill, to foster an attitude or all three.

The media center, discussed above, is generally found in an elementary school or a high school. The relationship between the center at the school and the center at the district office or regional center is a relationship which needs to be looked at when you are considering what a media center is. Some school centers exist with a minimum of assistance from a district center. Other school centers exist with almost all materials supplied by the district center. Still others

From *Audiovisual Instruction*, Vol. 14 (September 1969), pp. 21-23. Reprinted by permission of the publisher and author.

have worked out an arrangement where the district center is an integral part of the school center and acts as a production agency and as a temporary storage agency for excess materials and materials which are not being used in the school center. If we were to describe a function of both centers, we might say they are pumping stations, pumping materials into the educational process as needed.

DESIGN CONSIDERATIONS

What are some of the considerations necessary when you are thinking of building or creating some kind of media center?

It is imperative that you have a large measure of agreement on the educational goals of the school district, the role of each school and each teacher in accomplishing these objectives. The diagram below indicates how these goal relationships might be charted.

SOME RELATIONSHIPS OF THE VALUES, AIMS, PURPOSES,
OBJECTIVES AND PROCEDURES TO LEVELS OF DECISION MAKING

VALUES

Societal	←	AIMS	PROCEDURES	←	Board of Education
			Superintendent		
Institutional	→	PURPOSES	PROCEDURES	→	Central Office
			Principals		
Instructional	→	OBJECTIVES	PROCEDURES	→	Building
			Teachers		
Learner	→	NEEDS	PROCEDURES	→	Classroom or Learning Space

It is apparent that there are four levels of purposes and procedures. There must be a good deal of agreement in the direction these goals take or you will have an uncoordinated, undirected, and fragmented program.

The Fountain Valley School District in California has demonstrated in its publication entitled *A Plan for Educational Reform* how these levels would appear in writing—district goals, district objectives, school objectives, and classroom objectives.

District Goal No. 9

THE CONSTRUCTIVE USE OF PERSONAL TIME

District Objective: When given unscheduled time blocks, students (institutional objective) will demonstrate their respect for the use of personal time (instructional objective) by their response (behavioral objective) in the learning center.

School Objective: Following classroom instruction regarding the use of personal time (instructional objective) students (institutional objective) will demonstrate their response (behavioral objective) to the concept by applying learned skills in the learning centers when given unscheduled blocks of time (evaluative objective).

Classroom Objective: When assigned unscheduled blocks of time in the learning centers, students (institutional objective) will demonstrate response (behavioral objective) to the use of personal time (instructional objective) by selecting with greater frequency activities that require independent study rather than activities directed by the coordinating teacher (evaluative objective).

Another factor which you must consider when building a media center is where are you going to focus your effort? Is your effort going to be teacher-centered or learner-centered?

One might call a teacher-centered focus "The Ptolemaic Theory" as illustrated in the photo.

If you subscribe to the learner-centered focus, you might be inclined to call this the "Copernican Theory," also illustrated.

The activities in a media center at a school and the relationship of the media center of a school and district will be considerably dif-

Planning Team

According to Ptolemaic Theory, the sun and planets revolved about the earth, which was the center of the solar system. By analogy, the teacher has been viewed as the center of the school system.

In Copernican Theory, the earth revolves around the sun, which is a small star in the universe. By analogy, the student is the center, around which the teacher and other members of the school "solar" system revolve.

ferent if your organization is learner-centered rather than teacher-centered. Being learner-centered, you pay much more attention to the successes and failures of students than if you are teacher-centered. The objectives on all four levels are considerably different. How you plan to integrate instructional materials is also considerably different.

Let's take a look at the place or role of instructional materials in the learning process.

In Diagram 1, instructional materials or audiovisual materials were selected by teachers as visual or auditory aids. They were generally appliqued onto the learning process.

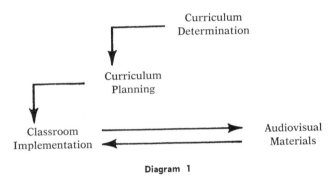

Diagram 1

In Diagram 2, you will note that instructional technology, which is a systematic application of knowledge to the solution of practical problems, has moved up to the curriculum planning level. When curricula are built, materials are considered an integral part of instruction and actually planned for in the curriculum. Philosophically, that is quite a difference from letting the teacher choose from a storehouse or warehouse of materials. (Note: Diagrams 1 and 2 are by Robert Heinich in "The Teacher in an Instructional System," *Instructional Technology*, F. Knirk and J. Childs (editors), New York: Holt, Rinehart and Winston, 1968.)

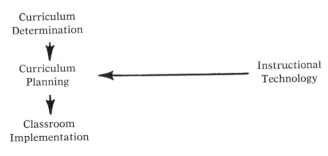

Diagram 2

In Diagram 3 we have what promises to be a fruitful direction for the application of technology. The media faculty will consist of teachers, student representatives, administrators, curriculum people

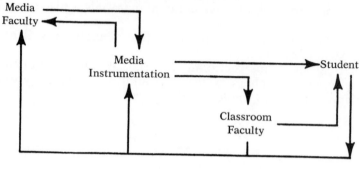

Diagram 3

augmented with specialists such as sociologists, psychologists, anthropologists, and specialists in content areas such as science mathematics, or social studies. They will plan an entire program for a student or a given group of students. Then they will plan the processes by which the student will obtain the objectives as defined. Note that the classroom faculty members are not necessarily always between the media instrumentation and the student. The classroom faculty will have an opportunity to perform on a much higher professional plane in connection with the learning process than it has up to this time.

A chart for an individual school might look like this:

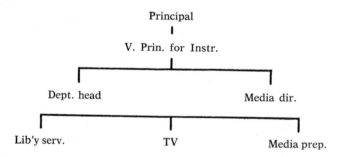

The media director is a person who may have come through the library, through television, or through the media preparation area or one of any other subsystem. I do not think that there should be any argument between audiovisual people and librarians over who should head up the programs. There are many factors to be considered when a person is selected to head a unit in a school such as skill, knowledge, ability, credentials, and even politics. It will take all of the skills and knowledges of all people concerned to solve the educational problems. The application of technology requires a major effort with strong leadership in order for it to succeed.

A fourth consideration is the kind of teaching situation in which the materials will be used.

One kind of teaching situation is the self-contained classroom. Students in a self-contained classroom do not all move through the instructional program at the same rate of speed. This has been obvious for many years. Classroom teachers have set up interest centers, divided the class into special groups, and have made many other arrangements to take care of individual differences. There are students whose needs have not been met with the self-contained classroom. Many educators are suggesting other kinds of teaching situations than the self-contained school.

In the self-contained school, students may progress through self-progress or self-direction through an ungraded arrangement. It is possible for students to be at many different places in connection with the learning process with which they are concerned. All of the results from experiments in the ungraded, self-progress or self-directed schools are not in. There are many management and learning problems still being considered and there are many instructional programs not yet available for students with a great variety of needs.

Apparently even the self-contained school is not a complete answer for meeting needs of all youngsters. In the May 17, 1969, issue of the *Saturday Review*, Donald Cox reported on Philadelphia's new school without walls. In an article entitled "Learning on the Road," Mr. Cox reports on one of the most unusual educational experiments now underway. The Parkway Project "opened its doors" to 142 high school students. "There is no single building in which these students learn; instead, they go to nongraded classes in two dozen different public and private institutions located along or near the mile-and-a-half length of the city's tree-lined Benjamin Franklin Parkway."

When you consider the relationship of a media center to this concept, the prospects are staggering. No format or pattern is now available to help identify the kinds of materials required in this new situation.

This discussion raises the question, "Where do we go from here?" How do we organize for the best instruction? What is the relationship of a media center to some of these new ideas? Perhaps we're at a place where the following quotation might be valid, "You must be free to take a path whose end I have no need to know."

81 | Flexible Scheduling

Nelson L. Haggerson

A major reason for most of the changes and innovations in education today is to focus on the individual. Individualize instruction, provide for individual differences, respect the individuality of the pupil, utilize the individual capabilities of the teacher, are popular phrases of the day which manifest this emphasis.

In recent years we have seen a number of changes designed to implement this philosophy. An emphasis on different and differentiated materials, programmed learning materials designed for the individual to be able to learn at his own rate, units (unipacs) designed for individuals, and a host of suggestions for determining individual needs and interests are some approaches. Team-teaching, large-group instruction, small-group instruction, independent study, and laboratory exploration are other approaches. Nongraded schools and continuous progress are both terms representing ways of respecting the individuality of each pupil. New school plants contain large and small rooms, folding walls and portable furniture, instructional and learning centers, acoustically treated surfaces and easily accessible spaces, once again to provide many alternative ways to "individualize" instruction. A key concept in providing for individual differences is flexibility.

The vehicle through which courses, materials, pupils, teachers, facilities, time and space are related in the school is the schedule. In order to relate these elements to best provide for the individual differences upon which we are focusing, we need a flexible schedule. We also need flexible teachers and administrators.

While the term "flexible scheduling" can be used at any level it is most commonly thought of and written about as relating to the junior and senior high school levels. The following comments will probably seem more pertinent to junior and senior high schools, but the principles involved are applicable at all levels of schooling.

The impetus for flexible scheduling seems to come from the following notions: Pupils do not all learn at the same rate; pupils are interested in a wide variety of subjects and topics within subjects; various modes of instruction—large-group, small-group, and independent study—are appropriate to serve different instructional purposes; all students do not need to learn the same amount of subject matter in order to be successful; different time and facility arrangements are needed to fulfill different purposes; subjects differ greatly in nature and purpose, to mention a few variations.

From *Arizona Teacher*, Vol. 56 (September 1967), pp. 14-16. Reprinted by permission of the author and publisher.

If all of these variables are to be handled within the confines of the school a flexible schedule is surely needed. This need is succinctly stated by Bush and Allen in *A New Design for High School Education.*

Class size, length of class meeting, and the number and spacing of classes ought to vary according to the nature and aim of the subject, the type of instruction, the level of ability and interest of the pupils, and the aim and purpose of teaching. (p. 17)

Before the age of the computer the schedule-maker would have thrown up his hands in horror if asked to account for all of these variables in the schedule. With the development of the computer, however, we must now assume that handling all of these variables is possible. The question then becomes: Do we want to schedule flexibly enough to take care of the individual needs and interests of students? Part of the answer to this question is concerned with the education of teachers and administrators.

Assuming, then, that flexible scheduling is a possibility and that we want to schedule flexibly, how do we start? Perhaps the best approach is to ask what decisions must be made before relating all the elements through the schedule.

One decision to be made is about the most desirable unit of time in the school day. We have typically used 40 to 55 minute periods of time and have assigned that much time each day to each subject. Some schools have now moved to units of 10, 15 or 20 minutes. This represents the shortest amount of time needed to meet with any group of students for any subject. When more time is needed it is allocated in multiples of the basic unit.

Another decision is about the smallest number of students deemed wise for small group work. Typically we have talked about (indeed built classrooms to hold) 30 students. Schools using flexible scheduling are now using groups of from 5 to 15 students. Decisions also must be made about the largest number for large-group instruction, 100, 300, 500?

When you relate the shortest amount of time and the smallest number of students for small groups you have what Bush and Allen refer to as a modular unit. Put two of each together and you have 4 modular units.

The modular unit, then, is used as a basic in building a flexible schedule.

The type of instruction required for any task is another decision that must be made. For instance, if a lecture to a large group of 300 is to last for 40 minutes, appropriate space and time arrangements must be made. If, on the other hand, small-group instruction for 300 students in groups of 15 pupils is desired, still other arrangements must be made. The schedule-maker makes these arrangements according to a number of modular units. Besides deciding that a certain number of small groups will be needed, the basis upon which the pupils are grouped must be decided. Are they interest groups or ability groups? What is the objective of the group?

To provide for student needs and interests, decisions must be made about how many required and how many elective subjects are offered. What is the minimum amount of knowledge a student must learn in any one subject? What does he do when he has learned the minimum? Those who are interested and have abilities in that subject may go on to learn in more depth in that subject. Those who are not interested and/or have less ability in that area may become involved in another subject area.

How often do we have large-group instruction in any given subject? How about small-group? How much time for independent study? Since students learn at different rates and need different amounts of repetition we must provide many alternatives to fulfill the many needs.

If a student is not attending class, where does he go? Is the library equipped to assist him? Are the assignments made to him open-ended so that he has plenty of challenge? Must he stay at school? May he study at home during the school day? Can he be counted as present for average daily attendance purposes if he does his independent project at home? At the public library? At a nearby college?

Suppose the student, moving at his own rate of learning, meets the minimum requirements in less than the usual time? Is he allowed to leave school? Graduate? If not, what does he do? There are decisions which must be made before moving into the flexible scheduling being discussed in the literature today.

In view of the daily changes in learners, teachers and knowledge, how often must the schedule be changed? Another question is: How often does the cycle of activities repeat itself? In most schools every day's schedule is the same, so the cycle repeats itself daily. In some schools the cycle of activities is scheduled for a week, each day during the week being different. The next week the cycle repeats itself. An ultimately flexible schedule would have every day of every semester scheduled to meet the needs of that day, and the cycle would not repeat itself. The realities of schedule-making at this time, however, cause most schools on flexible schedules to repeat the cycle of activities at least weekly.

Once the staff has made these decisions (and many others) they are ready to make the schedule for a given time.

When we think of the complexity of the preparation for and the operation of a flexible schedule we realize the need for computer help. (It must be said, however, that some schools have been "hand scheduled" to meet all of these variables.) We also recognize the need for teachers and administrators and others of the instructional team to have knowledge about what they are doing and want to do, and just as important, if not more so, to be flexible persons. As you will conclude from reading this account (and others) the school operating on a flexible schedule will not be as orderly, as neat, or as predictable as a school run on a "tight" regular schedule. The important question is, however, are the individual needs, interests and capabilities of each pupil being better met? If we can answer yes to this question, then the effort put into making a flexible schedule is well expended.

Recognizing the need on the part of teachers and administrators to have knowledge of and get the "feel" for flexible scheduling, team teaching, continuous progress and individualized instruction, we at Arizona State University have designed several experiences to help teachers and administrators in their endeavors to become "flexible."

One set of experiences during the summer of 1967 was a series of workshops conducted by Mr. Gardner Swenson of the Kettering Foundation staff, Dayton, Ohio. There were three two-week workshops on team teaching, flexible scheduling, and individualizing instruction through development of materials. Using the fine facilities furnished by Tempe Elementary School District No. 3, Mr. Swenson teamed with an unusually talented group of consultants to conduct the workshops.

Once we determined the great amount of interest in the topics of the workshops we made some basic assumptions. The first was that we would take all graduate students who were interested. We enrolled 118 for the first two weeks, 55 for the second and 88 for the third.

The second assumption was that we could "individualize instruction" to meet the needs of all enrollees. In attempting to do this Mr. Swenson and his staff spent untold hours in conferences, interviews, and discussions with individuals and small groups, as well as making many large-group presentations. He also taught them to make the very ingenious "unipac." The unipac is a combination of a unit and a package of materials. It is centered around one concept and a limited number of behavioral objectives which the student is to attain. Mr. Swenson's contention was that if teachers know how to make and use unipacs they are well on the way to being able to "individualize instruction." Not only did the participants make unipacs, but the staff read them all carefully, tested some of them out on children, and selected some of them for publication.

The third assumption was that the goal of helping teachers to become knowledgeable about team teaching, flexible scheduling, continuous progress and individualizing instruction, as well as having a feeling for these innovations, could be reached by using the concepts themselves as teaching methods. That is, teach about team-teaching by team teaching; teach about flexible scheduling by scheduling flexibly (many conferences were held on pool-side); teach about continuous progress by taking all comers where they are and helping them move as far and as fast as they can move; teach how to individualize instruction by individualizing instruction; teach how to make appropriate materials by constructing unipacs.

It must be said that individualizing instruction is very difficult, and some found it frustrating not to be in a 55-minute class every day with a lecturer doing the work. Most, however, picked up the idea quickly and became extremely productive. The acid test of the experience, however, will come when teachers and administrators enter their schools this fall.

The Future of | 82
Educational Technology

Norton F. Kristy

As every educator is aware, public education has been sharply impacted by science and technology during the past decade or two. We can expect that in the near future this influence will continue to increase, taking the form of a convergence between three forces— computer technology, information systems, and changing educational requirements and practices. Children today must simply learn more —*much* more— in order to keep pace with the knowledge explosion. If we strip away the mystique of public education and view the instructional process in the cold light of this increasing demand for educational efficiency, some of the possibilities of the application of technology to education become clearer.

First, planning as a tool is available to education. It now frequently comes under the label of system analysis. System analysis is a technique that was invented about 25 years ago in order to assure that the many elements of military aircraft or military ships would in fact fit together. It was belatedly discovered that complex ships, airplanes, and other weapon systems had independently designed elements such as guns, navigation systems, and power plants which simply did not work well together without a prior integrated overall system design. The system analysis technique applied to education seeks first to define *educational objectives* such as custodial care, socializing or acculturating children, learning basic skills, and acquiring vocational skills. It then relates the resources or operational elements of the educational system in a way that best satisfies these objectives. Resources of an educational system include the teaching and learning strategies (usually called curriculum), instructional tools (new and old), administrative and management support activities, facilities, in-house training programs, etc.

Usually, however, the application of system analysis techniques to an educational system has rather limited objectives. It ordinarily does not seek to redefine, reconstruct, or redesign a total educational system. In the study which forms the basis for this article we undertook to define computer applications to a large urban school district. This was to our knowledge the most comprehensive study yet undertaken on computer system support for a large city school system. The study sought to answer several basic questions:

From *Phi Delta Kappan* Vol. 58 (January 1967). pp. 240-243.

- What does electronic data processing offer to the school district?
- How can it better perform jobs that are presently being performed manually?
- What kind of jobs can it do that are presently left undone?
- What will it cost and what will it require in time, leadership, special training, and organizational change?

The most powerful single conclusion of the study is that large urban school districts must plan to acquire comprehensive electronic data processing support for operation. That is, education is to some extent becoming an *information transmission* activity with growing requirements for computer application. (Although the adult-to-child influence is still a most significant human relationship in education, the realities of economics, numbers, teacher training problems, and student hostility or apathy afford a large role for learning techniques or devices which motivate, stimulate, and facilitate education.

In general, the support of education by large-scale electronic data processing systems is a development that is already well under way. Inexorably, such systems are coming into the central operational settings of many school districts, particularly those in the large cities. They are coming first to those central city school districts that are feeling the impact of seemingly irresolvable problems of ghetto slum living. But more important, the best and most advanced systems are being implemented in school districts that are willing to innovate, experiment, and undertake some modest risk. However, this innovation and experimentation should be undertaken on the basis of a substantial measure of prudent planning. Some school districts may plunge into the purchase of large computer support systems in an unplanned or short-sighted way, with the result that frustration and disappointment may cause them to shun continuation (thus delaying the effective application of these systems for an extended period). However, carefully planned and well-managed developmental programs can offer a central city school district a completely new range of capability in meeting its educational responsibilities.

Over the next 10 to 15 years, computer systems are likely to revolutionize education. For the first time, truly individualized instruction can be afforded to young people in a form that amplifies personal motivation by whole orders of magnitude. This possibility has profound implications for all children, but its greatest benefits may come from its effects on culturally deprived children—the student population often of most concern to the central city school district. Computer systems will also provide a capability for teacher monitoring and responsiveness to individual students that is impossible to achieve at the present time. For both pupil and teacher, and ultimately to the benefit of society as a whole, the educational environment can be so enhanced that it provides better outcomes, more rewards, and more satisfaction. However, these revolutionary changes in the capability of educational systems will not come about without a great deal of effort, planning, and leadership.

DATA PROCESSING APPLICATIONS

The remarkable capabilities of computer systems are often combined with frightening complexities. The complexity and the changing state of computer science and art require skilled and knowledgeable technical planning for implementation.

Computer based systems can, however, provide greatly augmented and (in some cases) new capability in the following areas:

1. *Computer Assisted Scheduling.* With methodological and procedural techniques now developing, the computer can be an indispensable tool for the scheduling of complex interactions. A computer subsystem can schedule curriculum, instructor assignment, facility assignment, student work load, courses of variable length, and all other interactive elements to support and facilitate individualized and flexible learning. Many such programs are in operation in Iowa, Florida, Illinois (Chicago), and elsewhere around the nation.

2. *Student Data Processing.* This computer use offers the teacher, counselor, or school administrator immediate access to a wide range of highly relevant information about any single student. Such information can facilitate early and appropriate responses to behavior problems, educational difficulties, attitudinal or motivational issues, or related administrative problems. In the next three to five years student data banks can be made more specifically responsive to the needs of the school personnel who use them; ultimately, they will become finely sensitive tools available to support the kinds of relationships that are necessary if each student is to be treated as an individual human being. This is one of the ways in which large school districts can deal with their huge aggregations of students in human terms.

3. *System Data Files.* An educational system can be viewed as a large, complex information-processing system. It requires more and more records on ever-larger numbers of students, teachers, and administrative personnel. Complete records on learning, health, and administrative actions are vital, of course, but efficiency requires that they be progressively automated, both in their generation and in their storage and retrieval. Computer systems increase the efficiency with which this necessary information can be developed, stored, and retrieved. They make it possible to analyze and collate these data automatically or on demand. Even more important, they enable teachers and administrators to make more useful and meaningful predictions based on the data.

4. *Computer Centered Learning.* The new computerized learning center offers the first real opportunity for individualizing the educational experience of millions of children. In almost infinite variety and form, the computer as a teaching tool can stimulate and motivate a new degree of excitement in learning. It can allow children to engage in individual learning games; it can respond directly and immediately to the child's own temperament and learning style. It can be the equivalent of a "master instructor" who is totally responsive to the learning needs of the particular child. As a direct teaching and learning tool, the computer offers the likelihood—over the next decade or two—of making learning an exciting and welcome experience for *every child* in the school system! A half dozen computer centered learning systems are in prototype development and testing at this moment.

5. *Management Data Processing.* The well-defined tools and techniques of management control information systems that have been developed in many other aspects of the American economy and in military areas are now available to the schools. They afford the capability for immediate access to information and analysis on personnel administration, purchasing and procurement, administrative control, financial planning, and other management subsystems.

6. *Educational Research.* Research has been severely constrained in public schools because the data necessary for significant findings have been fragmented and difficult to obtain. Computer centered learning and the availability of data on all the other computerized educational subsystems offer the opportunity to do really significant research on human learning in the classroom and in the public school environment. Computer centered educational support systems may provide a capability for answering fundamental questions about *how children learn.* Certainly the related research and planning issues concerning optimum school layout, teacher-student ratios, and facilities design can be answered in far more effective ways than they are at present.

7. *Vocational Education.* This field in particular will be profoundly influenced by computer technology. The computer offers a new capability for planning vocational education so that training in the schools is closely matched with job requirements and job opportunities in the community. It offers the possibility of computer-centered vocational education, that is, training for vocational skills in a high-motivation, accelerated-learning environment. Already, computer controlled simulation of a job environment is being integrated with a computer tutorial teaching system so that young people can learn a vocation in both theoretical and on-the-job contexts. Varied forms of simulation and learning games can enormously facilitate and expedite vocational education.

PLANNING FOR COMPUTER SYSTEMS

Many large school districts are already spending substantial funds on the purchase of electronic data processing systems. However, for the most part, school districts are buying these systems on a piecemeal basis. They perceive a need and respond to it by purchasing what seems to be an appropriate computer system to service the given need. Our study indicates that this approach can turn out to be almost incredibly inefficient. In connection with the major urban school system we studied, our data showed that a reasonable application of electronic data processing (computer systems), *if purchased individually and separately*, would have cost at least five times as much as a carefully developed central system. Put in other terms, a well-designed and sensibly implemented centralized system can offer five times as much computing power, actual application, and payoff on school district problems for a given sum of money as can a number of individually purchased electronic data processing systems.

If a school district purchases computer systems individually as perceived needs arise, the system components will probably be incapable of communicating with one another. That is to say, it would be extremely difficult to get data from independent student data bank subsystems into a computer assisted scheduling subsystem. It would be difficult or even impossible to get data from a computer assisted instruction subsystem into an educational research subsystem. Individually purchased systems will most likely have incompatible software (computer programming), incompatible hardware (usually tape units will be incompatible), and the several computers and their memories will be inefficiently utilized. It is almost impossible to tie together separately designed computer systems once they come into being. These disconnected systems will often have little or no growth potential, thus leading to the possibility that they may have to be discarded after a very few years and completely repurchased. The result of such unplanned computer system acquisition will at an early point become tragically apparent to the managers of a large school district.

WHAT IS NEEDED?

The results of our study indicate several requirements if effective and economical electronic data processing is to be implemented for a major urban school district.

The first requirement is for a *centralized system design* covering the full range of requirements and services sought by the school district. The second need is for a *development* plan extending over a number of years for purchasing and integrating the elements of the total centralized system. In the study, we devised such a development plan, really a menu of subsystem options for the school district. These subsystems can be purchased in the quantity and at the rate deemed most desirable by the responsible officials of the school district.

The third requirement is for a knowledgeable, experienced *system manager* who can monitor and direct the implementation of the system.

A fourth requirement is that of developing a *complete program for training* school district personnel in electronic data processing and in the use of each of the computer subsystems.

The final requirement is, of course, for *strong leadership* and support on the part of the responsible officials of the school district. In order to achieve the efficiencies and economics of a centralized computer system, it is necessary for the officials of the school district to decide as early as possible what they want and where they are going with regard to electronic data processing.

The huge investment of this nation in large military information systems has provided us with a beginning understanding of how humans *learn* in a complex information environment. These same billions of dollars have helped give us sophisticated analytical tools and advanced technology, especially in computers and communications.

A fresh look at the objectives and methods of public education clearly indicates the explosive application of computers and information systems in the next decade. If these tools are developed and used in a thoughtful, planned, and economically sensible manner, they can bring a powerful new force to bear on the central city problem, on the pressing requirement to increase the efficiency and effectiveness of human learning, and on the need to upgrade the human resources of our nation.

index

Paraprofessional staff, 256
  recruitment of, 256
  selection of, 256
  training of, 256
Personnel administration
  precepts for, 286
Personnel services, 224
  in-service training in, 227
  outside consultants in, 227
  and programs, 228
  selecting personnel for, 225
  utilizing staff in, 226
Philosophy of Education
  shifts in, 18
Pressure Groups
  accountability by, 496
  civil rights, 495
  negotiating with, 495
  non-employee, 497, 499
  political accommodations with, 498
  spokesman for, 495
Principal
  as administrative leader, 224
  and administrative team, 215
  delegation of duties of, 216
  and human behavior, 200
  and part-time assistants, 216
  and research, 119
  selection and training of, 350
  and supervision, 200
Principalship
  inner-city, 31
Professionalism, 60
Professional team, 98
Public education, 4
  threat to, 13
Public relations, 25
Pursuit of excellence, 104

Racial Imbalance Law, 14
Racial isolation, 460
Racial tension, 335
Rating forms, 196
Regional laboratories, 120
Relevance or revolt, 332
Remote access system, 515
Remuneration
  professional, 23
Research
  designs, 121
  language, 120

Rights
  extra-legal, 53

School-Community relations, 487
  in decision making, 493
  mediating service in, 498
  and the power system, 491
  a report of the National Advisory Committee on Civil Disorders, 490
School organization, 175
  open system in, 178
School parks
  administration, 475
  for equal opportunities, 467
Secondary school administrators
  importance of, 151, 152
Segregation
  residential, 12
Sex Education
  how, when, by whom, 379
  national study on, 373
  objective of, 379
  pilot program in, 383
  policy-making in, 372
  a school responsibility, 377
  team approach to, 383
Social systems, 247
Specially-oriented student, 229
Staff involvement, 113
Staff-student relations, 365
Student
  behavior and dress, 69
  controlled organization, 55
  discipline, 216
  dissent, 70
  load, 24
  newspaper, 367
  personalized activities of, 360
  protests, 338, 346, 349
  responsibility, 92
Student skills, 22
Student teaching
  principal's role in, 261
Students for a Democratic Society, 53
Sub-professional staff, 254
  recruitment of, 254
  selection of, 254
  training of, 254
Suburban deprivation, 434
Supervising teachers, 132